PREFACE

The last 25 years have witnessed an unprecedented increase in competition in both national and world markets. In this competitive environment, managers must make increasingly complex business decisions that will determine whether the firm will prosper or even survive. Today, economic analysis is more important than ever as a tool for decision making.

OBJECTIVES OF THIS BOOK

The aims of this textbook are to illustrate the central decision problems managers face and to provide the economic analysis they need to guide these decisions. It was written with the conviction that an effective managerial economics textbook must go beyond the "nuts and bolts" of economic analysis; it should also show how practicing managers use these economic methods. Our experience teaching managerial economics to undergraduates, MBAs, and executives alike shows that a focus on applications is essential.

KEY FEATURES

Managerial Decision Making

The main feature that distinguishes *Managerial Economics*, Eighth Edition, is its consistent emphasis on managerial decision making. In a quest to explain economics per se, many current texts defer analysis of basic managerial decisions such as optimal output and pricing policies until later chapters—as special applications or as relevant only to particular market structures. In contrast, decision making is woven throughout every chapter in this book. Each chapter begins with a description of a real managerial problem that challenges students to ponder possible choices and is concluded by revisiting and analyzing the decision in light of the concepts introduced in the chapter. Without exception, the principles of managerial economics are introduced and analyzed by extended decision-making examples. Some of these examples include pricing airline seats (Chapter 3), competing as a commercial day-care provider (Chapter 7), fighting global warming (Chapter 11), choosing between risky research and development projects (Chapter 12), and negotiating David Letterman's *Late Show* contract (Chapter 15). In addition to reviewing important concepts, the summary at the end of each chapter lists essential decision-making principles.

The analysis of optimal decisions is presented early in the book. Chapter 2 introduces and analyzes the basic profit-maximization problem of the firm. Chapter 3 begins with a traditional treatment of demand and goes on to apply demand analysis to the firm's optimal pricing problem. Chapters 5 and 6 take a closer look at production and cost as guides to making optimal managerial decisions. The emphasis on decision making continues throughout the remainder of the book because, in our view, this is the best way to teach managerial economics. The decision-making approach also provides a direct answer to students' perennial question: How and why is this concept useful? A list of real-world applications used throughout the text appears on the inside of the front cover.

New Topics

At one time, managerial economics books most closely resembled intermediate microeconomics texts with topics reworked here and there. Due to the advance of modern management techniques, the days when this was sufficient are long past. This text goes far beyond current alternatives by integrating the most important of these advances with the principal topic areas of managerial economics. Perhaps the most significant advance is the use of game theory to illuminate the firm's strategic choices. Game theoretic principles are essential to understanding strategic behavior. An entire chapter (Chapter 10) is devoted to this topic. Other chapters apply the game-theoretic approach to settings of oligopoly (Chapter 9), asymmetric information and organization design (Chapter 14), and negotiation (Chapter 15).

A second innovation of the text is its treatment of decision making under uncertainty. Managerial success—whether measured by a particular firm's profitability or by the international competitiveness of our nation's businesses as a whole—depends on making decisions that involve risk and uncertainty. Managers must strive to envision the future outcomes of today's decisions, measure and weigh competing risks, and determine which risks are acceptable. Other managerial economics textbooks typically devote a single, short chapter to decision making under uncertainty after devoting a dozen chapters to portraying demand and cost curves as if they were certain.

Decision making under uncertainty is a prominent part of *Managerial Economics,* Eighth Edition. Chapter 12 shows how decision trees can be used to structure decisions in high-risk environments. Chapter 13 examines the value of acquiring information about relevant risks, including competing in high-risk auction and procurement settings. Subsequent chapters apply the techniques of decision making under uncertainty to topics that are on the cutting edge of managerial economics: organization design and negotiation.

A third innovation is the expanded coverage of international topics and applications. In place of a stand-alone chapter on global economic issues, we have chosen to integrate international applications throughout the text. For instance, early applications in Chapters 2 and 3 include responding to exchange-rate changes and multinational pricing. Comparative advantage, tariffs and quotas, and the risks of doing international business are additional applications taken up in later chapters. In all, 14 of the 16 chapters contain international applications. In short, our aim is to leave the student with a first-hand appreciation of business decisions within the global economic environment.

A fourth innovation is the inclusion of end-of-chapter spreadsheet problems. In the last 25 years, spreadsheets have become the manager's single most important quantitative tool. It is our view that spreadsheets provide a natural means of modeling managerial

EIGHTH EDITION

Managerial Economics

William F. Samuelson
Boston University

Stephen G. Marks
Boston University

VICE PRESIDENT AND EXECUTIVE PUBLISHER: George Hoffman
EXECUTIVE EDITOR: Joel Hollenbeck
SPONSORING EDITOR: Marian Provenzano
PROJECT EDITOR: Brian Baker
ASSOCIATE EDITOR: Christina Volpe
ASSISTANT EDITOR: Courtney Luzzi
EDITORIAL ASSISTANT: Jacqueline Hughes
EDITORIAL ASSISTANT: Tai Harriss
PRODUCTION MANAGER: Michael Olivo
ASSISTANT PRODUCTION EDITOR: Wanqian Ye
SENIOR MARKETING MANAGER: Karolina Zarychta
COVER DESIGNER: Thomas Nery
COVER CREDIT: Ulli Seer/LOOK/Getty Images

This book is printed on acid-free paper. ∞

Library of Congress Cataloging-in-Publication Data
Samuelson, William.
  Managerial economics / William F. Samuelson, Stephen G. Marks. — Eighth edition.
    pages cm
  Includes index.
    ISBN 978-1-118-80894-8 (paperback)
1. Managerial economics.   2. Decision making. I. Marks, Stephen G. (Stephen Gary)
II. Title.
  HD30.22.S26 2015
  338.5'024658—dc23
                        2014031372

Printed in the United States of America
10 9 8 7 6 5 4 3

decisions. In their own way, they are as valuable as the traditional modeling approaches using equations and graphs. (This admission comes from a long-ago college math major who first saw spreadsheets as nothing more than "trivial" arithmetic and a far cry from "true" programming.) Optimization is one hallmark of quantitative decision making, and with the advent of optimizer tools, managers can use spreadsheets to model problems and to find and explore profit-maximizing solutions. A second hallmark is equilibrium analysis. Again, spreadsheet tools allow immediate solutions of what otherwise would be daunting sets of simultaneous equations.

Spreadsheets offer a powerful way of portraying economic decisions and finding optimal solutions without a large investment in calculus methods. We have worked hard to provide a rich array of spreadsheet problems in 14 of the 15 principal chapters. Some of these applications include optimal production and pricing, cost analysis with fixed and variable inputs, competitive market equilibrium in the short and long runs, monopoly practices, Nash equilibrium behavior, identifying superior mutual fund performance, and the welfare effects of externalities. In each case, students are asked to build and analyze a simple spreadsheet based on an example provided for them. In addition, a special appendix in Chapter 2 provides a self-contained summary of spreadsheet optimization. In short, using spreadsheets provides new insights into managerial economics and teaches career-long modeling skills.

Organization, Coverage, and Level

This textbook can be used by a wide range of students, from undergraduate business majors in second-level courses to MBA students and executive program participants. The presentation of all topics is self-contained. Although most students will have taken an economics principles course in their recent, or not so recent, past, no prior economic tools are presumed. The presentations begin simply and are progressively applied to more and more challenging applications. Each chapter contains a range of problems designed to test students' basic understanding. A number of problems explore advanced applications and are indicated by an asterisk. Suggested references at the end of each chapter direct students to extensions and advanced applications of the core topics presented in the chapter.

Although this text has many unique features, its organization and coverage are reasonably standard. All of the topics that usually find a home in managerial economics are covered and are in the usual sequence. As noted earlier, the analytics of profit maximization and optimal pricing are presented up front in Chapter 2 and the second part of Chapter 3. If the instructor wishes, he or she can defer these optimization topics until after the chapters on demand and cost. In addition, the book is organized so that specific chapters can be omitted without loss of continuity. In the first section of the book, Chapters 4 and 5 fit into this category. In the second section of the book, Chapters 7, 8, and 9 are core chapters that can stand alone or be followed by any combination of the remaining chapters. The book concludes with applications chapters, including chapters on decision making under uncertainty, asymmetric information, negotiation, and linear programming that are suitable for many broad-based managerial economics courses.

Analyzing managerial decisions requires a modest amount of quantitative proficiency. In our view, understanding the *logic* of profit-maximizing behavior is more important than mathematical sophistication; therefore, *Managerial Economics,* Eighth Edition, uses only the most basic techniques of differential calculus. These concepts are explained and summarized in the appendix to Chapter 2. Numerical examples and applications abound throughout all of the chapters. In our view, the best way for students to master the material is to learn by example. Four to six "Check Stations"—mini-problems that force students to test themselves on their quantitative understanding—appear throughout each chapter. In short, the text takes a quantitative approach to managerial decision making without drowning students in mathematics.

THE EIGHTH EDITION

While continuing to emphasize managerial decision making, the Eighth Edition of *Managerial Economics* contains several changes.

First, we have extensively revised and updated the many applications in the text. Analyzing the pricing of Amazon's Kindle; using regression analysis to estimate box-office revenues for film releases; assessing the impact of OPEC's oil cartel; judging the government's antitrust case against Microsoft; or weighing the challenges of corporate governance in the aftermath of the financial crisis—these are all important and timely economic applications.

Second, we have highlighted and expanded an applications feature called *Business Behavior.* The rapidly growing area of behavioral economics asks: How does actual decision making behavior and practice compare with the prescriptions of economics and decision analysis? In many cases, the answer is that decisions rely on psychological responses, heuristic methods, and bounded rationality as much as on logic and analysis. In almost every chapter, we take deliberate time to provide an assessment (based on cutting-edge research findings) of real-world decision-making behavior, noting the most common pitfalls to avoid.

Throughout the text, we have included a wide range of end-of-chapter problems, from basic to advanced. Each chapter also contains a wide-ranging discussion question designed to frame broader economic issues. We have also updated each chapter's suggested bibliographic references, including numerous Internet sites where students can access and retrieve troves of economic information and data on almost any topic.

The Eighth Edition examines the economics of information goods, e-commerce, and the Internet—topics first introduced in previous editions. While some commentators have claimed that the emergence of e-commerce has overturned the traditional rules of economics, this text takes a more balanced view. In fact, e-commerce provides a dramatic illustration of the power of economic analysis in analyzing new market forces. Any analysis of e-commerce must consider such issues as network and information externalities, reduced marginal costs and transaction costs, pricing and revenue sources, control of standards, e-commerce strategies, product versioning, and market segmentation, to name just a few topics. E-commerce applications appear throughout the text in Chapter 3 (demand), Chapter 6 (cost), Chapters 7 and 9 (competitive effects), and Chapter 14 (organization of the firm).

Finally, the Eighth Edition is significantly slimmer than earlier editions. Inevitably, editions of textbooks grow longer and longer as authors include more and more concepts, applications, and current examples. By pruning less important material, we have worked hard to focus student attention on the most important economic and decision-making principles. In our view, it is better to be shorter and clearer than to be comprehensive and overwhelming. Moreover, most of the interesting examples have not been lost, but rather have been moved to the Samuelson and Marks website at www.wiley.com/college/samuelson, where they can be accessed by instructors and students.

ANCILLARY MATERIALS

Study Guide   The student study guide is designed to teach the concepts and problem-solving skills needed to master the material in the text. Each chapter contains multiple-choice questions, quantitative problems, essay questions, and mini-cases.

Instructor's Manual, Test Bank, and PowerPoints   The Instructor's Manual includes suggestions for teaching managerial economics, additional examples to supplement in-text examples, suggested cases, references to current articles in the business press, anecdotes, follow-up on text applications, and answers to the back-of-chapter problems. The test bank contains over 500 multiple-choice questions, quantitative problems, essay questions, and mini-cases.

Respondus Test Bank   The test bank is available electronically in Respondus format on the book companion site.

Online Chapter   Chapter 17 is now available on the book companion site at www.wiley.com/college/samuelson.

All instructor materials are available by accessing Wiley's website at www.wiley.com/college/samuelson

Wiley E-Text
Powered by VitalSource®
The **Wiley E-Text: Powered by VitalSource** gives students anytime, anywhere access to the best economics content when and where they study: on their desktop, laptop, tablet, or smartphone. Students can search across content, highlight, and take notes that they can share with teachers and classmates.

   Wiley's E-Text for *Managerial Economics, 8th edition* takes learning from traditional to cutting edge by integrating inline interactive multimedia with market-leading content. This exciting new learning model brings textbook pages to life—no longer just a static e-book, the E-Text enriches the study experience with dynamic features:

- **Interactive Tables and Graphs** allow students to access additional rich layers and "hot areas" of explanation by manipulating slider controls or clicking on embedded "hotspots" incorporated into select tables and graphs

- **Practice Quizzes** allow students to practice as they read and thereby receive instant feedback on their progress
- **Audio-Enhanced Graphics** provide further explanations for key graphs in the form of short audio clips.

ACKNOWLEDGMENTS

In preparing this revision, we have benefited from suggestions from the following reviewers and survey respondents: Richard Beil, Auburn University; Shawn Carter, Jacksonville State University; Ann Garnett, Murdoch University; Koushik Ghosh, Central Washington University; Theodore Groves, University of California–San Diego; Duncan Holthausen, North Carolina State University; John R. McNamara, Lehigh University; Kofi O. Nti, Pennsylvania State University; Nicola Persico, University of Pennsylvania; Franklin Robeson, College of William and Mary; Don Stengel, California State University–Fresno; Charles B. Wagoner, Delta State University; Craig Walker, Delta State University; Ron Wilder, University of South Carolina, and Chris Woodruff, University of California–San Diego.

We have also had valuable help from colleagues and students who have commented on parts of the manuscript. Among them are Alan J. Daskin; Cliff Dobitz, North Dakota State University; Howard Dye, University of South Florida; David Ely, San Diego State University; Steven Felgran, Northeastern University; William Gunther, University of Alabama; Robert Hansen, Dartmouth College; George Hoffer, Virginia Commonwealth University; Yannis Ioannides, Tufts University; Sarah Lane; Darwin Neher; Albert Okunade, Memphis State University; Mary Jean Rivers, Seattle University; Patricia Sanderson, Mississippi State University; Frank Slesnick, Bellarmine College; Leonard Tashman, University of Vermont; Rafael Tenorio, University of Notre Dame; Lawrence White, New York University; Mokhlis Zaki, Northern Michigan University; and Richard Zeckhauser, Harvard University. Other colleagues provided input on early teaching and research materials that later found prominent places in the text: Max Bazerman, Harvard University; John Riley, University of California–Los Angeles; James Sebenius, Harvard University; and Robert Weber, Northwestern University.

In addition, we have received many detailed comments and suggestions from our colleagues at Boston University, Shulamit Kahn, Michael Salinger, and David Weil. The feedback from students in Boston University's MBA and executive programs has been invaluable. Special thanks to Diane Herbert and Robert Maurer for their comments and suggestions.

Finally, to Susan and Mary Ellen: We cannot thank you enough.

William F. Samuelson
Stephen G. Marks

About the Authors

William F. Samuelson is professor of economics and finance at Boston University School of Management. He received his BA and PhD from Harvard University. His research interests include game theory, decision theory, bidding, bargaining, and experimental economics. He has published a variety of articles in leading economics and management science journals including *The American Economic Review, The Quarterly Journal of Economics, Econometrica, The Journal of Finance, Management Science,* and *Operations Research.* His teaching and research have been sponsored by the National Science Foundation and the National Institute for Dispute Resolution, among others. He currently serves on the editorial board of *Group Decision and Negotiation.*

Stephen G. Marks is associate professor of law at Boston University. He received his JD, MA, and PhD from the University of California–Berkeley. He has taught in the areas of managerial economics, finance, corporate law, and securities regulation. His research interests include corporate governance, law and economics, finance, and information theory. He has published his research in various law reviews and in such journals as *The American Economic Review, The Journal of Legal Studies,* and *The Journal of Financial and Quantitative Analysis.*

BRIEF CONTENTS

CHAPTER 1   Introduction to Economic Decision Making   1

CHAPTER 2   Optimal Decisions Using Marginal Analysis   19

CHAPTER 3   Demand Analysis and Optimal Pricing   59

CHAPTER 4   Estimating and Forecasting Demand   100

CHAPTER 5   Production   146

CHAPTER 6   Cost Analysis   175

CHAPTER 7   Perfect Competition   214

CHAPTER 8   Monopoly   244

CHAPTER 9   Oligopoly   266

CHAPTER 10   Game Theory and Competitive Strategy   303

CHAPTER 11   Regulation, Public Goods, and Benefit-Cost Analysis   341

CHAPTER 12   Decision Making under Uncertainty   378

CHAPTER 13   The Value of Information   413

CHAPTER 14   Asymmetric Information and Organizational Design   445

CHAPTER 15   Bargaining and Negotiation   475

CHAPTER 16   Linear Programming   503

CHAPTER 17   Auctions and Competitive Bidding   available online

Index   539

CONTENTS

CHAPTER 1 Introduction to Economic Decision Making 1

SEVEN EXAMPLES OF MANAGERIAL DECISIONS 2

SIX STEPS TO DECISION MAKING 5
Step 1: Define the Problem 5
Step 2: Determine the Objective 6
Step 3: Explore the Alternatives 8
Step 4: Predict the Consequences 8
Step 5: Make a Choice 9
Step 6: Perform Sensitivity Analysis 10

PRIVATE AND PUBLIC DECISIONS: AN ECONOMIC VIEW 11
Public Decisions 14

THINGS TO COME 15

CHAPTER 2 Optimal Decisions Using Marginal Analysis 19

A SIMPLE MODEL 20
A Microchip Manufacturer 21

MARGINAL ANALYSIS 27
Marginal Analysis and Calculus 28

MARGINAL REVENUE AND MARGINAL COST 31
Marginal Revenue 31
Marginal Cost 33
Profit Maximization Revisited 33

SENSITIVITY ANALYSIS 35
Asking What If 36

APPENDIX TO CHAPTER 2: CALCULUS AND OPTIMIZATION TECHNIQUES 47

SPECIAL APPENDIX TO CHAPTER 2: OPTIMIZATION USING SPREADSHEETS 56

CHAPTER 3 Demand Analysis and Optimal Pricing 59

DETERMINANTS OF DEMAND 60
The Demand Function 60
The Demand Curve and Shifting Demand 61
General Determinants of Demand 63

ELASTICITY OF DEMAND 64
Price Elasticity 64
Factors Affecting Price Elasticity 68
Other Elasticities 69
Price Elasticity and Prediction 70

DEMAND ANALYSIS AND OPTIMAL PRICING 71
Price Elasticity, Revenue, and Marginal Revenue 71

Maximizing Revenue   74
Optimal Markup Pricing   75
Price Discrimination   78
Information Goods   81

APPENDIX TO CHAPTER 3: CONSUMER PREFERENCES AND DEMAND   93

CHAPTER 4   **Estimating and Forecasting Demand**   100

COLLECTING DATA   101
Consumer Surveys   101
Controlled Market Studies   102
Uncontrolled Market Data   103

REGRESSION ANALYSIS   104
Ordinary Least-Squares Regression   104
Interpreting Regression Statistics   109
Potential Problems in Regression   114

FORECASTING   118
Time-Series Models   118
Fitting a Simple Trend   120
Barometric Models   127
Forecasting Performance   128
Final Thoughts   131

APPENDIX TO CHAPTER 4: REGRESSION USING SPREADSHEETS   140

SPECIAL APPENDIX TO CHAPTER 4: STATISTICAL TABLES   144

CHAPTER 5   **Production**   146

BASIC PRODUCTION CONCEPTS   147

PRODUCTION IN THE SHORT RUN   147
Optimal Use of an Input   151

PRODUCTION IN THE LONG RUN   153
Returns to Scale   153
Least-Cost Production   154

MEASURING PRODUCTION FUNCTIONS   160
Linear Production   160
Production with Fixed Proportions   161
Polynomial Functions   161
The Cobb-Douglas Function   162

OTHER PRODUCTION DECISIONS   164
Multiple Plants   164
Multiple Products   166

CHAPTER 6   **Cost Analysis**   175

RELEVANT COSTS   176
Opportunity Costs and Economic Profits   176
Fixed and Sunk Costs   179

THE COST OF PRODUCTION   182
Short-Run Costs   183
Long-Run Costs   187

RETURNS TO SCALE AND SCOPE   191
Returns to Scale   191
Economies of Scope   196

COST ANALYSIS AND OPTIMAL DECISIONS   199
A Single Product   199
The Shut-Down Rule   200
Multiple Products   202

APPENDIX TO CHAPTER 6: TRANSFER PRICING   211

CHAPTER 7   **Perfect Competition**   214

THE BASICS OF SUPPLY AND DEMAND   216
Shifts in Demand and Supply   217

COMPETITIVE EQUILIBRIUM   219
Decisions of the Competitive Firm   220
Market Equilibrium   223

MARKET EFFICIENCY   225
Private Markets: Benefits and Costs   225

INTERNATIONAL TRADE   234
Tariffs and Quotas   235

CHAPTER 8   **Monopoly**   244

PURE MONOPOLY   244
Monopoly Behavior   245
Barriers to Entry   247

PERFECT COMPETITION VERSUS PURE MONOPOLY   250
Cartels   252
Natural Monopolies   255

MONOPOLISTIC COMPETITION   257

CHAPTER 9   **Oligopoly**   266

OLIGOPOLY   268
Five-Forces Framework   268
Industry Concentration   269
Concentration and Prices   273

QUANTITY COMPETITION   276
A Dominant Firm   276
Competition among Symmetric Firms   278

PRICE COMPETITION   280
Price Rigidity and Kinked Demand   280
Price Wars and the Prisoner's Dilemma   282

OTHER DIMENSIONS OF COMPETITION   287
Strategic Commitments   288
Advertising   290

APPENDIX TO CHAPTER 9: BUNDLING AND TYING   299

CHAPTER 10   Game Theory and Competitive Strategy   303
SIZING UP COMPETITIVE SITUATIONS   304

ANALYZING PAYOFF TABLES   307
Equilibrium Strategies   310

COMPETITIVE STRATEGY   315
Market Entry   317
Bargaining   318
Sequential Competition   319
Repeated Competition   323

APPENDIX TO CHAPTER 10: MIXED STRATEGIES   336

CHAPTER 11   Regulation, Public Goods, and Benefit–Cost Analysis   341
I. MARKET FAILURES AND REGULATION   342

MARKET FAILURE DUE TO MONOPOLY   343
Government Responses   344

MARKET FAILURE DUE TO EXTERNALITIES   349
Remedying Externalities   351
Promoting Positive Externalities   356

MARKET FAILURE DUE TO IMPERFECT INFORMATION   358

II. BENEFIT–COST ANALYSIS AND PUBLIC GOODS PROVISION   359

PUBLIC GOODS   359
Public Goods and Efficiency   359

THE BASICS OF BENEFIT–COST ANALYSIS   361
Applying the Net Benefit Rule   362
Dollar Values   362
Efficiency versus Equity   362

EVALUATING A PUBLIC PROJECT   363
Public Investment in a Bridge   363

VALUING BENEFITS AND COSTS   366
Market Values   366
Nonmarketed Benefits and Costs   366

CHAPTER 12   Decision Making under Uncertainty   378
UNCERTAINTY, PROBABILITY, AND EXPECTED VALUE   379
Probability   379
Expected Value   381

DECISION TREES   381
An Oil Drilling Decision   382
Features of the Expected-Value Criterion   384

SEQUENTIAL DECISIONS   388

RISK AVERSION   395
Expected Utility   398
Why the Expected-Utility Method Works   400
Expected Utility and Risk Aversion   402

CHAPTER 13   **The Value of Information**   413

THE VALUE OF INFORMATION   414
The Oil Wildcatter Revisited   414
Imperfect Information   416

REVISING PROBABILITIES   418
Bayes' Theorem   419

OTHER APPLICATIONS   422
Predicting Credit Risks   423
Business Behavior and Decision Pitfalls   424

AUCTIONS AND COMPETITIVE BIDDING   429
Private-Value Auctions   429
Common-Value Auctions   431
Expected Auction Revenue   433

CHAPTER 14   **Asymmetric Information and Organizational Design**   445

ASYMMETRIC INFORMATION   446
Adverse Selection   446
Signaling   448
Principals, Agents, and Moral Hazard   449

ORGANIZATIONAL DESIGN   454
The Nature of the Firm   454
The Boundaries of the Firm   455
Assigning Decision-Making Responsibilities   456
Monitoring and Rewarding Performance   460
Separation of Ownership and Control in the Modern Corporation   464

CHAPTER 15   **Bargaining and Negotiation**   475

THE ECONOMIC SOURCES OF BENEFICIAL AGREEMENTS   476
Resolving Disputes   479
Differences in Values   481
Contingent Contracts   483

MULTIPLE-ISSUE NEGOTIATIONS   484

NEGOTIATION STRATEGY   489
Perfect Information   490
Imperfect Information   491
Repetition and Reputation   492

CHAPTER 16   Linear Programming   503

LINEAR PROGRAMS   504
Graphing the LP Problem   506
A Minimization Problem   510

SENSITIVITY ANALYSIS AND SHADOW PRICES   513
Changes in the Objective Function   513
Shadow Prices   515
Optimal Decisions and Shadow Prices   517

FORMULATION AND COMPUTER SOLUTION FOR LARGER LP PROBLEMS   520
Production Decisions   520
Computer Solutions   523

CHAPTER 17   Auctions and Competitive Bidding   available online

THE ADVANTAGES OF AUCTIONS

BIDDER STRATEGIES
English and Dutch Auctions
Sealed-Bid Auctions
Common Values and the Winner's Curse

OPTIMAL AUCTIONS
Expected Auction Revenue
Competitive Procurement

INDEX   539

LIST OF REAL-WORLD APPLICATIONS

1 Maximizing Value
2 Lower Drug Prices in Africa
3 Conflict in Fast-Food Franchising
4 Siting a Shopping Mall*
5 Manufacturing Microchips
6 Responding to Exchange Rate Changes
7 Pricing Amazon's Kindle
8 Airline Ticket Pricing
9 Ticket Pricing for a Sports Franchise
10 Pricing in Practice
11 Multinational Production and Pricing
12 Information Goods
13 The Economics of Groupon*
14 Estimating Movie Demand
15 Data-Driven Business
16 New Coke
17 Estimating the Demand for Air Travel
18 Forecasting Cable TV Customers
19 The Demand for Toys
20 Forecasting the Fate of Euro Disney
21 Forecasting Performance
22 Forecasting the Demand for Nickel*
23 Allocating a Sales Force
24 A Production Function for Auto Parts
25 Returns to Scale in Coal Mining*
26 Winning in Football and Baseball
27 Estimating Production Functions
28 Allocating Production between Refineries
29 Aluminum vs. Steel in Cars and Trucks
30 Allocating Costs
31 Starting a New Business
32 Sunk Costs
33 Ordering a Best-Seller*
34 Pricing E-books
35 Comparative Advantage and International Trade
36 E-Commerce and Cost Economies
37 Flexibility and Innovation
38 Betting the Planet
39 The Market for Day Care
40 Market Competition and the Internet
41 Tariffs and Quotas
42 New York City's Taxicabs
43 Intel's Monopoly
44 The OPEC Cartel
45 A "Natural" Telecommunications Monopoly?*
46 Collusion in the Infant Formula Industry
47 The Five-Forces Model
48 Concentration Ratios in U.S. Industry
49 Global Airfares
50 A Price War
51 Attack on a Skater*
52 When to Cut Price
53 Strategic Commitments
54 Bundling Films
55 A Battle for Air Passengers
56 Jockeying in the TV Ratings Game
57 Market-Share Competition
58 Two-Tiered Tender Offers
59 A Common Standard for High-Definition DVDs
60 The Platform Wars Continue*
61 Staples versus Office Depot
62 An International Mineral Lease
63 Entry Deterrence
64 Establishing a Reputation
65 A Game of Trust
66 The FDA, AZT, and AIDS
67 Rent Seeking
68 Too Big to Fail
69 The United States versus Microsoft
70 Global Warming
71 Regulatory Reform and Deregulation
72 Assessing Risks*
73 Expanding a Highway
74 Building a Bridge
75 Gearing Down for a Recession
76 An Oil Drilling Decision
77 The Perils of International Business

78 Developing a Drug
79 Risking a New York Blackout*
80 Risky Decisions
81 The BP Oil Spill Disaster
82 The Demand for Insurance
83 Risk Management at Microsoft
84 The Stock Market and the Economy
85 Evaluating a Seismic Test
86 Predicting Credit Risks
87 Decision Pitfalls
88 The *Challenger* Disaster and NASA's Risk Analysis
89 Searching for the Best Price*
90 English and Sealed-Bid Auctions*
91 Private-Value and Common-Value Auctions*
92 The Winner's Curse*
93 Real-Life Bidding*
94 Competitive Procurement*
95 Incentive Pay at DuPont's Fiber Division
96 A Loss-Making Benefits Plan
97 A "Lemons" Market
98 A Building Contract
99 Health Insurance and Medical Costs
100 The Financial Meltdown

101 Airbus's Dysfunctional Organization
102 DHL Worldwide Express
103 Integration or Franchising?
104 Information Technology and Organizational Structure
105 Motivating Workers
106 Executive Compensation and Incentives
107 Enron, WorldCom, and Tyco
108 Sanofi's Bid for Genzyme
109 Selling a Warehouse
110 The Paperback Rights for *In Search of Excellence*
111 A Patent Conflict
112 A Complex Procurement
113 Wooing David Letterman
114 Making a Tender Offer
115 Failed Agreements
116 Texaco versus Pennzoil*
117 An Investment Problem
118 An Optimal Computer Mix
119 Clean-Water Funding
120 Allocating HIV Resources
121 Staffing a Police Force
122 Clean Coal
123 A School Bussing Problem

Items indicated with an asterisk (*) are located in the text's online companion site.

CHAPTER 1

Introduction to Economic Decision Making

The crucial step in tackling almost all important business and government decisions begins with a single question: What is the alternative?

ANONYMOUS

LO#1. Describe seven different kinds of decisions that managers face.

LO#2. Outline the six steps in the decision-making process.

LO#3. Contrast decision making in the private and public sectors.

Decision making lies at the heart of most important business and government problems. The range of business decisions is vast: Should a high-tech company undertake a promising but expensive research and development program? Should a petrochemical manufacturer cut the price of its best-selling industrial chemical in response to a new competitor's entry into the market? Should management of a food products company launch a new product after mixed test-marketing results?

Likewise, government decisions range far and wide: Should the Department of Transportation impose stricter rollover standards for sports utility vehicles? Should a city allocate funds for construction of a harbor tunnel to provide easy airport and commuter access? These are all economic decisions. In each case, a sensible analysis of what decision to make requires a careful comparison of the advantages and disadvantages (often, but not always, measured in dollars) of alternative courses of action.

Managerial economics is the analysis of major management decisions using the tools of economics. Managerial economics applies many familiar concepts from economics—demand and cost, monopoly and competition, the allocation of resources, and economic trade-offs—to aid managers in making better decisions. This book provides the framework and the economic tools needed to fulfill this goal.

In this chapter, we begin our study of managerial economics by stressing decision-making applications. In the first section, we introduce seven decision examples, all of which we will analyze in detail later in the text. Although these examples cover only some applications of economic analysis, they represent the breadth of managerial economics and are intended to whet the reader's appetite. Next, we present a basic model of the decision-making process as a framework in which to apply economic analysis. This model proposes six steps to help structure complicated decisions so that they may be clearly analyzed.

After presenting the six steps, we outline a basic theory of the firm and of government decisions and objectives. In the concluding section, we present a brief overview of the topics covered in the chapters to come.

SEVEN EXAMPLES OF MANAGERIAL DECISIONS

The best way to become acquainted with managerial economics is to come face to face with real-world decision-making problems. The seven examples that follow represent the different kinds of decisions that private- and public-sector managers face. All of them are revisited and examined in detail in later chapters.

The examples follow a logical progression. In the first example, a global carmaker faces the most basic problem in managerial economics: determining prices and outputs to maximize profit. As we shall see in Chapters 2 through 6, making decisions requires a careful analysis of revenues and costs.

The second example highlights competition between firms, the subject of Chapters 7 through 10. Here, three large office supply chains are battling for market share in a multitude of regional markets. Each is trying to secure a monopoly, but when rivals build superstores in the same city, they frequently get caught up in price wars.

The next two examples illustrate public-sector decisions: The first concerns funding a public project, the second is a regulatory decision. Here, a shift occurs both in the decision maker—from private to public manager—and in the objectives. As we argue in Chapter 11, government decisions are guided by the criterion of benefit–cost analysis rather than by profit considerations.

The final three examples involve decision making under uncertainty. In the fifth example, the failure of BP to identify and manage exploration risks culminated in the 2010 explosion of its *Deepwater Horizon* drilling rig in the Gulf of Mexico. In the next example, a pharmaceutical company is poised between alternative risky research and development (R&D) programs. Decision making under uncertainty is the focus of Chapters 12 and 13. In the final example, David Letterman and two rival television networks are locked in a high-stakes negotiation as to which company will land his profitable late-night show. Competitive risk in the context of negotiation is taken up in Chapter 15.

Multinational Production and Pricing

Almost all firms face the problem of pricing their products. Consider a US multinational carmaker that produces and sells its output in two geographic regions. It can produce cars in its home plant or in its foreign subsidiary. It sells cars in the domestic market and in the foreign market. For the next year, it must determine the prices to set at home and abroad, estimate sales for each market, and establish production quantities in each facility to supply those sales. It recognizes that the markets for vehicles at home and abroad differ with respect to demand (i.e., how many cars can be sold at different prices). Also, the production facilities have different costs and capacities. Finally, at a cost, it can ship vehicles from the home facility to help supply the foreign market, or vice versa. Based on the available information, how can the company determine a profit-maximizing pricing and production plan for the coming year?

For the last 25 years, three giant office supply chains—Staples, Office Depot, and Office Max—have engaged in a cutthroat retail battle. In major city after major city, the rivals have opened superstores, often within blocks of each other.

    This ongoing competition raises a number of questions: How do the chains assess the profitability of new markets? Where and when should each enter new markets? What if a region's office-supply demand is sufficient to support only one superstore? What measures might be taken by an incumbent to erect entry barriers to a would-be entrant? In view of accelerating office supply sales via the Internet, can mega bricks-and-mortar office supply stores survive?

Market Entry

As chief city planner of a rapidly growing Sun Belt city, you face the single biggest decision of your tenure: whether to recommend the construction of a new harbor bridge to connect downtown with the surrounding suburbs located on a northern peninsula. Currently, suburban residents commute to the city via a ferry or by driving a long-distance circular route. Preliminary studies have shown that there is considerable need and demand for the bridge. Indeed, the bridge is expected to spur economic activity in the region as a whole. The projected cost of the bridge is $75 million to $100 million. Toll charges on commuting automobiles and particularly on trucks could be instituted to recoup a portion of the bridge's costs. But, if bridge use falls short of projections, the city will be saddled with a very expensive white elephant. What would you recommend?

Building a New Bridge

Environmental regulations have a significant effect on business decisions and consumer behavior. Charles Schultze, former chairperson of the President's Council of Economic Advisers, describes the myriad problems associated with the regulations causing electric utilities to convert from oil to coal.

A Regulatory Problem

> Petroleum imports can be conserved by switching [utilities] from oil-fired to coal-fired generation. But barring other measures, burning high-sulfur Eastern coal substantially increases pollution. Sulfur can be "scrubbed" from coal smoke in the stack, but at a heavy cost, with devices that turn out huge volumes of sulfur wastes that must be disposed of and about whose reliability there is some question. Intermittent control techniques (installing high smoke stacks and turning off burners when meteorological conditions are adverse) can, at a lower cost, reduce local concentrations of sulfur oxides in the air, but cannot cope with the growing problem of sulfates and widespread acid rainfall. Use of low-sulfur Western coal would avoid many of these problems, but this coal is obtained by strip mining. Strip-mine reclamation is possible but substantially hindered in large areas of the West by lack of rainfall. Moreover, in some coal-rich areas the coal beds form the underlying aquifer, and their removal could wreck adjacent farming or ranching economies. Large coal-burning plants might be located in remote areas far from highly populated urban centers in order to minimize the human effects of pollution. But such areas are among the few left that are unspoiled by pollution, and both environmentalists and the residents (relatively few in number compared to

those in metropolitan localities but large among the voting populations in the particular states) strongly object to this policy. Fears, realistic or imaginary, about safety and accumulation of radioactive waste have increasingly hampered the nuclear option.[1]

Schultze's points apply directly to today's energy and environmental trade-offs. Actually, he penned this discussion in 1977! Important questions persist. How, when, and where should the government intervene to achieve and balance its energy and environmental objectives? How would one go about quantifying the benefits and costs of a particular program of intervention?

BP and Oil Exploration Risks

BP (known as British Petroleum prior to 2001) is in the business of taking risks. As the third largest energy company in the world, its main operations involve oil exploration, refining, and sale. The risks it faces begin with the uncertainty about where to find oil deposits (including drilling offshore more than a mile under the ocean floor), mastering the complex, risky methods of extracting petroleum, cost-effectively refining that oil, and selling those refined products at wildly fluctuating world prices. In short, the company runs the whole gamut of risk: geological, technological, safety, regulatory, legal, and market related.

Priding itself on 17 straight years of 100 percent oil reserve replacement, BP is an aggressive and successful oil discoverer. But the dark side of its strategic aspirations is its troubling safety and environmental record, culminating in the explosion of its *Deepwater Horizon* drilling rig in the Gulf of Mexico in April 2010. This raises the question: What types of decisions should oil companies like BP take to identify, quantify, manage, and hedge against the inevitable risks they face?

An R&D Decision

A five-year-old pharmaceutical company faces a major research and development decision. It already has spent a year of preliminary research toward producing a protein that dissolves blood clots. Such a drug would be of tremendous value in the treatment of heart attacks, some 80 percent of which are caused by clots. The primary method the company has been pursuing relies on conventional, state-of-the-art biochemistry. Continuing this approach will require an estimated $100 million additional investment and should lead to a commercially successful product, although the exact profit is highly uncertain. Two of the company's most brilliant research scientists are aggressively advocating a second R&D approach. This new biogenetic method relies on gene splicing to create a version of the human body's own anticlotting agent and is considerably riskier than the biochemical alternative. It will require a $200 million investment and has only a 20 percent chance of commercial success. However, if the company accomplishes the necessary breakthroughs, the anti-clotting agent will represent its first blockbuster, genetically engineered drug. If successful, the method will entail minimal production costs and generate annual profits two to five times greater than a biochemically based drug would. Which method should the firm choose for its R&D investment?

---

[1]C. L. Schultze, *The Public Use of Private Interest* (Washington, DC: The Brookings Institution, 1977), 9–10.

In January 1993, David Letterman made it official—he would be leaving *Late Night* on NBC for a new 11:30 P.M. show on CBS beginning in the fall. A tangled web of negotiations preceded the move. In 1992, NBC chose the comedian Jay Leno, instead of Letterman, to succeed Johnny Carson as the host of *The Tonight Show* in an effort to keep its lock on late-night programming. Accordingly, CBS, a nonentity in late-night television, saw its chance to woo David Letterman.

After extensive negotiations, CBS offered Letterman a $14 million salary to do the new show (a $10 million raise over his salary at NBC). In addition, Letterman's own production company would be paid $25 million annually to produce the show. But, NBC was unwilling to surrender Letterman to CBS without a fight. The network entered into secret negotiations with Letterman's representative, Michael Ovitz, exploring the possibility of dumping Leno and giving *The Tonight Show* to Letterman.

One group of NBC executives stood firmly behind Leno. Another group preferred replacing Leno to losing Letterman to CBS. In the end, NBC offered *The Tonight Show* to Letterman—but with the condition that he wait a year until Leno's current contract was up. David Letterman faced the most difficult decision of his life. Should he make up and stay with NBC or take a new path with CBS? In the end, he chose to leave.

The Letterman negotiations raise a number of questions. How well did Michael Ovitz do in squeezing the most out of CBS on behalf of Letterman? In its negotiations, what (if anything) could NBC have done differently to keep its star?

SIX STEPS TO DECISION MAKING

The examples just given represent the breadth of the decisions in managerial economics. Different as they may seem, each decision can be framed and analyzed using a common approach based on six steps, as Figure 1.1 indicates. With the examples as a backdrop, we will briefly outline each step. Later in the text, we will refer to these steps when analyzing managerial decisions.

Step 1: Define the Problem

What is the problem the manager faces? Who is the decision maker? What is the decision setting or context, and how does it influence managerial objectives or options?

Decisions do not occur in a vacuum. Many come about as part of the firm's planning process. Others are prompted by new opportunities or new problems. It is natural to ask, what brought about the need for the decision? What is the decision all about? In each of the examples given earlier, the decision problem is reasonably well defined. In practice, however, managerial decisions do not come so neatly packaged; rather, they are messy and poorly defined. Thus, problem definition is a prerequisite for problem management. In fact, the decision in the fourth example—the conversion of utilities to coal—raises interesting issues concerning problem definition. How narrowly does one define the problem? Is the crux of the problem minimizing pollution from utilities? Presumably,

FIGURE 1.1

The Basic Steps in Decision Making

The process of decision making can be broken down into six basic steps.

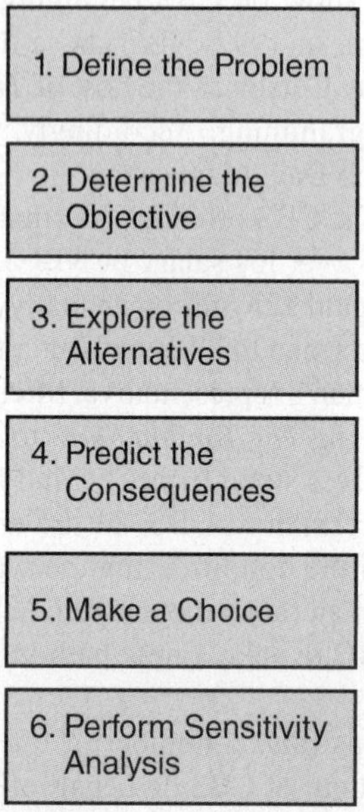

1. Define the Problem
2. Determine the Objective
3. Explore the Alternatives
4. Predict the Consequences
5. Make a Choice
6. Perform Sensitivity Analysis

cost is also important. Thus, the problem involves determining how much pollution to clean up, by what means, and at what cost. Or is the problem much broader: reducing US dependence on foreign energy sources? If so, which domestic energy initiatives (besides or instead of utility conversion to coal) should be undertaken?

A key part of problem definition involves identifying the context. The majority of the decisions we study take place in the private sector. Managers representing their respective firms are responsible for the decisions made in five of the examples. By contrast, the third and fourth examples occur in the public sector, where decisions are made at all levels of government: local, state, and national. The recommendation concerning construction of a new bridge is made by a city agency and must be approved by the state government. Similarly, the chain of decisions accompanying the conversion of utilities from oil to coal involves numerous public-sector authorities. As one might imagine, the larger the number of bodies that share policy responsibility and the pursuit of different goals, the greater is the likelihood that decision-making problems and conflicts will occur.

Step 2: Determine the Objective

What is the decision maker's goal? How should the decision maker value outcomes with respect to this goal? What if he or she is pursuing multiple, conflicting objectives?

When it comes to economic decisions, it is a truism that "you can't always get what you want."[2] But to make any progress at all in your choice, you have to know what you want. In most private-sector decisions, **profit** is the principal objective of the firm and the usual barometer of its performance. Thus, among alternative courses of action, the manager will select the one that will maximize the profit of the firm. Attainment of maximum profit worldwide is the natural objective of the multinational carmaker, the drug company, and the management and shareholders of Staples, Office Depot, Office Max, BP, NBC, and CBS.

The objective in a public-sector decision, whether building a bridge or regulating a utility, is broader than the private-sector profit standard. The government decision maker should weigh all benefits and costs, not solely revenues and expenses. According to this benefit-cost criterion, the bridge in the fourth example may be worth building even if it fails to generate a profit for the government authority. In turn, regulating the production decisions of the utility depends on a careful comparison of benefits (mainly in the form of energy conservation and independence) and costs (in dollar and environmental terms).

In practice, profit maximization and benefit–cost analysis are not always unambiguous guides to decision making. One difficulty is posed by the timing of benefits and costs. Should a firm (the drug company, for example) make an investment (sacrifice profits today) for greater profits 5 or 10 years from now? Are the future benefits to commuters worth the current capital expense of building the bridge? Both private and public investments involve trade-offs between present and future benefits and costs.

Uncertainty poses a second difficulty. In some economic decisions, risks are minimal. For instance, a fast-food chain might know that it can construct a new outlet in 75 days at a cost of $75 per square foot. The cost and timing of construction are not entirely certain, but the margin of error is small enough to be safely ignored. In contrast, the cost and date of completing a mammoth petrochemical plant are highly uncertain (due to unanticipated design changes, cost overruns, schedule delays, government regulations, and the like). At best, the plant owners may be able to estimate a range of cost outcomes and completion dates and assess probabilities for these possible outcomes.

The presence of risk and uncertainty has a direct bearing on the way the decision maker thinks about his or her objective. Both BP and the pharmaceutical company seek to maximize company profit, but there is no simple way to apply the profit criterion to determine their best actions and strategies. BP might pay $50 million to acquire a promising site it believes is worth $150 million and find, after thorough drilling and exploration, that the site is devoid of oil or natural gas. Similarly, the drug company cannot use the simple rule of "Choose the method that will yield the greater profit," because the ultimate profit from either method cannot be pinned down ahead of time. There are no profit guarantees; rather, the drug company faces a choice between two risky research options. Similarly, public programs and regulatory policies generate future benefits and costs that cannot be predicted with certainty.

---

[2]Many readers will recognize this quote as a lyric penned by Mick Jagger of the Rolling Stones. What many may not know is that Jagger briefly attended the London School of Economics before pursuing the path to rock stardom.

Step 3: Explore the Alternatives

What are the alternative courses of action? What are the variables under the decision maker's control? What constraints limit the choice of options?

After addressing the question, "What do we want?" it is natural to ask, "What are our options?" Given human limitations, decision makers cannot hope to identify and evaluate all possible options. Still, attractive options should not be overlooked or, if discovered, not mistakenly dismissed. Moreover, a sound decision framework should be able to uncover options in the course of the analysis.

In our examples, the main work of problem definition has already been carried out, greatly simplifying the identification of decision options. In the first example, the carmaker is free to set prices at home and abroad. These prices will largely determine the numbers of vehicles the firm can expect to sell in each market. It still remains for the firm to determine a production plan to supply its total projected sales; that is, the firm's other two decision variables are the quantities to produce in each facility. The firm's task is to find optimal values of these four decision variables—values that will generate a maximum level of profit.

In the other examples, the decision maker faces a choice from a relatively small number of alternatives. But even when the choices are limited, there may be more alternatives than first meet the eye. BP faces a myriad of choices as to how and where to explore for oil, how to manage its wells and refineries, and how to sell its petroleum products. Similarly, the utilities example illustrates the way in which options can multiply. There, the limitations and repercussions of the "obvious" alternatives lead to a wider consideration of other choices, which, unfortunately, have their own side effects.

The drug company might appear to have a simple either/or choice: pursue the biochemical R&D program or proceed with the biogenetic program. But there are other alternatives. For instance, the company could pursue both programs simultaneously. This strategy means investing resources and money in both but allows the firm to commercialize the superior program that emerges from the R&D competition.

Most managerial decisions involve more than a once-and-for-all choice from among a set of options. Typically, the manager faces a sequence of decisions from among alternatives. For instance, in the battle for David Letterman, each side had to formulate its current negotiation stance (in light of how much value it might expect to get out of alternative deals). How aggressive or conciliatory an offer should it make? How much can it expect the other side to concede? Thus, a commonly acknowledged fact about negotiation is that the main purpose of an opening offer is not to have the offer accepted (if it were, the offer probably was far too generous); rather, the offer should direct the course of the offers to follow. To sum up, in view of the myriad uncertainties facing managers, most ongoing decisions should best be viewed as *contingent* plans.

Step 4: Predict the Consequences

What are the consequences of each alternative action? Should conditions change, how would this affect outcomes? If outcomes are uncertain, what is the likelihood of each? Can better information be acquired to predict outcomes?

Depending on the situation, the task of predicting the consequences may be straight-forward or formidable. Sometimes elementary arithmetic suffices. For instance, the simplest profit calculation requires only subtracting costs from revenues. The choice between two safety programs might be made according to which saves the greater number of lives per dollar expended. Here the use of arithmetic division is the key to identifying the preferred alternative.

In more complicated situations, however, the decision maker often must rely on a model to describe how options translate into outcomes. A **model** is a simplified description of a process, relationship, or other phenomenon. By deliberate intent, a model focuses on a few key features of a problem to examine carefully how they work while ignoring other complicating and less important factors. The main purposes of models are to explain and to predict—to account for past outcomes and to forecast future ones.

The kinds of predictive models are as varied as the decision problems to which they are applied. Many models rest on economic relationships. Suppose the multinational carmaker predicts that a 10 percent price cut will increase unit sales by 15 percent in the foreign market. The basis for this prediction is the most fundamental relationship in economics: the demand curve. Staples' decision of when and how to enter a new market depends on predictions of demand and cost and of how its rivals might be expected to respond. These elements may be captured with a model of competitive behavior among oligopolists.

Other models rest on statistical, legal, and scientific relationships. The construction and configuration of the new bridge (and its likely environmental impact) and the plan to convert utilities to coal depend in large part on engineering predictions. Evaluations of test-marketing results rely heavily on statistical models. Legal models, interpretations of statutes, precedents, and the like are pertinent to predictions of a firm's potential patent liability and to the outcome in other legal disputes. Finally, the drug company's assessment of the relative merits of competing R&D methods rests on scientific and biological models.

A key distinction can be drawn between deterministic and probabilistic models. A **deterministic model** is one in which the outcome is certain (or close enough to a sure thing that it can be taken as certain). For instance, a soft-drink manufacturer may wish to predict the numbers of individuals in the 10-to-25 age group over the next five years. There are ample demographic statistics with which to make this prediction. Obviously, the numbers in this age group five years from now will consist of those who today are between ages 5 and 20, minus a predictable small number of deaths. Thus, a simple deterministic model suffices for the prediction. However, the forecast becomes much less certain when it comes to estimating the total consumption of soft drinks by this age group or the market share of a particular product brand. The share of a particular drink will depend on many unpredictable factors, including the advertising, promotion, and price decisions of the firm and its competitors, as well as consumer preferences. As the term suggests, a **probabilistic model** accounts for a range of possible future outcomes, each with a probability attached.

Step 5: Make a Choice

After all the analysis is done, what is the preferred course of action? For obvious reasons, this step (along with step 4) occupies the lion's share of the analysis and discussion in this book. Once the decision maker has put the problem in context, formalized key objectives, and identified available alternatives, how does he or she go about finding a preferred course of action?

In the majority of decisions we take up, the objectives and outcomes are directly quantifiable. Thus, a private firm (such as the carmaker) can compute the profit results of alternative price and output plans. Analogously, a government decision maker may know the computed net benefits (benefits minus costs) of different program options. The decision maker could determine a preferred course of action by **enumeration**, that is, by testing a number of alternatives and selecting the one that best meets the objective. This is fine for decisions involving a small number of choices, but it is impractical for more complex problems. For instance, what if the car company drew up a list of two dozen different pricing and production plans, computed the profits of each, and settled on the best of the lot? How could management be sure this choice is truly the best of all possible plans? What if a more profitable plan, say, the twenty-fifth candidate, was overlooked? Expanding the enumerated list could reduce this risk, but at considerable cost.

Fortunately, the decision maker need not rely on the painstaking method of enumeration to solve such problems. A variety of methods can identify and cut directly to the best, or **optimal**, decision. These methods rely to varying extents on marginal analysis, decision trees, game theory, benefit–cost analysis, and linear programming, all of which we take up later in this book. These approaches are important not only for computing optimal decisions but also for checking why they are optimal.

Step 6: Perform Sensitivity Analysis

What features of the problem determine the optimal choice of action? How does the optimal decision change if conditions in the problem are altered? Is the choice sensitive to key economic variables about which the decision maker is uncertain?

In tackling and solving a decision problem, it is important to understand and be able to explain to others the "why" of your decision. The solution, after all, did not come out of thin air. It depended on your stated objectives, the way you structured the problem (including the set of options you considered), and your method of predicting outcomes. Thus, **sensitivity analysis** considers how an optimal decision is affected if key economic facts or conditions vary.

Here is a simple example of the use of sensitivity analysis. Senior management of a consumer products firm is conducting a third-year review of one of its new products. Two of the firm's business economists have prepared an extensive report that projects significant profits from the product over the next two years. These profit estimates suggest a clear course of action: Continue marketing the product. As a member of senior management, would you accept this recommendation uncritically? Probably not. After all, you may be well aware that the product has not yet earned a profit in its first two years. (Although it sold reasonably well, it also had high advertising and promotion costs and a low introductory price.) What lies behind the new profit projection? Greater sales, a higher price, or both? A significant cost reduction? The process of tracking down the basic determinants of profit is a key aspect of sensitivity analysis.[3]

These decision steps offer a guide. In actual practice, how well do individuals and business people do in analyzing and making decisions? Much of economic analysis is built on a description of ultra-rational self-interested individuals and profit-maximizing businesses. While this framework does an admirable job of describing many of the decisions occurring in markets and within organizations, we all know that real-world human behavior is much more complicated than this. The ultra-rational analyzer and calculator (e.g., Mr. Spock of *Star Trek*) is an extreme type, a caricature.

Behavioral Economics

Over the last 25 years, research in behavioral economics has shown that beyond economic motives, human actions and decisions are shaped by psychological factors, cognitive constraints, and altruistic and cooperative motives.[4] For instance, credit card use encourages extra spending because it is psychologically less painful to pay on credit than to part with cold cash. Many of us, whether age 25 or 55, lack the foresight, self-control, and financial acumen to plan for and save enough for retirement. And not all our actions are governed by dollars and cents. I'm happy to snow-blow the driveway of the elderly widow next door (because it is the right thing to do), and she is happy to look after my kids in a pinch. Neighbors help neighbors; altruism and reciprocity are the norm alongside everyday monetary transactions.

Twin lessons emerge from behavioral economics. On the one hand, personal and business decisions are frequently marked by biases, mistakes, and pitfalls. We're not as smart or as efficient as we think we are. On the other, decision makers can gain from their experience, learn from their mistakes, benefit from thoughtful analysis—all of which make for better decision making.

PRIVATE AND PUBLIC DECISIONS: AN ECONOMIC VIEW

Our approach to managerial economics is based on a model of the firm: how firms behave and what objectives they pursue. The main tenet of this model, or **theory of the firm,** is that management strives to maximize the firm's profits. This objective is unambiguous for decisions involving predictable revenues and costs occurring during the same period of time. However, a more precise profit criterion is needed when a firm's

---

[3]Sensitivity analysis is also invaluable in testing the effects of uncertainty. Management should recognize that the revenue and cost projections of its consumer product are highly uncertain. Accordingly, it should investigate the profit effects if outcomes differ from the report's forecasts. What if sales are 12 percent lower than expected? What if projected cost reductions are not realized? What if the price of a competing product is slashed? By answering these what-if questions, management can determine the degree to which its profit projections are sensitive to the uncertain outcomes of key economic variables.

[4]For a discussion of behavioral economics, see D. Kahneman, "Maps of Bounded Rationality: Psychology for Behavioral Economics," *The American Economic Review* (September 2003): pp. 1,449-1,475; and D. Brooks, "The Nudge Debate," *The New York Times*, August 9, 2013, p. A19.

revenues and costs are uncertain and accrue at different times in the future. The most general theory of the firm states that

❙ Management's primary goal is to maximize the value of the firm. ❙

Here, the firm's value is defined as the present value of its expected future profits. Thus, in making any decision, the manager must attempt to predict its impact on future profit flows and determine whether, indeed, it will add to the value of the firm.

Business Behavior Maximizing Value

Value maximization is a compelling *prescription* concerning how managerial decisions *should* be made. Although this tenet is a useful norm in describing actual managerial behavior, it is not a perfect yardstick. After all, large-scale firms consist of many levels of authority and myriad decision makers. Even if value maximization is the ultimate corporate goal, actual decision making within this complex organization may look quite different. There are several reasons for this:

1. Managers may have individual incentives (such as job security, career advancement, increasing a division's budget, resources, power) that are at odds with value maximization of the total firm. For instance, it sometimes is claimed that company executives are apt to focus on short-term value maximization (increasing next year's earnings) at the expense of long-run firm value.

2. Managers may lack the information (or fail to carry out the analysis) necessary for value-maximizing decisions.

3. Managers may formulate but fail to implement optimal decisions.

Although value maximization is the standard assumption in managerial economics, three other decision models should be noted. The model of **satisficing** behavior posits that the typical firm strives for a satisfactory level of performance rather than attempting to maximize its objective. Thus, a firm might aspire to a level of annual profit, say $40 million, and be satisfied with policies that achieve this benchmark. More generally, the firm may seek to achieve acceptable levels of performance with respect to multiple objectives (profitability being only one such objective).

A second behavioral model posits that the firm attempts to **maximize total sales** subject to achieving an acceptable level of profit. Total dollar sales are a visible benchmark of managerial success. For instance, the business press puts particular emphasis on the firm's sales revenue and market share.[5] In addition, a variety of studies show a close link between executive compensation and company sales. Thus, top management's self-interest sometimes lies as much in sales maximization as in value maximization.

A third issue centers on the **social responsibility of business**. In modern capitalist economies, business firms contribute significantly to economic welfare. Within free markets, firms compete to supply the goods and services that consumers demand. Pursuing the profit motive, they constantly strive to produce goods of higher quality

---

[5]Business analysts sometimes claim that raising the firm's current market share is the best prescription for increasing long-run profitability. In particular circumstances (for instance, when learning-curve effects are important), share increases may indeed promote profitability. But this does not mean that the firm's ultimate objective is gaining market share. Rather, gaining market share remains a means toward the firm's ultimate end: maximum value.

at lower costs. By investing in research and development and pursuing technological innovation, they endeavor to create new and improved goods and services. In the large majority of cases, the economic actions of firms (spurred by the profit motive) promote social welfare as well: business production contributes to economic growth, provides widespread employment, and raises standards of living.

The objective of value maximization implies that management's primary responsibility is to the firm's shareholders. But the firm has other stakeholders as well: its customers, its workers, even the local community to which it might pay taxes. This observation raises an important question: To what extent might management decisions be influenced by the likely effects of its actions on these parties? For instance, suppose management believes that downsizing its workforce is necessary to increase profitability. Should it uncompromisingly pursue maximum profits even if this significantly increases unemployment? Alternatively, suppose that because of weakened international competition, the firm has the opportunity to profit by significantly raising prices. Should it do so? Finally, suppose that the firm could dramatically cut its production costs with the side effect of generating a modest amount of pollution. How should it weigh such adverse environmental side effects?

All of these examples suggest potential trade-offs between value maximization and other possible objectives and social values. Thus, there are circumstances in which business leaders choose to pursue other objectives at the expense of some forgone profits. For instance, management might decide that retaining 100 jobs at a regional factory is worth a modest reduction in profit. To sum up, value maximization is not the only model of managerial behavior. Nonetheless, the available evidence suggests that it offers the best description of a private firm's ultimate objectives and actions.

Over the last decade, in response to growing international outcries, major American and European pharmaceutical companies have dramatically reduced the prices of AIDS drugs in Africa. Drug companies such as Abbott Laboratories, Bristol-Myers Squibb Co., GlaxoSmithKline PLC, and Merck & Co. have variously pledged to cut prices by 50 percent or more, sell the drugs at or below cost, or in some cases even supply the drugs for free.[6] In 2005, Glaxo offered its powerful cocktail of AIDS drugs at a price of $1,300 per year in Africa (whereas the price was greater than $11,000 in the United States). Since then, there have been further rounds of price cuts.

Lower Drug Prices in Africa

The problem of health and disease in the developing world presents a stark conflict between the private profit motive and social welfare. The outbreak of disease in sub-Saharan Africa is considered to be the world's number one health problem. Some 30 million African inhabitants are infected with HIV, the virus that causes AIDS. Millions of others suffer from a host of tropical diseases including malaria, river blindness, and sleeping sickness. Over the last decade, such groups as the World Health Organization, Doctors without Borders, and national governments of developing countries have argued for low

[6]This account is based on many published reports including, G. Harris and K. Thomas, "Low-Cost Drugs in Poor Nations Get a Lift in Indian Court," *The New York Times*, April 2, 2013, p. A1; J. Whelan, "Glaxo Cuts Price of HIV Drugs for World's Poorest Countries," *The Wall Street Journal*, February 20, 2008, p. D7; "A Gathering Storm," *The Economist*, June 9, 2007, p. 71; "Aids: The End of the Beginning?" *The Economist*, July 17, 2004, p. 76.

drug prices and abundant drug supplies to deliver the greatest possible health benefits. However, global pharmaceutical companies have little profit incentive to invest in drugs for tropical diseases since those afflicted are too poor to pay for the drugs. Given the enormous R&D costs (not to mention marketing costs) of commercializing new drugs, multinational companies maximize their profits by selling drugs at high prices to high-income nations.

What accounts for the dramatic change in the drug companies' position since the turn of the millennium? Pharmaceutical executives professed their willingness to cut prices and therefore sacrifice profit only after being convinced of the magnitude of Africa's health problem. In addition, the "voluntary" cuts in drug prices were spurred by two other factors. First was the competitive threat of two Indian companies that already were promoting and selling generic (copycat) versions of a host of AIDS drugs and other drugs in Africa. Second, several national governments, notably South Africa, Thailand, and Brazil, have threatened to revoke or ignore drug patents. (From the 1970s to the present, the Indian government has refused to acknowledge international drug patents.) In return for the companies' price concessions, the World Health Organization has reaffirmed the validity of the companies' patents. The major multinational drug companies seem willing to make targeted price cuts (they are unwilling to cut prices for the poor in industrial economies) in return for patent assurances.

The ultimate solution for the health crisis in developing nations will require additional initiatives such as (1) resources for more doctors and hospitals as well as for disease prevention and drug distribution, (2) improved economic conditions, education, and in many regions the end of civil war, and (3) monetary aid from world health organizations and foreign governments.

Public Decisions

In government decisions, the question of objectives is much broader than simply an assessment of profit. The purpose of public decisions is to promote the welfare of society, where the term *society* is meant to include all the people whose interests are affected when a particular decision is made. However, difficulties arise because inevitably some groups will gain and others will lose from any public decision. In our earlier example of the bridge, businesses and commuters in the region can expect to gain, but nearby neighbors who suffer extra traffic, noise, and exhaust emissions will lose. The program to convert utilities from oil to coal will benefit the nation by reducing our dependence on foreign oil. However, it will increase many utilities' costs of producing electricity, which will mean higher electric bills for many residents. The accompanying air pollution will bring adverse health and aesthetic effects in urban areas. Strip mining has its own economic costs and environmental risks, as does nuclear power. In short, any significant government program will bring a variety of new benefits and costs to different affected groups.

The important question is: How do we weigh these benefits and costs to make a decision that is best for society as a whole? One answer is provided by benefit-cost analysis, the principal analytical framework used in guiding public decisions. **Benefit-cost analysis** begins with the systematic enumeration of all of the potential benefits and costs of a particular public decision. It goes on to measure or estimate the dollar magnitudes of these benefits and costs. Finally, it follows the decision rule: Undertake the project or program if and only if its total benefits exceed its total costs. Benefit-cost analysis is similar to the profit calculation of the private firm with one key difference: Whereas the firm considers only the revenue it accrues and the cost it incurs, public decisions account for all benefits—whether or not recipients pay for them (i.e., regardless of whether revenue is generated)—and all costs (direct and indirect).

THINGS TO COME

Figure 1.2 presents a schematic diagram of the topics and decision settings to come. As the figure indicates, the central focus of managerial economics is the private firm and how it should go about maximizing its profit. Chapters 2 and 3 begin the analysis by presenting a basic model of the firm and considering the case of profit maximization *under certainty—* that is, under the assumption that revenues and costs can be predicted perfectly. Specifically, the chapters show how the firm can apply the logic of marginal analysis to determine

FIGURE 1.2

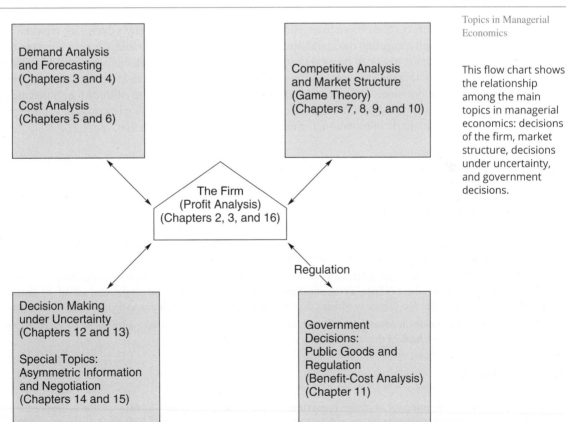

Topics in Managerial Economics

This flow chart shows the relationship among the main topics in managerial economics: decisions of the firm, market structure, decisions under uncertainty, and government decisions.

Demand Analysis and Forecasting (Chapters 3 and 4)

Cost Analysis (Chapters 5 and 6)

Competitive Analysis and Market Structure (Game Theory) (Chapters 7, 8, 9, and 10)

The Firm (Profit Analysis) (Chapters 2, 3, and 16)

Regulation

Decision Making under Uncertainty (Chapters 12 and 13)

Special Topics: Asymmetric Information and Negotiation (Chapters 14 and 15)

Government Decisions: Public Goods and Regulation (Benefit-Cost Analysis) (Chapter 11)

optimal outputs and prices. Chapters 3 and 4 present an in-depth study of demand analysis and forecasting. Chapters 5 and 6 present analogous treatments of production and cost. The firm's resource allocations using linear programming are deferred to Chapter 16.

Chapters 7 through 11 focus on market structure and competitive analysis and constitute the second major section of the text. This discussion stresses a key point: The firm does not maximize profit in a vacuum; rather, the market environment it inhabits has a profound influence on its output, pricing, and profitability. Chapters 7 and 8 present overviews of perfect competition and pure monopoly, while Chapter 9 examines the case of oligopoly and provides a rich treatment of competitive strategy. Chapter 10 applies the discipline of game theory to analyze strategic behavior.

Chapter 11 considers the regulation of private markets and government provision of goods and services. These topics are particularly important in light of the divergent views of government held by the person on the street. Some see government as the essential engine to promote social welfare and to check private greed. Others call for "less" government, insisting that "for every action, there is an equal and opposite government regulation." Our discussion focuses on the discipline of benefit-cost analysis to help evaluate how well government programs and regulations function.

Chapters 12 and 13 extend the core study of management decisions by incorporating risk and uncertainty. Managerial success increasingly depends on taking calculated risks. Managers must strive to envision the future outcomes of today's decisions, measure and weigh competing risks, and determine which risks are acceptable. Chapter 12 shows how decision trees can be used to structure decisions in high-risk environments. Chapter 13 examines the value of acquiring information about relevant risks prior to making important decisions. Chapters 14 and 15 present thorough analyses of three topics that are on the cutting edge of managerial economics and are of increasing importance to managers: asymmetric information, organizational design, and negotiation.

SUMMARY

Decision-Making Principles

1. Decision making lies at the heart of most important problems managers face. Managerial economics applies the principles of economics to analyze business and government decisions.

2. The prescription for sound managerial decisions involves six steps: (1) Define the problem; (2) determine the objective; (3) explore the alternatives; (4) predict the consequences; (5) make a choice; and (6) perform sensitivity analysis. This framework is flexible. The degree to which a decision is analyzed is itself a choice to be made by the manager.

3. Experience, judgment, common sense, intuition, and rules of thumb all make potential contributions to the decision-making process. However, none of these can take the place of a sound analysis.

Nuts and Bolts

1. In the private sector, the principal objective is maximizing the value of the firm. The firm's value is the present value of its expected future profits. In the public sector, government programs and projects are evaluated on the basis of net social benefit, the difference between total benefits and costs of all kinds. According to the criterion

of benefit-cost analysis, a public program should be undertaken if and only if its total dollar benefits exceed its total dollar costs.

2. Models offer simplified descriptions of a process or relationship. Models are essential for explaining past phenomena and for generating forecasts of the future. Deterministic models take the predicted outcome as certain. Probabilistic models identify a range of possible outcomes with probabilities attached.

3. Besides maximizing the value of the firm, other management goals sometimes include maximizing sales or taking actions in the interests of stakeholders (its workers, customers, neighbors).

4. Sensitivity analysis considers how an optimal decision would change if key economic facts or conditions are altered.

Questions and Problems

1. What is managerial economics? What role does it play in shaping business decisions?

2. Management sometimes is described as the art and science of making decisions with too little information. What kinds of additional information would a manager want in the seven examples cited in the chapter?

3. Suppose a soft-drink firm is grappling with the decision about whether to market a new carbonated beverage with 25 percent real fruit juice. How might it use the six decision steps to guide its course of action?

4. Listed here are several examples of bad, or at least questionable, decisions. Evaluate the decision maker's approach or logic. In which of the six decision steps might the decision maker have gone wrong?
   a. Mr. and Mrs. A recently bought a house, the very first one they viewed.
   b. Firm B has invested five years and $6 million in developing a new product. Even now, it is not clear whether the product can compete profitably in the market. Nonetheless, top management decides to commercialize it so that the development cost will not be wasted.
   c. You are traveling on a highway with two traffic lanes in each direction. Usually traffic flows smoothly, but tonight traffic moving in your direction is backed up for half a mile. After crawling for 15 minutes, you reach the source of the tie-up: a mattress is lying on the road, blocking one lane. Like other motorists before you, you shrug and drive on.
   d. The sedative thalidomide was withdrawn from drug markets in 1962 only after it was found to be the cause of over 10,000 birth defects worldwide, many of which resulted in death. (An exception was the United States, where the use of thalidomide was severely restricted.)
   e. A couple, nervous about boarding their airline flight on time, patiently wait together in one of three baggage check-in lines.
   f. While devoting himself to successfully leading his company, the CEO's marriage broke up.
   g. Each year, State F allocates $400,000 to provide special ambulance service for heart attack victims and $1,200,000 for improvements in highway safety (better lighting, grading, and the like). The former program saves an estimated 20 lives per year; the latter saves 40 lives. Recently, the ambulance budget was cut by 40 percent, and the highway safety budget increased by 10 percent.
   h. In August 2001, the Federal Emergency Management Agency judged the two likeliest natural catastrophes to be a massive earthquake in San Francisco and a hurricane in New Orleans causing its levees to be breached. In August 2005, Hurricane Katrina struck New Orleans, flooding the city and causing an estimated $125 billion in economic damage.
   i. "After 9/11, to do nothing would constitute an abject surrender to terrorism. On the other hand, the United States cannot fight multiple wars against terrorist factions everywhere in the world. The only sane alternative, then, is to identify and stop terrorists from operating in the United States, even if this means sacrificing certain civil liberties."
   j. Mr. G is debating how to spend his summer vacation. Should he spend a quiet week at home, go to the beach, or go to the mountains, where his parents and several other relatives live? Unable to make up his mind, he decides to list the pros and cons of each option. The points he cares about are (1) relaxation and quiet, (2) some exercise, and (3) seeing family and old friends. With respect to these points, he ranks the alternatives as shown in the table:

	Relaxation	Exercise	Family/Friends
Home	1st	3rd	2nd
Beach	2nd	1st	3rd
Mountains	3rd	2nd	1st

Now he is ready to compare the options. Which is his better choice: home or beach? Since home ranks higher than beach on two of the three points, he gives it two pros and one con and judges it the better choice. What about home versus mountains? Mountains versus beach?

Discussion Question   A town planning board must decide how to deal with the Kendall Elementary School building. Twenty years ago, the Kendall school (one of four in the town) was closed due to falling enrollment. For the last 20 years, the town has rented 60 percent of the building space to a nonprofit organization that offers classes in the creative and performing arts. The group's lease is up, and now the board is mulling other options:

a. Renew the current lease agreement. This will generate a small but steady cash flow and free the town of building maintenance expenses (which under the lease are the tenant's responsibility).
b. Renegotiate the lease and solicit other tenants.
c. Use the building for needed additional town office space. (A minimal conversion would allow reconversion to a school in 5 to 10 years, when the elementary school population is expected to swell.)
d. Sell the building to a private developer, if one can be found.
e. Convert the building to condominiums to be sold by the town.
f. Raze the building and sell the site and all or part of the surrounding playing fields as building lots (from 6 to 12 lots, depending on how much land is sold).

Apply the six decision-making steps presented in the chapter to the town's decision. What objectives might the town pursue in making its decision? What additional information would the planning board need in carrying out the various steps? What kind of analysis might the board undertake?

Suggested References

A number of valuable references chart different approaches to analyzing and making decisions.

Bazerman, M., and D. Moore. *Judgment in Managerial Decision Making,* Chapters 1 and 9. New York: John Wiley & Sons, 2013.

Belsky, G., and T. Gilovich. *Why Smart People Make Big Money Mistakes and How to Correct Them.* New York: Simon & Schuster, 2000.

Kahneman, D., *Thinking Fast and Slow.* New York: Farrar, Straus, and Giroux, 2011.

Russo, J. E., M. Hittleman, and P. J. Schoemaker. *Winning Decisions.* New York: Bantam Dell Publishers, 2001.

For a comprehensive Web site about economics, firms, markets, government regulation, and much more (with links to many other sites), see: http://economics.about.com.

C H A P T E R 2

Optimal Decisions Using Marginal Analysis

Government and business leaders should pursue the path to new programs and policies the way a climber ascends a formidable mountain or the way a soldier makes his way through a mine field: with small and very careful steps.

ANONYMOUS

LO#1. Explain how—in a simple model of profit maximization—revenues and costs depend on price and output decisions.

LO#2. Describe how marginal analysis looks at the change in profit that results from making a small change in a decision variable.

LO#3. Discuss the concepts of marginal revenue and marginal cost.

LO#4. Understand the use of marginal revenue and marginal cost in sensitivity analysis.

Conflict in Fast-Food Franchising[1]

The rapid growth in franchising during the last three decades can be explained in large part by the mutual benefits the franchising partners receive. The franchiser (parent company) increases sales via an ever-expanding network of franchisees. The parent collects a fixed percentage of the revenue each franchise earns (as high as 15 to 20 percent, depending on the contract terms). The individual franchisee benefits from the acquired know-how of the parent, from the parent's advertising and promotional support, and from the ability to sell a well-established product or service. Nonetheless, economic conflicts frequently arise between the parent and an individual franchisee. Disputes even occur in the loftiest of franchising realms: the fast-food industry. For some two decades, there have been ongoing conflicts between franchise operators and parent management of McDonald's, Subway, and Burger King, among others.

These conflicts have centered on a number of recurring issues. First, the parent insists on periodic remodeling of the premises; the franchisee resists. Second, the franchisee favors raising prices on best-selling items; the parent opposes the change and wants to expand promotional discounts. Third, the parent seeks longer store hours and multiple express lines to cut down on lunchtime congestion; many franchisees resist both moves.

---

[1]We begin this and the remaining chapters by presenting a managerial decision. Your first job is to familiarize yourself with the manager's problem. As you read the chapter, think about how the principles presented could be applied to this decision. At the chapter's conclusion, we revisit the problem and discuss possible solutions.

How does one explain these conflicts? What is their economic source? What can the parent and the franchisee do to promote cooperation? At the conclusion of the chapter, we will revisit the franchising setting and offer explanations for these conflicts.

This chapter introduces the analysis of managerial decision making that will occupy us for the remainder of the book. The focus is on two main topics. The first is a simple economic model (i.e., a description) of the private, profit-maximizing firm. The second is an introduction to marginal analysis, an important tool for arriving at optimal decisions. Indeed, it is fair to say that the subsequent chapters provide extensions or variations on these two themes. The present chapter employs marginal analysis as a guide to output and pricing decisions in the case of a single product line under the simplest demand and cost conditions. In Chapters 3 and 4, we extend marginal analysis to the cases of complex demand conditions, multiple markets, and price discrimination. In Chapters 5 and 6, we apply the same approach to settings that involve more complicated production technologies and cost conditions, multiple production facilities, and multiple products. In Chapters 7, 8, and 9, we analyze the key market environments—competition, oligopoly, and monopoly—in which the profit-maximizing firm operates. Together, these chapters demonstrate the great power of marginal analysis as a tool for solving complex decisions. Consequently, it is important to master the logic of marginal analysis at the outset.

A SIMPLE MODEL

The decision setting we will investigate can be described as follows:

1. A firm produces a single good or service for a single market with the objective of maximizing profit.
2. Its task is to determine the quantity of the good to produce and sell and to set a sales price.
3. The firm can predict the revenue and cost consequences of its price and output decisions with certainty. (We will deal with uncertainty in Chapters 12 and 13.)

Together, these three statements fulfill the first four fundamental decision-making steps described in Chapter 1. Statement 1 specifies the problem and objective. Statement 2 lays out the firm's possible decision alternatives. Statement 3 (along with some specific quantitative information supplied shortly) links the actions and the ultimate objective—that is, the consequences, namely, profit. It remains for the firm's manager to choose the "solution" and explore this decision problem using marginal analysis as well as sensitivity analysis (steps 5 and 6).

Before turning to this task, note the simplifying facts embodied in statement 1. Typically, a firm produces a variety of goods or services. Nonetheless, even for the multi-product firm, examining products one at a time has significant decision advantages. For one thing, it constitutes an efficient managerial division of labor. Thus, multiproduct firms, such as Procter & Gamble, assign product managers to specific consumer products. A product manager is responsible for charting the future of the brand (pricing, advertising, promotion, and production policies). Similarly, most large companies make profit-maximizing decisions along product lines. This product-by-product strategy is feasible and appropriate as long as the revenues and costs of the firm's products are independent of one another. (As we shall see in Chapters 3 and 6, things become more complicated if actions taken with respect to one product affect the revenues or costs, or both, of the firm's other products.) In short, the firm can maximize its total profit by separately maximizing the profit derived from each of its product lines.

A Microchip Manufacturer

Here, as a motivating example, let's consider a firm that produces and sells a highly sophisticated microchip. The firm's main problem is to determine the quantity of chips to produce and sell (now and in the immediate future) and the price. To tackle this problem, we begin by examining the manager's basic objective: profit. A simple accounting identity states that profit is the difference between revenue and cost. In algebraic terms, we have $\pi = R - C$, where the Greek letter pi (π) stands for profit. To see how profit depends on the firm's price and output decisions, let's examine the revenue and cost components in turn.

REVENUE   The analysis of revenue rests on the most basic empirical relationship in economics: the law of demand. This law states:

All other factors held constant, the higher the unit price of a good, the fewer the number of units demanded by consumers and, consequently, sold by firms.

The law of demand operates at several levels. Consider the microchip industry as a whole, consisting of the manufacturer in question and a half-dozen major competitors. Suppose the leading firms raise their chip prices due to the increased cost of silicon. According to the law of demand, the industry's total sales of chips will fall. Of course, the law applies equally to a single chip manufacturer. An individual firm competes directly or indirectly with the other leading suppliers selling similar chips.

Let's suppose that currently there is a stable pattern of (different) prices and market shares for the leading firms in the industry. Consider what would happen if *one* of the firms unilaterally instituted a significant reduction in the price of its chips. The law of demand predicts that its microchip sales would increase. The sources of the increase are threefold: (1) increased sales to the firm's current customers; (2) sales gained from rival firms; and (3) sales to new buyers. Of course, each of these factors might be important to a greater or lesser degree.

Figure 2.1 illustrates the law of demand by depicting the individual firm's downward-sloping **demand curve**. The horizontal axis lists the quantity of microchips demanded by customers and sold by the firm each week. The quantity of chips is measured in lots consisting of 100 chips. The vertical axis lists the price per lot (measured in thousands of dollars) charged by the firm. Three particular points along the downward-sloping demand curve are noted. Point A corresponds to a quantity of 2 lots and a price of $130 thousand; this means that if the firm charges $130 thousand per lot, its weekly sales will be 2 lots (or 200 chips). If the firm cut its price to $100 thousand, its sales would increase to 3.5 lots (point B). A dramatic reduction to a price of $50 thousand would increase sales to 6 lots (point C). Thus, the demand curve shows the firm's predicted sales over a range of possible prices. The downward slope of the curve embodies the law of demand: A lower price brings forth an increased quantity of sales.

Demand curves and demand equations have a wide variety of uses in economics. Predicting the profit consequences of selective fare discounts by airlines, the impact of higher gasoline prices on automobile travel, and the effect of government day-care subsidies for working mothers all require the use of demand curves. The properties of demand curves and the ways of estimating demand equations are important topics in Chapters 3 and 4. At present, we will focus on the firm's main use of the demand relationship:

> The firm uses the demand curve as the basis for predicting the revenue consequences of alternative output and pricing policies.

The demand curve allows the firm to predict its quantity of sales for any price it charges. In turn, revenue can be computed as the product of price and quantity. The most useful way to begin the revenue estimation task is to work with the mathematical representation of the demand curve. An algebraic representation of the demand curve in Figure 2.1 is

$$Q = 8.5 - .05P, \qquad [2.1]$$

where Q is the quantity of lots demanded per week and P denotes the price per lot (in thousands of dollars). In this form, the demand equation predicts the quantity of microchips sold at any given price. For instance, if P equals $50 thousand, then, according to Equation 2.1, $Q = 8.5 - (.05)(50) = 6$ lots after substituting 50 for P in Equation 2.1. (The combination of $P = $50 thousand and $Q = 6$ lots corresponds to point C in the figure.) If P equals $130 thousand, Q equals 2 lots, and so on. *For any price the firm charges, the demand equation predicts the resulting quantity of the good that will be sold.* Setting different prices and computing the respective quantities traces out the demand curve in Figure 2.1.

With a bit of algebraic rearrangement, we can derive an equivalent version of Equation 2.1, namely,

$$P = 170 - 20Q. \qquad [2.2]$$

Here, we have isolated P on the left side of the equation. This equation generates exactly the same price-quantity pairs as Equation 2.1; thus, the two equations are equivalent. The only difference is the variable chosen for placement on the left-hand side. Note the interpretation of Equation 2.2. For any quantity of microchips the firm plans to sell, Equation 2.2 indicates the price needed to sell exactly this quantity. For instance, setting $Q = 3.5$ lots in Equation 2.2, we find that P equals $100 thousand (point B in Figure 2.2). This price equation usually is referred to as the firm's *inverse demand equation.*[2]

---

[2] An important special case occurs when the firm produces for a perfectly competitive market. (An extensive discussion appears in Chapter 7.) There the firm faces a horizontal demand curve instead of a downward-sloping curve. For example, suppose the inverse demand equation is $P = 170$. The firm can sell as much or as little output as it wishes at $170 thousand per lot, the competitive price, and its level of output will have no effect on this price.

FIGURE 2.1

The Demand Curve
for Microchips

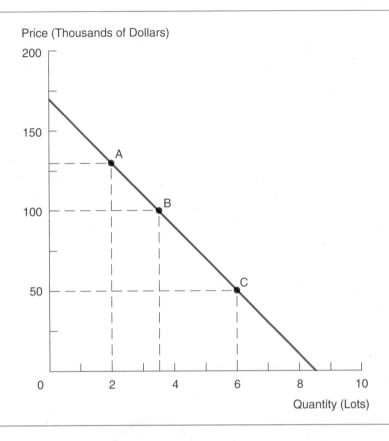

Price (Thousands of Dollars)

The demand curve
shows the total
number of micro-
chips that will be
demanded (i.e.,
purchased) by buyers
at different prices.

Quantity (Lots)

Equation 2.1 (or the equivalent, Equation 2.2) contains all the information the firm needs to predict revenue. However, before launching into the revenue analysis, we should pause to make two points. First, the demand equation furnishes a quantitative snapshot of the *current* demand for the firm's product as it depends on price. Of course, many other factors, including competing firms' products and prices and the general strength of the computer industry, affect the firm's chip sales. The demand prediction of Equation 2.1 is based on the current state of these factors. If economic conditions change, so too will the firm's sales at any given price; that is, Equation 2.1 would no longer be a valid representation of the new demand conditions. Throughout this discussion, our use of the demand equation takes other demand-relevant factors as *given,* that is, unchanged. (Chapters 3 and 9 take up the effects of changing market conditions and competitor behavior on a firm's demand.)

The second point is that we view the demand curve as **deterministic***;* that is, at any given price, the quantity sold can be predicted with certainty. For a given price, Equation 2.1 furnishes a precise sales quantity. Conversely, for any targeted sales quantity, Equation 2.2 provides a precise market-clearing price. We acknowledge that such certainty is hardly the norm in the real world. Nonetheless, the demand equation representation remains valid as long as the margin of error in the price–quantity relationship is relatively small. To become comfortable with the demand equations, think of a product with a long and stable history, allowing sales predictions to be made with very little error. (A deterministic demand equation would be inappropriate in the case of a new product launch. Other methods, discussed in Chapters 12 and 13, would be used to provide probability forecasts of possible sales levels.)

Let's use Equation 2.2 to predict the revenues generated by alternative sales policies of the microchip manufacturer. Figure 2.2 contains the pertinent information and provides a graph of revenue. Column 1 of the tabular portion lists a spectrum of possible sales quantities ranging from 0 to 8.5 lots. It will be convenient to think of the sales quantity, Q, as the firm's decision variable, that is, the variable it explicitly chooses. For each alternative choice of Q, column 2 lists the corresponding sales price obtained from Equation 2.2. (Be sure you understand that the firm *cannot* set both Q and P independently. Once one is set, the other is determined by the forces of demand embodied in the demand equation.) Finally, column 3 lists the resulting revenue earned by the firm, where revenue is defined as follows:

$$R = P \cdot Q.$$

From the table, we observe that revenue is zero when sales are zero (obviously). Then as Q increases, revenue initially rises, peaks, and eventually begins to fall, finally falling

FIGURE 2.2

Revenue from Microchips

The table and graph show the amount of total revenue the firm will earn for different quantities of microchips that it sells.

Quantity (Lots)	Price ($000s)	Revenue ($000s)
0.0	170	0
1.0	150	150
2.0	130	260
3.0	110	330
4.0	90	360
5.0	70	350
6.0	50	300
7.0	30	210
8.0	10	80
8.5	0	0

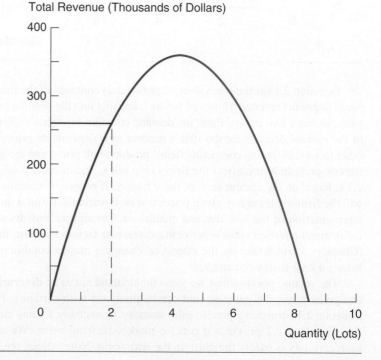

to zero at $Q = 8.5$ lots. (Note that to sell 8.5 lots, the requisite sales price from Equation 2.2 is zero; that is, the lots would have to be given away.) In short, the law of demand means that there is a fundamental trade-off between P and Q in generating revenue. An increase in Q requires a cut in P, the former effect raising revenue but the latter lowering it. Operating at either extreme—selling a small quantity at high prices or a large quantity at very low prices—will raise little revenue.

The revenue results in Figure 2.2 can be obtained more directly using basic algebra. From Equation 2.3, we know that $R = P \cdot Q$, and from Equation 2.2 that the market-clearing price satisfies $P = 170 - 20Q$. Substituting the latter equation into the former yields the **revenue function**

$$R = P \cdot Q = (170 - 20Q)Q = 170Q - 20Q^2 \qquad [2.3]$$

Figure 2.2 also shows the graph of revenue as it depends on the quantity of chips sold. At the sales quantity of 2 lots, the market-clearing price is \$130,000; therefore, revenue is \$260,000. The graph clearly indicates that the firm's revenue rises, peaks, and then falls as the sales quantity increases. (Some readers will recognize Equation 2.3 as a quadratic function. Accordingly, the graph in Figure 2.2 is a simple parabola.)

Let the inverse demand function be $P = 340 - .8Q$. Find the revenue function.   **CHECK STATION 1**

COST   To produce chips, the firm requires a plant, equipment, and labor. The firm estimates that it costs \$380 (in materials, labor, and so on) for each chip it produces; this is \$38,000 per lot. In addition, it incurs fixed costs of \$100,000 per week to run the plant, whether or not chips are produced. For our highly simplified example, these are the only costs. The total cost of producing a given quantity of output is given by the equation

$$C = 100 + 38Q \qquad [2.4]$$

where C is the weekly cost of production (in thousands of dollars) and Q is the number of lots produced each week. This equation is called the **cost function**, because it shows how total cost depends on quantity. By substituting in a given quantity, we can find the resulting total cost. Thus, the cost of producing $Q = 2$ lots is \$176 thousand. Other quantities and costs are listed in Figure 2.3, which also shows the graph of cost versus output. As the graph shows, in this simple example the firm's total cost of production increases with output at a steady rate; that is, the slope of the cost function is constant.

PROFIT   From the preceding analysis of revenue and cost, we now have enough information to compute profit for any given output of microchips the firm might choose to produce and sell. These profit calculations are listed in Figure 2.4, where the profit column is computed as the difference between the revenue and cost columns reproduced from earlier figures. The graph in Figure 2.4 shows profit (on the vertical axis) as it varies with quantity (on the horizontal axis). Observe that the graph depicts the level of profit over a wide range of output choices, not just for the round-lot choices listed in the tabular portion of the figure. In effect, the graph allows us to determine visually the profit-maximizing, or optimal, output level from among all possible sales plans. In this case, the optimal output appears to be about 3.3 lots (or 330 microchips) per week.

FIGURE 2.3

The Cost of Microchips

The table and graph
show the firm's total
cost of producing
different quantities
of microchips.

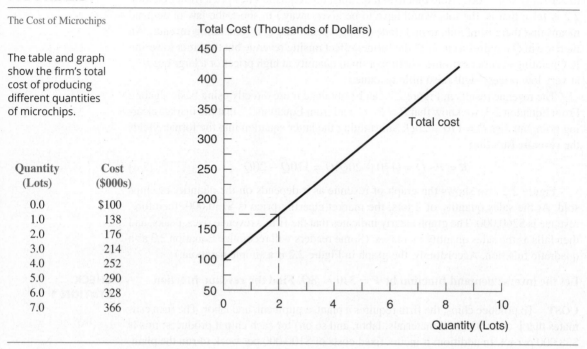

Quantity (Lots)	Cost ($000s)
0.0	$100
1.0	138
2.0	176
3.0	214
4.0	252
5.0	290
6.0	328
7.0	366

How were we able to graph the profit curve in Figure 2.4 so precisely? The graph was constructed from the following basic profit equation, often called the **profit function**:

$$\pi = R - C$$

$$= (170Q - 20Q^2) - (100 + 38Q)$$

$$= -100 + 132Q - 20Q^2.$$

[2.5]

In the second line, we have substituted the right-hand sides of the revenue and cost equations (Equations 2.3 and 2.4) to express profit in terms of Q, the firm's decision variable. In the third line, we have collected terms. The important point about the profit equation is that it provides a numerical prediction of profit for any given quantity Q. To check that the equation is correct, simply substitute in a value for Q, say, two lots, and calculate profit: $\pi = -100 + (132)(2) - (20)(2)^2 = \$84$ thousand, the same result as in Figure 2.4.

CHECK STATION 2   Suppose the inverse demand function is $P = 340 - .8Q$ and the cost function is $C = 120 + 100Q$. Write down the profit function.

FIGURE 2.4

Profit from Microchips

Total Profit (Thousands of Dollars)

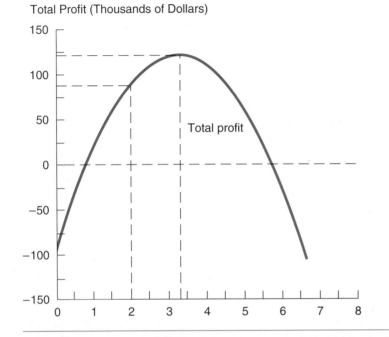

Profit is the difference between the firm's total revenue and total cost. The table and graph show the amount of profit the firm will earn for different quantities of microchips that it produces and sells.

Quantity (Lots)	Profit ($000s)	Revenue ($000s)	Cost ($000s)
0.0	−100	0	100
1.0	12	150	138
2.0	84	260	176
3.0	116	330	214
4.0	108	360	252
5.0	60	350	290
6.0	−28	300	328
7.0	−156	210	366

MARGINAL ANALYSIS

Consider the problem of finding the output level that will maximize the firm's profit. One approach is to use the preceding profit formula and solve the problem by *enumeration,* that is, by calculating the profits associated with a range of outputs and identifying the one with the greatest profit. Enumeration is a viable approach if there are only a few output levels to test. However, when the number of options is large, enumeration (and the numerous calculations it requires) is not practical. Instead, we will use the method of *marginal analysis* to find the "optimal" output level.

   Marginal analysis looks at the change in profit that results from making a small change in a decision variable. To illustrate, suppose the firm first considers producing 3 lots, forecasting its resulting profit to be $116,000 as in Figure 2.4. Could it do better than this? To answer this question, the firm considers increasing production slightly, to, say, 3.1 lots. (One-tenth of a lot qualifies as a "small" change. The exact size of the change does not matter as long as it is small.) By substituting $Q = 3.1$ into Equation 2.5, we see that the new profit is $117,000. Thus, profit has increased by $1,000. The *rate* at which profit has changed is a $1,000 increase per .1 lot increase, or $1,000/.1 = $10,000 per lot.

   Marginal profit is the change in profit resulting from a small increase in any managerial decision variable. Thus, we say that the marginal profit from a small (.1 lot) increase in output starting from 3.0 lots is $10,000 per lot. The algebraic expression for marginal profit is

$$\text{Marginal profit} = [\text{Change in Profit}]/[\text{Change in Output}]$$

$$= \Delta\pi/\Delta Q = [\pi_1 - \pi_0]/[Q_1 - Q_0],$$

where the Greek letter delta (Δ) stands for "change in" and Q_0 denotes the original output level and π_0 the associated profit. The variables Q_1 and π_1 denote the new levels of output and profit. We abbreviate marginal profit by the notation $M\pi$.

CHECK STATION 3   **Using the profit function you found in Check Station 2, find the marginal profit of increasing output from 99 to 100 units.**

In Table 2.1, we have calculated marginal profits for various output levels. The marginal profit associated with a given change in output is calculated based on a .1-lot increase from the next lowest output. Thus, the $M\pi$ for an increase in output from 2.9 to 3.0 lots is ($116,000 - $114,600)/.1 = $14,000.

How can the decision maker use profit changes as signposts pointing toward the optimal output level? The answer is found by applying the maxim of marginal analysis:

> Make a small change in the level of output if and only if this generates an increase in profit. Keep moving, always in the direction of increased profits, and stop when no further output change will help.

Starting from a production level of 2.5 lots, the microchip firm should increase output to 2.6 because marginal profit from the move ($30,000) is positive. Marginal profit continues to be positive up to 3.3 lots. Therefore, output should be increased up to and including a final step going from 3.2 to 3.3 lots. What about increasing output from 3.3 to 3.4 lots? Since the marginal profit associated with a move to 3.4 is negative (−$2,000), this action would decrease profit. Having reached 3.3 lots, then, no further profit gains (positive marginal profits) are possible. Note that the final output, 3.3, could have been reached starting from a "high" output level such as 3.7 lots. As long as marginal profit is negative, one should reduce output (i.e., reverse field) to increase profit.

Marginal Analysis and Calculus

The key to pinpointing the firm's optimal quantity (i.e., the *exact* output level at which maximum profit is attained) is to compute marginal profit *at* any given level of output rather than *between* two nearby output levels. At a particular output, Q, marginal profit is given by the slope of the *tangent* line to the profit graph *at* that output level. Figure 2.5 shows an enlarged profit graph with tangent lines drawn at outputs of 3.1 and 3.3 lots. From viewing the tangents, we draw the following simple conclusions. At 3.1 lots, the tangent is upward sloping. Obviously, marginal profit is positive; that is, raising output by a small amount increases total profit. Conversely, at 3.4 lots, the curve is downward sloping. Here marginal profit is negative, so a small reduction in output (not an increase) would increase total profit. Finally, at 3.3 lots, the tangent is horizontal; that is, the tangent's slope and marginal profit are zero. Maximum profit is attained at precisely this level of

TABLE 2.1

Quantity	Profit	Marginal Profit (per Lot)
2.5	$105,000	
		$30,000
2.6	108,000	
		26,000
2.7	110,600	
		22,000
2.8	112,800	
		18,000
2.9	114,600	
		14,000
3.0	116,000	
		10,000
3.1	117,000	
		6,000
3.2	117,600	
		2,000
3.3	117,800	
		-2,000
3.4	117,600	
		-6,000
3.5	117,000	
		-10,000
3.6	116,000	
		-14,000
3.7	114,600	

Marginal Profit

Marginal profit is the extra profit the firm earns from producing and selling an additional unit of output.

output. Indeed, the condition that marginal profit is zero marks this point as the optimal level of output. Remember: If $M\pi$ were positive or negative, total profit could be raised by appropriately increasing or decreasing output. Only when $M\pi$ is exactly zero have all profit-augmenting opportunities been exhausted. In short, when the profit function's slope just becomes zero, we know we are at the precise peak of the profit curve.[3] Thus, we have demonstrated a basic optimization rule:

I Maximum profit is attained at the output level at which marginal profit is zero ($M\pi = 0$). I

A practical method for calculating marginal profit at any level of output is afforded by the simple rules of differential calculus. (For a thorough review, read the appendix to this chapter.) Consider once again the firm's profit equation:

$$\pi = -100 + 132Q - 20Q^2. \qquad [2.6]$$

Marginal profit (the slope of the corresponding profit graph) is found by taking the derivative of this equation with respect to Q. The result is

$$M\pi = d\pi/dQ = 132 - 40Q. \qquad [2.7]$$

[3]In some cases, the $M\pi = 0$ rule requires modification. For example, suppose demand and cost conditions are such that $M\pi > 0$ for all output quantities up to the firm's current production capacity. Clearly, the rule $M\pi = 0$ does not apply. However, the marginal profit message is clear: The firm should increase output up to capacity, raising profit all the while. (For further discussion, see the appendix to this chapter and Problem 5 at the end of the chapter.)

FIGURE 2.5

A Close-Up View of Profit

Maximum profit
occurs at an output
where marginal
profit is zero, that is,
the slope of the
tangent line is zero.

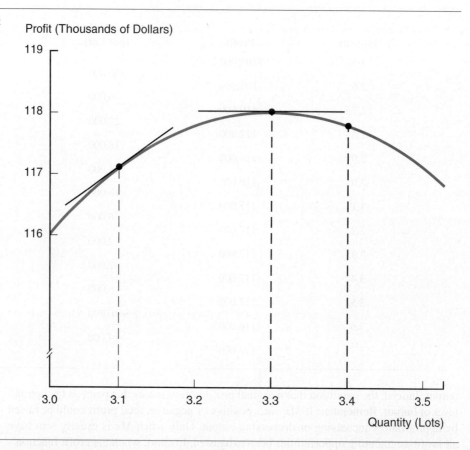

Profit (Thousands of Dollars)

With this formula in hand, we can find the marginal profit at any output level simply by substituting the specified quantity into the equation. For example, the marginal profit at $Q = 3.0$ is $12 thousand per lot.[4] In turn, we can immediately determine the firm's profit-maximizing level of output. Using Equation 2.7, we simply set $M\pi = 0$ and solve for Q:

$$M\pi = 132 - 40Q = 0.$$

Therefore, we find that $Q = 132/40 = 3.3$ lots. At 3.3 lots per week, the firm's marginal profit is zero. This is the output that maximizes profit.

[4]The difference between Equation 2.7 and Table 2.1 is that the table lists marginal profit over small, discrete intervals of output, whereas the equation lists marginal profit *at* particular output levels. When we use a very small interval, the discrete marginal profit between two output levels is a very close approximation to marginal profit at either output. For example, with an interval of .01, the discrete marginal profit at $Q = 3$ is the slope of the line connecting the points $Q = 2.99$ and $Q = 3.00$. This line is nearly identical to the tangent line (representing marginal profit) *at* $Q = 3$. Thus,

Using a .01 interval:	$M\pi = \$12,200$
Via calculus (Equation 2.7)	$M\pi = \$12,000$

Figure 2.6 graphs the firm's total profit (part a) as well as the firm's marginal profit (part b). Note that at the optimal output, $Q = 3.3$ lots, total profit reaches a peak in Figure 2.6a, whereas marginal profit is exactly zero (i.e., the marginal profit graph just cuts the horizontal axis) in Figure 2.6b.

A complete solution to the firm's decision problem requires two additional steps. We know the optimal quantity is $Q = 3.3$ lots. What price is required for the firm to sell this quantity? The answer is found by substituting $Q = 3.3$ into Equation 2.2: $P = 170 - (20)(3.3) = \$104$ thousand. What is the firm's final profit from its optimal output and price decision? At this point, we can separately compute total revenue as \$343,200 and total cost as \$225,400. Alternatively, we can compute profit directly from Equation 2.6 (with $Q = 3.3$). Either way, we arrive at $\pi = \$117,800$. This completes the algebraic solution.

Once again, consider the inverse demand curve $P = 340 - .8Q$ and the cost function $C = 120 + 100Q$. Derive the formula for $M\pi$, as it depends on Q. Set $M\pi = 0$ to find the firm's optimal output.   **CHECK STATION 4**

MARGINAL REVENUE AND MARGINAL COST

The concept of marginal profit yields two key dividends. The general concept instructs the manager that optimal decisions are found by making small changes in decisions, observing the resulting effect on profit, and always moving in the direction of greater profit. A second virtue of the approach is that it provides an efficient tool for calculating the firm's optimal decision. The discussion in this section underscores a third virtue: Marginal analysis is a powerful way to identify the factors that determine profits and, more important, profit changes. We will look once again at the two components of profit— revenue and cost—and highlight the key features of *marginal revenue* and *marginal cost.*

Marginal Revenue

Marginal revenue is the amount of additional revenue that comes with a unit increase in output and sales. Marginal revenue *at* a given sales quantity has as its graphic counterpart the slope of the tangent line touching the revenue graph. To calculate the marginal revenue at a given sales output, we start with the revenue expression (Equation 2.3), $R = 170Q - 20Q^2$, and take the derivative with respect to quantity:

$$MR = 170 - 40Q \qquad [2.8]$$

We can use this formula to compute MR at any particular sales quantity. For example, marginal revenue at $Q = 3$ is $MR = 170 - (40)(3) = \$50$ thousand; that is, at this sales quantity, a small increase in sales increases revenue at the rate of \$50,000 per additional lot sold.

A SIMPLIFYING FACT   Recall that the firm's market-clearing price is given by Equation 2.2:

$$P = 170 - 20Q.$$

FIGURE 2.6

Total Profit and
Marginal Profit

The point of maxi-
mum total profit in
part (a) corresponds
to the point at which
marginal profit is
zero in part (b). In
each case, the firm's
optimal output is
3.3 lots.

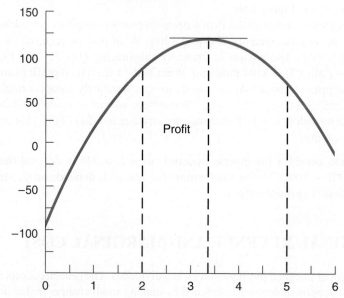

(a)   Total Profit (Thousands of Dollars)

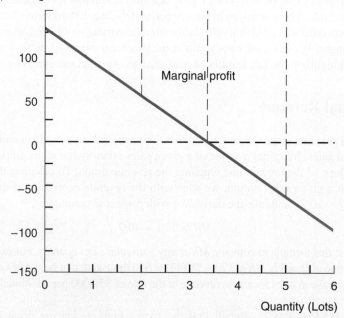

(b)   Marginal Profit

Quantity (Lots)

Note the close similarity between the MR expression in Equation 2.8 and the firm's selling price in Equation 2.2. This similarity is no coincidence. The following result holds:

| For any linear (i.e., straight-line) demand curve with an inverse demand equation of the form $P = a - bQ$, the resulting marginal revenue is $MR = a - 2bQ$. |

In short, the MR equation has the same intercept and twice the slope as the firm's price equation.[5]

Marginal Cost

Marginal cost (MC) is the additional cost of producing an extra unit of output. The computation of MC is particularly easy for the microchip manufacturer's cost function in Equation 2.4. From the cost equation, $C = 100 + 38Q$, it is apparent that producing an extra lot (increasing Q by a unit) will increase cost by $38 thousand. Thus, marginal cost is simply $38 thousand per lot. Note that regardless of how large or small the level of output, marginal cost is always constant. The cost function in Equation 2.4 has a constant slope and thus also an unchanging marginal cost. (We can directly confirm the MC result by taking the derivative of the cost equation.)

Profit Maximization Revisited

In view of the fact that $\pi = R - C$, it should not be surprising that

$$M\pi = MR - MC. \qquad [2.9]$$

In other words, marginal profit is simply the difference between marginal revenue and marginal cost.

The logic of this relationship is simple enough. Suppose the firm produces and sells an extra unit. Then its change in profit is simply the extra revenue it earns from the extra unit net of its additional cost of production. But the extra revenue is MR and the extra cost is MC, so $M\pi = MR - MC$.

Thus far, we have emphasized the role of marginal profit in characterizing the firm's optimal decision. In particular, profits are maximized when marginal profit equals zero. Thus, using the fact that $M\pi = MR - MC$, an equivalent statement is $MR - MC = 0$. This leads to the following basic rule:

| The firm's profit-maximizing level of output occurs when the additional revenue from selling an extra unit just equals the extra cost of producing it, that is, when $MR = MC$. |

There are a number of ways to check the logic of the $MR = MC$ decision rule. Figure 2.7 provides a graphical confirmation. Part (a) reproduces the microchip manufacturer's revenue and cost functions (from Equations 2.3 and 2.4) in a single graph.

---

[5]If $P = a - bQ$, it follows that $R = PQ = aQ - bQ^2$. Taking the derivative with respect to Q, we find that $MR = dR/dQ = a - 2bQ$. This confirms the result described.

FIGURE 2.7

Marginal Revenue and
Marginal Cost

In part (a), total profit
is shown as the
difference between
total revenue and
total cost. In part (b),
the firm's optimal
output occurs where
the marginal revenue
and marginal cost
curves intersect.

(a) Total Revenue, Cost, and Profit (Thousands of Dollars)

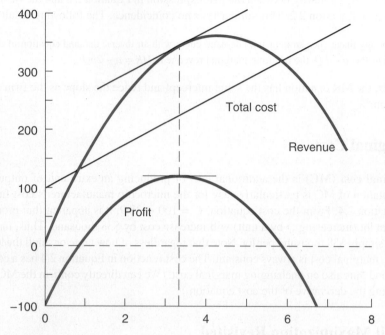

(b) Marginal Revenue and Cost (Thousands of Dollars)

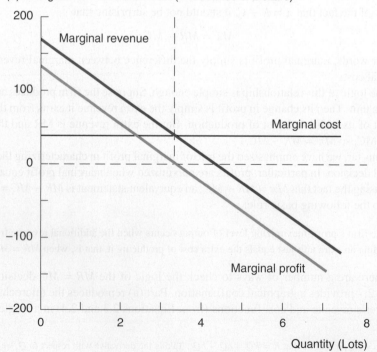

For any level of output, the firm's profit is measured as the vertical distance between the revenue and cost curves. The firm's break-even outputs occur at the two crossings of the revenue and cost curves. At these outputs, revenue just matches cost, so profit is zero. Positive profits are earned for quantities between these two output levels. In addition, the graph of profit is shown in Figure 2.7a (and, except for scale, is identical to Figure 2.4). From the profit curve, we observe the profit peak at an output of $Q = 3.3$ lots.

Using the $MR = MC$ rule, how can we confirm that the output level $Q = 3.3$ is profit maximizing? A simple answer is provided by appealing to the revenue and cost curves in Figure 2.7a. Suppose for the moment that the firm produces a lower quantity, say, $Q = 2$ lots. At this output, the revenue curve is steeper than the cost line; thus, $MR > MC$. Hence, the firm could increase its profit by producing extra units of output. On the graph, the move to a greater output widens the profit gap. The reverse argument holds for a proposed higher quantity, such as 4 lots. In this case, revenue rises less steeply than cost: $MR < MC$. Therefore, a reduction in output results in a greater cost saved than revenue sacrificed. Again, profit increases.

Combining these arguments, we conclude that profit always can be increased so long as a small change in output results in *different* changes in revenue and cost. Only at $Q = 3.3$ is it true that revenue and cost increase at exactly the same rate. At this quantity, the slopes of the revenue and cost functions are equal; the revenue tangent is parallel to the cost line. But this simply says that marginal revenue equals marginal cost. At this optimal output, the gap between revenue and cost is neither widening nor narrowing. Maximum profit is attained.

It is important to remember that the $M\pi = 0$ and $MR = MC$ rules are exactly equivalent. Both rules pinpoint the *same* profit-maximizing level of output. Figure 2.7b shows this clearly. At $Q = 3.3$ lots, where the profit function reaches a peak (and the profit tangent is horizontal) in part (a), we note that the MR line exactly intersects the MC line in part (b). This provides visual confirmation that profit is maximized at the output level at which marginal revenue just equals marginal cost.

The $MR = MC$ rule often is the shortest path to finding the firm's optimal output. Instead of finding the marginal profit function and setting it equal to zero, we simply take the marginal revenue and marginal cost functions and set them equal to each other. In the microchip manufacturer's problem, we know that $MR = 170 - 40Q$ and $MC = 38$. Setting $MR = MC$ implies that $170 - 40Q = 38$. Solving for Q, we find that $Q = 3.3$ lots. Of course, this is precisely the same result we obtained by setting marginal profit equal to zero.

Once again, let us consider the price equation $P = 340 - .8Q$ and the cost equation $C = 120 + 100Q$. Apply the $MR = MC$ rule to find the firm's optimal output. From the inverse demand curve, find its optimal price.   **CHECK STATION 5**

SENSITIVITY ANALYSIS

As we saw in Chapter 1, sensitivity analysis addresses the basic question: How should the decision maker alter his or her course of action in light of changes in economic conditions? Marginal analysis offers a powerful answer to this question:

For any change in economic conditions, we can trace the impact (if any) on the firm's marginal revenue or marginal cost. Once we have identified this impact, we can appeal to the *MR = MC* rule to determine the new, optimal decision.

Figure 2.8 illustrates the application of this rule for the microchip firm's basic problem. Consider part (a). As before, the firm's decision variable, its output quantity, is listed on the horizontal axis. In turn, levels of MR and MC are shown on the vertical axis, and the respective curves have been graphed. How do we explain the shapes of these curves? For MC, the answer is easy. The marginal cost of producing an extra lot of chips is $38,000 regardless of the starting output level. Thus, the MC line is horizontal, fixed at a level of $38,000. In turn, the graph of the MR curve from Equation 2.8 is

$$MR = 170 - 40Q.$$

We make the following observations about the MR equation and graph. Starting from a zero sales quantity, the firm gets a great deal of extra revenue from selling additional units ($MR = 170$ at $Q = 0$). As sales increase, the extra revenue from additional units falls (although MR is still positive). Indeed, at a quantity of 4.25 lots (see Figure 2.9) MR is zero, and for higher outputs MR is negative; that is, selling extra units causes total revenue to fall. (Don't be surprised by this. Turn back to Figure 2.2 and see that revenue peaks, then falls. When volume already is very large, selling extra units requires a price cut on so many units that total revenue drops.)

In Figure 2.8a, the intersection of the MR and MC curves establishes the firm's optimal production and sales quantity, $Q = 3.3$ lots. At an output less than 3.3 units, MR is greater than MC, so the firm could make additional profit producing extra units. (Why? Because its extra revenue exceeds its extra cost.) At an output above 3.3 units, MR is smaller than MC. Here the firm can increase its profit by cutting back its production. (Why? Because the firm's cost saving exceeds the revenue it gives up.) Thus, profit is maximized only at the quantity where *MR = MC*.

Asking What If

The following examples trace the possible effects of changes in economic conditions on the firm's marginal revenue and marginal cost.

INCREASED OVERHEAD   Suppose the microchip manufacturer's overhead costs (for the physical plant and administration) increase. Fixed costs were $100,000 per week; now they are $112,000. How will this affect the firm's operating decisions? The simple, albeit surprising, answer is that the increase in fixed costs will have no effect whatsoever. The firm should produce and sell the same output at the same price as before. There are several ways to see this.

First, note that the firm's profit is reduced by $12,000 (relative to its profit before the cost increase) *whatever its level of output.* Thus, whatever output was profit-maximizing before the cost increase must be profit-maximizing after it. Second, the revenue and cost graphs in Figure 2.7a provide a visual confirmation of the same reasoning. An increase in fixed cost causes the cost line to shift upward (parallel to the old one) by the amount

FIGURE 2.8

(a) Marginal Revenue and Cost (Thousands of Dollars)

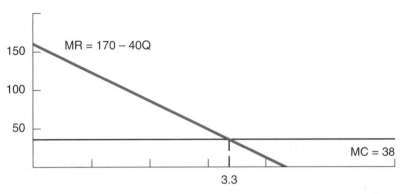

Shifts in Marginal
Revenue and Marginal
Cost

Part (b) depicts an
increase in marginal
cost as an upward
shift in the marginal
cost curve. As a
result, the firm's
optimal output level
declines. Part (c)
shows an upward
(rightward) shift in
marginal revenue
resulting from an
increase in demand.
As a result, the firm's
optimal output level
increases.

(b) Marginal Revenue and Cost (Thousands of Dollars)

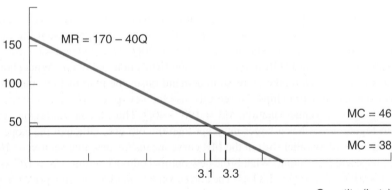

(c) Marginal Revenue and Cost (Thousands of Dollars)

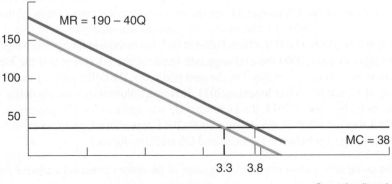

of the increase. At any output, the revenue-cost gap is smaller than before. But note that the point of equal slopes—where $MR = MC$ and the profit gap is maximized—is unchanged. Profit is still maximized at the same output as before, $Q = 3.3$. Finally, the MR and MC curves in Figure 2.8a make the same point. Has the increase in fixed cost changed the MR or MC curves? No! Thus, the firm's optimal output, where the MR and MC lines intersect, is unchanged.

INCREASED MATERIAL COSTS   Silicon is the main raw material from which micro-chips are made. Suppose an increase in the price of silicon causes the firm's estimated cost per lot to rise from \$38,000 to \$46,000. How should the firm respond? Once again, the answer depends on an appeal to marginal analysis. In this case, the firm's MC per chip has changed. In Figure 2.8b, the new MC line lies above and parallel to the old MC line. The intersection of MR and MC occurs at a lower level of output. Because produc-ing extra output has become more expensive, the firm's optimal response is to cut back the level of production. What is the new optimal output? Setting $MR = MC$, we obtain $170 - 40Q = 46$, so $Q = 3.1$ lots. In turn, the market-clearing price (using Equation 2.2) is found to be \$108,000. The increase in cost has been partially passed on to buyers via a higher price.

INCREASED DEMAND   Suppose demand for the firm's chips increases dramatically. Whereas the former price equation was $P = 170 - 20Q$, let's represent the demand increase by the "new" price equation, $P = 190 - 20Q$. This demand increase means an upward and rightward shift in position of the firm's demand curve. What should be the firm's response? Here, the increase in demand raises the marginal revenue the firm obtains from selling extra chips. To see this, use the new price equation to write down the new marginal revenue equation, $MR = 190 - 40Q$. Thus, the new marginal revenue curve in Figure 2.8(c) has a larger intercept than the old one, although the slope is the same. The upward, parallel shift in the MR curve means the new intersection of MR and MC occurs at a higher output. What is the new optimal output? Setting $MR = MC$, we find that $190 - 40Q = 38$, so $Q = 3.8$ lots. The corresponding market-clearing price (using the *new* price equation) is \$114 thousand. The firm takes optimal advantage of the increase in demand by selling a larger output (380 chips per week) at a higher price per lot.

Responding to Changes in Exchange Rates

Domestic steel producers have long competed vigorously with foreign steel manufac-turers for shares of the US market. Given the intensity of price competition, global steel producers constantly strive to trim production costs to maintain profits. In recent years, the competitive playing field has been buffeted by large swings in foreign exchange rates. For instance, in early 2009 the exchange rate between the US dollar and the Japanese yen was about 100 yen per dollar. For the next two years, the dollar steadily depreciated, standing at 82 yen per dollar in spring 2011.This was followed by a steady dollar appre-ciation, so by November 2013, the exchange rate was again about 100 yen per dollar.

What was the effect of the dollar's 2009–2011 depreciation on the competition for our domestic market between Japanese and US steel producers?

The dollar depreciation (the fall in the value of the dollar) conferred a relative cost advantage on US steel producers to the disadvantage of Japanese producers.

To see this, suppose that based on its current costs, a Japanese steel maker sets its 2009 price for a unit of specialty steel at 10,000 yen. At an exchange rate of 100 yen per dollar, this translates into a price charged to US buyers of 10,000/100 = $100 per unit, a level competitive with the prices of US steel producers. Two years later, suppose that the Japanese supplier's costs and targeted price in yen are unchanged. However, with an exchange rate of 82 yen per dollar, the equivalent dollar price of its steel is now 10,000/82 = $122. For US buyers, Japanese steel is now much more expensive and less competitive. The demand curve for imported steel from Japan has effectively shifted inward (i.e., downward and to the left) to Japan's detriment. Correspondingly, the domestic demand curve facing US steel producers has shifted outward, as has the Japanese demand curve for steel exports from the United States. (US steel produced at a cost of $100 per unit now costs only 8,200 yen when exported and sold in Japan.)

How should US steel producers respond to the favorable demand shift caused by the dollar's depreciation? Using the example of increased demand displayed in Figure 2.8c, we find that domestic firms should plan to increase their outputs as well as to raise their dollar prices.

Pricing Amazon's Kindle

In November 2007, Amazon introduced the Kindle, the first successful reading device for electronic books. The price was a daunting $399. In 2009, the company dropped the Kindle's price to $259 and in mid-2010 to $189. (Today, minimalist versions of the Kindle are priced under $100.) Though Amazon is notoriously secretive about the Kindle's sales, revenues, and costs, financial analysts estimated annual sales to be approximately 1 million units at the $259 price.

At the time, there was some second guessing as to whether the price cut to $189 made sense for the company—indeed whether the marginal revenue from additional units sold exceeded Amazon's marginal cost of producing the Kindle. Amazon CEO Jeff Bezos appeared to be playing a market-share strategy, predicated on establishing the Kindle as *the* dominant platform for e-books and counting on maximizing profits from e-book sales (rather than profits from the Kindle itself). Bezos reported that the price cut was successful in igniting Kindle sales, claiming that the price cut to $189 had tripled the rate of sales (implying annual sales of 3 million units at this lower price). Furthermore, it was estimated that Amazon earned a contribution margin of $4 on each e-book and that each Kindle sold generated the equivalent of 25 e-book sales over the Kindle's life. In other words, besides the marginal revenue Amazon earned for each Kindle sold, it gained an additional MR (per Kindle) of $100 due to new e-book sales.

CHECK STATION 6

a. The sales figures listed above imply that the Kindle's (linear) inverse demand curve is described by the equation: $P = 294 - 35Q$. Check that the two quantity-price points ($Q = 1$ million at $P = \$259$ and $Q = 3$ million at $P = \$189$) satisfy this equation.

b. In 2010, the marginal cost of producing the Kindle was estimated at $126 per unit. Apply the $MR = MC$ rule to find the output and price that maximize Kindle profits.

c. Considering that each Kindle sold generates $100 in e-book profits, determine Amazon's optimal quantity and price with respect to the *total* profit generated by Kindle and e-book sales. What is the implication for Amazon's pricing strategy?

**Conflict in Fast-Food
Franchising
Revisited**

The example that opened this chapter recounted the numerous kinds of conflicts between fast-food parents and individual franchise operators.[6] Despite the best intentions, bitter disputes have erupted from time to time at such chains as McDonald's, Burger King, and Subway. A key source for many of these conflicts is the basic contract arrangement between parent and individual franchisee. Virtually all such contracts call for the franchisee to pay back to the parent a specified percentage of revenue earned. This total royalty comprises a base percentage plus additional percentages for marketing and advertising and rent (if the parent owns the outlet). The franchisee's profit begins only after this royalty (typically ranging anywhere from 5 to 20 percent depending on the type of franchise) and all other costs have been paid.

Thus, a key source of conflict emerges. Under the contract agreement, the parent's monetary return depends on (indeed, is a percentage of) the revenues the franchisee takes in. Accordingly, the parent wants the franchisee to operate so as to maximize revenue. What does the pursuit of maximum revenue imply about the franchisee's volume of sales? Suppose the revenue and cost curves for the franchisee are configured as in Figure 2.7a. (Ignore the numerical values and reinterpret the quantity scale as numbers of burgers sold rather than microchips.) We observe that the revenue-maximizing output is well past the franchisee's optimal (i.e., profit-maximizing) output. The range of economic conflict occurs between these two outputs—the franchisee unwilling to budge from the lower output and the parent pushing for the higher output.

The same point can be made by appealing to the forces of MR and MC. The parent always wants to increase revenue, even if doing so means extra costs to the franchisee. Thus, the parent wishes to push output to the point where $MR = 0$. (Make sure you understand why.) But the franchisee prefers to limit output to the point where extra costs match extra revenues ($MR = MC$). Past this point, the extra revenues are not worth the extra costs: $MR < MC$. In Figure 2.7b, the franchisee's preferred output occurs where $MR = MC$ and the parent's occurs at the larger output where $MR = 0$.

The conflict in objectives explains each of the various disputes. In the parent company's view, all its preferred policies—longer operating hours, more order lines, remodeling, lower prices—are revenue increasing. In each case, however, the individual franchisee resists the move because the extra cost of the change would exceed the extra revenue. From its point of view (the bottom line), none of the changes would be profitable.

To this day, conflicts between parent and individual franchisees continue. The Quiznos sandwich shop chain and the Steak 'n Shake chain have experienced repeated franchisee revolts. Dunkin' Donuts franchisees have strongly opposed its

[6]Franchise conflicts are discussed in J. Jargon, "Battle over Menu Prices Heats Up," *Wall Street Journal* (August 23, 2013): p. B6; R. Gibson, "Franchisee v. Franchiser," *The Wall Street Journal* (February 14, 2011): p. R3; and R. Gibson, "Burger King Franchisees Can't Have It Their Way," *The Wall Street Journal* (January 21, 2010): p. B1.

parent's deals to allow Procter & Gamble, Sara Lee Foods, and Hess gas stations to sell the chain's branded coffee, reporting that this has cut into their own stores' coffee sales. In 2010, a group of Burger King franchisees sued the franchiser to stop imposing a $1 value price for a double cheeseburger, a promotion on which franchisees claimed to be losing money. Even McDonald's Corp., long considered the gold standard of the franchise business, is feeling the heat. McDonald's efforts to increase market share have been fiercely resisted by a number of franchisees. What's good for the parent's market share and revenue may not be good for the individual franchisee's profit. Franchise owners have resisted the company's efforts to enforce value pricing (i.e., discounting). McDonald's strategy of accelerating the opening of new restaurants to claim market share means that new outlets inevitably cannibalize sales of existing stores. Such conflicts are always just below the surface.

SUMMARY

Decision-Making Principles

1. The fundamental decision problem of the firm is to determine the profit-maximizing price and output for the good or service it sells.
2. The firm's profit from any decision is the difference between predicted revenues and costs. Increasing output and sales will increase profit, as long as the extra revenue gained exceeds the extra cost incurred. Conversely, the firm will profit by cutting output if the cost saved exceeds the revenue given up.
3. If economic conditions change, the firm's optimal price and output will change according to the impact on its marginal revenues and marginal costs.

Nuts and Bolts

1. The basic building blocks of the firm's price and output problem are its demand curve and cost function. The demand curve describes (1) the quantity of sales for a given price or, conversely, (2) the price needed to generate a given level of sales. Multiplying prices and quantities along the demand curve produces the revenue function. The cost function estimates the cost of producing a given level of output. Combining the revenue and cost functions generates a profit prediction for any output Q.
2. The next step in finding the firm's optimal decision is to determine the firm's marginal profit, marginal revenue, and marginal cost:
   a. Marginal profit is the extra profit earned from producing and selling an additional unit of output.
   b. Marginal revenue is the extra revenue earned from selling an additional unit of output.
   c. Marginal cost is the extra cost of producing an additional unit of output.
   d. By definition, marginal profit is the difference between marginal revenue and marginal cost: $M\pi = MR - MC$. The $M\pi$, MR, and MC expressions can be found by taking the derivatives of the respective profit, revenue, and cost functions.
3. The firm's optimal output is characterized by the following conditions: (1) $M\pi = 0$ or, equivalently, (2) $MR = MC$. Once output has been determined, the firm's optimal price is found from the price equation, and profit can be estimated accordingly.

Questions and Problems

1. A manager makes the statement that output should be expanded as long as average revenue exceeds average cost. Does this strategy make sense? Explain.

2. The original revenue function for the microchip producer is $R = 170Q - 20Q^2$. Derive the expression for marginal revenue, and use it to find the output level at which *revenue is maximized.* Confirm that this is greater than the firm's profit-maximizing output, and explain why.

3. Because of changing demographics, a small, private liberal arts college predicts a fall in enrollments over the next five years. How would it apply marginal analysis to plan for the decreased enrollment? (The college is a nonprofit institution, so think broadly about its objectives.)

4. Suppose a firm's inverse demand curve is given by $P = 120 - .5Q$ and its cost equation is $C = 420 + 60Q + Q^2$.
   a. Find the firm's optimal quantity, price, and profit (1) by using the profit and marginal profit equations and (2) by setting MR equal to MC. Also provide a graph of MR and MC.
   b. Suppose instead that the firm can sell any and all of its output at the fixed market price $P = 120$. Find the firm's optimal output.

5. a. As in Problem 4, demand continues to be given by $P = 120$, but the firm's cost equation is linear: $C = 420 + 60Q$. Graph the firm's revenue and cost curves. At what quantity does the firm break even—that is, earn exactly a zero profit?
   b. In general, suppose the firm faces the fixed price P and has cost equation $C = F + cQ$, where F denotes the firm's fixed cost and c is its marginal cost per unit. Write down a formula for the firm's profit. Set this expression equal to zero and solve for the firm's break-even quantity (in terms of P, F, and c). Give an intuitive explanation for this break-even equation.
   c. In this case, what difficulty arises in trying to apply the $MR = MC$ rule to maximize profit? By applying the logic of marginal analysis, state the modified rule applicable to this case.

6. A television station is considering the sale of promotional videos. It can have the videos produced by one of two suppliers. Supplier A will charge the station a setup fee of $1,200 plus $2 for each DVD; supplier B has no setup fee and will charge $4 per DVD. The station estimates its demand for the DVDs to be given by $Q = 1,600 - 200P$, where P is the price in dollars and Q is the number of DVDs. (The equivalent price equation is $P = 8 - Q/200$.)
   a. Suppose the station plans to give away the videos. How many DVDs should it order? From which supplier?
   b. Suppose instead that the station seeks to maximize its profit from sales of the DVDs. What price should it charge? How many DVDs should it order from which supplier? (*Hint:* Solve two separate problems, one with supplier A and one with supplier B, and then compare profits. In each case, apply the $MR = MC$ rule.)

7. The college and graduate-school textbook market is one of the most profitable segments for book publishers. A best-selling accounting text—published by Old School Inc (OS)—has a demand curve: $P = 150 - Q$, where Q denotes yearly sales (in thousands) of books. The cost of producing, handling, and shipping each additional book is about $40, and the publisher pays a $10 per book royalty to the author. Finally, the publisher's overall marketing and promotion spending (set annually) accounts for an average cost of about $10 per book.
   a. Determine OS's profit-maximizing output and price for the accounting text.
   b. A rival publisher has raised the price of its best-selling accounting text by $15. One option is to exactly match this price hike and so exactly preserve your level of sales. Do you endorse this price increase? (Explain briefly why or why not.)
   c. To save significantly on fixed costs, Old School plans to contract out the actual printing of its textbooks to outside vendors. OS expects to pay a somewhat higher printing cost per book (than in part a) from the outside vendor (who marks up price above its cost to make a profit). How would outsourcing affect the output and pricing decisions in part (a)?

8. Firm Z is developing a new product. An early introduction (beating rivals to market) would greatly enhance the company's revenues. However, the intensive development effort needed to expedite the introduction can be very expensive. Suppose total revenues and costs associated with the new product's introduction are given by
$$R = 720 - 8t \qquad \text{and} \qquad C = 600 - 20t + .25t^2,$$

where t is the introduction date (in months from now). Some executives have argued for an expedited introduction date, 12 months from now ($t = 12$). Do you agree? What introduction date is most profitable? Explain.

9. As the exclusive carrier on a local air route, a regional airline must determine the number of flights it will provide per week and the fare it will charge. Taking into account operating and fuel costs, airport charges, and so on, the estimated cost per flight is \$2,000. It expects to fly full flights (100 passengers), so its marginal cost *on a per-passenger basis* is \$20. Finally, the airline's estimated demand curve is $P = 120 - .1Q$, where P is the fare in dollars and Q is the number of passengers per week.

   a. What is the airline's profit-maximizing fare? How many passengers does it carry per week, using how many flights? What is its weekly profit?

   b. Suppose the airline is offered \$4,000 per week to haul freight along the route for a local firm. This will mean replacing one of the weekly passenger flights with a freight flight (at the same operating cost). Should the airline carry freight for the local firm? Explain.

10. A producer of photocopiers derives profits from two sources: the immediate profit it makes on each copier sold and the additional profit it gains from servicing its copiers and selling toner and other supplies. The firm estimates that its additional profit from service and supplies is about \$300 over the life of *each copier sold.*

   There is disagreement in management about the implication of this tie-in profit. One group argues that this extra profit (though significant for the firm's bottom line) should have no effect on the firm's optimal output and price. A second group argues that the firm should maximize total profit by lowering price to sell additional units (even though this reduces its profit margin at the point of sale). Which view (if either) is correct?

11. Suppose a firm's inverse demand and cost equations are of the general forms $P = a - bQ$ and $C = F + cQ$, where the parameters a and b denote the intercept and slope of the inverse demand function and the parameters F and c are the firm's fixed and marginal costs, respectively. Apply the $MR = MC$ rule to confirm that the firm's optimal output and price are: $Q = (a - c)/2b$ and $P = (a + c)/2$. Provide explanations for the ways P and Q depend on the underlying economic parameters.

*12. Under the terms of the current contractual agreement, Burger Queen (BQ) is entitled to 20 percent of the revenue earned by each of its franchises. BQ's best-selling item is the Slopper (it slops out of the bun). BQ supplies the ingredients for the Slopper (bun, mystery meat, etc.) at cost to the franchise. The franchisee's average cost per Slopper (including ingredients, labor cost, and so on) is \$.80. At a particular franchise restaurant, weekly demand for Sloppers is given by $P = 3.00 - Q/800$.

   a. If BQ sets the price and weekly sales quantity of Sloppers, what quantity and price would it set? How much does BQ receive? What is the franchisee's net profit?

   b. Suppose the franchise owner sets the price and sales quantity. What price and quantity will the owner set? (*Hint:* Remember that the owner keeps only \$.80 of each extra dollar of revenue earned.) How does the total profit earned by the two parties compare to their total profit in part (a)?

   c. Now, suppose BQ and an individual franchise owner enter into an agreement in which BQ is entitled to a share of the franchisee's profit. Will profit sharing remove the conflict between BQ and the franchise operator? Under profit sharing, what will be the price and quantity of Sloppers? (Does the exact split of the profit affect your answer? Explain briefly.) What is the resulting total profit?

   d. Profit sharing is not widely practiced in the franchise business. What are its disadvantages relative to revenue sharing?

Discussion Question   As vice president of sales for a rapidly growing company, you are grappling with the question of expanding your direct sales force (from its current level of 60 national salespeople) by hiring 5 to 10 additional personnel.

   How would you estimate the additional dollar cost of each additional salesperson? Based on your company's past sales experience, how would you estimate the expected net revenue generated by an additional salesperson? (Be specific about the information you might use to derive this estimate.) How would you use these cost and revenue estimates to determine whether a sales force increase (or possibly a decrease) is warranted?

*Starred problems are more challenging.

Spreadsheet Problems

S1. A manufacturer of spare parts faces the demand curve,

$$P = 800 - 2Q,$$

and produces output according to the cost function,

$$C = 20,000 + 200Q + .5Q^2.$$

a. Create a spreadsheet modeled on the example shown.[7] (The only numerical value you should enter is the quantity in cell B7. Enter appropriate formulas to compute all other numerical entries.)
b. What is the firm's profit-maximizing quantity and price? First, determine the solution by hand—that is, by changing the quantity value in cell B7. (*Hint*: Keep an eye on marginal revenue and marginal cost in finding your way to the optimal output.)
c. Use your spreadsheet's optimizer to confirm your answer to part a.

	A	B	C	D	E	F	G
1							
2			THE OPTIMAL OUTPUT OF SPARE PARTS				
3							
4							
5		Quantity	Price	Revenue	Cost	Profit	
6							
7		20	760	15,200	24,200	−9,000	
8							
9							
10				MR	MC	Mπ	
11							
12				720	220	500	
13							

S2. Your firm competes with a close rival for shares of a $20 million per year market. Your main decision concerns how much to spend on advertising each year. Your rival is currently spending $8 million on advertising. The best estimate of your profit is given by the equation

$$\pi = 20[A/(A + 8)] - A,$$

where A is your firm's advertising expenditure (in millions of dollars). According to this equation, the firms' shares of the $20 million market are in proportion to their advertising spending. (If the firms spend equal amounts, $A = 8$, they have equal shares of the market, and so on.)

---

[7]This chapter's special appendix reviews the basics of creating, using, and optimizing spreadsheets.

a. Create a spreadsheet modeled on the example shown. Determine the firm's optimal advertising expenditure. Refer to the appendix of this chapter, if you are unsure about finding *MR*—that is, taking the derivative of the quotient, $A/(A + 8)$.

b. Use your spreadsheet's optimizer to confirm your answer in part a. Is matching your rival's spending your best policy?

	A	B	C	D	E	F
1						
2		AN OPTIMAL ADVERTISING BUDGET				
3						
4						
5		Advertising	Revenue	Cost	Profit	
6						
7		8.00	10.00	8.00	2.00	
8						
9						
10			MR	MC	Mπ	
11						
12			0.625	1.000	−0.375	
13						

S3. a. Create a spreadsheet describing Amazon's output and pricing choices with respect to the Kindle e-reader. (Use the template from Problem S1 with price equation: $P = 294 − 35Q$ and $MC = \$126$.) Use your spreadsheet optimizer to find the combination of output and price that maximizes profit.

b. Now include the extra net revenue from e-book sales, $100 per Kindle. (Compute this total in cell G9 according to the formula: $= 100*B7$.) Finally, in cell H9, compute total profit (from both Kindles and e-book sales). What combination of Kindle output and price maximizes Amazon's total profit? Explain why Amazon should cut its price relative to the price in part (a).

Suggested References

The following references provide advanced treatments of marginal analysis using differential calculus.

Baldani, J., J. Bradford, and R. Turner. *Mathematical Economics, 3rd Edition.* Ronkonkoma, NY: Linus Publications, 2011.

Besanko, D., and W. R. Braeutigam. *Microeconomics.* Hoboken, NJ: John Wiley & Sons, 2010.

Valuable references on optimization methods include:

Fourer, R., and J.-P. Goux. "Optimization as an Internet Resource." *Interfaces* (March–April 2001): 130–150.

Can a disastrous decision result from mistaking a minimum for a maximum? For a dramatic example, see:

Biddle, W. "Skeleton Alleged in the Stealth Bomber's Closet." *Science* (May 12, 1989): 650–651.

A guide to optimization software and resources on the World Wide Web is provided by H. D. Mittelmann, "Decision Tree for Optimization Software." http://plato.asu.edu/guide.html, 2013.

Check Station Answers

1. The revenue function is $R = 340Q - .8Q^2$.
2. The profit function is $\pi = R - C = -120 + 240Q - .8Q^2$.
3. At $Q = 100$, $\pi = -120 + (240)(100) - .8(100)^2 = 15,880$.
   At $Q = 99$, $\pi = -120 + (240)(99) - .8(99)^2 = 15,799.2$.
   Thus, $M\pi = (15,880 - 15,799.2)/(100 - 99) = 80.8$.
4. Marginal profit is $M\pi = d\pi/dQ = 240 - 1.6Q$. Setting this equal to zero implies that $240 - 1.6Q = 0$, or $Q = 150$.
5. Setting $MR = MC$ implies that $340 - 1.6Q = 100$. Therefore, $Q = 150$. Substituting $Q = 150$ into the price equation implies that $P = 340 - .8(150) = \$220$.
6. a. Plugging each quantity value into the inverse demand equation generates the corresponding market-clearing price.
   b. From the price equation $P = 294 - 35Q$, it follows that $MR = 294 - 70Q$. Setting $MR = MC = \$126$ implies $Q^* = 2.4$ million units and $P^* = \$210$.
   c. Adding \$100 in e-book net revenue means that Amazon's MR equation is now: $MR = 394 - 70Q$. Setting $MR = MC$ implies $Q^* = 3.829$ million units. In order to sell this volume, Amazon must lower its price to: $P^* = 294 - (35)(3.829) = \$160$. (To find this price, we have used the *unchanged* demand curve $P = \$294 - 35Q$.) By lowering its price margin, Amazon is deliberately sacrificing profit at the point of sale. But it is more than making up for it by way of additional e-book profit.

Calculus
and Optimization
Techniques

LO#1. Review the use of calculus in optimization problems.

The study of managerial economics emphasizes that decisions are taken to optimize certain objectives. This appendix introduces and reviews the use of calculus in optimization problems. These techniques will be applied throughout the book. Let's begin with an example.

Maximizing Profit   A manager who is in charge of a single product line is trying to determine the quantity of output to produce and sell to maximize the product's profit. Based on marketing and production studies, she has estimated the product's profit function to be

$$\pi = 2Q - .1Q^2 - 3.6 \qquad [2A.1]$$

where π is profit (thousands of dollars) and Q is quantity of output (thousands of units). Here the level of output, Q, is identified as the manager's *decision variable*, the item the decision maker controls. The profit function shows the relationship between the manager's decision variable and her objective. (For this reason, it often is referred to as the *objective function.*)

Figure 2A.1 presents a table listing the profit consequences of different output choices and graphs the profit function. (The graph plots profits across a continuum of possible output levels. Remember that output is measured in thousands of units. Thus, $Q = 6.123$ and $Q = 6.124$ are both legitimate output candidates.) According to convention, the graph plots the decision variable (also commonly referred to as the *independent* variable) on the horizontal axis and the objective (or *dependent* variable) on the vertical axis.

From either the table or the graph, we see that at very low output levels profit is negative. As the level of output increases, profit rises, becomes positive, and peaks. For still higher outputs, profit declines and eventually turns negative. The goal of management is to set production to generate positive profits—in particular, to attain maximum profit.

FIGURE 2A.1

The Firm's Profit Function

Marginal profit at a particular output is determined by the slope of the line drawn tangent to the profit graph.

Quantity (000s)	Profit ($000s)
0.0	−3.6
2.0	0
4.0	2.8
6.0	4.8
8.0	6.0
10.0	6.4
12.0	6.0
14.0	4.8
16.0	2.8
18.0	0
20.0	−3.6

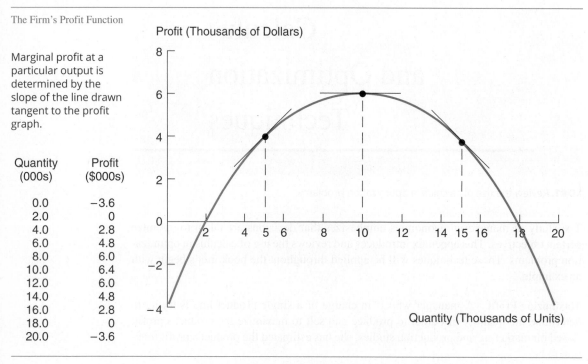

Marginal Analysis

The marginal value of any variable is the change in that variable per unit change in a given decision variable. In our example, marginal profit is the change in profit from an increase in output. A direct way to express marginal profit is to find the slope of the profit function at a given level of output. The graph in Figure 2A.1 shows how this is done. We start by specifying a particular level of output, say, $Q = 5$. Next, we draw a tangent line that just touches the profit graph at this output level. Finally, we find the slope of the tangent line. By careful measurement (taking the ratio of the "rise over the run" along the line), we find the slope to be exactly 1 (i.e., the tangent happens to be a 45° line). Thus, the marginal profit at $Q = 5$ is measured as $1,000 per additional 1,000 units or, equivalently, $1 per unit.

The upward-sloping tangent shows that profit rises as output increases. Marginal profit measures the steepness of this slope, that is, how quickly profit rises with additional output. In the graph in Figure 2A.1, tangents also are drawn at output levels $Q = 10$ and $Q = 15$. At $Q = 15$, profit falls with increases in output; marginal profit (the slope of the tangent) is negative. At $Q = 10$, the tangent line is horizontal; marginal profit (again its slope) is exactly zero.

Marginal analysis can identify the optimal output level directly, dispensing with tedious enumeration of candidates. The principle is this:

> The manager's objective is maximized when the marginal value with respect to that objective becomes zero (turning from positive to negative).

To maximize profit, the marginal principle instructs us to find the output for which marginal profit is zero. To see why this is so, suppose we are considering an output level at which marginal profit is positive. Clearly, this output cannot be optimal because a small increase would raise profit. Conversely, if marginal profit is negative at a given output, output should be decreased to raise profit. In Figure 2A.1, profit can be increased (we can move toward the revenue peak) if current output is in either the upward- or downward-sloping region. Consequently, the point of maximum profit occurs when marginal profit is neither positive nor negative; that is, it must be zero. This occurs at output $Q = 10$ thousand, where the tangent's slope is flat, that is, exactly zero.

DIFFERENTIAL CALCULUS   To apply the marginal principle, we need a simple method to compute marginal values. (It would be tedious to have to compute rates of change by measuring tangent slopes by hand.) Fortunately, the rules of differential calculus can be applied directly to any functional equation to *derive* marginal values. The process of finding the tangent slope commonly is referred to as *taking the derivative of* (or *differentiating*) the functional equation.[1] To illustrate the basic calculus rules, let y denote the dependent variable and x the independent variable. We write $y = f(x)$, where $f(x)$ represents the (unspecified) functional relationship between the variables. The notation dy/dx represents the derivative of the function, that is, the rate of change or slope of the function at a particular value of x. (The d in this notation is derived from the Greek letter delta, which has come to mean "change in.") We list the following basic rules.

Rule 1. The derivative of a constant is zero. If $y = 7$, for example, $dy/dx = 0$. Note that $y = 7$ is graphed as a horizontal line (of height 7); naturally this has a zero slope for all values of x.

Rule 2. The derivative of a constant times a variable is simply the constant. If $y = bx$, then $dy/dx = b$. For example, if $y = 13x$, then $dy/dx = 13$. In words, the function $y = 13x$ is a straight line with a slope of 13.

Rule 3. A power function has the form $y = ax^n$, where a and n are constants. The derivative of a power function is

$$dy/dx = n \cdot ax^{n-1}.$$

For instance, if $y = 4x^3$, then $dy/dx = 12x^2$.

---

[1]The following are all equivalent statements:
1. The slope of the profit function at $Q = 5$ is \$1 per unit of output.
2. The derivative of the profit function at $Q = 5$ is \$1 per unit of output.
3. The marginal profit at $Q = 5$ is \$1 per unit of output.
4. At $Q = 5$, profit is rising at a rate of \$1 per unit of output.

It is important to recognize that the power function includes many important special cases.[2] For instance, $y = 1/x^2$ is equivalently written as $y = x^{-2}$. Similarly, $y = \sqrt{x}$ becomes $y = x^{1/2}$. According to Rule 3, the respective derivatives are $dy/dx = -2x^{-3} = -2/x^3$ and $dy/dx = .5x^{-1/2} = .5/\sqrt{x}$.

Rule 4. The derivative of a sum of functions is equal to the sum of the derivatives; that is, if $y = f(x) + g(x)$, then $dy/dx = df/dx + dg/dx$. This simply means we can take the derivative of functions term by term. For example, given that $y = .1x^2 - 2x^3$, then $dy/dx = .2x - 6x^2$.

Rule 5. Suppose y is the product of two functions: $y = f(x)g(x)$. Then we have

$$dy/dx = (df/dx)g + (dg/dx)f.$$

For example, suppose we have $y = (4x)(3x^2)$. Then $dy/dx = (4)(3x^2) + (4x)(6x) = 36x^2$. (Note that this example can also be written as $y = 12x^3$; we confirm that $dy/dx = 36x^2$ using Rule 3.)

Rule 6. Suppose y is a quotient: $y = f(x)/g(x)$. Then we have

$$dy/dx = [(df/dx)g - (dg/dx)f]/g^2.$$

For example, suppose we have $y = x/(8 + x)$. Then

$$dy/dx = [1 \cdot (8 + x) - 1 \cdot (x)]/(8 + x)^2 = 8/(8 + x)^2.$$

Let's derive an expression for marginal profit (denoted by $M\pi$) applying these calculus rules to our profit function:

$$\pi = 2Q - .1Q^2 - 3.6.$$

From Rule 4, we know we can proceed term by term. From Rule 2, the derivative of the first term is 2. According to Rule 3, the derivative of the second term is $-.2Q$. From Rule 1, the derivative of the third term is zero. Thus,

$$M\pi = d\pi/dx = 2 - .2Q.$$

Notice the elegance of this approach. By substituting specific values of Q, we can find marginal profit at any desired level of output. For instance, at $Q = 5$, we find that $M\pi = 2 - (.2)(5) = 1$; at $Q = 12$, $M\pi = -.4$; and so on.

To determine the firm's optimal output level, we set $M\pi = 0$. Thus,

$$2 - .2Q = 0.$$

Solving this equation for Q, we find $Q = 10$. This confirms that the profit-maximizing level of output is 10 thousand units.

---

[2]Notice that Rules 1 and 2 are actually special cases of Rule 3. Setting $n = 0$ implies that $y = a$, and, therefore, $dy/dx = 0$ (Rule 1). Setting $n = 1$ implies that $y = ax$ and, therefore, $dy/dx = a$ (Rule 2).

THE SECOND DERIVATIVE   In general, one must be careful to check that a maximum, not a minimum, has been found. In the previous example, the graph makes it clear that we have found a maximum. But suppose the profit expression is more complicated, say:

$$\pi = 1.8Q^2 - .1Q^3 - 6Q - 10. \qquad\qquad [2A.2]$$

Figure 2A.2 shows the associated profit graph. Notice that there are two quantities at which the slope is zero: one is a maximum and the other is a minimum. It would be disastrous if we confused the two. Taking the derivative of the profit function, we find

$$M\pi = d\pi/dx = 3.6Q - .3Q^2 - 6.$$

FIGURE 2A.2

A Second Profit Function

The manager must be careful to distinguish a maximum from a minimum.

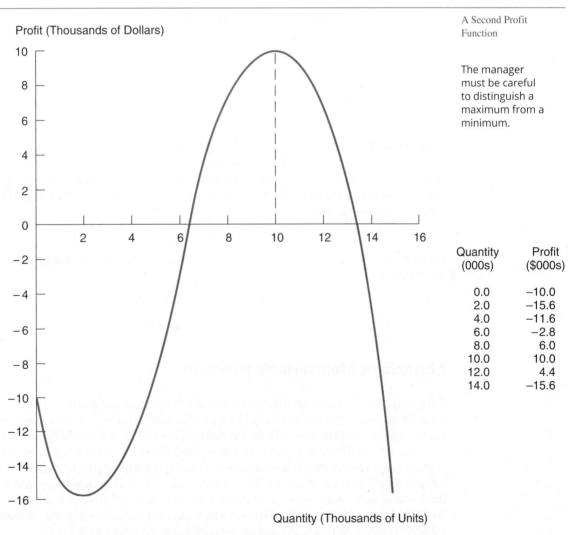

Profit (Thousands of Dollars)

Quantity (Thousands of Units)

Quantity (000s)	Profit ($000s)
0.0	−10.0
2.0	−15.6
4.0	−11.6
6.0	−2.8
8.0	6.0
10.0	10.0
12.0	4.4
14.0	−15.6

Substitution confirms that marginal profit is zero at the quantities $Q = 2$ and $Q = 10$. The graph shows that $Q = 2$ *minimizes* profit, whereas $Q = 10$ *maximizes* profit.

There is a direct way to distinguish between a maximum and a minimum. At a maximum, the slope of the profit function changes from positive to zero to negative as output increases; that is, the slope of the profit function decreases as output increases around the maximum. In contrast, at a minimum, the slope changes from negative to zero to positive; the slope is increasing. Because of this difference, the *second* derivative of the profit function can be used to distinguish between the two cases. The second derivative is found by taking the derivative of $d\pi/dt$. If the second derivative is negative (i.e., the slope is decreasing), the point in question is a local maximum; if the second derivative is positive, the point is a local minimum. Taking the derivative of $d\pi/dQ$, we find the second derivative to be

$$d^2\pi/dQ^2 = d(d\pi/dQ)dQ$$
$$= dM\pi/dQ = d(3.6Q - 0.3Q^2 - 6)/dQ$$
$$= 3.6 - .6Q$$

take the derivative *twice*. At $Q = 2$, we find that $d^2\pi/dQ^2 = 3.6 - .6(2) = 2.4$. Since this is positive, $Q = 2$ represents a local minimum. At $Q = 10$, we find that $d^2\pi/dQ^2 = 3.6 - .6(10) = -2.4$. Since this is negative, $Q = 10$ represents a local maximum.

MARGINAL REVENUE AND MARGINAL COST   We have seen that maximum profit is achieved at the point such that marginal profit equals zero, $d\pi/dQ = 0$. The same condition can be expressed in a different form by separating profit into its two components. Profit is defined as the difference between revenues and costs. Thus, the profit function can be written as

$$\pi(Q) = R(Q) - C(Q),$$

the difference between revenues and costs. In turn, the condition that marginal profit equal zero is

$$d\pi/dQ = dR/dQ - dC/dQ = MR - MC = 0.$$

In short, profit is maximized when marginal revenue equals marginal cost.

Maximizing Multivariable Functions

Frequently, the manager must determine optimal values for several decision variables at once, for instance, a product's price and its associated advertising budget. In this case, the product's profit would be expressed by the function, $\pi = \pi(P, A)$, where P is the product's price and A is its advertising budget in dollars. Here the key to maximizing profit is to apply a double dose of marginal reasoning. Marginal profit with respect to each decision variable should be equated to zero. The optimal value of P is found where the "partial" derivative of profit with respect to P equals zero. This partial derivative is denoted by $\partial\pi/\partial P$ and is found by taking the derivative with respect to P, holding A (the other decision variable) constant. Similarly, the optimal value of A is found where $\partial\pi/\partial A = 0$.

PRICE AND ADVERTISING   Suppose the firm's profit function is

$$\pi = 20 + 2P - 2P^2 + 4A - A^2 + 2PA.$$

The partial derivative of profit with respect to P is

$$\partial\pi/\pi P = 2 - 4P + 2A.$$

Notice that when we take the partial derivative with respect to P, we are treating A as a constant. Thus, $4A$ and A^2 disappear (Rule 1) and $2PA$ becomes $2A$ (Rule 2). The partial derivative of profit with respect to A is

$$\partial\pi/\partial A = 4 - 2A + 2P.$$

Setting each of these expressions equal to zero produces two equations in two unknowns. Solving these simultaneously, we find that $P = 3$ and $A = 5$. Thus, profit is maximized at these values of P and A.

Constrained Optimization

In the previous examples, the decision variables were unconstrained, that is, free to take on any values. Frequently, however, decision variables can be changed only within certain constraints. Consider the following example.

A SUPPLY COMMITMENT   A firm is trying to identify its profit-maximizing level of output. By contract, it already is committed to supplying at least seven units to its customer. Suppose that its predicted profit function is given by $\pi = 40Q - 4Q^2$. The firm seeks to maximize π subject to $Q \geq 7$. Setting marginal profit equal to zero, we have $d\pi/dQ = 40 - 8Q = 0$ so that $Q = 5$. But this value is *infeasible*; it violates the contract constraint. The constrained maximum occurs at $Q = 7$, where $d\pi/dQ = -6$. Note that, since marginal profit is negative, profit would decline if Q were increased. Thus, the firm would like to raise profit by decreasing Q, but this is impossible due to the binding contract constraint.

Another kind of constrained optimization problem occurs when there are multiple decision variables.

Profits from Multiple Markets   A firm has a limited amount of output and must decide what quantities (Q_1 and Q_2) to sell to two different market segments. For example, suppose it seeks to maximize total profit given by

$$\pi = (20Q_1 - .5Q_1^2) + (40Q_2 - Q_2^2),$$

subject to $Q_1 + Q_2 \leq 25$. Setting marginal profit equal to zero for each quantity, we find that $Q_1 = 20$ and $Q_2 = 20$. But these desired quantities are infeasible; the total (40) exceeds the available supply (25). The manager must cut back one or both outputs. But how should she do this while maintaining as high a level of profit as possible? To answer this question, observe that if output is cut back in each market, the marginal profit in each market will be positive. What if the manager chose outputs such that marginal profit differed across the two markets, say, $M\pi_1 > M\pi_2 > 0$? If this were the case, the manager could increase her total profit by selling one more unit in market 1 and one less unit in market 2. She would continue to switch units as long as the marginal profits differed across the markets. At the optimal solution, marginal profits must be equal. Thus, $\partial\pi/\partial Q_1 = \partial\pi/\partial Q_2$ must hold as well as $Q_1 + Q_2 = 25$. Taking derivatives, we find the first condition to be $20 - Q_1 = 40 - 2Q_2$. Solving this equation and the quantity constraint simultaneously, we find that $Q_1 = 10$ and $Q_2 = 15$. This is the firm's optimal solution.

THE METHOD OF LAGRANGE MULTIPLIERS   The last two problems can be solved by an alternative means known as the *method of Lagrange multipliers.* To use the method, we create a new variable, the Lagrange multiplier, for each constraint. In the subsequent solution, we determine optimal values for the relevant decision variables and the Lagrange multipliers. For instance, in the supply commitment example, there is one constraint, $Q = 7$. (We know the constraint is binding from our discussion.) To apply the method, we rewrite this constraint as $7 - Q = 0$, create a new variable, call it z, and write

$$L = \pi + z(7 - Q)$$
$$= 40Q - 4Q^2 + z(7 - Q)$$

In short, we have formed L (denoted the Lagrangian) by taking the original objective function and adding to it the binding constraint (multiplied by z). We then find the partial derivatives with respect to the two variables, Q and z, and set them equal to zero:

$$\partial L/\partial Q = 40 - 8Q - z = 0;$$
$$\partial L/\partial z = 7 - Q = 0.$$

Solving these equations simultaneously, we find that $Q = 7$ and $z = -16$. The value of Q is hardly surprising; we already know this is the best the manager can do. The interpretation of the Lagrange multiplier, z, is of some interest. The value of the multiplier measures the marginal profit ($M\pi = -16$) at the constrained optimum.

To apply the method in the multiple-market example, we write

$$L = (20Q_1 - 0.5Q_1^2) + (40Q_2 - Q_2^2) + z(25 - Q_1 - Q_2),$$

where the binding constraint is $Q_1 + Q_2 = 25$ and z again denotes the Lagrange multiplier. Setting the appropriate partial derivatives equal to zero, we find

$$\partial L/\partial Q_1 = 20 - Q_1 - z = 0;$$
$$\partial L/\partial Q_2 = 40 - 2Q_2 - z = 0;$$
$$\partial L/\partial z = 25 - Q_1 - Q_2 = 0.$$

Notice that the third condition is simply the original constraint. We now find values that satisfy these three equations simultaneously: $Q_1 = 10$, $Q_2 = 15$, and $z = 10$. The values for Q_1 and Q_2 confirm our original solution. In addition, note that the first two equations can be written as $z = 20 - Q_1 = 40 - 2Q_2$, or $z = M\pi_1 = M\pi_2$. In other words, the multiplier z represents the common value of marginal profit (equalized across the two markets). The actual value of $M\pi$ in each market is $z = 10$. Thus, if the manager could increase total sales (above 25), he would increase profit by 10 per unit of additional capacity.

To sum up, the use of Lagrange multipliers is a powerful method. It effectively allows us to treat constrained problems as though they were unconstrained.[3]

Questions and Problems

1. Suppose a firm assesses its profit function as

$$\pi = -10 - 48Q + 15Q^2 - Q^3.$$

   a. Compute the firm's profit for the following levels of output:

$$Q = 2, 8, \text{ and } 14.$$

   b. Derive an expression for marginal profit. Compute marginal profit at $Q = 2, 8$, and 14. Confirm that profit is maximized at $Q = 8$. (Why is profit not maximized at $Q = 2$?)

2. The economist Arthur Laffer has long argued that *lower* tax rates, by stimulating employment and investment, can lead to *increased* tax revenue to the government. If this prediction is correct, a tax rate reduction would be a win-win policy, good for both taxpayers and the government. Laffer went on to sketch a tax revenue curve in the shape of an upside-down U.

   In general, the government's tax revenue can be expressed as $R = t \cdot B(t)$, where t denotes the tax rate ranging between 0 and 1 (i.e., between 0 and 100 percent) and B denotes the tax base. Explain why the tax base is likely to shrink as tax rates become very high. How might this lead to a U-shaped tax revenue curve?

3. The economic staff of the US Department of the Treasury has been asked to recommend a new tax policy concerning the treatment of the foreign earnings of US firms. Currently the foreign earnings of U.S. multinational companies are taxed only when the income is returned to the United States. Taxes are deferred if the income is reinvested abroad. The department seeks a tax rate that will maximize total tax revenue from foreign earnings. Find the optimal tax rate if
   a. $B(t) = 80 - 100t$
   b. $B(t) = 80 - 240t^2$
   c. $B(t) = 80 - 80\sqrt{t}$, where B(t) is the foreign earnings of US multinational companies returned to the United States and t is the tax rate.

4. A firm's total profit is given by $\pi = 20x - x^2 + 16y - 2y^2$.
   a. What values of x and y will maximize the firm's profit?
   b. Repeat part a assuming the firm faces the constraint $x + y \le 8$.
   c. Repeat part a assuming the constraint is $x + .5y \le 7.5$.

---

[3]It is important to note that the method of Lagrange multipliers is relevant only in the case of binding constraints. Typically, we begin by seeking an unconstrained optimum. If such an optimum satisfies all of the constraints, we are done. If one or more constraints are violated, however, we apply the method of Lagrange multipliers for the solution.

Optimization
Using Spreadsheets

LO#1. Review the use of spreadsheets in optimization problems.

We have already encountered several quantitative approaches to optimizing a given objective: enumeration, graphic solutions, and (in the preceding appendix) calculus. To these we can add a fourth approach: spreadsheet-based optimization. Over the past 30 years, spreadsheets have become powerful management tools. Modeling a quantitative decision on a spreadsheet harnesses the power of computer calculation instead of laborious pencil-and-paper figuring. Besides helping to define and manage decision problems, spreadsheets also compute optimal solutions with no more than a click of a mouse. There are many leading spreadsheet programs—Excel, Google Docs, Calc, Lotus 123, Quattro Pro, to name a few—and all work nearly the same way. To review the fundamentals of spreadsheet use, let's revisit the microchip example.

Table 2A.1 shows this example depicted in an Excel spreadsheet. The spreadsheet consists of a table of cells. Besides the title in row 2, we have typed labels (Quantity, Price, MR) in rows 5 and 10. We have also entered the number 2.0 in cell B7 (highlighted in colored type). This cell houses our basic decision variable, output. For the moment, we have set microchip output at 2.0 lots. Cells C7 to F7 show the price, revenue, cost, and profit results of producing 2.0 lots. These cells are linked via formulas to our output cell. For instance, consider cell C7 showing a price of 130. When we created the spreadsheet, we typed the formula:

$$= 170 - 20*B7,$$

into cell C7 (and then pressed return). This formula embodies the price equation, $P = 170 - 20Q$. By entering the preceding spreadsheet formula, we are telling the computer to subtract 20 times the value of cell B7 from 170 and to enter the resulting numerical value in cell C7. (*Note*: We entered a formula, *not* the number 130, into this cell.)

The other numerical values are similarly determined by formulas. Thus, in cell D7, we entered the formula: =B7*C7, instructing the spreadsheet to compute revenue as the product of the price and quantity cells. In cell E7, we entered the cost formula: =100 + 38*B7. In cell F7, we computed profit by entering: = D7 − E7, and in cell D12, we computed MR by entering: =170 − 40*B7. Indeed, to gain experience with the ways of spreadsheets, we suggest that you start with a blank spreadsheet and re-create Table 2A.1 for yourself.

TABLE 2A.1

Optimizing a
Spreadsheet

	A	B	C	D	E	F	G
1							
2			THE OPTIMAL OUTPUT OF MICROCHIPS				
3							
4				.			
5		Quantity	Price	Revenue	Cost	Profit	
6							
7		2.0	130	260	176	84	
8							
9							
10				MR	MC	Mπ	
11							
12				90	38	52	
13							
14							

That is, type in labels, numerical values, and formulas as indicated. (Note: Typing in cell addresses is not the only way to enter formulas. The quickest way is to mouse click on the cell that is part of the formula.)

With the spreadsheet in hand, there are several ways to determine the microchip firm's profit-maximizing output. The most primitive way is to try various numerical values in cell B7, observe the resulting profit results in cell F7, and, thereby, identify the optimal output. This represents solution by enumeration. A second, more expeditious approach uses MR and MC as guides. Again, values in cell B7 are varied by hand, but this time systematically. Output should be increased as long as MR exceeds MC; it should be cut if MC exceeds MR. When MR equals MC, the profit-maximizing level of output has been attained.

A third approach is to direct the computer to optimize the spreadsheet. The top menu in Table 2A.2 illustrates Excel's optimizer, called "Solver," which is called by clicking on the "Solver" listing found under the "Tools" menu. By completing the menu in Table 2A.2, one instructs the computer to optimize the spreadsheet. In the menu, we have (1) entered target cell F7 (the profit cell), (2) to be maximized, (3) by varying cell B7. Then, after one clicks on the solve box, the computer finds a new numerical value in cell B7 that maximizes cell F7. (The value one starts with in cell B7 doesn't matter; the computer will replace it with the optimal value it finds.) Using an internal mathematical algorithm, Solver finds the optimal level of output, 3.3 lots, places this value in cell B7, and the other cells (price, revenue, cost, and so on) change accordingly.

This simple example illustrates but does not do full justice to the power of spreadsheet optimization. In fact, optimizers are designed to solve complex problems involving

TABLE 2A.2

Optimizing a Spreadsheet

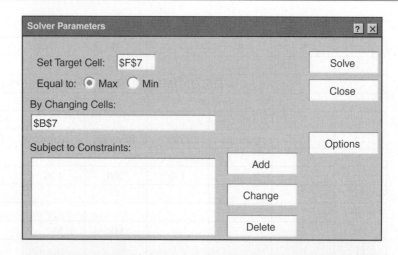

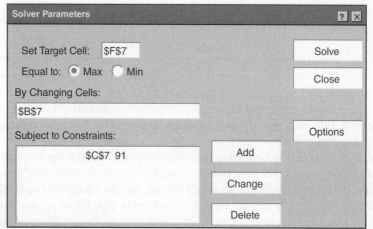

many decision variables and multiple constraints. For instance, the firm's profit might well depend on several decision variables: output, advertising spending, the size of its direct sales force. Here, in order to maximize profit, the manager would specify multiple variable cells in the solver menu. In addition, the firm might face various constraints in its quest for maximum profit. For instance, suppose the microchip producer was quite sure that setting a price greater than $91,000 per lot would attract a cutthroat competitor whose sales of "cloned" chips would decimate the firm's own profit. In this case, management's *constrained* optimization problem would include the requirement that the value in price cell C7 should not exceed 91. The bottom menu in Table 2A.2 includes this new constraint. The spreadsheet's new optimal solution (not shown) becomes 3.95 lots, implying exactly a $91,000 price and a reduced profit of $109,350.

To sum up, the beauty of any spreadsheet-based optimization program is that, upon execution, it instantly computes all optimal values consistent with satisfying all constraints.

CHAPTER 3

Demand Analysis
and Optimal Pricing

*There's no brand loyalty so strong that the offer of "penny off"
can't overcome it.*

A MARKETING APHORISM

LO#1. Describe the key determinants of demand.

LO#2. Introduce elasticity as the key quantitative measure of demand.

LO#3. Demonstrate how demand analysis is used in decisions involving revenue maximization, optimal markup pricing, and price discrimination.

Anyone who has traveled via commercial airline, even on an infrequent basis, knows there is a bewildering plethora of fares for the same route. Besides the standard first-class, business, and coach fares, there are discount fares for round-trip travel and for travelers who book well in advance, travel on off-peak days, or bundle their flight with a vacation package. The fare structure is daunting not only for travelers but also for the airlines. In determining the standard coach fare on a particular route, the airline has to consider (1) the cost of the flight (including fuel, labor, and administrative costs), (2) the historical pattern of business and leisure use on the route, (3) overall economic conditions (which affect travel demand), and (4) the prices charged by competing airlines. Together, the airlines mount some 85,000 domestic flights each day, and they repeatedly alter prices on their computerized reservation systems as conditions change.

Among airlines, the name of the game is yield management: how to price seat by seat to generate the greatest possible profit. For instance, airlines typically sell higher-priced tickets to business travelers who cannot take advantage of supersaver and other discount fares. At the same time, they sell other seats on the same flight at sharply lower prices to attract price-sensitive vacation travelers. A classic example of yield management is the competitive route between Los Angeles and Kennedy Airport in New York. For a typical March departure, the cabin of a 158-seat aircraft along this route featured scores of fares, ranging from first-class round-trip tickets at $4,800 to discount tickets below $300. On average, half the tickets might be sold for fares below $500, some 20 percent of tickets above $900, with the remainder priced in between. For the same economy class seat, some travelers cashed in frequent flier miles; some purchased at discounts from third-party providers; others received lower fares for restricted tickets. In general, early buyers paid less, but fares typically fluctuated day to day, depending on demand.

The question here is: How can demand analysis help the airlines win the game of yield management?

**Airline Ticket
Pricing**

In Chapter 2, we presented a simple model of profit maximization. There the manager began with demand and cost functions and used them to determine the profit-maximizing price and output level for a given product or service. In this chapter, we will take a closer look at demand and the role it plays in managerial decision making.

DETERMINANTS OF DEMAND

The notion of demand is much richer than the simple formulation given in the previous chapter. Up until now we have studied the dependence of demand on a single factor: price. We begin this chapter by considering the *multiple* determinants of demand. Next, we look more closely at the responsiveness of demand to these factors, a concept captured in the basic definition of *elasticity*. In the remaining sections, we show how demand can be used to guide managers in their goal of maximizing profits. We will refine our optimization techniques to account for more complicated demand conditions—those that include the possibilities of market segmentation and price discrimination.

The Demand Function

To illustrate the basic quantitative aspects of demand, let's start with a concrete example: the demand for air travel. Put yourself in the position of a manager for a leading regional airline. One of your specific responsibilities is to analyze the state of travel demand for a nonstop route between Houston, Texas, and a rapidly growing city in Florida. Your airline flies one daily departure from each city to the other (two flights in all) and faces a single competitor that offers two daily flights from each city. Your task is complicated by the fact that the number of travelers on your airline (and therefore the revenue your company earns) has fluctuated considerably in the past three years. Reviewing this past experience, you realize the main determinants of your airline's traffic are your own price and the price of your competitor. In addition, traffic between the two cities was brisk during years in which the Texas and Florida economies enjoyed rapid expansion. But, during the Great Recession beginning in 2008, air travel fell between the two cities.

Your immediate goal is to analyze demand for coach-class travel between the cities. (The small aircraft used on this route does not accommodate first-class seating.) You begin by writing down the following demand function:

$$Q = f(P, P^c, Y). \qquad [3.1]$$

This expression reads, "The number of your airline's coach seats sold per flight (Q) depends on (is a function of) your airline's coach fare (P), your competitor's fare (P^c), and income in the region (Y)." In short, the **demand function** shows, in equation form, the relationship between the quantity sold of a good or service and one or more variables.

The demand function is useful shorthand, but does not indicate the exact quantitative relationship between Q and P, P^c, and Y. For this we need to write the demand function in a particular form. Suppose the economic forecasting unit of your airline has supplied you with the following equation which best describes demand:

$$Q = 25 + 3Y + P^c - 2P. \qquad [3.2]$$

Like the demand equations in Chapter 2, Equation 3.2 predicts sales quantity once one has specified values of the explanatory variables appearing on the right-hand side.[1] What does the equation say about the current state of demand? Currently, your airline and your competitor are charging the same one-way fare, \$240. The current level of income in the region is 105.[2] Putting these values into Equation 3.2, we find that

$$Q = 25 + 3(105) + 1(240) - 2(240)$$
$$= 100 \text{ seats.}$$

A comparison of this prediction with your airline's recent experience shows this equation to be quite accurate. In the past three months, the average number of coach seats sold per flight (week by week) consistently fell in the 90- to 105-seat range. Since 180 coach seats are available on the flight, the airline's load factor is $100/180 = 55.5$ percent.

The demand equation can be used to test the effect of changes in any of the explanatory variables. From Equation 3.2, we see the following:

1. For each point increase in the income index, 3 additional seats will be sold.
2. For each \$10 increase in the airline's fare, 20 fewer seats will be sold.
3. For each \$10 increase in the competitor's fare, 10 additional seats will be sold.

Each of these results assumes that the effect in question is the *only* change that occurs; that is, all other factors are held constant. In fact, the *total change* in demand caused by simultaneous changes in the explanatory variables can be expressed as

$$\Delta Q = 3\Delta Y + 1\Delta P^c - 2\Delta P, \qquad [3.3]$$

where Δ means "change in." Thus, if income increases by 5 index points while both airline prices are cut by \$15, we find $\Delta Q = 3(5) + 1(-15) - 2(-15) = 30$ seats. Your airline would expect to sell 30 additional seats on each flight.

Use Equation 3.3 to compute the change in sales, ΔQ, that will result from $\Delta Y = -8$, $\Delta P^c = 12$, and $\Delta P = 20$.

CHECK STATION 1

The Demand Curve and Shifting Demand

Suppose that, in the immediate future, regional income is expected to remain at 105 and the competitor's fare will stay at \$240. However, your airline's fare is not set in stone,

[1]Methods of estimating and forecasting demand are presented in Chapter 4.

[2]This value is an *index* of aggregate income—business profits and personal income—in Texas and Florida. The index is set such that *real* income (i.e., after accounting for inflation) in 2005 (the so-called base year) equals 100. Thus, a current value of 105 means that regional income has increased 5 percent in real terms since then. In the depth of the Texas recession, the index stood at 87, a 13 percent reduction in real income relative to the base year.

and you naturally are interested in testing the effect of different possible coach prices. Substituting the values of Y and P^c into Equation 3.2's demand function, we find that

$$Q = 25 + 3(105) + 1(240) - 2P \qquad [3.4]$$
$$= 580 - 2P.$$

Like the basic demand equation facing the microchip producer in Chapter 2, Equation 3.4 relates the quantity of the good or service sold to its price. Here, however, it is important to remember that, in the background, all other factors affecting demand are held constant (at the values $Y = 105$ and $P^c = 240$). Of course, it is a simple matter to graph this demand equation as a demand curve. (Do this yourself as practice.) As usual, the demand curve is downward sloping.[3]

Starting from an initial price, by varying the coach fare up or down, we move *along* (respectively, up and down) the demand curve. A higher price means lower sales. But what happens if there is a change in one of the other factors that affect demand? As we now show, *such a change causes a shift in the demand curve.* To illustrate, suppose that a year from now P^c is expected to be unchanged but Y is forecast to grow to 119. What will the demand curve look like a year hence? To answer this question, we substitute the new value, $Y = 119$ (along with $P^c = 240$), into the demand function:

$$Q = 622 - 2P. \qquad [3.5]$$

Now compare the new and old demand equations. Observe that they are of the same form, with one key difference: The constant term of the new demand curve is larger than that of the old. Therefore, if your airline were to leave its own fare unchanged a year from now, you would enjoy a greater volume of coach traffic. Figure 3.1 underscores this point by graphing both the old and new demand curves. Note that the new demand curve constitutes a parallel shift to the right (toward greater sales quantities) of the old demand curve. At $P = \$240$, current demand is 100 seats per flight. At the same fare, coach demand one year from now is forecast to be 142 seats (due to the increase in regional income), a gain of 42 seats. In fact, for *any* fare your airline might set (and leave unchanged), demand a year from now is predicted to grow by 42 seats. Thus, we confirm that there is a 42-unit rightward shift in the demand curve from old to new demand.

Another way to think about the effect of the increase in regional income is to write down the equations for the market-clearing price for the old and new demand curves. After rearranging Equations 3.4 and 3.5, these are

$$P = 290 - Q/2 \text{ (old)} \qquad [3.6]$$
$$P = 311 - Q/2 \text{ (new)}.$$

Thus, if your airline seeks to sell the same number of seats a year from now that it does today, it can do so while raising the coach ticket price by \$21 (the difference between 311 and 290). To see this in Figure 3.1, fix the quantity and read the higher price off the new demand curve.

---

[3]We can graph the demand *curve* (by putting quantity and price on the respective axes), but we cannot graph the demand *function* (because this involves four variables and we do not have four axes). Thus, graphing a particular demand curve requires holding all other factors constant.

FIGURE 3.1

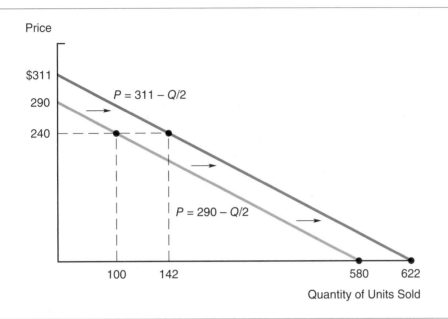

Price

$311

290

240

$P = 311 - Q/2$

$P = 290 - Q/2$

100   142

580   622

Quantity of Units Sold

A Shift in Demand

Due to growth in regional income, the airline's demand curve in one year's time lies to the right of its current demand curve. At an unchanged price a year from now, it expects to sell 42 additional seats on each flight.

General Determinants of Demand

The example of demand for air travel is representative of the results found for most goods or services. Obviously, the *good's own price* is a key determinant of demand. Close behind in importance is the *level of income* of the potential purchasers of the good or service. A basic definition is useful in describing the effect of income on sales: A product is called a **normal good** if an increase in income raises its sales. In our example, air travel is a normal good. For any normal good, sales vary directly with income; that is, the coefficient on income in the demand equation is positive. As an empirical matter, most goods and services are normal. (Of course, the extra spending on a given good may be small or even nearly zero.) Likewise, when income is reduced in an economy experiencing a recession, demand falls across the spectrum of normal goods. For a small category of goods (such as certain food staples), an increase in income causes a reduction in spending. These are termed **inferior goods**. For instance, an individual of moderate means may regularly consume a large quantity of beans, rice, and ground meat. But, after experiencing an increase in income, the individual can better afford other foods and therefore reduces his consumption of the old staples.

A third set of factors affecting demand are the prices of *substitute* and *complementary* goods. As the term suggests, a **substitute good** competes with and can substitute for the good in question. In the airline example, travel on one airline serving the same intercity route is a very close substitute for travel on the other. Accordingly, *an increase in the price of the substitute good or service causes an increase in demand for the good in question* (by making it relatively more attractive to purchase). Note that substitution in demand can occur at many levels. For instance, the airline's sales along the route are affected not only by changes in competing airline fares but also by train and bus fares and auto-operating costs. To a greater or lesser degree, these other modes of transportation are substitutes for air travel.

A pair of goods is **complementary** if an increase in demand for one causes an increase in demand for the other. For instance, an increase in the sales of new automobiles will have a positive effect on the sales of new tires. In particular, tire manufacturers are very interested in the prices car manufacturers announce for new models. They know that discount auto prices will spur not only the sales of cars but also the sales of tires. The price of a complementary good enters negatively into the demand function; that is, *an increase in the price of a complementary good reduces demand for the good in question.* For example, Florida resort packages and travel between Houston and Florida are to some extent complementary. Thus, the price of resort packages would enter with a negative coefficient into the demand function for travel along the route.[4]

Finally, a wide variety of other factors may affect the demand for particular goods and services. Normal *population* growth of prime groups that consume the good or service will increase demand. As the populations of Houston and the Florida city grow, so will air travel between them. The main determinant of soft-drink sales is the number of individuals in the 10-to-25 age group. Changes in preferences and tastes are another important factor. Various trends over the past 20 years have supported growth in demand for new foods (diet, natural, organic), new electronic products (smart phones, digital cameras, MP3 players, DVD players, and iPads), and new recreation services (exercise, travel, tanning salons, and so on). The list is endless.

ELASTICITY OF DEMAND

Price Elasticity

Price elasticity measures the responsiveness of a good's sales to changes in its price. This concept is important for two reasons. First, knowledge of a good's price elasticity allows firms to predict the impact of price changes on unit sales. Second, price elasticity guides the firm's profit-maximizing pricing decisions.

Let's begin with a basic definition: The **price elasticity of demand** is the ratio of the percentage change in quantity and the percentage change in the good's price, all other factors held constant. In algebraic terms:

$$E_P = \frac{\% \text{ change in } Q}{\% \text{ change in } P}, \qquad [3.7]$$

$$= \frac{\Delta Q/Q}{\Delta P/P} = \frac{(Q_1 - Q_0)/Q_0}{(P_1 - P_0)/P_0}$$

---

[4]Although we say that autos and tires are complementary goods, the cross-price effects need not be of comparable magnitudes. Auto prices have a large impact on tire sales, but tire prices have a very minor impact on auto sales because they are a small fraction of the full cost of a new car.

where P_0 and Q_0 are the initial price and quantity, respectively. For example, consider the airline's demand curve as described in Equation 3.4. At the current \$240 fare, 100 coach seats are sold. If the airline cut its price to \$235, 110 seats would be demanded. Therefore, we find

$$E_P = \frac{(110 - 100)/100}{(235 - 240)/240} = \frac{10.0\%}{-2.1\%} = -4.8.$$

In this example, price was cut by 2.1 percent (the denominator), with the result that quantity increased by 10 percent (the numerator). Therefore, the price elasticity (the ratio of these two effects) is −4.8. Notice that the change in quantity was due solely to the price change. The other factors that potentially could affect sales (income and the competitor's price) did not change. (The requirement "all other factors held constant" in the definition is essential for a meaningful notion of price elasticity.) We observe that there is a large percentage quantity change for a relatively small price change. The ratio is almost fivefold. Demand is very responsive to price.

Price elasticity is a key ingredient in applying marginal analysis to determine optimal prices. Because marginal analysis works by evaluating "small" changes taken with respect to an initial decision, it is useful to measure elasticity with respect to an infinitesimally small change in price. In this instance, we write elasticity as

$$E_P = \frac{dQ/Q}{dP/P}. \qquad [3.8a]$$

We can rearrange this expression to read

$$E_P = \left(\frac{dQ}{dP}\right)\left(\frac{P}{Q}\right). \qquad [3.8b]$$

In words, the elasticity (measured at price P) depends directly on dQ/dP, the derivative of the demand function with respect to P (as well as on the ratio of P to Q).

The algebraic expressions in Equations 3.7 and 3.8a are referred to as *point elasticities* because they link percentage quantity and price changes *at a price-quantity point on the demand curve*. Although most widely used, point elasticity measures are not the only way to describe changes in price and quantity. A closely related measure is *arc* price elasticity, which is defined as

$$E_P = \frac{\Delta Q/\overline{Q}}{\Delta P/\overline{P}},$$

where $\overline{Q}$ is the average of the two quantities, $\overline{Q} = (Q_0 + Q_1)/2$, and $\overline{P}$ is the average of the two prices, $\overline{P} = (P_0 + P_1)/2$. In the airline example, the average quantity is 105 seats, the average price is \$237.50, and the arc price elasticity is $(10/105)/(-5/237.5) = -4.5$.

The main advantage of the arc elasticity measure is that it treats the prices and quantities symmetrically; that is, it does not distinguish between the "initial" and "final" prices and quantities. Regardless of the starting point, the elasticity is the same. In contrast, in computing the elasticity via Equation 3.7, one must be careful to specify P_0 and Q_0. To illustrate, suppose the initial airfare is \$235 and 110 seats are filled. The elasticity associated with a price hike to \$240 (and a drop to 100 seats) is $E_P = (-10/110)/(5/235) = -4.3$. Thus, we see that the elasticity associated with the change is -4.8 or -4.3, depending on the starting point.

The overriding advantage of point elasticities (Equation 3.8a) is their application in conjunction with marginal analysis. For instance, a firm's optimal pricing policy depends directly on its estimate of the price elasticity, $E_P = (dQ/Q)/(dP/P)$. In this and later chapters, we will focus on point elasticities in our analysis of optimal decisions.[5]

Elasticity measures the sensitivity of demand with respect to price. In describing elasticities, it is useful to start with a basic benchmark. First, demand is said to be **unitary elastic** if $E_P = -1$. In this case, the percentage change in price is exactly matched by the resulting percentage change in quantity, but in the opposite direction. Second, demand is **inelastic** if $-1 < E_P \leq 0$. The term *inelastic* suggests that demand is relatively unresponsive to price: The percentage change in quantity is less (in absolute value) than the percentage change in price. Finally, demand is **elastic** if $E_P < -1$. In this case, an initial change in price causes a larger percentage change in quantity. In short, elastic demand is highly responsive, or sensitive, to changes in price.

The easiest way to understand the meaning of inelastic and elastic demand is to examine two extreme cases. Figure 3.2a depicts a vertical demand curve representing **perfectly inelastic** demand, $E_P = 0$. Here sales are constant (at $Q = 100$) no matter how high the price charged. Thus, for any price change, the quantity change is zero and therefore so is the elasticity.[6] Figure 3.2b depicts the opposite extreme: a horizontal demand curve where demand is **perfectly elastic**, $E_P = -\infty$. The horizontal curve indicates that the firm can sell as much output as it likes at the given price; whether it sells a large or small output quantity will have no effect on its price. In this case, we say that the market determines the firm's price. (Note, also, that the firm can sell nothing at a higher-than-market price.) Demand is called perfectly elastic because sales are infinitely sensitive to price. To see this, consider the nearly horizontal demand curve in Figure 3.2 and observe that any small price change causes a very large quantity change in the opposite direction. For horizontal demand, the quantity change becomes infinite for any price change, even one approaching zero; thus, the elasticity ratio becomes infinite, $E_P = -\infty$.

CHECK STATION 2   **"The demand for automobiles must be less elastic than the demand for videogame players because a \$50 reduction in the price of cars does not affect the number sold nearly as much as a \$50 reduction in the price of players." Is this statement correct? Explain.**

[5] As long as the price change is very small, the point elasticity calculated via Equation 3.7 will vary little whether the higher or lower price is taken as the starting point. Furthermore, this value will closely approximate the exact measure of elasticity given by Equation 3.8a.

[6] *Caution*: The strictly vertical demand curve should be thought of as a hypothetical, limiting case, not something that could occur in practice. If it did occur, the firm could raise the good's price as high as it wished, maintaining an unchanged level of sales. By doing so, it would earn unlimited profit. We all know, however, that there is no such "free lunch" in the business world.

FIGURE 3.2

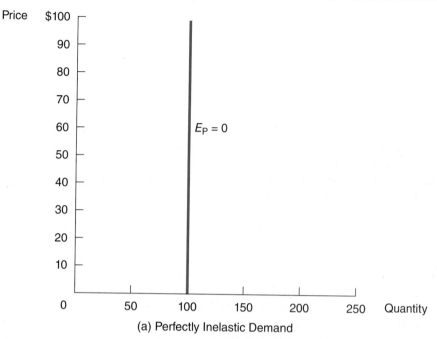

(a) Perfectly Inelastic Demand

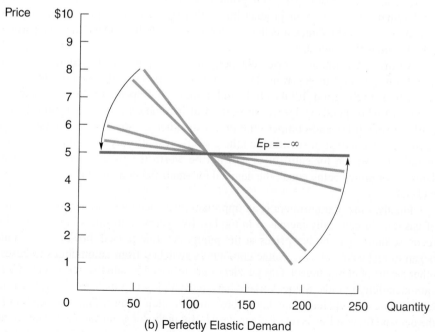

(b) Perfectly Elastic Demand

Two Extreme Cases

The vertical demand curve in part (a) represents perfectly inelastic demand, $E_P = 0$. The horizontal demand curve in part (b) represents perfectly elastic demand, $E_P = -\infty$.

Factors Affecting Price Elasticity

Four important factors determine whether the demand for a good is price elastic or price inelastic: (1) the degree to which the good is a necessity; (2) the availability of substitutes; (3) the proportion of income a consumer spends on the good; and (4) the time available for adjustment.

A first factor is the degree to which the good is a necessity. If a good or service is not considered essential, the purchaser can easily do without it—if and when the price becomes too high—even if there are no close substitutes. In that case, demand is elastic. If the good is a necessary component of consumption, it is more difficult to do without it in the face of a price increase. In this case, demand tends to be price inelastic.

A second factor is the availability of substitutes. With many substitutes, consumers easily can shift to other alternatives if the price of one good becomes too high; demand is elastic. Without close substitutes, switching becomes more difficult; demand is more inelastic. For this reason, *industry demand tends to be much less elastic than the demand facing a particular firm in the industry.* If one firm's price increases, consumers are able to go to other firms quite easily. Thus, the demand facing a single firm in an industry may be quite elastic because competitors produce goods that are close substitutes. But consider what happens if the *industry* price goes up—that is, all firms in the industry increase their prices in unison. In this case, price-sensitive consumers are limited in their course of action: to do without the good or to find a good in another industry to replace it. If these options are infeasible, the third option is to pay the higher price. Thus, industry demand is less elastic. The same point applies to the case where a single monopolist dominates an industry or product line. Other things being equal, the monopolist's demand is less elastic (since it is the sole producer) than the demand facing a particular firm in a multifirm industry.

A third determinant of price elasticity is the proportion of income a consumer spends on the good in question. The issue here is the cost of searching for suitable alternatives to the good. It takes time and money to compare substitute products. An individual who spends a significant portion of income on a good will find it worthwhile to search for and compare the prices of other goods. This consumer is price sensitive. By contrast, if spending on the good represents only a small portion of total income, the search for substitutes will not be worth the time, effort, and expense. Thus, other things being equal, the demand for small-ticket items tends to be relatively inelastic.

Finally, time of adjustment is an important influence on elasticity. When the price of gasoline dramatically increased in the last five years, consumers initially had little recourse but to pay higher prices at the pump. As time passed, however, consumers began to make adjustments. Some commuters switched from automobiles to buses or other means of public transit. Gas guzzlers were replaced by smaller, more fuel-efficient cars including hybrids. Some workers have moved closer to their jobs, and when jobs turned over, workers have found new jobs closer to their homes. Thus, in the short run, the demand for gasoline is relatively inelastic. But in the long run, demand is much more elastic as people are able to cut back consumption by a surprising amount. As a general rule, demand is more elastic in the long run than in the short run.

Other Elasticities

The elasticity concept can be applied to any explanatory variable that affects sales. Many of these variables—income, the prices of substitutes and complements, and changes in population or preferences—have already been mentioned. (An additional important variable affecting sales is the firm's spending on advertising and promotion.)

INCOME ELASTICITY **Income elasticity** links percentage changes in sales to changes in income, *all other factors held constant.* It is defined as

$$E_Y = \frac{\% \text{ change in } Q}{\% \text{ change in } Y} = \frac{\Delta Q/Q}{\Delta Y/Y}$$

in a manner exactly analogous to the earlier price elasticity definition.[7] For example, the income elasticity of demand for spending on groceries is about .25; that is, a 10 percent increase in income results in only about a 2.5 percent increase in spending in this category. In other words, a household's consumption of groceries is relatively insensitive to changes in income. In contrast, restaurant expenditures are highly sensitive to income changes. The income elasticity for this type of spending is about 3.0.

A main impact on the sales outlook for an industry, a firm, or a particular good or service is the overall strength of the economy. When the economy grows strongly, so do personal income, business profits, and government income. Gains in these income categories generate increased spending on a wide variety of goods and services. Conversely, when income falls during a recession, so do sales across the economy. Income elasticity thus provides an important measure of the sensitivity of sales for a given product to swings in the economy. For instance, if $E_Y = 1$, sales move exactly in step with changes in income. If $E_Y > 1$, sales are highly *cyclical,* that is, sensitive to income. For an inferior good, sales are *countercyclical,* that is, move in the opposite direction of income and $E_Y < 0$.

CROSS-PRICE ELASTICITY   A final, commonly used elasticity links changes in a good's sales to changes in the prices of related goods. **Cross-price elasticity** is defined as

$$E_P = \frac{\Delta Q/Q}{\Delta P_0/P_0},$$

where P_0 denotes the price of a related good or service. If the goods in question are substitutes, the cross-elasticity will be positive. For instance, if a 5 percent cut in a competitor's intercity fare is expected to reduce the airline's ticket sales by 2 percent, we

---

[7]If an infinitesimal change is considered, the corresponding elasticity expression is $E_Y = (dQ/Q)/(dY/Y)$. In addition, when multiple factors affect demand, the "partial derivative" notation emphasizes the separate effect of income changes on demand, all other factors held constant. In this case, we write $E_Y = (\partial Q/Q)/(\partial Y/Y)$.

TABLE 3.1

Estimated Price and
Income Elasticities for
Selected Goods and
Services

Good or Service	Price Elasticity	Income Elasticity
Air travel:		
Business	−.7	1.1
Nonbusiness	−1.5	1.8
Automobiles:		1.9
Subcompact	−.81	
Luxury	−2.1	
Beef	−.5	.51
Beer	−.36	1.0
Wine	−.57	1.0
Cigarettes:		
All smokers	−.7	
Ages 15–18	−1.4	
Gasoline (1-year)	−0.20	.20
Housing		.34
Telephone calls		
Long distance	−.5	1.0

Source: Elasticities were compiled by the authors from articles in economic journals and other published sources.

find $E_{P^\circ} = (-2\%)/(-5\%) = 0.4$. The magnitude of E_{P° provides a useful measure of the substitutability of the two goods.[8] For example, if $E_{P^\circ} = .05$, sales of the two goods are almost unrelated. If E_{P° is very large, however, the two goods are nearly perfect substitutes. Finally, if two goods are complements, the cross-elasticity is negative. An increase in the complementary good's price will adversely affect sales.

Table 3.1 provides estimated price and income elasticities for selected goods and services.

Price Elasticity and Prediction

Price elasticity is an essential tool for estimating the sales response to possible price changes. A simple rearrangement of the elasticity definition (Equation 3.7) gives the predictive equation:

$$\Delta Q/Q = E_P(\Delta P/P).$$ [3.9]

[8]We could also examine the effect of a change in the airline's fare on the competitor's ticket sales. Note that the two cross-price elasticities may be very different in magnitude. For instance, in our example the airline flies only half as many flights as its competitor. Given its smaller market share and presence, one would predict that changes in the airline's price would have a much smaller impact on the sales of its larger rival than vice versa.

For instance, in Table 3.1, the short-term (i.e., one-year) price elasticity of demand for gasoline is −.2. This indicates that if the average price of gasoline were to increase from $2.50 to $3.00 per gallon (a 20 percent increase), then consumption of gasoline (in gallons) would fall by only 4 percent (−.2 × 20%). The table also shows that the price elasticity of demand for luxury cars is −2.1. A modest 5 percent increase in their average sticker price implies a 10.5 percent drop in sales. (*Caution*: Equation 3.9 is exact for very small changes but only an approximation for large percentage changes, over which elasticities may vary.)

How does one estimate the impact on sales from changes in two or more factors that affect demand? A simple example can illustrate the method. In Table 3.1, the price and income elasticities for nonbusiness air travel are estimated to be $E_P = -1.5$ and $E_Y = 1.8$, respectively. In the coming year, average airline fares are expected to rise by 4 percent and income by 5 percent. What will be the impact on the number of tickets sold to nonbusiness travelers? The answer is found by adding the separate effects due to each change:

$$\Delta Q/Q = E_P(\Delta P/P) + E_Y(\Delta Y/Y). \quad\quad [3.10]$$

Therefore, $\Delta Q/Q = (-1.5)(4\%) + (1.8)(5\%) = 3\%$. Sales are expected to increase by about 3 percent.

DEMAND ANALYSIS AND OPTIMAL PRICING

In this section, we put demand analysis to work by examining three important managerial decisions: (1) the special case of revenue maximization, (2) optimal markup pricing, and (3) price discrimination.

Price Elasticity, Revenue, and Marginal Revenue

What can we say about the elasticity along any downward-sloping, linear demand curve? First, we must be careful to specify the starting quantity and price (the point on the demand curve) from which percentage changes are measured. From Equation 3.8b, we know that $E_P = (dQ/dP)(P/Q)$. The slope of the demand curve is dP/dQ (as it is conventionally drawn with price on the vertical axis). Thus, the first term in the elasticity expression, dQ/dP, is simply the inverse of this slope and is constant everywhere along the curve. The term P/Q decreases as one moves downward along the curve. Thus, along a linear demand curve, moving to lower prices and greater quantities reduces elasticity; that is, demand becomes more inelastic.

As a concrete illustration of this point, consider a software firm that is trying to determine the optimal price for one of its popular software programs. Management estimates this product's demand curve to be

$$Q = 1,600 - 4P$$

where Q is copies sold per week and P is in dollars. We note for future reference that $dQ/dP = -4$. Figure 3.3a shows this demand curve as well as the associated marginal

FIGURE 3.3

Demand, Revenue, and Marginal Revenue

In part (a), elasticity varies along a linear demand curve. The point of maximum revenue occurs at a price and quantity such that $MR = 0$ or, equivalently, $E_P = -1$

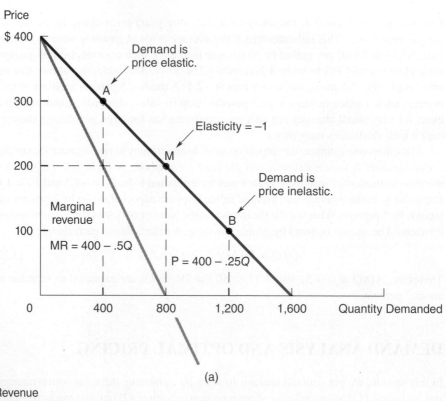

(a)

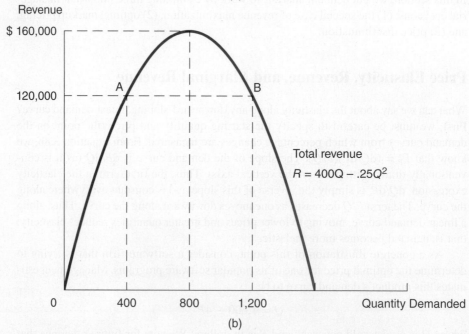

(b)

revenue curve. In the figure, the midpoint of the demand curve is marked by point M: $Q = 800$ and $P = \$200$. Two other points, A and B, along the demand curve also are shown.

Figure 3.3a depicts a useful result. Any linear demand curve can be divided into two regions. *Exactly midway along the linear demand curve, price elasticity is unity.* To the northwest (at higher prices and lower quantities), demand is elastic. To the southeast (at lower prices and greater quantities), demand is inelastic. For example, consider a point on the inelastic part of the curve such as B: $P = \$100$ and $Q = 1,200$. Here, the point elasticity is $E_P = (dQ/dP)(P/Q) = (-4)(100/1,200) = -.33$. Conversely, at a point on the elastic portion of the demand curve such as A ($P = \$300$ and $Q = 400$), the point elasticity is $E_P = (-4)(300/400) = -3.0$.

Compute the price elasticity at point M. Show that the elasticity is unity. This result holds for the midpoint of any linear demand curve.   **CHECK STATION 3**

Figure 3.3b depicts the firm's total revenue curve for different sales volumes. It displays the familiar shape of an upside-down U. Total revenue increases as quantity increases up to the revenue peak; at still higher quantities, revenue falls.

Let's carefully trace the relationship between price elasticity and changes in revenue. Suppose that management of the software firm is operating at point A on the demand curve in Figure 3.3a. Its price is $300, it sells 400 copies of the software program, and it earns $120,000 in revenue per week. Could the firm increase its revenue by cutting its price to spur greater sales? If demand is elastic, the answer is yes. Under elastic demand, the percentage increase in quantity is greater than the percentage fall in price. Thus, revenue—the product of price and quantity—must increase. The positive change in quantity more than compensates for the fall in price. Figure 3.3b shows clearly that starting from point A, revenue increases when the firm moves to greater quantities (and lower prices). Starting from any point of elastic demand, the firm can increase revenue by reducing its price.

Now suppose the software firm is operating originally at point B, where demand is inelastic. In this case, the firm can increase revenue by raising its price. Because demand is inelastic, the percentage drop in quantity of sales is smaller than the percentage increase in price. With price rising by more than quantity falls, revenue necessarily increases. Again, the revenue graph in Figure 3.3b tells the story. Starting from point B, the firm increases its revenue by reducing its quantity (and raising its price). As long as demand is inelastic, revenue moves in the same direction as price. By raising price and reducing quantity, the firm moves back toward the revenue peak.

Putting these two results together, we see that when demand is inelastic or elastic, revenue can be increased (by a price hike or cut, respectively). Therefore, revenue is maximized when neither a price hike nor a cut will help; that is, when demand is unitary elastic, $E_P = -1$. In the software example illustrated in Figure 3.3b, the revenue-maximizing quantity is $Q = 800$. This quantity (along with the price, $P = \$200$) is the point of unitary elasticity (in Figure 3.3a).

Our discussion has suggested an interesting and important relationship between marginal revenue and price elasticity. The same point can be made mathematically. By definition, $MR = dR/dQ = d(PQ)/dQ$. The derivative of this product (see Rule 5 of the appendix to Chapter 2) is

$$MR = P(dQ/dQ) + (dP/dQ)Q \qquad [3.11]$$
$$= P + P(dP/dQ)(Q/P)$$
$$= P[1 + (dP/dQ)(Q/P)]$$
$$= P[1 + 1/E_P].$$

For instance, if demand is elastic (say, $E_P = -3$), MR is positive; that is, an increase in quantity (via a reduction in price) will increase total revenue. If demand is inelastic (say, $E_P = -.6$), MR is negative; an increase in quantity causes total revenue to decline. If elasticity is precisely -1, MR is zero. Figure 3.3a summarizes the relationship between marginal revenue and price elasticity.

Maximizing Revenue

As we saw in Chapter 2, there generally is a conflict between the goals of maximizing revenue and maximizing profit. Clearly, maximizing profit is the appropriate objective because it takes into account not only revenues but also relevant costs. In some important special cases, however, the two goals coincide or are equivalent. This occurs when the firm faces what is sometimes called a **pure selling problem**: a situation where it supplies a good or service while incurring *no* variable cost (or a variable cost so small that it safely can be ignored). Without any variable costs, the firm maximizes its ultimate profit by setting price and output to gain as much revenue as possible (from which any *fixed* costs then are paid). The following pricing problems serve as examples:

- A software firm is deciding the optimal selling price for its software.
- A manufacturer must sell (or otherwise dispose of) an inventory of unsold merchandise.
- A professional sports franchise must set its ticket prices for its home games.
- An airline is attempting to fill its empty seats on a regularly scheduled flight.

In each of these examples, variable costs are absent (or very small). The cost of producing an additional software copy is trivial. In the case of airline or sports tickets, the cost of an additional passenger or spectator is negligible once the flight or event has been scheduled. As for inventory, production costs are sunk; selling costs are negligible or very small. Thus, in each case the firm maximizes profits by setting price and output to maximize revenue.

How does the firm determine its revenue-maximizing price and output? There are two equivalent answers to this question. The first answer is to apply Chapter 2's fundamental rule: $MR = MC$. In the case of a pure selling problem, marginal cost is zero. Thus, the rule becomes $MR = 0$, exactly as one would expect. This rule instructs the manager to push sales to the point where there is no more additional revenue to be had ($MR = 0$) and no further.

From the preceding discussion, we have established a second, equivalent answer: Revenue is maximized at the point of unitary elasticity. If demand were inelastic or elastic, revenue could be increased by raising or lowering price, respectively. The following proposition sums up these results.

> Revenue is maximized at the price and quantity for which marginal revenue is zero or, equivalently, the price elasticity of demand is unity (-1).

Note that this result confirms that the point of unitary elasticity occurs at the midpoint of a linear demand curve. For the sales quantity at the midpoint, marginal revenue is exactly zero (since the *MR* curve cuts the horizontal axis at the midpoint quantity). But when $MR = 0$, it is also true that $E_P = -1$.

The management of a professional sports team has a 36,000-seat stadium it wishes to fill. It recognizes, however, that the number of seats sold (Q) is very sensitive to average ticket prices (P). It estimates demand to be $Q = 60,000 - 3,000P$. Assuming the team's costs are known and do not vary with attendance, what is management's optimal pricing policy? **CHECK STATION 4**

Optimal Markup Pricing

There is a close link between demand for a firm's product and the firm's optimal pricing policy. In the remainder of this chapter, we will take a close and careful look at the trade-off between price and profit. Recall that in Chapter 2, the focus was squarely on the firm's quantity decision. Once the firm determined its optimal output by weighing marginal revenue and marginal cost, it was a simple matter to set price in order to sell exactly that much output. Now we shift our focus to price and consider a related trade-off.

To illustrate this trade-off, we can write the firm's contribution as

$$\text{Contribution} = (P - MC)Q,$$

where, for simplicity, *MC* is assumed to be constant. How should the firm set its price to maximize its contribution (and, therefore, its profit)? The answer depends on how responsive demand is to changes in price, that is, on price elasticity of demand. Raising price increases the firm's contribution per unit (or margin), $P - MC$. But to a greater or lesser degree, a price hike also reduces the total volume of sales Q. If sales are relatively unresponsive to price (i.e., demand is relatively inelastic), the firm can raise its price and increase its margin without significantly reducing quantity. In this instance, the underlying trade-off works in favor of high prices.

Alternatively, suppose demand is very elastic. In this instance, a price increase would bring a large drop in sales to the detriment of total contribution. Here, the way to maximize contribution (and profit) is to play the other side of the trade-off. The firm should pursue a policy of discount pricing to maximize profitability. As we shall see, the correct pricing policy depends on a careful analysis of the price elasticity of demand. Indeed, when the firm has the ability to segment markets, it may benefit by trading on demand differences. As noted in this chapter's opening example, airlines set a variety of different ticket prices—charging high fares to less price-sensitive business travelers and discounting prices to economy-minded vacation travelers.

In Chapter 2, we focused on the application of the $MR = MC$ rule as a way to determine the firm's optimal level of output. It is possible to apply a modified (but exactly equivalent) version of the $MR = MC$ rule to derive a simple rule for the firm's profit-maximizing *price*. The firm's optimal price is determined as follows:

$$\frac{P - MC}{P} = \frac{1}{-E_P}. \qquad [3.12]$$

This equation, called the **markup rule**, indicates that

| The size of the firm's markup (above marginal cost and expressed as a percentage of price) depends inversely on the price elasticity of demand for a good or service. |

The markup is always positive. (Note that E_P is negative, so the right-hand side is positive.) What happens as demand becomes more and more price elastic (i.e., price sensitive)? The right-hand side of the markup rule becomes smaller, and so does the optimal markup on the left-hand side. In short, the more elastic is demand, then the smaller is the markup above marginal cost.[9]

The markup rule is intuitively appealing and is the most commonly noted form of the optimal pricing rule. Nonetheless, to make computations easier, it is useful to rearrange the rule:

$$P = \left(\frac{E_P}{1 + E_P}\right)MC. \qquad [3.13]$$

Using this formula, Table 3.2 lists optimal prices by elasticity. Again, we see that greater elasticities imply lower prices.

CAUTION   The markup rule is applicable only in the case of *elastic* demand. Why not inelastic demand? The simple fact is that *the firm's current price cannot be profit maximizing if demand is inelastic.* Under inelastic demand, the firm could raise its price and

TABLE 3.2

Elasticities and Optimal Prices	Elasticity	Markup Factor $E_P/(1 + E_P)$	MC	Price
The markup of price above marginal cost varies inversely with the elasticity of demand.	−1.5	3.0	100	300
	−2.0	2.0	100	200
	−3.0	1.5	100	150
	−5.0	1.25	100	125
	−11.0	1.1	100	110
	−∞	1.0	100	100

[9]Here is how the markup rule is derived. From Equation 3.11, we know that $MR = P[1 + 1/E_P]$. Setting $MR = MC$, we have $P + P/E_P = MC$. This can be written as $P - MC = -P/E_P$ and, finally, $[P - MC]/P = -1/E_P$, the markup rule. Thus, the markup rule is derived from and equivalent to the $MR = MC$ rule.

increase its revenue. Because it would sell less output at the higher price, it also would lower its production cost at the same time. Thus, profit would increase. In short, the firm should never operate on the inelastic portion of its demand curve. It should increase profit by raising price and moving to the elastic portion; the optimal markup rule tells it exactly how far it should move into the elastic region of demand.

The markup rule is a formal expression of the conventional wisdom that *price should depend on both demand and cost.* The rule prescribes how prices should be determined in principle. In practice, managers often adopt other pricing policies. The most common practice is to use *full-cost pricing*. With this method, price is expressed in this form:

$$P = (1 + m)AC, \qquad\qquad [3.14]$$

Business Behavior
Pricing in
Practice

where AC denotes total average cost (defined as total cost divided by total output) and m denotes the markup of price above average cost.

Our study of optimal managerial decisions suggests two points of criticism about full-cost pricing. First, full-cost pricing uses average cost—the incorrect measure of relevant cost—as its base. The logic of marginal analysis in general and the optimal markup rule (Equation 3.13) in particular show that optimal price and quantity depend on marginal cost. Fixed costs, which are counted in AC but not in MC, have no effect on the choice of optimal price and quantity.[10] Thus, to the extent that AC differs from MC, the full-cost method can lead to pricing errors.

Second, the percentage markup should depend on the elasticity of demand. There is considerable evidence that firms vary their markups in rough accord with price elasticity.[11] Gourmet frozen foods carry much higher markups than generic food items. Inexpensive digital watches ($15 and under) have lower markups than fine Swiss watches or jewelers' watches. Designer dresses and wedding dresses carry much higher markups than off-the-rack dresses. In short, producers' markups are linked to elasticities, at least in a qualitative sense. Nonetheless, it is unlikely that firms' full-cost markups exactly duplicate optimal markups. Obviously, a firm that sets a fixed markup *irrespective* of elasticity is needlessly sacrificing profit.

The US cigarette industry has negotiated with Congress and government agencies to settle liability claims against it. Under the proposed settlement, cigarette companies will make fixed annual payments to the government based on their historic market shares. Suppose a manufacturer estimates its marginal cost at $2.00 per pack, its own price elasticity at −1.5, and sets its price at $6.00. The company's settlement obligations are expected to raise its average total cost per pack by about $.50. What effect will this have on its optimal price?

CHECK
STATION 5

---

[10]Fixed costs obviously are important for the decision about whether to produce the good. For production to be profitable in the long run, price must exceed average cost, $P \geq AC$. If not, the firm should cease production and shut down. Chapter 6 provides an extensive discussion of this so-called shutdown rule for firms producing single and multiple products.

[11]In evaluating the practice of full-cost pricing, the real issue is how close it comes to duplicating optimal markup pricing. Even if firms do not apply the optimal markup rule, they may price as though they did. For instance, a firm that experiments with different full-cost markups may soon "discover" the profit-maximizing price (without ever computing an elasticity).

Price Discrimination

Price discrimination occurs when a firm sells the same good or service to different buyers at different prices.[12] As the following examples suggest, price discrimination is a common business practice.

- Airlines charge full fares to business travelers, while offering discount fares to vacationers.
- Firms sell the same products under different brand names or labels at different prices.
- Providers of professional services (doctors, consultants, lawyers, etc.) set different rates for different clients.
- Manufacturers introduce products at high prices before gradually dropping price over time.
- Publishers of academic journals charge much higher subscription rates to libraries and institutions than to individual subscribers.
- Businesses offer student and senior citizen discounts for many goods and services.
- Manufacturers sell the same products at higher prices in the retail market than in the wholesale market.
- Movies play in "first-run" theaters at higher ticket prices before being released to suburban theaters at lower prices.

When a firm practices price discrimination, it sets different prices for different market segments, even though its costs of serving each customer group are the same. Thus, price discrimination is purely demand based. Of course, firms may also charge different prices for the "same" good or service because of cost differences. (For instance, transportation cost may be one reason why the same make and model of automobile sells for significantly different prices on the west and east coasts.) But cost-based pricing does not fall under the heading of price discrimination.

Price discrimination is a departure from the pricing model we have examined up to this point. Thus far, the firm has been presumed to set a *single* market-clearing price. Obviously, charging different prices to different market segments, as in the examples just listed, allows the firm considerably more pricing flexibility. More to the point, the firm can increase its profit with a policy of optimal price discrimination (when the opportunity exists).

Two conditions must hold for a firm to practice price discrimination profitably. First, the firm must be able to identify market segments that differ with respect to price elasticity of demand. As we show shortly, the firm profits by charging a higher price to the more inelastic (i.e., less price-sensitive) market segment(s). Second, it must be

---

[12]Here, we are discussing legal methods of price discrimination; that is, we are using the term *discrimination* in its neutral sense. Obviously, many laws prohibit economic discrimination (including unfair pricing practices) based on gender, race, or national origin. The antitrust statutes also limit specific cases of price discrimination that can be shown to significantly reduce competition.

possible to enforce the different prices paid by different segments. This means that market segments receiving higher prices must be unable to take advantage of lower prices. (In particular, a low-price buyer must be unable to resell the good or service profitably to a high-price buyer.) The conditions necessary to ensure different prices exist in the preceding examples. Sometimes the conditions are quite subtle. Business travelers rarely can purchase discount air tickets because they cannot meet advance-booking or minimum-stay requirements. First-run moviegoers pay a high ticket price because they are unwilling to wait until the film comes to a lower-price theater.

How can the firm maximize its profit via price discrimination? There are several (related) ways to answer this question. The markup rule provides a ready explanation of this practice. To illustrate, suppose a firm has identified two market segments, each with its own demand curve. (Chapter 4 discusses the means by which these different demand curves can be identified and estimated.) Then the firm can treat the different segments as separate markets for the good. The firm simply applies the markup rule twice to determine its optimal price and sales for each market segment. Thus, it sets price according to $P = [E_P/(1 + E_P)]MC$ (Equation 3.13) separately for each market segment. Presumably, the marginal cost of producing for each market is the same. With the same MC inserted into the markup rule, the difference in the price charged to each segment is due solely to differences in elasticities of demand.

For instance, suppose a firm identifies two market segments with price elasticities of -5 and -3, respectively. The firm's marginal cost of selling to either segment is $200. Then, according to the markup rule, the firm's optimal prices are $250 and $300, respectively. (Be sure to check these calculations.) We see that the segment with the more inelastic demand pays the higher price. The firm charges the higher price to less price-sensitive buyers (with little danger of losing sales). At the same time, it attracts the more price-sensitive customers (who would buy relatively little of the good at the higher price) by offering them a discounted price. Thus, by means of optimal price discrimination, the firm maximizes its profit.

Like the method just described, a second approach to price discrimination treats different segments as distinct markets and sets out to maximize profit separately in each. The difference is that the manager's focus is on optimal sales quantities rather than prices. The optimal sales quantity for each market is determined by setting the extra revenue from selling an extra unit in that market equal to the marginal cost of production. In short, the firm sets $MR = MC$ in each market.

In the first example in Chapter 1, an automobile producer faced the problem of pricing its output at home and abroad. We are now ready to put demand analysis to work to determine the firm's optimal decisions. The facts are as follows: The producer faces relatively little competition at home; it is one of the most efficient domestic producers, and trade barriers limit the import of foreign cars. However, it competes in the foreign market with many local and foreign manufacturers. Under these circumstances, demand at home is likely to be much more inelastic than demand in the foreign country. Suppose that the price equations at home (H) and abroad (F) are, respectively,

Multinational Production and Pricing Revisited

$$P_H = 30{,}000 - 50Q_H \quad \text{and} \quad P_F = 25{,}000 - 70Q_F,$$

where price is in dollars per vehicle and quantities are annual sales of vehicles in thousands. Automobiles are produced in a single domestic facility at a marginal cost of $10,000 per vehicle. This is the MC relevant to vehicles sold in the domestic market. Shipping vehicles to the foreign market halfway around the world involves additional transport costs of $1,000 per vehicle. What are the firm's optimal sales quantities and prices?

Addressing this question is straightforward, but the answer may come as a surprise. The quantities of cars sold to the respective markets are determined by the conditions $MR_H = MC_H$ and $MR_F = MC_F$. Therefore, $30,000 - 100Q_H = 10,000$ and $25,000 - 140Q_F = 11,000$. The optimal quantities and prices (after substituting back into the demand curves) are $Q_H = 200$ thousand and $P_H = \$20,000$ in the domestic market and $Q_F = 100$ thousand and $P_F = \$18,000$ in the foreign market. The surprise comes when we compare domestic and foreign prices. Even though the marginal cost of vehicles sold in the foreign market is 10 percent higher than that of cars sold domestically, the foreign price is *lower*—by some 10 percent—than the domestic price. Why is it profitable for the company to sell on the foreign market at a much lower price than at home? It is because demand is much more elastic abroad than it is domestically. Accordingly, the company's pricing policy is a textbook case of an optimal dual-pricing strategy.

DEMAND-BASED PRICING   As these examples indicate, the ways in which firms price discriminate are varied. Indeed, there are many forms of demand-based pricing that are closely related to price discrimination (although not always called by that name). For instance, resorts in Florida and the Caribbean set much higher nightly rates during the high season (December to March) than at off-peak times. The difference in rates is demand based. (The resorts' operating costs differ little by season.) Vacationers are willing to pay a much higher price for warm climes during the North American winter. Similarly, a convenience store, open 24 hours a day and located along a high-traffic route or intersection, will set premium prices for its merchandise. (Again, the high markups are predominantly demand based and only partly based on higher costs.) Likewise, golf courses charge much higher prices on weekends than on weekdays. Each of these examples illustrates demand-based pricing.

FORMS OF PRICE DISCRIMINATION   It is useful to distinguish three forms of price discrimination. The practice of charging different prices to different market segments (for which the firm's costs are identical) is often referred to as **third-degree price discrimination**. Airline and movie ticket pricing are examples. Prices differ across market segments, but customers within a market segment pay the same price.

Now suppose the firm could distinguish among different consumers within a market segment. What if the firm knew each customer's demand curve? Then it could practice perfect price discrimination. **First-degree**, or **perfect, price discrimination** occurs when a firm sets a different price for each customer and by doing so extracts the maximum possible sales revenue. As an example, consider an auto dealer who has a large stock of used cars for sale and expects 10 serious potential buyers to enter her showroom each week. She posts different model prices, but she knows (and customers know) that the sticker price is a starting point in subsequent negotiations. Each customer knows the maximum price he or she is personally willing to pay for the car in question. If the dealer is a shrewd judge of character, she can guess the range of each buyer's maximum price and, via the negotiations, extract almost this full value. For instance, if four buyers' maximum prices are \$6,100, \$6,450, \$5,950, and \$6,200, the perfectly discriminating dealer will negotiate prices nearly equal to these values. In this way, the dealer will sell the four cars for the maximum possible revenue. As this example illustrates, perfect discrimination is fine in principle but much more difficult in practice. Clearly, such discrimination requires that the seller have an unrealistic amount of information. Thus, it serves mainly as a benchmark—a limiting case, at best.

Finally, **second-degree price discrimination** occurs when the firm offers different price schedules, and customers choose the terms that best fit their needs. The most common example is the offer of quantity discounts: For large volumes, the seller charges a lower price per unit, so the buyer purchases a larger quantity. With a little thought, one readily recognizes this as a form of profitable price discrimination. High-volume, price-sensitive buyers will choose to purchase larger quantities at a lower unit price, whereas low-volume users will purchase fewer units at a higher unit price. Perhaps the most common form of quantity discounts is the practice of *two-part pricing*. As the term suggests, the total price paid by a customer is

$$P = A + pQ,$$

where A is a fixed fee (paid irrespective of quantity) and p is the additional price per unit. Telephone service, electricity, and residential gas all carry two-part prices. Taxi service, photocopy rental agreements, and amusement park admissions are other examples. Notice that two-part pricing implies a quantity discount; the average price per unit, $P/Q = A/Q + p$, declines as Q increases. Two-part pricing allows the firm to charge customers for access to valuable services (via A) while promoting volume purchases (via low p).

Information Goods

The last 20 years have witnessed explosive growth in the provision of **information goods and services**. The business press speaks of Internet industries and e-business markets. The "information" label is meant to be both more broad based and more precise. An information good could be a database, game cartridge, news article (in electronic or paper form), piece of music, or piece of software. Information services range from e-mail and instant messaging, to electronic exchanges and auctions, to brokerage and other financial services, to job placements. Of course, information services also include all manner of Internet-based transactions, such as purchasing airline tickets, procuring industrial inputs, and gathering extensive data on potential customers.[13]

Although the information category is broad, all of the preceding examples share a common feature: *Information is costly to create but cheap (often costless) to reproduce.* In short, any information good or service is characterized by high fixed costs but low or negligible marginal costs. With marginal costs at or near zero, the firm's total costs vary little with output volume, so that average cost per unit sharply declines as output increases. (Creating a \$1 million database to serve 1,000 end users implies an average

---

[13]A superb discussion of the economics of information goods can be found in C. Shapiro and H. R. Varian, *Information Rules*, Chapters 1–3, 7 (Boston: Harvard Business School Press, 1999).

cost of $1,000 per user. If, instead, it served 500,000 end-users, the average cost drops to $2 per user.) Moreover, with marginal costs negligible, a supplier of an information good once again faces a pure selling problem: how to market, promote, and price its product to maximize revenue (and thereby profit).

The early history of e-business activities was characterized by high up-front costs and the pursuit of customers, revenues, and profits, in that order. In 1999 and 2000, Internet startups were the beneficiaries of enormous capital infusions by investors and spectacular market valuations, sometimes before a trace of revenue had been earned. These early Internet ventures were properly regarded as investments, and risky ones at that. Early losses were expected to be balanced by significant future revenues. For instance, strong revenue growth has been the pattern for such information goods as videotapes, CDs, MP3 players, videogames, and music downloads (once a critical mass of consumers adopt the new technologies).

In many respects, information providers face special revenue issues. First, revenues can be earned in numerous ways. The most familiar means is simply setting a price per unit, as in the sale of a music CD, a movie DVD, or a piece of software. Maximizing total revenue from sales means identifying the unit price such that $E_P = -1$. However, there are myriad other pricing options. Alternatively, software may be sold via site license, allowing group users to enjoy a kind of quantity discount. Internet services are sold by monthly subscription, by pay per use (or per download), or in some combination. Many information services, particularly search engines such as Google and high-traffic Web portals, earn the bulk of their cash flows from advertising revenues. Internet advertising includes sponsored search links, banner ads, pop-up ads, e-mail advertisements, and mobile ads. In addition, there are all kinds of indirect revenues. In 2014, Rovio Entertainment, the company behind the Angry Birds franchise, decided to make its games free—charging nothing for downloads but including features that users must pay to access (such as ways to speed up play) and aiming to profit by increasing its customer base for related "Bird-themed" paid products. Some information suppliers sell their customer lists to third parties. Finally, there are numerous trade-offs between these different revenue sources. Outright DVD sales compete with DVD rentals. Raising subscription prices lowers traffic and therefore reduces the effectiveness of Web advertising. Obviously, these trade-offs complicate the task of maximizing total revenue. In short, the information supplier faces multiple, interdependent, and imprecise demand curves.

Second, most information goods exhibit positive **network externalities**. This means that customers of a given information good obtain greater value with a larger network of other connected customers. For instance, wireless telephone customers benefit from the most fully developed nationwide (or worldwide) network, and air travelers benefit from airlines with integrated national and international routes offering multiple daily flights. Facebook members and Twitter followers benefit from extensive networks of like-minded participants. The network need not be physical. For example, the global network of Microsoft's Windows-based operating system and Office applications allows easy file and software transfers among users. By contrast, the separate network of Apple Mac users is much more limited. eBay, the highly successful online auction company, has attracted thousands of sellers and millions of buyers. This enormous network is valuable, not only for sellers who seek the greatest number of potential buyers (and vice versa) but also for eBay, which earns a percentage fee on all auction listings. In all these instances, positive network externalities imply that customer values and, therefore, underlying demand curves, shift outward over time as the customer network expands.

What are the strategic implications of network externalities for information providers? Clearly, there is a potential "first-mover" advantage in enlisting the greatest number of users of the information good in question. (We will say more about first-mover strategies in Chapter 10.) Users "in hand" are valuable to the firm not only for the revenue they directly generate, but also because they enhance the value of other current and future users (from which the firm also gains revenue). Well aware of this dynamic, e-business firms have aggressively sought customers, not only via advertising and promotions, but also by significant price cuts. The extreme cases of cutthroat competition have bred *free* information services of all kinds: electronic greeting cards, e-mail, Internet connections, and online newspapers and magazines. Interestingly, offering free services is a viable business strategy as long as the expanded customer base generates revenue through advertising or from any of the avenues mentioned earlier. In numerous instances, free downloadable versions of stripped-down software or Web content have enticed consumers to trade up to "professional" or "deluxe" versions, for which dollar fees are charged. In other cases, information providers have been locked in savage price wars or battles over free content that have decimated company revenues, thereby degenerating into "wars of attrition." National newspapers have been especially hard hit by younger demographic groups that prefer to get their news for free from online sources. After much internal debate, in 2011 the *New York Times* set its digital subscription price at $15 per month (print subscribers have digital access for free. The *Wall Street Journal* has adopted a similar online subscription policy. To date, readers of these publications have proved willing to pay for top-notch journalism.

CUSTOMIZED PRICING AND PRODUCTS   The emergence of electronic commerce and online transactions has greatly expanded the opportunities for market segmentation and price discrimination. From management's point of view, the beauty of information goods and services is that they can be sold over and over again (at negligible marginal cost). Moreover, unlike a traditional good sold at a posted price from a store shelf, the price of an information good (transacted electronically) can be changed minute by minute, customer by customer. Sellers of sophisticated databases—from Reuters to Lexis-Nexis to Bloomberg financial information—set scores of different prices to different customers. As always, prices are set according to elasticities; the most price-sensitive (elastic) customers receive the steepest discounted prices. Consider the ways in which an airline website (such as www.delta.com) can price its airline seats. Each time a customer enters a possible itinerary with departure and return dates, the webpage responds with possible flights and prices. These electronic prices already reflect many features: the class of seat; 30-day, 14-day, or 7-day advanced booking; and so on. By booking in advance, pleasure travelers can take advantage of discounted fares. Business travelers, whose itineraries are not able to meet these restrictions, pay much higher prices. Moreover, the airline can modify prices instantly to reflect changes in demand. If there is a surplus of unsold discount seats as the departure date approaches, the airline can further cut their price or sell the seats as part of a vacation package (hotel stay, rentacar included) at an even steeper discount. (Airlines also release seats to discount sellers, such as Priceline.com, Hotwire.com, and lastminute.com, who sell tickets at steep discounts to the most price-sensitive fliers.) Alternatively, some discount seats might be reassigned as full-fare seats if last-minute business demand for the flight is particularly brisk. Online, the pricing possibilities are endless.

Closely akin to customized pricing is the practice of **versioning**—selling different versions of a given information good or service. Whether it be software, hardware, database access, or other Internet services, this typically means a "standard" version offered at a lower price and a "professional" or "deluxe" version at a premium price. The versions are designed and priced to ensure that different market segments self-select with respect to the product offerings. The inelastic demand segment eagerly elects to pay the premium price to obtain the more powerful version. The more elastic demand segment purchases the stripped-down version at the discounted price. Although customers may not know it, the firm's costs for the different versions are usually indistinguishable. In this respect, versioning is closely akin to third-degree price discrimination. In fact, some software firms begin by designing their premium products and then simply disable key features to create the standard version.

Airline Ticket Pricing Revisited

We are now ready to take a closer look at the pricing policy of the airline in the chapter-opening example and to suggest how it might succeed at yield management. Consider again Equation 3.4, which describes current demand:

$$Q = 580 - 2P.$$

At its current price, $240, the airline sells 100 coach seats (of the 180 such seats available per flight). Assuming the airline will continue its single daily departure from each city (we presume this is not an issue), what is its optimal fare?

The first step in answering this question is to recognize this as a pure selling problem. With the airline committed to the flight, all associated costs are fixed. The marginal cost of flying 180 passengers versus 100 passengers (a few extra snacks, a bit more fuel, and so on) is negligible. Thus, the airline seeks the pricing policy that will generate the most revenue.

The next step is to appeal to marginal revenue to determine the optimal fare. The price equation is $P = 290 - Q/2$. (Check this.) Consequently, $MR = 290 - Q$. *Note*: Even at a 100 percent load ($Q = 180$), marginal revenue is positive ($MR = \$110$). If more seats were available, the airline would like to ticket them and increase its revenue. Lacking these extra seats, however, the best the airline can do is set $Q = 180$. From the price equation, $200 is the price needed to sell this number of seats. The airline should institute a $40 price cut. By doing so, its revenue will increase from $24,000 to $36,000 per flight.

Now let's extend (and complicate) the airline's pricing problem by introducing the possibility of profitable price discrimination. Two distinct market segments purchase coach tickets—business travelers (B) and pleasure travelers (T)—and these groups differ with respect to their demands. Indeed, business travelers (who are willing and able to pay higher fares) are well in the majority on the flight. Suppose the equations that best represent these segments' demands are $Q_B = 330 - P_B$ and $Q_T = 250 - P_T$. Note that these demand equations are consistent with Equation 3.4; that is, if both groups are charged price P, total demand is $Q = Q_B + Q_T = (330 - P) + (250 - P) = 580 - 2P$, which is exactly Equation 3.4. The airline's task is to determine Q_B and Q_T to maximize total revenue from the 180 coach seats.

The key to solving this problem is to appeal to the logic of marginal analysis. With the number of seats limited, the airline attains maximum revenue by setting $MR_B = MR_T$. The marginal revenue from selling the last ticket to a business traveler must equal the marginal revenue from selling the last ticket to a pleasure traveler. Why must this be so? Suppose to the contrary that the marginal revenues differ: $MR_B > MR_T$. Then, the airline can increase its revenue simply by selling one less seat to pleasure travelers and one more seat to business travelers. As long as marginal revenues differ across the segments, seats should be transferred from the low-MR segment to the high-MR segment, increasing revenue all the while. Revenue is maximized only when $MR_B = MR_T$.

After writing down the price equations ($P_B = 330 - Q_B$ and $P_T = 250 - Q_T$), deriving the associated marginal revenue expressions, and equating them, we have:

$$330 - 2Q_B = 250 - 2Q_T,$$

which can be simplified to $Q_B = 40 + Q_T$. The maximum-revenue plan always allocates 40 more seats to business travelers than to pleasure travelers. Since the plane capacity is 180, sales are constrained by $Q_B + Q_T = 180$. Therefore, the optimal quantities are $Q_B = 110$ and $Q_T = 70$. Optimal prices are $P_B = \$220$ and $P_T = \$180$. In turn, if we substitute $Q_B = 110$ into the expression $MR_B = 330 - 2Q_B$, we find that $MR_B = \$110$ per additional seat. (Of course, MR_T is also \$110 per seat.) Finally, total revenue is computed as $R = R_B + R_T = (\$220)(110) + (\$180)(70) = \$36,800$. Recall that maximum revenue under a single price system was \$36,000. Optimal yield management (price discrimination) has squeezed an additional \$800 out of passengers on the flight. As the chapter-opening example suggests, additional revenue can be gained by increasing the number of different fares, from 2 to as many as 12 or more.

Suppose the airline's management is considering adding an extra flight every second day. Therefore, average daily capacity would increase from 180 to 270 seats. The additional cost of offering this extra flight is estimated at \$50 per seat. Show that adding this "second-day" flight would be profitable but that an additional "everyday" flight would not. Determine the new ticket prices for the two classes.   **CHECK STATION 6**

SUMMARY

Decision-Making Principles

1. Optimal managerial decisions depend on an analysis of demand.
2. The firm's optimal uniform price is determined by the markup rule. This price depends on marginal cost and the price elasticity of demand.
3. Where the opportunity exists, the firm can increase its profit by practicing price discrimination.

Nuts and Bolts

1. The demand function shows, in equation form, the relationship between the unit sales of a good or service and one or more economic variables.
   a. The demand curve depicts the relationship between quantity and price. A change in price is represented by a movement along the demand curve. A change in any other economic variable shifts the demand curve.
   b. A pair of goods are substitutes if an increase in demand for one causes a fall in demand for the other. In particular, a price cut for one good reduces sales of the other.
   c. Two goods are complements if an increase in demand for one causes an increase in demand for the other. In particular, a price cut for one good increases sales of the other.
   d. A good is normal if its sales increase with increases in income.

2. The price elasticity of demand measures the percentage change in sales for a given percentage change in the good's price, all other factors held constant: $E_P = (\Delta Q/Q)/(\Delta P/P)$.
   a. Demand is unitary elastic if $E_P = -1$. In turn, demand is elastic if $E_P < -1$. Finally, demand is inelastic if $-1 < E_P \leq 0$.
   b. Revenue is maximized at the price and quantity for which marginal revenue is zero or, equivalently, the price elasticity of demand is unity.

3. The optimal markup rule is: $(P - MC)/P = -1/E_P$. The firm's optimal markup (above marginal cost and expressed as a percentage of price) varies inversely with the price elasticity of demand for the good or service. (Remember that the firm's price cannot be profit maximizing if demand is inelastic.)

4. Price discrimination occurs when a firm sells the same good or service to different buyers at different prices (based on different price elasticities of demand). Prices in various market segments are determined according to the optimal markup rule.

Questions and Problems

1. During a five-year period, the ticket sales of a city's professional basketball team have increased 30 percent at the same time that average ticket prices have risen by 50 percent. Do these changes imply an upward-sloping demand curve? Explain.

2. A retail store faces a demand equation for Roller Blades given by:

$$Q = 180 - 1.5P,$$

   where Q is the number of pairs sold per month and P is the price per pair in dollars.
   a. The store currently charges $P = \$80$ per pair. At this price, determine the number of pairs sold.
   b. If management were to raise the price to $100, what would be the impact on pairs sold? On the store's revenue from Roller Blades?
   c. Compute the point elasticity of demand first at $P = \$80$, and then at $P = \$100$. At which price is demand more price sensitive?

3. Management of McPablo's Food Shops has completed a study of weekly demand for its "old-fashioned" tacos in 53 regional markets. The study revealed that

$$Q = 400 - 1{,}200P + .8A + 55Pop + 800P^c,$$

   where Q is the number of tacos sold per store per week, A is the level of local advertising expenditure (in dollars), Pop denotes the local population (in thousands), and P^c is the average taco price of local competitors. For a particular McPablo's outlet, $P = \$1.50$, $A = \$1,000$, $Pop = 40$, and $P^c = \$1$.
   a. Estimate the weekly sales for this McPablo's outlet.
   b. What is the current price elasticity for tacos? What is the advertising elasticity?
   c. Should McPablo's raise its taco prices? Why or why not?

4. Four firms have roughly equal shares of the market for farm-raised catfish. The price elasticity of demand for the market as a whole is estimated at −1.5.
   a. If all firms raised their prices by 5 percent, by how much would total demand fall?
   b. What is the price elasticity if a *single* firm raises its price with other firms' prices unchanged? *Hint:* Use the expression for elasticity in Equation 3.8(b), $E_P = (dQ/dP)(P/Q)$, and note that the individual firm's output is only one-quarter as large as total output.
   c. Suppose that the quantity supplied by the four firms is forecast to increase by 9 percent. Assuming that the demand curve for catfish is not expected to change, what is your forecast for the change in market price (i.e., what percentage price drop will be needed to absorb the increased supply)?

5. As economic consultant to the dominant firm in a particular market, you have discovered that, at the current price and output, demand for your client's product is price inelastic. What advice regarding pricing would you give?

6. A minor league baseball team is trying to predict ticket sales for the upcoming season and is considering changing ticket prices.
   a. The elasticity of ticket sales with respect to the size of the local population is estimated to be about .7. Briefly explain what this number means. If the local population increases from 60,000 to 61,500, what is the predicted change in ticket sales?
   b. Currently, a typical fan pays an average ticket price of $10. The price elasticity of demand for tickets is −.6. Management is thinking of raising the average ticket price to $11. Compute the predicted percentage change in tickets sold. Would you expect ticket revenue to rise or fall?
   c. The typical fan also consumes $8 worth of refreshments at the game. Thus, at the original $10 average price, each admission generates $18 in *total* revenue for team management. Would raising ticket prices to $11 increase or reduce *total* revenue? Provide a careful explanation of your finding. (*Hint:* If you wish, you may assume a certain number of tickets sold per game, say 2,000. However, to answer the question the precise number of tickets need not be specified.)

7. a. Triplecast was NBC's and Cablevision's joint venture to provide pay-per-view cable coverage of the 1992 Summer Olympics in Barcelona. Based on extensive surveys of potential demand, the partners hoped to raise $250 million in revenue by attracting some 2 million subscribers for three channels of nonstop Olympics coverage over 15 days. NBC set the average package price at $125 for complete coverage and offered a separate price of $29.95 per day. However, as the games began, fewer than 400,000 homes had subscribed.
      i. In general, what goal should NBC have followed in setting its program prices? Explain.
      ii. After experiencing the unexpectedly lukewarm response prior to the games, what strategy would you recommend that NBC had pursued?
   b. In 1997, America Online (AOL) overhauled its pricing of Internet access. Formerly, subscribers paid a monthly fee of $9.95 (good for a limited number of access hours) and paid an additional fee for each hour exceeding the limit. In a bid to increase its customer base, AOL offered a new plan allowing unlimited access at a fixed monthly fee of $19.95. (The company estimated that the new plan would deliver a cheaper effective rate per hour for the vast majority of its current customers.)
      i. In terms of impact on revenue, what are the pros and cons of AOL's unlimited access pricing plan?
      ii. What might the cost consequences be?

8. During the 1990s, Apple Computer saw its global share of the personal computer market fall from above 10 percent to less than 5 percent. Despite a keenly loyal customer base, Apple found it more and more difficult to compete in a market dominated by the majority standard: PCs with Microsoft's Windows-based operating system and Intel's microchips. Accordingly, software developers put a lower priority on writing Mac applications than on Windows applications.
   a. Apple vigorously protected its proprietary hardware and software and refused to license Mac clones. What effect did this decision have on long-run demand?
   b. In the early 1990s, Apple enjoyed high markups on its units. In 1995 Apple's chief, John Sculley, insisted on keeping Mac's gross profit margin at 50 to 55 percent, even in the face of falling demand. (Gross profit margin is

measured as total revenue minus total variable costs expressed as a percentage of total revenue.) At this time, the business of selling PCs was becoming more and more "commodity-like." Indeed, the price elasticity facing a particular company was estimated in the neighborhood of $E_P = -4$. Using the markup rule of Equation 3.12, carefully assess Sculley's strategy.

c. In the last decade, Apple has discontinued several of its lower-priced models and has expanded its efforts in the education and desktop publishing markets. In addition, software innovations allow Macs to read most documents, data, and spreadsheets generated on other PCs. Do these initiatives make sense? Do they support Apple's core pricing strategy?

9. a. General Motors (GM) produces light trucks in several Michigan factories, where its annual fixed costs are $180 million, and its marginal cost per truck is approximately $20,000. Regional demand for the trucks is given by: $P = 30,000 - .1Q$, where P denotes price in dollars and Q denotes annual sales of trucks. Find GM's profit-maximizing output level and price. Find the annual profit generated by light trucks.

b. GM is getting ready to export trucks to several markets in South America. Based on several marketing surveys, GM has found the elasticity of demand in these foreign markets to be $E_P = -9$ for a wide range of prices (between $20,000 and $30,000). The additional cost of shipping (including paying some import fees) is about $800 per truck. One manager argues that the foreign price should be set at $800 above the domestic price (in part a) to cover the transportation cost. Do you agree that this is the optimal price for foreign sales? Justify your answer.

c. GM also produces an economy ("no frills") version of its light truck at a marginal cost of $12,000 per vehicle. However, at the price set by GM, $20,000 per truck, customer demand has been very disappointing. GM has recently discontinued production of this model but still finds itself with an inventory of 18,000 unsold trucks. The best estimate of demand for the remaining trucks is:

$$P = 30,000 - Q.$$

One manager recommends keeping the price at $20,000; another favors cutting the price to sell the entire inventory. What price (one of these or some other price) should GM set and how many trucks should it sell? Justify your answer.

10. A New Hampshire resort offers year-round activities: in winter, skiing, and other cold-weather activities and, in summer, golf, tennis, and hiking. The resort's operating costs are essentially the same in winter and summer. Management charges higher nightly rates in the winter, when its average occupancy rate is 75 percent, than in the summer, when its occupancy rate is 85 percent. Can this policy be consistent with profit maximization? Explain.

11. Often, firms charge a range of prices for essentially the same good or service because of cost differences. For instance, filling a customer's one-time small order for a product may be much more expensive than supplying "regular" orders. Services often are more expensive to deliver during peak-load periods. (Typically it is very expensive for a utility to provide electricity to meet peak demand during a hot August.) Insurance companies recognize that the expected cost of insuring different customers under the same policy may vary significantly. How should a profit-maximizing manager take different costs into account in setting prices?

12. Explain how a firm can increase its profit by price discriminating. How does it determine optimal prices? How does the existence of substitute products affect the firm's pricing policy?

*13. A private-garage owner has identified two distinct market segments: short-term parkers and all-day parkers with respective demand curves of $P_S = 3 - (Q_S/200)$ and $P_C = 2 - (Q_C/200)$. Here P is the average hourly rate and Q is the number of cars parked at this price. The garage owner is considering charging different prices (on a per-hour basis) for short-term parking and all-day parking. The capacity of the garage is 600 cars, and the cost associated with adding extra cars in the garage (up to this limit) is negligible.

a. Given these facts, what is the owner's appropriate objective? How can he ensure that members of each market segment effectively pay a different hourly price?

*Starred problems are more challenging.

b. What price should he charge for each type of parker? How many of each type of parker will use the garage at these prices? Will the garage be full?

c. Answer the questions in part (b) assuming the garage capacity is 400 cars.

14. In what respects are the following common practices subtle (or not-so-subtle) forms of price discrimination?

a. Frequent-flier and frequent-stay programs

b. Manufacturers' discount coupon programs

c. A retailer's guarantee to match a lower competing price

Discussion Question   The notion of elasticity is essential whenever the multiplicative product of two variables involves a trade-off. (Thus, we have already appealed to price elasticity to maximize revenue given the trade-off between price and output.) With this in mind, consider the following examples.

a. Why might a bumper crop (for instance, a 10 percent increase in a crop's output) be detrimental for overall farm revenue?

b. Court and legal reforms (to speed the process of litigation and lower its cost) will encourage more disputants to use the court system. Under what circumstances could this cause an *increase* in total litigation spending?

c. Despite technological advances in fishing methods and more numerous fishing boats, total catches of many fish species have declined over time. Explain.

d. Predict the impact on smoking behavior (and the incidence of lung disease) as more and more producers market low-tar and low-nicotine cigarettes.

Spreadsheet Problems

S1. Let's revisit the maker of spare parts in Problem S1 of Chapter 2 to determine its optimal price. The firm's demand curve is given by: $Q = 400 - .5P$, and its cost function by: $C = 20,000 + 200Q + .5Q^2$.

a. Treating price as the relevant decision variable, create a spreadsheet (based on the example shown) to model this setting. Compute the price elasticity in cell B12 according to $E_P = (dQ/dP)(P/Q)$.

b. Find the optimal price by hand. (*Hint*: Vary price while comparing cells E12 and F12. When $(P - MC)/P$ exactly equals $-1/E_P$, the markup rule is satisfied and the optimal price has been identified.)

c. Use your spreadsheet's optimizer to confirm the optimal price.

	A	B	C	D	E	F	G
1							
2			THE OPTIMAL PRICE FOR SPARE PARTS				
3							
4							
5		Price	Quantity	Revenue	Cost	Profit	
6							
7		780	10	7,800	22,050	−14,250	
8							
9							
10		Elasticity	MC		$(P - MC)/P$	$-1/E_P$	
11							
12		−39.0	210		0.7308	0.0256	
13							

S2. On a popular air route, an airline offers two classes of service: business class (B) and economy class (E). The respective demands are given by:

$$P_B = 540 - .5Q_B \quad \text{and} \quad P_E = 380 - .25Q_E.$$

Because of ticketing restrictions, business travelers cannot take advantage of economy's low fares. The airline operates two flights daily. Each flight has a capacity of 200 passengers. The cost per flight is $20,000.

a. The airline seeks to maximize the total revenue it obtains from the two flights. To address this question, create a spreadsheet patterned on the example shown. (In your spreadsheet, only cells E2, E3, E4, C9, and D9 should contain numerical values. The numbers in all other cells are computed by using spreadsheet formulas. For instance, the total available seats in cell E5 is defined as the product of cells E2 and E3.)

b. What fares should the airline charge, and how many passengers will buy tickets of each type? Remember that maximum revenue is obtained by setting MR_B equal to MR_E. After you have explored the decision by hand, confirm your answer using your spreadsheet's optimizer. (*Hint*: Be sure to include the constraint that the total number of seats sold must be no greater than the total number of seats available—that is, cell E9 must be less than or equal to cell E5.

c. Suppose the airline is considering promoting a single "value fare" to all passengers along the route. Find the optimal single fare using your spreadsheet's optimizer. (*Hint*: Simply modify the optimizer instructions from part (b) by adding the constraint that the prices in cells C11 and D11 must be equal.)

	A	B	C	D	E	F
1						
2	DUAL AIRFARES			Planes	2	
3				Seats/Plane	200	
4				Cost/Plane	20,000	
5				Total Seats	400	
6						
7			Business	Non-Bus.	Total	
8						
9	Number of Seats		200	200	400	
10						
11	One-way Fare		440	330	—	
12						
13	Revenue		88,000	66,000	154,000	
14	MR		340	280		
15						
16	MC		100	Total Cost	40,000	
17						
18				Total Profit	114,000	
19						

S3. Now suppose the airline in Problem S2 can vary the number of daily departures.

a. Use marginal analysis to find the airline's profit-maximizing number of flights, and how many passengers of each type it should it carry. (*Hint*: The optimal numbers of passengers, Q_B and Q_E, can be found by setting

$MR_B = MR_E = MC$ per seat. Be sure to translate the $20,000 marginal cost per flight into the relevant MC per seat.)

b. Confirm your algebraic answer by using the spreadsheet you created in Problem S2. (*Hint*: The easiest way to find a solution by hand is to vary the number of passengers of each type to equate *MR*s and *MC*; then adjust the number of planes to carry the necessary total number of passengers.)

c. Use your spreadsheet's optimizer to confirm the optimal solution. (*Hint*: When maximizing total profit in cell E18, be sure to list cell E2, the number of planes, as an adjustable cell. Also, there is no need to include any "*MR* equal to *MC*" constraints; these will automatically be satisfied in the optimizer solution.)

Suggested References

The following references illustrate the various uses of demand analysis, including the computation and application of elasticities.

Baye, M. R., D. W. Jansen, and J. W. Lee. "Advertising Effects in Complete Demand Systems." *Applied Economics* 24 (1992): 1087–1096.

Becker, G. S., M. Grossman, and K. M. Murphy. "An Empirical Analysis of Cigarette Addiction." *The American Economic Review* 84 (June 1994): 396–418.

Bordley, R. F. "Estimating Automotive Elasticities from Segment Elasticities and First Choice/Second Choice Data." *The Review of Economics and Statistics* 75 (August 1993): 455–462.

Fogarty, J. "The Demand for Beer, Wine, and Spirits." *AAWE,* Working Paper 31 (November 2008).

Hughes, J. E., C. R. Knittel, and D. Sperling. "Evidence of a Shift in the Short-Run Price Elasticity of Gasoline Demand." Working Paper 12530, *National Bureau of Economic Research* (September 2006).

Hunt-McCool, J., B. F. Kiker, and Y. C. Ng. "Estimates of the Demand for Medical Care Under Different Functional Forms." *Journal of Applied Econometrics* 9 (1994): 201–218.

McCarthy, P. S. "Market Price and Income Elasticities of New Vehicles Demand." *Review of Economics and Statistics* 78 (August 1996): 543–547.

Pagoulatos, E., and R. Sorenson. "What Determines the Elasticity of Industry Demand?" *International Journal of Industrial Organization*, 4 (1986): 237–250.

Silk, J. I., and F. L. Joutz. "Short- and Long-Run Elasticities in US Residential Electricity Demand: A Co-integration Approach." *Energy Economics* 19 (October 1997): 493–513.

Smith, M., and B. Pierce. "Air Travel Demand." *TIATA Economics Briefing, 9* (April 2008).

Subramanian, S., and A. Deaton. "The Demand for Food and Calories." *The Journal of Political Economy* 104 (February 1996): 133–162.

The following references contain discussions of optimal pricing, price discrimination, and advertising.

Anderson, J. C., M. Wouters, and W. Van Rossum, "Why the Highest Price Isn't the Best Price." *Sloan Management Review* (Winter 2010): 67–76.

Knetter, M. M. "International Comparisons of Pricing-to-Market Behavior." *The American Economic Review* 83 (June 1993): 473–486.

"The Price Is Right, but Maybe It's Not and How Do You Know?" *Knowledge@Wharton* (October 3, 2007), http://knowledge.wharton.upenn.edu/article.cfm?articleid=1813.

Demand characteristics and selling strategies for information goods and services are analyzed in:

Shapiro, C., and H. Varian. *Information Rules*, Chapters 1–3, 7. Boston: Harvard Business School Press, 1999, and at the associated website, www.inforules.com.

Check Station Answers

1. $\Delta Q = -24 + 12 - 40 = -52$ seats.

2. The facts in the second part of the statement are correct, but this does not mean that auto demand is less elastic. Elasticity measures the effect of a percentage change in price, not an absolute change. The change in any good's sales is given by $\Delta Q/Q = E_P(\Delta P/P)$; that is, it depends both on the elasticity and the magnitude of the percentage price change. After all, a $50 auto price cut is trivial in percentage terms. Even if auto demand is very elastic, the change in sales will be small. By contrast, a $50 price cut for a videogame player is large in percentage terms. So there may be a large jump in sales even if player demand is quite inelastic.

3. $E_P = (dQ/Q)/(dP/P) = (dQ/dP)(P/Q)$. With $dQ/dP = -4$, the elasticity at $P = \$200$ and $Q = 800$ is
   $E_P = (-4)(200)/800 = -1$.

4. Since costs are assumed to be fixed, the team's management should set a price to maximize ticket revenue. We know that $Q = 60,000 - 3,000P$ or, equivalently, $P = 20 - Q/3,000$. Setting $MR = 0$, we have $20 - Q/1,500 = 0$, or $Q = 30,000$ seats. In turn, $P = \$10$ and revenue = $\$300,000$ per game. Note that management should *not* set a price to fill the stadium (36,000 seats). To fill the stadium, the necessary average price would be $8 and would generate only $288,000 in revenue.

5. Before the settlement, the cigarette company is setting an optimal price called for by the markup rule: $P = [-1.5/(-1.5 + 1)]2.00 = \$6.00$. The settlement payment takes the form of a fixed cost (based on past sales). It does not vary with respect to current or future production levels. Therefore, it does not affect the firm's marginal cost and should not affect the firm's markup. Note also that the *individual* firm faces *elastic* demand (because smokers can switch to other brands if the firm unilaterally raises prices), whereas industry demand (according to Table 3.1) is *inelastic*. If all firms raise prices by 10 percent, total demand will decline by only 7 percent.

6. The new seat allocations satisfy $MR_B = MR_T$ and $Q_B + Q_T = 270$. The solution is $Q_B = 155$ and $Q_T = 115$. In turn, $P_B = \$175$, $P_T = \$135$, and total revenue is $\$42,650$ — approximately $6,000 greater than current revenue ($36,800). Since the extra cost of the "second day" is only $4,500 (90 × $50), this expansion is profitable. Note, however, that the common value of marginal revenue has dropped to $20. (To see this, compute $MR_B = 330 - 2(155) = \$20$.) Because the marginal revenue per seat has fallen below the marginal cost ($50), any further expansion would be unprofitable.

Consumer Preferences and Demand

In this appendix, we provide a brief overview of the foundations of consumer demand—how consumers allocate their spending among desired goods and services. The analysis is important in its own right as a basis for downward-sloping demand curves. Perhaps its greater importance lies in the broader decision-making principle it illustrates. As we shall see, an optimal decision—made either by a consumer or a manager—depends on a careful analysis of preferences and trade-offs among available alternatives.

The Consumer's Problem

Consider an individual who must decide how to allocate her spending between desirable goods and services. To keep things simple, let's limit our attention to the case of two goods, X and Y. These goods could be anything from specific items (soft drinks versus bread) to general budget categories (groceries versus restaurant meals or food expenditures versus travel spending). The consumer faces a basic question: Given a limited amount of money to spend on the two goods, and given their prices, what quantities should she purchase?

INDIFFERENCE CURVES To answer this question, we will use a simple graphical device to describe the individual's preferences. Imagine that we have asked the consumer what her preferences are for alternative bundles of goods. Which do you prefer, 5 units of X and 10 units of Y, or 7 units of X and 6 units of Y? The answers to enough of such questions generate a preference ranking for a wide range of possible bundles of goods. Figure 3A.1 shows these possible bundles by listing the quantities of the goods on the respective axes. The figure also depicts a number of the consumer's indifference curves as a way of representing her preferences.

As its name suggests, an **indifference curve** shows all combinations of the goods among which the individual is indifferent. The consumer is indifferent between all bundles on the same curve. Using the middle indifference curve in the figure, we see that the consumer is indifferent between the bundle containing 15 units of Y and 2 units of X (point A), 10 units of Y and 3 units of X (point B), and 4 units of Y and 6 units of X (point D). The bundles corresponding to points C, E, and F lie on the same indifference curve and are equally preferred by the consumer.

We can make three observations about the consumer's indifference curves. First, as we move to greater quantities of *both* goods, we move to higher and higher indifference

FIGURE 3A.1

A Consumer's Indifference
Curves

Each indifference curve
shows combinations of
the goods that provide
the consumer with the
same level of welfare.

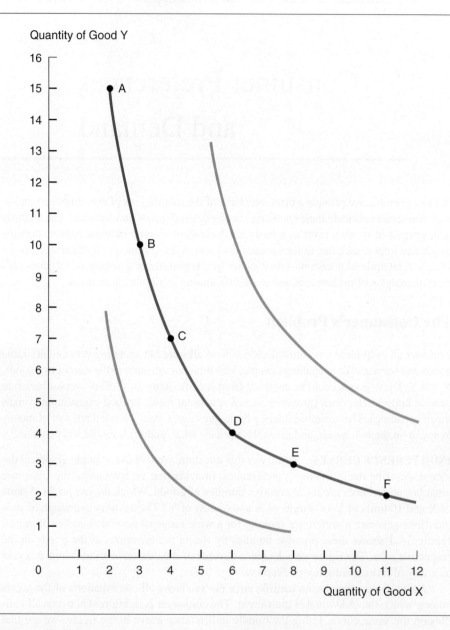

Quantity of Good Y

curves. The figure depicts three different indifference curves. The consumer's welfare
increases as we move to curves farther to the northeast in the figure.[1] Second, we note

---

[1]One way to think about the indifference curve is to view it as a contour elevation map. Such a map has contour
lines that connect points of equal elevation. Theoretically, there is a line for every elevation. Practically, we
cannot have an infinite number of lines, so we draw them for only a few elevations. Similarly, we draw a few
representative indifference curves for the consumer. Bundles of goods lying on "higher" indifference curves
generate greater welfare.

that the indifference curve is downward sloping. Since both goods are valued by the consumer, a decrease in one good must be compensated by an increase in the other to maintain the same level of welfare (or utility) for the consumer.

Third, we note that the slope of each curve goes from steep to flat, moving southeast along its length. This means that the trade-off between the goods changes as their relative quantities change. For instance, consider a movement from A to B. At point A, the consumer has 15 units of Y (a relative abundance) and 2 units of X. By switching to point B, she is willing to give up 5 units of Y to gain a single additional unit of X. Thus, the trade-off is five to one. By moving from point B (where Y is still relatively abundant) to point C, the consumer is willing to give up another 3 units of Y to get an additional unit of X. Now the trade-off between the goods (while leaving the consumer indifferent) is three to one. The trade-offs between the goods continue to diminish by movements from C to D to E. Thus, the indifference curve is bowed. This shape represents a general result about consumer preferences:

> The greater the amount of a good a consumer has, the less an additional unit is worth to him or her.

This result usually is referred to as the *law of diminishing marginal utility*. In our example, moving southeast along the indifference curve means going from a relative abundance of Y and a scarcity of X to the opposite proportions. When X is scarce, the consumer is willing to trade many units of Y for an additional unit of X. As X becomes more abundant and Y more scarce, X's relative value diminishes and Y's relative value increases.

THE BUDGET CONSTRAINT   Having described her preferences, next we determine the consumer's alternatives. The amount of goods she can purchase depends on her available income and the goods' prices. Suppose the consumer sets aside $20 each week to spend on the two goods. The price of good X is $4 per unit, and the price of Y is $2 per unit. Then she is able to buy any quantities of the goods (call these quantities *X* and *Y*) so long as she does not exceed her income. If she spends the entire $20, her purchases must satisfy

$$4X + 2Y = 20. \qquad\qquad [3A.1]$$

This equation's left side expresses the total amount the consumer spends on the goods. The right side is her available income. According to the equation, her spending just exhausts her available income.[2] This equation is called the consumer's **budget constraint**. Figure 3A.2 depicts the graph of this constraint. For instance, the consumer could purchase 5 units of X and no units of Y (point A), 10 units of Y and no units of X (point C), 3 units of X and 4 units of Y (point B) or any other combination along the budget line shown. Note that bundles of goods to the northeast of the budget line are infeasible; they cost more than the $20 that the consumer has to spend.

---

[2]Because both goods are valuable to the consumer, she will never spend *less* than her allotted income on the goods. To do so would unnecessarily reduce her level of welfare.

FIGURE 3A.2

The Consumer's
Budget Line

The budget
line shows the
combinations of
goods X and Y that
can be purchased
with the consumer's
available income.

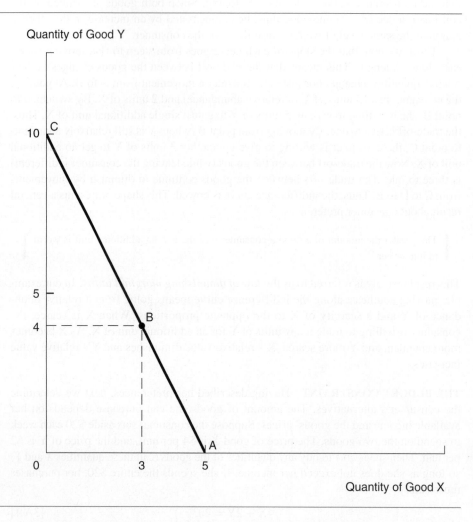

OPTIMAL CONSUMPTION We are now ready to combine the consumer's indifference curves with her budget constraint to determine her optimal purchase quantities of the goods. Figure 3A.3 shows that the consumer's optimal combination of goods lies at point B, 3 units of X and 4 units of Y. Bundle B is optimal precisely because it lies on the consumer's "highest" attainable indifference curve while satisfying the budget constraint. (Check that all other bundles along the budget line lie on lower indifference curves.)

Observe that, at point B, the indifference curve is tangent to the budget line. This means that at B the slope of the indifference curve is exactly equal to the slope of the budget line. Let's consider each slope in turn. The slope of the budget line (the "rise over the run") is −2. This slope can be obtained from the graph directly or found by

The Consumer's Optimal
Consumption Bundle

Quantity of Good Y

The consumer
attains her highest
level of welfare at
point B, where her
indifference curve
is tangent to the
budget line.

Quantity of Good X

rearranging the budget equation in the form $Y = 10 - 2X$. As a result, $\Delta Y/\Delta X = -2$. More generally, we can write the budget equation in the form:

$$P_X X + P_Y Y = I,$$

where P_X and P_Y denote the goods' prices and I is the consumer's income. Rearranging the budget equation, we find $Y = I/P_Y - (P_X/P_Y)X$. Therefore, we have $\Delta Y/\Delta X = -P_X/P_Y$. The trade-off between the goods along the budget line is the *inverse* of the ratio of the goods' prices. Since the price of X is twice that of Y, by purchasing one less unit of X the consumer can purchase two additional units of Y. In short, $\Delta Y/\Delta X = -2$.

We already have commented on the slope of the consumer's indifference curve. Unlike the budget line, the indifference curve's slope is not constant. Rather, it flattens as one moves southeast along its length. The **marginal rate of substitution (MRS)** measures the amount of one good the consumer is willing to give up to obtain a unit of the other good. In other words, MRS measures the trade-off between the goods in terms of the consumer's preferences. To be specific, MRS measures the slope of the indifference curve at any bundle, that is, $MRS = -\Delta Y/\Delta X$ along the indifference curve. In the present example, the MRS at point B is 2.

Now we are ready to state a general result:

> The consumer's optimal consumption bundle is found where the marginal rate of substitution is exactly equal to the ratio of the product prices, $MRS = P_X/P_Y$.

Another way of saying this is that the consumer's preference trade-off between the goods should exactly equal the price trade-off she faces. The MRS represents the *value* of X in terms of Y, whereas P_X/P_Y is the *price* of X in terms of Y. If the relative value of X were greater than its relative price (such as is the case at point D), the consumer would shift to additional purchases of X and thereby move to higher indifference curves. At point E, the situation is reversed. The relative value of X falls short of its relative price, so the consumer would purchase less of X. The consumer's optimal purchase quantities (3 units of X and 4 units of Y) occur at point B. Here, $MRS = P_X/P_Y = 2$. No change in purchases could increase the consumer's welfare.

Demand Curves

The demand curve graphs the relationship between a good's price and the quantity demanded, holding all other factors constant. Consider the consumer's purchase of good X as its price is varied (holding income and the price of Y constant). What if the price falls from $4 per unit to $2 per unit to $1 per unit? Figure 3A.4 shows the effect of these price changes on the consumer's budget line. As the price falls from $4 to $2, the budget line flattens and pivots around its vertical intercept. (Note that, with the price of Y unchanged, the maximum amount of Y the consumer can purchase remains the same.) The figure shows the new budget lines and new points of optimal consumption at the lower prices.

As one would expect, reduction in price brings forth greater purchases of good X and increases the consumer's welfare (i.e., she moves to higher indifference curves). The figure also shows a **price-consumption curve** that passes through the optimal consumption points. This curve shows the consumer's optimal consumption as the price of X is varied continuously. Using this curve, we can record the consumption of X at each price. If we plot the quantity of X demanded versus its price, we arrive at the consumer's demand curve for X; it has the usual downward slope. The consumer increases her optimal consumption of X in response to lower prices.

Of course, different individuals will have varying preferences for goods and varying incomes. For these reasons, they obviously will have different demand curves. How do we arrive at the market demand curve (the total demand by all consumers as price varies)? The answer is found by summing the quantities demanded by all consumers at any given price. Graphically, this amounts to *horizontally* summing the individual demand curves. The result is the market demand curve.[3]

---

[3]Of course, market researchers do not investigate demand individual by individual. Rather, they survey random, representative samples of potential consumers. The main point is that properties of individual demand curves—their downward slope stemming from optimal consumption behavior—carry over to the market demand curve itself.

FIGURE 3A.4

The Price-Consumption Curve

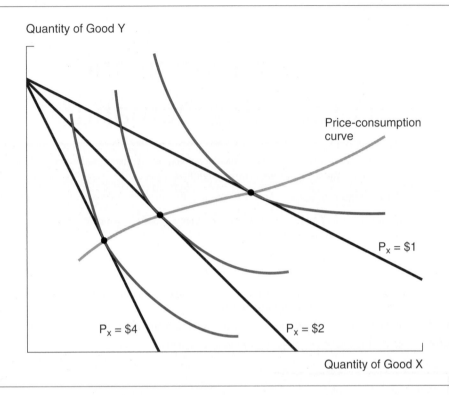

Quantity of Good Y

Price-consumption curve

$P_X = \$1$

$P_X = \$4$

$P_X = \$2$

Quantity of Good X

The price-consumption curve shows that the consumer's demand for X increases as its price falls.

Questions and Problems

1. a. Consider a different consumer who has much steeper indifference curves than those depicted in Figure 3A.1. Draw a graph showing such curves. What do these curves imply about his relative valuation for good X versus good Y?
    b. Using the curves from part a and the budget line in Equation 3A.1, graph the consumer's optimal consumption bundle. How does his consumption bundle compare with that of the original consumer? Is it still true that $MRS = P_X/P_Y = 2$?

2. a. Suppose the income the consumer has available to spend on goods increases to $30. Graph the new budget line and sketch a new indifference curve to pinpoint the consumer's new optimal consumption bundle. According to your graph, does the consumer purchase more of each good?
    b. Sketch a graph (with an appropriate indifference curve) in which one of the goods is inferior. That is, the rise in income causes the consumer to purchase less of one of the goods.

3. Suppose that the price of good X rises and the price of good Y falls in such a way that the consumer's new optimal consumption bundle lies on the same indifference curve as his old bundle. Graph this situation. Compare the quantities demanded between the old and new bundles.

CHAPTER 4

Estimating and Forecasting Demand

To count is a modern practice, the ancient method was to guess; and when numbers are guessed, they are always magnified.

SAMUEL JOHNSON

If today were half as good as tomorrow is supposed to be, it would probably be twice as good as yesterday was.

NORMAN AUGUSTINE, AUGUSTINE'S LAWS

LO#1. Compare survey methods, controlled market studies, and uncontrolled market data as sources of information for forecasting demand.

LO#2. Identify the statistical techniques used in regression analysis and the purpose of each.

LO#3. Describe the two main categories of models used in forecasting.

Estimating Movie Demand

Making movies is a risky business. Even if you find the most promising screenplay, assemble the best actors, and finish the film on time and on budget, your film may still bomb. Yet studios continue to produce movies and theaters continue to book them.

To succeed, studios and theaters must forecast a film's potential box office revenue. This forecasting has evolved from a subjective "art" to a hard-nosed, statistical "science." Numerous variables—the film's genre, its cast and director, the timing of its release, the breadth of its release (limited release or mass release nationwide), the advertising campaign, reviews, and social media "buzz"—all influence the film's expected gross receipts and profits.

Given this risky forecasting environment, how can film producers and exhibitors derive sound predictions of likely box-office revenues?

In previous chapters, we used demand equations, but we did not explain where they came from. Here, we discuss various techniques for collecting data and using it to estimate and forecast demand.

This chapter is organized as follows. We begin by examining sources of information that provide data for forecasts. These include consumer interviews and surveys, controlled market studies, and uncontrolled market data. Next, we explore regression analysis, a statistical method widely used in demand estimation. Finally, we consider a number of important forecasting methods.

COLLECTING DATA

Data and *knowledge* aren't synonymous. The key is to be able to gather and economically analyze data to obtain knowledge. This section examines some valuable tools for collecting data.

Consumer Surveys

One way to get information is to ask. Face to face, by telephone, online, or via direct mail, researchers ask a host of questions: How much product will you buy this year? What if the price increased by 10 percent? Do rebates influence your purchase decisions? What features do you value most? Have you seen our current advertising campaign? Do you purchase competing products? What do you like about them?

Consumer product companies use surveys extensively. In a given year, Campbell Soup Company questions over 100,000 consumers about foods and uses the responses to modify and improve its product offerings and to construct demand equations. Marriott Corporation used this method to design the Courtyard by Marriott hotel chain, asking hundreds of interviewees to compare features and prices. Today, online surveys bring thousands of responses (often highly detailed) at very low cost.

SURVEY PITFALLS   Though useful, surveys have limitations. Market researchers may ask the right questions, but of the wrong people. Economists call this **sample bias**. Sometimes, random sampling protects against sample bias. However, researchers must take care to target representative samples of the relevant market segments.

A second problem is **response bias**. Respondents might report what they believe the questioner wants to hear. ("Your product is terrific, and I intend to buy it.") Alternatively, the customer may attempt to influence decision making. ("If you raise prices, I won't buy.") Neither response may reflect the potential customer's true preferences.[1]

A third problem is **response accuracy**. Potential customers often do not know how they will react to a price increase or to new advertising. Their guesses may be inaccurate. A final difficulty is cost. Extensive consumer surveys are costly. These costs must be weighed against the benefits.

An alternative to consumer surveys is the use of controlled consumer experiments. For example, consumers are given money (real or script) and must make purchasing decisions. Researchers then vary key demand variables (and hold others constant) to determine how the variables affect consumer purchases. Because consumers make actual decisions, their results are likely to be more accurate than those of consumer surveys. Nonetheless, this approach has its own difficulties. Subjects know they are participating in an experiment and this may affect their responses. For example, they may react to price much more in an experiment than they do in real life. In addition, controlled

---

[1]Consumer products firms and retailers such as Walmart actively monitor social media "chatter" to gain information on consumer perceptions. Monitoring conversations among customers is a valuable alternative to asking people directly (and worrying about whether they are telling you the true story). In addition, both proprietary and third-party websites allow consumers to express their views on their purchasing experiences.

experiments are expensive. Consequently, they generally are small (few subjects) and short, and this limits their accuracy. The following is a cautionary tale.

Business Behavior New Coke

In April 1985, the Coca-Cola Company announced it would change the formulation of the world's best-selling soft drink to an improved formula: New Coke. This move followed nearly five years of market research and planning. In some 190,000 taste tests conducted by the company, consumers favored New Coke consistently over the old (by 55 to 45 percent in blind tests) and, perhaps more important, over Pepsi. (In the 1980s, Coke was losing market share to Pepsi and also losing in highly publicized taste tests.)

With the advantage of 20-20 hindsight, we know that the taste tests were wrong. (It just goes to show that you can succeed in doing the wrong thing, even with 190,000 people backing you up.) New Coke did not replace the old Coke in the hearts and mouths of soft-drink consumers. Why? The tests failed to measure how attached Coke drinkers were to their product. Coke drinkers protested. Old Coke outsold New Coke by four to one, causing the Coca-Cola Company to revive the old Coke three months later and to apologize to its customers. With its quick about-face, Coca-Cola minimized the damage to its flagship product, now called Coke Classic. Since then, Coca-Cola has greatly expanded its cola offerings: Diet Coke, Cherry Coke, Caffeine-free Coke, among other offerings. On the advertising, image, taste, and new-product fronts, the cola wars" continue.

Controlled Market Studies

Firms can also generate data on product demand by selling their product in several test markets while varying key demand determinants. The firm might set a high price with high advertising spending in one market, a high price and low advertising in another, a low price and high advertising in another, and so on. In this way, the firm can learn how various pricing and advertising policies affect demand.

To draw valid conclusions from such market studies, all other, uncontrolled factors affecting demand should vary as little as possible. These factors include population size, consumer incomes and tastes, competitors' prices, and even differences in climate. Unfortunately, regional and cultural differences, built-up brand loyalties, and the like may thwart the search for uniform markets. In practice, researchers seek to identify and account for as many of these extraneous factors as possible.

Market studies typically generate **cross-sectional data**—observations in different regions or markets during the same time period. Another type of study relies on **time-series data**. Here, the firm chooses a single geographic area and varies its key decision variables over time. The firm might begin by setting a high price and a low advertising expenditure and observe the market response. Later, it might increase advertising; later still, it might lower price; and so on. Time-series experiments test a single population, thus avoiding some of the problems of uncontrolled factors, but they suffer the problem that consumers may be influenced by the sequence of changes. Whether cross-section or time-series, controlled market tests are extremely expensive. A very rough rule of thumb holds that it costs $1 million for a market test in 1 percent of the United States.

In the last decade, the use of Internet-based controlled market tests has grown exponentially. For instance, Google can randomly assign Internet visitors to different types of ads and compare the average response rates. The company Omniture provides clients immediate feedback on different Web page designs through this method. The credit-card company Capital One does much the same thing when it runs controlled tests of different credit-card solicitations, systematically varying interest rates and cash-back percentages. These newest kinds of controlled experiments are run at ever-decreasing costs.[2]

An airline is considering expanding its business-class seating. Which method, survey or controlled market study, would you recommend to gather information for this decision?

CHECK STATION 1

Uncontrolled Market Data

In its everyday operation, the market itself produces a large amount of data. Many firms operate in multiple markets. Population, income, product features, product quality, prices, and advertising vary across markets and over time. This creates both opportunity and difficulty. Change allows researchers to see how factors affect demand. Unfortunately, many factors change at the same time. How, then, can we judge the effect of any single factor? Fortunately, statisticians have developed methods to handle this very problem.

Today, firms increasingly use computers to gather information. More than three-quarters of all supermarkets employ checkout scanners that provide enormous quantities of data. The drugstore chain CVS uses such data extensively to identify its best customers, to determine which products to stock, and where to locate products in the store. Online purchases generate even more data on consumer preferences and purchasing behavior. Gathering this data is quick and cheap—as little as one-tenth the cost of controlled market tests. With massive computing power at its disposal, a company can search through and analyze terabytes of data about customers and their buying habits, a technique known as *data mining*.[3]

In today's computerized world, almost everything is monitored and measured. With the right analysis, so called "Big Data" is there for the taking. Google, Amazon and others employ thousands of data analysts and pay them six-figure salaries to track and analyze millions of customers online. Data analysis has made headlines, from baseball to

Data-Driven Business

[2]For a detailed discussion of controlled randomized market tests, see I. Ayres, *Super Crunchers: Why Thinking-by-Numbers Is the New Way to Be Smart*, Chapter 2 (New York: Bantam Dell Publishing Group, 2007). Of course, controlled market tests are not new. Fifty years ago, David Ogilvy, the lion of advertising, extolled the virtue of mail-order advertising because its impact was immediately testable. Either readers clipped the coupon, or they didn't.

[3]Firms also seek out publicly available information and often purchase key data. For example, the University of Michigan publishes surveys of consumer buying plans for durable items, and the US Bureau of the Census disseminates *Consumer Buying Intentions*. In estimating its sales, a firm is well aware that consumer income (proxied by gross domestic product) is a key determinant. Accordingly, the firm purchases GDP forecasts that are better and cheaper than it could produce itself.

politics, and has been employed in areas as diverse as venture capital and crime fighting. The detailed behavior of millions of customers can be tracked online. For instance, Google uses scores of statistical techniques to improve its search engine, monitor search behavior, and to fine-tune its search rankings for the most popular sites.

Yet, Big Data isn't knowledge. From enormous databases we must extract relevant relationships such as the firm's demand curve. There are numerous, powerful statistics and forecasting programs; these are spreadsheet based, user-friendly, and readily available at low cost. This permits a wonderful division of labor. Statistical software programs are very good at uncovering patterns from huge amounts of data, while humans are good at explaining and exploiting those patterns.

What's the best advice for a college student preparing for a business career or for life in general? After learning some economics, be sure to learn enough statistics.[4]

REGRESSION ANALYSIS

Regression analysis is a set of statistical techniques using past observations to find (or estimate) the equation that best summarizes the relationships among key economic variables. The method requires that analysts (1) collect data on the variables in question, (2) specify the form of the equation relating the variables, (3) estimate the equation coefficients, and (4) evaluate the accuracy of the equation. Let's begin with a concrete example.

Ordinary Least-Squares Regression

In Chapter 3, an airline's management used a demand equation to predict ticket sales and to make operating decisions along a Texas–Florida air route. Let's examine how the airline can use regression analysis to estimate such an equation. The airline begins by collecting data. The second column of Table 4.1 shows the average number of coach seats sold per flight for each quarter (i.e., 90 days) over the last four years.

Consider a number of key measures of the data. The **mean** is computed as the simple average of the quarterly sales results. Here, the mean is 87.2 seats sold per flight. Next we would like some idea of how much sales vary around the mean. The usual measure of variability is the **sample variance** defined as:

$$s^2 = \frac{\sum_{i=1}^{n}(Q_i - \overline{Q})^2}{n - 1}.$$

[4]According to the McKinsey Global Institute (http://www.mckinsey.com/features/big_data), the United States needs 140,000 to 190,000 more data experts and 1.5 million more data-savvy managers. Political data analysts had a particularly good year in 2012 soundly trouncing the Washington pundits. See R. Thaler, "Applause for the Numbers Machine," *The New York Times* (November 18, 2012), p. BU4. See also C. C. Miller, "Google Ventures Stress Science of the Deal, Not Art of the Deal," *The New York Times* (June 24, 2013), p. B1; S. Sengupta, "In Hot Pursuit of Numbers to Ward Off Crime," *The New York Times* (June 20, 2013), p. F6; S. Lohr, "Sizing Up Big Data, Broadening Beyond the Internet," *The New York Times* (June 20, 2013), p. F1; and G. Mankiw, "A Course Load for the Game of Life," *The New York Times* (September 5, 2010), p. BU5.

TABLE 4.1

Year and Quarter		Average Number of Coach Seats	Average Price	
Y1	Q1	64.8	250	Ticket Prices and Ticket Sales along an Air Route
	Q2	33.6	265	
	Q3	37.8	265	
	Q4	83.3	240	
Y2	Q1	111.7	230	
	Q2	137.5	225	
	Q3	109.6	225	
	Q4	96.8	220	
Y3	Q1	59.5	230	
	Q2	83.2	235	
	Q3	90.5	245	
	Q4	105.5	240	
Y4	Q1	75.7	250	
	Q2	91.6	240	
	Q3	112.7	240	
	Q4	102.2	235	
Mean		87.2	239.7	
Standard deviation		28.0	12.7	

Here, Q_i denotes each of the quarterly sales figures, $\overline{Q}$ is the overall mean, and n is the number of observations. In short, we take the difference between each observation and the mean, square these differences, and then average them. (We use $n - 1$ instead of n for technical reasons.) As the dispersion of the observations increases, so does the variance.

The sample **standard deviation**, s, is the square root of the variance. It is measured in the same units (seats) as the data. In the present example, the sample variance is $s^2 = 11{,}706/15 = 780.4$ and the standard deviation is $s = \sqrt{780.4} = 28.0$ seats.

With these data, how can we best predict next quarter's sales, and how good will this prediction be? We might use the sample mean, 87.2 seats, as an estimate of next quarter's demand. Given our data, this is better than any other estimate. Why? Recall that the sum of squared differences (errors) from the mean was 11,706. But what if we had chosen some other value, say 83 or 92, as our estimate? The sum of squared errors around either of these values would be much larger than around the mean. It turns out that using the sample mean always *minimizes* the sum of squared errors. In this sense, the sample mean is the most accurate estimate of sales. Of course, there is a considerable chance of error in using 87.2 as next quarter's forecast. Next quarter's sales are very likely to fluctuate above or below 87.2. As a rough rule of thumb, we can expect sales to be within two standard deviations of the mean 95 percent of the time. In our example, this means we can expect sales to be 87.2 plus or minus 56 seats (with a 5 percent chance that sales might fall outside this range).

Let's now try to improve our sales estimate by appealing to additional data. We begin with the past record of the airline's prices. These prices (quarterly averages) are listed in the third column of Table 4.1. Again there is considerable variability. At high prices, the airline sold relatively few seats; with lower prices, sales increased. Figure 4.1 provides a visual picture. Each of the 16 points represents a price-quantity pair for a particular quarter. The scatter of observations slopes downward: high prices generally imply low ticket sales, and vice versa.

The next step is to translate this scatter plot of points into a demand equation. A *linear* demand equation has the form

$$Q = a + bP.$$

The left-hand variable Q (the one being predicted or explained) is the *dependent* variable. The right-hand variable P (the one doing the explaining) is the *independent* (or explanatory) variable. The coefficient a is called the constant term. The coefficient b (which we expect to be negative) is the slope of the demand equation. We have selected the *form* of the equation (linear) but we do not yet know the values of a and b. For this, we use regression analysis.

FIGURE 4.1

Four Years of Prices and Quantities

The figure plots the average number of seats sold at different average prices over the last 16 quarters. A "guesstimated" demand curve also is shown.

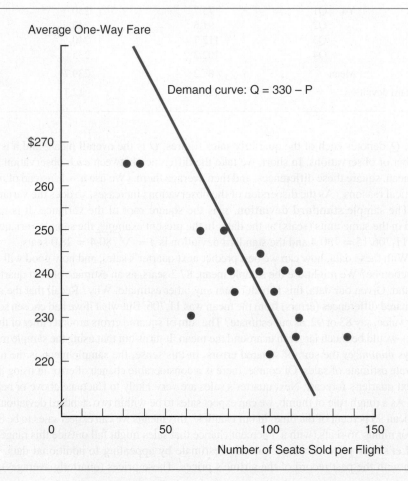

Average One-Way Fare

Demand curve: Q = 330 − P

Number of Seats Sold per Flight

The most common method of computing coefficients is called **ordinary least-squares (OLS) regression**. To illustrate the method, let's start by arbitrarily selecting particular values of a and b. Suppose $a = 330$ and $b = -1$. With these values, the demand equation becomes

$$Q = 330 - 1P. \qquad [4.1]$$

We plot this demand equation in Figure 4.1. Notice that the demand curve lies roughly along the scatter of observations. The equation provides a "reasonable fit" with the data. But how good is this fit? Table 4.2's second column lists Equation 4.1's sales predictions quarter by quarter. For instance, the first quarter's sales prediction (at a price of $250) is computed as $330 - 250 = 80$. The third column lists actual sales. The fourth column lists the differences between predicted sales (column 2) and actual sales (column 3). This difference (positive or negative) is the *estimation error*.

To measure the overall accuracy of the equation, we square each error and then add them up. The final column of Table 4.2 lists the squared errors. The total sum of squared errors (SSE) comes to 6,027.7. It measures the equation's accuracy. The smaller the SSE, the more accurate the regression equation. We square the errors for two reasons. First, by squaring, we treat negative errors and positive errors equally. (Both are bad and should not cancel each other out.) Second, large errors are much worse than small ones. Squaring the errors makes large errors count much more than small errors in SSE. (In addition, there are also important statistical reasons for using the sum of squares.)

TABLE 4.2

Year and Quarter		Predicted Sales (Q^*)	Actual Sales (Q)	$Q^* - Q$	$(Q^* - Q)^2$	Predicted versus Actual Ticket Sales Using $Q = 330 - P$
Y1	Q1	80	64.8	15.2	231.0	
	Q2	65	33.6	31.4	986.0	
	Q3	65	37.8	27.2	739.8	
	Q4	90	83.3	6.7	44.9	
Y2	Q1	100	111.7	−11.7	136.9	
	Q2	105	137.5	−32.5	1,056.3	
	Q3	105	109.5	−4.5	20.3	
	Q4	110	96.8	13.2	174.2	
Y3	Q1	100	59.5	40.5	1,640.3	
	Q2	95	83.2	11.8	139.2	
	Q3	85	90.5	−5.5	30.3	
	Q4	90	105.5	−15.5	240.3	
Y4	Q1	80	75.7	4.3	18.5	
	Q2	90	91.6	−1.6	2.6	
	Q3	90	112.7	−22.7	513.3	
	Q4	95	102.2	−7.2	51.8	
Mean		90.3	87.2	+3.1	376.7	
			Sum of squared errors		6,027.7	

As the term suggests, *ordinary least-squares regression* computes coefficient values that give the smallest sum of squared errors. Using calculus techniques, statisticians have derived standard formulas for these least-squares estimates of the coefficients.[5] Based on our data, the least-squares estimates are: $a = 478.6$ and $b = -1.63$. Thus, the estimated OLS equation is

$$Q = 478.6 - 1.63P. \qquad [4.2]$$

Table 4.3 shows that the sum of squared errors (SSE) is 4,847.2, which is significantly smaller than the SSE (6,027.7) associated with Equation 4.1.

MULTIPLE REGRESSION   Price is not the only factor that affects sales. Suppose the airline also has data on its competitor's average price and regional income. Table 4.4 lists these data. Management would like to use this information to estimate a **multiple-regression** equation of the form

$$Q = a + bP + cP^c + dY.$$

In this equation, quantity depends on own price (P), competitor's price (P^c), and income (Y). We now need to estimate four coefficients. As before, the objective is to find coefficients that will minimize SSE. The OLS equation that does this is

$$Q = 28.84 - 2.12P + 1.03P^c + 3.09Y. \qquad [4.3]$$

TABLE 4.3

Predicted versus Actual Ticket Sales Using $Q = 478.6 - 1.63P$

Year and Quarter		Predicted Sales (Q^*)	Actual Sales (Q)	$Q^* - Q$	$(Q^* - Q)^2$
Y1	Q1	71.1	64.8	6.3	39.7
	Q2	46.6	33.6	13.0	170.3
	Q3	46.6	37.8	8.9	78.3
	Q4	87.4	83.3	4.1	16.8
Y2	Q1	103.7	111.7	-8.0	64.0
	Q2	111.8	137.5	-25.7	657.9
	Q3	111.8	109.5	2.3	5.5
	Q4	120	96.8	23.2	538.2
Y3	Q1	103.7	59.5	44.2	1,953.6
	Q2	95.5	83.2	12.3	152.5
	Q3	79.3	90.5	-11.2	126.6
	Q4	87.4	105.5	-18.1	327.6
Y4	Q1	71.1	75.7	-4.6	21.2
	Q2	87.4	91.6	-4.2	17.6
	Q3	87.4	112.7	-25.3	640.1
	Q4	95.5	102.2	-6.7	44.2
			Sum of squared errors		4,847.2

[5]We provide the general formulas for the least-squares estimators for the interested reader. Suppose that the estimated equation is of the form $y = a + bx$ and that the data to be fitted consist of n pairs of x-y observations (x_i, y_i), $i = 1, 2, \ldots, n$. Then the least-squares estimators are $b = [\Sigma(y_i - \bar{y})(x_i - \bar{x})]/[\Sigma(x_i - \bar{x})^2]$ and $a = \bar{y} - b\bar{x}$. (Here, $\bar{y}$ and $\bar{x}$ are the mean values of the variables, and the summation is over the n observations.)

TABLE 4.4

Year and Quarter		Average Number of Coach Seats	Average Price	Average Competitor Price	Average Income	Airline Sales, Prices, and Income
Y1	Q1	64.8	250	250	104.0	
	Q2	33.6	265	250	101.5	
	Q3	37.8	265	240	103.0	
	Q4	83.3	240	240	105.0	
Y2	Q1	111.7	230	240	100.0	
	Q2	137.5	225	260	96.5	
	Q3	109.5	225	250	93.3	
	Q4	96.8	220	240	95.0	
Y3	Q1	59.5	230	240	97.0	
	Q2	83.2	235	250	99.0	
	Q3	90.5	245	250	102.5	
	Q4	105.5	240	240	105.0	
Y4	Q1	75.7	250	220	108.5	
	Q2	91.6	240	230	108.5	
	Q3	112.7	240	250	108.0	
	Q4	102.2	235	240	109.0	

Table 4.5 lists the predictions, prediction errors, and squared errors for this regression equation. The equation's sum of squared errors is 2,616.4, much smaller than the SSE of any of the previously estimated equations. The additional variables have significantly increased the accuracy of the equation. By and large, the equation's predictions correspond closely to actual ticket sales.

This example suggests the elegance and power of the regression approach. We start with uncontrolled market data. The airline's own price, the competitor's price, and regional income all varied simultaneously from quarter to quarter over the period. Nonetheless, the regression approach has produced an equation (a surprisingly accurate one) that allows us to measure the separate influences of each factor. For instance, according to Equation 4.3, a $10 cut in the competitor's price would draw about 10 passengers per flight from the airline. In turn, a drop of about $5 in the airline's own price would be needed to regain those passengers. Regression analysis sees through the tangle of compounding and conflicting factors that affect demand and thus isolates *separate* demand effects.

Management believes price changes will have an immediate effect on ticket sales, but the effects of income changes will take longer (as much as three months) to play out. How would one test this delayed income effect using regression analysis?   **CHECK STATION 2**

Interpreting Regression Statistics

Many computer programs are available to carry out regression analysis. (In fact, almost all of the best-selling spreadsheet programs include regression features.) The user specifies

TABLE 4.5

Predicted versus Actual Ticket Sales Using $Q = 28.84 - 2.12P + 1.03P^c + 3.09Y$	Year and Quarter		Predicted Sales (Q^*)	Actual Sales (Q)	$Q^* - Q$	$(Q^* - Q)^2$
	Y1	Q1	77.7	64.8	12.9	166.4
		Q2	38.2	33.6	4.6	20.9
		Q3	32.5	37.8	−5.3	28.0
		Q4	91.7	83.3	8.4	70.4
	Y2	Q1	97.4	111.7	−14.3	203.3
		Q2	117.8	137.5	−19.7	387.1
		Q3	97.6	109.5	−11.9	140.7
		Q4	103.2	96.8	6.4	40.8
	Y3	Q1	88.2	59.5	28.7	822.0
		Q2	94.0	83.2	10.8	117.7
		Q3	83.7	90.5	−6.8	46.7
		Q4	91.7	105.5	−13.8	190.7
	Y4	Q1	60.7	75.7	−15.0	224.9
		Q2	92.2	91.6	.6	.4
		Q3	111.3	112.7	−1.4	2.1
		Q4	114.7	102.2	12.5	155.0
				Sum of squared errors		2,616.4

the form of the regression equation and inputs the necessary data. The program estimates coefficients and produces a set of statistics indicating how well the OLS equation performs. Table 4.6 lists the standard computer output for the airline's multiple regression. The regression coefficients and constant term are listed in the third-to-last line. Using these, we obtained the regression equation:

$$Q = 28.84 - 2.12P + 1.03P^c + 3.09Y.$$

To evaluate how well this equation fits the data, we must learn how to interpret the other statistics in the table.

R-SQUARED   The **R-squared** statistic (also known as the *coefficient of determination*) measures the proportion of the variation in the dependent variable (Q in our example) that is explained by the multiple-regression equation. Sometimes we say that it is a measure of *goodness of fit*, that is, how well the equation fits the data. The total variation in the dependent variable is computed as $\Sigma(Q - \bar{Q})^2$, that is, as the sum across the data set of squared differences between the values of Q and the mean of Q. In our example, this total sum of squares (labeled TSS) happens to be 11,706. The R^2 statistic is computed as

$$R^2 = \frac{TSS - SSE}{TSS} \qquad [4.4]$$

The sum of squared errors, *SSE*, embodies the variation in Q *not* accounted for by the regression equation. Thus, the numerator is the amount of explained variation and

TABLE 4.6

Airline Demand
Regression Output

Regression Output

	Constant	P	P^c	Y
Dependent variable: Q				
Sum of squared errors	2616.40			
Standard error of the regression	14.77			
R-squared	0.78			
Adjusted R-squared	0.72			
F-statistic	13.9			
Number of observations	16			
Degrees of freedom	12			
	Constant	**P**	**P^c**	**Y**
Coefficients	28.84	−2.12	1.03	3.09
Standard error of coefficients		0.34	.47	1.00
t-statistic		−6.24	2.20	3.09
P-value		.00004	.047	.0093

R-squared is simply the ratio of explained to total variation. In our example, we can calculate that $R^2 = (11{,}706 - 2{,}616)/11{,}706 = 0.78$. We can also rewrite Equation 4.4 as

$$R^2 = 1 - (SSE/TSS). \qquad [4.5]$$

Clearly, R^2 always lies between zero and one. If the regression equation predicts the data perfectly (i.e., the predicted and actual values coincide), then $SSE = 0$, and $R^2 = 1$. If the equation explains nothing (i.e., the individual explanatory variables did not affect the dependent variable), $SSE = TSS$, implying $R^2 = 0$. In our case, the regression equation explains 78 percent of the total variation.

Although R^2 is a simple and convenient measure of goodness of fit, it suffers from certain limitations. Primarily, it is sensitive to the number of explanatory variables in the regression equation. Adding more variables always results in a lower (or, at least, no higher) SSE, with the result that R^2 increases. Thus, it is a mistake to regard the main goal of regression analysis as finding the equation with the highest R^2. We can always jack up the R^2 by throwing more variables into the right-hand side of the regression equation even if the *added variables have no real explanatory power.*

ADJUSTED R-SQUARED   A partial remedy for this problem is to adjust R-squared according to the number of variables in the regression. The *degrees of freedom* is the number of observations (N) minus the number of estimated coefficients (k). In the airline regression, the number of observations is 16, and the number of coefficients (including the constant term) is 4. Thus, the degrees of freedom are: $N - k = 16 - 4 = 12$. The adjusted R-squared is given by

$$\hat{R}^2 = 1 - \frac{SSE/(N - k)}{TSS/(N - 1)}. \qquad [4.6]$$

The difference between R^2 and $\hat{R}^2$ is the adjustment for the *degrees of freedom* in the latter. One can show that $\hat{R}^2$ always is smaller than R^2. In our example, $\hat{R}^2 = 0.72$. Adding another variable to the equation will increase $\hat{R}^2$ (and therefore, be deemed worthwhile) only if it lowers SSE sufficiently.

CHECK STATION 3   **Suppose the airline's management had only eight quarters of data. How would this affect the quality of the regression? Would it adversely affect R^2? The adjusted R-squared?**

THE *F*-STATISTIC   The *F-statistic* is computed as

$$F = \frac{R^2/(k-1)}{(1-R^2)/(N-k)}. \tag{4.7}$$

The more accurate the predictions of the regression equation (the higher the R^2), then the larger is the value of F.

The *F*-statistic has the advantage that we can use it to test the overall statistical significance of the regression equation. Suppose someone asserts that the coefficients b, c, and d are all really equal to zero. If this were true, then the so-called explanatory variables would have no effect on the dependent variable—they would explain nothing. Note, however, that even if this were true, regression *estimates* of b, c, and d, would not be exactly zero, and both R^2 and F would almost certainly be above zero (though small) due to small accidental correlations in the data. In other words, R^2 and F must be high enough to convince us that the right-hand-side variables collectively have explanatory power.

How high does the *F*-statistic need to be? The most common standard is to insist on 95 percent confidence for the validity of any estimated relationship. Table 4B.1 in the chapter appendix lists critical values for the F distribution at the 95 percent confidence level. These critical values depend on the degrees of freedom, $k-1$ and $N-k$. If the *F*-statistic exceeds the 95 percent critical value, we can be (more than) 95 percent confident that the right-hand-side variables have real explanatory power. In our example, the *F*-statistic is $(.776/3)/(.224/12) = 13.86$ and has 3 and 12 degrees of freedom. From Table 4B.1, the 95 percent critical value is 3.49. Because F is greater than this, we are (more than) 95 percent confident that the equation as a whole has explanatory power—that is, the coefficients are highly unlikely all to be zero. Equivalently, we say that the equation is "statistically significant."

STANDARD ERRORS OF THE COEFFICIENTS   From the regression, we obtain estimates of the coefficients. But how accurate are these estimates? OLS coefficient estimates are unbiased; on average, they neither overestimate nor underestimate the true coefficients. Nonetheless, the estimates will not be 100 percent accurate.

The **standard error of a coefficient** is the estimated standard deviation of the estimated coefficient. The lower the standard error, the more accurate is the estimate. Roughly speaking, there is a 95 percent chance that the true coefficient lies within two standard errors of the estimated coefficient. For example, the estimate for the price coefficient is -2.12 and its standard error is 0.34. Two times the standard error is .68. Thus, there is roughly a 95 percent chance that the true coefficient lies in the range of -2.12 plus or minus .68—that is, between -2.80 and -1.44.

THE *t*-STATISTIC   The *t*-*statistic* is the value of the coefficient estimate divided by its standard error. The *t*-statistic tells us how many standard errors the coefficient estimate is above or below zero. For example, if the *t*-statistic is 3, then the coefficient estimate is three standard errors greater than zero. If the *t*-statistic is −1.5, then the coefficient estimate is one and one-half standard errors below zero. As we just noted, the estimated price coefficient is −2.12 and its standard error is .34. We now use the *t*-statistic to show that the price variable has true explanatory power (i.e., to reject any claim that the price coefficient equals zero, $b = 0$). The computed *t*-statistic is: $t = -2.12/.34 = -6.24$. The estimated coefficient is 6.24 standard errors less than zero. We now use the table of the *t*-distribution (Table 4B.2), noting that the *t*-statistic has $n - k = 16 - 4 = 12$ degrees of freedom. From the table, we find that 2.18 is the critical value to assure 95 percent confidence. Because the value of *t*, 6.34 in absolute value, is greater than 2.18, we can be (more than) 95 percent confident that the price variable has explanatory power (the true price coefficient is not zero).[6]

We apply the *t*-test to each explanatory variable to determine whether it truly affects airline sales. From Table 4.6, we see that all of the coefficients have *t*-values that are greater than 2.18 in absolute value. Thus we are 95 percent confident that each variable has explanatory power. If we found that a given coefficient were not significantly different than zero, we would drop that explanatory variable from the equation (absent a compelling reason to keep it).

We can use this same method to test other hypotheses. Suppose the airline's managers hypothesize that the coefficient of the competitor's price is 1. The appropriate *t*-statistic for testing this hypothesis is

$$t = \frac{c - 1}{\text{standard error of } c}$$

$$= \frac{1.035 - 1}{.47} = .085.$$

Since this is near zero, that is, smaller than 2.18, we cannot reject the hypothesis, $c = 1$. Applying similar tests to the other coefficients, it is clear that there is little to choose between Equation 4.3 and the "rounded" regression equation, $Q = 29 - 2P + P^c + 3Y$, used in Chapter 3.

Again, suppose we estimate the demand equation using only eight quarterly observations. How will this affect the equation's *F*-statistic? The standard errors of the coefficients?   CHECK STATION 4

THE *P*-VALUE   Standard regression programs now save users the steps of comparing *t*-values to tables of critical values in determining whether economic variables have explanatory power. Instead, they supply *P*-values for each estimated coefficient (and for the *F*-statistic). The *P*-value gives the probability that the estimated coefficient would

[6]From Table 4B.2 in the chapter appendix, we note that as the number of observations increases, the 95 percent critical value approaches 1.96. This justifies the benchmark of 2 as the rough boundary of the 95 percent confidence interval.

be as large as it is (in absolute value) if in fact the variable had no true effect. In other words, if we are exactly 95 percent confident that the coefficient is statistically significant (that is, truly different than zero), then the *P*-value is .05, meaning that there is a 5 percent chance that the coefficient is, indeed, truly zero. For instance, the competitor's price coefficient is 1.03, and its associated *P*-value is .047. This means that even if in reality seats sold were unaffected by the rival's price, there is still a 4.7 percent probability that the coefficient would be as large or larger than 1.03 (or as small or smaller than −1.03) due to chance alone. Accordingly, we are 95.3 percent confident that the rival's price affects seat sales.

STANDARD ERROR OF THE REGRESSION   The standard error of the regression is computed as

$$s = \sqrt{SSE/(N - k)}.$$ [4.8]

The standard error is an estimate of the standard deviation of the unexplained variation in the dependent variable. Accordingly, it is useful in constructing confidence intervals for forecasts. For instance, for regressions based on large samples, the 95 percent confidence interval for predicting the dependent variable (Q in our example) is given by the predicted value from the regression equation (Q^*) plus or minus two standard errors.

Potential Problems in Regression

Regression analysis can be quite powerful. Nonetheless, it does have certain limitations and potential problems.

EQUATION SPECIFICATION   In our example, we assumed a linear form. However, relations do not always follow straight lines.[7] Thus, we may be making a *specification error*, which can lead to poorer predictions.

   An alternative specification is to use the **constant elasticity** demand equation, which takes the form

$$Q = aP^b(P^c)^c Y^d,$$ [4.9]

where, *a*, *b*, *c*, and *d* are coefficients to be estimated. One can show mathematically that the coefficients *b*, *c*, and *d* represent the (constant) elasticity of demand with respect to the explanatory variables. For instance, if the estimated demand equation were $Q = 100P^{-2}(P^c)^{.8}Y^{1.2}$, then the price elasticity of demand would be −2, the cross-price elasticity would be 0.8, and the income elasticity would be 1.2.

   We can rewrite Equation 4.9 as

$$\log(Q) = \log(a) + b\log(P) + c\log(P^c) + d\log(Y)$$ [4.10]

after taking logarithms of each side. This log-linear form is then estimated using the ordinary least-squares method applied to the "logs" of all the variables.

---

[7]An alternative specification is the quadratic form, $Q = a + bP + cP^2$, because this allows for a curvilinear relationship among the variables.

OMITTED VARIABLES   A related problem is that of **omitted variables**. Recall that we began the analysis of airline demand with price as the only explanatory variable. When we added competitor's price and income, the equation did far better. In short, leaving out key variables worsens prediction performance. In fact, omitting key variables also affects the coefficients of the included variables. The price coefficient was -1.63 when it was the sole explanatory variable, quite different from the estimated multiple regression coefficient, -2.12. Thus, the single-variable regression underestimates the magnitude of the true price effect.

MULTICOLLINEARITY   When two or more explanatory variables move together, we say that the regression suffers from **multicollinearity**. With multicollinearity, it is difficult to tell which of the variables is affecting the dependent variable. Consider two factors that may affect demand: price and advertising. Suppose that whenever the firm increased advertising, it decreased price and that this resulted in increased sales. Later, when it decreased advertising, it also increased price, and sales dropped. Between price and advertising, which is affecting demand, and by how much? With this track record, it is impossible to tell, even with regression. If two right-hand variables move together, regression cannot separate the effects. Regression does *not* require that we hold one of the factors constant as we vary the other, but it does require that the two factors vary in different ways.

What happens when the forecaster runs a regression based on the previous data? If the right-hand variables are perfectly correlated, the computerized regression program will send back an error message. If the right-hand variables are not perfectly correlated, but move very closely together (either directly or inversely), the regression output will provide very imprecise coefficient estimates with large standard errors. In this case, additional data may improve the estimates. If not, the forecaster must live with the imprecise estimates.

Can the firm still use the equation to forecast? Yes and no. It can if it plans to continue the pattern of lowering price whenever it increases advertising. In that case, it need not care about the separate effects. However, if it plans to lower price without an advertising campaign, or to advertise more without lowering price, the forecast will be very unreliable.

SIMULTANEITY AND IDENTIFICATION   This brings us to a subtle, but interesting and important, issue. In the preceding discussion, we assumed that the firm had control over its price. In many settings, however, price is determined by overall demand and supply conditions, not by the individual firm. Here, the firm must take the price the market dictates or else sell nothing. Such settings are called *perfectly competitive markets*, which we will discuss in detail in Chapter 7. For now, note that price and quantity in competitive markets are determined *simultaneously* by supply and demand. Let's consider the implications of this with a simple example.

Suppose both the quantity supplied and the quantity demanded depend only on price, except for some random terms:

$$Q_D = a + bP + \varepsilon,$$
$$Q_s = c + dP + v$$

where ε and v are random variables. The random terms indicate that both the supply and demand curves jump around a bit. The equilibrium is determined by the intersection of the supply and demand curves. Figure 4.2a shows these curves with random shifts, as well as the price-quantity outcomes that these curves generate.

Now, look only at the points in Figure 4.2a and try to use these points to estimate either supply or demand. The "best line" appears in Figure 4.2b. Is this an estimate of the supply curve, the demand curve, or what? Because price and quantity are determined simultaneously, we cannot tell whether two points differ because of randomness in supply, in demand, or in both; that is, we cannot *identify* which curve is responsible. **Simultaneity** (in the determination of price and quantity) means that the regression approach may fail to identify the separate (and simultaneous) influences of supply and demand.

When is identification possible? If supply fluctuates randomly, but demand does not, this leads to a situation shown in Figure 4.2c. where all of the points lie along a stationary demand curve. In this case, we can estimate demand, although estimating supply remains impossible. We say that demand is identified, but supply is not. In the converse case, where demand fluctuates but supply does not, only the supply curve is identified. If both demand and supply fluctuate but if one or the other or both also depend on other variables, we can use more advanced techniques (beyond the scope of this book) to identify one or both curves. Our lesson here is that we must look carefully at the relationships being estimated and be on the lookout for simultaneously determined variables.

OTHER PROBLEMS   Finally, it is important to recognize that the regression approach depends on certain assumptions about randomness. Let us rewrite the multiple-regression equation as

$$Q = a + bP + cP^c + dY + \varepsilon \qquad [4.11]$$

Here, we have added the term ε. In words, sales depend on various variables plus some randomness. In regression, we make certain assumptions about the random term, ε. The key assumption is that the random term is normally distributed with a mean of zero and a constant variance and that it is completely independent of everything else. If this assumption is not true, then we must modify the OLS method to get good estimates.

Two main problems concerning random errors can be identified. First, **heteroscedasticity** occurs when the variance of the random error changes over the sample. For example, demand fluctuations may be much larger in recessions (low income levels Y) than in good times. To determine if this is true, we can divide the data into two groups, one associated with high income and one with low income and find the sum of squared errors for each subgroup. If these are significantly different, this is evidence of heteroscedasticity.

Serial correlation occurs when the errors run in patterns—that is, the distribution of the random error in one period depends on its value in the previous period. For instance, the presence of positive correlation means that prediction errors tend to persist: Overestimates are followed by overestimates and underestimates by underestimates. There are standard statistical tests to detect serial correlation (either positive or negative). The best-known test uses the **Durbin-Watson statistic** (which most regression

FIGURE 4.2

Shifts in Supply and Demand

Price

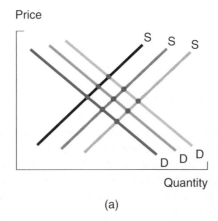

(a)

The scatter of points
in parts (a) and (b) is
caused by shifts in
both supply and
demand. To estimate
a demand curve as
in part (c), shifts in
supply are crucial.

Price

(b)

Price

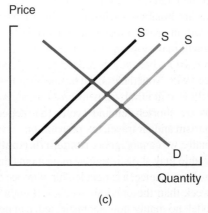

(c)

programs compute). A value of approximately 2 for this statistic indicates the absence of serial correlation. Large deviations from 2 (either positive or negative) indicate serial correlation.

FORECASTING

Forecasting uses both structural and nonstructural models. *Structural models identify how variables depend on each other.* The airline demand equation (4.1) is a single-equation structural model. Sophisticated large-scale structural models of the economy often contain scores of equations and hundreds of variables.

Nonstructural models look at patterns over time. *Time-series analysis* attempts to describe these patterns explicitly. Another method, *barometric analysis*, identifies leading indicators—economic variables that signal future economic developments. (The stock market is one of the best-known leading indicators of the course of the economy.)

Time-Series Models

Time-series models extrapolate past behavior into the future. Time-series patterns can be categorized as follows:

1. Trends
2. Business cycles
3. Seasonal variations
4. Random fluctuations

A **trend** is a steady movement over time. For example, the total production of goods and services in the United States has moved steadily upward over the years. Conversely, the number of farmers in the United States has steadily declined.

On top of such trends are **business cycles**. Economies experience periods of expansion marked by rapid growth in gross domestic product (GDP), investment, and employment. Then economic growth may slow and even fall. A sustained fall in (real) GDP and employment is called a *recession*. For the US economy, recessions have become less frequent and less severe since 1945. Nonetheless, the business cycle—with periods of growth followed by recessions, followed in turn by expansions—remains an economic fact of life.

Seasonal variations are shorter demand cycles that depend on the time of year. Seasonal factors affect tourism and air travel, tax preparation services, clothing, and other products and services. Finally, we cannot ignore **random fluctuations**. In any short period of time, an economic variable may show irregular movements due to essentially random (or unpredictable) factors. For instance, a car dealership may see 50 more customers walk into its showroom one week than the previous week, sell eight more automobiles, and have no idea why. No model, no matter how sophisticated, can perfectly explain the data.

Figure 4.3 shows how a time series (a company's sales, let's say) can be decomposed into its component parts. Part (a) depicts a smooth upward trend. Part (b) adds business

FIGURE 4.3

The Component Parts
of a Time Series

A typical time series
contains a trend,
cycles, seasonal
variations, and
random fluctuations.

(a) A Simple Upward Trend

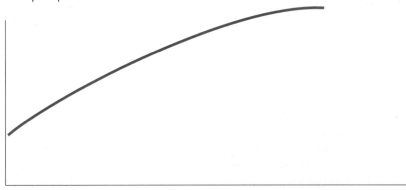

Time

(b) Cyclical Movements
around a Trend

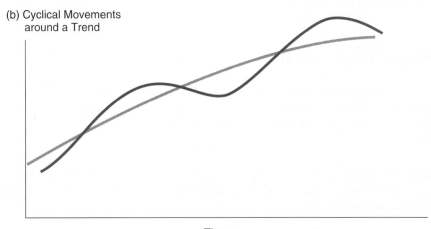

Time

(c) Seasonal Variations

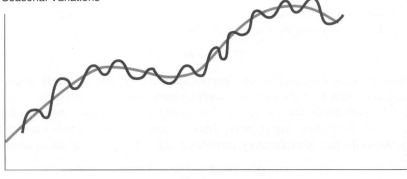

Time

cycles to the trend. Part (c) adds the regular seasonal fluctuations over the course of the year. We do not show the random fluctuations, but if we took an even "finer" look at the data (plotted it week by week, let's say), the time series would look even more rough and jagged.

The relative importance of the components—trends, cycles, seasonal variations, and random fluctuations—will vary according to the time series in question. Sales of men's plain black socks creep smoothly upward (due to population increases) and show little cyclical or seasonal fluctuations. By contrast, the number of lift tickets sold at a ski resort depends on cyclical, seasonal, and random factors. The components' relative importance also depends on the length of the time period being considered. For instance, data on day-to-day sales over a period of several months may show a great deal of randomness. The short period precludes looking for seasonal, cyclical, or trend patterns. By contrast, if one looks at monthly sales over a three-year period, not only will day-to-day randomness get averaged out, but we may see seasonal patterns and even some evidence of the business cycle. Finally, annual data over a 10-year horizon will let us observe trends and cyclical movements but will average out, and thus mask, seasonal variation.

Fitting a Simple Trend

Figure 4.4 plots a product's level of annual sales over a dozen years. The time series displays a smooth upward trend. Let's first estimate a linear trend, that is, a straight line to fit the data. We represent this linear relationship by

$$Q_t = a + bt, \qquad\qquad [4.12]$$

where t denotes time and Q_t denotes sales at time t. We can use OLS regression to estimate coefficients a and b. We first number the periods: year 1, year 2, and so on. Regression analysis then produces the equation:

$$Q_t = 98.2 + 8.6t.$$

Figure 4.4a shows this estimated trend line along with the data. We can see that the trend line fits the data quite closely.

A linear time trend assumes that sales increase by the same number of units each period. Instead we could use the quadratic form

$$Q_t = a + bt + ct^2. \qquad\qquad [4.13]$$

A positive value of the coefficient c implies an increasing rate of growth in sales over time, that is, sales tend to turn more steeply upward over time. Conversely, if c is negative, sales grow more slowly over time. The quadratic form includes the linear equation as a special case (when c equals zero). Thus, suppose the manager runs a regression of sales versus the pair of explanatory variables, t and t^2, and arrives at the equation

$$Q_t = 101.8 + 7.0t + .12t^2.$$

According to the t-tests, the constant term and both coefficients are statistically significant. Thus, it turns out that the quadratic specification fits the past time-series data better

FIGURE 4.4

Fitting a Trend to a
Time Series

Candidates include
linear and nonlinear
trends.

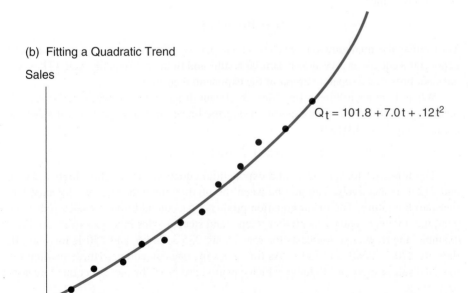

(a) Fitting a Linear Trend

Sales

$Q_t = 98.2 + 8.6t$

Time

(b) Fitting a Quadratic Trend

Sales

$Q_t = 101.8 + 7.0t + .12t^2$

Time

than the linear specification. The bottom portion of Figure 4.4 shows the time series and the fitted quadratic equation.

Besides the quadratic equation, forecasters often use the exponential form,

$$Q_t = br^t, \qquad\qquad [4.14]$$

where the coefficients b and r are to be estimated. Here, the coefficient r is raised to the power t. Thus, if r is greater than 1, then sales, Q_t, grow proportionally. For instance, if r equals 1.04, then sales grow by 4 percent each year. Alternatively, if the estimated r falls short of 1, then sales decrease proportionally. If r equals .94, then sales fall by 6 percent per period.

By taking the natural log of both sides of the equation, we can convert this into a linear form so that we can apply OLS:

$$\log(Q_t) = \log(b) + \log(r)t, \qquad\qquad [4.15]$$

Note that we must compute values of $\log(Q_t)$ to use as the dependent variable in this regression. To illustrate, suppose that the manager decides to fit an exponential equation to the time series in Figure 4.4. The resulting least-squares equation is

$$\log(Q_t) = 4.652 + .0545t,$$

with both coefficients statistically significant. Thus, our estimate of $\log(b)$ is 4.652 and our estimate of $\log(r)$ is .0545. We now take the antilog of each coefficient: $b = $ antilog(4.652) $= 104.8$ and $r = $ antilog(.0545) $= 1.056$. Thus, the fitted exponential equation becomes

$$Q_t = 104.8(1.056)^t.$$

The estimated annual growth rate is 5.6 percent per year. With our data, the quadratic and exponential equations give closely similar results and fit the data equally well. (Thus, we have not provided a separate graph of the exponential curve.)

When it comes to forecasting, the significant difference is between the linear and nonlinear specifications. For example, using the linear equation, we forecast sales for the next year (year 13) to be

$$Q_{13} = 98.2 + (8.6)(13) = 210.0.$$

The forecasts for quadratic and exponential equations are slightly higher, 213.1 and 212.4, respectively. The gap between the predictions widens as we forecast farther into the future. The linear equation predicts constant additions to sales year after year; the nonlinear equations predict steeper and steeper sales increases over time. For example, the respective forecasts for year 16 are 235.8, 244.5, and 250.1; for year 20, they are 270.2, 289.8, and 311.0. As time goes by, one can compare these predictions to actual sales experience to judge which equation produces the more accurate forecasts on average.

CHECK STATION 5   **In 1980, the common stock of both Company A and Company B sold for $50 per share. Over the next 35 years, the value of A's stock increased at an average rate of 5 percent per year; the value of B's stock increased by 6 percent per year on average. Find the 2015 price for each company's stock. Comment on your findings.**

In many economic settings, the value of a variable today influences the value of the same variable tomorrow. Increased sales in one month frequently mean increased sales in the following month. An elevated rate of inflation in the current quarter is likely to spell higher rates in succeeding quarters. Suppose that a firm's sales in the current period depend on its sales in the previous period according to

$$Q_t = a + bQ_{t-1}.$$

We can estimate the coefficients a and b by OLS regression using last period's sales (or sales "lagged" one period) as the explanatory variable.

As an example, suppose that a cable television company has 500,000 subscribers in hand and wants to predict how many additional subscribers it will have in the future. The company has the following facts. (1) Each quarter, about 98 percent of current subscribers retain the service. (2) The size of the potential market is about 1,000,000 households, so there are 500,000 potential customers not yet enlisted. (3) Each quarter, about 8 percent of unaffiliated customers become new subscribers to the company. These facts imply the following equation for total subscribers in quarter t:

$$Q_t = .98Q_{t-1} + .08(1,000,000 - Q_{t-1}).$$

The first term on the right side of the equation is the number of retained customers from last quarter; the second term is the number of new subscribers.

Notice that this equation can be simplified to: $Q_t = 80,000 + .90Q_{t-1}$. Starting from $Q_0 = 500,000$, next quarter's subscriptions are predicted to be: $Q_1 = 80,000 + (.9)(500,000) = 530,000$. Future quarterly forecasts are found recursively. Having computed 530,000, the forecast for two quarters in the future is: $Q_2 = 80,000 + (.9)(530,000) = 557,000$. The forecasts for one year ahead (Q_4), two years ahead (Q_8), and five years ahead (Q_{20}) are 603,170, 670,860, and 763,527, respectively. Subscriptions are expected to grow but at a diminishing rate.[8] Finally, if the cable company did not have the specific facts in items (1) to (3), it could instead use the record of its past quarterly subscriptions to fit the best regression equation of the form $Q_t = a + bQ_{t-1}$, estimate the coefficients a and b directly, and then use these estimates for forecasting future numbers of subscribers.

THE DEMAND FOR TOYS   To illustrate some of the issues involved in time-series modeling, consider the market for children's toys. The tabular portion of Figure 4.5 shows these hypothetical data. We see an unmistakable upward trend and some obvious seasonal behavior. The pattern does not seem completely regular, however, which indicates the presence of a random element.

Let's first estimate the long-term trend in toy sales, assuming a linear trend. The OLS regression equation is:

$$Q_t = 141.16 + 1.998t.$$

We have labeled the first quarter (winter 2005) as period one, the second quarter (spring 2005) as period two, and so on. We list the complete regression statistics

---

[8]In general, if the coefficient of Q_{-1} is less than 1, then sales grow but at a decreasing rate. Alternatively, if the coefficient is greater than one, sales grow at an increasing rate.

FIGURE 4.5

Seasonal Toy Sales over
Ten Years

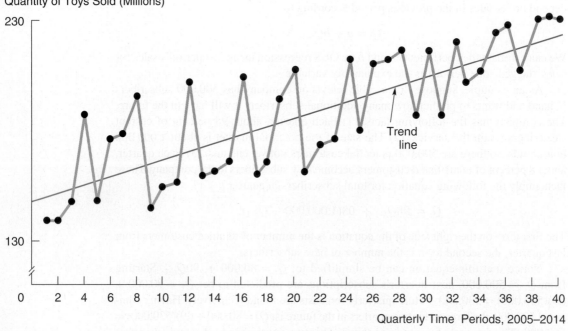

Seasonal Toy Sales over 10 Years

1	Winter 2005	133		21	Winter 2010	158
2	Spring 2005	135		22	Spring 2010	169
3	Summer 2005	140		23	Summer 2010	171
4	Fall 2005	181		24	Fall 2010	209
5	Winter 2006	141		25	Winter 2011	172
6	Spring 2006	170		26	Spring 2011	207
7	Summer 2006	172		27	Summer 2011	209
8	Fall 2006	186		28	Fall 2011	214
9	Winter 2007	143		29	Winter 2012	183
10	Spring 2007	148		30	Spring 2012	212
11	Summer 2007	150		31	Summer 2012	184
12	Fall 2007	194		32	Fall 2012	219
13	Winter 2008	154		33	Winter 2013	185
14	Spring 2008	156		34	Spring 2013	190
15	Summer 2008	158		35	Summer 2013	222
16	Fall 2008	196		36	Fall 2013	227
17	Winter 2009	153		37	Winter 2014	199
18	Spring 2009	161		38	Spring 2014	228
19	Summer 2009	193		39	Summer 2014	230
20	Fall 2009	204		40	Fall 2014	229

in Table 4.7. The high *F*-statistic indicates that the equation has considerable explanatory power and the time coefficient is statistically significant. Roughly, sales have gone up an average of 2 million per quarter.

We can use this equation to forecast future sales. For instance, winter 2015 corresponds to $t = 41$. Inserting this value into the equation implies the forecast $Q_{41} = 223.08$.

SEASONAL VARIATION   Now we must account for seasonality. We expect most sales to occur in the fall quarter (October to December) prior to the holidays and the fewest sales in the winter quarter (following the holidays). Indeed, this is exactly what we see. Figure 4.5 depicts the quarterly sales as well as the trend line. The trend line consistently underpredicts fall sales and overpredicts winter sales.

We can account for seasonality by using dummy variables. Consider this equation:

$$Q_t = bt + cW + dS + eU + fF.$$

The dummy variables, *W*, *S*, *U*, and *F*, represent the seasons of the year (*U* denotes summer). They take on only the values 0 and 1. For instance, the winter dummy (*W*) takes on the value 1 if the particular sales observation occurs in the winter quarter and 0 otherwise. When we perform an OLS regression to estimate the coefficients *b*, *c*, *d*, *e*, and *f*, we obtain:

$$Q_t = 1.89t + 126.24W + 139.85S + 143.26U + 164.38F.$$

As we expect, the coefficient for fall is greatest and the coefficient for winter is lowest. To forecast winter toy sales, we set $W = 1$, $S = U = F = 0$, generating the equation $Q_t = 1.89t + 126.24$. Analogously, the predictive equation for fall toy sales is $Q_t = 1.89t + 164.38$. In essence, we have a different constant term for each season. To generate a forecast for winter 2015, we use the winter equation while setting

TABLE 4.7

Time Trend of Toy Sales

Regression Output		
Dependent variable: Q		
Sum of squared errors	11,968.8	
Standard error of the regression	17.75	
R-squared	0.64	
Adjusted R-squared	0.63	
F-statistic	67.59	
Number of observations	40	
Degrees of freedom	38	
	Constant	*t*
Coefficient(s)	141.16	1.998
Standard error of coefficients	5.72	.24
T-statistic	24.68	8.22

$t = 41$. The computed value is $Q_{41} = 203.73$. Contrast this with the prediction of 223.08 based on the simple trend. Accounting for seasonality via dummy variables provides a better prediction.

**CHECK
STATION 6**

A utility that supplies electricity in Wisconsin is attempting to track differences in the demand for electricity in the winter (October through March) and the summer (April through September). Using quarterly data from the last five years, it estimates the regression equation $Q = 80.5 + 2.6t + 12.4W$, where W is a dummy variable (equal to 1 in the winter quarters, 0 otherwise). Has the utility made a mistake by not including a summer dummy variable? Now, suppose the utility believes that the rate of increase in demand differs in the winter and the summer. Think of an equation (using an additional dummy variable) that incorporates this difference.

**The Housing
Bubble and Crash**

Realtors will tell you that buying a house is a no-lose investment. By owning your dream home, you not only enjoy the housing services you would otherwise have to pay for in the form of rent, but you also have an asset that is sure to appreciate in value. After all, housing prices never go down.

With the benefit of hindsight, we know that the last statement is untrue (housing prices can crash) and that the case for home ownership was way oversold. By looking at the past pattern of house prices, could we have recognized the unusual nature of escalating house prices over the last 20 years? Should we have been concerned that the housing price bubble might pop and prices plummet? Figure 4.6 depicts an index of average housing prices for the period 1975 to 2010. The figure shows the level of *real* housing prices after netting out the underlying rate of inflation in the US economy.[9] The message of the figure is very clear. Between the mid-1970s and the mid-1990s, real housing prices were nearly constant (home prices simply increased with the rate of inflation in the greater economy). But between 1995 and 2006, housing prices took off like a rocket, nearly doubling in 10 years. Indeed, the rate of price increase was even greater in most major cities on the East and West coasts.

Which pattern was the exception and which was the rule? Two economic facts would suggest a norm of housing prices doing no better than keeping pace with inflation. First, looking back as far as 1950 shows a similar stable pricing pattern. (Indeed, real housing prices in 1900 were at similar levels to those in 1950, with a lengthy period of depressed housing prices during the Great Depression.) Second, the cost of renting homes shows a similar pattern of rising in line with the rate of inflation—a relatively stable pattern that has continued over the last decade. Therefore, the exploding cost of owning a house in the last 15 years is out of line with the historic pattern of rents and with previous housing price trends. High housing prices were not based on economic fundamentals but due to buyers and sellers who believed prices could not fall—until they did.[10]

---

[9] So an annual change in the index from 100 to 101.5 means that average house prices rose 1.5 percent faster than the rate of inflation. If inflation averaged 2.5 percent, then nominal house prices increased by 4 percent.

[10] This discussion is based on R. J. Shiller, *The Subprime Solution: How Today's Global Financial Crisis Happened and What to Do About It*, (Princeton, NJ: Princeton University Press, 2008); and D. Streitfeld, "Housing Fades as a Means to Build Wealth, Analysts Say," *The New York Times* (August 22, 2010), A1.

FIGURE 4.6

Thirty-Six Years of
Housing Prices

Of course, the speculative runup in housing prices, after peaking in 2006, culmi-nated in unprecedented price declines over the next two years of 30 to 50 percent. Why did so many homebuyers, homeowners, lenders, and financial institutions believe that housing prices could go nowhere but up? Simple psychology accounts for a large part of the answer. Such beliefs are supported by a strong (often unconscious) bias toward overoptimism. According to surveys taken over the last 20 years, homeowners report that they expect housing prices to increase in the future by some 10 percent per year. These predictions have been very stable—before and during the price run up and even after housing prices plunged. Moreover, individuals selectively cling to reasons—more qualified buyers, high demand in growing cities, the scarcity of land and housing in the most desirable locations—that support these beliefs, while overlooking or dismissing disconfirming evidence. To sum up, the way to overcome these psychological biases is to keep firmly in mind the 50-year "big picture" of house price movements.

Barometric Models

Barometric models search for patterns among different variables over time. Consider a firm that produces oil-drilling equipment. Management naturally would like to forecast demand for its product. It turns out that the *seismic crew count*, an index of the number of teams surveying possible drilling sites, gives a good indication as to changes in future demand for drilling equipment. We say that the seismic crew count is a **leading indicator** of the demand for drilling equipment.

Economists have identified many well-known leading indicators. The number of building permits leads the number of housing starts. Stock market indices (such as the Dow Jones Industrial Average) indicate future increases and decreases in economic activity (expansions or recessions). Such indicators, however, are not without certain problems:

1. Leading indicators are not always accurate. According to one humorous economic saying, declines in the stock market have predicted 12 of the last 7 recessions.
2. Leading indicators may say a change is coming, but they often cannot pinpoint exactly when.
3. The leading indicators rarely tell us the size of the change in the forecasted series.

Frequently, leading indicators are averaged to form a *composite* leading indicator. This helps eliminate some of the randomness and makes the indicator more accurate. The US Bureau of Economic Analysis has developed and publishes the **Index of Leading Indicators**. This index signals future changes in the course of the economy. The index is a weighted average of 11 economic series:

1. Weekly hours of manufacturing workers
2. Manufacturers' new orders
3. Changes in manufacturers' unfilled orders
4. Plant and equipment orders
5. The number of housing building permits
6. Changes in sensitive materials prices
7. Percentage of companies receiving slower deliveries
8. The money supply
9. The index of consumer confidence
10. The index of 500 companies' common-stock prices
11. Average weekly claims for unemployment insurance

Positive changes in the first 10 indicators (and a decline in the last) indicate future economic growth. Declines in the index presage a weak economy and possible recession. On average, the composite index tends to turn down nine months before the onset of recession. The index increases about four to five months before the economy bottoms out and begins to grow.

Forecasting Performance

When macroeconomic and microeconomic risks loom large, a firm's decisions are only as good as its economic forecasts.

Forecasting the Fate of Euro Disney

In 1987, Walt Disney Co. embarked on an ambitious project to open a $2 billion theme park outside of Paris. Besides the park, Disney's investment encompassed over 5,000 hotel rooms, office space, hundreds of private homes, and a golf course. When it opened in April 1992, Euro Disney floundered with lower-than-expected revenues and elevated costs. In the low season (November through March), Disney's luxury hotels averaged only 10 percent occupancy rates. Indeed, there were no buyers for the additional hotels that the company planned to build and sell. The average European visitor spent far less on food, lodging, and merchandise than the average visitor to the company's American parks.

In making its decision to build the park, Disney faced a monumental task of economic forecasting and came up short. For example, it did not anticipate the length and depth of the recession in Europe, even though the slowdown was foreseen and predicted by most international forecasters. The recession meant fewer visitors, less spending, and a disastrous fall in real-estate prices.

Microeconomic forecasts were also poor. The company relied heavily on its previous successful experience in opening its Tokyo theme park. But work rules, effective in Japan, did not suit the French labor environment. In addition, the Japanese visitor, with a higher income than its European counterpart, happily spent two to five days at the park. Europeans did not. Nor were Euro Disney's visitors as willing to wait in long lines. French visitors insisted on sit-down, high-quality meals. When it first opened, Euro Disney delivered snack food and did not serve beer or wine. Not surprisingly, European visitors preferred Parisian hotels 30 minutes away to Disney's high-priced "fantasy" accommodations.

In short, most of Disney's problems stemmed from the company's inability to forecast demand for its services and products. The company has since instituted many changes. It has lowered ticket prices and hotel rates, revamped its restaurant service, loosened stringent employee work rules, and changed its marketing campaign. Nevertheless, Euro Disney, now called Disneyland Paris, continues to struggle. In 2012, the company reported losses of over 50 million euros and almost 2 billion euros of debt.[11]

FORECASTING ACCURACY Forecast accuracy is measured by tracking how closely predictions match actual realizations. A frequently quoted performance measure is the average absolute error (AAE):

$$AAE = \frac{\Sigma|Q - Q^*|}{m},$$

where Q^* denotes the forecast, Q is the realized value, and m is the number of forecasts. An equation's root mean squared error (RMSE) is similarly defined:

$$RMSE = \sqrt{\frac{\Sigma(Q - Q^*)^2}{m - k}}.$$

Here, $m - k$ denotes the degrees of freedom (with k the number of coefficients that are estimated). Like the goodness of fit measures discussed earlier in this chapter, the RMSE depends on the sum of squared errors. Here, however, we are looking at the error in forecasting *future* values rather than how well the equation fits the *past* data.

---

[11]This account is based on F. Norris, "Euro Disney," *The New York Times, Norris Blog* (December 3, 2007); F. Norris, "Euro Disney Secures Plan to Ward Off Bankruptcy," *The New York Times* (September 29, 2004), p. C4; and other published reports.

Forecasts suffer from the same sources of error as estimated regression equations. These include errors due to (1) random fluctuations, (2) imprecise estimates of coefficients, (3) equation misspecification, and (4) omitted variables. Forecasting also introduces two new potential sources of error. First, the true economic relationship may change over the forecast period. An equation that was highly accurate in the past may not continue to be accurate in the future. Second, to compute a forecast, one must specify values of all explanatory variables. For instance, to predict demand in the future, we would need our own price, which we can set, but also competitor prices, the incomes of consumers, and the like. Uncertainty about these variables contributes to errors in demand forecasts. One of Disney's problems was its mistake about the income of customers during the recession. Indeed, an astute management team may put considerable effort into accurately forecasting key explanatory variables.

Forecasting Performance

How well do professional forecasters perform? Do some forecasting methods outperform others? Has forecasting accuracy improved over time? The track records of major forecasters and forecasting organizations have been analyzed in an effort to answer these questions. The forecasting methods examined include sophisticated econometric models, barometric methods, time-series analysis, and informal judgmental forecasts. Here are the main conclusions.[12]

First, forecast accuracy has improved over time as a result of better data and better models. Forecasts of the most important macroeconomic variables such as GDP were better in the 1990s than in the 1980s or 1970s. Energy forecasts have improved dramatically. However, since 2000, further incremental gains in accuracy have been small. Moreover, few major forecasters anticipated the onset of major recessions across the globe starting in 2007, nor how slow the recovery would be.

Second, many economic variables still elude accurate forecasting. For instance, changes in asset prices—stock market wealth, housing values, energy prices, and exchange rates—are inherently unpredictable. In turn, key spending behavior and future investment become harder to forecast to the extent that they are influenced by these asset prices. One way to appreciate this uncertainty is to survey a great many forecasters and observe the range of forecasts for the same economic variable.

Third, the time period matters. Accuracy falls as the forecasters try to predict farther into the future. The interval forecasted also matters. (Forecasts of annual changes tend to be more accurate than forecasts of quarterly changes.) Fourth, no forecast method consistently outperforms any other. Rather, the most accurate method depends on the economic variable being predicted, how it is measured, and the time horizon. But the differences in accuracy across the different methods are quite small. Macromodels based on structural models performed better than purely extrapolative models, but, for many economic variables, the advantage (if any) was small. Indeed, combining forecasts generated by different methods has been found to increase overall accuracy.

---

[12]For assessments of forecasting performance, see R. Fair, "Reflections on Macroeconometric Modeling," Cowles Foundation Discussion Paper #1908, Yale University, 2013; J. S. Armstrong, K. C. Green, and A. Graefe, "Golden Rule of Forecasting: Be Conservative," Working Paper, 2014; S. K. McNees, "An Assessment of the 'Official' Economic Forecasts." *New England Economic Review* (July–August 1995): 13–23, and S. K. McNees, "How Large Are Economic Forecast Errors?" *New England Economic Review* (July–August 1992): 25–42.

Final Thoughts

Estimating and forecasting demand are as much art as science. Judgment plays as important a role as statistics in evaluating demand equations. Consequently, statistical techniques alone must never be the final arbiter of the quality of demand estimates and forecasts. We should always ask a number of key questions:

1. Does the equation make economic sense? Are the "right" explanatory variables included in the equation? What form of the equation is suggested by economic principles?

2. Are the signs and magnitudes of the estimated coefficients reasonable? Do they make economic sense?

3. Based on an intelligent interpretation of the statistics, does the model have explanatory power? How well did it track the past data?

If the equation successfully answers these questions, the manager can be confident that it makes good economic sense.

Estimating Movie Demand Revisited

Top management of a movie theater chain seeks to produce the best-possible prediction of a film's weekly gross revenue per screen. The chain's profit directly depends on this prediction. For instance, paying the producers $4,500 per screen per week (for a four-week guaranteed run) will be a bargain if the film turns out to be a megahit and earns gross revenue of $8,000 per screen per week but a losing proposition if the film bombs and brings in only $1,500 per screen per week.

The theater chain used data for 204 films released in the previous year collected from the weekly entertainment magazine *Variety* to estimate the following regression equation to predict average revenues for a typical film:

$$AR = 12{,}697 N^{-.197}(1.31)^S(1.27)^H(1.22)^C(1.15)^A. \qquad [4.16]$$

AR is the average revenue per screen per week (during the first four weeks of the film's release). In turn, *N* denotes the number of nationwide screens on which the film is playing. The other explanatory variables are dummy variables: $S = 1$ for a summer release, $H = 1$ for a holiday release, $C = 1$ if the cast contains one or more proven blockbuster stars, and $A = 1$ if the film is a large-budget action film. (Otherwise, the dummy variable is assigned the value of 0.)

According to Equation 4.16, a nondescript film ($S = H = C = A = 0$) released in 2,000 theaters nationwide would generate revenue per screen per week of $AR = 12{,}697(2{,}000)^{-.197} = \$2{,}841$. Consider the effect of varying the number of screens. The negative exponent $-.197$ means that average revenue *per screen* falls with the number of screens playing the film. A film in narrow release (for instance, in an exclusive engagement on single screens in major cities) earns much more revenue *per screen* than a film in the widest release.

Thus, the same nondescript film released on only 100 screens nationwide would earn $AR = 12,697(100)^{-.197} = \$5,125$ per screen per week. Next, note the effect of each dummy variable. The multiplicative factor associated with S (1.31) means that, other things equal, a summer release ($S = 1$) will increase AR by a factor of $(1.31)^1$, or 31 percent. Similarly, a starry cast will increase predicted AR by 22 percent, and an action film will raise AR by 15 percent. Releasing a summer action film with a starry cast increases revenue by a factor of $(1.31)(1.22)(1.15) = 1.84$, or 84 percent.

To estimate equation 4.16, OLS regression was applied to the log linear form of the equation, with the following result:

$$\log(AR) = 9.45 - .197\log(N) + .27S + .23H + .20C + .14A. \qquad [4.17]$$

To go from Equation 4.17 to Equation 4.16, we took the antilog of Equation 4.17's coefficients. Thus, antilog(9.45) = 12,697, antilog(.27) = 1.31, antilog(.23) = 1.27, and so on. All the explanatory variables are statistically significant at the 95-percent confidence level. The variables N, S, and C exhibit a moderate degree of multicollinearity (summer films tend to have starry casts and very wide releases), but, given the large sample (204 observations), the regression is still able to isolate the effects of the individual explanatory variables.

The R^2 of the regression equation is only .31—that is, the equation explains only 31 percent of the variation in revenues for the films released that year. This should not be very surprising. Film revenues are inherently unpredictable. To explain 31 percent of these variations is a solid achievement. The theater chain's economists might make a better forecast with information about the magnitude of the studio's advertising budget, the reviews the film will receive, and the strengths of competing films being released at the same time.[13] However, at the time that management must contract for films, this information is unavailable. Given the large standard error of the regression, the margin of error surrounding AR is in the neighborhood of plus or minus 33 percent. Predicting movie revenues will always be a risky proposition.

[13]Conspicuously missing as explanatory variables in Equation 4.16 are price and income. These variables have no demand effects because both are essentially fixed over the one-year time period (and theaters do not vary ticket prices across films).

SUMMARY

Decision-Making Principles

1. Accurate demand forecasts are crucial for sound managerial decision making.

2. The margin of error surrounding a forecast is as important as the forecast itself. Disasters in planning frequently occur when management is overly confident of its ability to predict the future.

3. Important questions to ask when evaluating a demand equation are the following: Does the estimated equation make economic sense? How well does the equation track past data? To what extent is the recent past a predictable guide to the future?

Nuts and Bolts

1. Demand estimation and forecasting can provide the manager with valuable information to aid in planning and pricing. Ideally, the forecasting process should provide (1) the forecast, (2) an explicit description (an equation) of the dependency relationships, and (3) an estimate of its accuracy.

2. Data can be collected from a variety of sources, including surveys, controlled market studies, and uncontrolled market data.

3. Regression analysis is a set of statistical techniques that quantify the dependence of a given economic variable on one or more other variables. The first step in regression is to formulate a model of this relationship in terms of an equation to be estimated. The second step is to estimate an equation that best fits the data. The usual criterion is based on minimizing squared errors (so-called ordinary least squares). The third step is to evaluate the accuracy of the equation.

4. Regression analysis provides both coefficient estimates and statistics that reflect the accuracy and explanatory power of the equation. Important statistics include the equation's R^2, F-statistic, and standard error, and the standard errors and t-statistics for individual coefficients.

5. There are two main categories of forecasting methods. Structural forecasts rely on estimated equations describing relationships between economic variables. Nonstructural methods (such as time-series analysis and barometric methods) track observed patterns in economic variables over time. Time-series analysis relies on the identification of trends, cyclical fluctuations, and seasonal variations to predict the course of economic variables. Barometric methods (leading indicators) recognize that changes in some variables presage changes in others.

6. Forecasting accuracy has improved over time, but incremental gains have been small.

Questions and Problems

1. Discuss and compare the advantages and disadvantages of survey methods and test marketing.

2. Coca-Cola Company introduced New Coke largely because of Pepsi's success in taste tests head to head with Coke Classic.
   a. Consider the following hypothetical information: (1) In blind taste tests, 58 percent of subjects preferred Pepsi to Coke Classic; (2) in similar tests, 58 percent of subjects preferred the taste of New Coke to Pepsi. From these findings, what can Coca-Cola's management conclude about consumers' preferences between Coke Classic and New Coke?
   b. Consider the following preference rankings of three different types of consumers A, B, and C:

	A (42%)	B (42%)	C (16%)
Most preferred	Pepsi	Coke Classic	New Coke
Second choice	Coke Classic	New Coke	Pepsi
Least preferred	New Coke	Pepsi	Coke Classic

   As the table shows, 42 percent of consumers are "type A," whose top preference is Pepsi, followed by Coke Classic and New Coke. Are these preferences consistent with the information in part (a)? What do you predict would be the result of a blind taste test between Coke Classic and New Coke?
   c. From the information in part (b), what brand strategy would you recommend to Coca-Cola's management? What additional information about consumer preferences might be useful?

3. In preparation for their 2008 merger, Delta Airlines and Northwest Airlines undertook a comparative study of their on-time performance. The following table shows each airline's on-time record for a common two-month period for three cities where they both operated.

	Delta Airlines Flights		Northwest Airlines Flights	
	Total	**Late**	**Total**	**Late**
New York	1987	484	399	120
Chicago	718	118	1123	222
Memphis	193	24	536	70
Total	2898	626	2058	412

    a. Northwest's operations executives claim to have superior *overall* on-time results. Does the data support this claim?

    b. Delta's executives respond by pointing to its superior performance at key cities. Does the data support this claim?

    c. Explain carefully how to reconcile your answers in parts (a) and (b). In your view, which is the better measure of performance—an aggregate measure or disaggregate measures?

4. To what extent do you agree with the following statements?

    a. The best test of the performance of two different regression equations is their respective values of R^2.

    b. Time-series regressions should be run using as many years of data as possible; more data means more reliable coefficient estimates.

    c. Including additional variables (even if they lack individual significance) does no harm and might raise R^2.

    d. Equations that perform well in explaining past data are likely to generate accurate forecasts looking forward.

5. A study of cigarette demand resulted in the following logarithmic regression equation:

$$\log(Q) = -2.55 - .29\log(P) - .09\log(Y) + .08\log(A) - .1W.$$

$$(-2.07)\qquad (-1.05)\quad (4.48)\qquad (-5.2)$$

Here, Q denotes annual cigarette consumption, P is the average price of cigarettes, Y is per capita income, A is total spending on cigarette advertising, and W is a dummy variable whose value is 1 for years after 1963 (when the American Cancer Society linked smoking to lung cancer) and 0 for earlier years. The t-statistic for each coefficient is shown in parentheses. The R^2 of the equation is .94.

    a. Which of the explanatory variables have real effects on cigarette consumption? Explain.

    b. What does the coefficient of $\log(P)$ represent? If cigarette prices increase by 20 percent, how will this affect consumption?

    c. Are cigarette purchases sensitive to income? Explain.

6. A financial analyst seeks to determine the relationship between the return on PepsiCo's common stock and the return on the stock market as a whole. She has collected data on the monthly returns of PepsiCo's stock and the monthly returns of the Standard & Poor's stock index for the last five years. Using these data, she has estimated the following regression equation:

$$R_{\text{Pep}} = .06 + .92R_{\text{S\&P}}.$$

Here, returns are expressed in percentage terms. The t-values for the coefficients are 2.78 and 3.4, respectively, and the equation's R^2 is .28.

    a. Do the respective coefficients differ significantly from zero?

    b. The value of R^2 seems quite low. Does this mean the equation is invalid? Given the setting, why might one expect a low R^2?

    c. Suppose the S&P index is expected to fall by 1 percent over the next month. What is the expected return on PepsiCo's stock?

7. A water expert was asked whether the water table in a California community was falling. To answer this question, the expert estimated a linear regression equation of the form

$$W = a + bt,$$

where W = height of the water table and t = time measured from the start of the study period. (He used 10 years of water-table measurements.) The estimate for b was $b = -.4$ with a t-value of -1.4.

a. From this evidence, would you conclude that the water table was falling?

b. A second expert suggests yearly rainfall might affect the water table. The first expert agrees but argues that total rainfall fluctuates randomly from year to year. Rainy years would cancel out dry years and would not affect the results of the regression. Do you agree?

8. A food-products company has recently introduced a new line of fruit pies in six US cities: Atlanta, Baltimore, Chicago, Denver, St. Louis, and Fort Lauderdale. Based on the pie's apparent success, the company is considering a nationwide launch. Before doing so, it has decided to use data collected during a two-year market test to guide it in setting prices and forecasting future demand.

For each of the six markets, the firm has collected eight quarters of data for a total of 48 observations. Each observation consists of data on quantity demanded (number of pies purchased per week), price per pie, competitors' average price per pie, income, and population. The company has also included a time-trend variable. A value of 1 denotes the first quarter observation, 2 the second quarter, and so on, up to 8 for the eighth and last quarter.

A company forecaster has run a regression on the data, obtaining the results displayed in the accompanying table.

a. Which of the explanatory variables in the regression are statistically significant? Explain. How much of the total variation in pie sales does the regression model explain?

	Coefficient	Standard Error of Coefficient	Mean Value of Variable
Intercept	−4,516.3	4,988.2	—
Price (dollars)	−3,590.6	702.8	7.50
Competitors' price (dollars)	4,226.5	851.0	6.50
Income ($000)	777.1	66.4	40
Population (000)	.40	.31	2,300
Time (1 to 8)	356.1	92.3	—
$N = 48$.	$R^2 = .93$.	Standard error of regression = 1,442	

b. Compute the price elasticity of demand for pies at the firm's mean price ($7.50) and mean weekly sales quantity (20,000 pies). Next, compute the cross-price elasticity of demand. Comment on these estimates.

c. Other things equal, how much do we expect sales to grow (or fall) over the next year?

d. How accurate is the regression equation in predicting sales next quarter? Two years from now? Why might these answers differ?

e. How confident are you about applying these test-market results to decisions concerning *national* pricing strategies for pies?

9. Studies of automobile demand suggest that unit sales of compact cars depend principally on their average price and consumers' real personal income. Consider the historical record of sales shown in the table.

a. Estimate the point elasticity of demand with respect to price. (Be sure to choose two years in which all other factors are constant.)

b. Estimate the income elasticity of demand.

Year	Sales (Millions of Cars)	Average Price (Thousands of Dollars)	Personal Income (2011 = 100)
2011	2.00	20.0	100
2012	1.86	20.8	95
2013	1.94	20.0	97
2014	1.90	22.0	100
2015	1.90	24.0	105

c. Given the elasticities in parts (a) and (b), what change in sales do you expect between 2014 and 2015? How closely does your prediction match the actual sales?

d. Estimate a linear demand equation that best fits the data using a regression program. Comment on the accuracy of your equation. Is this degree of accuracy realistic?

10. The following table lists your company's sales during the last four years.

	Year 1	Year 2	Year 3	Year 4
Sales	100	110	105	120

a. A fellow manager points to the 15-unit increase between year 3 and year 4. Extrapolating this trend, he predicts 135 units will be sold in the coming year (year 5). Do you agree? Explain.

b. A second manager notes that annual sales increases have averaged $(120 - 100)/3 = 6.67$ units per year. Accordingly, her forecast for the coming year is 126.67 units sold. Do you agree with this prediction? Explain.

11. Consider again the data in Problem 10.

a. Using a computer program, estimate the linear increasing trend equation, $S = a + bt$, using OLS regression.

b. According to your regression statistics, how well does your estimated equation explain past variations in sales?

c. Use your equation to forecast sales in the coming year. What margin of error would you attach to your forecast?

12. As the name suggests, a lagging indicator is an economic variable whose movements occur *after* movements in the overall economy.

a. A number of employment measures are lagging indicators. Consider the following variables: (1) increased use of temporary workers, (2) increases in new hires, (3) a decline in the number of workers laid off, and (4) an increase in overtime hours. In an economic recovery from a recession, which of these variables would have the shortest and longest lags?

b. Top management of a company that produces luxury yachts has been waiting anxiously for the end of the recession and a resurgence in orders. Why might the company pay more attention to lagging indicators than to leading indicators? Explain.

13. The following regression was estimated for 23 quarters between 2007 and 2013 to test the hypothesis that tire sales (*T*) depend on new-automobile sales (*A*) and total miles driven (*M*). Standard errors are listed in parentheses.

$$\%\Delta T = .45 + 1.41(\%\Delta M) + 1.12(\%\Delta A)$$

$$(.32) \qquad (.19) \qquad\qquad (.41)$$

Note that the relationship is between percentage changes in the variables. Here, $N = 23$, corrected $R^2 = .83$, $F = 408$, standard error of the regression $= 1.2$, and the Durbin-Watson statistic $= 1.92$.

a. Does the regression equation (and its estimated coefficients) make economic sense? Explain.

b. Based on the regression output, discuss the statistical validity of the equation.

c. Do the coefficients on "miles driven" and "new-auto sales" significantly differ from 1.0? Explain why we might use unity as a benchmark for these coefficients.

d. Suppose that we expect "miles driven" to fall by 2 percent and "new-auto sales" by 13 percent (due to a predicted recession). What is the predicted change in the sales quantity of tires? If actual tire sales dropped by 18 percent, would this be surprising?

Discussion Question   There is an ongoing debate about the roles of quantitative and qualitative inputs in demand estimation and forecasting. Those in the qualitative camp argue that statistical analysis can only go so far. Demand estimates can be further improved by incorporating purely qualitative factors. Quantitative advocates insist that qualitative, intuitive, holistic approaches only serve to introduce errors, biases, and extraneous factors into the estimation task.

Suppose the head of a theater chain is convinced that any number of bits of qualitative information (the identity of the director, the film's terrific script and rock-music sound track, the Hollywood "buzz" about the film during production, even the easing of his ulcer) influence the film's ultimate box-office revenue.

How might one test which approach—purely qualitative or statistical— provides better demand or revenue estimates? Are there ways to combine the two approaches? Provide concrete suggestions.

Spreadsheet Problems

S1. To help settle the scientific debate in Problem 7, an expert has provided annual data on the water table and rainfall over the last decade.

					Year					
	1	2	3	4	5	6	7	8	9	10
Water Table	17.6	19.2	14.8	18.1	13.2	15.1	20	14.6	13.9	13.5
Rainfall	36	52	34	44	26	48	56	45	39	42

a. Using the 10 years of data, estimate the equation, $W = a + bt$, where W is the water table and t is time in years. Comment on the statistical validity of your equation. Can you conclude that the water table level is dropping over time?

b. Did the region have greater yearly rainfall in the first five years or the last five years of the decade? Should rainfall be added as an explanatory variable in your regression equation? If it were, what would be the effect on the estimate of coefficient b? Explain.

c. Now estimate the equation, $W = a + bt + cR$, where R denotes annual rainfall. Answer the questions posed in part (a) above. Is this equation scientifically superior to the equation in part (a)?

S2. A soft-drink bottler collected the following monthly data on its sales of 12-ounce cans at different prices.

						Month						
	1	2	3	4	5	6	7	8	9	10	11	12
Price	.45	.50	.45	.40	.35	.35	.50	.55	.45	.50	.40	.40
Quantity	98	80	95	123	163	168	82	68	96	77	130	125

a. Use a regression program to estimate a linear demand equation. If price is cut by $.10, by how much will the volume of sales increase?

b. Plot the 12 data points and the estimated regression line on a quantity-price graph. Does the scatter of points look linear?

c. Use a log-linear regression to estimate a demand curve of the form: $Q = kP^\beta$. What is the price elasticity of demand? Does this equation fit the data better than the linear equation in part (b)? Explain.

S3. Your company's sales have been growing steadily over the last 17 quarters, as shown in the following table.

Quarter	Quantity Sales	Quarter	Quantity Sales
1	103.2	9	137.1
2	105.7	10	140.9
3	111.3	11	142.7
4	113.8	12	149.3
5	116.9	13	154.4
6	121.8	14	158.1
7	125.0	15	164.8
8	132.4	16	172.0
		17	181.3

You wish to predict the next four quarters' sales. (You are aware that your product's sales have no seasonal component.)

a. Using regression techniques, find the linear time trend that best fits the sales data. How well does this equation fit the past data?

b. Now estimate the constant-growth equation, $Q = br^t$. Find the coefficients for b and r. Does this equation perform better than the linear form in part (a)? Explain.

c. Predict sales for the next four quarters using both equations.

S4. The accompanying table, compiled by economists Karl Case and Robert Shiller, lists average US housing prices (in the form of a real, inflation-adjusted index) from 1975 to 2010.

Year	Real House Price Index	Year	Real House Price Index	Year	Real House Price Index
1975	104.4	1987	118.3	1999	119.5
1976	105.2	1988	122.5	2000	126.6
1977	110.5	1989	125.3	2001	133.5
1978	117.1	1990	121.0	2002	143.4
1979	120.5	1991	114.1	2003	154.5
1980	114.5	1992	111.5	2004	171.4
1981	109.0	1993	109.0	2005	191.0
1982	105.1	1994	109.3	2006	194.7
1983	105.4	1995	108.2	2007	181.1
1984	105.5	1996	107.6	2008	146.1
1985	107.5	1997	108.6	2009	130.3
1986	112.7	1998	113.4	2010	128.2

a. Using the years 1975 to 2006 (and denoting the time variable by the integers 1 to 32 for simplicity), estimate the linear time trend of housing prices. Use the same data to estimate an exponential trend. How well does either trend fit the data?

b. Now estimate two separate linear regressions—one for years 1975 to 1996 and one for 1996 to 2006. Does dividing the time series in this way make sense? How well does the trend equation estimated for 1996 to 2006 predict actual housing prices over the next five years?

Suggested References

For an assessment of market experimentation see:

Harrison, G., and J. A. List. "Field Experiments." *Journal of Economic Literature* 42 (December 2004): 1013–1059.

The following are valuable references on demand estimation and forecasting.

Winston, W. L. *Microsoft Excel 2013: Data Analysis and Business Modeling*. Microsoft Press, 2014.

Stock, J. H., and M. Watson, *Introduction to Econometrics*. Third Edition, Boston: Addison-Wesley, 2010.

Armstrong, J. S. (Ed.), *Principles of Forecasting*. Boston: Kluwer Academic Publishers, 2002.

Pindyck, R. S., and D. L. Rubinfeld. *Econometric Models and Economic Forecasts*, Chapters 1-6. New York: McGraw-Hill, 1997.

Granger, C. W. J., and P. Newbold. *Forecasting in Business and Economics*. New York: Academic Press, 1989.

The following references discuss macroeconomic forecasting, the business cycle, and forecast accuracy.

McNees, S. K. "An Assessment of the 'Official' Economic Forecasts." *New England Economic Review* (July-August 1995): 13–23.

Stock, J. H., and M. Watson (Eds.), *Business Cycles, Indicators, and Forecasting*, Chicago: University of Chicago Press, 1993.

Zarnowitz, V. "Theory and History Behind Business Cycles: Are the 1990s the Onset of a Golden Age?" *Journal of Economic Perspectives* (Spring 1999): 13, 69–90.

Forecasting websites include: The Conference Board http://www.conference-board.org/, and www.oecd.org (statistics and forecasts for the major countries of the world), and Professor Ray Fair of Yale University http://fairmodel.econ.yale.edu/

For an assessment and survey of computer programs for statistical analysis and forecasting, see,

Swain, J. "Software Survey: Statistical Analysis," *ORMS Today* (February 2013): 44–51, and

Yurkiwicz, J., "Software Survey: Forecasting," *ORMS Today* (June 2012): 38–45.

Check Station Answers

1. Both surveys and test marketing would appear to be feasible. Since the target population (business travelers) is specific and easy to identify, surveying should be relatively accurate and inexpensive. For instance, we could distribute a questionnaire to passengers on flights known to be dominated by business travelers or send it to the airline's frequent fliers. In addition, business travelers probably would have more incentive than the typical respondent to express their true preferences about air travel. The airline also could test different types of business-class seating (at different fares) on various flights. Obviously, the company must extend the test long enough and publicize it adequately so that business travelers will have time to make up their minds about the new options. Although information from the actual test may be more accurate than that gleaned from surveys, it is also likely to be much more expensive.

2. The most direct way is to estimate the equation

$$Q = a + bP + cP^c + dY_{-1},$$

   where Y_{-1} denotes last quarter's income. For instance, the relevant data for the second quarter of year 1 is $Q = 33.6$, $P = 265$, $P^c = 250$, and $Y_{-1} = 104$ (i.e., first quarter's income).

3. Reducing the number of data points typically worsens the quality of the estimated regression equation. R^2 may decrease or increase. (By luck, the remaining points may or may not lie more nearly along a straight line.) The reduction in observations tends to produce a reduction in the adjusted R-squared. For instance, using only the odd-numbered quarters in Table 4.4 to estimate air travel demand, R^2 falls to .72 and adjusted R-squared is .65.

4. With fewer data points for estimation, one would expect the F-statistic to fall (because of fewer degrees of freedom), the coefficient estimates to change, and their standard errors to increase. The regression output based on odd-numbered quarters confirms this: $F = 3.43$. Since the critical F-value (3 and 4 degrees of freedom) is 6.59, the equation lacks overall explanatory power at the 95 percent confidence level. The estimated equation is

$$Q = 71.7 - 2.81P + .74P^c + 3.5Y.$$

   The respective standard errors are 19.4, .72, .76, and 1.9. Applying a t-test shows that P^c and Y are not significantly different than zero. With so little data, it is impossible to detect the real effects of these two variables. Finally, the standard error of the regression increases to 19.4.

5. The value of Company A's stock after 35 years will be $P_A = 50(1.05)^{35} = \$275.8$. The value of Company B's stock will be $P_B = 50(1.06)^{35} = \$384.3$. Small differences in average growth rates (when compounded over long periods of time) can lead to very large differences in value.

6. The utility has not erred in using only a single dummy. By setting $W = 0$, the utility obtains the summer equation, $Q_t = 80.5 + 2.6t$. By setting $W = 1$, it has the winter equation, $Q_t = (80.5 + 12.4) + 2.6t = 92.9 + 2.6t$. Thus, the coefficient 12.4 represents the difference in the constant terms between summer and winter. To allow different rates of increase, the company could estimate the equation $Q_t = a + cW + bt + d(Wt)$. The last term includes an additional explanatory variable, the product of the winter dummy and the time variable. To illustrate, suppose the estimated equation is found to be $Q_t = 78.4 + 2.9t + 13.2W - .7(Wt)$. Then the summer equation (setting $W = 0$) is $Q_t = 78.4 + 2.9t$, and the winter equation (setting $W = 1$) is $Q_t = 91.6 + 2.2t$. Here, the winter and summer seasons display different constant terms and different time coefficients.

Regression Using Spreadsheets

LO#1. Review the use of spreadsheets in regression analysis.

Today most spreadsheet programs give you the power to run multiple regression programs. In this appendix we use Microsoft's Excel spreadsheet program for the airline example in the text.

Simple Regression

Step 1: Enter the data. Recall that in Table 4.1, the average number of coach seats is the *dependent variable,* and the average price is the *independent variable*. We enter this data into the spreadsheet as columns, as Table 4A.1 shows.

Step 2: Call up the regression program. The method for calling up a regression program may vary a bit, depending on the version of the program. In Excel, calling up the regression program involves these steps: Under the Tools menu select Data Analysis, then select Regression, and click OK. A regression dialog box will appear, such as the one depicted in the bottom part of Table 4A.1.

Step 3: Designate the columns of data to be used in the regression. Next we tell the regression program where to find the data. This is done by entering the cells in the boxes labeled "Y Input Range" and "X Input Range." The Y input range refers to the dependent variable. In our case, the Y data range from cell A3 to cell A18. Thus we could simply type A3:A18 into the box.

Alternatively, we could select the range, pointing the mouse at A3, clicking, holding, and dragging to cell A18. There will appear in the Input Range box the entry $A$3:$A$18. (Do not worry about the dollar signs.) If you wish to include the column label in cell A2, simply select the range $A$2:$A$18. Then click on the label box. (In our example, we chose to include the label.) The advantage of using the label is it will appear in the output statistics, making these statistics easier to read.

The X input range refers to the independent variable. In our case, the X Input Range is from cell B3 to cell B18.

Step 4: Inform the program where you want the output. The regression program needs to be told where to put the output. This is known as the output range. Simply type

	A	B	C	D	E
1					
2	Seats	Price	C Price	Income	
3	64.8	250	250	104.0	
4	33.6	265	250	101.5	
5	37.8	265	240	103.0	
6	83.3	240	240	105.0	
7	111.7	230	240	100.0	
8	137.5	225	260	96.5	
9	109.5	225	250	93.3	
10	96.8	220	240	95.0	
11	59.5	230	240	97.0	
12	83.2	235	250	99.0	
13	90.5	245	250	102.5	
14	105.5	240	240	105.0	
15	75.7	250	220	108.5	
16	91.6	240	230	108.5	
17	112.7	240	250	108.0	
18	102.2	235	240	109.0	
19					

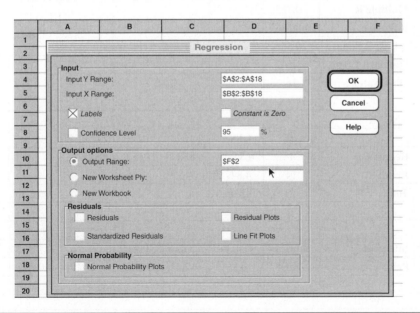

The Regression Menu

in a cell name (or point and click). The program will start with that cell and work to the right and down. It really does not matter where you put the output except that you do not want to put it over the data, thereby destroying the data. Thus you should put the output either below or to the right of the data. We specified F2 as the output range. Excel will also allow you to put the output in a separate spreadsheet.

Step 5: Run the regression.   Simply click OK. For the airline example, the program produces the output shown in Table 4A.2.

Multiple Regression

Performing multiple-regression analysis involves virtually the same steps as performing simple regression. Recall that the data in Table 4.4 include income and competitors' price as explanatory variables in addition to the airline's own price. The first step is to

TABLE 4A.2

Simple Regression Results

	E	F	G	H	I	J	K	L	M
1									
2		SUMMARY OUTPUT							
3									
4									
5		*Regression Statistics*							
6		**Multiple R**	0.765						
7		**R Square**	0.586						
8		**Adjust R Square**	0.556						
9		**Standard Error**	18.607						
10		**Observations**	16						
11									
12		**ANOVA**							
13			*df*	*SS*	*MS*	*F*	*Signif F*		
14		**Regression**	1	6,858.8	6,858.8	19.81	0.00055		
15		**Residual**	14	4,847.2	346.2				
16		**Total**	15	11,706.0					
17									
18			*Coefficients*	*Stand Error*	*t Stat*	*P-value*	*Lower 95%*	*Upper 95%*	
19		**Intercept**	478.55	88.039	5.436	0.00009			
20		**Price**	−1.633	0.367	−4.451	0.00055	−2.419	−0.846	
21									

enter the income and competitive price data in columns C and D of the spreadsheet. After calling up the regression menu, we again enter cells A2 to A18 for the Y range. However, next we enter cells B2 to D18 for the X range. (We designate the three columns of data by selecting the upper left and the lower right cells of the range containing the data. All explanatory variables must be listed in adjacent columns.) The regression program recognizes each column of data as a separate explanatory variable. Next, we specify the output range to begin in cell F2. Finally, we execute the regression program by clicking OK. The multiple-regression output is displayed in Table 4A.3.

TABLE 4A.3

Multiple-Regression Results

	E	F	G	H	I	J	K	L	M
1									
2		SUMMARY OUTPUT							
3									
4									
5		*Regression Statistics*							
6		**Multiple R**	0.881						
7		**R Square**	0.776						
8		**Adjust R Square**	0.721						
9		**Standard Error**	14.766						
10		**Observations**	16						
11									
12		**ANOVA**							
13			*df*	*SS*	*MS*	*F*	*Signif F*		
14		**Regression**	3	9,089.6	3,029.9	13.90	0.0003		
15		**Residual**	12	2,616.4	218.0				
16		**Total**	15	11,706.0					
17									
18			*Coefficients*	*Stand Error*	*t Stat*	*P-value*	*Lower 95%*	*Upper 95%*	
19		**Intercept**	28.84	174.67	0.165	0.872			
20		**Price**	−2.124	0.340	−6.238	0.00004	−2.865	−1.382	
21		**Competitor's P**	1.035	0.467	2.218	0.04664	0.018	2.051	
22		**Income**	3.089	0.999	3.093	0.00931	0.913	5.266	
23									

Statistical Tables

TABLE 4B.1

Critical Values of the
F-Distribution

$k - 1 =$	1	2	3	4	5	6	7
			.95 Critical Values				
$N - k = 1$	161.40	199.50	215.70	224.60	230.20	234.00	236.80
2	18.51	19.00	19.16	19.25	19.30	19.33	19.35
3	10.13	9.55	9.28	9.12	9.01	8.94	8.89
4	7.71	6.94	6.59	6.39	6.26	6.16	6.09
5	6.61	5.79	5.41	5.19	5.05	4.95	4.88
6	5.99	5.14	4.76	4.53	4.39	4.28	4.21
7	5.59	4.74	4.35	4.12	3.97	3.87	3.79
8	5.32	4.46	4.07	3.84	3.69	3.58	3.50
9	5.12	4.26	3.86	3.63	3.48	3.37	3.29
10	4.96	4.10	3.71	3.48	3.33	3.22	3.14
11	4.84	3.98	3.59	3.36	3.20	3.09	3.01
12	4.75	3.89	3.49	3.26	3.11	3.00	2.91
13	4.67	3.81	3.41	3.18	3.03	2.92	2.83
14	4.60	3.74	3.34	3.11	2.96	2.85	2.76
15	4.54	3.68	3.29	3.06	2.90	2.79	2.71
16	4.49	3.63	3.24	3.01	2.85	2.74	2.66
17	4.45	3.59	3.20	2.96	2.81	2.70	2.61
18	4.41	3.55	3.16	2.93	2.77	2.66	2.58
19	4.38	3.52	3.13	2.90	2.74	2.63	2.54
20	4.35	3.49	3.10	2.87	2.71	2.60	2.51
21	4.32	3.47	3.07	2.84	2.68	2.57	2.49
22	4.30	3.44	3.05	2.82	2.66	2.55	2.46
23	4.28	3.42	3.03	2.80	2.64	2.53	2.44
24	4.26	3.40	3.01	2.78	2.62	2.51	2.42
25	4.24	3.39	2.99	2.76	2.60	2.49	2.40
30	4.17	3.32	2.92	2.69	2.53	2.42	2.33
40	4.08	3.23	2.84	2.61	2.45	2.34	2.25
60	4.00	3.15	2.76	2.53	2.37	2.25	2.17
120	3.92	3.07	2.68	2.45	2.29	2.17	2.09
∞	3.84	3.00	2.60	2.37	2.21	2.10	2.01

Source: This table is abridged from Table 18 of the Biometrika Tables for Statisticians, Vol. 1, with the kind permission of E. S. Pearson and the trustees of Biometrika.

144

TABLE 4B.2

Critical Values of the
t-Distribution

Degrees of Freedom	Critical Values .95
1	12.71
2	4.30
3	3.18
4	2.78
5	2.57
6	2.45
7	2.36
8	2.31
9	2.26
10	2.23
11	2.20
12	2.18
13	2.16
14	2.14
15	2.13
16	2.12
17	2.11
18	2.10
19	2.09
20	2.09
40	2.02
60	2.00
∞	1.96

*Note to Instructor: The listed critical values are based on the usual "two-tailed" significant test. Accordingly, the critical value corresponding to 95 percent confidence is measured by the .975 fractile of the t-distribution.

CHAPTER 5

Production

One-tenth of the participants produce over one-third of the output. Increasing the number of participants merely reduces the average output.

NORMAN AUGUSTINE, AUGUSTINE'S LAWS

LO#1. Explore the production function.

LO#2. Discuss how to find the optimal use of a single input in the short run.

LO#3. Discuss how to choose the best mix of inputs in the long run.

LO#4. Understand how to estimate and measure various types of production functions.

LO#5. Describe additional production decisions involving the allocation of inputs.

Allocating a Sales Force

To a greater or lesser extent, almost all firms face the task of finding and retaining customers for their goods. For many service-intensive companies, the sales force is as important as—and indeed may outnumber—the production workforce.

Consider an office equipment company that leases copiers, word processors, computers, and various types of office furniture to large and small firms. In this business, equipment leases rarely last more than one year. Thus, the firm's sales force must continually reenlist current customers and find new customers. A key question faces the company's sales and marketing director: Of the firm's current sales force (18 strong), how many "reps" should specialize in servicing and retaining current leases and how many should devote themselves to new prospective accounts? Could a reallocation of the sales force increase the firm's total sales?

Production and cost are closely linked. The production manager strives to produce any given level of output at minimal total cost and continually seeks less costly ways to produce the firm's goods and services.

We open this chapter by examining the production function, a quantitative summary of the firm's production possibilities. Next, we look closely at production in the short run and examine the impact on output of changing a single input. Then we consider production in the long run, when the firm has the flexibility to vary the amounts of all inputs. Next, we turn to the various types of production functions and discuss the means by which they are estimated. Finally, we consider a number of constrained production decisions involving the allocation of inputs (in fixed supply) to multiple plants or products, or both.

BASIC PRODUCTION CONCEPTS

Production transforms inputs into outputs. For instance, producing automobiles requires a variety of inputs (also called factors of production): raw materials (steel, plastic, rubber, and so on), factories, machines, land, and many different categories of workers. For analysis, it is convenient to refer to two main categories of inputs—labor and materials on the one hand and long-term capital on the other—with each category broadly defined. Labor and materials includes production workers, marketers, and managers at all levels as well as raw materials and intermediate goods, including parts, water, and electricity. Capital includes buildings, equipment, and inventories.

The firm's **production function** indicates the maximum level of output the firm can produce for any combination of inputs. We will start by considering a production function with two inputs, labor and capital.[1] A shorthand description of such a production function is

$$Q = F(L, K). \qquad\qquad [5.1]$$

This states that the firm's quantity of output depends on the respective quantities of labor (L) and capital (K). For instance, a major domestic automobile manufacturer might plan to produce 3 million passenger cars per year, using materials (of all kinds) that cost $24 billion, a total nationwide labor force of 80,000 workers, and a total capital stock valued at $100 billion. Note that the firm's production function specifies the *maximum* output for a given combination of inputs. It assumes that managers use inputs efficiently. Obviously, production technologies improve over time, and efficient firms vigorously pursue these improvements.

PRODUCTION IN THE SHORT RUN

Our analysis of production and cost makes an important distinction between the short run and the long run. In the **short run,** one or more of the firm's inputs is fixed, that is, they cannot be varied. In the **long run,** the firm can vary *all* of its inputs. There is no universal rule for distinguishing between the short and long run; rather, the dividing line must be drawn on a case-by-case basis. For a petrochemical refinery, the short run might be any period less than five years since it takes roughly this long to build a new refinery. For a fast-food chain, six months (the time it takes to obtain zoning approvals and construct new restaurants) may be the dividing line between the short and long run.

Inputs that cannot be changed in the short run are called **fixed inputs**. A firm's production facility is a typical example. In the long run, the firm could vary the size and scale of its plant, whereas in the short run the size of this plant would be fixed at its existing capacity. If a firm operates under restrictive, long-term labor contracts, its

---

[1]As we have said, production also requires material inputs. For now, we assume that the firm has little or no flexibility with respect to this input. Each part requires a fixed amount of raw materials; producing twice as many parts requires twice as much raw materials and so on. Accordingly, the production function focuses on labor and capital and does *not* list the implicit amount of raw materials associated with each level of output. A more detailed production function might disaggregate materials into scores of categories, separate labor into numerous job descriptions, and disaggregate capital expenditures.

TABLE 5.1

A Production Function
for a Specialty Part

Number of Workers	Plant Size (Thousands of Square Feet)			
	10	20	30	40
10	93	120	145	165
20	135	190	235	264
30	180	255	300	337
40	230	315	365	410
50	263	360	425	460
60	293	395	478	510
70	321	430	520	555
80	346	460	552	600
90	368	485	580	645
100	388	508	605	680

This production function shows the quantity of output that can be obtained from various combinations of plant size and labor.

ability to reduce its labor force may be limited over the contract duration, perhaps up to three years. In this case, labor could be a fixed input in the short run.

A PRODUCTION FUNCTION FOR AUTO PARTS   Consider a multiproduct firm that supplies parts to several US automobile manufacturers. Table 5.1 tabulates the firm's production function for one such specialty part. The table lists the quantities of output that can be produced using different combinations of two inputs, labor and capital. For instance, the first entry indicates that an output of 93 specialty parts per day can be produced employing 10 workers in a 10,000-square-foot plant.

Let's consider the production decisions of the auto parts firm. Currently it is operating with a 10,000-square-foot plant. In the short run, this capital input is fixed. However, labor is a **variable input**; that is, the firm can freely vary its number of workers. Table 5.2 shows the amount of output obtainable using different numbers of workers. (This information is reproduced from the earlier production function and expanded slightly.) Notice that output steadily increases as the workforce increases, up to 120 workers. Beyond that point, output declines. It appears that too many workers within a plant of limited size are counterproductive to the task of producing parts.

The last column of Table 5.2 lists the marginal product of labor (MP_L). This **marginal product** is the additional output produced by an additional unit of labor, all other inputs held constant. For instance, increasing labor from 20 to 30 workers increases output by $180 - 135 = 45$ units, or $45/10 = 4.5$ units per worker. A further increase from 30 to 40 workers implies an MP_L of 5.0 units per worker. Mathematically, labor's marginal product is $MP_L = dQ/dL$. In other words, labor's marginal product is the change in output per unit change in labor input.

In our example, MP_L first rises (for increases up to 40 workers), then declines.[2] Why does MP_L rise initially? With a small workforce, the typical worker must be a

---

[2]Indeed, labor's marginal product becomes negative for additional workers beyond 120; that is, total product actually declines when "too many" workers are employed.

TABLE 5.2

Number of Workers	Total Product	Marginal Product	Production of Specialty Parts (10,000-Square-Foot Plant)
10	93		The second column
		4.2	shows the amount of
20	135		total output gen-
		4.5	erated by different
30	180		amounts of labor.
		5.0	The third column
40	230		shows the marginal
		3.3	product of labor—
50	263		the extra output
		3.0	produced by an
60	293		additional worker.
		2.8	
70	321		
		2.5	
80	346		
		2.2	
90	368		
		2.0	
100	388		
		1.2	
110	400		
		0.3	
120	403		
		−1.2	
130	391		
		−1.1	
140	380		

jack-of-all-trades (and master of none). Increasing the number of workers allows for *specialization* of labor—workers devoting themselves to particular tasks—which results in increased output per worker. Furthermore, additional workers can use underutilized machinery and capital equipment.

Figure 5.1a graphs labor's total product. Consider the total product curve for a 10,000-square-foot plant. Initially, the total product curve increases rapidly. As the number of workers increases, the curve's slope becomes less steep, then reaches a peak and declines. This reflects labor's marginal productivity. When MP_L is large (see Figure 5.1b), the total product curve is steep. As MP_L declines, the curve becomes less steep. The product curve peaks when MP_L approaches zero and begins to decline when MP_L becomes negative. Figure 5.1a also displays labor's total product curve for a 20,000-square-foot plant (with output rates taken from Table 5.1). As indicated, the larger plant generates an increased rate of output for the same workforce. Finally, Figure 5.1b graphs labor's marginal product for a 10,000-square-foot plant.

FIGURE 5.1

Total Product and
Marginal Product

Part a graphs labor's
total product; part b
depicts labor's mar-
ginal product.

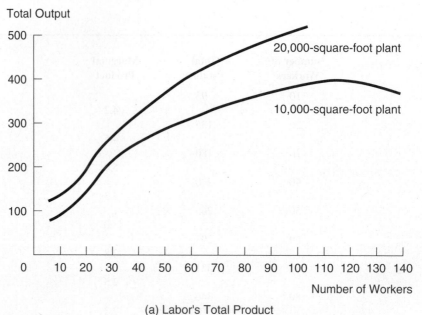

(a) Labor's Total Product

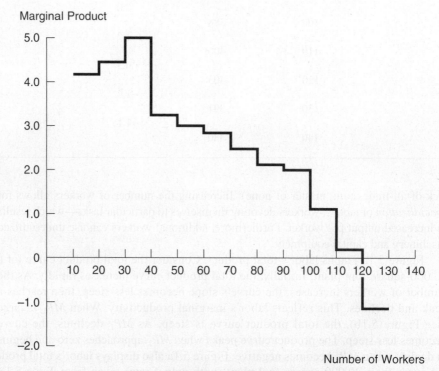

(b) Labor's Marginal Product (10,000-Square-Foot Plant)

Graph the marginal product of labor if the firm produces output using a 30,000-square-foot plant. Compare this with the MP_L using a 10,000-square-foot plant. Explain the difference.

Check Station 1

THE LAW OF DIMINISHING MARGINAL RETURNS   The declining marginal product of an input (like labor) represents one of the best-known and most important empirical "laws" of production:

> *The Law of Diminishing Marginal Returns.* As units of one input are added (with all other inputs held constant), resulting additions to output will eventually begin to decrease; that is, marginal product will decline.

In the preceding example, diminishing returns to labor occur beyond 40 workers. At this point the most productive jobs already are filled, specialization is being fully exploited, and the plant and equipment are being used efficiently. Extra workers are assigned to less productive tasks. These workers generate additional output but at a diminishing rate.

Optimal Use of an Input

The law of diminishing returns means that the firm faces a basic trade-off in determining its level of production. By using more of a variable input, the firm obtains a direct benefit—increased output—in return for incurring an additional input cost. What level of the input maximizes profits? As before, we look at the firm's marginal profit, but this time we look at marginal profit *per unit of input*. We increase the input until the marginal profit per unit of input is zero.

In analyzing this input decision, a definition is helpful. Marginal revenue product is the formal name for the marginal revenue associated with increased use of an input. An input's **marginal revenue product** is the extra revenue that results from a unit increase in the input. To illustrate, suppose the auto parts supplier is considering increasing labor from 20 to 30 workers. According to Table 5.2, the resulting marginal product is 4.5 parts per worker. Suppose further that the supplier's marginal revenue per part is constant. It can sell as many parts as it wants at a going market price of $40 per part. Therefore, labor's marginal revenue product (MRP_L) is ($40)(4.5) = $180 per worker. Similarly, the MRP_L for a move from 30 to 40 workers is ($40)(5.0) = $200 per worker. More generally, labor's marginal revenue product can be expressed as

$$MRP_L = (MR)(MP_L),\qquad\qquad [5.2]$$

where *MR* denotes marginal revenue per unit of output.[3]

---

[3] In calculus terms, $MRP_L = dR/dL = (dR/dQ)(dQ/dL) = (MR)(MP_L)$.

Now consider the marginal cost of using additional labor. The **marginal cost of an input** is simply the amount an additional unit of the input adds to the firm's total cost.[4] If the firm can hire as many additional workers as it wishes at a constant wage (say, $160 per day), then the marginal cost of labor is $MC_L = \$160$. (In some cases, however, the firm may have to bid up the price of labor to obtain additional workers.)

Now note that the additional profit from adding one more worker is the revenue generated by adding the worker less the worker's marginal cost.

$$M\pi_L = MRP_L - MC_L.$$

The firm should continue to increase its labor force as long as the amount of additional profit from doing so is positive—that is, as long as the additional revenue (MRP_L) is greater than the additional cost (MC_L). Due to diminishing marginal returns, labor's marginal revenue product eventually will fall. When MRP_L exactly matches MC_L (that is, when $M\pi_L = 0$), increasing the labor force any further will be unprofitable, which leads to the following principle:

> To maximize profit, the firm should increase the amount of a variable input up to the point at which the input's marginal revenue product equals its marginal cost, that is, until:

$$MRP_L = MC_L. \qquad [5.3]$$

After this point, the marginal cost of labor will exceed the marginal revenue product of labor, and profits will decline.

EXAMPLE 1 The human resources manager of the auto parts firm with a 10,000-square-foot plant estimates that the marginal cost of hiring an extra worker is $P_L = \$160$ per day. Earlier we noted that a move from 20 to 30 workers implies $MRP_L = \$180$ per worker (per day). Since this exceeds the daily cost per worker, $160, this move is profitable. So, too, is a move from 30 to 40 workers ($MRP_L = \$200$). But an increase from 40 to 50 workers is unprofitable because $MRP_L = (\$40)(3.3) = \$132$, falls well short of the marginal labor cost. After this, MRP_L continues to decline due to diminishing returns. Thus, the optimal size of the firm's labor force is 40 workers.

What would be the firm's optimal labor force if it had in place a 30,000-square-foot plant? From Table 5.1, we see that a move from 50 to 60 workers results in an MRP_L of $212, a move from 60 to 70 workers an MRP_L of $168, and a move from 70 to 80 workers an MRP_L of $128. Given a labor price of $160 per day, the firm profits by increasing its labor force up to a total of 70 workers (since $MRP_L > MC_L$ in this range). But an increase beyond this level reduces profitability ($MRP_L < MC_L$). The firm would best utilize the 30,000-square-foot plant by using 70 workers and producing 520 parts per day.

Check Station 2   Let *MR* = $40 and MC_L = $160 per day. Using the relevant information from Table 5.1, determine the firm's optimal number of workers for a 20,000-square-foot plant. Repeat the calculation for a 40,000-square-foot plant.

---

[4]It is important to distinguish between the marginal cost of an input and the marginal cost of an additional unit of output. Taking labor as an example, MC_L is defined as $\Delta C/\Delta L$, the cost of hiring an extra worker. In contrast, the added cost of producing an extra unit of *output* is $MC = \Delta C/\Delta Q$.

EXAMPLE 2   Suppose that a firm's production function is described by

$$Q = 60L - L^2,$$

where Q measures units of output and L is the number of labor hours. Suppose that output sells for \$2 per unit, and the cost of labor is $MC_L = \$16$ per hour. How many hours of labor should the firm hire, and how much output should it produce?

To answer these questions, we apply the fundamental rule

$$MRP_L = MC_L.$$

First, observe that labor's marginal product is $MP_L = dQ/dL = 60 - 2L$. In turn, labor's marginal revenue product is $MRP_L = (\$2)(60 - 2L) = 120 - 4L$. Setting this equal to \$16, we obtain $120 - 4L = 16$. The optimal amount of labor is $L = 26$ hours. From the production function, the resulting output is 884 units. Finally, the firm's operating profit (net of its labor cost) is $(\$2)(884) - (\$16)(26) = \$1,352$.

PRODUCTION IN THE LONG RUN

In the long run, a firm has the freedom to vary all of its inputs. Two aspects of this flexibility are important. First, a firm must choose the proportion of inputs to use. For instance, a law firm may vary the proportion of its inputs to economize on the size of its clerical staff by investing in computers and software specifically designed for the legal profession. In effect, it is substituting capital for labor. Steeply rising fuel prices have caused many of the major airlines to modify their fleets, shifting from larger aircraft to smaller, fuel-efficient aircraft.

Second, a firm must determine the scale of its operations. Would building and operating a new facility twice the size of the firm's existing plants achieve a doubling (or more than doubling) of output? Are there limits to the size of the firm beyond which efficiency drastically declines? These are all important questions that can be addressed using the concept of returns to scale.

Returns to Scale

The *scale* of a firm's operations denotes the levels of all the firm's inputs. A *change in scale* refers to a given percentage change in *all* inputs. At a 15 percent scale increase, the firm would use 15 percent more of each of its inputs. A key question for the manager is how the change in scale affects the firm's output. **Returns to scale** measure the percentage change in output resulting from a given percentage change in inputs. There are three important cases.

Constant returns to scale occur if a given percentage change in all inputs results in an equal percentage change in output. For instance, if all inputs are doubled, output also doubles; a 10 percent increase in inputs results in a 10 percent increase in output; and so on. A common example of constant returns to scale occurs when a firm can easily replicate its production process. For instance, a manufacturer of electrical components might find that it can double its output by replicating its current plant and labor force, that is, by building an identical plant beside the old one.

Increasing returns to scale occur if a given percentage increase in all inputs results in a greater percentage change in output. For example, a 10 percent increase in all inputs causes a 20 percent increase in output. How can the firm do better than constant returns to scale? By increasing its scale, the firm might be able to use new production methods that were infeasible at the smaller scale. For instance, the firm might utilize sophisticated, highly efficient, large-scale factories. It also might find it advantageous to exploit specialization of labor at the larger scale. As an example, there is considerable evidence of increasing returns to scale in automobile manufacturing: An assembly plant with a capacity of 200,000 cars per year uses significantly less than twice the input quantities of a plant having a 100,000-car capacity. Frequently, returns to scale result from fundamental engineering relationships. Consider the economics of an oil pipeline from well sites in Alaska to refineries in the contiguous United States. Doubling the circumference of the pipe increases the pipe's cross-sectional area *fourfold*—allowing a like increase in the flow capacity of the pipeline. To sum up, as long as there are increasing returns, it is better to use larger production facilities to supply output instead of many smaller facilities.

Decreasing returns to scale occur if a given percentage increase in all inputs results in a smaller percentage increase in output. The most common explanations for decreasing returns involve organizational factors in very large firms. As the scale of the firm increases, so do the difficulties in coordinating and monitoring the many management functions. As a result, proportional increases in output require more than proportional increases in inputs.

Output elasticity is the percentage change in output resulting from a 1 percent increase in all inputs. For constant returns to scale, the output elasticity is 1; for increasing returns, it is greater than 1; and for decreasing returns, it is less than 1. For instance, an output elasticity of 1.5 means that a 1 percent scale increase generates a 1.5 percent output increase, a 10 percent scale increase generates a 15 percent output increase, and so on.

Check Station 3   Reexamine the production function in Table 5.1. Check that production exhibits increasing returns for low levels of input usage and decreasing returns for high levels of usage. Can you find instances of constant returns in the medium-input range?

Least-Cost Production

In the long run, the firm can vary all of its inputs. Because inputs are costly, this flexibility raises the question: How can the firm determine the mix of inputs that will minimize the cost of producing a given level of output? To answer this question, let's return to the case of two inputs, labor and capital. Here the firm's production function is of the form

$$Q = F(L, K),$$

where L is the number of labor hours per month and K is the amount of capital used per month. There are possibly many different ways to produce a given level of output (call this Q_0), utilizing more capital and less labor or vice versa.

The optimal mix of labor and capital in producing output Q_0 depends on the costs and marginal products of the inputs. Let's denote the firm's labor cost per hour by P_L and its cost per unit of capital by P_K. Then the firm's total cost of using L and K units of inputs is

$$TC = P_L L + P_K K.$$

The firm seeks to minimize this cost, subject to the requirement that it use enough L and K to produce Q_0. We now state the following important result concerning optimal long-run production:

In the long run, the firm produces at least cost when the ratios of marginal products to input costs are equal across all inputs.

For the case of two inputs, we have

$$MP_L/P_L = MP_K/P_K. \hspace{2cm} [5.4]$$

Equation 5.4 shows that when total cost is minimized, the extra output per dollar of input must be the same for all inputs. To see why this must be true, assume to the contrary that the ratios in Equation 5.4 differ. As an example, let MP_L be 30 units per hour and P_L be $15 per hour; in turn, let MP_K be 60 and P_K be $40. Then $MP_L/P_L = 30/15 = 2$ units per dollar of labor, while $MP_K/P_K = 60/40 = 1.5$ units per dollar of capital. Because labor's productivity per dollar exceeds capital's, it is advantageous for the firm to increase its use of labor and reduce its use of capital. The firm could maintain its present output level *by using two extra units of labor in place of one fewer unit of capital.* (The 60 units of output given up by reducing capital is exactly matched by $(2)(30) = 60$ units of output provided by the additional labor.) The net savings in total cost is $40 (the saved capital cost) minus $30 (the cost of two labor hours), or $10. If one input's productivity per dollar exceeds another's, the firm can produce the same output at lower cost by switching toward greater use of the more productive input. It should continue to make such switches until the ratios in Equation 5.4 come into equality. At that point, the firm will have found its least-cost input mix.

Suppose that initially $MP_L/P_L > MP_K/P_K$. Explain why the ratios will move toward equality as the firm switches to more labor and less capital.   **Check Station 4**

EXAMPLE 3   A manufacturer of home appliances faces the production function $Q = 40L - L^2 + 54K - 1.5K^2$ and input costs of $P_L = \$10$ and $P_K = \$15$. Thus, the inputs' respective marginal products are

$$MP_L = \partial Q/\partial L = 40 - 2L$$

and

$$MP_K = \partial Q/\partial L = 54 - 3K.$$

We know that the firm's least-cost combination of inputs must satisfy $MP_L/P_L = MP_K/P_K$. This implies that

$$[40 - 2L]/10 = [54 - 3K]/15.$$

Solving for L, we find $L = K + 2$. This relation prescribes the optimal combination of capital and labor. For instance, the input mix $K = 8$ and $L = 10$ satisfies this relationship. The resulting output is $Q = (40)(10) - (10)^2 + (54)(8) - 1.5(8)^2 = 636$. The firm's total input cost is $TC = (\$10)(10) + (\$15)(8) = \$220$. In other words, the minimum cost of producing 636 units is $220 using 10 units of labor and 8 units of capital.

Winning in Football and Baseball

The National Football League (NFL) lives by the golden rule of team parity. Large-market teams in New York, Miami, or Dallas command greater revenues from ticket sales, concessions, TV and cable contracts, team products, and promotional deals. But small-market teams in Green Bay, Kansas City, and Cincinnati can nonetheless field winning teams. To achieve parity, the NFL has instituted a cap on team salaries, a system of revenue sharing, and more favorable player draft positions and schedules for weaker teams.[5]

How can a sports franchise construct a winning team with a strictly limited player budget ($123 million per team in 2013)? Coach Bill Belichick of the New England Patriots (once an economics major at Wesleyan University) assembled teams that won the Super Bowl in 2002, 2004, and 2005, by carefully considering not only player performance, but also price. The Patriots deliberately avoided superstars (considered to be overpriced) and relied instead on a mix of moderate-priced veterans and undervalued free agents and draft choices. For instance, Lawyer Milloy, an outstanding defensive player, was replaced with free-agent veteran Rodney Harrison, trading a $5.8 million salary for $3.2 million. Though Milloy's marginal product (i.e., ability and winning impact) was likely higher than Harrison's, this gain was not worth the salary price. Harrison was acquired and Milloy replaced because $MP_H/P_H > MP_M/P_M$.

By contrast, Major League Baseball, lacking a salary cap and having limited revenue sharing, suffers from severe competitive inequalities. The richest large-market teams are able to sign the established top players at gargantuan salaries and, thus, assemble the best teams. Championship teams bring extra revenues, and strong players help bring championships. During the fall of 2007, the Yankees re-signed free-agent superstar Alex Rodriguez for $175 million (plus incentive bonuses) for 10 years. With no salary cap, the signing makes economic sense as long as the player's marginal revenue product is greater than his salary: $MRP_L > P_L$. And since championships produce greater marginal revenues for large-market teams than for small-market teams, the marginal revenue product is much greater for the Yankees than for other teams. Thus the Yankees were probably one of a few teams in baseball willing to pay A-Rod this much money.

In sum, under their respective ground rules, baseball's rich tend to get richer, while football's middle-class teams operate on the same level playing field.

A GRAPHICAL APPROACH   Consider once again the production function of Example 3: $Q = 40L - L^2 + 54K - 1.5K^2$. We saw that the firm could produce $Q = 636$ units of output using $L = 10$ and $K = 8$ units of inputs. The same output, $Q = 636$, can be produced using different combinations of labor and capital: 6 units of labor and 12 units of capital, for instance. (Check this.)

---

[5]This account is based in part on L. Zinser, "Path to Super Bowl No Longer Paved with Stars," *The New York Times* (February 4, 2004), A1.

An **isoquant** is a curve that shows all possible combinations of inputs that can produce a given level of output. The isoquant corresponding to $Q = 636$ is drawn in Figure 5.2a. The amounts of the inputs are listed on the axes. Three input combinations along the $Q = 636$ isoquant, $(L = 6, K = 12)$, $(L = 10, K = 8)$, and $(L = 14.2, K = 6)$, are indicated by points A, B, and C, respectively. A separate isoquant has been drawn for the output $Q = 800$ units. This isoquant lies above and to the right of the isoquant for $Q = 636$ because producing a greater output requires larger amounts of the inputs.

The isoquant's negative slope embodies the basic trade-off between inputs. If a firm uses less of one input, it must use more of the other to maintain a given level of output. For example, consider a movement from point B to point A in Figure 5.2a—a shift in mix from $(L = 10, K = 8)$ to $(L = 6, K = 12)$. Here an additional $12 - 8 = 4$ units of capital substitute for $10 - 6 = 4$ units of labor. But moving from point B to point C implies quite a different trade-off between inputs. Here 4.2 units of labor are needed to compensate for a reduction of only 2 units of capital. The changing ratio of input requirements directly reflects diminishing marginal productivity in each input. As the firm continually decreases the use of one input, the resulting decline in output becomes greater and greater. As a result, greater and greater amounts of the other input are needed to maintain a constant level of output.

Using the production function, we can obtain a precise measure of the isoquant's slope. The slope of an isoquant is just the change in K over the change in L (symbolically, $\Delta K/\Delta L$), holding output constant. Consider again point B, where 10 units of labor and 8 units of capital are used. Recall from Example 3 that $MP_L = 40 - 2L$ and $MP_K = 54 - 3K$. Thus, at these input amounts, $MP_L = 40 - 2(10) = 20$ and $MP_K = 54 - 3(8) = 30$. This means that a decrease in labor of one unit can be made up by a two-thirds unit increase in capital. Therefore, the slope of the isoquant at point B is:

$$\Delta K/\Delta L = [+2/3 \text{ capital units}]/[-1 \text{ labor units}] = -2/3.$$

The general rule is that the slope of the isoquant at any point is measured by the ratio of the inputs' marginal products:

$$\Delta K/\Delta L \text{ (for } Q \text{ constant)} = -MP_L/MP_K.$$

Notice that the ratio is $-MP_L/MP_K$ and not the other way around. The greater is labor's marginal product (and the smaller capital's), the greater the amount of capital needed to substitute for a unit of labor, that is, the greater the ratio $\Delta K/\Delta L$. This ratio is important enough to warrant its own terminology. The **marginal rate of technical substitution (MRTS)** denotes the rate at which one input substitutes for the other and is defined as

$$MRTS = -\Delta K/\Delta L \text{ (for } Q \text{ constant)} = MP_L/MP_K.$$

For example, at point B, the MRTS is $20/30 = .667$ units of capital per unit of labor. At point A $(L = 6, K = 12)$, the marginal products are $MP_L = 28$ and $MP_K = 18$. At this input combination, the MRTS is $28/18 = 1.55$ and the slope of the isoquant is -1.55 (much steeper).

Suppose the manager sets out to produce an output of 636 units at least cost. Which combination of inputs along the isoquant will accomplish this objective? The answer is

FIGURE 5.2

Isoquants

These two isoquants
show the different
combinations of
labor and capital
needed to produce
636 and 880 units of
output.

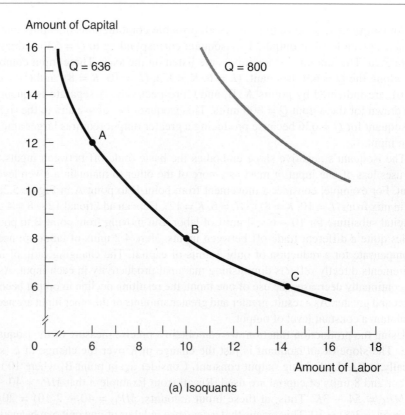

(a) Isoquants

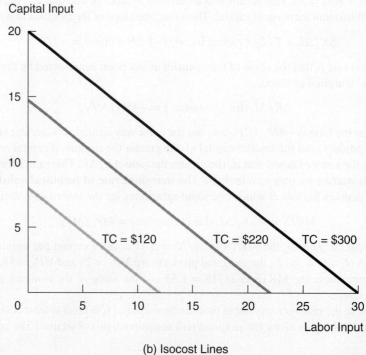

(b) Isocost Lines

provided by portraying the firm's least-cost goal in graphic terms. Recall that the firm's total cost of using L and K units of input is

$$TC = P_{L}L + P_{K}K.$$

Using this equation, let's determine the various combinations of inputs the firm can obtain at a given level of total cost (i.e., expenditure). To do this, we rearrange the cost equation to read

$$K = TC/P_{K} - (P_{L}/P_{K})L.$$

To illustrate, suppose the firm faces the input prices of Example 3, $P_{L} = \$10$ and $P_{K} = \$15$. If it limits its total expenditures to $TC = \$120$, the firm can use any mix of inputs satisfying $K = 120/15 - (10/15)L$ or $K = 8 - (2/3)L$. This equation is plotted in Figure 5.2b. This line is called an **isocost line** because it shows the combination of inputs the firm can acquire at a given total cost. We can draw a host of isocost lines corresponding to different levels of expenditures on inputs. In the figure, the isocost lines corresponding to $TC = \$220$ and $TC = \$300$ are shown. The slope of any of these lines is given by the ratio of input prices, $\Delta K/\Delta L = -P_{L}/P_{K}$. The higher the price of capital (relative to labor), the *lower* the amount of capital that can be substituted for labor while keeping the firm's total cost constant.

By superimposing isocost lines on the same graph with the appropriate isoquant, we can determine the firm's least-cost mix of inputs. We simply find the lowest isocost line that still touches the given isoquant. This is shown in Figure 5.3. For instance, to produce 636 units of output at minimum cost, we must identify the point along the isoquant that lies on the *lowest* isocost line. The figure shows that this is point B, the point at which the isocost line is tangent to the isoquant. Point B confirms Example 3's original solution: The optimal combination of inputs is 10 units of labor and 8 units of capital. Since point B lies on the \$220 isocost line, we observe that this is the minimum possible cost of producing the 636 units.

Note that at the point of tangency, the slope of the isoquant and the slope of the isocost line are the same. The isoquant's slope is $-MP_{L}/MP_{K}$. In turn, the isocost line's slope is $-P_{L}/P_{K}$. Thus, the least-cost combination of inputs is characterized by the condition

$$MRTS = MP_{L}/MP_{K} = P_{L}/P_{K}.$$

The ratio of marginal products exactly matches the ratio of input prices.[6] (If one input is twice as expensive as another, optimal usage requires that it have twice the marginal product.) This relationship can be rearranged to read

$$MP_{L}/P_{L} = MP_{K}/P_{K}.$$

This is exactly the condition established in Equation 5.4. The marginal product per dollar of input should be the same across all inputs.

---

[6]The same condition is derived readily using the method of Lagrange multipliers introduced in the appendix to Chapter 2. The problem is to minimize $TC = P_{L}L + P_{K}K$ subject to $F(L, K) = Q_{0}$, where Q_{0} denotes a given level of output. The Lagrangian is $\pounds = P_{L}L + P_{K}K + z(Q_{0} - F(L, K))$. The optimality conditions are $\partial\pounds/\partial L = P_{L} - z(\partial F/\partial L) = 0$, $\partial\pounds/\partial K = P_{K} - z(\partial F/\partial K) = 0$, and $\partial\pounds/\partial z = Q_{0} - F(L, K) = 0$. Dividing the first condition by the second yields $P_{L}/P_{K} - (\partial F/\partial L)/(\partial F/\partial K) = 0$. It follows that $P_{L}/P_{K} = MP_{L}/MP_{K}$, after recognizing that $MP_{L} = \partial F/\partial L$ and $MP_{K} = \partial F/\partial K$.

FIGURE 5.3

Producing Output at
Minimum Cost

The firm produces
636 units at minimum
cost at point B, where
the isoquant is tangent
to the lowest possible
isocost line. Point B
corresponds to
10 units of labor and
8 units of capital.

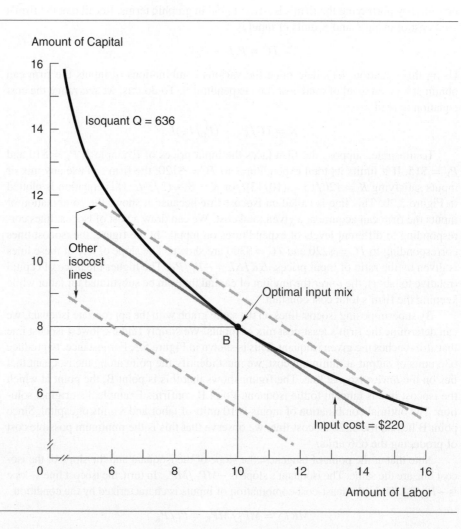

MEASURING PRODUCTION FUNCTIONS

In this section, we briefly discuss ways in which managers can estimate and measure
production functions based on engineering or economic data. Let us begin by considering four common specifications.

Linear Production

As the term suggests, a **linear production function** takes the form

$$Q = aL + bK + c,$$ [5.5]

where a, b, and c are coefficients that must be estimated from the data. An immediate implication of linearity is that each input's marginal product is constant: $MP_L = a$ and $MP_K = b$. Constant marginal productivity may approximate production over a limited range of input usage, but at sufficiently high levels of inputs it is at odds with the law of diminishing marginal productivity. In this sense, the linear form is too simple and should be viewed as a somewhat extreme case.

Because of the constant marginal products, the inputs are *perfect substitutes* for one another. Suppose, for example, that the production function is $Q = 20L + 40K$. In this case, one can always substitute two units of labor for one of capital to maintain the same level of production, and vice versa. Given fixed input prices, production will be "all or nothing" in the long run. If the unit cost of capital is less than the twice wage per unit of labor, the firm's least-cost means of production is to use only capital. In contrast, if labor is the less expensive option, production should use labor exclusively. In general, as long as $MP_K/P_K > MP_L/P_L$, the firm should use capital exclusively (and vice versa if the inequality is reversed).

Production with Fixed Proportions

Production with fixed proportions is the opposite extreme from linear production; fixed-proportions production allows no input substitution. Output can only be produced with a fixed proportion of inputs. Simple examples include a taxi and its driver or a construction crane and its operator. In both cases, the required mix of labor to capital is one to one. An excess of either input—a machine without an operator or vice versa—does no good. Expansion of production requires balanced increases in the necessary inputs. Like linear production, fixed-proportions production should be thought of as an extreme case. Rarely is there no opportunity for input substitution. (For example, it is true that a crane needs an operator but, at a more general level, extra construction workers can substitute for construction equipment.)

However, fixed-proportions production has an important implication. In the face of an increase in an input's price, the firm *cannot* economize on its use, that is, substitute away from it. Thus, a petrochemical firm that uses fixed proportions of different chemicals to produce its specialty products is at the mercy of market forces that drive up the prices of some of these inputs.

Polynomial Functions

In the *polynomial form*, variables in the production function are raised to positive integer powers. As a simple example, consider the quadratic form

$$Q = aLK - bL^2K^2,$$

where a and b are positive coefficients. It is easy to check that each input shows diminishing returns. (For example, $MP_L = \partial Q/\partial L = aK - 2bK^2L$, which declines as L increases.) The quadratic form also displays decreasing returns to scale. A more flexible representation is the cubic form,

$$Q = aLK + bL^2K + cLK^2 - dL^3K - eLK^3,$$

where all coefficients are positive. We can show that this function displays increasing returns for low output levels and then decreasing returns for high output levels. The marginal product of an input (say, labor) takes the form

$$MP_{\mathrm{L}} = \partial Q / \partial L = (aK + cK^2 - eK^3) + 2bKL - 3dKL^2.$$

We see that marginal product is a quadratic function in the amount of labor; that is, it is a parabola that rises, peaks, and then falls. Thus, this functional form includes an initial region of increasing marginal productivity followed by diminishing returns.

The Cobb-Douglas Function

Perhaps the most common production function specification is the **Cobb-Douglas function**

$$Q = cL^\alpha K^\beta, \qquad\qquad [5.6]$$

where c, α, and β denote parameters to be estimated. (Furthermore, α and β are between 0 and 1.) The Cobb-Douglas function is quite flexible and has a number of appealing properties. First, it exhibits diminishing returns to each input. To see this, note that $MP_{\mathrm{L}} = \partial Q / \partial L = c\alpha K^\beta L^{\alpha-1}$ and $MP_{\mathrm{k}} = \partial Q / \partial K = c\beta L^\alpha K^{\beta-1}$. Labor's marginal product depends on both L and K. It declines as labor increases, since L is raised to a negative power ($\alpha - 1 < 0$). However, labor's marginal product shifts upward with increases in the use of capital, a complementary input. (Analogous results pertain to capital.)

Second, the nature of returns to scale in production depends on the sum of the exponents, $\alpha + \beta$. Constant returns prevail if $\alpha + \beta = 1$; increasing returns exist if $\alpha + \beta > 1$; decreasing returns exist if $\alpha + \beta < 1$. We can check these effects as follows. Set the amounts of capital and labor at specific levels, say, L_0 and K_0. Total output is $Q_0 = cL_0^\alpha K_0^\beta$. Now suppose the inputs are increased to new levels, zL_0 and zK_0, for $z > 1$. According to Equation 5.6, the new output level is

$$
\begin{aligned}
Q_1 &= c(zL_0)^\alpha (zK_0)^\beta \\
&= cz^{\alpha+\beta}L_0^\alpha K_0^\beta \\
&= z^{\alpha+\beta}Q_0,
\end{aligned}
$$

after regrouping terms and using the definition of Q_0. If the scale increase in the firm's inputs is z, the increase in output is $z^{\alpha+\beta}$. Under constant returns ($\alpha + \beta = 1$), the increase in output is z; that is, it is identical to the scale increase in the firm's inputs. For instance, if inputs double (so that $z = 2$), output doubles as well. Under increasing returns ($\alpha + \beta > 1$), output increases in a greater proportion than inputs (since $z^{\alpha+\beta} > z$). Under decreasing returns ($\alpha + \beta < 1$), output increases in a smaller proportion than inputs.[7]

---

[7]One disadvantage of the Cobb-Douglas function is that it cannot allow simultaneously for different returns to scale. For instance, actual production processes often display increasing returns to scale up to certain levels of output, constant returns for intermediate output levels, and decreasing returns for very large output levels. The Cobb-Douglas function cannot capture this variation (because its returns are "all or nothing").

Third, the Cobb-Douglas function can be conveniently estimated in its logarithmic form. By taking logs of both sides of Equation 5.6, we derive the equivalent linear equation:

$$\log(Q) = \log(c) + \alpha\log(L) + \beta\log(K).$$

With data on outputs and inputs, the manager can employ the linear regression techniques of Chapter 4 using $\log(L)$ and $\log(K)$ as independent variables and $\log(Q)$ as the dependent variable. The statistical output of this analysis includes estimates of $\log(c)$ (the constant term) and the coefficients α and β.

EXAMPLE 4   Suppose the firm faces the production function $Q = L^{.5}K^{.5}$ and input prices are $P_L = \$12$ and $P_K = \$24$. (The inputs are equally productive, but capital is twice as expensive as labor.) The optimal input mix satisfies Equation 5.4 so that

$$[.5L^{-.5}K^{.5}]/12 = [.5L^{.5}K^{-.5}]/24.$$

After collecting terms, we get $K^{.5}/K^{-.5} = (12/24)L^{.5}/L^{-.5}$, or

$$K = .5L.$$

As noted, capital is twice as expensive as labor. As a result, for the Cobb-Douglas function, the firm employs half the number of units of capital as it does of labor.

Data for estimating production functions come in a number of forms. Engineering data can provide direct answers to a number of production questions: On average, how much output can be produced by a certain type of machine under different operating conditions? How many bushels of a particular crop can be grown and harvested on land (of known quality) using specified amounts of labor, capital, and materials (such as fertilizer)? Such information usually is based on experience with respect to similar (or not so similar) production processes. Consequently, the estimated production function is only as accurate as the past production experience on which it is based. The development of new weapons systems is a case in point. Although production and cost estimates are based on the best available engineering estimates (and possibly on tests of prototypes), they nonetheless are highly uncertain.[8]

A second source of production information is production data. For example, in a production time-series analysis, the firm's managers compile a production history, month by month or year by year, recording the amounts of inputs (capital, labor, land, materials, and so on) used in production and the resulting level of output. Alternatively, the economic data may come in the form of a *cross section*. In this case, information is gathered for different plants and firms in a given industry during a single period of time. For instance, by observing production in the auto industry, one can address a number of important questions: For

Estimating Production Functions

---

[8]Another limitation of engineering data is that they apply only to parts of the firm's activities, typically physical production operations. Thus, such data shed little light on the firm's marketing, advertising, or financial activities.

plants of fixed size (possibly employing different degrees of automation), what is the effect on output of expanding the labor force (for instance, adding extra shifts)? Does the industry exhibit economies of scale and, if so, over what range of outputs? (That is, will a 40 percent increase in plant scale deliver more than a 40 percent increase in output?)

Production data—although subject to measurement errors—are very useful to managers. Based on these data, the manager (often with the help of an operations research specialist) can estimate the mathematical relationship between levels of inputs and quantity of output. The principal statistical method for carrying out this task is regression analysis (the most important elements of which were discussed in Chapter 4). The end product of this analysis is a tangible representation of the firm's production function.

OTHER PRODUCTION DECISIONS

Within the limits of its production technology, the firm's managers face a number of important decisions. We have already discussed finding the optimal use of single input in the short run and choosing the best mix of inputs in the long run. We now consider two other decisions: (1) the allocation of a single input among multiple production facilities; and (2) the use of an input across multiple products.

Multiple Plants

Consider an oil company that buys crude oil and transforms it into gasoline at two of its refineries. Currently, it has 10 thousand barrels of oil under long-term contract and must decide how to allocate it between its two refineries. The company's goal is to allocate supplies to maximize total output from the refineries. Let M_A and M_B represent the crude input at each refinery and Q_A and Q_B the gasoline outputs. The firm's problem is:

Maximize $Q = Q_A + Q_B$, subject to $M_A + M_B = 10$ thousand.

The key to maximizing total output is to compare marginal products at the two refineries. Barrels of crude first should be allocated to the refinery whose marginal product is greater. Let's say this is refinery A. As additional barrels are allocated to this refinery, its marginal product diminishes, and it becomes worthwhile to allocate oil to refinery B as well.

In the final allocation of all 10,000 barrels, output is maximized if and only if *the marginal products of both refineries are equal*, that is, when

$$MP_A = MP_B.$$

Why must this be the case? If marginal products differed (say, $MP_A < MP_B$), barrels should be shifted from the low-MP plant (refinery A) to the high-MP plant (refinery B).

EXAMPLE 5   Based on extensive studies, suppose that management has estimated the following production functions for the refineries:

Refinery A: $Q_A = 24M_A - .5M_A^2$

Refinery B: $Q_B = 20M_B - M_B^2,$

where gasoline outputs are measured in thousands of gallons and quantities of crude oils are measured in thousands of barrels. Marginal products are

$$\text{Refinery A:} \quad MP_A = 24 - M_A$$

$$\text{Refinery B:} \quad MP_B = 20 - 2M_B.$$

Figure 5.4 shows the marginal product curve for each refinery and two possible allocations. One is a "naive" allocation calling for an equal split between the two facilities: $M_A = M_B = 5$ thousand barrels. Using the production functions, we find total output to be 182.5 thousand gallons. However, the figure immediately points out the inefficiency of such a split. At this division, the marginal product of the last barrel of crude at refinery A greatly exceeds the marginal product of the last barrel at refinery B (19 > 10). Barrels should be reallocated toward refinery A.

We can readily identify the optimal solution from Figure 5.4: $M_A = 8$ thousand barrels and $M_B = 2$ thousand barrels.[9] At these allocations, each refinery's marginal product is 16. (To check this, refer to the marginal product expressions just given.) The total output of gasoline from this allocation is 196 thousand gallons—a considerable improvement on the naive allocation. Furthermore, no other allocation can deliver a greater total output.

FIGURE 5.4

Splitting Production between Two Plants

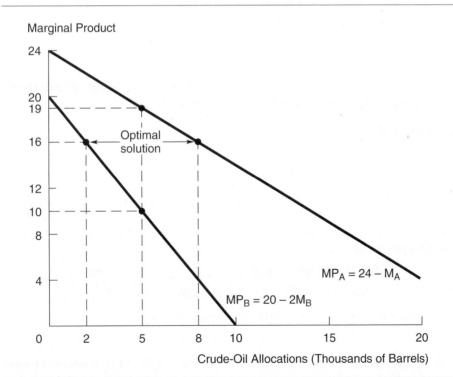

Marginal Product

Crude-Oil Allocations (Thousands of Barrels)

To produce a given amount of output at least cost, the firm divides output between the plants in order to equate the plants' marginal products.

[9] We can find these allocations directly using the facts that $MP_A = MP_B$ and $M_A + M_B = 10$. Equating marginal products implies $24 - M_A = 20 - 2M_B$. Solving this equation and the quantity constraint simultaneously gives the solution, $M_A = 8$ thousand barrels and $M_B = 2$ thousand barrels.

Multiple Products

Firms often face the problem of allocating an input in fixed supply among different products. The input may be a raw material—for instance, DRAM computer chips allocated to the various models of personal computers manufactured by the firm—or it may be capital. Frequently, the input in shortest supply is managerial labor itself. Which products of the firm are in greatest need of managerial attention? Which top-level managers are best suited to improve performance in a given product line?

Consider a variation on the oil company's decision. Suppose two of the company's product managers are engaged in a heated debate. The first manager oversees the company's production and sale of gasoline; the second is responsible for production of synthetic fiber. Both products use crude oil as an essential input. The problem is that the current demands of the managers for this input exceed the firm's available crude oil supply, 20 thousand barrels. Each manager is arguing for a greater share of the input.

How can economic analysis be used to resolve this dispute? Given a limited resource and two products, gasoline and fiber, management's ultimate goal must be to allocate the crude oil to each product (in quantities M_G and M_F) to maximize total profit subject to the constraint of 20 thousand total barrels.

The form of this decision is very similar to that of the multiplant decision. Here, total profit is maximized if and only if the input is allocated such that *the products generate identical marginal profits per unit of input*.[10]

$$M\pi_G = M\pi_F.$$

If fibers had a higher marginal profit per unit input than gasoline, gallons of crude should be switched from gasoline production to fiber production.

EXAMPLE 6   Suppose the production functions are

$$\text{Gasoline:} \quad G = 72M_G - 1.5M_G^2,$$
$$\text{Fiber:} \quad F = 80M_F - 2M_F^2.$$

Here, gasoline output is measured in thousands of gallons, fiber output in thousands of square feet, and crude oil in thousands of barrels. The products' profits per unit output are $.50 per gallon for gasoline and $.75 per square foot for fiber. Then the respective marginal profits are

$$M\pi_G = (\$.50)MP_G = (\$0.50)(72 - 3M_G) = 36 - 1.5M_G,$$
$$M\pi_F = (\$.75)MP_F = (\$.75)(80 - 4M_F) = 60 - 3M_F.$$

Setting these equal to each other and rearranging gives

$$M_F = .5M_G + 8.$$

Solving this equation and the constraint $M_G + M_F = 20$ implies $M_G = 8$ thousand barrels and $M_F = 12$ thousand barrels. This allocation generates 480 thousand gallons of gasoline and 672 thousand square feet of fiber. The firm's total profit is $744 thousand (less the cost of the crude).

---

[10]Here marginal profit is calculated *per unit input* because input is the appropriate decision variable.

Find the optimal crude oil allocation in the preceding example if the profit associated with fiber were cut in half, that is, fell to $.375 per square foot.

Check
Station 5

FINAL REMARKS   With respect to both the plant and product decisions, two comments are in order. First, the appropriate marginal conditions can be extended to the case of multiple (more than two) plants and decisions. (For instance, if there are three plants, the marginal product condition becomes $MP_A = MP_B = MP_C$.) Second, the decision framework changes significantly if management is able to vary the amount of the input. If management has access to as much crude oil as it wants (at a price), the problem can be dealt with plant by plant or product by product. Indeed, we have already considered the solution to this decision earlier: For each plant or each product, use of the input should be expanded to the point where its marginal revenue product equals its marginal cost per unit input (i.e., the input's price).

Pushed by stricter fuel-efficiency standards, steel and aluminum companies are fighting to build the next generation of lightweight cars and trucks. The more manufacturers can reduce the weight of vehicles, the more they can raise the mileage per gallon (MPG) rating. By replacing steel with aluminum (which is 10 to 30 percent lighter) in myriad parts throughout vehicle bodies, manufacturers are hoping to trim as much as 500 or 700 pounds per vehicle and, consequently, raise fuel efficiency by 5 to 10 MPG. By 2016, Corporate Average Fuel economy (CAFE) standards will require carmakers' vehicles and trucks to achieve an average of 35.6 MPG.[11]

Aluminum vs. Steel in Cars and Trucks

Like the multiplant and multiproduct problems already discussed, carmakers face an important constraint. However, here the constraint relates to average fuel efficiency (rather than limited inputs). To meet tougher CAFE standards, carmakers have two main options: (1) They can lighten the weight of various model cars and trucks by substituting aluminum for steel; and (2) they can tilt their production mix of vehicles toward lightweight compact cars and away from heavier trucks. However, both options are expensive. Even after a recent narrowing of the price gap, aluminum is still about 30 percent more expensive than steel in vehicles. In many instances, assembly-line processes must be modified to accommodate aluminum. In turn, carmakers earn significantly higher margins and profit on heavier vehicles—full-size luxury sedans, roomy minivans and SUVs, and trucks.

Thus, in seeking maximum profit subject to meeting stricter CAFE standards, carmakers face a number of complicated tradeoffs. To what degree is it best for aluminum to replace steel in various models? In addition, how should carmakers fine-tune their mix of vehicles to maximize their overall profit? In all this, there is one piece of good news. Aluminum producers are jumping at the chance to overturn steel's seven-to-one usage advantage in favor of something closer to a 50–50 split. In fiercely fighting for the auto business, aluminum and steel producers have already begun offering significant price reductions to auto makers.

Recall that the key issue for the office supply firm was how to divide its 18-person sales force between large accounts (firms already under contract with the company or a competitor) and new accounts (firms without a current rental contract).

Allocating a Sales Force Revisited

[11]This account is based in part on M. Ramsey, "Fuel Goal Tests Ford's Mettle," *The Wall Street Journal* (January, 13, 2014): B1; and R. G. Mathews, "Aluminum Tests Its Mettle Against Steel in Drive for Lighter Cars," *The Wall Street Journal* (March 16, 2011): B1.

To address this problem, five senior sales managers have put to paper their best estimate of the profit functions for both types of accounts; these functions are shown
in Figure 5.5. There is general agreement that the large accounts are more profitable than the new accounts. In Figure 5.5, the profit function for large accounts is
uniformly greater than that for new accounts. (For instance, assigning five salespeople to the former generates $800,000, whereas assigning the same number to
new accounts generates only $400,000.) In light of the profit curves, would senior
sales managers be justified in allocating all 18 salespeople to large accounts?

The answer is a resounding no! Management's objective is to assign its sales
force to maximize total profit. This is just a fixed-input/multiple-product decision.
Thus, the company should assign salespersons to the category of account that generates the greater marginal profit per unit input. For convenience, Figure 5.5 lists
marginal profits (in parentheses) for each type of account and for the different sizes
of sales force. The profit function for large accounts indicates that a two-person
sales force raises profit from $200,000 to $500,000, implying a marginal profit of
$150,000 per person (presumably this minimal sales force is essential for retaining

FIGURE 5.5

Profit Functions for an
Office Supply Firm

The optimal division
of salespeople is 8
individuals to "large"
accounts and 10 to
"new" accounts.

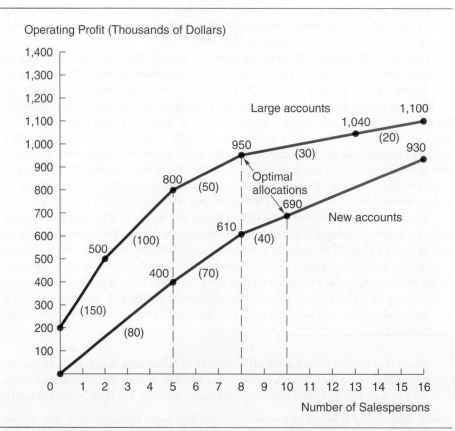

the firm's most loyal current clients); going from two to five salespeople increases profit by $100,000 per individual; and so on.

The optimal allocation is 8 salespeople to large accounts and 10 to new accounts. We assign salespersons to accounts in order of marginal profits; that is, the highest marginal profit assignments are made first. The "first" five individuals serve large accounts. (Marginal profit is $150,000 and then $100,000 per person.) The "next" eight individuals serve new accounts. (Marginal profit is $80,000 and then $70,000 per person.) The "next" three individuals go to large accounts (marginal profit is $50,000). The "last" two salespeople serve new accounts (marginal profit is $40,000). By assigning 8 and 10 salespeople to large and new accounts, respectively, the firm earns a total operating profit of $950,000 + $690,000 = $1,640,000.

New accounts have a lower average profit per salesperson but claim a majority of the sales force. The intuitive explanation is that these accounts offer better profit opportunities at the margin. Once five salespeople have been assigned to maintain the large accounts, there is relatively little opportunity to increase profit in this area. In contrast, there is a relatively steady marginal profit to be earned in new accounts. Thus, this is where the majority of the salespeople should be placed.

SUMMARY

Decision-Making Principles

1. Production is the process of turning inputs into outputs.
2. To maximize profit, the firm should increase usage of a variable input up to the point where the input's marginal cost equals its marginal revenue product.
3. To minimize the cost of producing a particular amount of output, the firm should choose an input mix such that the ratio of the marginal product to the input's cost is the same across all inputs.
4. In allocating an input among multiple plants, the firm maximizes total output when marginal products are equal across facilities.
5. In allocating an input among multiple products, the firm maximizes total profit when marginal profits per unit input are equal across products.

Nuts and Bolts

1. The production function indicates the maximum amount of output the firm can produce for any combination of inputs.
2. The short run is a period of time in which the amount of one or more of the firm's inputs is fixed, that is, cannot be varied.
   a. Marginal product (*MP*) is the additional output produced by an additional unit of an input, all other inputs held constant.
   b. The law of diminishing returns states that, as units of one input are added (with all other inputs held constant), a point will be reached where the resulting additions to output will begin to decrease; that is, marginal product will decline.
   c. An input's marginal revenue product (*MRP*) is the extra revenue generated by a unit increase in the input. For input A, $MRP_A = (MR)(MP_A)$.
3. The long run is an amount of time long enough to allow the firm to vary all of its inputs.
   a. Constant returns to scale occur if a given percentage change in all inputs results in an equal percentage change in output.

b. Increasing (decreasing) returns to scale occur if a given increase in all inputs results in a greater (lesser) proportionate change in output.

4. Production functions are estimated by specifying a variety of mathematical forms and fitting them to production data derived from engineering studies, economic time series, or cross sections.

Questions and Problems

1. Does optimal use of an input (such as labor) mean maximizing average output (per unit of input)? Explain.

2. Consider the production function $Q = 10L - .5L^2 + 24K - K^2$ for L and K in the range 0 to 10 units. Does this production function exhibit diminishing returns to each input? Does it exhibit decreasing returns to scale? Explain.

3. a. Suppose the inputs in Problem 2 can be purchased at the same price per unit. Will production be relatively labor intensive or capital intensive? Explain.
   b. Suppose input prices are $P_L = 40$ and $P_K = 80$ and the price of output is 10. Determine the optimal quantity of each input.

4. Making dresses is a labor-intensive process. Indeed, the production function of a dressmaking firm is well described by the equation $Q = L - L^2/800$, where Q denotes the number of dresses per week and L is the number of labor hours per week. The firm's additional cost of hiring an extra hour of labor is about $20 per hour (wage plus fringe benefits). The firm faces the fixed selling price, $P = \$40$.
   a. How much labor should the firm employ? What is its resulting output and profit?
   b. Over the next two years, labor costs are expected to be unchanged, but dress prices are expected to increase to $50. What effect will this have on the firm's optimal output? Explain. Suppose, instead, that inflation is expected to increase the firm's labor cost and output price by identical (percentage) amounts. What effect would this have on the firm's output?
   c. Finally, suppose once again that $MC_L = \$20$ and $P = \$50$ but that labor productivity (i.e., output per labor hour) is expected to increase by 25 percent over the next five years. What effect would this have on the firm's optimal output? Explain.

5. Explain the difference between diminishing returns and decreasing returns to scale.

6. A trendy French restaurant is one of the first businesses to open in a small corner of a commercial building still under construction. The restaurant has received rave reviews and has lines of diners waiting for tables most nights.
   a. In the short run (next few months), what measures should the restaurant take to maximize its profit? Explain.
   b. In the long run (next six months and beyond), how can it maximize its profit? (Assume that the impressive state of demand is permanent.)

7. A 200-pound steer can be sustained on a diet calling for various proportions of grass and grain. These combinations are shown in the table.

Pounds of Grass	Pounds of Grain
50	80
56	70
60	65
68	60
80	54
88	52

   a. Plot the isoquant corresponding to the inputs necessary to sustain a 200-pound steer. Comment on its shape.

b. The rancher's cost of grass is $.10 per pound; the cost of grain is $.07 per pound. He prefers a feed mix of 68 pounds of grass and 60 pounds of grain. Is this a least-cost mix? If not, what is? Explain.

c. The rancher believes there are constant returns to scale in fattening cattle. At current feed prices, what input quantities should he choose if he wants to raise the steer's weight to 250 pounds?

8. In recent years, Chrysler Corporation initiated three-shift or nearly continuous (21-hours-per-day) production at a number of its plants. Explain why Chrysler's decision might have been prompted by movements in its wage costs or capital costs, or both. Why would Chrysler have instituted this production change for its most popular (and profitable) vehicles, its minivans and Jeep Cherokee? What risks might such a plan pose?

9. Steel can be produced using three different methods: (1) a basic process using coke that produces steel ingots, (2) continuous casting, or (3) an electric furnace using steel scrap. The following table lists the average cost per ton of steel for each method.

Type of Cost	Basic Process	Continuous Casting	Electric Furnace
Materials	$150	$140	$120
Labor	$ 80	$ 75	$ 70
Capital	$100	$100	$ 60
Energy	$ 20	$ 15	$ 50
Other	$ 45	$ 40	$ 25

a. Production of steel by electric furnace is a relatively new development (beginning in the late 1970s) and accounts for a growing fraction of total steel sold. What is your prediction about the future production share of this method? Explain.

b. If there were a new energy crisis (causing energy prices to triple), how would this affect steelmakers' choices of production methods?

c. Suppose the price of steel scrap is expected to fall significantly over the next five years. What effect would this have on the choice of production method?

10. A firm is producing a given amount of output at least cost using a mix of labor and capital (which exhibit some degree of substitutability). Using an isoquant graph, show that if one input price increases, least-cost production calls for the firm to reduce that input (and increase the use of the other).

11. In her last-minute preparations for final exams, a student has set aside five hours to split between studying for two subjects, finance and economics. Her goal is to maximize the average grade received in the two courses. (Note that maximizing the average grade and maximizing the sum of the grades are equivalent goals.) According to her best guesses, grades vary with study as follows:

Study Hours	Finance Grade	Study Hours	Economics Grade
0	70	0	75
1	78	1	81
2	83	2	85
3	88	3	87
4	90	4	89
5	92	5	90

a. List the marginal values of additional hours worked for each subject.

b. How much time should the student spend studying each subject?

c. Suppose the student also is taking an accounting exam and estimates that each hour of studying will raise her grade by three points. She has allotted two hours for studying accounting (in addition to the five hours already mentioned). Is this an optimal decision? Explain. (Assume her objective is to maximize her average grade across the three courses.)

*12. Let $Q = L^\alpha K^\beta$. Suppose the firm seeks to produce a given output while minimizing its total input cost: $TC = P_L L + P_K K$. Show that the optimal quantities of labor and capital satisfy $L/K = (\alpha/\beta)(P_K/P_L)$. Provide an intuitive explanation for this result.

*13. In a particular region, there are two lakes rich in fish. The quantity of fish caught in each lake depends on the number of persons who fish in each, according to $Q_1 = 10N_1 - .1N_1^2$ and $Q_2 = 16N_2 - .4N_2^2$, where N_1 and N_2 denote the number of fishers at each lake. In all, there are 40 fishers.
   a. Suppose $N_1 = 16$ and $N_2 = 24$. At which lake is the average catch per fisher greater? In light of this fact, how would you expect the fishers to redeploy themselves?
   b. How many fishers will settle at each lake? (*Hint:* Find N_1 and N_2 such that the average catch is equal between the lakes.)
   c. The commissioner of fisheries seeks a division of fishers that will maximize the total catch at the two lakes. Explain how the commissioner should use information on the marginal catch at each lake to accomplish this goal. What division of the 40 fishers would you recommend?

Spreadsheet Problems

S1. A firm's production function is well described by the equation

$$Q = 2L - .01L^2 + 3K - .02K^2.$$

Input prices are $10 per labor hour and $20 per machine hour, and the firm sells its output at a fixed price of $10 per unit.
   a. In the short run, the firm has an installed capacity of $K = 50$ machine hours per day, and this capacity cannot be varied. Create a spreadsheet (based on the example below) to model this production setting. Determine the firm's profit-maximizing employment of labor. Use the spreadsheet to probe the solution by hand before using your spreadsheet's optimizer. Confirm that $MRP_L = MC_L$.

	A	B	C	D	E	F	G	H	I
1									
2			**OPTIMAL INPUTS**						
3								Output	136.0
4								Price	10.0
5		Labor	20.0		Capital	50.0			
6		MPL	1.600		MPK	1.000		MR	10.0
7								Revenue	1360.0
8		MRPL	16.0		MRPK	10.0			
9		MCL	10.0		MCK	20.0		Cost	1200.0
10								Ave Cost	8.8
11									
12								Profit	160.0
13									

   b. In the long run, the firm seeks to produce the output found in part (a) by adjusting its use of both labor and capital. Use your spreadsheet's optimizer to find the least-cost input amounts. (*Hint:* Be sure to include the appropriate output constraint for cell I3.)

*Starred problems are more challenging.

c. Suppose the firm were to downsize in the long run, cutting its use of both inputs by 50 percent (relative to part (b)). How much output would it now be able to produce? Comment on the nature of returns to scale in production. Has the firm's profitability improved? Is it currently achieving least-cost production?

S2. A second firm's production function is given by the equation

$$Q = 12L^5K^5.$$

Input prices are $36 per labor unit and $16 per capital unit, and $P = \$10$.

a. In the short run, the firm has a fixed amount of capital, $K = 9$. Create a spreadsheet to model this production setting. Determine the firm's profit-maximizing employment of labor. Use the spreadsheet to probe the solution by hand before using your spreadsheet's optimizer.

b. Once again, the firm seeks to produce the level of output found in part (a) by adjusting both labor and capital in the long run. Find the least-cost input proportions. Confirm that $MP_L/P_L = MP_K/P_K$.

c. Suppose the input price of labor falls to 18. Determine the new least-cost input amounts in the long run. Provide an intuitive explanation for the change in inputs caused by the lower labor price.

S3. The accompanying spreadsheet captures the profit-maximizing decisions of a carmaker facing stricter fuel-efficiency standards as discussed earlier in the chapter. The carmaker in question must decide how much aluminum to use in its trucks and sedans so as to lower their weight and improve their fuel efficiency. Cells C8 and C9 list these decision variables (expressed as percentages in decimal form, so that a value such as .10 means that the proportion of aluminum has increased by 10 percentage points). The company also must determine its mix of trucks and sedans by setting the proportion of trucks (again as a decimal) in cell D8 with cell D10 computed as: $= 1 - D8$.

Because of aluminum's extra cost, each vehicle's contribution per unit declines as more aluminum is used. Truck contribution (cell E8) is given by the Excel formula: $=10 - 80*H8*C8^2$. The cost impact of using aluminum depends on the relative cost of aluminum (cell H8) and increases quadratically as more and more aluminum is used. In turn, sedan contribution is given by the Excel formula: $= 6 - 80*H8*C8^2$. These formulas imply that current contribution margins for trucks and sedans (with cells C8 and C10 set to zero) are $10 thousand and $6 thousand, respectively. At the same time, each vehicle's fuel efficiency increases directly with its aluminum content. For trucks (cell F8), the Excel formula is: $=18 + 60*C8$, while for sedans (cell F10), the formula is: $38 + 80*C10$. These formulas imply that current fuel efficiency ratings for trucks and sedans (with cells C8 and C10 set to zero) are 18 miles per gallon and 38 miles per gallon, respectively. Finally, the fleet averages in row 12 are computed by weighting the vehicle values by the fleet shares in column D.

	A	B	C	D	E	F	G	H	I
1									
2		IMPROVING FUEL ECONOMY							
3									
4									
5			Δ Aluminum	Fleet Share	Contrib/unit	Fuel Eff.		A's relative	
6			(%)	(%)	($ 000)	(MPG)		Cost	
7									
8		Truck	0	.30	10.0	18.0		1.3	
9									
10		Sedan	0	.70	6.0	38.0			
11									
12			Fleet Average:		7.2	32.0			
13									
14					Requirement:	32			
15									

a. The company seeks to maintain a fleetwide average of 32 miles per gallon. To maximize its fleetwide average contribution (cell E12), how much aluminum should the maker add to each vehicle, and what mix of vehicles should it produce?

b. Re-answer the questions in part (a) if price cuts mean that aluminum is only 10 percent more costly than steel, that is, cell H8 takes the value 1.1.

c. Finally, what is the company's optimal production response if the fuel-efficiency standard is raised to 36 miles per gallon?

Suggested References

The following references offer case studies of production and economies of scale.

Basu, S., and J. G. Fernald. "Returns to Scale in U.S. Production: Estimates and Implications." *Journal of Political Economy* 105 (April 1997): 249–283.

Boyd, G. A. "Factor Intensity and Site Geology as Determinants of Returns to Scale in Coal Mining." *Review of Economics and Statistics* (1987): 18–23.

Cookenboo, L. "Production Functions and Cost Functions: A Case Study." in E. Mansfield (Ed.), *Managerial Economics and Operations Research*. New York: Norton, 1993.

Noulas, A. G., S. C. Ray, and S. M. Miller. "Returns to Scale and Input Substitution for Large U. S. Banks." *Journal of Money, Credit and Banking* 22 (February 1990): 94–108.

Managers' production strategies are discussed in:

Womack, J. P. "From Lean Production to Lean Enterprise." *Harvard Business Review* (March–April 1994): 93–103.

Check Station Answers

1. Labor's marginal product is uniformly greater (i.e., greater for any size of labor force) at a 30,000-square-foot plant than at a 10,000-square-foot plant.

2. At a 20,000-square-foot plant, the optimal labor force is 50 workers. (Here the MRP_L changes from $180 to $140.) At a 40,000-square-foot plant, the optimal labor force is 90 workers. (The MRP_L changes from $180 to $140.)

3. Doubling scale (starting from 10 workers and a 10,000-square-foot plant) more than doubles output. The same is true starting from 20 workers and a 20,000-square-foot plant. In contrast, doubling scale (starting from 50 workers and a 20,000-square-foot plant) produces less than double the output. Constant returns occur for a doubling of scale starting from 40 workers and a 10,000-square-foot plant or 30 workers and a 20,000-square-foot plant.

4. Given diminishing returns, using additional labor and less capital will lower the marginal product of labor and raise the marginal product of capital. Using extra labor also might bid up the price of labor. These effects move MP_L/P_L and MP_K/P_K into equality.

5. If fiber's profit is $.375 per square foot, fiber's marginal profit becomes $M\pi_F = 30 - 1.5M_F$. Equating this to $M\pi_G$ implies $M_F = M_G - 4$. Together with $M_F + M_G = 20$, the solution is $M_F = 8$ thousand barrels and $M_G = 12$ thousand barrels. Given the reduced profit from fiber, the allocation of crude oil to this product is lowered (from 12 thousand to 8 thousand barrels).

CHAPTER 6

Cost Analysis

Delete each element of capability until system capability is totally gone and 30 percent of the cost will still remain.

NORMAN AUGUSTINE, AUGUSTINE'S LAWS

LO#1. Define relevant costs and summarize their role in decision making.

LO#2. Compare and contrast the cost of production in the short run and in the long run.

LO#3. Discuss the importance of economies of scale and scope in the determination of average cost.

LO#4. Give examples of the use of relevant costs in decision making (including when to shut down operations) for single-product and multiproduct firms.

Allocating Costs

A sporting goods firm recently experimented with producing a new line of shoes: cross-training shoes for boys 10 to 16 years old. The boys' shoe is very similar to the firm's main product, a best-selling women's athletic shoe. (The sizes are virtually the same; only the colors and logos differ.) Thus, the new line of shoes is easy and inexpensive to produce; indeed, there is excess production-line capacity to do so. Production of the women's shoe runs about 8,000 pairs per week, and the company recently began producing 2,400 pairs of boys' shoes per week. The firm's production managers estimate that the factory overhead cost shared between the two shoe lines comes to about $90,000 per week. (Overhead costs include shared factory space, machines, electricity, and some sales and support staff.) The company's policy is to allocate these shared fixed costs in proportion to the numbers of pairs of each line of shoes.

Currently the company charges an average price of $36 per pair for the boys' shoe. However, the total revenues generated at that price fail to cover the shoe's total costs: its direct cost (primarily materials and labor) and the allocated overhead cost just mentioned. Faced with this apparent loss, top management is considering various options to achieve profitability.

- The firm's chief accountant suggests raising the price on the new line (say, to $40 per pair) to improve margins and better cover production costs.
- The marketing manager agrees this might be reasonable but cautions that sales are bound to drop.
- The head of production adds that unit costs will vary with volume as well. He advocates producing at an output level at which direct costs per unit will be minimized.

In light of this conflicting advice, what type of cost analysis could guide the firm in determining its profit-maximizing course of action?

Cost analysis is the bedrock on which many managerial decisions are grounded. Reckoning costs accurately is essential to determining a firm's current level of profitability. Moreover, profit-maximizing decisions depend on projections of costs at other (untried) levels of output. Thus, production managers frequently pose such questions as, what would be the cost of increasing production by 25 percent? What is the impact on cost of rising input prices? What production changes can be made to reduce or at least contain costs? In short, managers must pay close attention to the ways output and costs are interrelated.

In this chapter, we build on Chapter 5's analysis of production to provide an overview of these crucial cost concepts. In the first section, we discuss the basic principles of *relevant costs*—considering the concepts of opportunity costs and fixed costs in turn. Next, we examine the relationship between cost and output in the short run and the long run. Then we turn to economies of scale and economies of scope. Finally, we consider the importance of cost analysis for a number of key managerial decisions.

RELEVANT COSTS

A continuing theme of previous chapters is that optimal decision making depends crucially on a comparison of relevant alternatives. Roughly speaking, the manager must consider the relevant pros and cons of one alternative versus another. The precise decision-making principle is as follows:

> In deciding among different courses of action, the manager need only consider the differential revenues and costs of the alternatives.

Thus, the only relevant costs are those that differ across alternative courses of action. In many managerial decisions, the pertinent cost differences are readily apparent. In others, issues of relevant cost are more subtle. The notions of opportunity costs and fixed costs are crucial for managerial decisions. We will consider each topic in turn.

Opportunity Costs and Economic Profits

The concept of opportunity cost focuses explicitly on a comparison of relative pros and cons. The **opportunity cost** associated with choosing a particular decision is measured by the benefits forgone in the next-best alternative. Typical examples of decisions involving opportunity cost include the following:

- What is the opportunity cost of pursuing an MBA degree?
- What is the opportunity cost of using excess factory capacity to supply specialty orders?
- What is the opportunity cost that should be imputed to city-owned land that is to be the site of a public parking garage downtown?

As the definition suggests, an estimate of the opportunity cost in each case depends on identifying the next-best alternative to the current decision. Consider the first example.

Suppose the MBA aspirant has been working in business for five years. What is the person giving up by pursuing an MBA degree full time? Presumably, it is the income he could have earned from the present job. (This opportunity cost is larger or smaller depending on how remunerative the job is and on the chances for immediate advancement.) Therefore, the total cost of taking an MBA degree is the explicit, out-of-pocket tuition cost and other related expenses plus the implicit (but equally real) opportunity cost.[1]

Next, consider the case of excess factory space. Assuming this space otherwise would go unused, its opportunity cost is zero! In other words, nothing is given up if the extra space is used to supply the specialty orders. (Perhaps, one would assign a small opportunity cost to the capacity; committing the space to the specialty order might preclude using it for a more profitable "regular" order that might arrive unexpectedly.)

Finally, consider the case of the city-owned land. Here the opportunity cost is whatever dollar value the land could bring in its next-best alternative. This might mean a different, more profitable city project. In general, an accurate estimate of the land's alternative value is simply its current market price. This price reflects what potential buyers are willing to pay for comparable downtown real estate. Unless the city has a better alternative for the land, its next-best option will be to sell the land on the open market.

As the first and third examples illustrate, opportunity costs for goods, services, or inputs often are determined by market prices (assuming such markets exist). For instance, the opportunity cost of the full-time MBA student's time is his forgone wage income (determined, of course, by labor-market conditions). The cost of the city-owned land is its market price. Note that if the city did not own the land, its cost would be explicit; it would have to pay the market price to obtain it. The fact of ownership doesn't change this cost; opportunity cost is still determined by the market price.

The concept of opportunity cost is simply another way of comparing pros and cons. The basic rule for optimal decision making is this:

| Undertake a given course of action if and only if its incremental benefits exceed its incremental costs (including opportunity costs). |

Thus, pursuing the MBA degree makes sense only if the associated benefits—acquisition of knowledge, career advancement, future higher earnings—exceed the total costs. Likewise, the factory space should be used only if the direct increase in cash flows exceeds the opportunity cost. Finally, the garage should be built only if its total benefits exceed its costs, including land value.

How would one estimate the full cost to an airline if one of its planes is held over for 24 hours in a western airport for repair?

CHECK STATION 1

ECONOMIC PROFIT   At a general level, the notion of profit would appear unambiguous. Profit is the difference between revenues and costs. On closer examination,

---

[1]Here are some questions to consider: What is the opportunity cost of pursuing an MBA degree part time at night while holding one's current job? For a 19-year-old, what is the opportunity cost of pursuing an undergraduate business degree?

however, one must be careful to distinguish between two definitions of profit. **Accounting profit** is the difference between revenues obtained and expenses incurred. The profit figures reported by firms almost always are based on accounting profits; it is the job of accountants to keep a careful watch on revenues and explicit expenses. This information is useful for both internal and external purposes: for managers, shareholders, and the government (particularly for tax purposes). With respect to managerial decision making, however, the accounting measure does not present the complete story concerning profitability. In this case, the notion of economic profit is essential. **Economic profit** is the difference between revenues and all economic costs (explicit and implicit), including opportunity costs. In particular, economic profit involves costs associated with capital and with managerial labor. Here is a simplified illustration.

STARTING A BUSINESS   After working five years at her current firm, a money manager decides to start her own investment management service. She has developed the following estimates of annual revenues and costs (on average) over the first three years of business:

Management fees	$225,000
Miscellaneous revenues	40,000
Office expenses (excluding rent)	−86,000
Office utilities	−20,000
Staff wages (excluding self)	−44,000

From this list, the new venture's accounting profit, the difference between total revenues ($265,000) and total expenses ($150,000), would be reckoned at $115,000. Notice that the list contains no item for office rent. Instead of renting office space, the money manager has made a capital investment in her venture by purchasing a small office suite at a price of $250,000. Nor is there any line item for the money manager's own compensation.

Is going into business on one's own truly profitable? The correct answer depends on recognizing all relevant opportunity costs. First, suppose the manager's compensation (annual salary plus benefits) in her current position is valued at $90,000. Presumably, this current position is her next best alternative. Thus, $90,000 is the appropriate cost to assign to her human capital. Deducting this imputed compensation from the accounting profit of $115,000 leaves an annual net gain of $25,000.

Second, what about her $250,000 investment in the office condominium? Suppose she borrows this amount from a financial institution at a 6 percent interest rate. Consequently, the annual cost of capital for the venture is: $(.06)($250,000) = $15,000$. (If she decided to end the venture after a year, she'd sell the office condominium at a price of $250,000, absent any speculative gain or loss, and recover her investment. Her out-of-pocket cost would simply be the $15,000.) Thus, accounting for the cost of capital, her final economic profit is: $$25,000 − $15,000 = $10,000$ per year. Because it is positive (she earns more than her next best alternative), she should go out on her own.

Alternatively, suppose that the manager possessed ample accumulated savings and had used these to pay for the office condominium with 100 percent cash instead of borrowing. What cost of capital should she impute to *her own* $250,000 investment? The answer is that she should use the same 6 percent rate that the banker would have charged as her opportunity cost of capital. Presumably, this interest rate represents the *normal* return to capital invested in this particular venture. Here, *normal return* means the return required to compensate the suppliers of capital for bearing the risk (if any) of the investment. In making the investment she owes herself this same normal rate of return.

An equivalent way of making the same point is to speak in financial terms. After accounting for her $90,000 in compensation, she expects to earn an annual profit of $25,000 (before subtracting any capital costs). Given her $250,000 investment, she is earning an actual 10 percent (25,000/250,000) annual rate of return. Comparing this to the normal 6 percent rate, she is earning an "above normal" or excess rate of return. Any time a venture generates a positive economic profit, it is necessarily earning an above-normal rate of return. By contrast, the manager's venture would look very different if her current compensation were much greater—say, $110,000. Her annual net profit falls to $5,000, her rate of return falls to 2 percent (5,000/250,000), and her economic profit becomes −$10,000. Now, opening her own business is a losing proposition. Equivalently, her venture delivers a below normal rate of return (2% < 6%) and so does not warrant an investment (hers or the bank's).[2]

Finally, consider the knife-edge case of exactly a zero economic profit. Suppose that the manager's annual profit is projected to be exactly $15,000 so that economic profit is $0 after subtracting the $15,000 cost of capital. Her rate of return is 6 percent (15,000/250,000)—exactly equal to the normal (required) rate of return. To sum up, a venture earning a zero economic profit is a break-even proposition; it earns just enough accounting profit to cover its required cost of capital (but does *not* command even a penny extra above a normal rate of return).

Fixed and Sunk Costs

Costs that are **fixed**—that is, do not vary—with respect to different courses of action under consideration are irrelevant and need not be considered by the manager. The reason is simple enough: If the manager computes each alternative's profit (or benefit), the same fixed cost is subtracted in each case. Therefore, the fixed cost itself plays no role in determining the relative merits of the actions. Consider once again the recent graduate who is deciding whether to begin work immediately or to take an MBA degree. In his deliberations, he is concerned about the cost of purchasing his first car. Is this relevant? The answer is no, assuming he will need (and will purchase) a car whether he takes a job or pursues the degree.

Now consider a typical business example. A production manager must decide whether to retain the company's current production method or switch to a new method.

[2]A fundamental tenet of finance is that investors require higher rates of return for riskier investments. For instance, suppose that 12 percent were the appropriate *normal* rate of return for the manager's $250,000 investment (much higher than 6 percent because of much greater risk, let's say). Now, the annual cost of capital is: (0.12)($250,000) = $30,000. Economic profit—accounting profit minus the costs of the manager's compensation and invested capital—is now $115,000 − $90,000 − $30,000 = −$5,000. (Equivalently, the actual rate of return on her investment, 10 percent, falls short of the 12 percent required rate.) Because economic profit is negative, she should not go out on her own.

The new method requires an equipment modification (at some expense) but saves on the use of labor. Which production method is more profitable? The hard (and tedious) way to answer this question is to compute the bottom-line profit for each method. The easier and far more insightful approach is to ignore all fixed costs. The original equipment cost, costs of raw materials, selling expenses, and so on are all fixed (i.e., do not vary) with respect to the choice of production method. The only differential costs concern the equipment modification and the reduction in labor. Clearly, the new method should be chosen if and only if its labor savings exceed the extra equipment cost.

Notice that the issue of relevant costs would be very different if management were tackling the larger decision of whether to continue production (by either method) *or shut down.* With respect to a shut-down decision, many (if not all) of the previous fixed costs become variable. Here the firm's optimal decision depends on the magnitudes of costs saved versus revenues sacrificed from discontinuing production.

Ignoring fixed costs is important not only because it saves considerable computation but also because it forces managers to focus on the differential costs that are relevant. Be warned that ignoring fixed costs is easier in principle than in practice. The case of sunk costs is particularly important. A **sunk cost** is an expense that has already been incurred and cannot be recovered. For instance, in the earlier factory example, plant space may have been originally built at a high price. But this historic cost is sunk and is irrelevant to the firm's current decision. As we observed earlier, in the case of excess, unused factory capacity, the relevant opportunity cost is near zero.

More generally, sunk costs cast their shadows in sequential investment decisions. Consider a firm that has spent $20 million in research and development on a new product. The R&D effort to date has been a success, but an additional $15 million is needed to complete a prototype product that (because of delays) may not be first to market. Should the firm make the additional investment in the product? The correct answer depends on whether the product's expected future revenue exceeds the total *additional* costs of developing and producing the product. (Of course, the firm's task is to forecast accurately these future revenues and costs.) The $20 million sum spent to date is sunk and, therefore, irrelevant for the firm's decision. If the product's future prospects are unfavorable, the firm should cease R&D.

Perhaps the last word on sunk cost is provided by the story of the seventeenth-century warship *Vassa.* When first launched in Stockholm before a huge crowd that included Swedish royalty, the ship floated momentarily, overturned, and ignominiously (and literally) became a sunk cost.

Business Behavior
Sunk Costs

Sunk costs are easy to recognize in principle but frequently distort decisions in practice. The ongoing construction of nuclear power plants in the 1980s amidst declining revenues, cost overruns, and safety problems is a case in point. In light of uncertain profits and looming losses, making the right decision—to continue construction or abandon the effort—wasn't easy. (As the unrepentant actress Mae West once said, "In a choice between two evils, my general rule is to pick the one I haven't tried yet.") In some cases, utilities abandoned plants that were 85 percent complete after having spent more than $1 billion. Yet looking forward, this was a perfectly rational decision. By contrast, construction of the Shoreham nuclear plant on Long Island continued to completion despite severe cost escalation and safety concerns. It never received regulatory approval to operate, and the $6 billion spent was a complete loss.

Sunk costs are also important in new product development. In 2013, after heavy investments in development and marketing, Barnes & Noble abandoned manufacturing the Nook color tablet only after sustaining annual losses of $261 million and $475 million in the previous two years.

Research by psychologists testing the decision behavior of individuals including business managers clearly shows that sunk costs can adversely affect judgment.[3] For instance, executives will choose rightly to make a substantial initial investment in a simulated project, such as new product development, an R&D effort, or a capital investment. Yet, they continue to make cash investments even when new information in the simulation is highly unfavorable. By contrast, executives who enter the simulation only at the second decision with the same information (here, previous management has made the initial decision) are much more likely to pull the plug and write off the investment. The moral is clear; it's difficult to be objective when one is already psychologically invested in the initial decision (the more so the larger the initial sunk cost). Initial investors tend to maintain an overly optimistic outlook (despite the unfavorable new information) and adhere to the status quo established by their initial decision. Sunk costs also have effects in other contexts. For instance, in ongoing business disputes ranging from labor impasses to law suits, the rival parties frequently dig in as costs accumulate and refuse to settle (even when it is in their self-interest), thereby escalating the conflict.

Government spending programs, particularly in energy, defense, and basic science face similar challenges. Twenty-five years ago, Congress authorized the largest pure science project ever undertaken, the Supercollider program. Unhappily, the project's cost estimates obeyed their own law of acceleration, rising over the years from $4.4 billion to $6 billion to $8.2 billion to $11 billion to $13 billion. In 1993, with $2 billion already spent and 15 miles of underground tunnels dug, Congress voted to abandon the program. However, some weapons programs seem to have nine lives—refusing to die even when their original Defense Department sponsors have recommended cancellation. The futuristic Airborne Laser, conceived in the 1980s to shoot down enemy ballistic missiles, is a case in point.[4] Starting in 1996, the Pentagon spent some $5.2 billion on the program with only a poorly performing test aircraft to show for it. Believing the concept to be unworkable, the Clinton, Bush, and Obama administrations all recommended cancellation, while proponents in Congress lobbied hard to continue funding. Only in 2012 was the program finally killed for good.

In recent years, the budget axe has been used effectively in scrapping a number of uneconomical large-scale programs. Nonetheless, as critics point out, many government programs, once begun, seem to have lives of their own.

---

[3] For research on decision making and sunk costs, see H. Arkes and C. Blumer, "The Psychology of Sunk Cost," *Organizational Behavior and Human Decision Process*, 1985, 124–140; and W. Samuelson and R. Zeckhauser, "Status Quo Bias in Decision Making," *Journal of Risk and Uncertainty* (1988): 7–59.

[4] This discussion is based on N. Hodge, "Pentagon Loses War to Zap Airborne Laser from Budget," *The Wall Street Journal* (February 11, 2011): A1.

**CHECK
STATION 2**   A firm spent $10 million to develop a product for market. In the product's first two years, its profit was $6 million. Recently, there has been an influx of comparable products offered by competitors (imitators in the firm's view). Now the firm is reassessing the product. If it drops the product, it can recover $2 million of its original investment by selling its production facility. If it continues to produce the product, its estimated revenues for successive two-year periods will be $5 million and $3 million and its costs will be $4 million and $2.5 million. (After four years, the profit potential of the product will be exhausted and the plant will have zero resale value.) What is the firm's best course of action?

**Pricing
E-books**   For book publishers, the penetration of e-books represents both an opportunity and a threat. On the one hand, this new platform has the potential to spur overall book sales. On the other, e-books threaten to cannibalize sales of higher-margin print books. E-book sales have been accelerating, growing from 3 percent of total sales in 2009 to 14 percent in 2013. Book publishers face the key question: How should they market and price print books and e-books to maximize overall profit?

   Book publishers share (with Amazon and other online sellers) the revenue generated by e-books, and they are happy to add this to their bottom line. (After all, the marginal cost of producing an e-book is negligible.) However, publishers readily recognize the *opportunity cost* associated with aggressive e-book pricing. Yes, selling additional e-books means additional revenue. But it also means selling fewer print books and forgoing some of the associated profit from that high-margin business. Accordingly, publishers prefer a loftier $14.99 price for e-books. By contrast, Amazon prefers the lower $9.99 pricing strategy—not only to maximize its e-book revenue but also to help seize dominant control of the e-book market. At prices this low, print book sales begin to take a beating. Thus, it should hardly be surprising that book publishers and online sellers experience the same kinds of conflicts as franchisers and franchisees (discussed earlier in Chapter 2), with book publishers preferring higher e-book prices than online sellers.

THE COST OF PRODUCTION

As we noted in Chapter 5, production and cost are very closely related. In a sense, cost information is a distillation of production information. It combines the information in the production function with information about input prices. The end result can be summarized in the following important concept: The **cost function** indicates the firm's total cost of producing any given level of output. The concept of a cost function was first introduced in Chapter 2. In this section, we take a much closer look at the factors that determine costs. A key point to remember is that the concept of the cost function presupposes that the firm's managers have determined the least-cost method of producing any given level of output. (Clearly, inefficient or incompetent managers could contrive to produce a given level of output at some—possibly inflated—cost, but this would hardly be profit maximizing. Nor would the resulting cost schedule foster optimal managerial decision making.) In short, the cost function should always be thought of as a *least-cost function*. It usually is denoted as $C = C(Q)$ and can be described by means of a table, a graph, or an equation.

As in our study of production, our analysis of cost distinguishes between the short run and the long run. Recall that the short run is a period of time so limited that the firm is unable to vary the use of some of its inputs. In the long run, all inputs—labor, equipment, factories—can be varied freely. Our investigation of cost begins with the short run.

Short-Run Costs

In the basic model of Chapter 5, we focused on two inputs, capital and labor. In the short run, capital is a fixed input (i.e., cannot be varied) and labor is the sole variable input. Production of additional output is achieved by using additional hours of labor in combination with a fixed stock of capital equipment in the firm's current plant. Of course, the firm's cost is found by totaling its expenditures on labor, capital, materials, and any other inputs and including any relevant opportunity costs, as discussed in the previous section. For concreteness, consider a firm that provides a service—say, electronic repair. Figure 6.1 provides a summary of the repair firm's costs as they vary for different quantities of output (number of repair jobs completed).

The total cost of achieving any given level of output can be divided into two parts: fixed and variable costs. As the term suggests, **fixed costs** result from the firm's expenditures on fixed inputs. These costs are incurred regardless of the firm's level of output. Most overhead expenses fall into this category. Such costs might include the firm's lease payments for its factory, the cost of equipment, some portion of energy costs, and various kinds of administrative costs (payment for support staff, taxes, and so on). According to the table in Figure 6.1, the repair firm's total fixed costs come to $270,000 per year. These costs are incurred regardless of the actual level of output (i.e., even if no output were produced).

Variable costs represent the firm's expenditures on variable inputs. With respect to the short-run operations of the repair firm, labor is the sole variable input. Thus, in this example, variable costs represent the additional wages paid by the firm for extra hours of labor. To achieve additional output (i.e., to increase the volume of repair jobs completed), the firm must incur additional variable costs. Naturally, we observe that total variable costs rise with increases in the quantity of output. In fact, a careful look at Figure 6.1 shows that variable costs rise increasingly rapidly as the quantity of output is pushed higher and higher. Note that the firm's total cost exhibits exactly the same behavior. (With fixed costs "locked in" at $270,000, total cost increases are due solely to changes in variable cost.) The graph in Figure 6.1 shows that the total cost curve becomes increasingly steep at higher output levels.

Average total cost (or simply **average cost**) is total cost divided by the total quantity of output. Figure 6.2 shows average costs for the repair company over different levels of output. (Check that the average cost values are computed as the ratio of total cost in column 2 of the table and total output in column 1.) The graph displays the behavior of average cost. Both the table and graph show that short-run average cost is U-shaped. Increases in output first cause average cost (per unit) to decline. At 30,000 units of output, average cost achieves a minimum (at the bottom of the U). As output continues to increase, average unit costs steadily rise. (We will discuss the factors underlying this average cost behavior shortly.) Finally, **average variable cost** is variable cost divided

FIGURE 6.1

A Firm's Total Costs

Total cost is the sum
of fixed cost and
variable cost.

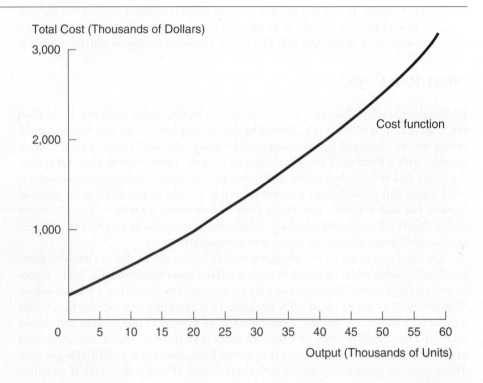

Annual Output (Repairs Thousands)	Total Cost ($ Thousands)	Fixed Cost ($ Thousands)	Variable Cost ($ Thousands)
0	270.0	270	0.0
5	427.5	270	157.5
10	600.0	270	330.0
15	787.5	270	517.5
20	990.0	270	720.0
25	1,207.5	270	937.5
30	1,440.0	270	1,170.0
35	1,687.5	270	1,417.5
40	1,950.0	270	1,680.0
45	2,227.5	270	1,957.5
50	2,520.0	270	2,250.0
55	2,827.5	270	2,557.5
60	3,150.0	270	2,880.0

by total output. Because it excludes fixed costs, average variable cost is always smaller than average total cost.

Marginal cost is the addition to total cost that results from increasing output by one unit. We already are acquainted with the concept of marginal cost from the analyses of the firm's output and pricing decisions in Chapters 2 and 3. Now we take a closer look at the determinants of marginal cost. The last column of the table in Figure 6.2 lists the repair company's marginal costs for output increments of 5,000 units. For instance, consider an output increase from 25,000 to 30,000 units. According to Figure 6.2, the result is a total cost increase of $1,440,000 − $1,207,500 = $232,500. Consequently, the marginal cost (*on a per-unit basis*) is $232,500/5,000 = $46.50/unit. The other entries in the last column are computed in an analogous fashion. From either the graph or the table, we observe that the firm's marginal cost rises steadily with increases in output. Expanding output starting from a level of 40,000 units per month is much more expensive than starting from 20,000 units.

What factors underlie the firm's increasing short-run marginal cost (SMC)? The explanation is simple. With labor the only variable input, SMC can be expressed as

$$SMC = P_L/MP_L, \hspace{3cm} [6.1]$$

where P_L denotes the price of hiring additional labor (i.e., wage per hour) and MP_L denotes the marginal product of labor.[5] To illustrate, suppose the prevailing wage is $20 per hour and labor's marginal product is .5 units per hour (one-half of a typical repair job is completed in one hour). Then the firm's marginal (labor) cost is $20/.5 = $40 per additional completed job.

According to Equation 6.1, the firm's marginal cost will increase if there is an increase in the price of labor or a decrease in labor's marginal product. Moreover, as the firm uses additional labor to produce additional output, the *law of diminishing returns* applies. With other inputs fixed, adding increased amounts of a variable input (in this case, labor) generates smaller amounts of additional output; that is, after a point, *labor's marginal product declines.* As a result, marginal cost rises with the level of output. (Clearly, material costs are also variable and, therefore, are included in SMC. However, because these costs typically vary in proportion to output, they do not affect the shape of SMC.)

Now we can explain the behavior of short-run average cost (SAC). When output is very low (say 5,000 units), total cost consists mainly of fixed cost (since variable costs are low). SAC is high because total cost is divided by a small number of units. As output increases, total costs (which are mostly fixed) are "spread over" a larger number of units, so SAC declines.

In the graph in Figure 6.2, notice that SMC lies well below SAC for low levels of output. As long as extra units can be added at a marginal cost that is lower than the average cost of the current output level, increasing output must reduce overall average cost. But what happens to average cost as marginal cost continues to rise? Eventually there comes a point at which SMC becomes greater than SAC. As soon as extra units become

---

[5]The mathematical justification is as follows. Marginal cost can be expressed as $MC = \Delta C/\Delta Q = (\Delta C/\Delta L)/(\Delta Q/\Delta L) = P_L/MP_L$. As the notation indicates, here we are looking at discrete changes in output and input. The same relationship holds with respect to infinitesimal changes, (dC/dQ).

FIGURE 6.2

A Firm's Average and
Marginal Costs

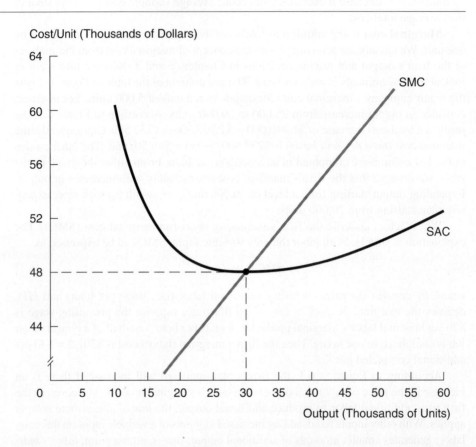

Annual Output (Repairs Thousands)	Total Cost (Thousands of Dollars)	Average Cost (Dollars/Unit)	Marginal Cost (Dollars/Unit)
0	270.0	∞	
5	427.5	85.5	31.5
10	600.0	60	34.5
15	787.5	52.5	37.5
20	990.0	49.5	40.5
25	1,207.5	48.3	43.5
30	1,440.0	48	46.5
35	1,687.5	48.2	49.5
40	1,950.0	48.8	52.5
45	2,227.5	49.5	55.5
50	2,520.0	50.4	58.5
55	2,827.5	51.4	61.5
60	3,150.0	52.5	64.5

more expensive than current units (on average), the overall average begins to increase. This explains the upward arc of the U-shaped SAC curve. This argument also confirms an interesting result: *The firm's marginal cost curve intersects its average cost curve at the minimum point of SAC.*

We have described the firm's short-run cost function in tabular and graphic forms. The cost function also can be represented in equation form. The repair company's short-run cost function is

$$C = C(Q) = 270 + (30Q + .3Q^2), \qquad [6.2]$$

where output is measured in thousands of units and costs are in thousands of dollars. (You should check this equation against Figure 6.1 for various outputs.) The first term is the firm's fixed costs; the term in parentheses encompasses its variable costs. In turn, short-run average cost is $SAC = C/Q$, or

$$SAC = 270/Q + (30 + .3Q). \qquad [6.3]$$

The first term is referred to as **average fixed cost** (fixed cost divided by total output); the term in the parentheses is **average variable cost** (variable cost divided by total output). According to Equation 6.3, as output increases, average fixed cost steadily declines while average variable cost rises. The first effect dominates for low levels of output; the second prevails at sufficiently high levels. The combination of these two effects explains the U-shaped average cost curve. Finally, treating cost as a continuous function, we find marginal cost to be

$$SMC = dC/dQ = 30 + .6Q, \qquad [6.4]$$

after taking the derivative of Equation 6.2. We observe that marginal cost rises with the level of output.

Long-Run Costs

In the long run, the firm can freely vary all of its inputs. In other words, there are no fixed inputs or fixed costs; *all costs are variable.* Thus, there is no difference between total costs and variable costs. We begin our discussion by stressing two basic points. First, the ability to vary all inputs allows the firm to produce at lower cost in the long run than in the short run (when some inputs are fixed). In short, flexibility is valuable. As we saw in Chapter 5, the firm still faces the task of finding the least-cost combination of inputs.

Second, the shape of the long-run cost curve depends on returns to scale. To see this, suppose the firm's production function exhibits constant returns to scale. **Constant returns to scale** means that increasing all inputs by a given percentage (say, 20 percent) increases output by the same percentage. Assuming input prices are unchanged, the firm's total expenditure on inputs also will increase by 20 percent. Thus, the output increase is accompanied by an equal percentage increase in costs, with the result that average cost is unchanged. *As long as constant returns prevail, average cost is constant.*

Production exhibits **increasing returns to scale**, or equivalently, **economies of scale** if average cost falls as the firm's scale of operation increases. For instance, a 20 percent increase in all inputs generates a greater than 20 percent increase in output, causing average cost per unit to fall. *When increasing returns prevail, average cost falls as output increases.* Finally, **decreasing returns to scale** prevail if increasing all inputs by a given percentage amount results in a less than proportional increase in output. It follows that *the presence of decreasing returns to scale implies rising average costs as the firm's output and scale increase.*

SHORT-RUN VERSUS LONG-RUN COST   Consider a firm that produces output using two inputs, labor and capital. Management's immediate task is to plan for future production. It has not leased plant and equipment yet, nor has it hired labor. Thus, it is free to choose any amounts of these inputs it wishes. Management knows that production exhibits constant returns to scale. Consequently, the firm's long-run average cost (LAC) is constant, as shown by the horizontal line in Figure 6.3. Furthermore, we can show that the firm should plan to use the same optimal *ratio* of labor to capital in production, regardless of the level of output. If the firm plans to double its level of output, it should also double the use of each input, leaving the proportions unchanged. These input proportions (in combination with prevailing input prices) determine the firm's average cost per unit. In Figure 6.3, $LAC = C/Q = \$4$. The long-run total cost function is $C = 4Q$. Thus, long-run marginal cost (LMC) is also $4 per unit. As the figure shows, long-run marginal and average costs are constant and identical.

FIGURE 6.3

Short-Run versus
Long-Run Cost

Under constant
returns to scale, the
firm's long-run
average cost is
constant. However,
short-run average
costs depend on the
size of the firm's plant
and are U-shaped.

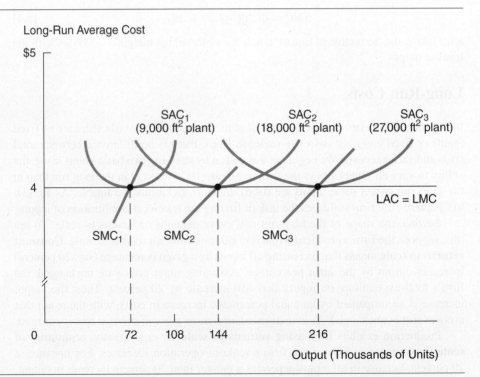

Figure 6.3 also shows the short-run average cost curves for three possible plants of varying sizes. The firm's plant (and equipment therein) represents the total capital input. The left curve is for a 9,000-square-foot plant, the middle curve for an 18,000-square-foot plant, and the right curve for a 27,000-square-foot plant. Notice that the smallest plant is optimal for producing 72,000 units of output. With such a plant in place (and using the right amount of labor), the firm can produce this output level at a minimum average cost of $4. If the firm planned to produce twice the level of output (144,000 units), it would use a plant twice the size (an 18,000-square-foot facility) and twice the labor. Finally, the largest plant is optimal for producing 216,000 units.

Once its plant is in place, however, the firm has considerably less flexibility. In the short run, its plant cannot be varied. Thus, if a 9,000-square-foot plant is in place, production of an output, such as 108,000 units (see Figure 6.3), means an increase in the average cost of production above $4. Why? To produce this output requires expanding the use of labor (since the plant is fixed). Because of diminishing returns, the extra output comes at an increasing marginal cost, and this drives up average cost as well.

Obviously, the firm may have many choices of plant size, not just three. Before its plant is in place, the firm has complete flexibility to produce *any* level of output at a $4 unit cost. It simply builds a plant of the proper scale and applies the right proportion of labor. In this long-run planning horizon, it can choose any scale of production. However, once the plant is built and in place, any change in planned output must be achieved by a change in labor (the sole variable input). The result is a movement either right or left up the U of the relevant SAC curve. In either case, there is an increase in average cost.

In a host of industries, such as electronics, automobiles, computers, aircraft, and agricultural products of all kinds, competition is worldwide. The major industrial countries of the world compete with one another for shares of global markets. For numerous goods, a US consumer has a choice of purchasing a domestically produced item or a comparable imported good made in a far-flung corner of the world—for instance, Europe, East Asia, or South America. Thus, a knowledge of international trade is essential for successful managers in increasingly global industries.

Comparative Advantage and International Trade

International trade is based on mutually beneficial specialization among countries. Why does one country concentrate on production and exports in certain goods and services, and another country specialize in others? Important reasons for varying patterns of specialization include different resource endowments, differences in the amount and productivity of labor, and differences in capital. For instance, a nation with abundant agricultural resources, predominantly unskilled labor, and little capital is likely to specialize in production of basic foods. By contrast, a nation, such as Japan, with a highly educated population and abundant capital but with relatively few natural resources, has an advantage in manufactured goods. Many observers believe that the United States' competitive advantage lies in high-tech goods and services. Relying on their research expertise and innovative ability, American firms excel in the development of technologically advanced goods and services. As these markets grow and mature, however, one would expect high-tech goods to evolve into commodity items, assembled and produced in large-scale facilities. It is not surprising that production of these goods tends to shift to other parts of the world over time.

To understand the basis for mutually beneficial trade, it is important to grasp the notion of comparative advantage. The easiest way to explain this concept is with a simple example. Table 6.1 offers a stylized depiction of trade involving two goods, digital electronic watches and pharmaceutical products, and two countries, the United States and Japan. Part (a) of the table shows the productivity of labor (that is, output per hour) in each country for each good. For instance, on average US workers produce 4 bottles of pills and 1 digital watch per labor-hour; their Japanese counterparts produce 2 bottles and .8 watches per labor-hour. According to the table, the United States is a more efficient manufacturer of both items; that is, US workers are more productive in both sectors.

However, labor productivity is only one factor influencing the cost of production. The other determinant is the price of the input, in this case, the price of labor. To compute the labor cost per unit of output, we need to know the prevailing hourly wage in each country. To keep things simple, suppose the US wage in both sectors is $15 per hour, whereas the Japanese wage in both sectors is 1,000 yen (¥) per hour. Naturally, the Japanese wage is denominated in that country's currency, the yen. Now consider the labor cost per unit of each good in each country. For the US pharmaceutical sector, this labor cost is simply ($15 per hour)/(4 bottles per hour) = $3.75 per bottle, using Equation 6.1. Part (b) of the table lists these costs for each country. For Japan, the cost in yen is shown in parentheses. For example, the labor cost per digital watch is 1,000/.8 = ¥1,250.

Finally, to make cross-country cost comparisons, we need one additional piece of information: the prevailing exchange rate between the two currencies. As its name suggests, the exchange rate denotes the amount of one country's currency that exchanges for a unit of another country's. Again, keeping things simple, suppose the current exchange rate in round numbers is 100 yen per dollar. (Furthermore, we suppose that this rate is expected to remain unchanged.) Using this exchange rate, it is a simple matter to convert the countries' costs per unit into a common currency, in this case the dollar. Japan's labor cost per bottle is ¥500, or $5.00 after dividing by the exchange rate of ¥100 per dollar. Similarly, its cost per digital watch is ¥1,250, or $12.50. Table 6.1b lists these conversions.

Table 6.1 conveys a specific message about the countries' relative costs for the goods. The United States has a unit labor cost advantage in producing pharmaceuticals ($3.75 compared to $5), whereas Japan has an advantage producing watches ($12.50 compared to $15). Thus, one would envision the United States specializing

TABLE 6.1

Relative Costs in the United States and Japan

a. Productivity

	Pharmaceuticals	Digital Watches
United States	4 per hour	1 per hour
Japan	2	.8

b. Costs

	Pharmaceuticals	Digital Watches
United States	$3.75 per bottle	$15 per watch
Japan	$5.00	$12.50
	(¥ 500)	(¥ 1,250)

in pharmaceuticals and Japan in digital watches. The predicted pattern of trade would have the United States exporting the former product and importing the latter from Japan. Indeed, actual trade flows between the two countries display exactly this pattern.

Table 6.1 also carries a general message: Productivity matters, but it is not the only thing that matters. After all, according to the table, the United States has an absolute productivity advantage in both goods. Yet Japan turns out to have a cost advantage in watches. The cost edge materializes because Japan has a **comparative advantage** in watches. That is, Japan's productivity disadvantage is much smaller in watches (where it is 80 percent as productive as the United States) than in pharmaceuticals (where it is only 50 percent as productive). After taking into account its lower wage rate, Japan indeed is the lower-cost watch producer.

Let us emphasize the point: Besides productivity, the countries' relative wages and the prevailing exchange rate also matter. For instance, if US wages increased more rapidly than Japanese wages over the coming year, the US cost advantage in pharmaceuticals would narrow, and Japan's cost advantage in watches would widen. Alternatively, suppose productivities and wages were unchanged in the two countries, but the exchange rate changed over the year. For instance, suppose the value of the dollar rose to ¥125 per dollar. (We say that the dollar has appreciated or, equivalently, that the yen has depreciated.) At this new exchange rate, Japan's labor costs per unit of output (converted into dollars) become $500/125 = \$4$ and $1,250/125 = \$10$ for the respective goods. With the appreciation of the dollar, Japanese goods become less costly (after converting into dollars). The US cost advantage in pharmaceuticals has narrowed significantly ($3.75 versus $4.00), whereas the Japanese cost advantage in watches has widened. Accordingly, US pharmaceutical exports should decline; these exports simply are not as attractive to Japanese consumers as before. In turn, a more expensive dollar (a cheaper yen) makes Japanese watch exports more attractive to US consumers.

To sum up, relative productivities, relative wages, and the prevailing exchange rate combine to determine the pattern of cost advantage and trade. With respect to the exchange rate, depreciation of a country's currency increases its exports and decreases its imports. A currency appreciation has exactly the opposite effect.

RETURNS TO SCALE AND SCOPE

Returns to Scale

Returns to scale are important because they directly determine the shape of long-run average cost. They also are crucial for answering such questions as these: Are large firms more efficient producers than small firms? Would a 50 percent increase in size reduce average cost per unit?

Although the exact nature of returns to scale varies widely across industries, a representative description is useful. Figure 6.4 depicts a long-run average cost curve that is U-shaped. This reflects increasing returns to scale (and falling LAC) for low output levels and decreasing returns (increasing LAC) for high levels. In the figure, the minimum level of long-run average cost is achieved at output level Q_{min}. As in Figure 6.3, SAC curves

FIGURE 6.4

U-shaped, Long-Run
Average Cost

The U shape is due
to increasing returns
at small outputs and
decreasing returns at
large outputs.

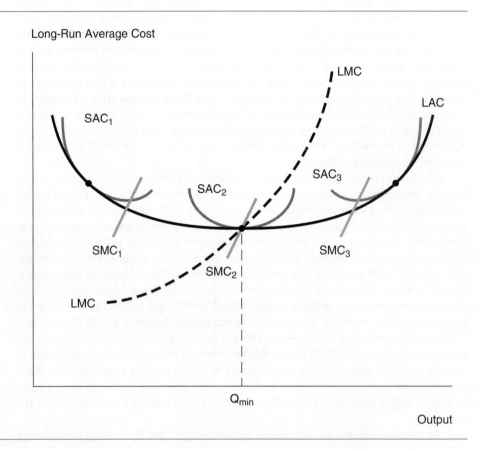

for three plants are shown. Thus, output Q_{min} is produced using the medium-sized plant. If the costs of *all* possible plants were depicted, the lower "envelope" of the many SAC curves would trace out the figure's LAC curve. To sum up, if the firm is free to use *any* size plant, its average production cost is exactly LAC.

As noted in Chapter 5, a number of factors influence returns to scale and, therefore, the shape of long-run average cost. First, *constant average cost* (due to constant returns to scale) occurs when a firm's production process can be replicated easily. For instance, the electronics repair firm may find it can double its rate of finished repair jobs simply by replicating its current plant and labor force—that is, by building an identical repair facility beside the existing one and proportionally increasing its labor force. By duplication, the firm could supply twice the level of service at an unchanged average cost per job.

Second, *declining average cost* stems from a number of factors, including capital-intensive mass production techniques, automation, labor specialization, advertising, and distribution. By increasing scale, the firm may be able to use new production methods that were infeasible at smaller outputs. It also may find it advantageous to exploit specialization of labor at the larger scale. The result of either kind of production innovation is a reduction in long-run average cost.

Fundamental engineering relationships may have the same effect. For instance, in 2011, Royal Caribbean International boasted the world's largest cruise liner, costing $1.1 billion, with capacity for 6,400 passengers and 2,300 crew. The largest cruise ships take full advantage of scale economies. At twice the tonnage, a super-cruise liner can carry significantly more than twice the number of passengers while requiring only a relatively modest increase in crew. Accordingly, the cost per passenger declines markedly.

Declining average cost also may be due to the presence of a variety of fixed expenses. Frequently, significant portions of a firm's advertising, promotional, and distributional expenses are fixed or (at least) vary little with the firm's level of output. (For instance, a 30-second television advertisement represents the same fixed cost to a large fast-food chain and a small chain alike. But this expense constitutes a much lower average cost per burger for the large chain.) Similarly, the costs to firms of many government regulations are (in the main) fixed. Accordingly, they represent a smaller average cost for the large firm. The US automobile industry, perhaps the most highly regulated sector in the world, is a case in point.

Finally, *increasing average cost* is explained by the problems of organization, information, and control in very large firms. As the firm's scale increases, so do the difficulties of coordinating and monitoring its many management functions. (For many goods and services, transportation costs are an important factor in explaining increasing LAC. At a small scale, the firm can efficiently serve a local market but serving a wider market becomes increasingly expensive.) The result is inefficiency, increased costs, and organizational overload.

A great many studies have investigated the shape of average cost curves for different industries in both the short and long runs.[6] One general finding is that, for most goods and services, there are significant economies of scale at low output levels, followed by a wide region of constant returns at higher levels. In short, for a great many industries, long-run average cost tends to be L-shaped, as depicted in Figure 6.5b. This is in contrast to the usual textbook depiction of U-shaped LAC shown in Figure 6.5a. A small number of products display continuously declining average costs. This case usually is described under the term *natural monopoly* and includes many (but not all) local utilities, local telephone service, and cable television. Figure 6.5c shows this case.

A useful way to summarize the degree of scale economies across industries is provided by the notion of efficient scale. **Minimum efficient scale (MES)** is the lowest output at which minimum average cost can be achieved. In parts (a) and (b) of Figure 6.5, minimum efficient scale is designated by Q_{min}. In Figure 6.5b, this occurs where the average cost curve first achieves a minimum. In Figure 6.5c, there is no minimum efficient scale because LAC continuously declines.

Minimum efficient scale is important in determining how many firms a particular market can support. For example, suppose market demand is 10 million units per year.

---

[6]Almost all of these studies use regression techniques to generate equations that explain total cost as a function of output and other relevant explanatory variables (such as wages and other input prices). The data for this analysis can come from either a time series (the same firm over a number of months or years) or a cross section (a cost comparison of different firms within a single time period). Despite difficulties in estimating costs from accounting data and controlling for changing inputs (especially capital), technology, and product characteristics, these studies have produced valuable information about costs.

FIGURE 6.5

Three Examples of
Long-Run Average Cost

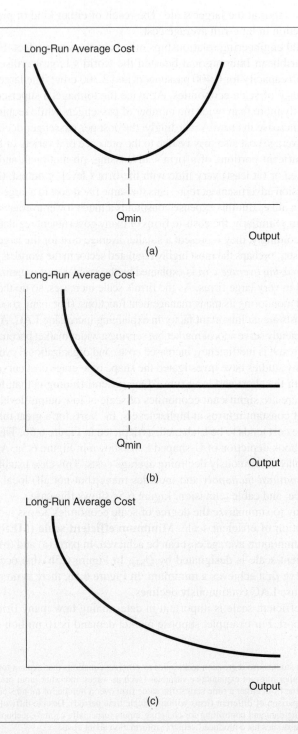

If minimum efficient scale for the typical firm occurs at 100,000 units per year, the market can support 100 firms, each producing at minimum efficient scale. In contrast, if minimum efficient scale is 5 million units, the market can support only two firms producing efficiently. Finally, if average cost declines for all outputs (up to 10 million units), the market may be able to support only one firm efficiently.

As one might expect, estimates of MES vary widely across industries.[7] For instance, in the production of sulfuric acid (a standard chemical), the MES for a plant is about 4 percent of total US consumption. The average cost disadvantage of producing at one-half of MES is only 1 percent. The clear implication is that there is ample room in the market for as many as 25 (1/.04) firms. By comparison, the MES for electric motors is about 15 percent of US consumption, and the cost disadvantage at one-half of MES is 15 percent. For production of commercial aircraft, MES is 10 percent of the US market, and the cost disadvantage at one-half of MES is 20 percent. This suggests that the industry could support as many as 10 manufacturers. Economies of scale would not seem to explain why Boeing and Airbus dominate the worldwide market. Rather, the rise of these two aviation giants and the demise of Lockheed and McDonnell-Douglas more aptly are attributed to differences in the companies' management strategies and technological capabilities.

E-Commerce and Cost Economies

As noted in Chapter 3, the Internet and the emergence of e-commerce have significant impacts on the structure of firm costs.[8] A wide-ranging research study by Washington's Brookings Institution estimated that across the whole of the US economy, the adoption of information technology and e-commerce methods was producing total annual cost savings of a magnitude equivalent to about 1 percent of annual gross domestic product. Increased efficiency stemmed from reengineering the firm's supply chain and from reducing transactions costs of all kinds. The greatest potential savings emerged in information-intensive industries such as health care, financial services, education, and public-sector operations.

Recall that the hallmark of information economics is the presence of high fixed costs accompanied by low or negligible marginal costs. As a result, average costs decline sharply with output. The fixed costs of business capital investments are increasingly found in computers, computing systems such as servers, software, and telecommunications (together constituting over 10 percent of capital expenditure), rather than in the traditional "bricks and mortar" of factories, assembly lines, and equipment. To date, a number of firms—Microsoft, Google, Cisco Systems, Oracle, eBay, Facebook, and YouTube, to name a few—have taken advantage of information economies to claim increasing shares of their respective markets, thus benefiting from sharply declining average unit costs.

[7]Estimates of plant-level economies of scale for different industries are collected in W. Shepherd and J. M. Shepherd, *The Economics of Industrial Organization* (Upper Saddle River, NJ: Prentice Hall, 2003).

[8]For discussions of e-commerce and cost economies, see J. Levin, "The Economics of the Internet," in D. Acemoglu, M. Arellano, and E. Dekel (Eds.), *Advances in Economics and Econometrics*, Cambridge University Press, 2013; G. Ellison and S. F. Ellison, "Lessons about Markets from the Internet," *Journal of Economic Perspectives* (Spring 2005): 139–158; S. Borenstein and G. Saloner, "Economics and Electronic Commerce," *Journal of Economic Perspectives* (Winter 2001): 3–12; and R. E. Litan and A. M. Rivlin, "Projecting the Economic Impact of the Internet," *American Economic Review*, Papers and Proceedings (May 2001): 313–317.

E-commerce also benefits from significant economies of scale in customer acquisition and service. In many e-commerce markets there has been a land-rush-like frenzy to acquire customers (often by offering a variety of free services). These customers come at a high initial fixed cost but have a very low marginal cost of servicing them. In addition, demand-side externalities mean that customers receive greater value as the population of other customers increase. This is true in online sites ranging from job-search to business-to-business commerce to online classified ads. For instance, such economies of scale provide eBay and Google with dominant positions in online auctions and search, respectively. In turn, economies of scale in distribution means that at large enough scale, taking orders online, holding inventories in centralized facilities, and shipping direct to customers is cheaper than selling the same item at a retail outlet. The online sales clout of Amazon is an obvious case in point.

Economies of Scope

Most firms produce a variety of goods. Computer firms, such as IBM and Toshiba, produce a wide range of computers from mainframes to personal computers. Consumer products firms, such as Procter & Gamble and General Foods, offer myriad personal, grocery, and household items. Entertainment firms, such as Walt Disney Corporation, produce movies, television programs, toys, theme park entertainment, and vacation services. In many cases, the justification for multiple products is the potential cost advantages of producing many closely related goods.

A production process exhibits **economies of scope** when the cost of producing multiple goods is less than the aggregate cost of producing each item separately. A convenient measure of such economies is

$$SC = \frac{C(Q_1) + C(Q_2) - C(Q_1, Q_2)}{C(Q_1) + C(Q_2)}.$$

Here, $C(Q_1, Q_2)$ denotes the firm's cost of jointly producing the goods in the respective quantities; $C(Q_1)$ denotes the cost of producing good 1 alone and similarly for $C(Q_2)$. For instance, suppose producing the goods separately means incurring costs of \$12 million and \$8 million, respectively. The total cost of jointly producing the goods in the same quantities is \$17 million. It follows that $SC = (12 + 8 - 17)/(12 + 8) = .15$. Joint production implies a 15 percent cost savings vis-a-vis separate production.

There are many sources for economies of scope. In some cases, a single production process yields multiple outputs. Cattle producers sell both beef and hides; indeed, producing cattle for beef or hides alone probably is not profitable. In other cases, production of a principal good is accompanied by the generation of unavoidable byproducts. Often, these byproducts can be fashioned into marketable products. Sawdust is a valuable byproduct of lumber production. Tiny plastic pellets (the byproduct of stamping out buttons) are used in sandblasting instead of sand. After the harvest, leftover cornstalks are used to produce alcohol for power generation. Still another source of economies is underutilization of inputs. An airline that carries passengers may find itself with unused cargo space; thus, it contracts to carry cargo as well as passengers. In recent years, many public school systems have made their classrooms available after hours for day-care, after-school, and community programs.

An important source of economies of scope is transferable know-how. Soft-drink companies produce many types of carbonated drinks, fruit juices, sparkling waters, and the like. Presumably, experience producing carbonated beverages confers cost advantages for the production of related drinks. Brokerage houses provide not only trading services but also investment advising and many bank-like services, such as mutual funds with check-writing privileges. Insurance companies provide both insurance and investment vehicles. In fact, whole-life insurance is a clever combination of these two services in an attractive package.

Scope economies also may be demand related. The consumption of many clusters of goods and services is complementary. For instance, the same company that sells or leases a piece of office equipment also offers service contracts. A select number of firms compete for the sales of cameras and photographic film. Sometimes the delivery of multiple services is so common and ubiquitous that it tends to be overlooked. Full-service banks provide a wide range of services to customers. The leading law firms in major cities provide extensive services in dozens of areas of the law. (Of course, smaller, specialty law firms coexist with these larger entities.) Many large hospitals provide care in all major medical specialties as well as in the related areas of emergency medicine, mental-health care, geriatrics, and rehabilitative therapy.

Toshiba America Information Systems (a subsidiary of the parent Japanese company) sells laptop computers, printers, disk drives, copiers, facsimile machines, and telephone equipment in North America. Would you expect there to be economies of scope in these product lines? If so, what are the sources of these economies?

CHECK STATION 3

Recent research has looked more closely at how firms in a variety of industries can successfully exploit economics of scale and scope. In the automobile industry, the advent of flexible manufacturing has begun to upend traditional thinking about the importance of returns to scale. In many circumstances, it is more profitable to be flexible than to be big.[9] At a new production facility, Honda workers can produce the Civic compact car on Tuesday and can switch production lines to produce the company's crossover SUV on Wednesday. When gasoline prices soar, causing demand for small fuel-efficient vehicles to rocket, the carmaker can immediately adjust its vehicle model production levels accordingly.

Flexibility and Innovation

By producing many different models under the same factory roof, Honda is exploiting economies of scope. Large-scale production runs aren't necessary to hold down average cost per vehicle. The same factory can combine large production runs of popular vehicles and much smaller runs of specialty or out-of-favor models. (A decade earlier, retooling a factory to produce a separate model could have required

[9]This discussion is drawn from various sources. including T. Bresnihan, S. Greenstein, and R. Henderson, "Schumpeterian Competition and Diseconomies of Scope: Illustrations from the Histories of Microsoft and IBM," *Harvard Business School*, Working Paper 11-077 (2011); C. Woodyard, "Ford Focuses on Flexibility," *USA Today* (February 28, 2011): 1B; J. Whalen, "Glaxo Tries Biotech Model to Spur Drug Innovation," *The Wall Street Journal* (July 1, 2010): A1.

as long as a year and hundreds of millions of dollars in changeover costs.) Honda is hardly alone. Ford Motor Company's state of the art plant in Wayne, Michigan, can produce multiple models. Changeovers mean switching the software programs that control nearly 700 assembly-line robots and reallocating the increasingly sophisticated responsibilities of the production-line workers. Costly capital and equipment changes are unnecessary.

Economies of scope are also demand driven. Consumer product firms have ample opportunities to provide related but differentiated and tailored products. Micromarketing is the process of differentiating products in order to targeting more markets. Years back, Procter & Gamble sold one type of Tide laundry detergent; now it sells a half-dozen kinds. E-commerce firms find it easy to customize the online buying experience. Amazon.com automatically recommends items based on a user's past purchase history. Retailers such as Nordstrom and the Gap offer much more clothing variety at their online sites than in their stores. Boeing uses computer-aided design to develop simultaneously several types of sophisticated aircraft for different buyers (domestic and international airlines).

By expanding its scope, the firm can frequently leverage its distinctive capabilities—brand name, reputation, control of a platform or industry standard, access to financing, to name a few—over a wide variety of activities. An interesting question is whether wider scope provides an *innovation* advantage in the development of new products and services. When it comes to *incremental* innovation (Gillette adding a fifth blade to its closer-shaving razor), the answer is typically yes. By contrast, *disruptive* innovation frequently presents a different story. Why is it the case that new firms and entrants—despite their startup disadvantages relative to industry leaders—spearhead some of the most dramatic innovations?

Recent research points to a number of possible reasons. First, the large multiproduct firm is understandably reluctant to risk cannibalizing its existing products by embracing and pursing promising but risky innovations. Second, behavioral factors can play a role—top management is psychologically invested in its current initiatives and consciously or unconsciously embraces the status quo. Finally, diseconomies of scale and scope may play a factor. At large pharmaceutical firms, the high levels of bureaucracy and internal red tape have been blamed for the declining rate of new drug discoveries during the last decade. Attempting to buck this trend, the drug company GlaxoSmithKline has carved dozens of small research units out of its thousand-strong R&D force—each small unit focusing on a single research initiative, with substantial freedom and monetary incentives to succeed. In attempting to emulate the success of biotech firms in basic research, smaller may be better. In turn, Microsoft arguably was held back by diseconomies of scope in extending its operations to browsers and Internet-based computing. Its reputation and inclination for controlling propriety standards made it very difficult to adopt open architectures needed to promote these new operating realms. It would have been better served if it had invested in an independent, stand-alone entity to pursue the browser and Internet-based software markets.

Many experts argue that relying on economies of scale—producing dedicated systems that are economical but inflexible—is no longer enough. The most successful firms in the future will also exploit the flexibility provided by economies of scope.

COST ANALYSIS AND OPTIMAL DECISIONS

Knowledge of the firm's relevant costs is essential for making sound managerial decisions. First, we consider decisions concerning a single product; then we examine decisions for multiproduct firms.

A Single Product

The profit-maximizing rule for a single-product firm is straightforward: As long as it is profitable to produce, the firm sets its optimal output where marginal revenue equals marginal cost. Figure 6.6 shows a single-product firm that faces a downward-sloping demand curve and a U-shaped average cost curve. The firm's profit-maximizing output is Q^* (where the MR and MC curves cross), and its optimal price is P^* (read off the demand curve). The firm's economic profit is measured by the area of the shaded rectangle in the figure. The rectangle's height represents the firm's profit per unit ($P^* - AC$), and its base is total output Q^*. (Remember that the firm's average cost includes a normal return on its invested capital. Therefore, a positive economic profit means that the firm is earning a greater-than-normal rate of return.) No alternative output and price could generate a greater economic profit.

By now, the application of marginal revenue and marginal cost should be very familiar. Nonetheless, it is worth pointing out two fallacies that occasionally find their way into managerial discussions. The first fallacy states that the firm can always increase its profit by exploiting economies of scale. Fully exploiting these economies means producing at minimum efficient scale—the point of minimum average cost. Figure 6.6 shows the problem with this contention: The profit-maximizing output Q^* falls well short of Q_{min}. In fact, if the firm were to produce at Q_{min}, it would suffer an economic loss. (The demand line falls below the average-cost curve at Q_{min}.)

The general point is that the firm's optimal output depends on *demand* as well as cost. In Figure 6.6, the level of demand for the firm's product is insufficient to justify exploiting all economies of scale. However, we easily could depict a much higher level of demand—one that pushes the firm to an output well above Q_{min}, that is, into the range of increasing average cost. The figure shows part of a (hypothetical) demand curve and the associated marginal revenue curve that intersects marginal cost at output Q'. For this level of demand, Q' (a quantity much greater than Q_{min}) is the profit-maximizing output.

The second fallacy works in the opposite direction of the first. It states that if the current output and price are unsatisfactory, the firm should raise its price to increase profits. The intuitive appeal of this "rule" is obvious. If price is too low relative to average cost, the remedy is to increase price. However, this contention is not necessarily so. In Figure 6.6, raising price is appropriate only if the current price is lower than P^* (with output greater than Q^*). If price is already greater than P^*, further price increases only reduce profits. In fact, the figure can readily demonstrate the classic fallacy of managing the product out of business. Suppose management makes the mistake of setting its output at $Q°$. Here the firm's price P^c is slightly below average cost, so the firm is incurring a loss. As a remedy, the firm raises price. Does this improve profits? No. The increase in

FIGURE 6.6

A Firm's Optimal Output

Regardless of the shape of its costs, a firm maximizes its profit by operating at Q*, where marginal revenue equals marginal cost.

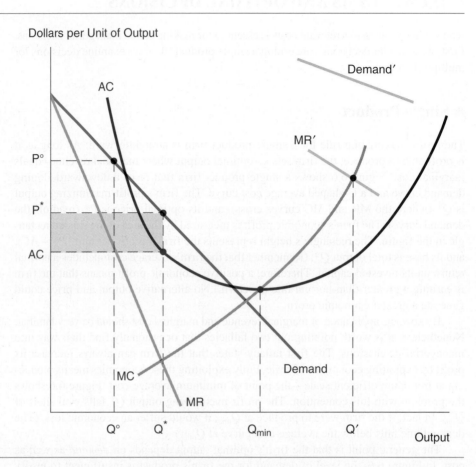

price causes a decrease in quantity (which is expected) but also an increase in average cost (perhaps unexpected). At a higher price and lower output, the firm still is generating a loss. If it raises price again, its volume will shrink further and its price still will fail to catch up with its increasing average cost. By using this strategy, the firm quickly would price itself out of the market.

The Shut-Down Rule

Under adverse economic conditions, managers face the decision of whether to cease production of a product altogether, that is, whether to shut down. Although the choice may appear obvious (shut down if the product is generating monetary losses), a correct decision requires a careful weighing of relevant options. These alternatives differ, depending on the firm's time horizon.

In the short run, many of the firm's inputs are fixed. Suppose the firm is producing a single item that is incurring economic losses—total cost exceeds revenues or,
equivalently, average total cost exceeds price. Figure 6.7 displays the situation. At the
firm's current output, average cost exceeds price: $AC > P^*$; the firm is earning negative
economic profit. Should the firm cease production and shut down? The answer is no. To
see this, write the firm's profit as

$$\pi = (R - VC) - FC = (P - AVC)Q - FC. \qquad [6.5]$$

The first term, $R - VC$, is referred to as the product's *contribution.* As long as revenue
exceeds variable costs (or, equivalently, $P > AVC$), the product is making a positive
contribution to the firm's fixed costs.

Observe that price exceeds average variable cost in Figure 6.7. (The average variable cost curve is U-shaped, and it lies below the AC curve because it excludes all fixed
costs.) Therefore, continuing to produce the good makes a contribution to fixed costs. (In
fact, output Q^* delivers maximum contribution because $MR = MC$.) If instead the firm
were to discontinue production ($Q = 0$), this contribution would be lost, and it would still

FIGURE 6.7

Shutting Down

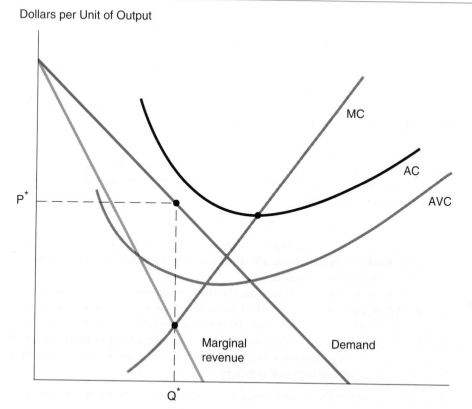

In the short run, the
firm should continue
to produce at Q^*
(even if it is suffering
a loss) so long as
price exceeds
average variable
cost. In the long run,
the firm should shut
down if price falls
short of average cost.

incur its fixed costs. If the firm shuts down, its profit will be $\pi = -FC$. The firm earns no revenues but pays its fixed costs. The firm suffers an economic loss in the short run; nevertheless, this is better than shutting down. Thus, we have the following general rule:

> In the short run, the firm should continue to produce as long as price exceeds average variable cost. Assuming it does produce, the firm maximizes contribution (and minimizes any losses) by setting marginal revenue equal to marginal cost.

In the long run, all inputs and all costs are variable. (For instance, a firm that leases its plant and equipment can shed these costs if it chooses not to renew its two-year lease. The firm can also downsize its workforce over time.) In the long run, the firm should continue operating only if it expects to earn a nonnegative economic profit. A firm that suffers persistent economic losses will be forced to exit the industry.

CHECK STATION 4   **Earlier we noted that the repair firm's cost function is $C = 270 + 30Q + .3Q^2$. Suppose demand is given by $P = 50 - .2Q$. What is the firm's optimal course of action in the short run? In the long run?**

Multiple Products

In the previous section, we noted that the prevalence of multiproduct firms is explained by economies of scope. The implication of such economies is that the firm can produce multiple products at a total cost that is lower than the sum of the items' costs if they were produced separately. As we shall see, managers must be careful to pay attention to relevant costs in a multiproduct environment.

To illustrate, consider a firm that produces two products in a common facility. The firm's total cost of production is described as

$$C = FC + VC_1 + VC_2,$$

where FC denotes the total fixed costs shared by the products. The separate variable costs for the products also are included and depend directly on the output levels of each product. The firm's total profit is

$$\pi = (R_1 - VC_1) + (R_2 - VC_2) - FC, \qquad [6.6]$$

where R_1 and R_2 denote the products' revenues. As noted earlier, each term in parentheses is the product's contribution. The firm's total profit is the sum of its products' contributions minus its total fixed costs.

As we saw in the single-product case, the firm should continue producing an item only if $R > VC$ or, equivalently, $P > AVC$. Exactly the same principle applies to the multiproduct case. Furthermore, in the long run the firm should continue in business only if the total profit in Equation 6.6 is nonnegative—that is, the total contribution from all of its activities covers its fixed costs; otherwise, it should shut down. The firm's output rule for multiple goods can be stated in two parts:

1. Each good should be produced if, and only if, it makes a positive contribution to the firm's fixed costs: $R_i > VC_i$ or, equivalently, $P_i > AVC_i$.

2. In the long run, the firm should continue operations if, and only if, it makes positive economic profits—the sum of its contributions fully covers its fixed costs.

In the example that opens this chapter, the managers of a sports shoe company were engaged in a debate over what strategy would lead to the greatest profit. Should production of the boys' shoes be increased? Cut back? Discontinued? The correct answers to these questions depend on a careful analysis of relevant costs. To clarify the situation, management has gathered cost information about different sales quantities. The firm's production managers have supplied the data on direct (i.e., variable) costs. Recall that production of women's and boys' running shoes share $90,000 in fixed costs. The firm's accountants allocate this cost to the two lines in proportion to numbers of pairs. The output of women's shoes is 8,000 pairs.

Allocating Costs Revisited

Pairs of Shoes	Price	Revenue	Direct Cost	Allocated Cost	Average Total Cost
1,600	$40	$64,000	$66,400	$15,000	$50.88
2,400	36	86,400	74,400	20,769	39.65
3,200	32	102,400	85,600	25,714	34.79
3,600	30	108,000	92,400	27,931	33.43
4,000	28	112,000	100,000	30,000	32.50

Thus, if the volume of boys' shoes is 4,000 pairs, the product's output is one-third of the total; hence, its allocation is $(1/3)(\$90,000) = \$30,000$. Allocations for other outputs are computed in the same way. Average total cost is the sum of direct and allocated costs divided by total output.

The firm currently is charging a price of $36 per pair and selling 2,400 pairs per week. How would management evaluate the current profitability of this strategy, and how might it improve its profits? First, consider the *wrong* method of approaching these questions. Management observes that when it sells 2,400 pairs, total average cost is $39.65 per pair. This exceeds the $36 selling price. Therefore, management believes its current strategy is unprofitable. What are its other options? An obvious possibility is to increase price to a level above $39.65, say, to $40. The table shows the results of this strategy. Volume drops to 1,600 pairs, but average total cost rises to $50.88. (Because the decline in volume is much greater than the reduction in total cost, average cost rises dramatically.) Price still falls well short of average cost. A price cut will do no better. The other prices in the table tell the same story: Average total cost exceeds price in all cases. Therefore, management concludes that the boys' running shoe cannot earn a profit and should be discontinued.

Let's now adopt the role of economic consultant and explain why management's current reasoning is in error. The problem lies with the allocation of the $90,000 in "shared" costs. Recall the economic "commandment": Do not allocate fixed costs. In a multiproduct firm, contribution is the correct measure of a product's profitability. A comparison of columns 3 and 4 in the table shows that the boys' shoe makes a positive contribution for four of the price and output combinations. Thus, the shoe should be retained. The firm's optimal strategy is to lower the price to $P = \$32$. The resulting sales volume is $Q = 3,200$. Maximum contribution is $\$102,400 - \$85,600 = \$16,800$. Beyond $P = \$32$, however, any further price reduction is counterproductive. (The additional cost of supplying these additional sales units exceeds the extra sales revenue.) Thus, the production manager would be wrong to advocate a policy of minimizing direct costs per unit of output. We can check that of the five output levels, average variable cost (AVC) is minimized at $Q = 4,000$. (Here AVC is $\$100,000/4,000 = \$25$ per pair.) Nonetheless, this volume of output delivers less contribution than $Q = 3,200$ because the accompanying drop in price is much greater than the decline in average variable cost. To sum up, the firm's correct strategy is to maximize the product's contribution.

SUMMARY

Decision-Making Principles

1. Cost is an important consideration in decision making. In deciding among different courses of action, the manager need only consider the differential revenues and costs of the various alternatives.

2. The opportunity cost associated with choosing a particular decision is measured by the forgone benefits of the next-best alternative.

3. Economic profit is the difference between total revenues and total costs (i.e., explicit costs and opportunity costs). Managerial decisions should be based on economic profit, not accounting profit.

4. Costs that are fixed (or sunk) with respect to alternative courses of action are irrelevant.

5. In the short run, the firm should continue to produce as long as price exceeds average variable cost. Assuming it does produce, the firm maximizes its profit (or minimizes its loss) by setting marginal revenue equal to marginal cost.

6. In the long run, all revenues and costs are variable. The firm should continue production if, and only if, it earns a positive economic profit. A multiproduct firm should continue operating in the long run only if total contribution exceeds its total fixed costs. There is no need to allocate shared fixed costs to specific products.

Nuts and Bolts

1. The firm's cost function indicates the (minimum) total cost of producing any level of output given existing production technology, input prices, and any relevant constraints.

2. In the short run, one or more of the firm's inputs are fixed. Short-run total cost is the sum of fixed cost and variable cost. Marginal cost is the additional cost of producing an extra unit of output. In the short run, there is an inverse relationship between marginal cost and the marginal product of the variable input: $MC = P_L/MP_L$. Marginal cost increases due to diminishing returns. The short-run average cost curve is U-shaped.

3. In the long run, all inputs are variable. The shape of the long-run average cost curve is determined by returns to scale. If there are constant returns to scale, long-run average cost is constant; under increasing returns, average cost decreases with output; and under decreasing returns, average cost rises. Empirical studies indicate L-shaped (or U-shaped) long-run average cost curves for many sectors and products.

4. Many firms supply multiple products. Economies of scope exist when the cost of producing multiple goods is less than the aggregate cost of producing each good separately.

5. Comparative advantage (not absolute advantage) is the source of mutually beneficial global trade. The pattern of comparative advantage between two countries depends on relative productivity, relative wages, and the exchange rate.

Questions and Problems

1. The development of a new product was much lengthier and more expensive than the company's management anticipated. Consequently, the firm's top accountants and financial managers argue that the firm should raise the price of the product 10 percent above its original target to help recoup some of these costs. Does such a strategy make sense? Explain carefully.

2. Comment on the following statement: "Average cost includes both fixed and variable costs, whereas marginal cost only includes variable costs. Therefore, marginal cost is never greater than average cost."

3. A company produces two main products: electronic control devices and specialty microchips. The average total cost of producing a microchip is $300; the firm then sells the chips to other high-tech manufacturers for $550. Currently, there are enough orders for microchips to keep its factory capacity fully utilized. The company also uses its own chips in the production of control devices. The average total cost (AC) of producing such a device is $500 plus the cost of two microchips. (Assume all of the $500 cost is variable and AC is constant at different output volumes.) Each control device sells for an average price of $1,500.
   a. Should the company produce control devices? Is this product profitable?
   b. Answer part (a) assuming outside orders for microchips are insufficient to keep the firm's production capacity fully utilized.
   c. Now suppose $200 of the average cost of control devices is fixed. Assume, as in part (a), that microchip capacity is fully utilized. Should control devices be produced in the short run? Explain.

4. The last 15 years have witnessed an unprecedented number of mega-mergers in the banking industry: Bank of America's acquisitions of Fleet Bank, MBNA, and U.S. Trust; Bank of New York's acquisition of Mellon Financial; and Wells Fargo's acquisition of Wachovia, to name several of the largest consolidations. Besides growth for its own sake, these super banks are able to offer one-stop shopping for financial services: everything from savings accounts to home mortgages, investment accounts, insurance vehicles, and financial planning.
   a. In the short run, what are the potential cost advantages of these mergers? Explain.
   b. Is a $300 billion national bank likely to be more efficient than a $30 billion regional bank or a $3 billion state-based bank? What economic evidence is needed to determine whether there are long-run increasing returns to scale in banking?
   c. Do you think these mergers are predicated on economies of scope?

5. An entrepreneur plans to convert a building she owns into a videogame arcade. Her main decision is how many games to purchase for the arcade. From survey information, she projects total revenue per year as $R = 10{,}000Q - 200Q^2$, where Q is the number of games. The cost for each game (leasing, electricity, maintenance, and so on) is $4,000 per year. The entrepreneur will run the arcade, but instead of paying herself a salary, she will collect profits. She has received offers of $100,000 to sell her building and a $20,000 offer to manage a rival's arcade. She recognizes that a normal return on a very risky investment such as the arcade is 20 percent.
   a. As a profit maximizer, how many games should she order?
   b. What is her economic profit?

6. Suppose the manufacturer of running shoes has collected the following quantitative information. Demand for the boys' shoe is estimated to be $Q = 9{,}600 - 200P$, or, equivalently, $P = 48 - Q/200$. The shoe's direct cost is: $C = \$60{,}000 + .0025Q^2$.
   a. Check that these demand and cost equations are consistent with the data presented in the "Allocating Costs Revisited" section.
   b. Find the firm's profit-maximizing price and output.

7. You are a theater owner fortunate enough to book a summer box office hit into your single theater. You are now planning the length of its run. Your share of the film's projected box office is $R = 10w - .25w^2$, where R is revenue in thousands of dollars and w is the number of weeks that the movie runs. The average operating cost of your theater is $AC = MC = \$5$ thousand per week.

   a. To maximize your profit, how many *weeks* should the movie run? What is your profit?

   b. You realize that your typical movie makes an average operating profit of $1.5 thousand per week. How does this fact affect your decision in part (a) if at all? Explain briefly.

   c. In the last 25 years, stand-alone movie theaters have given way to cineplexes with 4 to 10 screens and megaplexes with 10 to 30 screens under one roof. During the same period, total annual movie admissions have barely changed. What cost factors can explain this trend? In addition, what demand factors might also be relevant?

   d. The film's producer anticipates an extended theater run (through Labor Day) and accordingly has decided to move back the DVD release of the film by four weeks. Does the decision to delay make sense? Explain carefully.

8. A firm uses a single plant with costs $C = 160 + 16Q + .1Q^2$ and faces the price equation $P = 96 - .4Q$.

   a. Find the firm's profit-maximizing price and quantity. What is its profit?

   b. The firm's production manager claims that the firm's average cost of production is minimized at an output of 40 units. Furthermore, she claims that 40 units is the firm's profit-maximizing level of output. Explain whether these claims are correct.

   c. Could the firm increase its profit by using a second plant (with costs identical to the first) to produce the output in part (a)? Explain.

9. As noted in Problem 5 of Chapter 3, General Motors (GM) produces light trucks in its Michigan factories. Currently, its Michigan production is 50,000 trucks per month, and its marginal cost is $20,000 per truck. With regional demand given by: $P = 30,000 - .1Q$, GM sets a price of $25,000 per truck.

   a. Confirm that setting $Q = 50,000$ and $P = \$25,000$ is profit maximizing.

   b. GM also assembles light trucks in a West Coast facility, which is currently manufacturing 40,000 units per month. Because it produces multiple vehicle types at this mega-plant, the firm's standard practice is to allocate $160 million of factory-wide fixed costs to light trucks. Based on this allocation, the California production manager reports that the average total cost per light truck is $22,000 per unit. Given this report, what conclusion (if any) can you draw concerning the marginal cost per truck? If West Coast demand is similar to demand in Michigan, could the West Coast factory profit by changing its output from 40,000 units?

10. a. Firm K is a leading maker of water-proof outerwear. During the winter months, demand for its main line of waterproof coats is given by:

$$P = 800 - .15Q,$$

where P denotes price in dollars and Q is quantity of units sold per month. The firm produces coats in a single plant (which it leases by the year). The total monthly cost of producing these coats is estimated to be:

$$C = 175,000 + 300Q + .1Q^2.$$

(Leasing the plant accounts for almost all of the $175,000 fixed cost.) Find the firm's profit-maximizing output and price. If the firm's other outerwear products generate $50,000 in contribution, what is the firm's total monthly profit?

   b. From time to time, corporate customers place "special" orders for customized versions of Firm K's coat. Because they command premium prices, corporate orders generate an average contribution of $200 per coat. Firm K tends to receive these orders at short notice, usually during the winter when its factory is operating with little unused capacity. Firm K has just received an unexpected corporate order for 200 coats but has unused capacity to produce only 100. What would you recommend? In general, can you suggest ways to free up capacity in the winter?

c   Because of rival firms' successes in developing and selling comparable (sometimes superior) coats and outerwear, Firm K's winter demand *permanently* falls to $P = 600 - .2Q$. What is the firm's optimal operating policy during the next three winter months? When its plant lease expires in June?

11. Firm A makes and sells motorcycles. The total cost of each cycle is the sum of the costs of frames, assembly, and engine. The firm produces its own engines according to the cost equation:

$$C_E = 250,000 + 1,000Q + 5Q^2.$$

The cost of frames and assembly is $2,000 per cycle. Monthly demand for cycles is given by the inverse demand equation: $P = 10,000 - 30Q$.

a. What is the MC of producing an additional *engine?* What is the MC of producing an additional *cycle?* Find the firm's profit-maximizing quantity and price.

b. Now suppose the firm has the chance to buy an unlimited number of engines from another company at a price of $1,400 per engine. Will this option affect the number of *cycles* it plans to produce? Its price? Will the firm continue to produce engines itself? If so, how many?

*12. A firm produces digital watches on a single production line serviced during one daily shift. The total output of watches depends directly on the number of labor-hours employed on the line. Maximum capacity of the line is 120,000 watches per month; this output requires 60,000 hours of labor per month. Total fixed costs come to $600,000 per month, the wage rate averages $8 per hour, and other variable costs (e.g., materials) average $6 per watch. The marketing department's estimate of demand is $P = 28 - Q/20,000$, where P denotes price in dollars and Q is monthly demand.

a. How many additional watches can be produced by an extra hour of labor? What is the marginal cost of an additional watch? As a profit maximizer, what price and output should the firm set? Is production capacity fully utilized? What contribution does this product line provide?

b. The firm can increase capacity up to 100 percent by scheduling a night shift. The wage rate at night averages $12 per hour. Answer the questions in part (a) in light of this additional option.

c. Suppose demand for the firm's watches falls permanently to $P = 20 - Q/20,000$. In view of this fall in demand, what output should the firm produce in the short run? In the long run? Explain.

Discussion Question   Explain why the cost structure associated with many kinds of information goods and services might imply a market supplied by a small number of large firms. Could lower transaction costs in e-commerce ever make it easier for small suppliers to compete? As noted in Chapter 3, network externalities are often an important aspect of demand for information goods and services. (The benefits to customers of using software, participating in electronic markets, or using instant messaging increase with the number of other users.) How might network externalities affect firm operating strategies (pricing, output, and advertising) and firm size?

Spreadsheet Problems

S1. A firm's production function is given by the equation

$$Q = 12L^5K^5,$$

where L, K, and Q are measured in thousands of units. Input prices are 36 per labor unit and 16 per capital unit.

a. Create a spreadsheet (based on the example shown) to model this production setting. (You may have already completed this step if you answered Problem S2 of Chapter 5.)

---

*Starred problems are more challenging.

b. To explore the shape of short-run average cost, hold the amount of capital fixed at $K = 9$ thousand and vary the amount of labor from 1 thousand to 2.5 thousand to 4 thousand to 5.5 thousand to 7.5 thousand to 9 thousand units. What is the resulting behavior of SAC? Use the spreadsheet optimizer to find the amount of labor corresponding to minimum SAC. What is the value of SAC_{min}?

c. In your spreadsheet, set $L = 9$ thousand (keeping $K = 9$ thousand) and note the resulting output and total cost. Now suppose that the firm is free to produce this same level of output by adjusting both labor and capital in the long run. Use the optimizer to determine the firm's optimal inputs and LAC_{min}. (Remember to include an output constraint for cell I3.)

d. Confirm that the production function exhibits constant returns to scale and constant long-run average costs. For instance, recalculate the answer for part (c) after doubling both inputs.

e. Finally, suppose the firm's inverse demand curve is given by

$$P = 9 - Q/72.$$

With capital fixed at $K = 9$ (thousand) in the short run, use the optimizer to determine the firm's optimal labor usage and maximum profit. Then find the optimal amounts of both inputs in the long run. Explain the large differences in inputs, output, and profit between the short run and the long run.

	A	B	C	D	E	F	G	H	I	J
1										
2			COST ANALYSIS							
3								Output	36	
4								Price	8.50	
5		Labor	1.00		Capital	9.00				
6		MP_L	18.00		MP_K	2.00		MR	8.00	
7								Revenue	306	
8		MRP_L	144.00		MRP_K	16.00				
9		MC_L	36.00		MC_K	16.00		Cost	180	
10								Ave Cost	5.00	
11										
12								Profit	126	
13										

S2. A multinational firm produces microchips at a home facility and at a foreign subsidiary according to the respective cost functions:

$$C_H = 120Q_H \quad \text{and} \quad C_F = 50Q_F + .5Q_F^2.$$

The firm sells chips in the home market and the foreign market where the inverse demand curves are

$$P_H = 300 - D_H \quad \text{and} \quad P_F = 250 - .5D_F,$$

respectively. Here D denotes the quantity *sold* in each market, and Q denotes the quantity *produced* in each facility. Chips can be costlessly shipped between markets so that D_H need not equal Q_H (nor D_F equal Q_F). However, total production must match total sales: $Q_H + Q_F = D_H + D_F$.

a. Create a spreadsheet (based on the accompanying example) to model the firm's worldwide operations. Use the spreadsheet optimizer to find the firm's profit-maximizing outputs, sales quantities, and prices.

(Be sure to include the constraint that cell F9—extra output—must equal zero. That is, total sales must exactly equal total output.) Are chips shipped overseas? At the optimal solution, confirm that $MR_H = MR_F = MC_H = MC_F$.

	A	B	C	D	E	F	G	H
1								
2			WORLDWIDE CHIP DECISIONS					
3								
4			Set Sales & Output Quantities (000s)					
5								
6			Home	Abroad	Total			
7								
8		Sales	10	10	20		Extra	
9						0	< Output	
10		Output	10	10	20			
11								
12		Price	290	245		45	< Price Gap	
13								
14		Revenues	2,900	2,450	5,350			
15		MR	280	240	—			
16								
17		Costs	1,200	550	1,750			
18		MC	120	60	—			
19								
20		Profit	1,700	1,900	3,600			
21								

b. Answer the questions in part a under an "antidumping" constraint; that is, the company must charge the *same* price in both markets. (Include the additional constraint that cell F12, the price gap, must equal zero.)

Suggested References

The following articles examine the existence of scale and scope economies in a variety of settings.

Clark, J. "The Economies of Scale and Scope at Depository Financial Institutions: A Review of the Literature." *Economic Review* (Federal Reserve Bank of Kansas City, 1988): 16–33.

Koshal, R. K., and M. Koshal. "Do Liberal Arts Colleges Exhibit Economies of Scale and Scope?" *Education Economics* 8 (December 2000): 209–220.

Mosheim, R., and C. Lovell. "Scale Economies and Inefficiency of US Dairy Farms." *American Journal of Agricultural Economics* 91 (August 2009): 777–794.

Silk, A. J., and E. R. Berndt. "Scale and Scope Effects on Advertising Agency Costs." *Marketing Science* (Winter 1993): 53–72.

Sung, N., and M. Gort. "Economies of Scale and Natural Monopoly in the U.S. Local Telephone Industry." *Review of Economics and Statistics* 82 (November 2000): 694–697.

Wholey, D., et al. "Scale and Scope Economies among Health Maintenance Organizations." *Journal of Health Economics* 15 (December 1996): 657–684.

The following article reviews research estimating cost functions.

Panzar, J. "Determinants of Firm and Industry Structure." In R. Schmalensee and R. Willig (Eds.), *Handbook of Industrial Organization*. Amsterdam: North-Holland, 1989: 3–59.

Check Station Answers

1. The full cost to the airline of a grounded plane includes explicit costs—repair costs, overnight hangar costs, and the like. It also includes an opportunity cost: the lost profit on any canceled flights.

2. The past profits and development costs are irrelevant. If the firm drops the product, it recovers $2 million. If the firm continues the product, its additional profit is $5 + 3 - 4 - 2.5 = \$1.5$ million. Thus, the firm should drop the product.

3. The related electronics products would exhibit economies of scope for several reasons. First, they have many technological elements in common (e.g., expertise in copier technology carries over to facsimile machines). They also have some common components (microchips). Second, customers see the products as complementary. Thus, brand-name allegiance gained in computers could carry over to telephone equipment. Third, there are likely economies in joint advertising, promotion, and distribution. (Toshiba's sales force can pursue sales on any or all of its products.)

4. The repair firm's marginal revenue is $MR = 50 - .4Q$, and its marginal cost is $MC = 30 + .6Q$. Setting MR equal to MC, we find $Q^* = 20$. From the price equation, $P^* = 50 - (.2)(20) = 46$. In turn, profit is $\pi = 920 - 990 = -70$. The firm incurs a loss in the short run, but this is preferable to shutting down ($\pi = -270$). It is earning a maximum contribution toward overhead. In the long run, the firm should shut down unless conditions improve.

Transfer Pricing

LO#1. Determine the appropriate transfer price for sales among the divisions within a firm.

In the body of this chapter, we have focused on the production and sale of a firm's products to outside buyers. Although this is the most common case, products are also sold among divisions within large firms. For example, major automobile companies consist of many divisions. The division that produces parts will transfer its output to separate assembly divisions responsible for automobiles, trucks, and vans. In turn, assembled vehicles are transferred to different sales divisions and finally to dealers. In the same way, within a major chemical manufacturer, one division may produce a basic chemical that is used as an input in the production of specialty chemicals and plastics, each housed in separate divisions.

The price the selling division charges to the buying division within the company is called the **transfer price**. The firm's objective is to set the transfer price such that the buying and selling divisions take actions that maximize the firm's total profit. Accomplishing this task requires an accurate cost assessment. To illustrate the issues at stake, consider a large firm that sells a variety of office electronics products, such as telephones, printers, desktop computers, and copiers. One division specializes in the production of microchips that serve as the "electronic brains" for many of the firm's final products, including copiers, laser printers, and facsimile machines. For the time being, we assume there is no outside market for the firm's specialty chips; they are produced only for use in the firm's final products. (We relax this assumption in the following section.) What transfer price per unit should the chip division charge the copier (or any other) division?

The answer to this question is that *the firm should set the internal transfer price for the microchip exactly equal to its marginal cost of production.* Figure 6A.1 summarizes the demand and cost conditions associated with the production of copiers. The key point about the figure is understanding the "full" marginal cost of producing copiers. Managers of the copier division are well aware of the direct costs they incur in assembly. This marginal cost is shown as the upward-sloping MC_A curve in the figure. In addition, we must consider the marginal cost of producing the chips that are used in the copier. In Figure 6A.1, this marginal cost (labeled MC_M) is superimposed on the MC_A curve. The total marginal cost of producing copiers is the sum of the chip cost and the assembly cost. In the figure, this total marginal cost curve is denoted by $MC_T = MC_A + MC_M$ and is drawn as the vertical sum of the two curves. The firm maximizes the total profit it earns on copiers by setting the quantity such that marginal revenue equals total marginal

FIGURE 6A.1

Transfer Pricing

In the absence of an external market, the optimal transfer price for an intermediate product equals the item's marginal cost of production. Optimal output of the firm's final product occurs at Q*, where MR equals MC$_T$. Here MC$_T$ includes the intermediate good's transfer price.

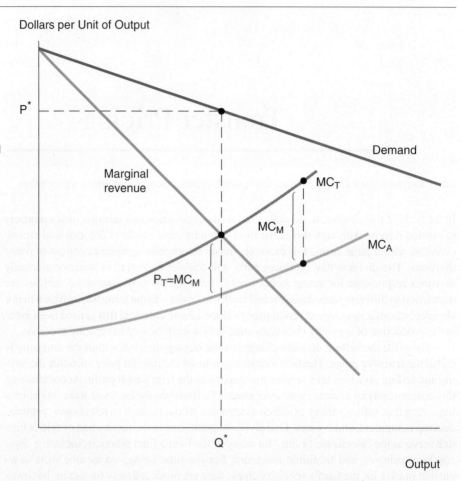

cost, $MR = MC_T$. In Figure 6A.1, the optimal quantity occurs at Q^*, and the associated optimal selling price for the copier is P^*. What transfer price for chips will lead to this outcome? The appropriate transfer price should be set at $P_T = MC_M$. By paying this transfer price, the copier division incurs an additional cost of $MC_A + P_T = MC_A + MC_M$ for each extra copier it produces. By taking into account the true "full" cost of producing additional output, the copier division automatically maximizes the firm's total profit.

A MARKET FOR CHIPS   If there is an external market in which microchips can be bought and sold, the profit-maximizing analysis must be modified. In this case, *the firm should set the internal transfer price for the microchip equal to the prevailing market price.* The reasoning is straightforward. Let $P°$ denote the prevailing market price. Obviously, the chip division cannot charge the copier division a transfer price that exceeds $P°$; the copier division would simply opt to buy chips from the outside market. Nor would the chip division be satisfied with a transfer price below $P°$; it would prefer to produce and sell chips exclusively for the outside market. Consequently, $P_T = P^\circ$ is the only price at which internal transfers will occur.

Here is another way to arrive at this conclusion. The correct price to impute to internally produced chips should reflect the firm's true opportunity cost. Each chip that goes into the "guts" of the firm's copiers is a chip that could have been sold on the outside market at price P°. Since it is this market price that the firm gives up, the internal transfer price should be set accordingly.

Transfer Pricing: A Numerical Example   Let the demand for copiers be given by $P = 4{,}000 - 3Q$, where Q is the number of copiers demanded per week and P is the price in dollars. The total cost of assembling copiers (excluding the cost of microchips) is given by $C_A = 360{,}000 + 1{,}000Q$. The cost of producing microchips is $C_M = 40{,}000 + 200Q_M + 0.5Q_M^2$, where Q_M is the quantity of chips. Suppose each copier uses *one* microchip. The total cost of producing copiers is $C_T = C_A + C_M = 400{,}000 + 1{,}200Q + 0.5Q^2$. In turn, the marginal cost of copiers is $MC_T = dC_T/dQ = 1{,}200 + Q$. Equivalently, $MC_T = MC_A + MC_M = 1{,}000 + (200 + Q) = 1{,}200 + Q$. Setting $MR = MC_T$ implies $4{,}000 - 6Q = 1{,}200 + Q$. The solution is: $Q^* = 400$ and $P^* = 4{,}000 - (3)(400) = \$2{,}800$. At a production rate of 400 microchips per week, marginal cost is $MC_M = 200 + 400 = \$600$. Thus, in the absence of an external market for microchips, the appropriate transfer price is $P_T = MC_M = \$600$. At an output of 400 chips, the average cost per chip is $AC_M = C_M/Q = 200{,}000/400 = \$500$. Thus, by selling its output to the copier division at $P_T = 600$, the chip division earns an internal profit of $(\$600 - \$500)(400) = \$40{,}000$ per week. The copier division's average total cost is $AC_A = C_A/Q + \$600 = \$2{,}500$ per copier. At $P^* = 2{,}800$, the division makes a profit of $\$300$ per copier, implying a total profit of $\$120{,}000$ per week. The combined profit of the divisions is $40{,}000 + 120{,}000 = \$160{,}000$.

Now, suppose an external market for chips exists and a chip's current market price is $P_M = \$900$. For each additional chip produced and sold, the chip division's marginal revenue equals $\$900$, the current market price. Setting $MR = MC$ implies $900 = 200 + Q_M$, where Q_M denotes the quantity of microchips. The solution is $Q_M = 700$. Next consider the copier division. The price it pays for chips is now $P_T = P_M = \$900$. Thus, its marginal cost (inclusive of the price of chips) is $MC_T = 1{,}000 + 900 = \$1{,}900$. Setting $MR = MC$ implies $4{,}000 - 6Q = \$1{,}900$. Thus, $Q^* = 350$ and $P^* = \$2{,}950$. To sum up, the chip division's total weekly output is 700 chips. Half of this output (350 chips) is transferred to the copier division; the other half is sold on the open market.

Questions and Problems

1. a. A senior manager argues that the chip division's main purpose is to serve the firm's final-product divisions. Accordingly, these services should be offered free of charge; that is, the transfer price for chips should be $P_T = 0$. Explain carefully what is wrong with this argument.

   b. Suppose the chip division treats the copier division as it would an outside buyer and marks up the transfer price above marginal cost. Explain what is wrong with this strategy.

2. In the numerical example, suppose the firm can purchase chips on the open market at a price of $300. What production decisions should the divisions make in this case?

CHAPTER 7

Perfect
Competition

Everything is worth what its purchaser will pay for it.

ANONYMOUS

LO#1. Review the basics of supply, demand, and market equilibrium.

LO#2. Describe the characteristics of perfect competition.

LO#3. Discuss the idea of market efficiency and its relationship to competitive markets.

LO#4. Explain why perfectly competitive global markets are efficient and why trade barriers reduce overall economic welfare.

**Betting
the Planet**

There has been an ongoing debate between economists and ecologists for the past 30 years about whether the world is running out of resources. (This is a renewal of a centuries-old debate that began with Malthus.) Many ecologists have argued that resources are limited and that economic growth and unchecked population increases are draining these resources (a barrel of oil consumed today means one less barrel available tomorrow) and polluting the environment. Leading economists have pointed out that the cry about limited resources is a false alarm. Technological innovation, human progress, and conservation have meant that the supply of resources has more than kept pace with population growth and can do so indefinitely. Living standards around the globe are higher today than at any time in the past.

One example of this debate was a bet made in 1981 between Paul Ehrlich, a well-known scientist, and Julian Simon, an eminent economist.[1] Simon challenged ecologists to pick any resources they wished and any future date. He then made a simple bet: The prices of the chosen resources would be lower at the future date than they were at the present time. With the help of economists and other scientists, Ehrlich selected five resources (copper, chrome, nickel, tin, and tungsten) for which he predicted increasing scarcity over the next decade. He hypothetically purchased $200 worth of each metal at 1981 prices. Then the two sides waited and watched price movements over the next 10 years.

What can the economics of supply and demand tell us about this debate (and this bet)? If the bet were to be made today, which side would you take?

---

[1]This account is based on John Tierney, "Betting the Planet," *The New York Times Magazine* (December 2, 1990), p. 52.

This chapter and the three that follow focus on the spectrum of industry structures. Markets are typically divided into four main categories: perfect competition, monopolistic competition, oligopoly, and pure monopoly. Table 7.1 provides a preview of these different settings by considering two dimensions of competition: the number of competing firms and the extent of entry barriers. At one extreme (the lower right cell of the table) is the case of perfect competition. Such a market is supplied by a large number of competitors. Because each firm claims only a very small market share, none has the power to control price. Rather, price is determined by supply and demand. As important, there are no barriers preventing new firms from entering the market.

At the other extreme (the upper left cell of the table) lies the case of pure monopoly. Here, a single firm supplies the market and has no direct competitors. Thus, as we shall see, the monopolist (if not constrained) has the ultimate power to raise prices and maximize its profit. Clearly, prohibitive entry barriers are a precondition for pure monopoly. Such barriers prevent rival firms from entering the market and competing evenhandedly with the incumbent monopolist.

Oligopoly (shown in the second row of Table 7.1) occupies a middle ground between the perfectly competitive and monopolistic extremes. In an oligopoly, a small number of large firms dominate the market. Each firm must anticipate the effect of its rivals' actions on its own profits and attempt to fashion profit-maximizing decisions in response. Again, moderate or high entry barriers are necessary to insulate the oligopolists from would-be entrants.

Finally, monopolistic competition (not shown in the table) shares several of the characteristics of perfect competition: many small firms competing in the market and an absence of entry barriers. In this sense, it would occupy the same cell as perfect competition. However, whereas perfect competition is characterized by firms producing identical standardized products, monopolistic competition is marked by product differentiation. In short, the two dimensions of competition shown in Table 7.1, although useful, do not do the full job in distinguishing different market structures.

TABLE 7.1

Comparing Market Structures

| | | Entry Barriers | | |
		High	**Moderate**	**None**
Number of Firms	**One**	Monopoly	Not Applicable	
	Few	Oligopoly		
	Very Many	Not Applicable		Perfect Competition

THE BASICS OF SUPPLY AND DEMAND

A thorough knowledge of the workings of supply and demand, and how they affect price and output in competitive markets, is essential for sound managerial decision making. In a perfectly competitive market, price is determined by the market demand and supply curves. We will consider each of these entities in turn.

The **demand curve** for a good or service shows the total quantities that consumers are willing and able to purchase at various prices, other factors held constant.[2] Figure 7.1 depicts a hypothetical demand curve D for shoes in a local market. As expected, the curve slopes downward to the right. Any change in price causes a movement along the demand curve.

The **supply curve** for a good or service shows the total quantities that producers are willing and able to supply at various prices, other factors held constant. In Figure 7.1,

FIGURE 7.1

Supply and Demand

The intersection of supply and demand determines the equilibrium price ($25) and quantity (8,000 pairs).

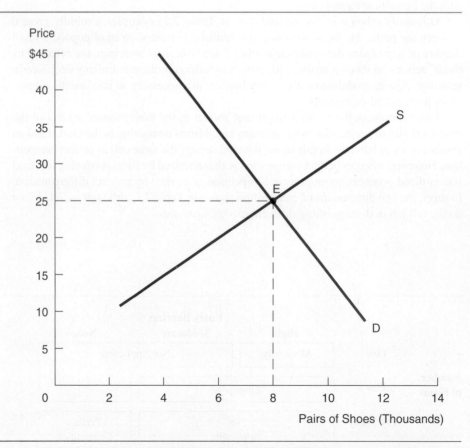

---

[2]In Chapters 2 and 3, we presented an extensive analysis of the demand curve facing an individual firm. In this discussion, we focus on total demand in the market as a whole. Except for this difference, all of the earlier analyses apply.

the supply curve for shoes (denoted by S) is upward sloping. As the price of shoes increases, firms are willing to produce greater quantities because of the greater profit available at the higher price. Any change in price represents a movement along the supply curve.

The **equilibrium price** in the market is determined at point E where market supply equals market demand. Figure 7.1 shows the equilibrium price to be $25 per pair of shoes, the price at which the demand and supply curves intersect. At the $25 price, the quantity of output demanded by consumers exactly matches the amount of output willingly offered by producers. The corresponding equilibrium quantity is 8,000 pairs. To see what lies behind the notion of demand–supply equilibrium, consider the situation at different prices. Suppose the market price were temporarily greater than $25 (say, $35). At this higher price, the amount of shoes firms supply would greatly exceed the amount consumers would purchase willingly. Given the surplus of supply relative to demand, producers would be forced to reduce their prices to sell their output. Price reductions would occur until equilibrium was restored at the $25 price. Similarly, if the price were temporarily lower than $25, consumer demand would outstrip the quantity supplied. The result would be upward pressure on price until the equilibrium price was restored.

If we augment the demand and supply graph with quantitative estimates of the curves, we can pinpoint equilibrium price and quantity more precisely. Suppose the market demand curve in Figure 7.1 is described by the equation

$$Q_D = 13 - .2P,$$

where Q_D denotes the quantity of shoes demanded (in thousands of pairs) and P is the dollar price per pair. Let the market supply curve be given by

$$Q_S = .4P - 2.$$

Then, if we set supply equal to demand ($Q_S = Q_D$), we have $13 - .2P = .4P - 2$, or $.6P = 15$; therefore, $P = 15/.6 = \$25$. Inserting $P = \$25$ into either the demand equation or the supply equation, we confirm that $Q_D = Q_S = 8$ thousand units.[3]

Shifts in Demand and Supply

Changes in key economic factors can shift the positions of the demand and/or supply curves, causing, in turn, predictable changes in equilibrium price and quantity. For example, suppose the local economy is coming out of a recession and that consumer incomes are rising. As a result, a greater quantity of shoes would be demanded even at an unchanged price. An increase in demand due to any non-price factor is depicted as a rightward shift in the demand curve. Shifting the entire curve means that we would expect an increase in the quantity demanded at *any* prevailing price.[4] Such a shift is shown in Figure 7.2a.

---

[3]The same answer would be found if we began with the curves expressed in the equivalent forms: $P = 65 - 5Q_D$ and $P = 5 + 2.5Q_S$. Setting these equations equal to one another, we find $65 - 5Q = 5 + 2.5Q$. It follows that $Q = 60/7.5 = 8$ thousand. Inserting this answer into either equation, we find $P = \$25$.

[4]It is important to distinguish between shifts in the demand curve and movements along the curve. The effect of a change in price is charted by a movement along the demand curve. (An increase in price means fewer units demanded, but the demand curve has not shifted.) By contrast, the demand curve shifts with a change in any *nonprice* factor that affects demand.

FIGURE 7.2

Shifts in Supply
and Demand

(a)   Price

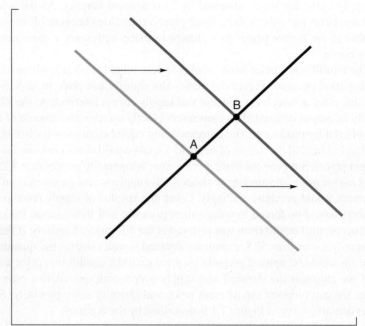

Quantity

(b)   Price

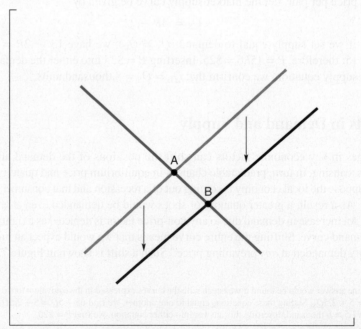

Quantity

What is the result of the shift in demand? We see from the figure that the new equilibrium occurs at a higher price and greater quantity of output. This is hardly surprising. The increase in demand causes price to be bid up. In the process, the amount supplied by firms also increases. The change from the old to the new market equilibrium represents a movement along the stationary supply curve (caused by a shift in demand).

Now consider economic conditions that might shift the position of the supply curve. Two principal factors are changes in input prices and technology improvements. For instance, increases in input prices will cause the supply curve to shift upward and to the left. (Any effect that increases the marginal cost of production means that the firm must receive a higher price to be induced to supply a given level of output.) Technological improvements, however, allow firms to reduce their unit costs of production. As a consequence, the supply curve shifts down and to the right. Such a shift is shown in Figure 7.2b. The result is a greater market output and a lower price. The favorable shift in supply has moved the equilibrium toward lower prices and greater quantities along the unchanged demand curve.

In 1999, the respective worldwide demand and supply curves for copper were: $Q_D = 15 - 10P$ and $Q_S = -3 + 14P$, where Q is measured in millions of metric tons per year. Find the competitive price and quantity. Suppose that in 2000 demand is expected to fall by 20 percent, so $Q_D = (.8)(15 - 10P) = 12 - 8P$. How much are world copper prices expected to fall?   **CHECK STATION 1**

COMPETITIVE EQUILIBRIUM

Perfect competition is commonly characterized by four conditions:

1. *A large number of firms supply a good or service* for a market consisting of a large number of consumers.

2. *There are no barriers with respect to new firms entering the market.* As a result, the typical competitive firm will earn a zero economic profit.

3. *All firms produce and sell identical standardized products.* Therefore, firms compete only with respect to price. In addition, all consumers have perfect information about competing prices. Thus, all goods must sell at a single market price.

4. *Firms and consumers are price takers.* Each firm sells a small share of total industry output, and, therefore, its actions have no impact on price. Each firm takes the price as given—indeed, determined by supply and demand. Similarly, each consumer is a price taker, having no influence on the market price.

It is important to remember that these conditions characterize an ideal model of perfect competition. Some competitive markets in the real world meet the letter of all four conditions. Many other real-world markets are effectively perfectly competitive because they approximate these conditions. At present, we will use the ideal model to make precise price and output predictions for perfectly competitive markets. Later in this and the following chapters, we will compare the model to real-world markets.

In exploring the model of perfect competition, we first focus on the individual decision problem the typical firm faces. Then we show how firm-level decisions influence total industry output and price.

Decisions of the Competitive Firm

The perfectly competitive firm is a **price taker;** that is, it has no influence on market price. Two key conditions are necessary for price taking. First, the competitive market is composed of a large number of sellers (and buyers), each of which is small relative to the total market. Second, the firms' outputs are perfect substitutes for one another; that is, each firm's output is perceived to be indistinguishable from any other's. Perfect substitutability usually requires that all firms produce a standard, homogeneous, undifferentiated product, and that buyers have perfect information about cost, price, and quality of competing goods.

Together, these two conditions ensure that the firm's demand curve is perfectly (or infinitely) elastic. In other words, it is horizontal like the solid price line in Figure 7.3a. Recall the meaning of *perfectly elastic demand.* The firm can sell as much or as little output as it likes along the horizontal price line ($8 in the figure). If it raises its price above $8 (even by a nickel), its sales go to zero. Consumers instead will purchase the good (a perfect substitute) from a competitor at the market price. When all firms' outputs are perfect substitutes, the "law of one price" holds: All market transactions take place at a single price. Thus, each firm faces the same horizontal demand curve given by the prevailing market price.

THE FIRM'S SUPPLY CURVE   Figure 7.3a also is useful in describing the supply of output by the perfectly competitive firm. It shows the cost characteristics of the typical firm in the competitive market. The individual firm produces output Q_F and faces a U-shaped, average cost curve (AC) and an increasing marginal cost curve (MC). (Recall that increasing marginal cost reflects diminishing marginal returns.)

Suppose the firm faces a market price of $8. (For the moment, we are not saying how this market price might have been established.) What is its optimal level of output? As always, the firm maximizes profit by applying the $MR = MC$ rule. In the case of perfectly elastic demand, the firm's marginal revenue from selling an extra unit is simply the price it receives for the unit: $MR = P$.

Here, the marginal revenue line and price line coincide. Thus, we have the following rule:

> A firm in a perfectly competitive market maximizes profit by producing up to an output such that its marginal cost equals the market price.

In Figure 7.3, the intersection of the horizontal price line and the rising marginal cost curve (where $P = MC$) identifies the firm's optimal output Q_F. At an $8 market

FIGURE 7.3

Price and Output under
Perfect Competition

Cost and Revenue per Unit

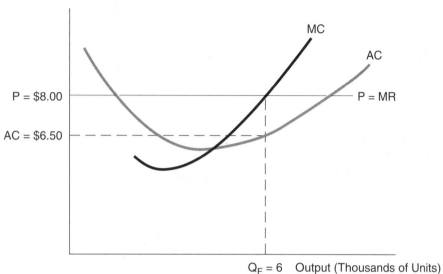

In part a, the firm
produces 6,000 units
(where $P = MC$) and
makes a positive
economic profit.
In part b, the entry
of new firms has
reduced the price to
$6, and the firm
earns zero economic
profit.

(a) A Competitive Firm's Optimal Output

Cost and Revenue per Unit

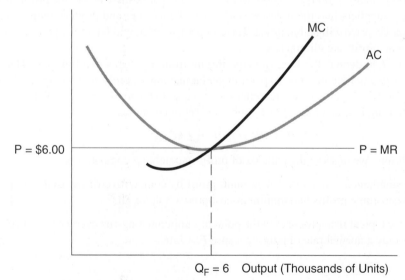

(b) Long-Run Equilibrium in a Competitive Market

price, the firm's optimal output is 6,000 units. (Check for yourself that the firm would sacrifice potential profit if it deviated from this output, by producing either slightly more or slightly less.) Notice that if the price rises above $8, the firm profitably can increase its output; the new optimal output lies at a higher point along the MC curve. A lower price implies a fall in the firm's optimal output. (Recall, however, that if price falls below average variable cost, the firm will produce nothing.) By varying price, we read the firm's optimal output off the marginal cost curve. The firm's **supply curve** is simply the portion of the MC curve lying above average variable cost.

CHECK STATION 2   The typical firm in a perfectly competitive market has a cost structure described by the equation

$$C = 25 - 4Q_F + Q_F^2,$$

where Q_F is measured in thousands of units. Using the profit-maximizing condition, $P = MC$, write an equation for the firm's supply curve. If 40 such firms serve the market, write down the equation of the market supply curve.

LONG-RUN EQUILIBRIUM   Perfectly competitive markets exhibit a third important condition: In the long run, firms can freely enter or exit the market. In light of this fact, it is important to recognize that the profit opportunity shown in Figure 7.3a is *temporary*. Here the typical firm is earning a positive economic profit that comes to: $\pi = (\$8.00 - \$6.50)(6,000) = \$9,000$. But the existence of positive economic profit will attract new suppliers into the industry, and as new firms enter and produce output, the current market price will be bid down. The competitive price will fall to the point where all economic profits are eliminated.

Figure 7.3b depicts the long-run equilibrium from the firm's point of view. Here, the firm faces a market price of $6 per unit, and it maximizes profit by producing 5,000 units. At this quantity, the firm's marginal cost is equal to the market price. In fact, long-run equilibrium is characterized by a "sublime" set of equalities:

$$P = MR = LMC = LAC_{MIN}.$$

In equilibrium, we observe the paradox of profit-maximizing competition:

The simultaneous pursuit of maximum profit by competitive firms results in zero economic profits and minimum-cost production for all.[5]

In short, the typical firm produces at the point of minimum long-run average cost (LAC) but earns only a normal rate of return because $P = LAC$.

---

[5]Remember that a zero economic profit affords the firm a normal rate of return on its capital investment. This normal return is already included in its estimated cost.

Market Equilibrium

Let's shift from the typical firm's point of view to that of the market as a whole. Figure 7.4 provides this marketwide perspective. The current equilibrium occurs at E, where the market price is $6 per unit (as in Figure 7.3b) and the industry's total quantity of output is 200,000 units. This output is supplied by exactly 40 competitive firms, each producing 5,000 units (each firm's point of minimum LAC). The market is in equilibrium. Industry demand exactly matches industry supply. All firms make zero economic profits; no firm has an incentive to alter its output. Furthermore, no firm has an incentive to enter or exit the industry.

In the perfectly competitive market described in Check Station 2, what is the equilibrium price in the long run? (*Hint*: Find the typical firm's point of minimum average cost by setting $AC = MC$.) Find the output level of the typical firm. Let industry demand be given by the equation $Q_D = 320 - 20P$. Find total output in the long run. How many firms can the market support?

CHECK STATION 3

FIGURE 7.4

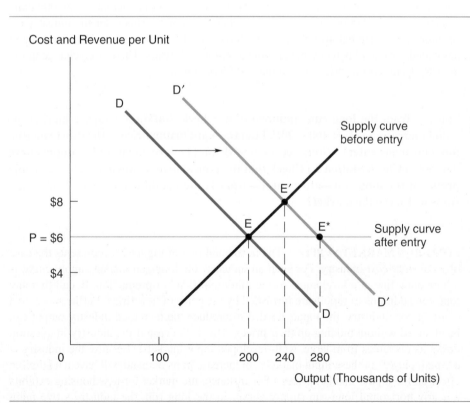

Cost and Revenue per Unit

Competitive Price and Output in the Long Run

An increase in demand from D to D' has two effects. In the short run, the outcome is E'; in the long run (after entry by new firms), the outcome is E*.

Now consider the effect of a permanent increase in market demand. This is shown as a rightward shift of the demand curve (from DD to D'D') in Figure 7.4. The first effect of the demand shift is to move the market equilibrium from E to E'. At the new equilibrium, the market price has risen from $6 to $8 and industry output has increased to 240,000 units. The higher level of output is supplied by the 40 incumbent firms, each having increased its production to 6,000 units. (According to Figure 7.3a, this is precisely each firm's profit-maximizing response to the $8 price.) The equilibrium at E' is determined by the intersection of the new demand curve and the total supply curve of the 40 firms currently in the industry. This supply curve also is shown in Figure 7.4 and is constructed by summing horizontally the individual firms' supply curves (i.e., marginal cost curves) in Figure 7.3. (Check Station 4 will ask you to derive the market equilibrium by equating demand and short-run supply.)

The shift in demand calls forth an immediate supply response (and a move from E to E'). But this is not the end of the story. Because the firms currently in the market are enjoying excess profits, new firms will be attracted into the industry. Price will be bid down below $8 and will continue to be bid down as long as excess profits exist. In Figure 7.4, the new long-run equilibrium result is at E*. Price is bid down to $6 per unit, its original level. At this price, total market demand is 280,000 units, a 40 percent increase above the 200,000 units sold at equilibrium E. In turn, industry supply increases to match this higher level of demand. How is this output supplied? With the price at $6 once again, each firm produces 5,000 units. Therefore, the total output of 280,000 units is supplied by 280,000/5,000 = 56 firms; that is, 16 new firms enter the industry (in addition to the original 40 firms). In the long run, the 40 percent increase in demand has called forth a 40 percent increase in the number of firms. There is no change in the industry's unit cost or price; both remain at $6 per unit.

CHECK STATION 4   **Starting from the long-run equilibrium in Check Station 3, suppose market demand increases to $Q_D = 400 - 20P$. Find the equilibrium price in the short run (before new firms enter). (*Hint*: Set the new demand curve equal to the supply curve derived in Check Station 2.) Check that the typical firm makes a positive economic profit. In the long run—after entry—what is the equilibrium price? How many firms will serve the market?**

LONG-RUN MARKET SUPPLY   The horizontal line in Figure 7.4 represents the case of a *constant-cost* industry. For such an industry, the long-run market supply curve is a horizontal line at a level equal to the minimum LAC of production. Recall that any long-run additions to supply are furnished by the entry of new firms. Furthermore, in a constant-cost industry, the inputs needed to produce the increased industry output can be obtained without bidding up their prices. This is the case if the industry in question draws its resources from large, well-developed input markets. (Because the industry is a "small player" in these input markets, an increase in its demand will have a negligible effect on the inputs' market prices.) For instance, the market for new housing exhibits a nearly horizontal long-run supply curve. In the long run, the industry's two main inputs—building materials and construction labor—are relatively abundant and provided by nationwide markets.[6]

For an *increasing-cost* industry, output expansion causes increases in the price of key inputs, thus raising minimum average costs. Here the industry relies on inputs in limited supply: land, skilled labor, and sophisticated capital equipment. For instance, if US drilling activity increased by 30 percent due to increases in world oil prices, let's say, the typical oil company's average cost per barrel of oil could be expected to rise, for a number of reasons. First, the increase in drilling would bid up the price of drilling rigs and sophisticated seismic equipment. Second, skilled labor (such as chemical engineering graduates), being in greater demand, would receive higher wages. Third, because the most promising sites are limited, oil companies would resort to drilling marginal sites, yielding less oil on average. For an increasing-cost industry, the result of such increases in average costs is an upward-sloping long-run supply curve.

MARKET EFFICIENCY

You might be familiar with one of the most famous statements in economics—Adam Smith's notion of an *invisible hand:*

> Every individual endeavors to employ his capital so that its produce may be of greatest value. He generally neither intends to promote the public interest, nor knows how much he is promoting it. He intends only his own security, only his gain. And he is in this led by an invisible hand to promote an end which was no part of his intention. By pursuing his own interest he frequently promotes that of society more effectively than when he really intends to promote it.[7]

One of the main accomplishments of modern economics has been to examine carefully the circumstances in which the profit incentive, as mediated by competitive markets, promotes social welfare. Here is a more precise statement: *Competitive markets provide efficient amounts of goods and services at minimum cost to the consumers who are most willing (and able) to pay for them.* The following example will explore the meaning of this proposition.

Private Markets: Benefits and Costs

The main step in our examination of market efficiency is the valuation (in dollar terms) of benefits and costs. We begin the analysis with a single transaction and move on to the thousands of transactions that take place within markets. Consider the following example.

---

[6]Here it is important to distinguish between long-run and short-run supply. In the short run, an increased local demand for new housing can bid up the wages of construction labor (and, to some extent, materials) until additional workers are attracted into the market. In addition, if available land is limited in rapidly growing metropolitan areas, its price may increase significantly.

[7]Adam Smith, *The Wealth of Nations* (1776).

THE DEMAND AND SUPPLY OF DAY CARE   A couple is seeking to obtain up to 10 hours of day care per week for their 2-year-old. Through informal inquiries in their neighborhood, they have found a grandmother who has done babysitting and day care in the past and comes highly recommended. Before any discussion has taken place, the couple has thought hard about their value for day care. They have decided that the maximum amount they are willing to pay is $8 per hour (that is, they would be indifferent to getting day care at this price and not getting it at all). In her own thinking, the grandmother has decided that her minimum acceptable price is $4 per hour. (Thus, $4 is the best estimate of her "cost" based on the value of her time and the strain of taking care of a 2-year-old. All things considered, she just breaks even at this price.) Can the couple and the grandmother conclude a mutually beneficial agreement? How can we measure the parties' gains from an agreement?

The answer to the first question clearly is yes. Any negotiated price between $4 and $8 per hour would be mutually beneficial. What about the second question? If the parties are equally matched bargainers, we might expect the final price to be $6. The grandmother makes a profit of $2 per hour, or $20 per week. Similarly, the couple makes a $2-per-hour "profit"; that is, they pay only $6 for a day-care hour that is worth $8 to them. Their "profit" per week is $20. The couple's gain (or any consumer's gain in general) is customarily labeled **consumer surplus.** Although it goes under a different name, the couple's gain is just as real (and here identical in amount) as the grandmother's profit.

Figure 7.5 makes the same point in graphical terms. The couple's $8 value is drawn as a horizontal demand curve (up to a maximum of 10 hours per week). The grandmother's $4 cost line and a $6 price line are also shown. The grandmother's profit is depicted as the area of the rectangle between the price and cost lines, while the couple's consumer surplus comprises the area of the rectangle between the value and price lines. The areas of the profit and consumer surplus rectangles are both $20. The total gain from trade—the sum of consumer surplus and profit—is shown as the area of the rectangle between the value and cost lines and comes to $40.

An agreement calling for 10 hours of day care per week delivers the maximum total gain to the parties together. For this reason, we call such a transaction *efficient.* In contrast, an agreement that called for only five hours of day care per week would furnish only $20 of total gain ($10 to each side). Although this agreement is better than nothing, it would rightly be labeled *inefficient* because it generates less than the maximum total gain. (More than 10 hours is infeasible because the grandmother is willing to supply 10 hours at most.)

We note two simple, but important, points about the efficiency concept. First, the actual price negotiated is *not* a matter of efficiency. An agreement calling for 10 hours of day care at a price of $7 (or at any other price between $4 and $8) would generate the same total profit, $40 per week. Of course, at $7 the total gain is redistributed. The grandmother's profit is $30 per week, and the couple's is $10. But the total gain has not changed.

Second, starting from any inefficient agreement, there is a different, efficient agreement that is better for both parties. In short, the best split of the proverbial pie for both parties is attained when the pie is made as big as possible in the first place. For

Now suppose the going price for day care is in fact $4 per hour, with the result that 8 million hours are purchased per week. What is the *total* consumer surplus enjoyed by purchasers? The answer is straightforward: Consumer surplus is measured by the triangle inscribed under the demand curve and above the price line. After all, the demand curve indicates what consumers are *willing* to pay, and the price line indicates what they *actually* pay, so the difference (added up over all units consumed) is their total surplus. Recall that the area of a triangle is given by one-half of its height times its base. Thus, the consumer surplus from 8 million hours demanded at a $4 price comes to $(.5)(12 − 4)(8) = 32 million.[11]

To complete the description of the market, let's consider the supply of day care. A day-care supply curve is shown in Figure 7.7. Notice that the main part of the supply

FIGURE 7.7

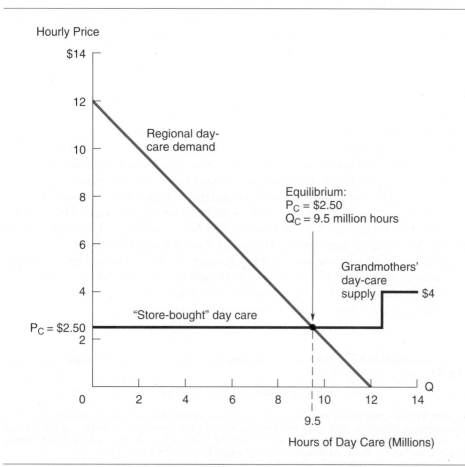

A Competitive Day-Care Market

The competitive price ($2.50) and output (9.5 million hours) are determined by the intersection of the supply and demand curves.

---

[11] An equivalent way to find consumer surplus is to reason as follows. The first unit consumed earns a surplus of $12 − 4 = 8$. The last (i.e., 8-millionth) unit consumed earns a surplus of $4 − 4 = 0$. Since demand is linear, the average surplus per unit is $(8 + 0)/2 = 4. We multiply this by 8 million units to arrive at a total surplus of $32 million.

curve is provided by low-cost suppliers at $2.50 per hour. Let's say these suppliers enjoy significant economies of scale while maintaining quality day care. In fact, as we shall see, less-efficient "grandmotherly" day care at $4 per hour will be priced out of the day-care market.

Now we are ready to take a closer look at market efficiency. To begin, we know that in a competitive day-care market, the intersection of supply and demand determines price and quantity. In Figure 7.7, the competitive price is $2.50 and quantity is 9.5 million hours per week. Now we can make our key point: *This competitive outcome is efficient; that is, it delivers the maximum total dollar benefit to consumers and producers together*. This is particularly easy to see in Figure 7.7, because day-care suppliers earn zero profits: Price equals average cost. All gain takes the form of consumer surplus. It is easy to check that the total surplus measures out to $(.5)($12 - $2.5)(9.5 \text{ million}) =$ $45.125 million.

An equivalent way to confirm that the competitive level of output is efficient is to appeal to the logic of marginal benefits and costs. We have argued that the height of the demand curve at a given output level, Q, measures the marginal benefit (in dollar terms) of consuming the last (Qth) unit. Similarly, the height of the supply curve indicates the marginal cost of producing the Qth unit. At a competitive equilibrium, demand equals supply. A direct consequence is that marginal benefit equals marginal cost. Equating marginal benefits and marginal costs ensures that the industry supplies the "right" quantity of the good—the precise output that maximizes the total net benefits (consumer benefits minus supplier costs) from production.

In contrast, at a noncompetitive price such as $4, only 8 million day-care hours would be demanded. At this reduced output, the marginal benefit (what consumers are willing to pay for additional day-care hours) is $4, and this is greater than the marginal cost of supplying extra hours, $2.50. Thus, there would be a net welfare gain of $4.00 - 2.50 =$ $1.50 for each additional day-care hour supplied. More generally, as long as the demand curve lies above the supply curve ($MB > MC$), there is a net gain ($MB - MC > 0$) from increasing the output of day care. Conversely, at any output level beyond the competitive quantity (say, 11 million hours), the marginal benefit of extra hours falls short of the marginal cost of supply ($MB < MC$). Producing these units is a "losing" proposition. Thus, there is a net gain from cutting output back to the competitive level.[12]

---

[12]In mathematical terms, consider the objective of maximizing the sum of consumer surplus and producer profit:

$$\text{Surplus} + \text{Profit} = (B - R) + (R - C) = B - C,$$

where B denotes the total consumer benefits associated with a given level of output, R is total revenue paid by consumers to producers, and C is the total cost of production. The revenue term is simply a transfer between consumers and producers and does not affect the objective. Thus, maximizing this sum is equivalent to maximizing net benefits, $B - C$. At the optimal level of output, it must be the case that $MB = MC$.

Furthermore, the competitive equilibrium achieves this optimal level of output. To see this, consider the demand and supply curves, denoted by the functions $D(Q)$ and $S(Q)$, respectively. The competitive price and output are determined by the intersection of supply and demand, $D(Q_C) = S(Q_C) = P_C$. By our earlier argument, $D(Q) \equiv MB(Q)$ and $S(Q) \equiv MC(Q)$ for all Q, where MB and MC denote the marginal benefit and cost functions, respectively. It follows that the price at which demand equals supply is also the price at which $MB(Q_C) = MC(Q_C) = P_C$. Thus, the combination of competitive price and output is efficient.

Figure 7.7 provides a visual depiction of our original proposition:

> Competitive markets provide efficient levels of goods and services at minimum cost to the consumers who are most willing (and able) to pay for them.

Think of this statement in three parts, focusing on production, consumption, and total output in turn. First, in a competitive market, the active firms are necessarily least-cost suppliers; all other higher-cost would-be suppliers are priced out of the market. (In our example, grandmothers cannot compete; "store-bought" day care is more efficiently supplied than "home-made.") The supply curve in Figure 7.7 is not drawn arbitrarily; rather, it describes the *lowest* possible costs of production. In this sense, *production is efficient.*

Second, competitive markets obey the "law of one price"; that is, all buyers and suppliers face the same price. In particular, this means that only consumers who are most willing (and able) to pay this price (i.e., those who reside on the highest portion of the demand curve) will actually end up with the goods. In this sense, *consumption is efficient.*

Third, given the market selection of minimum-cost producers and maximum-value consumers, the optimal output is achieved at the competitive intersection of supply and demand. Since $P_C = MB = MC$, it is impossible to alter output—above or below the competitive level—and increase net benefits. In this sense, *the level of output is efficient.*

What are the efficiency implications of a government program to provide universal, *free* day care?   **CHECK STATION 5**

DYNAMIC, MARKETWIDE EFFICIENCY   In our examination of competitive efficiency, we have focused on a *single* market and found that the efficient level of output occurs at the intersection of demand and supply, where $P_C = MB = MC$. Can this "invisible hand" result be extended to encompass at once all the innumerable markets in a modern economy? The generalization to multiple markets is more complicated than it might seem at first. When dealing with many markets, it is not quite correct to focus on them separately, one at a time. After all, demands for different goods and services in the economy are interdependent. Changing the price of one good affects not only its consumption but also the consumption of substitute and complementary goods. Given these interdependencies, can we draw any conclusions about the workings of private markets and economic efficiency?

Modern economic theory provides an elegant and important answer to this question: *If all markets in the economy are perfectly competitive, the economy as a whole is efficient; that is, it delivers an efficient quantity of each good and service to consumers at least cost.* In short, a system of competitive markets in which all goods and services and all inputs (including labor) can be freely bought and sold provides a solution to the economic problem of resource allocation.[13] Indeed, no matter how well intentioned, government measures that interfere with competitive markets can cause welfare losses.

---

[13]The proof of the "efficiency theorem" is beyond the scope of this book. It can be shown that a perfectly competitive economy is *Pareto efficient;* that is, it is impossible to reorganize the economy to make some economic agent (an individual or a firm) better off without making some other agent worse off.

A final virtue of competitive markets is that they are dynamically efficient; that is, they respond optimally to changes in economic conditions. If a new product or service can be supplied at a cost below the price that consumers are willing to pay, profit-seeking firms will create and supply a market where none formerly existed. If demand for an existing product rises, so will price, thus attracting new entrants and further supply. At the new equilibrium, the efficiency condition, $P = MB = MC$, will be restored. Alternatively, if costs decline, the efficient response is achieved via a fall in price, causing consumption to increase to a new, optimal level. Finally, markets encourage the pursuit of technological innovations. Firms have a continuous incentive to search for and adopt more profitable methods of production.

The "invisible hand" theorem—that perfectly competitive markets ensure maximum social benefits—is best thought of as a benchmark. Although many markets in the United States meet the requirements of perfect competition, notable cases of market failures also exist. Market failures usually can be traced to one of three causes: (1) the presence of monopoly power, (2) the existence of externalities, or (3) the absence of perfect information. In Chapter 11, we analyze each of these sources of market failure.

EFFICIENCY AND EQUITY   Finally, it is important to emphasize that efficient markets are not necessarily equitable or fair. The outcomes of competitive markets directly reflect the distribution of incomes of those who buy and sell in these markets. An inability to pay excludes many people from the economic equation. In trying to solve the problems of poverty, malnutrition, inadequate health care, and the like, the government has the responsibility of addressing equity issues (as well as efficiency issues).

Market Competition and the Internet

Is competition on the Internet one further step toward the textbook case of perfect competition?[14] The affirmative view holds that Internet competition, where consumers can easily find and identify the cheapest prices, should squeeze prices and profit margins to the bone. The early evidence suggests that the Internet can promote competition and efficiency in several respects. First, transacting online provides buyers and sellers much better information about available prices for competing goods. Clearly, the ability of customers to find better prices for standardized goods increases competition and induces more favorable prices. For instance, Internet prices for books and CDs tend to be 9 to 16 percent lower than traditional retail prices. New automobile prices are about 2 percent lower on average to buyers who enlist online comparison and referral services. Online insurance fees and brokerage charges are lower than charges for similar storefront products and services (and over time tend to exert downward pressure on storefront prices).

[14]For interesting discussions of market competition and the Internet, see J. D. Levin, "The Economics of Internet Markets." In D. Acemoglu, M. Arellano, and E. Dekel (eds.), *Advances in Economics and Econometrics*, Cambridge University Press, 2013; G. Ellison and S. F. Ellison, "Lessons about Markets from the Internet," *Journal of Economic Perspectives* (Spring 2005): 139–158; "A Perfect Market: Survey of E-commerce," *The Economist* (May 15, 2004), special supplement; E. Brynjolfsson, Y. Hu, and M. D. Smith, "Consumer Surplus in the Digital Economy: Estimating the Value of Increased Product Variety at Online Booksellers," *Management Science* (November 2003): 1580–1596; M. E. Porter, "Strategy and the Internet," *Harvard Business Review* (March 2001): 63–78; S. Borenstein and G. Saloner, "Economics and Electronic Commerce," *Journal of Economic Perspectives* (Winter 2001): 3–12; and R. E. Litan and A. M. Rivlin, "Projecting the Economic Impact of the Internet," *American Economic Review*, Papers and Proceedings (May 2001): 313–317.

Internet prices also display less dispersion than do retail prices. (However, online price dispersion persists. Competition is not so intense that all sellers are forced to charge the same market price.)

Second, the Internet increases the geographic range of markets and the variety of items sold in those markets. Hundreds of fragmented transactions are readily enlisted in unified markets. For example, a consumer could expend the time and effort to find a used copy of a John Grisham legal mystery by going to several bookstores and paying about $4.50 (half the new price in paperback). Or the consumer could use the Internet's unified used book market, where scores of the same title sell for about $3.50, shipping included. The important point is that unified markets directly increase overall economic efficiency. However, unified markets need not always imply lower prices. For instance, with numerous buyers seeking scarce copies of original Nancy Drew mysteries (dust jackets intact), the Internet price averages $20 to $30 per copy. By comparison, the rare buyer who is lucky enough to find the same book on a bookstore shelf might pay only $5 to $15. As always, the price effect of moving to a unified market depends on the relative increases in supply versus demand.

An additional key benefit of online markets is greater product variety. One research study discovered that some 45 percent of all books sold online at Amazon were "rare" titles (ranked below the top 100,000). Using fitted demand curves, the study estimated the associated consumer surplus for these purchases with dramatic results. Consumer surplus averaged about 70 percent of the purchase price of each rare title. In total, the ability to find a wide variety of rare books was worth about $1 billion in 2000. By comparison, Amazon's low prices saved consumers about $100 million. Item variety proved to be worth 10 times more than price reductions.

Third, in many important instances, a firm's use of the Internet lowers costs: from finding and serving customers to ordering and procuring inputs, to lowering inventories. Selling online also reduces the need for bricks-and-mortar investments, and online promotion and marketing may take the place of a direct sales force. Specific examples of cost savings abound: The cost of selling an airline ticket online is $20 cheaper than the cost of selling through a travel agent. Online automobile sales reduce the need for dealerships and vehicle inventories. Online stock trades are much less costly than brokered trades. Just as important, the Internet lowers the internal costs of the firm—by serving as a platform for sharing and disseminating information throughout the firm and for better managing all aspects of the supply chain. Of course, each firm is constantly in pursuit of lower costs—via online initiatives or in any other areas—as a way to gain a competitive advantage over its rivals. However, if all (or most) firms in a given market successfully exploit e-business methods to lower unit costs, the upshot is that the entire industry supply curve shifts downward. In a perfectly competitive market, these cost reductions are passed on, dollar for dollar, in lower prices to consumers. In the long run, only the most efficient firms will serve the market and economic profits again converge to zero.

Fourth, by lowering barriers to entry, online commerce moves markets closer to the perfectly competitive ideal. The e-business environment frequently means a reduced need for capital expenditures on plant, equipment, and inventories as well as for spending on highly trained direct sales forces. Elimination or reduction of these fixed costs makes it easier for numerous (perhaps small) firms to enter the market and compete evenhandedly with current competitors.

What aspects of the online business environment are at odds with perfect competition? First, numerous e-business goods and services are highly differentiated. (They do not fit the standardized designation of perfect competition.) Differentiation allows the firm to raise price without immediately losing all sales. (Its demand curve is downward sloping, not horizontal.) For example, the firm can potentially command higher prices for ease of use, better customer service and support, faster shipping, and customized offers and services. Even in cyberspace, a firm's ability to earn positive economic profits depends on how well it differentiates its product and how effectively it establishes a strong brand name. Thus, a loyal customer of Amazon.com will continue to shop there for the ease, convenience, and product selection, even if prices are somewhat higher than at other sites. (Moreover, information goods usually exhibit high switching costs: Consumers are reluctant to learn to use a new software system or to navigate through an unfamiliar website.) Second, network externalities and economies of scale confer market power. The firm with the largest user network (e.g., Google in search, Microsoft in PC operating systems, eBay in online auctions, America Online in instant messaging, Oracle in database software) will claim increasing market share and be able to command premium prices. In addition, the presence of economies of scale (due to high fixed costs and low marginal costs) means that market leaders (such as Google and Apple's iTunes) will command a significant average-cost advantage relative to smaller rivals. All of these factors create barriers to entry, preventing new rivals from penetrating the market. Thus, shielded from price competition, the market leaders are able to earn positive economic profits.

Although e-business offers obvious avenues for increased competition, it does not eliminate the potential for claiming and exploiting market power in a number of traditional ways. As management expert Michael Porter puts it, "Because the Internet tends to weaken industry profitability, it is more important than ever for companies to distinguish themselves through strategy."

INTERNATIONAL TRADE

As noted in Chapter 6, international trade is based on mutually beneficial specialization among countries, that is, on comparative advantage. The final section of this chapter underscores two additional points. First, when free trade is the norm, patterns of trade follow the rules of worldwide supply and demand. If a country's demand outstrips its available supply, it will make up the difference via imports from the rest of the world. Second, the proposition that competitive markets are efficient applies not only to individual markets within a nation but also to all global markets. Free trade is the basis for worldwide efficient production. When nations erect trade barriers, economic welfare is diminished.

To see why perfectly competitive global markets are efficient, we use exactly the same arguments as before. Under free trade, firms from all over the world compete for sales to consumers of different nations. Free competition means that the good in question will sell at a single world price (net of transport costs). Only the most efficient lowest-cost firms will supply the good. Only consumers willing and able to pay the world price will purchase the good. Finally, exactly the right amount of the good will be supplied and consumed worldwide. In competitive equilibrium, global output occurs at a quantity such that $P = MB = MC$. The quantity of output is efficient. In a nutshell, this is the efficiency argument for free trade.

Tariffs and Quotas

In reality, however, worldwide trade is far from free. Traditionally, nations have erected trade barriers to limit the quantities of imports from other countries. Most commonly, these import restrictions have taken the form of tariffs, that is, taxes on foreign goods, or direct quotas. The usual rationale for this is to protect particular industries and their workers from foreign competition. Since World War II, the industrialized nations of the world have pushed for reductions in all kinds of trade barriers. Under the General Agreement on Tariffs and Trade (GATT), member nations meet periodically to negotiate reciprocal cuts in tariffs.

Although there are a number of strategic reasons why a country might hope to profit from trade barriers, the larger problem is the efficiency harm imposed by these restrictions. To illustrate this point, we return to the digital watch example introduced in Chapter 6.

RESTRICTED TRADE IN WATCHES   Figure 7.8a depicts hypothetical US demand and supply curves for digital watches. Suppose that the world price is $12.50 per watch (shown in the figure by the horizontal price line at $P = \$12.50$). With free trade, the United States can import an unlimited number of watches at this price. At $P = \$12.50$, domestic demand is 25 million watches, which outstrips the domestic supply of 15 million watches. Therefore, the United States imports 10 million watches. In Figure 7.8a, the length of the line segment CD measures this volume of imports, the difference between US consumption and US production.

Now suppose the United States enacts trade restrictions prohibiting the import of watches altogether. Then, the no-trade equilibrium price would occur at the intersection of domestic supply and demand. In the figure, this price is $15, and total output is 20 million watches.

What is the net effect of prohibiting watch imports? Domestic watch producers benefit, while domestic consumers are harmed. We now show that the cost to consumers exceeds the benefit to producers, thus causing a net loss in the aggregate. To see this, note that the extra profit earned by domestic producers due to the price increase (from $12.50 to $15) is given by the area of trapezoid ABCE. (The extra profit lies between the old and new price lines and above the industry supply curve.) However, the increase in price has sliced into the total surplus of consumers. The reduction in consumer surplus is measured by trapezoid ABDE. (This is simply the area between the two price lines and under the demand curve.) When we compare trapezoids ABDE and ABCE, we see that consumer losses exceed producer gains by the shaded triangle ECD. This triangle measures the harm done to society, or the so-called deadweight loss attributable to the trade prohibition.[15]

---

[15]For more on deadweight loss, see the discussion of market failure in Chapter 11.

FIGURE 7.8

Trade Restrictions

Figure (a) shows a complete restriction on trade. Figure (b) shows a tariff.

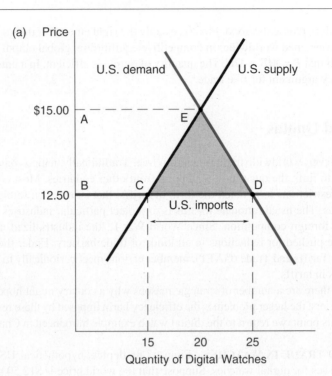

(a) Price

U.S. demand

U.S. supply

$15.00

A

E

12.50

B

C

D

U.S. imports

15   20   25

Quantity of Digital Watches

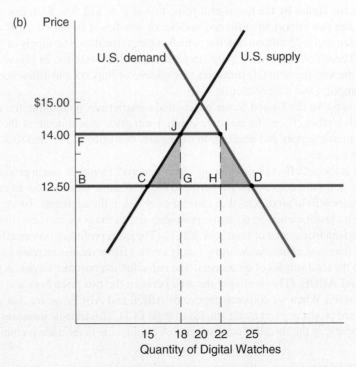

(b) Price

U.S. demand

U.S. supply

$15.00

14.00

J

I

F

B

C

G   H

D

12.50

15   18 20 22   25

Quantity of Digital Watches

Figure 7.8b depicts the effect of a less dramatic trade restriction. In this instance, US trade authorities have imposed a 12 percent tariff on Japanese imports, raising the price of watches to $(1.12)(\$12.50) = \$14$. As shown in the figure, the tariff reduces total US consumption to 22 million watches, while increasing domestic production to 18 million watches. Thus, US imports are $22 - 18 = 4$ million watches. Although less extreme, the impact of the tariff is qualitatively similar to that of a complete trade prohibition. Compared to free trade, consumer surplus is reduced by trapezoid FBDI (the area between the two price lines). Producer profits are increased by trapezoid FBCJ. The trade authority also collects tariff revenue, given by rectangle JGHI, on the 4 million watches imported. Comparing the loss in consumer surplus to these twin gains, we see that the nation as a whole suffers a net loss measured by the areas of the two shaded deadweight loss triangles.

We make two final observations. First, a tariff is superior to the alternative of a quota that achieves an equivalent reduction in imports. A quota of 4 million units would have exactly the same result as the 12 percent tariff, except that it would raise no revenue. After eliminating the revenue rectangle JGHI, we find the total deadweight loss of the quota to be trapezoid CDIJ. Second, moves to higher and higher tariffs steadily diminish imports, increase deadweight losses, and ultimately raise little revenue. In this example, as the tariff is raised toward 20 percent, the price of watches approaches $15, and imports fall closer and closer to zero. Obviously, tariff rates that eliminate nearly all imports generate very little revenue.

Betting the Planet Revisited

Simon's bet rested on the simple economics of supply and demand. If ecologists were correct in their assertion that the world was running out of essential resources, then the prices of these scarce resources should rise. Based on his own research, Simon was confident that the ecologists were wrong and that resources would be more abundant tomorrow than today so that their prices would fall.

Who was right? When the bet was settled in 1991, the prices of all five metals had declined over the decade. The same quantities of the metals that were worth $1,000 in 1981 had a total market value of only $618 in 1991. The explanations? Increases in supply kept up with increases in demand; mining companies found new deposits and used more efficient methods to recover and refine ores; the metals often were replaced by cheaper substitutes; and the tin cartel collapsed and tin prices collapsed with it. Ehrlich wrote Simon a check for the difference between the prices then and now—$382 plus accumulated interest over the decade. Using price as the market test, the "boomster" had won his bet with the "doomster."

Of course, the result of such a bet hardly settles the larger debate about the depletion of resources.[16] Although supplies of many resources are more abundant

---

[16]For discussions of the resource debate, see J. Lahart, P. Barta, and A. Batson, "New Limits to Growth Revive Malthusian Fears," *The Wall Street Journal* (March 24, 2008), p. A1; J. Diamond, "What's Your Consumption Factor?" *The Wall Street Journal* (March 24, 2008), p. A19; and K. Arrow et al., "Are We Consuming Too Much?" *Journal of Economic Perspectives* (Summer 2004): 147–172; and P. Kedrosky, "Relitigating the Simon/Ehrlich Bet," Infectious Greed Blog (February 18, 2010).

now than in the past, this does not mean that resource supplies will outstrip demand indefinitely. Indeed, dramatic economic growth in the developing world has greatly raised demand for essential resources. The emergence of high-consuming middle classes in China and India means exponential increases in food consumption, automobile purchases, and energy use *per capita*. Higher living standards per capita constitute a greater demand on resources than population growth per se.

Are we entering an era of markedly higher resource prices and greater scarcity? The last few years have seen significant price increases for oil, food, and many commodities. Financial expert Paul Kedrosky points out that had the same bet been made in any year from 1994 on, Ehrlich—not Simon—would have been the winner. In no small part, the aforementioned surge in commodity demand by China, India, and other fast-growing emerging nations has contributed to commodity price increases. (This effect reflects the increased *value* of commodities as engines of growth, rather than a sign of increased scarcity.)

In the longer term, much will depend on (1) technological innovations that enable the extraction of greater output from limited resources, (2) success in finding substitutes for today's most important scarce resources, and (3) better management and conservation. No doubt some combination of alternative fuels, wind, solar, and nuclear power will take the place of oil and coal in global energy supplies. A greater concern is the increasing scarcity of water (often wasted because it is priced much too low) and arable land and the long-term risks posed by global warming. Thus, the resource debate continues.

SUMMARY

Decision-Making Principles

1. Whatever the market environment, the firm maximizes profit by establishing a level of output such that marginal revenue equals marginal cost.

2. In perfect competition, the firm faces infinitely elastic demand: Marginal revenue equals the market price. Thus, the firm follows the optimal output rule, $P = MC$. In long-run equilibrium, the firm's output is marked by the equalities, $P = MR = MC = AC_{MIN}$, and the firm earns zero economic profit.

3. Economic transactions are voluntary. Buyers and sellers participate in them if and only if the transactions are mutually beneficial.

4. Competitive markets provide the efficient amounts of goods and services at minimum cost to the consumers who are most willing (and able) to pay for them. Worldwide competition and free trade promote global efficiency.

Nuts and Bolts

1. In a perfectly competitive market, a large number of firms sell identical products, and there are no barriers to entry by new suppliers. Price tends toward a level where the market demand curve intersects the market supply curve. In the long run, price coincides with minimum average cost, and all firms earn zero economic profits.

2. The total value associated with an economic transaction is the sum of consumer and producer surplus. Consumer surplus is the difference between what the individual is willing to pay and what she or he actually pays.

3. For any market, the height of the demand curve shows the monetary value that consumers are willing to pay for each unit. Consumer surplus in the market is given by the area under the demand curve and above the market price line.

4. In equilibrium, a competitive market generates maximum net benefits. The optimal level of output is determined by the intersection of demand and supply—that is, where marginal benefit exactly equals marginal cost.

Questions and Problems

1. The renowned Spaniard Pablo Picasso was a prolific artist. He created hundreds of paintings and sculptures, as well as drawings and sketches numbering in the thousands. (He is said to have settled restaurant bills by producing sketches on the spot.)
   a. What effect does the existence of this large body of work have on the monetary value of individual pieces of his art?
   b. Might his heirs suffer from being bequeathed too many of his works? As the heirs' financial adviser, what strategy would you advise them to pursue in selling pieces of his work?

2. Consider the regional supply curve of farmers who produce a particular crop.
   a. What does the supply curve look like at the time the crop is harvested? (Show a plausible graph.)
   b. Depict the crop's supply curve at the beginning of the growing season (when farmers must decide how many acres to cultivate).
   c. Depict the crop's supply curve in the long run (when farmers can enter or exit the market).

3. Potato farming (like farming of most agricultural products) is highly competitive. Price is determined by demand and supply. Based on Department of Agriculture statistics, US demand for potatoes is estimated to be: $Q_D = 184 - 20P$, where P is the farmer's wholesale price (per 100 pounds) and Q_D is consumption of potatoes per capita (in pounds). In turn, industry supply is: $Q_S = 124 + 4P$.
   a. Find the competitive market price and output.
   b. Potato farmers in Montana raise about 7 percent of total output. If these farmers enjoy bumper crops (10 percent greater harvests than normal), is this likely to have much effect on price? On Montana farmers' incomes?
   c. Suppose that, due to favorable weather conditions, US potato farmers as a whole have bumper crops. The total amount delivered to market is 10 percent higher than that calculated in part (a). Find the new market price. What has happened to total farm revenue? Is industry demand elastic or inelastic? In what sense do natural year-to-year changes in growing conditions make farming a boom-or-bust industry?

4. a. In 2009, the Japanese beer industry was affected by two economic events:
      (1) Japan's government imposed on producers a tax on all beer sold. (2) Consumer income fell due to the continuing economic recession. How would each factor affect (i.e., shift) demand or supply? What impact do you predict on industry output and price?
   b. In 2011, the US trucking industry faced the following economic conditions: (1) At last, the US economy was recovering from a prolonged slump during which trucking had shrunk its capacity by 14 percent. (2) The government instituted new regulations imposing more frequent equipment inspections and restricting operators' daily driving hours. (3) Year over year, diesel fuel prices were up by 9 percent.
      For each separate effect, show whether and how it would shift the industry demand curve or supply curve. What *overall* impact do you predict on industry output (measured in total volume and miles of goods transported) and trucking rates?

5. The Green Company produces chemicals in a perfectly competitive market. The current market price is $40; the firm's total cost is $C = 100 + 4Q + Q^2$.
   a. Determine the firm's profit-maximizing output. More generally, write down the equation for the firm's supply curve in terms of price P.
   b. Complying with more stringent environmental regulations increases the firm's fixed cost from 100 to 144. Would this affect the firm's output? Its supply curve?

c. How would the increase in fixed costs affect the market's long-run equilibrium price? The number of firms? (Assume that Green's costs are typical in the market.)

6. In 2009, dairy farmers faced an (equilibrium) wholesale price for their milk of about 1 cent per ounce. Because of changes in consumer preferences, the demand for milk has been declining slowly but steadily since then.
    a. In the short run, what effect would the drop in demand have on the price of milk? On the size of herds of current dairy producers? Explain.
    b. If milk production is a constant-cost industry, what long-term prediction would you make for the price of milk and the number of dairy farms?

7. In a perfectly competitive market, industry demand is given by $Q = 900 - 15P$. The typical firm's total cost is: $C = 300 + Q^2/3$.
    a. Confirm that $Q_{MIN} = 30$. (*Hint*: Set AC equal to MC.) What is AC_{MIN}?
    b. Suppose 10 firms serve the market. Find the individual firm's supply curve. Find the market supply curve. Set market supply equal to market demand to determine the competitive price and output. What is the typical firm's profit?
    c. Determine the long-run, zero-profit equilibrium. How many firms will serve the market?

8. Firm Z, operating in a perfectly competitive market, can sell as much or as little as it wants of a good at a price of \$16 per unit. Its cost function is $C = 50 + 4Q + 2Q^2$. The associated marginal cost is $MC = 4 + 4Q$ and the point of minimum average cost is $Q_{MIN} = 5$.
    a. Determine the firm's profit-maximizing level of output. Compute its profit.
    b. The industry demand curve is $Q = 200 - 5P$. What is the total market demand at the current \$16 price? If all firms in the industry have cost structures identical to that of firm Z, how many firms will supply the market?
    c. The outcomes in part (a) and (b) cannot persist in the long run. Explain why. Find the market's price, total output, number of firms, and output per firm in the long run.
    d. Comparing the short-run and long-run results, explain the changes in the price and in the number of firms.

9. Demand for microprocessors is given by $P = 35 - 5Q$, where Q is the quantity of microchips (in millions). The typical firm's total cost of producing a chip is $C_i = 5q_i$, where q_i is the output of firm i.
    a. Under perfect competition, what are the equilibrium price and quantity?
    b. Does the typical microchip firm display increasing, constant, or decreasing returns to scale? What would you expect about the real microchip industry? In general, what must be true about the underlying technology of production for competition to be viable?
    c. Under perfect competition, find total industry profit and consumer surplus.

10. In a competitive market, the industry demand and supply curves are: $P = 200 - .2Q_d$ and $P = 100 + .3Q_s$, respectively.
    a. Find the market's equilibrium price and output.
    b. Suppose the government imposes a tax of \$20 per unit of output on all firms in the industry. What effect does this have on the industry supply curve? Find the new competitive price and output. What portion of the tax has been passed on to consumers via a higher price?
    c. Suppose a \$20-per-unit sales tax is imposed on consumers. What effect does this have on the industry demand curve? Find the new competitive price and output. Compare this answer to your findings in part (b).

11. The market for rice in an East Asian country has demand and supply given by $Q_D = 28 - 4P$ and $Q_S = -12 + 6P$, where quantities denote millions of bushels per day.
    a. If the domestic market is perfectly competitive, find the equilibrium price and quantity of rice. Compute the triangular areas of consumer surplus and producer surplus.
    b. Now suppose that there are no trade barriers, and the world price of rice is \$3. Confirm that the country will import rice. Find Q_D, Q_S, and the level of imports, $Q_D - Q_S$. Show that the country is better off than in part (a), by again computing consumer surplus and producer surplus.
    c. The government authority believes strongly in free trade but feels political pressure to help domestic rice growers. Accordingly, it decides to provide a \$1 per bushel subsidy to domestic growers. Show that this subsidy induces the same domestic output as in part (a). Including the cost of the subsidy, is the country better off now than in part (b)? Explain.

Discussion Question   Over the last 30 years in the United States, the *real* price of a college education (i.e., after adjusting for inflation) has increased by almost 80 percent. Over the same period, an increasing number of high school graduates have sought a college education. (Nationwide, college enrollments almost doubled over this period.) Although faculty salaries have barely kept pace with inflation, administrative staffing (and expenditures) and capital costs have increased significantly. In addition, government support to universities (particularly research funding) has been cut.

a. College enrollments increased at the same time that average tuition rose dramatically. Does this contradict the law of downward-sloping demand? Explain briefly.

b. Use supply and demand curves (or shifts therein) to explain the dramatic rise in the price of a college education.

Spreadsheet Problems

S1. In a perfectly competitive market, the cost structure of the typical firm is given by: $C = 25 + Q^2 - 4Q$, and industry demand is given by: $Q = 400 - 20P$. Currently, 24 firms serve the market.

a. Create a spreadsheet (similar to the given example) to model the short-run and long-run dynamics of this market. (*Hint:* Enter numerical values for the Price, # Firms, and Q_F cells; all other cells should be linked by formulas to these three cells.)

b. What equilibrium price will prevail in the short run? (*Hint:* Use the spreadsheet's optimizer and specify cell F8, the difference between demand and supply, as the target cell. However, instead of maximizing this cell, instruct the optimizer to set it equal to zero. In addition, include the constraint that $P - MC$ in cell F14 must equal zero.)

c. What equilibrium price will prevail in the long run? (*Hint:* Include cell C8, the number of firms, as an adjustable cell, in addition to cells B8 and B14, and add the constraint that total profit in cell G8 must equal zero.)

	A	B	C	D	E	F	G	H
1								
2				EQUILIBRIUM IN A PERFECTLY				
3				COMPETITIVE MARKET				
4								
5				The Industry				
6		Price	# Firms	Supply	Demand	D − S	Tot Profit	
7								
8		10	24	192	200	8	552	
9								
10								
11				The Typical Firm				
12		Q_F	MC	Cost	AC	P − MC	Firm Profit	
13								
14		8	12	57	7.13	−2	23	
15								
16								
17				SR: (1) D − S = 0 and (2) $P = MC$; Adjust: P & Q_F				
18				LR: (1) and (2) and (3) $P = AC$; Adjust: P & Q_F & #Firms				
19								

S2. The industry demand curve in a perfectly competitive market is given by the equation: $P = 160 - 2Q$, and the supply curve is given by the equation: $P = 40 + Q$. The upward-sloping supply curve represents the increasing marginal cost of expanding *industry* output. The total *industry* cost of producing Q units of output is: $C = 800 + 40Q + .5Q^2$. (Note that taking the derivative of this equation produces the preceding industry MC equation.) In turn, the total benefit associated with consuming Q units of output is given by the equation: $B = 160Q - Q^2$. (Total benefit represents the trapezoidal area under the demand curve. It is also the sum of consumer surplus and revenue. Note that taking the derivative of the benefit equation produces the original industry demand curve: $MB = 160 - 2Q$.)

  a. Create a spreadsheet similar to the given example. Only the quantity cell (C5) contains a numerical value. All other cells are linked by formulas to the quantity cell.

  b. Find the intersection of competitive supply and demand by equating the demand and supply equations or by varying quantity in the spreadsheet until *MB* equals *MC*.

  c. Alternatively, find the optimal level of industry output by maximizing net benefits (cell F9) or, equivalently, the sum of consumer and producer gains (cell F10). Confirm that the perfectly competitive equilibrium of part (b) is efficient.

	A	B	C	D	E	F	G
1							
2			EFFICIENCY OF				
3			PERFECT COMPETITION				
4							
5		Quantity	32		Price	96	
6							
7		Benefit	4,096		Con Surplus	1,024	
8		P = MB	96				
9					B – C	1,504	
10		Revenue	3,072		CS + Profit	1,504	
11		MR	32				
12					Profit	480	
13		Cost	2,592				
14		MC	72				
15							

Suggested References

Brock, J. R. (Ed.). *The Structure of American Industry.* New York: Prentice-Hall, 2013, especially Chapter 1.

This volume devotes separate chapters to describing the market structures of the major sectors in the American economy—from agriculture to banking, from cigarettes to beer, from automobiles to computers.

The following readings discuss Internet and e-commerce competition:

Levin, J. D. "The Economics of Internet Markets." In D. Acemoglu, M. Arellano, and E. Dekel (eds.), *Advances in Economics and Econometrics.* Oxford, UK: Cambridge University Press, 2013.

Borenstein, S., and G. Saloner. "Economics and Electronic Comm
3–12.

Brynjolfsson, E., Y. Hu, and M. D. Smith. "From Niches to Riches: Ana
Review (Summer 2006): 67–71.

For more on the debate about diminishing resources, see:

P. Sabin, *The Bet: Paul Ehrlich, Julian Simon, and Our Gamble over Earth's Future*,
Press, 2013.

Kedrosky, P. "Relitigating the Simon/Ehrlich Bet," Infectious Greed Blog (February 18, 201
kedrosky.com/archives/2010/02/.

The following book and articles provide readable treatments of competitiveness, free trade, and pro

Bhagwati, J. *In Defense of Globalization*. Oxford, UK: Oxford University Press, 2004.

Samuelson, P. A. "Where Ricardo and Mill Rebut and Confirm Arguments of Mainstream Economists Supp
ization." *Journal of Economic Perspectives* 18 (Summer 2004): 135–146.

"A Special Report: The World Economy, the Gated Globe." *The Economist* (October 10, 2013).

The best Internet sources for analyzing free trade are the writings of Professor Jagdish Bhagwati of Columbia University
http://www.columbia.edu/~jb38/.

Check Station Answers

1. Equating $Q_D = 15 - 10P$ and $Q_S = -3 + 14P$ implies $18 = 24P$. Therefore, $P = 18/24 = \$.75$ per pound. Given the drop in demand, we equate $12 - 8P = -3 + 14P$, implying the new price $P = \$.68$. Although demand has fallen 20 percent, price has declined by just some 10 percent.

2. Setting $P = MC$ implies $P = 2Q_F - 4$, or $Q_F = (P + 4)/2$. With 40 firms, the supply curve is $Q_S = 40Q_F = 40(P + 4)/2 = 20P + 80$.

3. To find the point of minimum average cost, we set $AC = MC$. This implies $25/Q + Q - 4 = 2Q - 4$, or $25/Q = Q$. After multiplying both sides by Q, we have $Q^2 = 25$ or $Q_{MIN} = 5$. Thus, each firm will produce 5 thousand units. In turn, $AC_{MIN} = 6$. Thus, the long-run price is also $P = \$6$. At this price, $Q_D = 320 - (20)(6) = 200$ thousand units. The requisite number of firms to supply this demand is $200/5 = 40$. (This exactly matches the number of current firms.)

4. From Check Station 2, the short-run supply curve is: $Q_S = 20P + 80$. Setting Q_D equal to Q_S implies $400 - 20P = 20P + 80$. Therefore, we have $P = \$8$. In turn, $Q_F = (8 + 4)/2 = 6$ thousand units and $Q_S = (40)(6) = 240$ thousand units. With price greater than average cost, each firm is making a positive economic profit. In the long run, $P = AC_{MIN} = \$6$, implying $Q_D = 400 - (20)(6) = 280$ thousand units, supplied by $280/5 = 56$ firms.

5. If day care is free ($P = \$0$), the outcome will be inefficient: Too much day care will be demanded and consumed. The marginal benefit of the last hours consumed will be nearly zero—that is, much less than the hours' marginal cost, $MB < MC$. (However, there may be beneficial distributional consequences.)

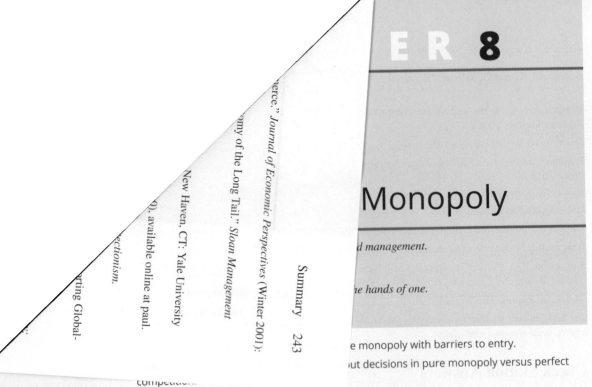

Monopoly

d management.

he hands of one.

e monopoly with barriers to entry.

ut decisions in pure monopoly versus perfect competition.

LO#3. Describe the characteristics and market results of monopolistic competition.

erce." *Journal of Economic Perspectives* (Winter 2001):

my of the Long Tail." *Sloan Management*

New Haven, CT: Yale University

0), available online at paul.

ectionism.

rting Global-

New York City's Taxicabs

Everyone has stories to tell, good and bad, about New York cabbies. However, the largely untold story is that New York's taxis (like those of most other major cities) are highly regulated. Minimum standards of service and fares are set by a city commission. Even more important, this commission directly limits the number of taxis via its licensing authority. By law, each authorized "yellow" cab must carry a medallion. The number of medallions has been nearly unchanged for 75 years. In 1937, the number for New York City was 11,787. This number increased only slightly until 2013 when the city sold 2,000 additional medallions at auction, bringing the total to slightly greater than 15,000.

The commission is caught in a continuous crossfire from consumer advocates, government officials, and representatives of taxi companies and drivers. Are fares too high or not high enough? Should additional medallions be issued, or would this be bad for the industry? Does the industry need tighter regulation, or is the regulatory burden already too great? How can competition be encouraged? Should new players such as Uber and Lyft be allowed to enter the local taxi market? As you read this chapter, think about the ways in which an economic analysis could be applied to address these questions.

PURE MONOPOLY

A **pure monopoly** is a market that has only one seller: a single firm. It is worth noting at the outset that pure monopolies are very rare. It is estimated that less than 3 percent of the US gross domestic product (the dollar value of all goods and services) is produced in monopolistic markets. (Here, a monopoly is defined as a market in which a single firm has 90 percent or more of the market.) Nonetheless, the case of pure monopoly is important not only in its own right but also because of its relevance for cases of near monopolies, in which a few firms dominate a market. The monopoly model also explains the behavior of cartels—groups of producers that set prices and outputs in concert.

There are two main issues to address in analyzing monopoly. First, one must understand monopoly behavior—how a profit-maximizing monopolist determines price and output. Second, one must appreciate that a precondition for monopoly is the presence of **barriers to entry,** factors that prevent other firms from entering the market and competing on an equal footing with the monopolist.

Monopoly Behavior

Let's start by considering a monopolist's price and output decision. Being the lone producer, the monopolist is free to raise price without worrying about losing sales to a competitor that might charge a lower price. Although the monopolist has complete control over industry output, this does not mean it can raise price indefinitely. Its optimal price and output policy depend on market demand. Because the monopolist *is* the industry, its demand curve is given simply by the industry demand curve. Figure 8.1

FIGURE 8.1

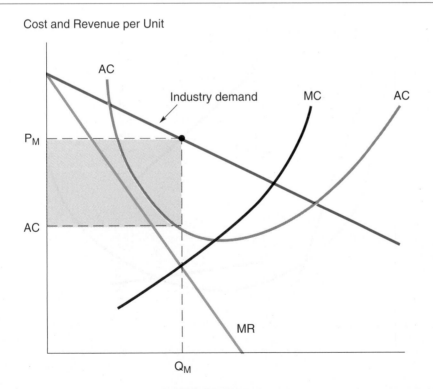

A Monopolist's Optimal Price and Output

The monopolist maximizes its profit by producing an output such that *MR* equals *MC.*

depicts the industry demand curve and long-run costs for the monopolist. Given information on demand and cost, it is straightforward to predict monopoly price and output. As a profit maximizer, the monopolist should set its output such that marginal revenue (derived from the industry demand curve) equals the marginal cost of production. In Figure 8.1, this output, Q_M, is shown where the monopolist's marginal revenue and marginal cost curves intersect. According to the industry demand curve, the corresponding monopoly price is P_M. The area of the shaded rectangle measures the monopolist's total excess profit. This profit is the product of the monopolist's profit per unit, $P_M - AC$ (the rectangle's height), and total output, Q_M (the rectangle's base).

We make two related remarks about the potential for excess profits under pure monopoly. First, monopoly confers a greater profit to the firm than it would earn if the firm shared the market with competitors. We have seen that economic profits in perfect competition are zero in the long run—not so for the monopolist. Second, even when the firm occupies a pure-monopoly position, its excess profits depend directly on the position of industry demand versus its cost. Figure 8.2 makes the point by depicting three different industry demand curves. It should be evident that only curve D_1 offers significant excess profits. Demand curves D_2 and D_3 offer very little in the way of profit possibilities. Although they differ with respect to elasticities, both curves barely exceed the monopolist's average cost. The lesson here is that pure monopoly enables the firm to

FIGURE 8.2

Possible Industry
Demand Curves

The industry demand
curve facing a
monopolist might be
D_1, D_2, or D_3. Only
the former curve
affords the
opportunity for
significant economic
profits.

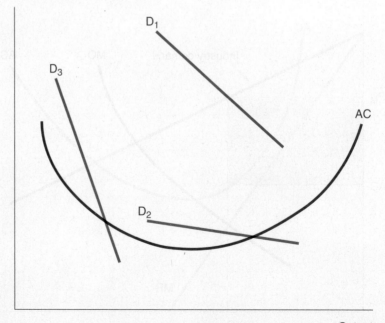

Dollars per Unit of Output

earn excess profit, but the actual size of this profit depends on a comparison of demand and cost. For instance, if other goods or services are close substitutes for the monopolist's product, industry demand may be relatively elastic and afford relatively little excess profit (curve D_2). If it is to increase its profit substantially, the monopolist must find a way to lower its average cost of production or to raise market demand. (Of course, there may be no demand at all for the monopolist's unique product. The US Patent Office overflows with "unique" inventions that have never earned a dime.)

A common measure of monopoly power is given by the Lerner index, defined as $L = (P_M - MC)/P_M$, where P_M denotes the monopolist's price and MC is marginal cost. For a profit-maximizing monopolist, how does the Lerner index depend on the elasticity of industry demand? (*Hint*: Recall the price-markup rule of Chapter 3.) What do you see as the advantages and disadvantages of using the Lerner index as a measure of monopoly power? **CHECK STATION 1**

Barriers to Entry

A **barrier** is any factor that blocks or impedes entry of new firms into a particular market. There are numerous kinds of barriers to entry that are more or less important, depending on the market under consideration. In some cases, one or more of these barriers are sufficient to support a single dominant firm in the market. In others, entry barriers are not absolute but limit the market to a small number of firms. It is also useful to speak of *barriers to competition*—that is, factors that, while not precluding rivals from the market, insulate a given firm from direct competition. Sources of entry barriers include the following.

ECONOMIES OF SCALE   When average cost falls significantly with increases in scale, a new firm must enter the market with a large market share to be competitive. If this addition to industry output requires a significant drop in market price, entry will be unprofitable. In so-called natural monopolies, average cost continually decreases with output, implying that a single firm achieves the lowest possible unit cost by supplying the entire market. For instance, it is cheaper for one company to lay a single network of cables to provide cable TV to a particular town or region.

CAPITAL REQUIREMENTS   In some industries (automobiles, defense, oil refining, deep-sea drilling), the capital requirements of production are enormous. In others (chemicals, pharmaceuticals, electronics), large investments in research and development are necessary. When large sunk costs are required, entry is particularly risky. (If, after entry, a firm finds itself suffering losses, it will be largely unable to recover its investment.)

PURE QUALITY AND COST ADVANTAGES   Sometimes a single firm has absolute quality or cost advantages over all potential competitors. Cost advantages may be due to superior technology, more efficient management, economies of scope, or learning. For these reasons, Intel dominates the market for microchips, Walmart is the world's leading chain of discount department stores, and Boeing and Airbus share the global aircraft market.

In many e-commerce markets, network externalities (making larger networks more valuable to customers) bestow an important quality advantage on the market leader (eBay in online auctions, for instance). Although there are many close substitutes, Coca-Cola continues to guard the secret for its best-selling soft drink. In the 1980s and 1990s, the Department of Defense used sole-source procurements to purchase major weapon systems, claiming that only a single qualified supplier existed. A dramatic expression of the monetary return to "being the best" is the annual income of a "superstar" such as Tiger Woods, LeBron James, Lady Gaga, George Clooney, or Angelina Jolie.

PRODUCT DIFFERENTIATION   Once an incumbent has created a preference for a unique product or brand name via advertising and marketing campaigns, it has erected considerable barriers to new entrants that seek to compete for its customers. Producers of retail goods and services thrive on product differentiation, real or perceived. Differentiation is the norm in products ranging from soft drinks to ready-to-eat breakfast cereals to toothpaste. *Switching costs* can be an important barrier to competition in markets for information-intensive goods and services. When customers have invested in learning to use a particular software program, navigate a website, or set up online accounts, they are less likely to switch to competitive (perhaps even superior) alternatives. Google's continuing dominance in Internet search depends in part on the learning costs of changing to an alternative search engine.

CONTROL OF RESOURCES   A barrier to entry exists when an incumbent firm (or firms) controls crucial resources—mineral deposits, oil supplies, even scientific talent. At the local level, a retailer's choice location may provide protection from entry by would-be competitors. Ownership of unique items (fine art, antiques) confers a degree of monopoly power (albeit limited by the availability of substitutes). For instance, the price of a unique item at auction is determined by what the market will bear, not by competitive supply. The best-known examples of monopoly power based on resource control include French champagne, De Beers (diamonds), and OPEC (crude oil).

PATENTS, COPYRIGHTS, AND OTHER LEGAL BARRIERS   A patent grants the holder exclusive rights to make, use, or sell an invention for 20 years. A patent can apply to an idea, process, or system as well as to an invention. A copyright prohibits the unauthorized copying of a particular work. (Currently, there is considerable controversy concerning whether computer software qualifies for copyright protection.) Patents and copyrights constitute important barriers to entry in computing, machinery, electronics, publishing, pharmaceuticals, defense, and chemicals. In many instances (local utilities, cable television firms, vendors on state highways and in national parks), the government grants legal monopolies for extended periods of time.

STRATEGIC BARRIERS   Finally, the dominant firm (or firms) may take actions explicitly aimed at erecting entry barriers. Securing legal protection (via patent or copyright) is only one example. A monopolist may exercise *limit* pricing—that is, keep price below monopoly levels to discourage new entry. It may threaten retaliatory pricing. For the same reasons, it may engage in extensive advertising and brand proliferation, not because this is profitable in itself (it may not be) but to raise the cost of entry for new competitors. Finally, the monopolist may intentionally create excess productive capacity as a warning that it can quickly expand output should a new firm attempt to enter. We will reexamine strategic barriers in Chapter 10.

Intel Corporation is by far the most powerful and profitable producer of microchips in the world. In the early 1970s, Intel invented the microprocessor, the computer on a chip that serves as the "brain" of the personal computer. Since then, it has produced numerous generations of chips, each faster and cheaper than the last. Currently, it accounts for about 80 percent of chips used in PCs, a share mainly unchanged over the past decades. In advanced microprocessors, its market dominance is well over 90 percent. Thus, Intel holds a near monopoly in many parts of the microchip market.[1]

> **Intel's Monopoly**

Over the years, however, new competitors have increasingly pushed into Intel's markets. During the last 20 years, other chips have emerged as competitors in particular market segments: the Power PC chip shared by IBM, Motorola, and Apple, Hewlett-Packard's RISC chip, and Sun's SPARC chip, to name a few. The most formidable challenge has come from Advanced Micro Devices, Inc. (AMD), which succeeded in developing compatible microchips while avoiding Intel's patents. Today, AMD competes head-to-head with Intel in developing technologically advanced chips.

To protect its monopoly position, Intel's main strategy has been to invest in research and development (over $6 billion annual spending) in order to accelerate the pace at which it introduces new chips. Remarkably, the company has been able to keep pace with Moore's law, the prediction that the number of (ever shrinking) transistors fitted on a chip would double every 18 months, driving a doubling of computer power as well. Both Intel and AMD raised the 32-bit standard by introducing 64-bit chips. Both have split the computing chores among multiple cores (first dual, then quad cores) on the same chip, thereby increasing efficiency and reducing energy consumption. Intel relies on continuous innovation to keep a "monopoly" step ahead of the competition. The company knows that today's chip will quickly be challenged by competitors' clones, causing prices and profits to erode. Indeed, Intel expects today's best-selling chip to be displaced by the company's next and newest chip. As a company spokesperson put it, "We eat our young."

In response to competitive challenges, Intel has not been a quiet or complacent monopolist. It has invested in the "Intel Inside" marketing and advertising campaign aimed at convincing computer purchasers that its chip is superior to the clones. In its most threatened segments, the company has preserved market share by aggressively cutting chip prices, even on its most advanced chips. It has repeatedly entered into litigation to protect its patent rights. In one antitrust action, the European Commission found that Intel restricted competition by offering rebates to computer makers who used fewer AMD chips.

While Intel has been the successful master of new technologies, it has been unable to control the emergence of new chip markets. Intel is the market leader in producing chips that power large servers, but it is an "also ran" in the exploding market for chips

---

[1]This account is drawn from industry reports and Q. Hardy, "Intel Tries to Secure Its Footing beyond PCs," *The New York Times* (April 15, 2013), B1; R. Winkler, "Getting an ARM Up on Intel," *The Wall Street Journal* (March 17, 2011), B5; and N. Wingfield, "A Bruising Fight for Survival," *The New York Times* (July 29, 2013), p. B1.

used in mobile devices, where chips by AMD, Qualcomm, and ARM dominate the market. Indeed, Intel's family of powerful, but less power-hungry processors called Atom has claimed less than 5 percent of the mobile market. Thus, Intel finds itself at a strategic crossroads—monopolizing an ever-shrinking market for PC chips, while trailing in the exploding mobile market.

CHECK STATION 2   **What kinds of entry barriers helped to protect Intel's monopoly position? What actions did Intel take to impede market entry?**

PERFECT COMPETITION VERSUS PURE MONOPOLY

Recall from Chapter 7 that a perfectly competitive market delivers output to consumers at the lowest sustainable price. (If prevailing prices were any lower, firms would incur losses and leave the market.) In a pure monopoly, in contrast, a single firm is the sole supplier of a good or service. The monopolist uses its market power to restrict output and raise price.

The simplest way to compare and contrast the basic price and output implications for purely monopolistic and purely competitive industries is by means of a graph. Figure 8.3 displays demand and cost curves for an unspecified good or service. The industry demand curve D has the usual downward slope. For any given industry price, it predicts total industry-wide sales. The horizontal cost line S depicts the long-run unit cost of supplying different industry levels of output. The cost line reflects the fact that output can be expanded in the long run at a constant cost (at least for the range of output shown in the graph). We can now use these demand and cost facts to predict long-run price and output for a perfectly competitive industry versus the *same* industry organized as a pure monopoly.

Under perfect competition, industry price and output are determined at the intersection of the demand and supply curves. The total industry output is split among a large number of firms, each producing at a constant cost per unit. Competitive price and output are P_C and Q_C, respectively. Note that P_C is identical to the typical supplier's cost per unit; that is, the typical competitive firm makes zero economic profit. If the market price ever rises above unit cost, opportunities for positive economic profits will induce suppliers, including new entrants, to increase output. This supply influx will drive price back down to the unit cost level.[2]

Now suppose that the *same* industry is controlled by a single firm, a monopolist. Because the monopolist is the industry, its demand curve is simply D. The monopolist

---

[2]We have spoken of the "typical" firm as though all competitive firms were identical. Of course, this need not be literally true. Some firms may be more efficient producers and, therefore, have lower costs than the average firm. For instance, suppose one firm owns an input (say, a piece of land) that is twice as productive as the comparable inputs of other firms. Although we could view this as a cost advantage, the likelihood is that the productivity edge already is reflected in the price of the input. (Land that is twice as productive carries double the market price.) Thus, many seeming cost advantages disappear. Any that remain can be incorporated easily into the supply curve. The supply curve begins with the production of the lowest-cost producers and then slopes upward until a horizontal segment of typical cost producers is reached.

FIGURE 8.3

Perfect Competition
versus Pure Monopoly

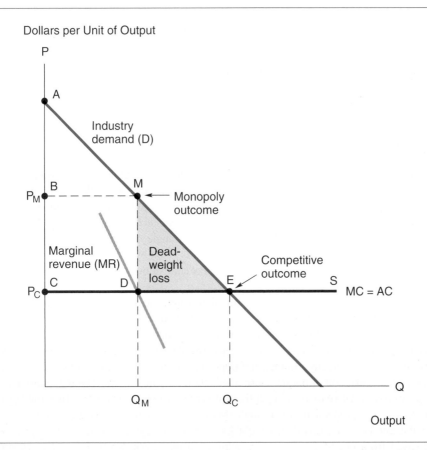

Dollars per Unit of Output

Under perfect
competition, market
equilibrium occurs at
point E, where supply
equals demand. If
the same industry
were controlled by
a monopolist, the
outcome would be
M. By restricting
output and raising
price, the monopolist
maximizes its profit.

can supply as much or as little output as it wishes at a constant unit cost given by S. What price and output will a profit-maximizing monopolist set? As always, marginal analysis supplies the answer: The firm will set output where industry-wide marginal revenue equals marginal cost. Figure 8.3 shows MR (derived from the industry demand curve in the usual way). The line S does double duty: Besides being a supply curve, it measures the monopolist's marginal cost curve. (The monopolist can produce additional units at this unit cost.) The monopolist's optimal output is Q_M (where $MR = MC$), and the required market-clearing price is P_M.

Figure 8.3 provides a graphical comparison of perfect competition and pure monopoly. Under competition, long-run price is driven down to the lowest sustainable level (where industry economic profit is zero). As a consequence, a competitive market delivers maximum benefits to consumers. In contrast, the monopolist has the opportunity to exercise market power, that is, to raise price above competitive levels. The monopolist does not set price and output capriciously. The key to maximizing monopoly profit is to restrict output to well below the competitive level and, in so doing, to raise price. The monopolist's optimal level of output occurs where marginal revenue equals marginal cost.

Note that monopoly output is always smaller than competitive output. In the figure, the intersection of MR and MC occurs to the left of the intersection of D and MC. Thus, we have the following summary comparison of perfect competition and pure monopoly:

$$P_M > P_C$$

$$Q_M < Q_C$$

and

$$(\text{maximum}) \ \pi_M > \pi_C = 0.$$

Competition delivers output at a minimum price and implies zero industry profits. Monopoly delivers maximum industry profits by limiting output and raising price.

Finally, the presence of monopoly represents a major deviation from the efficiency of perfect competition. In Figure 8.3, the net benefit attained under perfect competition is measured by the area of the large consumer-surplus triangle ACE. (Producers make zero economic profits because $P_C = AC$ in the long run.) By contrast, under pure monopoly, the monopolist raises price, thereby earning a pure economic profit (rectangle BCDM) but leaving a smaller triangle of surplus for the consumer (triangle ABM). Thus, under monopoly, the sum of consumer surplus and producer profit is given by the trapezoidal area ACDM, which is smaller than the total gains under perfect competition. The difference is measured by the triangle MDE.

The triangle MDE is referred to as the **deadweight loss** attributed to monopoly. The economic critique of monopoly is not simply that the firm gains at the expense of consumers when it elevates price. (In terms of total welfare, the firm's profit counts equally with the consumers' surplus. Indeed, consumers could well be shareholders of the monopolist and share in the profit directly.) Rather, the important point is that the monopolist's elevation of price and restriction of output cause a reduction in *total* welfare. The reduction in consumer surplus (relative to the competitive outcome) exceeds the excess profit earned by the monopolist. The deadweight-loss triangle (MDE) measures the size of the total welfare loss.

Put another way, this deadweight loss would be regained if market output were increased from Q_M to Q_C. For these additional units, *consumers' marginal benefits exceed suppliers' marginal costs.* Consequently, producing this output would increase social welfare. As we will see later in this chapter, the common government response to the case of "natural" monopoly is to regulate lower prices and increased output. Similarly, as will be noted in Chapter 11, the government undertakes a broad spectrum of antitrust initiatives to restrain or prohibit specific actions and behavior that would lead to monopolization of markets.

CHECK STATION 3   Suppose the industry demand curve in Figure 8.3 shifted up and to the right. What would be the effect on price, output, and profit under competition and under monopoly? Answer these questions again, supposing unit costs increased.

Cartels

A **cartel** is a group of producers that enter into a collusive agreement aimed at controlling price and output in a market. The intent of the cartel is to secure monopoly profits for its members. Successful maintenance of the cartel not only has an immediate profit advantage; it also reduces the competitive uncertainties for the firms and can raise additional entry barriers to new competitors.

In the United States, collusive agreements among producers (whether open or tacit) represent violations of antitrust laws and are illegal.[3] Some cartels outside the United States have the sanction of their host governments; in others, countries participate directly. The best-known and most powerful cartels are based on control of natural resources. Today, the Organization of Petroleum Exporting Countries (OPEC) controls about one-third of the world supply of oil. De Beers currently controls the sale of more than 90 percent of the world's gem-quality diamonds.

The monopoly model is the basis for understanding cartel behavior. The cartel's goal is to maximize its members' collective profit by acting as a single monopolist would. Based on the demand it faces, the cartel maximizes profit by restricting output and raising price. Ideally, the cartel establishes total output where the cartel's marginal revenue equals its marginal cost. For instance, if cartel members share constant and identical (average and marginal) costs of production, Figure 8.3's depiction of the monopoly outcome would apply equally to the cartel. The cartel maximizes its members' total profits by restricting output and raising price according to Q_M and P_M, where marginal revenue equals marginal cost.[4]

Output restriction is essential for a cartel to succeed in maximizing its members' profits. No matter how strong its control over a market, a cartel is not exempt from the law of demand. To maintain a targeted price, the cartel must carefully limit the total output it sells. Efforts to sell additional output lead to erosion of the cartel price. The larger the additions to supply, the greater is the fall in price and, therefore, the greater the decline in the cartel's total profit. This observation underscores the major problem cartels face: *Cartels are inherently unstable.* The reason lies in the basic conflict between behavior that maximizes the collective profits of the cartel and self-interested behavior by individual cartel members.

To see this, return to the cartel's optimal price and output, P_M and Q_M, in Figure 8.3. Suppose the cartel agrees to set total output at Q_M and assigns production quotas to members. The self-interest of each member is to *overproduce* its quota. The member can sell this additional output by cutting price very slightly. (Remember that one member's additional output is small enough to put little downward pressure on price.) What effect does this added output have on the member's profit? Figure 8.3 shows that the cartel price is well above marginal cost. Thus, even allowing for a slightly discounted selling price, selling the extra output is very profitable. Each member has an incentive to cheat on its agreed-upon output quota. But if all members overproduce, this behavior is self-defeating. If all members increase output (say, by 10 to 15 percent), flooding the market with extra output will have a significant downward effect on price. The total output of the cartel will be far greater than Q_M, price will fall below P_M, and the cartel's

[3]The law permits trade and professional associations; these organizations sometimes formulate and sanction industry practices that some observers deem anticompetitive. In the 1950s, widespread collusion among electrical manufacturers in contract bidding was uncovered and prosecuted.

[4]When costs differ across cartel members, there is more to determining the relevant marginal cost curve. To maximize profit, the cartel first should draw its production from the member(s) with the lowest marginal costs. As output increases, the cartel enlists additional supplies from members in ascending order of marginal cost. The cartel's marginal cost curve will be upward sloping and is found by horizontally summing the members' curves. This ensures that cartel output is obtained at minimum total cost.

total profit inevitably must drop. Thus, overproduction is a constant threat to the cartel's existence.[5] In the presence of wholesale cheating, the cartel may fall apart.

Business Behavior: The OPEC Cartel

The 12 member nations of OPEC meet twice a year to discuss the cartel's target price for crude oil and to allot members' production quotas.[6] Like a continuing drama with many acts, the OPEC negotiations center on (1) an assessment of the world demand for oil, (2) the appropriate limit on total OPEC supply, and (3) the division of this supply among cartel members.

Though recent oil prices have been sustained above $90 per barrel, OPEC has had a mixed long-term record in limiting its supply and maintaining high oil prices.[7] In the late 1990s, OPEC was largely successful in negotiating lower total output levels for the cartel (from 26 million down to 24.2 million barrels per day (mbd) and, therefore, maintaining high crude oil prices (a then-record high of $40 per barrel). However, the worldwide economic slowdown in 2002 and greatly increased supply by nonmember Russia contributed to falling oil prices. With OPEC members exceeding their quotas by an estimated 1 million total barrels per day, oil prices fell below $20 per barrel.

In the last decade, OPEC has prospered due to a combination of steadily increasing oil demand and limited supply. The surge in demand was led by the rapid economic growth in China and India and surprisingly strong consumption in the United States. Supply disruptions in Venezuela, Iraq, Iran, Libya, and Nigeria have contributed to supply shortfalls. In response to increasing demand, OPEC pursued a profit-maximizing strategy, raising its official supply quota from 24 mbd in 2003 to 26 mbd in 2005 and ultimately to 30 mbd in early 2008, where the quota remains today. Average crude oil prices climbed steadily, exceeding $40 per barrel in 2004, $60 per barrel in 2005, and $90 per barrel in 2007.

This growth in output and prices was abruptly interrupted by sharply curtailed worldwide oil demand, which caused oil prices to fall as low as $40 per barrel in 2009 and forced OPEC to slash its total production from 29.0 mbd to 24.8 mbd. Though worldwide demand has recovered, OPEC as a whole overproduced its quota by some 4 million barrels per day, holding oil prices at $80 per barrel in 2011.

Recent cartel discipline has boosted the oil price above $90 per barrel, but there are continuing challenges, including surprising increases in supply by non-OPEC producers including the United States, Canada, and Brazil. Iraq's production is also rebounding following the war. Venezuela and the poorer African members of OPEC insist on keeping prices high, while gulf state members worry about OPEC's falling global market share.

CHECK STATION 4   **Suppose that the demand curve facing OPEC is given by $P = 140 - 2Q$ and that each member's cost of producing oil is $AC = MC = \$20$. Find the cartel's profit-maximizing total output and price. If instead of keeping to this output, all members overproduced their quotas by 20 percent, what would be the effect on OPEC's total profit?**

[5]A related problem is that an oil producer is typically better off being outside the cartel, where it can take advantage of a high, cartel-maintained price without limiting its own output. Many oil producers, including Mexico, Malaysia, Gabon, Norway, Russia, and Egypt, support OPEC's initiatives while refusing membership.

[6] The 12 members of OPEC (in order of production) are Saudi Arabia, Iran, United Arab Emirates, Iraq, Kuwait, Venezuela, Nigeria, Libya, Algeria, Angola, Qatar, and Ecuador. Iraq, revovering from war, is not subject to the organization's quota.

[7]This synopsis is based on industry reports, OPEC's official communications, and on S. Reed and C. Krauss, "OPEC Leaves Production Quotas in Place," *The New York Times* (December 13, 2013), p. B2; and F. Norris, "Two Directions for the Prices of Oil and Natural Gas," *The New York Times* (February 26, 2011), p. B3.

Natural Monopolies

A **natural monopoly** occurs when the average cost of production declines throughout the relevant range of product demand. Utilities—water, electric power, gas, and telephone—typically fall into this category. Figure 8.4 shows a natural monopoly (say, in the generation of electricity) that displays steeply declining average cost.

Natural monopoly poses obvious difficulties for the maintenance of workable competition. First, it is costly and inefficient for multiple competing firms to share the market. A single firm can always produce a specified quantity of output—call this Q—at lower average cost than it could if the same total quantity were supplied by n firms, each producing Q/n. (Use Figure 8.4 to confirm this.) It is unnecessarily duplicative and costly for six local firms to make the large capital investment to supply electricity. With a facility of suitable capacity, a single firm is better suited to be the sole source of supply. Second, even if the market, in principle, could support more than one firm, the inevitable result would be the emergence of a single dominant monopolist. This is simply to say that any firm that increases output can achieve lower unit costs and so price

FIGURE 8.4

A Natural Monopoly

Regulators seek to implement average-cost pricing where the demand curve intersects the AC curve.

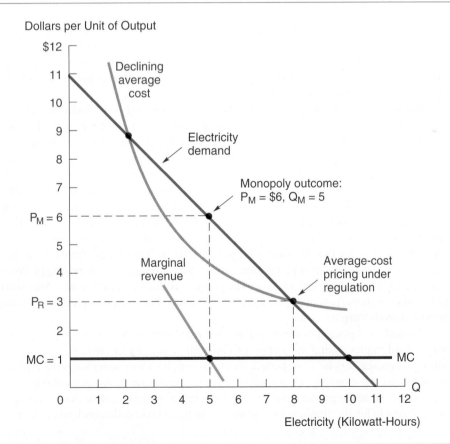

the competition out of the market. Thus, we would expect that the first firm to enter the market and expand its output will grow to control the industry.

Government decision makers play an active and direct role in the regulation of natural monopoly. The principal regulatory aim is to target industry price and output at the efficient competitive level. Let's use Figure 8.4 to display the natural-monopoly outcome, with and without price regulation. In the absence of any regulation (i.e., under a policy of laissez-faire), the firm acts as a pure monopolist. The resulting outcome is the price-quantity pair Q_M and P_M, where the firm's marginal revenue equals its marginal cost. Here the marginal benefit of the last unit consumed is equal to the monopoly price, which, of course, is well above the marginal cost of production. An increase in output from the monopoly level would improve welfare (since $MB > MC$).

The regulator can induce an increase in output by limiting the natural monopolist to a price that delivers a "fair" rate of return on the firm's investment. This is accomplished by instituting **average-cost pricing.** The appropriate price and quantity are determined by the intersection of the demand and average cost curves in Figure 8.4. At price P_R, the firm earns zero economic profit; that is, price exactly equals average cost, where AC includes a provision for a normal return on invested capital. Relative to the unregulated outcome, the lower average-cost-based price spurs a significant increase in output and, therefore, in welfare.

However, average-cost pricing does not exhaust the opportunities for welfare gains. At output $Q_R = 8$, the demand curve still lies above marginal cost; that is, $MB > MC$. Output should be expanded and price lowered. In fact, optimal price and output can be determined by the intersection of the demand and marginal cost curves. This outcome is referred to as **marginal-cost pricing** because it fulfills the efficiency condition $P = MB = MC$. Consumers are encouraged to purchase more output as long as their value exceeds the (low) marginal cost of production.

If marginal-cost pricing is efficient, why isn't it universally used? The practical difficulty with this pricing scheme should be evident. Price falls short of the firm's declining average cost, $P = MC < AC$, so the firm makes persistent losses. One way to maintain $P = MC$ while making good this loss is to have the government subsidize the decreasing-cost producer. (Government-owned utilities often follow this route, financing deficits from general tax revenues.) An alternative method is for the utility to institute so-called two-part pricing. Here, each customer pays a flat fee (per month) for access to output and then pays an additional fee, equal to marginal cost, according to actual usage. Thus, customers are encouraged to consume output at marginal cost. At the same time, the flat-fee charge allows the firm to cover average cost; that is, it covers the firm's large fixed costs. Though beneficial, two-part pricing is not a perfect remedy for the pricing problems associated with declining average cost. The problem is that the fixed fee may deter some potential customers from purchasing the service altogether, even though their marginal benefit exceeds marginal cost.

Average-cost pricing is the most common regulatory response, and it goes a long way toward implementing the virtues of competitive pricing in the natural-monopoly setting. However, it is far from perfect. First, the regulator/rate setter faces the problem of estimating the monopolist's true costs over the relevant range of potential output. At regulatory rate hearings, the natural monopolist has a strong incentive to exaggerate its average cost to justify a higher price. Imperfect or biased cost estimates lead to incorrect regulated price and output. Second, the regulated monopolist has a reduced incentive to minimize its cost of production. Indeed, if the regulatory agency were able to maintain $P_R = AC$ at all times, any cost change would prompt an equal price increase. The firm would have no economic incentive (although it might have a political one) to hold costs down. Interestingly, the presence of *regulatory lag*—the fact that prices are reset periodically, sometimes after long delay—bolsters the firm's cost-cutting incentives. In the typical case of escalating costs, the monopolist profits from cost-cutting measures during the period over which the regulated price is fixed.

Finally, critics of price regulation point out that over time, government intervention has spread into many areas that are a far cry from natural monopolies—trucking, airlines, and banking, for example. Furthermore, they point out that, by intention or not, regulation frequently reduces true competition: Regulated rates can hold prices *up* as well as down. In this sense, regulators can be "captured" by the firms over which they are supposed to exercise control, in effect maintaining a status quo protected from new competition. For instance, until the emergence of airline deregulation, the express purpose of the Civil Aeronautics Board (the governing regulator) was to fix prices and limit entry into the airline market. In the late 1970s, the CAB, under economist Alfred Kahn, changed course dramatically, freeing fares and allowing the entry of no-frills airlines. The result was the current era of significantly lower airfares.

MONOPOLISTIC COMPETITION

In perfect competition, all firms supply an identical standardized product. In monopoly, a single firm sells a unique product (albeit one that may have indirect substitutes). As the term suggests, **monopolistic competition** represents a mixture of these two cases. The main feature of monopolistic competition is *product differentiation*: Firms compete by selling products that differ slightly from one another. Product differentiation occurs to a greater or lesser degree in most consumer markets. Firms sell goods with different attributes (claimed to be superior to those of competitors). They also deliver varying levels of support and service to customers. Advertising and marketing, aimed at creating product or brand-name allegiance, reinforce (real or perceived) product differences.

Product differentiation means that competing firms have some control over price. Because competing products are close substitutes, demand is relatively elastic, but not perfectly elastic as in perfect competition. The firm has some discretion in raising price without losing its entire market to competitors. Conversely, lowering price will induce additional (but not unlimited) sales. In analyzing monopolistic competition, one often speaks of product groups. These are collections of similar products produced by competing firms. For instance, designer dresses would be a typical product group, within which there are significant perceived differences among competitors.

The determination of appropriate product groups always should be made on the basis of substitutability and relative price effects. Many, if not most, retail stores operate under monopolistic competition. Consider competition among supermarkets. Besides differences in store size, types of products stocked, and service, these stores are distinguished by locational convenience—arguably the most important factor. Owing to locational convenience and other service differences, a spectrum of different prices can persist across supermarkets without inducing enormous sales swings toward lower-priced stores.

Monopolistic competition is characterized by three features:

1. *Firms sell differentiated products.* Although these products are close substitutes, each firm has some control over its own price; demand is not perfectly elastic.

2. *The product group contains a large number of firms.* This number (be it 20 or 50) must be large enough so that each individual firm's actions have negligible effects on the market's average price and total output. In addition, firms act independently; that is, there is no collusion.

3. *There is free entry into the market.*

One observes that the last two conditions are elements drawn from perfect competition. Nonetheless, by virtue of product differentiation (condition 1), the typical firm retains some degree of monopoly power.

Let's consider the output and price implications of these conditions. Figure 8.5a shows a short-run equilibrium of a typical firm under monopolistic competition. Because of product differentiation, the firm faces a slightly downward-sloping demand curve. (If it raises price slightly, it loses some, but not all, customers to competitors.) Given this demand curve, the firm maximizes profit by setting its marginal revenue equal to its marginal cost in the usual way. In the figure, the resulting output and price are Q and P, respectively. Because price exceeds average cost, this typical firm is earning positive economic profits.

In a long-run equilibrium, the free entry (or exit) of firms ensures that all industry participants earn zero economic profits. Thus, in the long run, the outcome in Figure 8.5a is not sustainable. Attracted by positive economic profits, new firms will enter the market. Because it must share the market with a greater number of competitors, the typical firm will find that demand for its product will be reduced; that is, its demand curve will shift to the left.

Figure 8.5b shows the firm's new long-run demand curve. As in Figure 8.5a, the firm is profit maximizing. The firm's optimal output is Q_E, where marginal revenue equals marginal cost. However, even as a profit maximizer, the firm is earning *zero* economic profit. At this output, its price, P_E, exactly equals its average cost. In fact, the firm's demand curve is tangent to (and otherwise lies below) its average cost curve. Any output other than Q_E, greater or smaller, implies an economic loss for the firm.

A comparison of Figures 7.3 and 8.5 shows the close correspondence between the graphical depictions of monopolistic competition and perfect competition. The essential difference centers on the individual firm's demand curve—either downward sloping (reflecting differentiated products) or infinitely elastic (indicating standardized products that are perfect substitutes). In both cases, the long-run equilibrium is marked by the tangency of the demand line with the average cost curve. Under perfect competition, this occurs at the point of minimum average cost. In contrast, the typical firm in monopolistic competition (by virtue of its differentiated product) charges a higher price (one above minimum average cost) and supplies a smaller output than its counterpart in a competitive market.

FIGURE 8.5

Monopolistic Compe-
tition

Dollars per Unit of Output

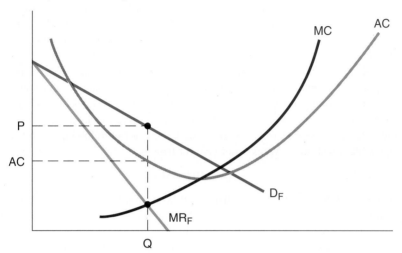

(a) The Firm Earns Excess Profit

In part (a), the firm
produces output
Q (where $MR = MC$)
and makes a positive
economic profit. In
part (b) the entry
of new firms has
reduced the firm's
demand curve to the
point where only a
zero economic profit
is available.

Dollars per Unit of Output

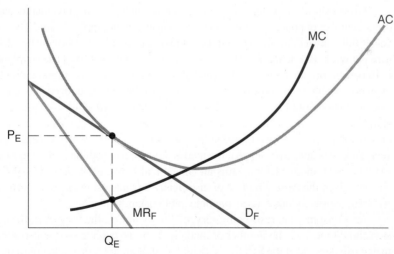

(b) Long-Run Equilibrium—The Firm Earns Zero Economic Profit

Over the last 75 years, New York City's taxi commission has kept the number of medallions (legally required to drive a taxi) nearly fixed. Currently, there are about 15,000 licensed cabs to serve a population of some 8 million. Cabs are never around when New Yorkers want them. Yet the market price of medallions (bought and sold weekly) is nearing $1 million. It would seem there is significant unfilled demand for taxi service and a substantial profit to be had from supplying it.

The New York taxi market is a classic case of a monopoly restriction on output—sanctioned and maintained by government regulation. Although there are economic grounds for government regulation in many aspects of this service (fare rates, safety and maintenance of cabs, conduct of drivers), an absolute restriction on entry does not appear to be one of them. Consider the following hypothetical, but plausible, illustration. Weekly demand for trips is

$$Q = 10 - .5P,$$

where Q denotes the number of trips in millions and P is the average price of a trip in dollars. The taxi meter rates currently established by the commission imply an average fare of $P = \$15$ per trip. The current number of licensed taxis is 15,000, and a taxi, if fully utilized, can make a maximum of 140 trips per week. The typical taxi's cost of carrying Q_t weekly trips is

$$C = 980 + 3Q_t.$$

This cost includes wages paid to the driver, a normal rate of return on the investment in the taxi, depreciation, and gasoline.

These facts allow us to prepare an economic analysis of the taxi market and to address a number of policy questions. Is there an insufficient supply of cabs? The answer is yes. If fully utilized, the current number of taxis can supply $(15,000)(140) = 2,100,000$ trips per week. But demand is $Q = 10 - .5(15) = 2.5$ million trips. (The supply shortfall is 16 percent of total demand.) Are medallion holders (fleet owners and individual taxi owners) earning excess profits? The answer is yes. For a fully utilized cab, the cost per week is: $980 + (3)(140) = \$1,400$. The average cost is $\$1,400/140 = \$10$ per trip. Thus, at full capacity, cab owners enjoy an excess profit of: $(\$15 - 10)(140) = \$700$ per week, or $\$36,400$ per year. A medallion entitles the owner to this excess profit each and every year. Thus, it is not surprising that the market value of a medallion is close to $1 million. (At this value, the medallion earns an annual real return of $36,400/1,000,000 = 3.64$ percent; given the current regime of historically low interest rates, this return is in line with real returns for other assets of comparable riskiness.)

Are consumer interests being served? Surely not. At the very least, the commission should increase the number of medallions by 16 percent so that trip supply can match trip demand at the $15 fare. Current medallion holders would continue to earn $700 excess profit per week (along with new holders), so they would feel no adverse effects. A far more dramatic policy change would be to do away with the medallion system and allow free entry into the taxi market by anyone who wishes to drive a cab. What would be the likely outcome of this deregulation? Attracted by excess profits, new taxis would enter the market. If fare regulations remained unchanged ($P = \$15$), the influx of taxis would mean fewer trips per taxi and zero economic profits for all taxis in equilibrium. Alternatively, the commission could set lower fares (say, $P = \$12$) in conjunction with free entry, allowing price to decline with the influx of supply. A third option would be to allow free entry and, at the same time, deregulate fares. Supply (augmented by free entry) and demand would then determine prevailing taxi fares—presumably at levels well below those set by regulation. Of course, completely free entry and unregulated fares would erode the economic profit associated with holding a medallion and, therefore, decrease the value of the medallion itself (in the extreme case, rendering it worthless).

In many cities today, the entrenched monopoly power afforded by limiting the number of licensed taxis is being challenged by a powerful new disruptive entrant, Uber, the high-tech startup that allows users to use a mobile app to find and summon the nearest affiliated car. It should not be surprising that incumbent owners of taxi fleets have mounted legal challenges to keep Uber from operating and disturbing the current medallion system.

SUMMARY

Decision-Making Principles

1. Whatever the market environment, the firm maximizes profit by establishing a level of output such that marginal revenue equals marginal cost.

2. A monopolist sets $MR = MC$, where marginal revenue is determined by the industry demand curve. The magnitude of monopoly profit depends on demand (the size and elasticity of market demand) and on the monopolist's average cost.

3. In monopolistic competition, the firm's long-run equilibrium is described by the conditions $MR = MC$ and $P = AC$.

Nuts and Bolts

1. Under pure monopoly, a single producer is shielded from market entrants by some form of barrier to entry. To maximize profit, the monopolist restricts output (relative to the competitive outcome) and raises price above the competitive level.

2. A cartel is a group of producers that enter into a collusive agreement aimed at controlling price and output in a market. The cartel restricts output and raises price to maximize the total profits of its members. The incentive for individual members to sell extra output (at discounted prices) is the main source of cartel instability.

3. A natural monopoly occurs when the average cost of production declines throughout the relevant range of product demand. Regulation via average-cost pricing is the most common response to natural monopoly.

4. In monopolistic competition, a large number of firms sell differentiated products and there are no barriers to entry by new suppliers. Because each firm faces a slightly downward-sloping demand curve, price exceeds minimum average cost.

Questions and Problems

1. In 2002, the *Atlanta Journal* and the *Atlanta Constitution*, once fierce competitors, merged to become the *Atlanta Journal-Constitution,* the only remaining daily newspaper in the city.
   a. Before the merger, each of the separate newspapers was losing about $10 million per year. What forecast would you make for the merged firms' profits? Explain.
   b. Before the merger, each newspaper cut advertising rates substantially. What explanation might there be for such a strategy? After the merger, what do you think happened to the *Atlanta Journal-Constitution's* advertising rates?
   c. What effect do you think the increased availability of online news sources has had on advertising rates?

2. A pharmaceutical company has a monopoly on a new medicine. Under pressure by regulators and consumers, the company is considering lowering the price of the medicine by 10 percent. The company has hired you to analyze the effect of such a cut on its profits. How would you carry out the analysis? What information would you need?

3. The ready-to-eat breakfast cereal industry is dominated by General Mills, Kellogg, Kraft Foods, and Quaker Oats that together account for 90 percent of sales. Each firm produces a bewildering proliferation of different brands (General Mills alone has over 75 cereal offerings), appealing to every conceivable market niche. Yet, the lowest brands on each company's long pecking list generate meager or no profits for the corporate bottom line. What strategic reasons might the dominant companies have for pursuing extreme brand proliferation? Explain.

4. Formerly, the market for air travel within Europe was highly regulated. Entry of new airlines was severely restricted, and air fares were set by regulation. Partly as a result, European air fares were and continue to be higher than US fares for routes of comparable distance. Suppose that, for a given European air route (say, London to Rome), annual air travel demand is estimated to be $Q = 1,500 - 3P$ (or, equivalently, $P = 500 - Q/3$), where Q is the number of trips in thousands and P is the one-way fare in dollars. (For example, 600 thousand annual trips are taken when the fare is $300.) In addition, the long-run average (one-way) cost per passenger along this route is estimated to be $200.
   a. Some economists have suggested that during the 1980s and 1990s there was an implicit cartel among European air carriers whereby the airlines charged monopoly fares under the shield of regulation. Given the preceding facts, find the profit-maximizing fare and the annual number of passenger trips.
   b. In the last 10 years, deregulation has been the norm in the European market, and this has spurred new entry and competition from discount air carriers such as Ryan Air and EasyJet. Find the price and quantity for the European air route if perfect competition becomes the norm.

5. Consider a natural monopoly with declining average costs summarized by the equation $AC = 16/Q + 1$, where AC is in dollars and Q is in millions of units. (The total cost function is $C = 16 + Q$.) Demand for the natural monopolist's service is given by the inverse demand equation $P = 11 - Q$.
   a. Determine the price and output of the unregulated natural monopolist.
   b. Suppose a regulator institutes average-cost pricing. What is the appropriate price and quantity?
   c. Answer part (b) assuming the regulator institutes marginal-cost pricing. What is the enterprise's deficit per unit of output? How might this deficit be made up?

6. Firm S is the only producer of a particular type of foam fire retardant and insulation used in the construction of commercial buildings. The inverse demand equation for the product is

$$P = 1,500 - .1Q,$$

where Q is the annual sales quantity in tons and P is the price per ton. The firm's total cost function (in dollars) is

$$C = 1,400,000 + 300Q + .05Q^2.$$

   a. To maximize profit, how much foam insulation should firm S plan to produce and sell? What price should it charge?
   b. Compute the firm's total profit.

7. Suppose that, over the short run (say, the next five years), demand for OPEC oil is given by the inverse demand curve: $P = 165 - 2.5Q$. (Here Q is measured in millions of barrels per day.) OPEC's marginal cost per barrel is $15.
   a. What is OPEC's optimal level of production? What is the prevailing price of oil at this level?
   b. Many experts contend that maximizing short-run profit is counterproductive for OPEC in the long run because high prices induce buyers to conserve energy and spur competition and new exploration that increases the overall supply of oil. Suppose that the demand curve just described will remain unchanged only if oil prices stabilize at $65 per barrel or below. If oil price exceeds this threshold, long-run demand (over a second five-year period) will be curtailed to: $P = 135 - 2.5Q$. OPEC seeks to maximize its total profit over the next decade. What is its optimal output and price policy? (Assume all values are present values.)

8. Consider once again the microchip market described in Problem 9 of Chapter 7. Demand for microprocessors is given by $P = 35 - 5Q$, where Q is the quantity of microchips (in millions). The typical firm's total cost of producing a chip is $C_i = 5q_i$, where q_i is the output of firm i.
   a. Suppose that one company acquires all the suppliers in the industry and thereby creates a monopoly. What are the monopolist's profit-maximizing price and total output?
   b. Compute the monopolist's profit and the total consumer surplus of purchasers.

9. Consider again the New York taxi market, where demand is given by $Q = 10 - .5P$, each taxi's cost is $C = 980 + 3Q_t$, and $AC_{MIN} = \$10$ at 140 trips per week.

   a. Suppose that, instead of limiting medallions, the commission charges a license fee to anyone wishing to drive a cab. With an average price of $P = \$15$, what is the maximum fee the commission could charge? How many taxis would serve the market?

   b. Suppose the commission seeks to set the average price P to maximize total profit in the taxi industry. (It plans to set a license fee to tax all this profit away for itself.) Find the profit-maximizing price, number of trips, and number of taxis. How much profit does the industry earn? (*Hint*: Solve by applying $MR = MC$. In finding MC, think about the extra cost of adding fully occupied taxis and express this on a cost-per-trip basis.)

   c. Now the city attempts to introduce competition into the taxi market. Instead of being regulated, fares will be determined by market conditions. The city will allow completely free entry into the taxi market. In a *perfectly competitive* taxi market, what price will prevail? How many trips will be delivered by how many taxis?

   d. Why might monopolistic competition provide a more realistic description of the free market in part (c)? In the resulting zero-profit equilibrium, suppose average price falls only to $12.80. At this price, how many trips would a typical taxi make per week? (Are taxis underutilized?) How many taxis would operate?

10. Firms A and B make up a cartel that monopolizes the market for a scarce natural resource. The firms' marginal costs are $MC_A = 6 + 2Q_A$ and $MC_B = 18 + Q_B$, respectively. The firms seek to maximize the cartel's total profit.

   a. The firms have decided to limit their total output to $Q = 18$. What outputs should the firms produce to achieve this level of output at minimum total cost? What is each firm's marginal cost?

   b. The market demand curve is $P = 86 - Q$, where Q is the total output of the cartel. Show that the cartel can increase its profit by expanding its total output. (*Hint*: Compare MR to MC at $Q = 18$.)

   c. Find the cartel's optimal outputs and optimal price. (*Hint*: At the optimum, $MR = MC_A = MC_B$.)

*11. a. When a best-selling book was first released in paperback, the Hercules Bookstore chain seized a profit opportunity by setting a selling price of $9 per book (well above Hercules' $5 average cost per book). With paperback demand given by: $P = 15 - .5Q$, and Q measured in thousands of books, the chain enjoyed sales of 12 thousand books per week. Draw the demand curve and compute the bookstore's profit and the total consumer surplus.

   b. For the first time, Hercules has begun selling books online—in response to competition from other online sellers and in its quest for new profit sources. The average cost per book sold online is only $4. As part of its online selling strategy, it sends weekly e-mails to preferred customers announcing which books are new in paperback. For this segment, it sets an average price (including shipping) of $12. According to the demand curve in part (a), only the highest-value consumers (whose willingness to pay is $12 or more) purchase at this price. Check that these are the first 6 thousand book buyers on the demand curve. In turn, because of increased competition, Hercules has reduced its store price to $7 per book.

      At $P = \$7$, how many books are bought in Hercules Bookstores? (Make sure to exclude online buyers from your demand curve calculation.) Compute Hercules' total profit. Then compute the sum of consumer surplus from online and in-store sales. Relative to part (a), has the emergence of online commerce improved the welfare of book buyers as a whole? Explain.

*12. Firm 1 is a member of a monopolistically competitive market. Its total cost function is $C = 900 + 60Q_1 + 9Q_1^2$. The demand curve for the firm's differentiated product is given by $P = 660 - 16Q_1$.

   a. Determine the firm's profit-maximizing output, price, and profit.

   b. Attracted by potential profits, new firms enter the market. A typical firm's demand curve (say, firm 1) is given by $P = 1,224 - 16(Q_2 + Q_3 + ... + Q_n) - 16Q_1$, where n is the total number of firms. (If competitors' outputs or numbers increase, firm 1's demand curve shifts inward.) The long-run equilibrium under monopolistic competition is claimed to consist of 10 firms, each producing 6 units at a price of $264. Is this claim correct? (*Hint*: For the typical firm, check the conditions $MR = MC$ and $P = AC$.)

   c. Based on the cost function given, what would be the outcome if the market were perfectly competitive? (Presume market demand is $P = 1,224 - 16Q$, where Q is total output.) Compare this outcome to the outcome in part (b).

*Starred problems are more challenging.

Discussion Question   Pharmaceutical companies can expect to earn large profits from blockbuster drugs (for high blood pressure, depression, ulcers, allergies, sexual dysfunction) while under patent protection. What is the source of these profits? Upon patent expiration, numerous rival drug companies offer generic versions of the drug to consumers. (The original developer continues to market the drug under its trade name and usually offers a second generic version of the drug as well.) Discuss the effect of patent expiration on market structure, pricing, and profitability for the drug.

Spreadsheet Problems

S1. Imagine that the perfectly competitive market described in Chapter 7, Problem S1, was transformed into a pure monopoly. (What were formerly independent small firms are now production units owned by the monopolist.) The cost structure of the typical unit continues to be given by $C = 25 + Q^2 - 4Q$, and industry demand is: $Q = 400 - 20P$ or, equivalently, $P = 20 - .05Q$. Currently, the monopolist has 30 production facilities in place.

   a. Create a spreadsheet similar to the example shown. Enter numerical values for cells B14 and C8; all other cells should be linked by formulas to these two cells.

   b. In the short run, the monopolist can change output level Q_F but cannot vary the number of production facilities. Use the spreadsheet optimizer to maximize the firm's short-run profit.

   c. In the long run, the monopolist can change output levels Q_F and the number of production facilities. Use the spreadsheet optimizer to maximize the firm's long-run profit.

	A	B	C	D	E	F	G
1							
2			Monopolist Controls				
3			the Market				
4							
5			The Industry				
6		Output	Plants	Price	MR	Tot Profit	
7							
8		180	30	11	2	870	
9							
10							
11			The Typical Production Unit				
12		Q_F	MC	Cost	AC		
13							
14		6	8	37	6.17		
15							
16		Short Run:	Maximize total profit: Adjust: Q_F				
17		Long Run:	Maximize total profit: Adjust Q_F & # Firms				
18							

S2. Suppose a monopolist controls the industry described in Problem S2 of Chapter 7. The industry demand curve remains: $P = 160 - 2Q$. In addition, total production costs are unchanged: $C = 800 + 40Q + .5Q^2$. Create the requisite spreadsheet and use the spreadsheet's optimizer to determine the monopolist's profit-maximizing output.

Suggested References

Carlton, D. W., and J. M. Perloff. *Modern Industrial Organization,* Chapters 4, 5, and 7. Reading, MA: Addison-Wesley, 2004.

Joskow, P. L. "Restructuring, Competition, and Regulatory Reform in the U.S. Electricity Sector." *Journal of Economic Perspectives* (Summer 1997): 119–138.

Joskow notes that natural monopoly elements are more important in electricity transmission than in generation and discusses opportunities for competition and deregulation.

Levenstein, M. C. "What Determines Cartel Success?" *Journal of Economic Literature* (March 2006): 43–95.

Tirole, J. *The Theory of Industrial Organization,* Chapter 1. Cambridge, MA: MIT Press, 1989.

Tirole's opening chapters provide a theoretical overview of pure monopoly.

OPEC's official website is www.opec.org.

Check Station Answers

1. Note that the Lerner index is just the monopolist's optimal markup. According to the markup rule in Chapter 3, $(P - MC)/P = -1/E_p$. In short, if the monopolist is profit maximizing, the Lerner index should be equal to the inverse of the industry's price elasticity of demand. This index indicates the degree to which the monopolist can elevate price above marginal cost. However, it does not measure the magnitude of monopoly profit (since no account is made for the firm's total quantity of output or its fixed costs).

2. Intel's entry barriers stemmed from (1) pure quality and cost advantages (Intel's chips were cheaper and faster than anyone else's), (2) patents (which the company vigorously defended), (3) product differentiation (the Intel Inside campaign), and possibly (4) economies of scale. Besides items (2) and (3), Intel impeded entry by cutting prices on its chips and expanding factory capacity for producing chips. Indeed, when Intel announced the development of its Pentium chip, it exaggerated its features, thereby deterring its major customers (computer manufacturers) from experimenting with rival chips.

3. In a competitive market, the increase in demand would generate an equal long-run increase in supply. There is no increase in price. Under monopoly, the demand shift causes a rightward shift in the *MR* curve. As a result, the monopolist increases output as well as price. What if there is a cost increase instead? In the competitive market, price increases dollar for dollar with cost. (Firms' economic profits remain zero.) The monopolist's optimal response is to cut output (*MR* = *MC* occurs at lower *Q*) and pass on only part of the cost increase in the form of a higher price. (For linear demand and cost, the price increase is one-half the cost increase.)

4. OPEC maximizes its profit by setting *MR* = *MC*. Thus, we have $140 - 4Q = 20$, implying $Q = 30$ million barrels per day. In turn, $P = 140 - 60 = \$80$ per barrel and $\pi = (80 - 20)(30) = \$1,800$ million per day. If the cartel overproduces by 20 percent, the new quantity is 36, the new price is $68, and OPEC's profit falls to $\pi = (68 - 20)(36) = \$1,728$ million, a 4 percent drop.

CHAPTER 9

Oligopoly

It is in rare moments that I see my business clearly: my customers, my organization, my markets and my costs. Then why do I still lie awake at night? I'm trying to figure the damn strategies of my competitors!

A MANAGER'S LAMENT

LO#1. Describe and analyze different types of oligopolies.

LO#2. Discuss quantity competition in oligopolies.

LO#3. Compare and contrast two basic models of price competition in oligopolies.

LO#4. Discuss the effects of advertising and of strategic precommitments in oligopolistic competition.

Collusion in the Infant Formula Industry

In the early 1990s, the infant-formula industry accounted for annual sales of some $2 billion. Abbott Laboratories, Mead Johnson (then owned by Bristol-Myers Squibb), and American Home Products Corp. dominated the market with 50 percent, 37 percent, and 9 percent market shares, respectively. However, with the rise in breast feeding, growth in the formula market had slowed significantly. Twenty-five years of research had convinced pediatricians that mother's milk is the optimum baby food. In the 1990s, about 50 percent of American mothers breastfed their babies, up from only 20 percent in the 1970s.

The three dominant companies employed strikingly similar business practices. The formulas they sold were nearly identical (and must have the same nutrients by federal law). The companies charged virtually the same wholesale prices. They increased prices by an average of 8 percent annually over the decade (while milk prices increased by 2 percent annually). They produced a 13-ounce can at a marginal cost of about $0.60 and sold it for an average wholesale price of $2.10. With average total cost estimated to be about $1.70 per can, the companies enjoyed nearly a 25 percent profit margin. The companies engaged in almost no advertising; instead, they promoted and marketed their formulas via giveaway programs to hospitals and doctors. Research showed that 90 percent of mothers stick to the formula brand the hospital gives them.

The cozy oligopoly enjoyed by the three companies attracted would-be entrants and government scrutiny. In the late 1980s, Carnation and Gerber entered the formula market by advertising directly to consumers. However, the American Academy of Pediatrics opposed this strategy, arguing that direct advertising would influence mothers not to breastfeed. Consequently, the two companies' sales constituted less than 5 percent of the market. In addition, the federal government took an interest in formula pricing. Under its Women, Infants, and Children (WIC) Program, the government subsidized formula for disadvantaged families. Administered by the states, the WIC program accounted for about one-third of all formula sales. In most states, families received WIC vouchers that could be exchanged for any brand of formula, with the companies giving the government a discount (about $0.50 per can) off the regular wholesale price. However, a number of states instituted competitive bidding—awarding all WIC sales in the state to the firm making the lowest price bid.

The history of the baby-formula industry raises a number of questions. Does viable competition exist in the industry? Are barriers to entry significant? Are prices excessive? What effect might competitive bidding have on market structure, pricing, and profitability in the infant-formula industry?

In the previous two chapters, we focused on perfect competition and pure monopoly, the polar cases of market structure. However, many important markets occupy positions between these extremes; that is, they are dominated by neither a single firm nor a plethora of firms. Oligopoly is the name for markets or industries consisting of a small number of firms. Because of oligopoly's importance and because no single model captures the many implications of firm behavior within oligopoly, we devote the entire chapter to this topic.

A firm within an oligopoly faces the following basic question: How can it determine a profit-maximizing course of action when it competes against an identifiable number of competitors similar to itself? This chapter and the succeeding chapter on game theory answer this question by introducing and analyzing competitive strategies. (Thus, we depart from the approach taken previously where the main focus was on a "single" firm, facing rivals whose actions are predictable and unchanging.) In crafting a competitive strategy, a firm's management must anticipate a range of competitor actions and be prepared to respond accordingly. Competitive strategy finds its most important applications within oligopoly settings. By contrast, in a pure monopoly, there are no immediate competitors to worry about. In pure competition, an individual firm's competitive options are strictly limited because industry price and output are set by supply and demand, and products are undifferentiated.

The strategic approach extends the single-firm point of view by recognizing that a firm's profit depends not only on the firm's own actions but also on the actions of competitors. To determine its own optimal action, the firm must correctly anticipate the actions and reactions of its rivals. The manager should put himself or herself in the competitor's place to analyze what the competitor's optimal decision might be. This approach is central to game theory and is often called *interactive* or *strategic* thinking.

The outline of this chapter is as follows. In the first section, we describe how to analyze different types of oligopolies, beginning with Michael Porter's Five-Forces model. Next, we introduce the concept of market concentration, as well as the link between concentration and industry prices. In the following section, we consider two kinds of quantity competition: when a market leader faces a number of smaller competitors and when competition is between equally positioned rivals. In the third section, we examine price competition, modeling settings supporting stable prices as well as price wars. In the final section, we explore two important dimensions of competition within oligopolies: advertising and strategic precommitments.

OLIGOPOLY

An **oligopoly** is a market dominated by a small number of firms, whose actions directly affect one another's profits, making the fates of oligopoly firms *interdependent*. It is useful to size up an oligopolistic industry along a number of important economic dimensions.

Five-Forces Framework

Michael Porter's Five-Forces model provides a powerful synthesis for describing the structures of different industries and guiding competitive strategy.[1] Figure 9.1 provides a summary of the Five-Forces framework. The core of Porter's analysis centers on internal industry rivalry: the set of major firms competing in the market and how they compete. Naturally, the number of close rivals, their relative size, and their power are crucial. Entry into the market is the second most important factor in sizing up the industry. We have already seen that free entry predisposes a perfectly competitive market to zero economic profits in the long run. Conversely, significant barriers to entry (as listed and described in Chapter 8) are a precondition for monopoly. Ease of entry is also crucial for analyzing oligopoly. Boeing and Airbus compete vigorously to sell new aircraft, but barriers to entry due to economies of scale protect them from new competitors. By contrast, numerous new discount airlines in Europe have dramatically changed the competitive landscape in the air travel market. Similarly, a small, independent studio (putting together a good script, directing talent, and up-and-coming actors) can produce a well-reviewed and profitable hit movie despite the formidable clout of the major studios.

The impacts of substitutes and complements directly affect industry demand, profitability, and competitive strategy. In a host of industries, this impact is ongoing, even relentless. For instance, trucking and railways are *substitutes*—competing modes of transport in the long-haul market. Soft-drink consumption suffers at the hands of bottled water, sports drinks, and new-age beverages. In other cases, the emerging threat of new substitutes is crucial. Cable companies have long challenged network television (with satellite TV a third option), and now vigorously compete for Internet subscribers

FIGURE 9.1

The Five-Forces
Framework

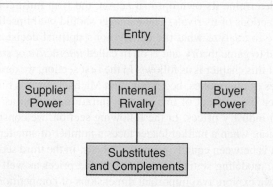

and local telephone customers. Since the millennium, online commerce has steadily increased its sales, often at the expense of bricks-and-mortar stores. The fast growth of hybrid automobiles poses a long-term threat to traditional gasoline-powered vehicles.

More recently, new attention and analysis has been paid to the industry impact of *complementary* goods and activities. Computer hardware and software are crucial complements. Steady growth in one market requires (and is fueled by) steady growth in the other. Sales of stores such as Walmart, Best Buy, and Target are enhanced by their significant online sales channels.

Coined by Adam Brandenberger and Barry Nalebuff, the term *coopetition* denotes cooperative behavior among industry "competitors." Thus, firms in the same industry often work together to set common technology standards (for high-definition television or DVDs, for instance) so as to promote overall market growth. Firms also join in shared research and development programs. Coopetition also occurs when a company and its input supplier cooperate to streamline the supply chain, improve product quality, or lower product cost. In short, oligopoly analysis embraces both the threat of substitutes and the positive impacts of complementary activities.

Finally, the potential *bargaining power* of buyers and suppliers should not be overlooked. For instance, the pricing behavior of a final goods manufacturer depends on the nature of the customers to whom it sells. At one extreme, its customers—say, a mass market of household consumers—may have little or no bargaining power. The manufacturer has full discretion to set its price as it wants (always taking into account, of course, overall product demand and the degree of competition from rival firms). At the other extreme, a large, multinational corporate buyer will have considerable bargaining clout. Typically, such a buyer will have the power to negotiate the final terms of any contract (including price), and indeed it might hold the balance of power in the negotiation. In the extreme, the buyer might ask for competitive bids from would-be goods producers so as to secure the best contract terms and price. The same analysis applies to the firm's relationships with its suppliers. We know from Chapter 7 that the firm will receive the best possible input prices if its suppliers compete in a perfectly competitive market. On the other hand, if the number of suppliers is limited or if actual inputs are in short supply, bargaining power shifts to the suppliers, who are able to command higher prices.

Industry Concentration

An oligopoly is dominated by a small number of firms. This "small number" is not precisely defined, but it may be as small as two (a duopoly) or as many as eight to a dozen. One way to grasp the numbers issue is to appeal to the most widely used measure of market structure: the **concentration ratio.** The four-firm concentration ratio is the percentage of sales accounted for by the *top* four firms in a market or industry. (Eight-firm and 20-firm ratios are defined analogously.) Concentration ratios can be computed from publicly available market-share information. Ratios also are compiled in the *US Census Bureau,* released by the government at five-year intervals. Table 9.1 lists concentration ratios for selected goods and services compiled from both sources.

Market concentration has a ready interpretation. The higher the concentration ratio, the greater is the degree of market dominance by a small number of firms. It is common to distinguish among different market structures by degree of concentration. For example,

TABLE 9.1

Concentration Ratios
for Selected Goods &
Services

Product or Service	Concentration Ratio		
	4 Firms	8 Firms	20 Firms
Laundry machines	98	100	
Warehouse clubs	94	100	
Refrigerators	92	98	
Web Search	91	95	
Aluminum Refining	90	99	
Beer	90	92	
Tobacco	90	95	
Glass containers	87	95	
Rental cars	87	96	
Personal computers	87	92	
Carbon black	84	99	
Cellular phone service	82	94	
Aircraft	81	94	
Breakfast foods	80	92	
Office supply stores	80	81	
Ammunition	79	89	
Tires	78	93	
Running shoes	77	96	
Metal cans	77	95	
Aircraft engines	74	81	
Burial caskets	74	83	
Computer Stores	73	77	
Bottled Water	72	85	
Vacuum cleaners	71	96	
Book stores	71	78	
Pet food	71	84	
Lawn equipment	71	84	
Flat glass	70	98	
Men's underwear	70	87	
Stockings	69	85	
Motor vehicles	68	86	
Domestic air flights	65	83	
Motion pictures	64	96	
Drug Stores	63	66	
Cable television	62	79	
Photocopying machines	61	83	
Farm machinery	59	65	
Men's shoes	57	82	
Elevators	56	70	
National Comm. Banks	56	69	
Snack foods	53	61	
Nuclear Power	53	76	
Investment Banking	52	77	
Mattresses	51	64	
Oil refining	48	73	
Soap	47	60	
Milk	46	58	
Paper mills	46	67	
Coffee	43	58	
Television broadcasting	43	56	
Rubber	43	65	

TABLE 9.1

(*continued*)

Product or Service	Concentration Ratio		
	4 Firms	8 Firms	20 Firms
Ski Facilities	42	53	
Paint	39	59	
Software	39	47	
Toys	36	51	
Boat building	35	43	
Internet Service	34	49	
Leather	34	42	
Book publishing	33	48	68
Basic chemicals	33	44	60
Supermarkets	32	46	59
Pumps	31	41	55
Internet Shopping	31	37	85
Pharmaceuticals	30	47	69
Newspapers	29	45	63
Jewelry	29	38	55
Women's dresses	28	39	69
Life Insurance	27	44	75
Office furniture	26	34	42
Advertising Agencies	24	29	33
Light Fixtures	23	34	49
Concrete	23	28	40
Hotels	23	28	35
Motor Vehicle Parts	19	28	42
Elder Care Homes	19	23	30
Funeral homes	16	17	18
Electric power	15	27	26
Metal Stamping	14	19	28
Furniture Stores	14	19	27
Management Consulting	14	19	26
Used car dealers	13	14	16
Portfolio Management	12	20	35
Printing	12	20	34
Furniture	11	19	30
Gasoline stations	10	17	31
Trucking	9	15	21
Lumber and wood	9	14	23
Bolts, nuts, screws	9	12	19
Restaurants	9	12	17
Liquor Stores	8	13	19
Musical groups & artists	7	11	20
Hospitals	7	11	19
Signs	7	10	18
Veterinary Services	7	8	9
Towing	6	9	12
Legal Offices	2.6	4.6	9.0
Florists	2.1	2.9	4.5
Machine Shops	2.0	3.4	6.1
Auto repair	1.7	2.6	4.3
Dry Cleaners	1.4	2.2	3.9

Source: US Bureau of the Census, 2007, and industry reports.

an **effective monopoly** is said to exist when the single-firm concentration ratio is above 90 percent, $CR_1 > 90$. A market is **effectively competitive** when CR_4 is below 40 percent. If $CR_4 < 40$ percent, the top firms have individual market shares averaging less than 10 percent, and they are joined by many firms with still smaller market shares. Finally, one often speaks of a **loose oligopoly** when 40 percent $< CR_4 < 60$ percent and a **tight oligopoly** when $CR_4 > 60$ percent. Monopolistic competition, discussed in the previous chapter, typically falls in the loose-oligopoly range.

About three-quarters of the total dollar value of goods and services (gross domestic product or GDP) produced by the US economy originate in competitive markets, that is, markets for which $CR_4 < 40$. Competitive markets included the lion's share (85 percent or more) of agriculture, forestry, fisheries, mining, and wholesale and retail trade. Competition is less prevalent in manufacturing, general services, and construction (making up between 60 percent and 80 percent of these sectors). In contrast, pure monopoly accounts for a small portion of GDP (between 2 and 3 percent). Tight oligopolies account for about 10 percent of GDP, whereas loose oligopolies comprise about 12 percent.[2] In short, as Table 9.1 shows, while concentrated markets are relatively rare in the US economy, specific industries and manufactured products are highly concentrated.

Because the notion of concentration ratio is used so widely, it is important to understand its limitations. One problem is the identification of the *relevant market*. A market is a collection of buyers and sellers exchanging goods or services that are very close substitutes for one another. (Recall that the cross-elasticity of demand is a direct measure of substitution. The larger the impact on a good's sales from changes in a competitor's price, the stronger the market competition.) Concentration ratios purport to summarize the size distribution of firms for relevant markets. However, it should be evident that market definitions vary, depending on how broadly or narrowly one draws product and geographic boundaries.

First, in many cases the market definitions used in government statistics are too broad. An industry grouping such as *pharmaceutical products* embraces many distinct, individual product markets. Numerous firms make up the overall consumer-drug market (concentration is low), but individual markets (drugs for ulcers and blood pressure) are highly concentrated. Similarly, government statistics encompass national markets and therefore cannot capture local monopolies. Based on CR_4, the newspaper industry would seem to be effectively competitive for the United States as a whole. But for most major cities, one or two firms account for nearly 100 percent of circulation.[3]

Second, the census data exclude imports—a serious omission considering that the importance of imports in the US economy has risen steadily (to some 13 percent of GDP today). In many industries (automobiles, televisions, electronics), the degree of concentration for US *sales* (including imports) is much less than the concentration for US *production*. Thus, many industries are far more competitive than domestic concentration ratios would indicate.

---

[2] The categorization of market structures by concentration is not hard and fast. The preceding data are based on W. G. Shepherd and J. M. Shepherd, *The Economics of Industrial Organization*, Chapter 3 (Upper Saddle River, NJ: Prentice-Hall, 2003).

[3] The Bureau of the Census presents concentration ratios starting for broad industry categories and progressing to narrower and narrower groups (so-called six-digit categories). The categories in Table 9.1 are at the five- and six-digit levels. As one would expect, concentration tends to increase as markets are defined more narrowly. Many researchers believe that five-digit categories best approximate actual market boundaries.

Finally, using a concentration ratio is not the only way to measure market dominance by a small number of firms. An alternative and widely used measure is the Herfindahl-Hirschman Index (HHI), defined as the sum of the squared market shares of all firms:

$$HHI = s_1^2 + s_2^2 + \cdots s_n^2$$

where s_i denotes the market share of firm i and n denotes the number of firms. For instance, if a market is supplied by five firms with market shares of 40, 30, 16, 10, and 4 percent, respectively, $HHI = 40^2 + 30^2 + 16^2 + 10^2 + 4^2 = 2{,}872$. The HHI index ranges between 10,000 for a pure monopolist (with 100 percent of the market) to near zero for an infinite number of small firms. If a market is shared *equally* by n firms, HHI is the n-fold sum of $(100/n)^2$, or $(n)(100/n)^2 = 10{,}000/n$. If the market has 5 identical firms, $HHI = 2{,}000$; if it has 10 identical firms, $HHI = 1{,}000$. The Herfindahl-Hirschman Index has a number of noteworthy properties:

1. The index counts the market shares of all firms, not merely the top four or eight.
2. The more unequal the market shares of a collection of firms, the greater is the index because shares are squared.
3. Other things being equal, the more numerous the firms, the lower is the index.

Because of these properties, the HHI has advantages over concentration ratios; indeed, the HHI is used as one factor in the Department of Justice's Merger Guidelines. (Under antitrust laws, the government can block a proposed merger if it will substantially reduce competition or tend to create a monopoly.) Nonetheless, concentration ratios, being more readily available, are quoted more frequently.

Concentration and Prices

Concentration is an important factor affecting pricing and profitability within markets.

Other things being equal, increases in concentration can be expected to be associated with increased prices and profits.

One way to make this point is to appeal to the extreme cases of pure competition and pure monopoly. Under pure competition, market price equals average cost, leaving all firms zero economic profits (i.e., normal rates of return). Low concentration leads to minimum prices and zero profits. Under a pure monopoly, in contrast, a single dominant firm earns maximum excess profit by optimally raising the market price. Between these polar cases, we find a positive relationship between an industry's degree of monopolization (as measured by concentration) and industry prices. For instance, the smaller the number of firms that dominate a market (the tighter the oligopoly), the greater is the likelihood that firms will avoid cutthroat competition and succeed in maintaining high prices. High prices may be a result of tacit collusion or coordination. But even without any form of collusion, fewer competitors can lead to higher prices. The models of price leadership and quantity competition (analyzed in the next section) make exactly this point.

There is considerable evidence that increases in concentration promote higher prices. This research focuses on particular markets and collects data on price (the dependent variable) and costs, demand conditions, and concentration (the explanatory variables). Price is viewed in the functional form

$$P = f(C, D, SC),$$

where C denotes a measure of cost, D a measure of demand, and SC seller concentration. Based on these data, regression techniques are used to estimate this price relationship in the form of an equation. Of particular interest is the separate influence of concentration on price, other things (costs and demand) being equal. The positive association between concentration and price has been confirmed for a wide variety of products, services, and markets—from retail grocery chains to air travel on intercity routes; from cement production to television advertising; from auctions of oil leases and timber rights to interest rates offered by commercial banks.[4]

Is an increase in monopoly power necessarily harmful to the interests of consumers? The foregoing discussion citing the evidence of higher prices would say yes. However, an alternative point of view claims that monopoly (i.e., large firms) offers significant efficiency advantages vis-a-vis small firms.[5] According to this hypothesis, monopoly reflects superior efficiency in product development, production, distribution, and marketing. A few firms grow large and become dominant *because* they are efficient. If these cost advantages are large enough, consumers can obtain lower prices from a market dominated by a small number of large firms than from a competitive market of small firms. Thus, a price comparison between a tight oligopoly and a competitive market depends on which is the greater effect: the oligopoly's cost reductions or its price increases. For example, suppose that in the competitive market $P_c = AC_c$, and, in the tight oligopoly $P_o = 1.15AC_o$. Absent a cost advantage, the oligopoly exhibits higher prices. But if the oligopoly's average cost advantage exceeds 15 percent, it will have the lower overall price.

The evidence concerning monopoly efficiency is mixed at best. It is hard to detect significant efficiency gains using either statistical approaches or case studies. Large firms and market leaders do not appear to be more efficient or to enjoy larger economies of scale than smaller rivals. (They do profit from higher sales and prices afforded by brand-name allegiance.) Nonetheless, the efficiency issue offers an important reminder that greater concentration per se need not be detrimental. Indeed, the government's antitrust guidelines mentioned earlier cover many factors—concentration, ease of entry, extent of ongoing price competition, and possible efficiency gains—in evaluating a particular industry.

---

[4]See C. Kelton and L. Weiss, "Change in Concentration, Change in Cost, Change in Demand, and Change in Price," in Leonard Weiss (Ed.), *Concentration and Price*. (Cambridge, MA: MIT Press, 1989). This book provides a comprehensive collection and critical analysis of the price-concentration research.

[5]This view often is referred to as the *University of Chicago-UCLA approach*, because much of the research originated at these schools. For discussion and critique, see M. Salinger, "The Concentration-Margins Relationship Reconsidered," *Brookings Papers: Microeconomics* (1990): 287–335.

Fares on air routes around the world offer a textbook case of the link between concentration and prices. Numerous research studies have shown that average fares on point-to-point air routes around the globe vary inversely with the number of carriers.[6] Indeed, the degree of competition on a particular route is a much stronger predictor of airfares than the distance actually traveled.

The effect of competition can be seen in several ways. Airline deregulation in the United States began in 1978. Fares were deregulated, and air routes were opened to all would-be carriers. In the first decade of deregulation, the average number of carriers per route increased from 1.5 to almost 2. During the same period, deregulated fares proved to be about 20 percent below what they would have been absent deregulation. For the next 20 years, average airfares have continued to decline (after adjusting for general inflation and higher fuel costs).

However, over the last 20 years, the advent of the hub-and-spoke system and industry consolidation via mergers have meant reduced competition on many routes. American Airlines accounts for about 70 percent of all flights to and from Dallas-Fort Worth. Delta Airlines controls over 75 percent of the traffic in Atlanta, Cincinnati, Detroit, Minneapolis, and Salt Lake City. Together, United Airlines and American Airlines account for some 85 percent of all flights at Chicago's O'Hare Airport. United and Southwest Airlines provide nearly 60 percent of the flights in Denver. Fares at hub airports dominated by a single airline tend to be more than 20 percent higher than those on comparable routes. Conversely, on routes where discount airlines have entered and compete successfully with incumbent carriers, fares have dropped by 30 to 50 percent. Nonetheless, discount carriers complain of barriers to entry (few or no takeoff and landing slots) and the predatory practices (incumbents' sudden price cuts and flight increases) that keep them from competing on key routes.

Air route competition in Europe and the rest of the world has been far behind developments in the United States. European governments have a long history of protecting national carriers from competition by foreign airlines. The result has been far fewer competing carriers on the major European air routes and, therefore, elevated fares. Because of protectionist policies, an intranational fare (Paris to Marseilles) may be higher than an intra-European fare (Paris to Athens), which, in turn, is comparable to an international fare (Paris to New York). Because of high wages and low labor productivity, operating costs at European airlines are more than 40 percent above those of US airlines. In short, high concentration within Europe coincides with high costs (not economies of scale) and meager profits. Only during the last decade have discount carriers like Ryanair, Norwegian Air, Air Berlin, and EasyJet begun to penetrate important European markets, spurring incumbent carriers to cut unnecessary costs and to reduce fares. As in the United States, new entry and greater competition are bringing lower fares to Europe.

---

[6]See C. Winston, *Last Exit: Privatization and Deregulation of the US Transportation System* (Washington, D.C.: Brookings Institution Press, 2010); S. Morrison and C. Winston, *The Economics of the Airline Industry* (Washington, D.C.: Brookings Institution Press, 1995); and S. Morrison, "Actual, Adjacent, and Potential Competition: Estimating the Full Effect of Southwest Airlines," *Journal of Transport Economics and Policy*, 2001: 239–256.

QUANTITY COMPETITION

There is no single ideal model of competition within oligopoly. This is hardly surprising in view of the different numbers of competitors (from two upward) and dimensions of competition (price, product attributes, capacity, technological innovation, marketing, and advertising) encompassed by oligopoly. In this section, we examine quantity competition in a pair of settings. In the following section, we take up different kinds of price competition.

A Dominant Firm

In many oligopolistic industries, one firm possesses a dominant market share and acts as a leader by setting price for the industry. Historically, one can point to dominant firms, such as General Motors in the automobile industry, Du Pont in chemicals, and U.S. Steel. Firms that currently hold dominant market shares include Walmart among discount stores, eBay in online auctions, FedEx in overnight delivery, Procter & Gamble in a variety of consumer products, Intel in microchips, and Microsoft in PC software, to name just a few.

What are the implications of price leadership for the oligopoly market? To supply a precise answer, we must construct a tractable and realistic model of price behavior. The accepted model assumes that the dominant firm establishes the price for the industry, and the remaining small suppliers sell all they want at this price. The small firms have no influence on price and behave competitively; that is, each produces a quantity at which its marginal cost equals the market price. Figure 9.2 depicts the resulting combined supply curve for these small firms. The demand curve for the price leader, labeled d in the figure, is found by subtracting the supply curve of the small firms from the total industry demand curve. In other words, for any given price (see P^* and P' in the figure), the leader's sales quantity is equal to total market demand minus the supply of the small firms—that is, the horizontal distance between curves D and S.

Once the dominant firm anticipates its *net demand curve*, it sets out to maximize its profits in the usual way: It establishes its quantity where marginal revenue (derived from curve d) equals marginal cost (curve MC). In Figure 9.2, the leader's optimal price is P^*, its output is Q^*, and the small firms' combined output is Q_S. A numerical example illustrates the result. Suppose that total market demand is given by $Q_D = 248 - 2P$ and that the total supply curve of the 10 small firms in the market is given by $Q_S = 48 + 3P$. The dominant firm's marginal cost is $MC = .1Q$. Then, the dominant firm determines its optimal quantity and price as follows. The firm identifies its net demand curve as $Q = Q_D - Q_S = [248 - 2P] - [48 + 3P] = 200 - 5P$, or equivalently, $P = 40 - .2Q$. Setting $MR = MC$ implies $40 - .4Q = .1Q$, or $Q^* = 80$ units. In turn, $P^* = 40 - (.2)(80) = \$24$. Therefore, $Q_S = 48 + (3)(24) = 120$; thus, each of the 10 small firms supplies 12 units.

In effect, the dominant firm makes the first (and most important) strategic move in the market, with the remaining smaller firms responding to its actions. The key strategic consideration for the dominant firm is to anticipate the supply response of the competitive fringe of firms. For instance, suppose the dominant firm anticipates that any increase in price will induce a significant increase in supply by the other firms and,

FIGURE 9.2

Optimal Output for a Dominant Firm.

The dominant firm's net demand curve is the difference between industry demand and the competitive supply of small firms.

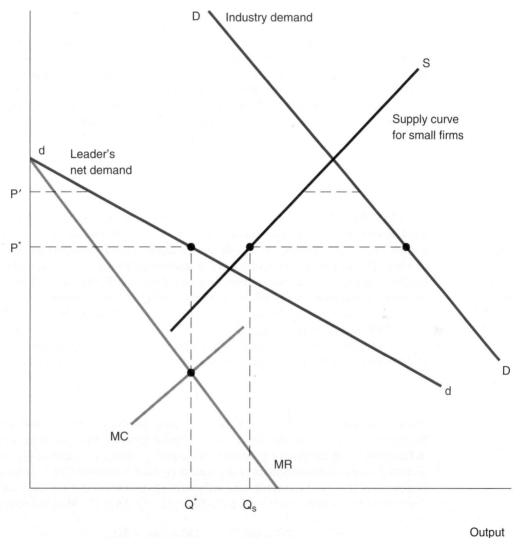

therefore, a sharp reduction in the dominant firm's own net demand. In other words, the more price elastic is the supply response of rivals, then the more elastic is the dominant firm's net demand. Under such circumstances, the dominant firm does best to refrain from raising the market price.

Competition among Symmetric Firms

Now let's modify the previous setting by considering an oligopoly consisting of a small number of *equally positioned* competitors. As before, a small number of firms produce a standardized, undifferentiated product. Thus, all firms are locked into the same price. The *total* quantity of output supplied by the firms determines the prevailing market price according to the industry demand curve. Via its quantity choice, an individual firm can affect total output and therefore influence market price.

A simple but important model of quantity competition between duopolists (i.e., two firms) was first developed by Augustin Cournot, a nineteenth-century French economist. To this day, the principal models of quantity competition bear his name. Knowing the industry demand curve, each firm must determine the quantity of output to produce—with these decisions made independently. As a profit maximizer, what quantity should each firm choose? To answer this question, let's consider the following example.

DUELING SUPPLIERS   A pair of firms compete by selling quantities of a standardized good. Each firm's average cost is constant at $6 per unit. Market demand is given by $P = 30 - (Q_1 + Q_2)$, where Q_1 and Q_2 denote the firms' respective outputs (in thousands of units). In short, the going market price is determined by the *total* amount of output produced and sold by the firms. Notice that each firm's profit depends on both firms' quantities. For instance, if $Q_1 = 5$ thousand units and $Q_2 = 8$ thousand units, the market price is $17. The firms' profits are $\pi_1 = (17 - 6)(5) = \$55$ thousand and $\pi_2 = (17 - 6)(8) = \$88$ thousand, respectively.

To determine each firm's profit-maximizing output, we begin by observing the effect on demand of the competitor's output. For instance, firm 1 faces the demand curve

$$P = (30 - Q_2) - Q_1. \qquad [9.1]$$

The demand curve (as a function of the firm's own quantity) is downward sloping in the usual way. In addition, the demand curve's price intercept, the term in parentheses in Equation 9.1, depends on the competitor's output quantity. Increases in Q_2 cause a parallel downward shift in demand; a decrease in Q_2 has the opposite effect. Given a prediction about Q_2, firm 1 can apply marginal analysis to maximize profit in the usual way. The firm's revenue is $R_1 = (30 - Q_2 - Q_1)Q_1 = (30 - Q_2)Q_1 - Q_1^2$. Marginal revenue is

$$MR = \partial R_1/\partial Q_1 = (30 - Q_2) - 2Q_1.$$

Setting marginal revenue equal to the $6 marginal cost, we find that $30 - Q_2 - 2Q_1 = 6$,

or $\qquad\qquad\qquad\qquad\qquad Q_1 = 12 - .5Q_2. \qquad\qquad\qquad\qquad\qquad [9.2]$

Firm 1's profit-maximizing output depends on its competitor's quantity. An increase in Q_2 reduces firm 1's (net) demand, its marginal revenue, and its optimal output. For example, if firm 1 anticipates $Q_2 = 6$, its optimal output is 9; if it expects $Q_2 = 10$, its optimal output falls to 7. Equation 9.2 sets a schedule of optimal quantities in response to different competitive outputs. For this reason, it is often referred to as the *optimal reaction function.* A similar profit maximization for firm 2 produces the analogous reaction function:

$$Q_2 = 12 - .5Q_1. \qquad [9.3]$$

Now we are ready to derive the quantity and price outcomes for the duopoly. The derivation rests on the notion of *equilibrium.*[7] In **equilibrium,** each firm makes a profit-maximizing decision, anticipating profit-maximizing decisions by all competitors. Let's determine the equilibrium quantities in the current example. To qualify as an equilibrium, the firms' quantities must be profit-maximizing against each other; that is, they must satisfy both Equations 9.2 and 9.3. Solving these equations simultaneously, we find $Q_1 = Q_2 = 8$ thousand units. (Check this.) These are the unique equilibrium quantities. Since the firms face the same demand and have the same costs, they produce the same optimal outputs. These outputs imply the market price, $P = 30 - 16 = \$14$ thousand. Each firm's profit is \$64,000, and total profit is \$128,000.

Suppose the duopoly example is as described earlier except that the second firm's average cost is \$9 per unit. Find the firms' equilibrium quantities.   **CHECK STATION 1**

The duopoly equilibrium lies between the pure-monopoly and purely competitive outcomes. The latter outcome occurs at a quantity sufficiently large that price is driven down to average cost, $P_c = AC = \$6$, so that industry profit is zero. According to the demand curve, the requisite total quantity is $Q_c = 24$ thousand units. In contrast, a monopolist—either a single firm or the two firms acting as a cartel—would limit total output (Q) to maximize industry profit:

$$\pi = (30 - Q)Q - 6Q.$$

Setting marginal revenue (with respect to *total* output) equal to marginal cost implies: $30 - 2Q = 6$. Thus, $Q_M = 12$ thousand units and $P_M = \$18$ thousand. Total industry profit is \$144,000. In sum, the duopoly equilibrium has a lower price, a larger total output, and a lower total profit than the pure-monopoly outcome.

The analysis behind the quantity equilibrium can be applied to any number of firms; it is not limited to the duopoly case. Suppose n firms serve the market and the market-clearing price is given by

$$P = 30 - (Q_1 + Q_2 + \cdots + Q_n).$$

Then firm 1's marginal revenue is $MR = [30 - (Q_2 + \cdots + Q_n)] - 2Q_1$. Setting MR equal to the firm's \$6 MC yields

$$Q_1 = 12 - .5(Q_2 + \cdots + Q_n). \qquad [9.4]$$

---

[7]This concept is called a Cournot equilibrium, also a Nash equilibrium, after John Nash, who demonstrated its general properties.

Analogous expressions hold for each of the other firms. The equilibrium is found by simultaneously solving n equations in n unknowns. In fact, the easiest method of solution is to recognize that the equilibrium must be symmetric. Because all firms have identical costs and face the same demand, all will produce the same output. Denoting each firm's output by Q^*, we can rewrite Equation 9.4 as

$$Q^* = 12 - .5(n - 1)Q^*,$$

implying the solution

$$Q^* = 24/[n + 1]. \tag{9.5}$$

Notice that in the duopoly case ($n = 2$), each firm's equilibrium output is 8 thousand, the same result we found earlier. As the number of firms increases, each firm's profit-maximizing output falls (becomes a smaller part of the market). What is the impact on *total* output? Total output is

$$Q = nQ^* = 24n/(n + 1)$$

and approaches 24 thousand units as the number of firms becomes large (say, 19 or more). In turn, the equilibrium market price approaches: $30 - 24 = \$6$; that is, *price steadily declines and approaches average cost.* It can be shown that this result is very general. (It holds for any symmetric equilibrium, not only in the case of linear demand.) The general result is as follows:

> As the number of firms increases, the quantity equilibrium played by identical oligopolists approaches the purely competitive (zero-profit) outcome.

In short, the Cournot quantity equilibrium has the attractive feature of being able to account for prices ranging from pure monopoly ($n = 1$) to pure competition (n being very large), with intermediate oligopoly cases in between.

PRICE COMPETITION

In this section, we consider two basic models of price competition. The first is a model of stable prices based on kinked demand. The second is a model of price wars based on the paradigm of the prisoner's dilemma.

Price Rigidity and Kinked Demand

Competition within an oligopoly is complicated by the fact that each firm's actions (with respect to output, pricing, advertising, and so on) affect the profitability of its rivals. Thus, actions by one or more firms typically will trigger competitive reactions by others; indeed, these actions may trigger "second-round" actions by the original firms. Where does this jockeying for competitive position settle down? (Or does it settle down?) We begin our discussion of pricing behavior by focusing on a model of *stable* prices and output. Many oligopolies—steel, automobiles, and cigarettes, to name a few—have enjoyed relatively stable prices over extended periods of time. (Prices simply adjust over time to reflect general inflation.) Even when a firm's cost or demand fluctuates, it may be reluctant to change prices.

Price rigidity can be explained by the existence of **kinked demand curves** for competing firms. Consider a typical oligopolist that currently is charging price P^*. Why might there be a kink in its estimated demand curve, as in Figure 9.3? Suppose the firm lowers its price. If price competition among firms is fierce, such a price cut is likely to be matched by rival firms staunchly defending their market shares. The upshot is that the firm's price reduction will generate only a small increase in its sales. (The firm will not succeed in gaining much market share from its rivals, although it could garner a portion of the increase in industry sales owing to lower market-wide prices.) In other words, when it comes to price reductions, demand is relatively inelastic. Conversely, suppose the firm raises its price above P^*. By holding to their current prices, rival firms can acquire market share from the price raiser. If the other firms do not follow, the firm

FIGURE 9.3

Optimal Output with Kinked Demand

If the demand curve is kinked, the firm's marginal revenue curve has a gap at quantity Q^*.

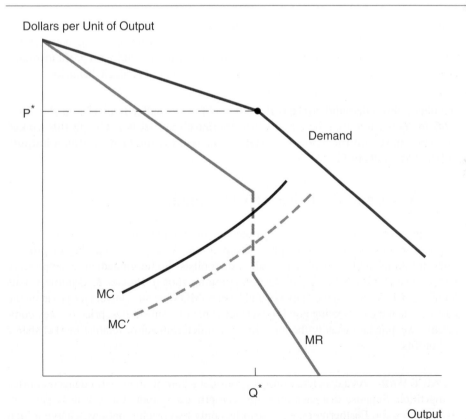

will find its sales falling precipitously for even small price increases. Demand is elastic for price increases. This explains the demand curve's kink at the firm's current price.

In view of kinked demand, the firm's profit-maximizing price and quantity are simply P^* and Q^*. This is confirmed by noting that the firm's marginal revenue curve in Figure 9.3 is discontinuous. The left part of the MR curve corresponds to the demand curve to the left of the kink. But MR drops discontinuously if price falls slightly below P^*. The presence of the vertical discontinuity in MR means that P^* and Q^* are optimal as long as the firm's marginal cost curve crosses MR within the gap. The dotted MC curve in the figure shows that marginal cost could decrease without changing the firm's optimal price. (Small shifts in demand that retain the kink at P^* would also leave the firm's optimal price unchanged.) In short, each firm's price remains constant over a range of changing market conditions. The result is stable industry-wide prices.

The kinked demand curve model presumes that the firm determines its price behavior based on a prediction about its rivals' reactions to potential price changes. This is one way to inject strategic considerations into the firm's decisions. Paradoxically, the willingness of firms to respond aggressively to price cuts is the very thing that sustains stable prices. Price cuts will not be attempted if they are expected to beget other cuts. However, the kinked demand curve model is incomplete. It does not explain why the kink occurs at the price P^*. Nor does it justify the price-cutting behavior of rivals. (Price cutting may not be in the best interests of these firms. For instance, a rival may prefer to hold to its price and sacrifice market share rather than cut price and slash profit margins.) A complete model needs to incorporate a richer treatment of strategic behavior.

CHECK STATION 2   An oligopolist's demand curve is $P = 30 - Q$ for Q smaller than 10 and $P = 36 - 1.6Q$ for Q greater than or equal to 10. Its marginal cost is 7. Graph this kinked demand curve and the associated MR curve. What is the firm's optimal output? What if MC falls to 5?

Price Wars and the Prisoner's Dilemma

Stable prices constitute one oligopoly outcome, but not the only one. In many markets, oligopolists engage in vigorous price competition. A surprising number of product lines are dominated by two firms, called duopolists. Some immediate examples are Pepsi versus Coke, Nike versus Reebok (running shoes), Procter & Gamble versus Kimberly-Clark (disposable diapers), and Disney-MGM versus Universal (movie theme parks). When the competing goods or services are close substitutes, price is a key competitive weapon and usually the most important determinant of relative market shares and profits.

A PRICE WAR   As a concrete example, consider a pair of duopolists engaged in price competition. Suppose that each duopolist can produce output at a cost of $4 per unit: $AC = MC = \$4$. Furthermore, each firm has only two pricing options: charge a high price of $8 or charge a low price of $6. If both firms set high prices, each can expect to sell 2.5 million units annually. If both set low prices, each firm's sales increase to 3.5 million units. Finally, if one firm sets a high price and the other a low price, the former sells 1.25 million units, the latter 6 million units.

Table 9.2 presents a payoff table summarizing the profit implications of the firms' different pricing strategies. Firm 1's two possible prices are listed in the first and second rows. Firm 2's options head the two columns. The upper-left cell shows that if both firms charge high prices, each will earn a profit of $10 million. (It is customary to list firm 1's payoff or profit first and firm 2's payoff second.) Each firm's profit is computed as: $\pi = (P - AC)Q = (8 - 4)(2.5) = \$10$ million. The other entries are computed in analogous fashion. (Check these.) Notice that firm profits are lower when both charge lower prices. (The price reduction increases the firms' total sales, but not by enough to compensate for lower margins. Demand is relatively inelastic.) Notice also that if one firm undercuts the other's price, it wins significant market share and profit at the expense of the other.

Each firm must determine its pricing decision privately and independently of the other with the aim of maximizing its profit. What pricing policy should each adopt? Setting a low price is each firm's more profitable alternative, regardless of what action its rival takes. To see this, let's look at the payoffs in Table 9.2 from firm 1's point of view. To find its best strategy, firm 1 asks a pair of "what if" questions about its rival. What if firm 2 were to charge a high price? Then, clearly, firm 1 does best by setting a low price, that is, undercutting. (A profit of 12 is superior to a profit of 10.) Alternatively, if firm 2 sets a low price, firm 1's profit-maximizing response is to set a low price, that is, to match. (Here, 7 is better than 5.) Because the firms face symmetric payoffs, exactly the same logic applies to firm 2. In short, self-interest dictates that each firm sets a low price.

The upshot of both sides charging low prices is profits of 7 for each—lower than the profits (10 each) if they both charged high prices. Both would prefer the larger profits enjoyed under a high-price regime. Yet the play of self-interested strategies is driving them to low prices and low profits. One might ask, Why can't the firms achieve the beneficial, high-price outcome? The answer is straightforward. To set a high price, anticipating that one's rival will do likewise, is simply wishful thinking. Although high prices are collectively beneficial, this outcome is *not* an equilibrium. Either firm could (and presumably would) profitably undercut the other's price. An initial high-price regime quickly gives way to low prices. As long as the firms act independently, the profit incentive drives down prices.

Before leaving this example, we make an additional point. The strategic behavior of rational firms can be expected to depend not only on the profit stakes as captured in the

TABLE 9.2

A Price War

		Firm 2	
		High Price	Low Price
Firm 1	High Price	10, 10	5, 12
	Low Price	12, 5	7, 7

Each firm's optimal strategy is to set a low price.

payoff table but also on the "rules" of the competition.[8] Here, the rules have the firms making their price decisions independently. There is no opportunity for communication or collusion. (In fact, any kind of price collusion is illegal under US antitrust laws.) We say that the firms behave *noncooperatively*. However, the "rules" would be quite different if the firms were the two largest members of an international cartel. Opportunities for communication and collusion would be freely available. Clearly, the firms would strive for a *cooperative* agreement that maintains high prices. However, it is worth remembering a lesson from Chapter 8's analysis of cartels: A collusive agreement can facilitate a mutually beneficial, cooperative outcome, but it hardly guarantees it. Cartels are unstable precisely because of the individual incentives to cut price and cheat. Even a collusive agreement is not ironclad.

CHECK STATION 3   **In the price war, suppose that some consumers display a strong brand allegiance for one firm or the other. Consequently, any price difference between the duopolists is expected to produce a much smaller swing in the firms' market shares. Specifically, suppose that if one firm charges a price of $6 and the other $8, the former sells 4 million units and the latter 2 million (instead of the original 6 million and 1.25 million sales). All other facts are as before. How does this change the payoffs in Table 9.2? What price should each firm set? Explain.**

THE PRISONER'S DILEMMA   So frequent are situations (like the preceding example) in which individual and collective interests are in conflict that they commonly are referred to as the **prisoner's dilemma.** The origin of the term comes from a well-known story of two accomplices arrested for a crime. The police isolate each suspect and ask each to confess and turn state's evidence on the other, in return for a shortened sentence. Table 9.3 shows the possible jail terms the suspects face. If the police can garner dual confessions, the suspects will be charged and convicted of a serious crime that carries a five-year sentence. Without confessions, convictions will be for much shorter jail terms.

Obviously, each suspect seeks to *minimize* time spent in jail. A careful look at Table 9.3 shows that each prisoner's best strategy is to confess. (If his or her accomplice stays mum, confessing brings the shortest sentence, one year. If the partner confesses and testifies against him, so too must the suspect, to avoid a maximum term.) Without the benefit of communication, there is no way for the partners to agree to stay mum.

TABLE 9.3

The Prisoner's Dilemma

Each suspect's optimal strategy is to confess and turn state's evidence on the other.

			Suspect 2	
			Stay Mum	**Confess**
Suspect 1		**Stay Mum**	2 years, 2 years	8 years, 1 year
		Confess	1 year, 8 years	5 years, 5 years

[8]The example of price competition also serves as an introduction to game theory. Payoff tables, the rules of the game, and the analysis of optimal strategies are all topics taken up in greater depth in Chapter 10.

The individual incentive is for each to turn against the other. By cleverly constructing the configuration of possible jail terms, the authorities can induce the suspects to make voluntary confessions, resulting in five-year prison terms.

The prisoner's dilemma should be viewed as a general model rather than as a special (perverse) case. Once one has the model in mind, it is easy to identify countless situations in which it applies:

- In the superpowers' arms race, it is advantageous for one country to have a larger nuclear arsenal than its rival. But arms escalation by *both* sides improves neither side's security (and probably worsens it).

- A cartel has a collective interest in restricting output to earn a monopoly profit. But, cartel members can increase their individual profits by cheating on the cartel, that is, exceeding their quotas. (Recall the discussion in Chapter 8.)

- Abnormally cold winter temperatures bring the threat of a shortage of natural gas for heating buildings and homes. State and city officials urge residents to turn down their thermostats to conserve natural gas. Unfortunately, the result is a negligible reduction in use. (Why should I suffer low temperatures when my personal energy saving will have no discernible impact on the shortage?)

- The use of public resources, most commonly natural resources, presents similar dilemmas. For instance, many countries fish the Georges Bank in the North Atlantic. Each country's fleet seeks to secure the greatest possible catch. But the simultaneous pursuit of maximum catches by all countries threatens depletion of the world's richest fishing grounds. Similarly, firms in many industries generate air and water pollution as manufacturing byproducts, and it is not in their self-interest to adopt costly pollution controls. Nonetheless, the collective, social benefit of reducing pollution may be well worth the cost.

- The more widely antibiotics are prescribed, the more rapidly drug-resistant microorganisms develop.

In each of these cases, there is a significant collective benefit from cooperation. However, the self-interest of individual decision makers leads to quite different, *non-cooperative*, behavior. The key to overcoming the prisoner's dilemma is to form an agreement that binds the parties to take the appropriate cooperative actions. To halt the arms race, the interested parties must bind themselves to a verifiable arms control treaty. Cartel members can agree to restrict output in order to maximize the collective profit of the cartel. A negotiated treaty on fishing quotas is one way to preserve Georges Bank. The American Medical Association has proposed guidelines calling for conservative practices in prescribing antibiotics. In the natural gas example, a binding agreement among consumers is impossible; rather, the way to encourage cuts in consumption is via higher natural gas prices.

In the prisoner's dilemma example, suppose that a minimum sentencing law requires that a defendant entering into a plea bargain must serve a minimum of three years. What entries will this affect in Table 9.3? Explain why this law is likely to backfire in the present instance.   **CHECK STATION 4**

BERTRAND PRICE COMPETITION   An extreme case of price competition originally was suggested by Joseph Bertrand, a nineteenth-century French economist. Suppose duopolists produce an undifferentiated good at an identical (and constant) marginal cost, say $6 per unit. Each can charge whatever price it wishes, but consumers are very astute and always purchase solely from the firm giving the lower price. In other words, the lower-price firm gains the entire market, and the higher-price firm sells nothing.

To analyze this situation, suppose that each firm seeks to determine a price that maximizes its own profit while anticipating the price set by its rival. In other words, as in the previous example of quantity competition, we focus on equilibrium strategies for the firms. (The difference is that here the firms compete via prices, whereas previously they competed via quantities.) What are the firms' equilibrium prices? A little reflection shows that the unique equilibrium is for each firm to set a price equal to marginal cost: $P_1 = P_2 = \$6$. This may appear to be a surprising outcome. In equilibrium, $P = AC = MC$ so that both firms earn zero economic profit. With the whole market on the line, as few as two firms compete the price down to the perfectly competitive, zero-profit level.

Why isn't there an equilibrium in which firms charge higher prices and earn positive profits? If firms charged different prices, the higher-price firm (currently with zero sales) could profit by slightly undercutting the other firm's price (thereby gaining the entire market). Thus, different prices cannot be in equilibrium. What if the firms were currently charging the same price and splitting the market equally? Now either firm could increase its profit by barely undercutting the price of the other—settling for a slightly smaller profit margin while doubling its market share. In summary, the possibilities for profitable price cutting are exhausted only when the firms already are charging $P = AC = MC$ and earning zero profits.

The Bertrand model generates the extreme result that price competition, by as few as two firms, can yield a perfectly competitive outcome. It should be emphasized that this result depends on two extreme assumptions—that (1) all competition is on the basis of price and (2) the lower-price firm always claims the entire market. We already have seen that quantity competition leads to quite a different outcome. Furthermore, even if price is the most important competitive dimension, market shares are unlikely to be all or nothing.[9] In models with some degree of product differentiation, competition leads to price reductions, but equilibrium prices remain above the perfectly competitive level.

When to Cut Price   Pricing has been a focus of attention throughout the first half of this book. Let's step back and take stock of the factors that dictate changes in pricing strategy, in particular, that call for price cuts.

Changes in Market Demand.   The surest rationale for a cut in price is an adverse shift in demand. As we've seen, facing a less-favorable demand curve means setting a lower optimal sales target and a lower price. Amid a fall in demand because of a growing recognition of health risks, tanning salons have responded by cutting prices.

---

[9]A good example of the Bertrand model is the case of competitive bidding. Here, the firm that submits the lowest bid price gains the exclusive award of a supply contract. Competitive bidding is discussed in Chapter 13.

Seeing buyer demand sapped by the ongoing US recession, Saks Fifth Avenue broke ranks with other upscale retailers by sharply discounting its prices at the start of the holiday buying season.

Market Skimming.   This strategy of price discriminating over time involves setting a high price to pioneer adopters (who have relatively inelastic demand), then later lowering the price to attract mass-market users (whose demand is more elastic). Apple's iPhone and iPad both saw significant price discounts during their first years on the market.

The Learning Curve.   As a firm gains cumulative experience producing a new product, it can expect to reduce its cost per unit by reengineering and improving the production process. Lower unit costs support lower prices. More important, it pays the firm to cut a product's price at the outset in order to induce a "virtuous circle" of profitability. The initial price cut spurs sales and production levels, speeding the learning process, thereby accelerating cost efficiencies, and, in turn, supporting further price reductions— with additional profit accruing to the firm at each stage. Strong learning curve effects have been documented for a range of assembly-line products: from aircraft to laptops to photocopiers.

Strategic Price Cuts.   Increased competition from competitors—whether in the form of advertising, quality improvements, or aggressive pricing—can be expected to have an adverse effect on the firm's demand and, therefore, might call for price cuts in response. For instance, Neiman Marcus Group, Gucci, Hermes, and several top fashion houses were compelled (albeit belatedly) to follow Saks' price discounting strategy. Major airlines routinely meet the challenge of a rival introducing additional flights along its routes by offering fare discounts.

Boosting Sales of Related Products.   When a firm sells complementary products, cutting the price of one spurs the demand for another, and more importantly, is the path to maximizing the firm's total profit. Gillette is happy to give away its multiblade razors at minimal cost because the company generates its real profit by selling packs of replacement blades at a price of upward of $3 per blade. As long as a consumer is locked into his favorite shaver, the money from blade purchases will keep on coming. Microsoft has long underpriced its Windows operating system because that platform generates significant demand for its applications software such as Microsoft Office. Google generates so much revenue (some $50 billion in 2013) from Internet advertising that it makes sense to tie consumers to Google by giving away free such key online features as e-mail, Google Maps, and its Chrome browser.

OTHER DIMENSIONS OF COMPETITION

Thus far, our focus has been on quantity and price competition within oligopolies. In this final section, we briefly consider two other forms of competition: strategic commitments and advertising.

Strategic Commitments

A comparison of quantity competition and price competition yields a number of general propositions about the strategic actions and reactions of competing firms. Consider once again the case of symmetric firms competing with respect to quantities. A key part of that example was the way in which one firm's quantity action affected the other's—that is, how the competitor would be expected to react. If one firm (for whatever reason) were to increase its quantity of output, then the profit-maximizing response of the other would be to *decrease* its output. (Roughly speaking, the greater is one firm's presence in the market, the less demand there is for the other.) Equation 9.3's reaction function shows this explicitly. We say that the firms' actions are **strategic substitutes** when increasing one firm's action causes the other firm's optimal reaction to decrease. Thus, the duopolists' quantity decisions are strategic substitutes.

By contrast, price competition works quite differently. If one firm changes its price (up or down), the optimal response for the competing firm is to change its price in the *same* direction. (One firm's price cut prompts a price cut by its rival. Conversely, if one firm raises its price, the other can afford to raise its price as well.) The earlier example of Bertrand (winner take all) price competition exhibits exactly this behavior. Similar (but less dramatic) price reactions occur when competition is between differentiated products. (Here, a price cut by one firm will attract only a portion of the other firm's customers and so prompts only a modest price reaction.) We say that the firms' actions are **strategic complements** when a change in one firm's action causes the other firm's optimal response to move in the *same* direction.

A comparison of competition between strategic substitutes and strategic complements leads to the following proposition:

> In a host of oligopoly models, competition involving prices (strategic complements) results in lower equilibrium profits than competition involving quantities (strategic substitutes).

This result underscores the key difference between firm strategies under price competition and quantity competition. When firms compete along the price dimension, a rival's lower price leads to the firm lowering its own price. In short, competition *begets* more competition. By contrast, under quantity competition, a rival's increase in output induces a lower quantity of output by the firm itself; an increase in output *deters* a competitive response. In general, price competition is more intense than quantity competition (which is self-limiting). The upshot is that equilibrium price setting tends to lead to lower profits for the firms than equilibrium quantity setting.

Of course, it is important to keep this result in perspective. Price competition is not always destructive; the particular equilibrium outcome depends, as always, on underlying demand and cost conditions. (For instance, Check Station 3 displays favorable demand conditions in which equilibrium behavior leads to *high* prices.) In other words, the comparison of equilibrium outcomes requires holding other factors constant. The result does suggest an interesting strategic message. Frequently, firms find themselves surveying any number of strategic dimensions—price, quantity, advertising, and so on—and have the opportunity to "pick their battles." Most oligopoly models suggest that it is wise to avoid price competition (because this involves strategic complements) and to compete on quantity and advertising (where both involve strategic substitutes).

COMMITMENTS   Suppose a firm is about to engage in quantity competition but also faces an earlier decision. For instance, the firm has the opportunity to invest in a new production process that has the advantage of lowering its marginal cost of production. Should the firm commit to this process investment? A complete answer to this question depends on anticipating the investment's effect on the subsequent quantity competition. Looking just at the firm's own behavior, we know that the lower marginal cost induces a higher optimal output. But the strategic effect also matters. Because the firms' quantities are strategic substitutes, an increased output by the first firm will induce a lower output by the rival. This reduction in competing output further spurs the firm to greater output and increases its profitability. (Check Station 1 provides a good example of these equilibrium output effects.) In short, the original commitment to invest in capacity might well be profitable exactly *because* of its strategic effect on subsequent competitor behavior.

Economists Drew Fudenberg and Jean Tirole have explored the general principles underlying this example.[10] When the subsequent competition involves strategic substitutes, a tough commitment by one of the firms will advantageously affect the ensuing equilibrium. Here, *tough* denotes any move that induces an increase in the firm's own output and (in turn) a decrease in the rival's output. Making product quality improvements, increasing advertising spending, and lowering unit costs would all qualify as tough commitments. Fudenberg and Tirole characterize any of these moves as part of a "Top-Dog" strategy, an aggressive strategy that induces the rival to back off. (Chapter 10 uses game theory to consider further instances that confer this kind of first-mover advantage.) The extreme case of this strategy occurs if the firm's first move has such a dramatic effect on the economics of its rival that the rival's best response is to exit the market altogether. The top dog has driven its rival from the market.

The logic of strategic commitment is exactly reversed when the subsequent competition involves strategic complements. Consider once again price competition. Here, a tough commitment that implies lower prices by the initiating firm also induces lower prices by the competitor. But a lower rival price is exactly what the first firm *does not want* to happen. (The tough first move would only make sense if it succeeded in driving the competitor out of the market altogether.) Instead, the firm in question should adopt a "Fat-Cat" strategy, to use Fudenberg and Tirole's label. This means making a *soft* first move, such as engaging in product differentiation—real (via product innovation) or perceived (via increased advertising spending). The effect of any soft move is to allow for a higher price for the firm itself and to induce a higher price by the competitor. The point of the initial commitment is to soften or blunt the subsequent price competition.

---

[10]See D. Fudenberg and J. Tirole, "The Fat-Cat Effect, the Puppy-Dog Ploy, and the Lean and Hungry Look," *American Economic Review* (1984): 361–366. An additional source is J. Bulow, J. Geanakopolos, and P. Klemperer, "Multimarket Oligopoly: Strategic Substitutes and Complements," *Journal of Political Economy* (1985): 488–511.

In summary, a tough strategic commitment is advantageous when the subsequent competition involves strategic substitutes; a soft commitment is appropriate when strategic complements are involved.

Advertising

In oligopolies, advertising can be a powerful means of promoting sales. Firms that sell differentiated goods spend enormous sums on advertising. We begin this section by analyzing a single firm's optimal advertising decision. Later, we consider advertising as a competitive weapon within oligopoly.

OPTIMAL ADVERTISING   Consider a consumer-products firm that must determine not only the price at which to sell one of its goods but also the associated level of advertising expenditure. At a given price, an increase in advertising will raise sales to a greater or lesser extent.

One way to picture the firm's decision problem is to write its demand function as $Q(P, A)$. Here the demand function, Q, shows that the quantity of sales depends on price, P, and advertising expenditure, A. The firm's total profit in terms of P and A can be written as

$$\pi = P \cdot Q(P, A) - C[Q(P, A)] - A. \qquad [9.6]$$

Profit is simply revenue minus production cost (that depends on Q) minus total advertising cost. We see that determining the level of advertising involves a basic trade-off: Raising A increases sales and profits (the net value of the first two terms) but is itself costly (the third term). As always, the optimal level of advertising is found where marginal profit with respect to A is zero. Taking the derivative of Equation 9.6 and setting this equal to zero, we find

$$M\pi_A = \partial\pi/\partial A = P(\partial Q/\partial A) - (dC/dQ)(\partial Q/\partial A) - 1 = 0$$

or

$$(P - MC)(\partial Q/\partial A) = 1. \qquad [9.7]$$

The left-hand side of this equation is the marginal profit of an extra dollar of advertising, computed as the increase in quantity ($\partial Q/\partial A$) times the profit contribution per unit. The right-hand side is the MC of advertising ($1). Optimal advertising spending occurs when its marginal benefit (in terms of profit) equals its marginal cost.

EXAMPLE   Let the demand for a good be given by $Q = 10{,}000P^{-5}A^{.5}$ and let $MC = \$.80$. Let's use marginal analysis to find the firm's optimal price, output, and level of advertising. We know that the price exponent measures price elasticity—that is, $E_P = -5$. So we can solve for price using the markup rule: $P = [E_P/(1 + E_P)]MC = (-5/-4)(.8) = \$1.00$. With $P = 1.00$ and $MC = .8$, the firm's contribution is $.20 per unit. Thus, net profit is

$$\pi = .2Q(P, A) - A$$
$$= (.2)(10,000A^{.5}) - A.$$

In turn, we find $M\pi_A = 1,000A^{-.5} - 1 = 0$. A rearrangement gives $A^{.5} = 1,000$. Therefore, $A = (1,000)^2 = \$1,000,000$. Finally, substituting $A = \$1,000,000$ into the demand equation yields $Q = 10,000,000$ units.

ADVERTISING WITHIN OLIGOPOLY   To consider the impact of advertising in an oligopoly, we must move from a single firm's point of view and ask: What is the effect when a small number of oligopolists simultaneously pursue optimal strategies? To illustrate the possibilities, we briefly consider two polar cases.

1. *Product differentiation.* One role of advertising is to underscore real or perceived differences between competing products, that is, to promote product differentiation and brand-name allegiance. Thus, the aim of a firm's advertising is to convince consumers that its product is different and better than competing goods, for example, "Coke is the real thing," "Only Rolaids spells relief," and "Tropicana Orange Juice tastes like fresh squeezed, not concentrate." The ideal result of such advertising is to create a large segment of loyal consumers—customers who will not defect to a rival product, even if the competitor offers a lower price or enhanced features.

    Increased product differentiation lessens the substitutability of other goods while reducing the cross-price elasticity of demand. In other words, it tends to blunt competition between oligopolists on such dimensions as price and performance. (For instance, because of heavy advertising, Dole pineapples and Chiquita bananas enjoy much higher price markups than generic fruit.) The individual oligopolistic firm finds it advantageous to differentiate its product. Moreover, the firms' simultaneous advertising expenditures may well result in increased profits for the oligopoly as a whole.[11]

2. *Informational advertising.* A second major role of advertising is to provide consumers better information about competing goods. Claims that "We offer the lowest price" (or "best financing" or "50 percent longer battery life" or "more convenient locations") clearly fall into this category. Advertising copy frequently provides direct descriptions of products, including photographs.

    The effect of informational advertising is to make consumers more aware of and sensitive to salient differences among competing products. When *imperfect information* is the norm, some firms might charge higher-than-average prices or

---

[11]To construct the most extreme case, suppose that a small amount of advertising has the power to create a mini-monopoly for each differentiated product. Then the profits from higher monopoly prices would far outweigh the cost of the advertising.

deliver lower-than-average quality and still maintain modest market shares. Informational advertising tends to eliminate those possibilities and forces firms to compete more vigorously for *informed* consumers, resulting in lower prices (and/or improved product quality) and lower industry profits.[12]

Across the spectrum of oligopoly, both reasons for advertising—to differentiate products and to provide information—are important. Both effects provide firms an economic incentive to advertise. (Only under perfect competition—where products are standardized and consumers already have perfect information—would we expect advertising to be absent.) However, the implications for firms and consumers (whether advertising enhances or blunts competition) tend to work in opposite directions. Commentators and policy makers have attacked pervasive advertising as anticompetitive. (In novelist F. Scott Fitzgerald's words, "Advertising is a racket. Its contribution to humanity is exactly minus zero.") But, it remains an empirical question as to which aspect of advertising—its procompetitive or anticompetitive effect—tends to be stronger and more important.

There have been numerous research studies concerning the effect of advertising in different industries over different time periods.[13] Overall, findings are mixed. Advertising about price has been found to lower average prices for consumer products, such as toys, gasoline, pharmaceuticals, and eyeglasses. (For instance, consumers in states that ban eyeglass advertising pay higher prices than consumers in states that allow it.) Advertising (once vigorously fought by state and national bar associations) can lower the price of legal services. In certain markets, advertising plays an important role in providing price information. However, there is also countervailing evidence that advertising and product differentiation can create entry barriers and increase industry concentration and profits. (Here, the evidence is somewhat mixed. Whether high levels of advertising cause increased concentration or are *caused by it* is an open question.)

Collusion in the Infant Formula Industry Revisited	We can use concepts developed in this chapter to shed light on the structure and conduct of the infant-formula industry in the 1990s. First, the industry was dominated by three large firms that made up 96 percent of total sales, a clear triopoly. Thus, there existed preconditions for the exercise of market power. Second, there is evidence that leading firms enjoyed excess profits in the 1980s and early 1990s, profit margins as much as 25 percent above average costs. Third, the three firms had nearly identical patterns of price increases well in excess of the cost of milk (the main ingredient in formula). The companies succeeded in these price increases

---

[12]To cite another extreme case, suppose that informational advertising's sole effect is to shuffle sales from one oligopolist to another; no amount of advertising can increase total industry sales. Furthermore, each oligopolist has some product feature for which it pays to advertise. The result is a classic prisoner's dilemma. Advertising is in each oligopolist's self-interest. But, collectively, advertising is self-defeating. Total sales do not increase and market shares remain unchanged. Thus, from the industry's point of view, the total sum spent on advertising is wasted.

[13]A fine survey and discussion of these studies can be found in D. W. Carlton and J. M. Perloff, *Modern Industrial Organization,* Chapter 14 (Reading, MA: Addison-Wesley, 2004).

despite some decline in formula use (and a resurgence in breastfeeding). This pricing behavior raises the suspicion of tacit collusion among the companies to maintain orderly (and increasing) prices. Indeed, the Federal Trade Commission undertook an investigation of these pricing practices for possible collusion.

The formula industry met a fourth acid test of entrenched oligopoly: The market was insulated from competition by new entrants. Despite their size and prowess in other markets, Carnation and Gerber made few inroads in the US infant-formula market. The major companies' direct giveaway programs to hospitals and doctors was an effective entry barrier. With 90 percent of mothers continuing to use the formula brought home from the hospital, the companies enjoyed the ideal captive market. Furthermore, the American Academy of Pediatrics allied itself with the dominant firms to press for a prohibition on all advertising of infant formula (so as to encourage breastfeeding. Carnation and Gerber advertised aggressively and insisted it was the only chance they had to bring their products before the public. Carnation filed a lawsuit against the academy and the formula producers, accusing them of conspiring to prevent it from marketing formula. A Bristol-Myers memo revealed in a Florida lawsuit stated, "It is probably in our best interests to forestall any form of consumer advertising." The chief of Florida's antitrust division added, "I have walked into my pediatrician's office and have had him try to convince me not to buy Carnation even though it is cheaper."

What is the likely economic impact of competitive bidding for formula sales under the Women, Infants, and Children (WIC) program? As noted, most states allow vouchers to be exchanged for any brand of formula. These states have seen company discounts averaging $.50 per can. Formula companies lobbied strongly against winner-take-all bidding, arguing that awarding the WIC contract to one bidder would restrict a family's choice of formula. The experience in states with winner-take-all bidding indicates why the companies resisted it. Competition was intense. With as much as one-third of the total market up for bid, winning discounts averaged $1.00 per can. Indeed, the winning discount reached a high of $1.50 per can in Michigan. (Here, the net price of $.60 roughly matched estimated marginal cost. Thus, this bidding outcome appears to have achieved the Bertrand equilibrium.) Overall, competitive bidding offered the advantage of lower prices and the real possibility of competition by new entrants.[14]

In the late 1990s, the three major formula producers reached a settlement with the Federal Trade Commission in its price-fixing investigation. While admitting no wrongdoing, the firms agreed to make reimbursements to formula customers in eight states. Since 2000, Nestle has entered the US market and slowly built its market share to about 10 percent. In addition, a number of generic formula makers have made small market-share gains.

---

[14] Accounts of the history of the formula market, the advertising controversy, and experiments with competitive bidding include B. P. Noble, "Price-Fixing and Other Charges Roil Once-Placid Market," *The New York Times,* July 28, 1991: p. C9; B. Meier, "Battle for Baby Formula Market," *The New York Times* (June 15, 1993): p. C1; M. Brick, "Makers of Generic Baby Formula Win Round in Court," *The New York Times*, May 2, 2001: p. C5; G. Retsinas, "The Marketing of a Superbaby Formula," *The New York Times*, June 1, 2003: p. BU1; and D. Betson, "Impact of the WIC Program on the Infant Formula Market," Final; Report for Grant Award 43-3AEM-3-80107, 2007.

SUMMARY

Decision-Making Principles

1. The key to making optimal decisions in an oligopoly is anticipating the actions of one's rivals.

2. In the dominant-firm model, smaller firms behave competitively, taking price as fixed when making their quantity decisions. Anticipating this behavior, the dominant firm maximizes its profit by setting quantity and price (and applying $MR = MC$) along its *net* demand curve.

3. When output competition is between symmetrically positioned oligopolists (the Cournot case), each firm maximizes its profit by anticipating the (profit-maximizing) quantities set by its rivals.

4. Intense price competition has the features of the prisoner's dilemma; optimal behavior implies mutual price cuts and reduced profits.

5. Advertising should be undertaken up to the point where increased profit from greater sales just covers the last advertising dollar spent.

Nuts and Bolts

1. An oligopoly is a market dominated by a small number of firms. Each firm's profit is affected not only by its own actions but also by actions of its rivals.

2. An industry's concentration ratio measures the percentage of total sales accounted for by the top 4 (or 8 or 20) firms in the market. Another measure of industry structure is the Herfindahl-Hirschman Index (HHI), defined as the sum of the squared market shares of all firms. The greater the concentration index or the HHI, the more significant the market dominance of a small number of firms. Other things being equal, increases in concentration can be expected to be associated with increases in prices and profits.

3. There are two main models of quantity rivalry: competition with a dominant firm or competition among equals. In each, equilibrium quantities are determined such that no firm can profit by altering its planned output. The industry equilibrium approaches the perfectly competitive outcome as the number of (identical) firms increases without bound.

4. If a firm expects price cuts (but not price increases) to be matched by its rivals, the result is a kink in the firm's demand curve. Prices will be relatively stable (because price changes will tend to be unprofitable).

5. The prisoner's dilemma embraces such diverse cases as price wars, cartel cheating, arms races, and resource depletion. Self-interested behavior by interacting parties leads to an inferior outcome for the group as a whole.

Questions and Problems

1. Venture capitalists provide funds to finance new companies (startups), usually in return for a share of the firm's initial profits (if any). Of course, venture capitalists look to back experienced entrepreneurs with strong products (or at least product blueprints). But potential competitors and the structure of the market into which the new firm enters also are important. According to the conventional wisdom, the best startup prospects involve entry into loose oligopolies. What economic factors might be behind this conventional wisdom?

2. In granting (or prohibiting) proposed acquisitions or mergers in an industry, government regulators consider a number of factors, including the acquisition's effect on concentration, ease of entry into the market, extent of ongoing price competition, and potential efficiency gains. In 2011, T-Mobile agreed to merge with AT&T at an acquisition price of $39 billion. However, facing opposition from the Department of Justice, the companies later abandoned their merger plans. In 2011, AT&T's market share of the US wireless market was 26.6 percent, with T-Mobile 12.2 percent, Verizon 31.3 percent, Sprint 11.9 percent, TracFone 5.0 percent, US Cellular 3.1 percent, MetroPCS 2.3 percent, Cricket 1.6 percent, and numerous small providers making up the remaining 4 percent.

a. What would be the effect of the merger on the market's concentration ratio? On the HHI?

b. Antitrust guidelines call for close scrutiny of mergers in moderately concentrated markets (HHI between 1,500 and 2,500) if the resulting HHI increase is more than 100 to 200 points. How would this rule apply to the AT&T merger with T-Mobile? (How would the rule apply to a hypothetical merger between T-Mobile and TracFone?)

c. AT&T argued that the merger would extend its network, providing more reliable and faster cell phone service (particularly to existing T-Mobile customers who on average have lower-grade service plans at cheaper rates). Market observers were worried that after the merger, AT&T would raise cellular rates to some customer segments. Briefly evaluate these pros and cons.

3. The OPEC cartel is trying to determine the total amount of oil to sell on the world market. It estimates world demand for oil to be $Q_W = 96 - .2P$, where Q_W denotes the quantity of oil (in millions of barrels per day) and P is price per barrel. OPEC's economists also recognize the importance of non-OPEC oil suppliers. These can be described by the estimated supply curve $Q_S = .3P + 26$.

a. Write down OPEC's net demand curve.

b. OPEC's marginal cost is estimated to be $20 per barrel. Determine OPEC's profit-maximizing output and price. What quantity of oil is supplied by non-OPEC sources? What percentage of the world's total oil supply comes from OPEC?

4. Firm A is the dominant firm in a market where industry demand is given by $Q_D = 48 - 4P$. There are four "follower" firms, each with long-run marginal cost given by $MC = 6 + Q_F$. Firm A's long-run marginal cost is 6.

a. Write the expression for the total supply curve of the followers (Q_S) as this depends on price. (Remember, each follower acts as a price taker.)

b. Find the net demand curve facing firm A. Determine A's optimal price and output. How much output do the other firms supply in total?

5. Two firms serve a market where demand is described by $P = 120 - 5(Q_1 + Q_2)$. Each firm's marginal cost is 60.

a. Suppose each firm maximizes its own profit, treating the other's quantity as constant. Find an expression for firm 1's optimal output as it depends on firm 2's. In equilibrium, what (common) level of output will each firm supply?

b. Suppose, instead, that the firms collude in setting their outputs. What outputs should they set and why?

6. Firms M and N compete for a market and must independently decide how much to advertise. Each can spend either $10 million or $20 million on advertising. If the firms spend equal amounts, they split the $120 million market equally. (For instance, if both choose to spend $20 million, each firm's net profit is 60 − 20 = $40 million.) If one firm spends $20 million and the other $10 million, the former claims two-thirds of the market and the latter one-third.

		Firm N's Advertising	
		$10 million	$20 million
Firm M's	$10 million	?, ?	?, ?
Advertising	$20 million	?, ?	40, 40

a. Fill in the profit entries in the payoff table.

b. If the firms act independently, what advertising level should each choose? Explain. Is a prisoner's dilemma present?

c. Could the firms profit by entering into an industry-wide agreement concerning the extent of advertising? Explain.

7. In each case, provide a brief explanation of whether a prisoner's dilemma is present. If so, suggest ways the dilemma can be overcome.

a. When there is a bumper crop (a large supply and, therefore, low prices), farmers incur losses.

b. Individual work effort has been observed to suffer when managers are grouped in teams with all team members receiving comparable compensation based on the overall performance of the group.

8. Economists Orley Ashenfelter and David Bloom studied disputes that were brought to arbitration between management and workers' unions. They found that being represented by a lawyer increased that side's chance of winning its arbitration case. The payoff table (listing the union's chance of winning the arbitration case) summarizes their empirical findings.

		Management	
		W/O Lawyer	Lawyer
Union	**W/O Lawyer**	.56	.27
	Lawyer	.77	.54

For instance, according to the upper-left entry, if neither side uses a lawyer, the union is expected to prevail in the arbitration case 56 percent of the time.

a. Determine each side's optimal action and the resulting outcome.

b. Does this situation constitute a prisoner's dilemma? Explain briefly.

9. Two firms produce differentiated products. Firm 1 faces the demand curve: $Q_1 = 75 - P_1 + .5P_2$. (Note that a lower competing price robs the firm of some, but not all, sales. Thus, price competition is not as extreme as in the Bertrand model.) Firm 2 faces the analogous demand curve $Q_2 = 75 - P_2 + .5P_1$. For each firm, $AC = MC = 30$.

a. Confirm that firm 1's optimal price depends on P_2 according to $P_1 = 52.5 + .25P_2$. (*Hint:* Set up the profit expression $\pi_1 = (P_1 - 30)Q_1 = (P_1 - 30)(75 - P_1 + .5P_2)$ and set $M\pi = \partial\pi_1/\partial P_1 = 0$ to solve for P_1 in terms of P_2. Alternatively, use the rearranged, inverse demand curve: $P_1 = 75 - Q_1 + .5P_2$. Then, set $MR_1 = MC$ and solve for Q_1 and then P_1 in terms of P_2.

b. Explain why the firm should lower its price in response to a lower price by its competitor.

c. In equilibrium, the firms set identical prices: $P_1 = P_2$. Find the firms' equilibrium prices, quantities, and profits.

10. In Problem 9, suppose that firm 2 acts as a price leader and can commit in advance to setting its price once and for all. In turn, firm 1 will react to firm 2's price, according to the profit-maximizing response found earlier, $P_1 = 52.5 + .25P_2$. In committing to a price, firm 2 is contemplating either a price increase to $P_2 = \$73$ or a price cut to $P_2 = \$67$. Which price constitutes firm 2's optimal commitment strategy? Justify your answer and explain *why* it makes sense.

11. Firm Z faces the price equation $P = 50 + A^5 - Q$, and the cost function $C = 20Q + A$, where A denotes advertising spending.

a. Other things (price) held constant, does an increase in advertising spending lead to greater sales? Does advertising spending represent a fixed cost or a variable cost?

b. Find the firm's profit-maximizing quantity as a function of A. (*Hint:* Treating A as fixed, we have $MR = 50 + A^5 - 2Q$.) Then, find the firm's optimal price (again, as it depends on A). Explain these results.

c. Using the results in part (b), write the firm's profit expression in terms of A alone. Find the firm's optimal level of advertising. Find its optimal quantity and price.

*12. a. Using the marginal condition in Equation 9.7, show that an equivalent condition for the optimal level of advertising is $(P - MC)Q/A = 1/E_A$, where $E_A = (\partial Q/Q)/(\partial A/A)$ is the elasticity of demand with respect to advertising. In words, the ratio of advertising spending to operating profit should equal E_A. Other things being equal, the greater this elasticity, the greater the spending on advertising.

b. Use the markup rule, $(P - MC)/P = -1/E_P$, and the equation in part (a) to show that $A/(PQ) = -E_A/E_P$. *Hint:* Divide the former by the latter. According to this result, the ratio of advertising spending to dollar sales is simply the ratio of the respective elasticities.

c McDonald's advertising spending constitutes about 3 percent of its total sales revenue. By contrast, Walt Disney Studios spends about 25 percent of its total revenue on advertising. Given the result in part (b), what must be true about the firms' respective price and advertising elasticities to explain this difference?

Discussion Question   Choose a good or service that is supplied by a small number of oligopoly firms. (Examples range from athletic shoes to aircraft to toothpaste, or choose a product from the industry list in Table 9.1.) Gather information on the good from public sources (business periodicals, the Internet, or government reports) to answer the following questions.

a. Who are the leading firms, and what are their market shares? Compute the concentration ratio for the relevant market.

*Starred problems are more challenging.

b. What are the most important dimensions (price, technological innovation, advertising and promotion, and so on) on which firms compete?

c. What has been the history of entry into the market? What kinds of barriers to entry exist?

Spreadsheet Problems

S1. A dominant firm in an industry has costs given by $C = 70 + 5q_L$. The dominant firm sets the market price, and the eight "small" firms coexisting in the market take this price as given. Each small firm has costs given by $C = 25 + q^2 - 4q$. Total industry demand is given by $Q_d = 400 - 20P$.

a. Create a spreadsheet similar to the accompanying example to model price setting by the dominant firm. (If you completed Problem S1 of Chapter 7, you need only make slight modifications in that spreadsheet.)

b. Experiment with prices between $P = 7$ and $P = 16$. For each price, determine the output supplied by the typical small firm by setting q such that $P = MC$. Taking into account the supply response of the eight other firms, what price seems to be most profitable for the dominant firm?

c. Use your spreadsheet's optimizer to find the dominant firm's optimal price. (*Hint*: Adjust cells B8 and B14 to maximize cell I8 subject to the constraint G14 equal to zero.)

	A	B	C	D	E	F	G	H	I	J
1										
2			Dominant Firm							
3			Price Leadership							
4										
5			Market Supply & Demand				Dominant Firm			
6		Price	# S. Firms	Q_s	Q_d		$Q_d - Q_s$	Cost	Profit	
7										
8		8	8	48	240		192	1030	506	
9										
10										
11					Small Firms					
12		q	MC	Cost	AC		P − MC	Firm Profit		
13										
14		6	8	37	6.167		0	11.0		
15										
16										
17			Small Firms' supply is determined by $P = MC$.							
18			Large Firm maximizes profit given net demand.							
19										

S2. A firm faces a price equation $P = 12.5 + .5A^{.5} - .25Q$ and a cost equation $C = 5Q + A$, where Q denotes its output and A denotes its level of advertising expenditure.

a. Create a spreadsheet to describe the firm's profit as it varies with output and advertising. Set advertising spending at 50 and find the firm's optimal level of output.

b. Use your spreadsheet's optimizer to find the firm's optimal output and level of advertising spending.

Suggested References

The following texts provide comprehensive treatments of market structure and oligopoly.

Besanko, D., D. Dranove, M. Shanley, and S. Schaefer. *Economics of Strategy*. New York: John Wiley & Sons, 2013. (See especially Chapters 5–8.)

Brock, J. (ed). *The Structure of American Industry*. Upper Saddle River, NJ: Prentice-Hall, 2013.

Carlton, D. W., and J. M. Perloff. *Modern Industrial Organization*. Reading, MA: Addison-Wesley, 2004.

Dixit, A., D. Reiley, and S. Skeath. *Games of Strategy*. New York: W. W. Norton, 2009.

McGahan, A. M., and M. E. Porter. "How Much Does Industry Matter Really?" *Strategic Management Journal* 18 (Summer 1997): 167–185.

The preceding article provides a statistical analysis of firm profitability. It finds that variations in profitability depend on firm characteristics and strategies (accounting for 32 percent of profit variations), market structure (19 percent), other factors (7 percent), and random fluctuations (42 percent).

Shepherd, J. M., and W. G. Shepherd. *The Economics of Industrial Organization*. Upper Saddle River, NJ: Prentice-Hall, 2008.

Tirole, J. *The Theory of Industrial Organization*, Chapters 3, 5, and 7. Cambridge, MA: MIT Press, 1989.

Powerful and intriguing analyses of the prisoner's dilemma include:

Axelrod, R. M. *The Complexity of Cooperation*. Princeton, NJ: Princeton University Press, 1997.

Axelrod, R. M. *The Evolution of Cooperation*. New York: Basic Books, 1985.

Fine articles on advertising include:

Greuner, M. R., D. R. Kamerschen, and P. G. Klein. "The Competitive Effects of Advertising in the US Automobile Industry, 1970–94." *International Journal of the Economics of Business* 7 (2000): 245–261.

Silk, A. J., L. R. Klein, and E. R. Berndt. "The Emerging Position of the Internet as an Advertising Medium." *Netnomics* 3 (2001): 129–148.

Concentration ratios gathered by the US Bureau of the Census are available online at: http://www.census.gov/epcd/www/concentration.html.

Check Station Answers

1. Firm 1's optimal reaction function remains $Q_1 = 12 - .5Q_2$. To determine its optimal output, firm 2 sets marginal revenue equal to 9 (its MC): $30 - Q_1 - 2Q_2 = 9$; therefore, $Q_2 = 10.5 - .5Q_1$. Solving these equations simultaneously, we find $Q_1 = 9$ and $Q_2 = 6$. In equilibrium, the lower-cost firm claims a majority market share.

2. The kink occurs at $Q = 10$. At outputs less than 10, $MR = 30 - 2Q$. For outputs greater than 10, $MR = 36 - 3.2Q$. Evaluating each expression at $Q = 10$, we see that MR drops from 10 to 4. As long as MC is between 10 and 4, the firm's optimal output is 10 and its optimal price is 20.

3. In the off-diagonal entries in Table 9.2, both the low-price firm and the high-price firm earn $8 million in profit. This change completely reverses the firms' incentives. Regardless of what action the other takes, each firm's profit-maximizing strategy is to set a *high* price. (Comparing possible profits, 10 is greater than 8, and 8 is greater than 7.) Strong brand allegiance removes the incentive to cut price.

4. The minimum sentencing law changes the off-diagonal payoffs in Table 9.3. Now a unilateral confession brings a three-year term (not a one-year term). It is in each prisoner's best interest to stay mum, provided he expects his partner to do likewise (two years is better than three years). By limiting the scope of plea bargaining, the law has impeded the prosecutor's ability to secure longer prison terms.

Bundling and Tying

LO#1. Explain how oligopolistic firms use bundling and tying.

Besides pricing its separate products, oligopolistic firms frequently choose to **bundle** their products, that is, to sell two or more products as a package. Under the right circumstances, bundling can be considerably more profitable than separate sales. Consider the following example.

BUNDLING FILMS A movie studio has two films ready for sale to two theater chains. Each chain consists of 500 multiscreen theaters. Table 9A.1a shows the values each chain places on each film. For instance, chain 1 is willing to pay up to $13,000 per screen per week for film X; chain 2 will pay only $7,000; and so on. (The differences in value reflect the respective geographic patterns of the chains' theaters and the fact that some films tend to "play better" in some regions and cities than others.)

The movie studio has a number of pricing options. If it sells film X separately and charges $7,000 per screen per week, it will sell to both chains, earning total revenue of $7 million per week.[1] If it charges $13,000 instead, it will sell only to chain 1, earning $6.5 million in revenue. Clearly, the $7,000 price is the better option. Similarly, the studio's optimal price for film Y is $6,000 per screen per week. At these prices, the films will be sold to both chains and will produce $13 million in total revenue.

What if the studio were to sell the films as a package at a bundled price? The last column of Table 9A.1 shows the combined value each chain puts on the film package. Clearly, the studio's optimal bundled price is $P_B = \$18,000$.

At this price, both chains purchase the bundle, and the studio earns $18 million per week, increasing the studio's revenue by $5 million, or some 38 percent. What is the source of this additional profit? The answer lies in the fact that each chain's values for the films are *negatively* correlated. The chain with the higher value for one film has the lower value for the other. Since higher and lower values are offsetting, the chains have very similar *total* values for the bundled package. By bundling films, the studio can set a

---

[1]Here and throughout, we are presuming that a chain will purchase the film at a price equal to its value; in fact, purchasing or not would be a matter of indifference. If you are worried about this knife-edge case, think of the studio as charging a slightly lower price, $6,995 say, in order to provide the chain a strictly positive incentive to buy. (Note that this makes no essential difference in the revenue calculations.)

TABLE 9A.1

Selling Films: Separate
Sales versus Bundling

Depending on the
circumstances, a
firm can increase its
revenue via bundling.

(a)

		Values ($000)		
		Film X	Film Y	Bundle
Theater Chains	**Chain 1**	13	6	19
	Chain 2	7	11	18

(b)

		Values ($000)		
		Film X	Film Y	Bundle
Theater Chains	**Chain 1**	13	6	19
	Chain 2	7	11	18
	Chain 3	15	2	17
	Marginal Cost	5	5	10

price ($18,000) that extracts nearly all of each chain's total value (or consumer surplus) for the films, without pricing either chain out of the market.

Notice that bundling holds no advantage over separate pricing if the chains' values for film Y are reversed. In this scenario, chain 1 puts higher values ($13,000 and $11,000) on both films. Each chain's values are *positively* correlated; that is, high values go with high values, low values with low values. Check for yourself that the studio's optimal bundled price is $P_B = \$7,000 + \$6,000 = \$13,000$. In other words, the bundled price is simply the sum of the separate film prices. Sold separately or as a bundle, the films deliver exactly the same revenue.

Bundling can be profitable even when the goods' values are *uncorrelated.* Consider once again the studio's pricing problem, but now let each chain have uncorrelated values. In particular, suppose that each of the 1,000 theaters that make up the two chains values film X at $13,000 or $7,000, with each value equally likely. In turn, each theater values film Y at $11,000 or $6,000, again with each value equally likely. (Like coin tosses, a theater's value for one film is independent of its value for the other.) Thus, the same numbers in Table 9A.1a apply, but with new interpretations. As before, the studio's optimal separate film prices are $P_X = \$7,000$ and $P_Y = \$6,000$, inducing all theaters to purchase both films. Now consider the demand for the films as a bundle. From the values in Table 9A.1, the possible bundled values are $13,000 (25 percent of theaters), $18,000, (25 percent), $19,000 (25 percent), and $24,000 (25 percent). If the studio sets $P_B = \$13,000$, all theaters purchase the film. However, the studio can do better by raising its price to $P_B = \$18,000$, inducing 75 percent of the theaters to purchase the bundle. To check this, note that only the "$13,000" theaters refuse to buy. The studio's revenue is ($18,000)(750) = $13,500,000. In short, even with independent demands, bundling has a revenue advantage over separate sales. (Check for yourself that raising the bundled price above $18,000 is counterproductive.)

MIXED BUNDLING   Thus far, our discussion has centered on the potential advantages of so-called pure bundling vis-a-vis separate sales. Of course, firms frequently offer customers both options: to purchase the bundle or to buy only one of the goods at a separate price. This policy is termed **mixed bundling**.

Table 9A.1b demonstrates the advantage of mixed bundling. Following our original interpretation, chains 1 and 2 have negatively correlated values for the films (the same values as before). We have modified the example in two ways. First, we have added a third buyer, chain 3, which places a very low value on film Y. (Think of chain 3's theaters as being spread throughout retirement communities. Film X is *Everyone Loves Gramma* and film Y is *Horror on Prom Night*.) Second, we have introduced a cost associated with producing and selling the film. (The $5,000 cost in the example reflects the studio's cost of creating extra prints of the film for distribution to theaters.)[2]

Now consider the studio's possible pricing strategies. Its most profitable pure-bundling strategy is to set $P_B = \$17,000$ and to sell to all three chains (1,500 theaters), giving it total profit: $\pi = (\$17,000 - \$10,000)(1,500) = \$10,500,000$. (Check for yourself that setting $P_B = \$18,000$ and selling only to chains 1 and 2 is less profitable.) Alternatively, the studio can pursue mixed bundling: pricing the bundle at $P_B = \$18,000$ and pricing the separate films at $P_X = \$15,000$ and $P_Y = \$12,000$. Given these prices, chains 1 and 2 purchase the bundle, while chain 3 purchases only film X. Therefore, the studio's total profit is: $(\$18,000 - \$10,000)(1,000) + (\$15,000 - \$5,000)(500) = \$13,000,000$. Relative to pure bundling, mixed bundling has increased the studio's profit by $2.5 million.

What is the source of this $2.5 million advantage? First, the studio gains by raising the bundled price paid by chains 1 and 2 from $17,000 (under pure bundling) to $18,000, thereby increasing its profit by $1 million. Second, under pure bundling, chain 3 was induced to buy film Y—a film that costs $5,000 per print but only returns $2,000 to chain 3 in value. Mixed bundling precludes this purchase and transfers the savings, $(\$5,000 - \$2,000)(500) = \$1,500,000$, to the studio in added profit. In short, these two gains, $1,000,000 + $1,500,000, account for the total $2,500,000 increase in profit.

In this example, mixed bundling is more profitable than pure bundling, but this need not be the case in general. As the example shows, the potential advantage of mixed bundling occurs when there are significant marginal costs associated with separate goods, and some consumers place very low values on some goods. In this case, allowing separate purchases via mixed bundling benefits both buyer and seller. Absent these conditions, pure bundling or even separate sales may be more profitable.

Finally, the case of mixed bundling clearly underscores a basic point: bundling (of either sort) is a form of price discrimination. In effect, bundling represents a quantity discount; the price of the package is far less than the sum of the separate goods' prices. As this example shows, a particular customer may put a much lower value on one item in the bundle than another. By offering the second item in the bundle at minimal extra cost, the firm lures additional purchasers and increases its revenue in the process.

TYING Closely related to bundling is **tying**, which occurs when a firm selling one product requires (or attempts to require) the purchase of another of its related products. For instance, 30 years ago, customers who leased Xerox copiers were required to buy

---

[2]In Table 9A.1a, we ignored marginal costs for the purpose of keeping things simple. It is easy to check (after computing profits rather than revenues) that pure bundling becomes even more advantageous if marginal costs are present.

Xerox paper. Although strict requirements are rare today, companies continue to try to induce customers to purchase related items. Microsoft Corporation claims that its applications programs work best with its Windows operating systems. General Motors insists that genuine GM replacement parts are essential for its cars and trucks.

A firm has several reasons for tying. First, it is one way to ensure peak performance for the good or service. By ensuring quality, the firm protects its brand name and reputation. For instance, McDonald's insists that all its franchise restaurants buy materials and food from itself. Second, the firm can use tie-in sales as a subtle form of price discrimination. By charging a price above marginal cost for the complementary product (copier paper, for instance), the firm can effectively require intensive users of its main product (the copier) to pay a higher (total) price than average users. Thus, the firm can effectively segment the market according to differing demands. Third, even if there are no differences in buyers, tying presents the opportunity to gain a captive audience of buyers for the complementary product. The result is relatively inelastic demand and substantial price markups and profits for the firm. (For instance, the average list price of an American-made automobile is about $20,000. But the cost of buying all its parts separately, at replacement part prices, would be over $50,000, even before assembly.) In some cases, a firm might well find it advantageous to discount its main product (even price it below average cost) in order to generate a customer base for highly profitable tie-in sales.

Problems

1. Peter's Restaurant lists separate prices for all the items on its dinner menu. Chez Pierre offers only a fixed-price complete dinner (with patrons choosing from a list of appetizers, entrees, and desserts). Casa Pedro offers complete dinners at a fixed price and an a la carte menu. Under what different circumstances might these respective pricing schemes make economic sense? Explain briefly.

*2. A firm sells two goods in a market consisting of three types of consumers. The accompanying table shows the values consumers place on the goods. The unit cost of producing each good is $10.

		Good X	Good Y
	A	$8	$20
Consumers	B	14	14
	C	20	8

Find the optimal prices for (1) selling the goods separately, (2) pure bundling, and (3) mixed bundling. Which pricing strategy is most profitable?

CHAPTER 10

Game Theory and Competitive Strategy

It is a remarkable fact that business strategies are played largely in the mind. Only a small part of the play appears in overt action. Its full scope and depth lie in the players' looking backward and forward and running through their minds their alternative moves and countermoves.

JOHN McDONALD, *THE GAME OF BUSINESS*

LO#1. Model the key features of competitive situations using game theory.

LO#2. Use payoff tables to analyze competitive situations using game theory.

LO#3. Discuss a selection of competitive strategies that blend competition and cooperation.

Three airlines (A, B, and C) are competing for passengers on a lucrative long-haul air route. At present, the carriers are charging identical fares ($225 for a one-way ticket), the result of a truce in recent price wars. The airlines currently compete for market share via the number of scheduled daily departures they offer. Each airline must make a decision on its desired number of departures for the coming month—without knowing its rivals' plans ahead of time. Each airline is aware of the following facts:

A Battle for Air Passengers

1. The size of the total daily passenger market is stable regardless of the number of departures offered. At current prices, an estimated 2,000 passengers fly the route each day.

2. Each airline's share of these total passengers equals its share of the total flights offered by the three airlines. (For example, if airline A offers twice as many flights as each of its rivals, it claims half of all passengers and B and C obtain 25 percent shares.)

3. The airlines fly identical planes and have identical operating costs. Each plane holds a maximum of 200 passengers. Regardless of the plane's loading (full, half full, and so on), each one-way trip on the route costs the airline $20,000.

As the manager of one of these airlines, how many departures should you schedule for the coming month? After seeing the first month's results (your rivals' choices and the resulting airline profits), what decisions would you make for the second month and subsequent months?

In pursuing his or her objectives, how should a decision maker choose a course of action in competition with rivals who are acting in their own interests? This is the essential question addressed by the discipline of **game theory**. We will apply this approach to the specific problem of firms competing within a market. In this context, we could just as well call our approach *strategic profit analysis*. Nonetheless, the more general term, *game theory*, remains apt. This name emphasizes the kind of logical analysis evident in games of pure strategy—chess, poker, even war games. As we shall see, strategic considerations are equally important when firms vie for market share, engage in patent races, wage price wars, and enter new markets. Indeed, it is fair to say that over the last 25 years, the game-theoretic approach has been at the heart of the most important advances in understanding competitive strategies.

The key presumption of game theory is that each decision maker (or player) acts rationally in pursuing his or her own interest and recognizes that competitors also act rationally.[1] Although rational behavior may be directed toward a variety of goals, the usual operational meaning is that all players pursue profit-maximizing strategies and expect competitors to do likewise. (In this sense, the models of quantity and price competition discussed in the preceding chapter are game-theoretic models.)

SIZING UP COMPETITIVE SITUATIONS

A convenient way to begin is with an overview of the basic game-theoretic elements of competitive situations. We begin with elements *common to all* competitive situations.

1. **Players and their actions.** If it is to have a strategic interest, the competitive situation must involve two or more players whose choices of actions affect each other. (It is customary to use *player* as a catch-all term. Depending on the context, a player may be an individual, a manager, a firm, a government decision maker, a military leader, a representative of a group or coalition, you name it.) In the example opening this chapter, the players are the managers of three competing airlines. Each must decide what action to take—what number of daily departures to fly along the air route in question. By deliberate intent, this example considers only one kind of action. Generally, an airline's operations on a single air route involve decisions about prices, plane scheduling, advertising, and so on. In broadest terms, an airline strategy would encompass marketing decisions, investment decisions (ordering planes, expanding terminals, and choosing hubs), labor decisions, and merger and acquisition strategies.

2. **Outcomes and payoffs.** The firm's action, together with actions taken by its rivals, determines the outcome of the competition. In the battle for air passengers, the three airlines' numbers of departures completely determine their market shares

---

[1]The publication in 1944 of *The Theory of Games and Economic Behavior,* by Oskar Morgenstern and John Von Neumann, launched the discipline of game theory. The first 35 years were marked by theoretical advancements and applications to economics, international relations, and conflict studies. The last 35 years have seen an explosion of interest in extending and applying game theory in such diverse areas as management science, economics, political science, evolutionary biology, and especially competitive strategy.

(and the number of tickets they sell). Associated with any outcome is a payoff that embodies each competitor's ultimate objective. For a private firm, such as an airline, this payoff usually is measured in terms of monetary profit. In other situations, payoffs take nonmonetary forms. In a war, payoffs might be expressed in terms of territory taken, number of enemy killed, and so on. In the race for the US presidency, payoffs might be counted in electoral college votes. In short, a payoff summarizes and measures the objective of a given player.

3. **Underlying "rules."** As important as the players, actions, outcomes, and payoffs are the formal and informal rules that govern the behavior of the competitors. One category of rules includes generally agreed-upon competitive practices, laws, and specific industry regulations. For instance, antitrust rules and regulations prohibit price collusion, unfair practices, and mergers that would increase monopoly power. A second category of "rules" provides a framework to model the competition. They specify whether competitors take actions simultaneously or sequentially. These rules also describe what each competitor knows about the others' preferences and previous moves at the time it takes action. In the battle for air passengers, airlines set their number of departures independently and without knowing their competitors' decisions.

Equally important, competitive situations *differ* across a number of dimensions.

1. **Number of competitors.** The number of competitors is one fundamental way to categorize competitive situations. We distinguish between settings with two competitors (so-called two-person games) and those with more than two (*n*-person or many-person games). In a two-person game, you and your adversary have conflicting interests to a greater or lesser degree. In the preceding chapter, we considered quantity and price competition between duopolists. In Chapter 15, we will examine two-party negotiations: between buyer and seller, management and labor, plaintiff and defendant. Frequently, one can analyze multi-competitor settings as if they involved only two parties: the firm in question versus all other competitors. This is true in the battle for air passengers. One airline's market share depends on its own number of departures and on the *total* departures by its competitors (not the particular breakdown). Thus, an airline need only anticipate the combined actions of its competitors to determine its own best response.

   When there are more than two interested players, one must distinguish the differing interests of the multiple parties. For instance, when a mediator or arbitrator intervenes in two-party disputes, this third party's actions and preferences influence the final outcome. Second, with multiple parties, there is the possibility that some of the competitors will form coalitions to deal more effectively with the others. Cartels form to attempt to exercise market power as a group; workers join unions; and nations sign mutual aid treaties. When coalitions are present, an important issue is their stability. How likely is it that members of one coalition will break with their original partners to join others, form new coalitions, or strike out on their own?

2. **Degree of mutual interest.** In some situations, the interests of the competitors are strictly opposed; one side's gain is the other side's loss. At the end of a poker game, for example, there is simply an exchange of dollars. Since winnings are

balanced by losses, the total net gain of the players together is equal to zero. In the terminology of game theory, this type of competitive situation is called a **zero-sum game**. The zero-sum game may be thought of as one extreme—that of pure conflict. At the other extreme are situations of pure common interest—situations in which "competitors" win or lose together, and both prefer the same outcome. Of course, real-world examples of either pure cooperation or pure conflict are the exception. In most settings, players exhibit varying degrees of common interest and competition. Because different outcomes can lead to very different (and non-offsetting) gains and losses for the competitors, these situations are designated **non-zero-sum games**.

The battle for air passengers is a non-zero-sum competition. Certainly, airlines are competing for passengers at their rivals' expense. But they also recognize that flooding the market with flights can be suicidal for all. (After all, total demand is limited and extra flights are costly.) In Chapter 15, labor and management find themselves in a similar position during contract negotiations. While each side seeks to secure better terms for itself, both have an interest in avoiding a costly strike. In short, a realistic description of managerial strategies in competitive settings must incorporate elements of common interest as well as conflict.

3. **Communication and agreement among competitors.** In the battle for passengers, the competing airlines make independent decisions. If all airlines set too many flights, the eventual outcome may well be losses for all carriers. By contrast, if rival airlines were allowed to communicate their intentions and coordinate their operations, one would expect them to agree to mutual flight reductions. (One also would expect cooperation on other dimensions, such as higher prices, less generous frequent-flier programs, and so on.)

A competitive situation is called **noncooperative** if players are unable (or are not allowed) to communicate and coordinate their behavior. The airlines, like almost all competing firms in the United States, are required by law to play noncooperatively; any form of collusion is prohibited. The situation is **cooperative** if players can communicate before taking action and form binding agreements about what joint actions to take. A cartel, such as OPEC, in which a group agrees on price and output policy, is an example of a cooperative setting.

In general, the more the players' interests coincide, the more significant is their ability (or inability) to communicate. In a two-person zero-sum game, communication cannot benefit either competitor. My gain is your loss, so there is nothing to agree about. In settings involving both common and conflicting interests, communication plays a complex role in determining the outcome. Frequently, these communications—threats, promises, or even bluffs—are intended to influence a competitor's behavior. Other times, firms take actions to signal their intent to one another, without explicitly communicating. In negotiation settings, parties are free to communicate as they please in attempting to reach an agreement.

4. **Repeated or one-shot competition.** Another important distinction is whether the competition is one shot or ongoing—that is, whether the same parties will be involved in similar situations in the future. For instance, competition among airlines

is ongoing. Similarly, when management and union representatives negotiate a contract, they recognize that the bargaining will repeat itself three or so years down the road when the new contract expires. By contrast, a buyer and seller negotiating a house sale are unlikely to meet again. In one-shot situations, competitors usually are out for all they can get. In an ongoing competition, they often behave much differently. All they can get now is tempered by the impact on what they might get in the future. As we shall see, if a noncooperative situation is repeated or ongoing, a clear opportunity is provided for tacit communication and understanding to take place over time.

5. **Amount of information.** The degree of information one competitor has about another is one of the most important factors in a competitive situation. In many industries, secrecy is crucial. Detroit's automakers carefully guard their new designs. At the same time, some firms invest large sums attempting to obtain information about their competitors. Management usually knows who its main rivals are, but it may have only sketchy knowledge of their intentions, views, and ultimate objectives. Normally, the firm has limited information about its competitors' organizations and costs. This raises the question: What would management like to know about its competitors?

In the rest of this chapter, we focus primarily on two-party settings under perfect information, that is, where the firms have all immediately relevant information about each other. (Examples of competitive settings with imperfect information and two or more players are presented in Chapter 15.) We take up zero-sum and non-zero-sum games and explore the implications of repetition and tacit communication.

ANALYZING PAYOFF TABLES

The starting point for a game-theoretic analysis of any competitive situation is a description of the players, their strategies, and their payoffs. Here is a motivating example.

JOCKEYING IN THE TV RATINGS GAME   The profits of the four major television networks—CBS, NBC, ABC, and FOX—depend significantly on the ratings achieved by their prime-time programs. The higher the ratings, the higher the price the network can charge for advertising and the greater the number of advertising spots it can sell. To keep things simple, we restrict our attention to NBC and CBS (two of the ratings leaders during the last decade) and focus on their programming decisions for the 8-to-9 P.M. and 9-to-10 P.M. slots on a particular weeknight. The networks must decide which hour-long programs from last season to pencil into the slots. Each network's main concern is when to schedule its hit show—at 8 P.M. or 9 P.M. The other time slot will be filled by a run-of-the-mill program.

Here, the focus of competition is between two players, NBC and CBS. Each network has two possible actions: to run its hit show at 8 P.M. or at 9 P.M. The essential elements of any two-player competitive decision can be described by a two-dimensional

TABLE 10.1

A TV Ratings Battle

Each network's dominant strategy is to schedule its "hit" at 8 P.M. The left-hand entry in each cell lists NBC's total number of viewers (in millions). The right-hand entry lists CBS's total viewers. Figures in parentheses divide total viewers between 8 P.M. and 9 P.M.

		CBS			
		Schedule Hit at 8 P.M.		Schedule Hit at 9 P.M.	
NBC	Schedule Hit at 8 P.M.	36 (21 + 15)	33 (19 + 14)	39 (25 + 14)	28 (11 + 17)
	Schedule Hit at 9 P.M.	30 (13 + 17)	36 (20 + 16)	32 (16 + 16)	30 (16 + 14)

payoff table. According to the standard format, the first player's actions are listed along the rows of the table; the second player's possible actions are listed along the columns. The payoff table in Table 10.1 is an example. NBC's possible actions are listed along the rows and CBS's actions along the columns. For any combination of actions, the resulting payoffs to the networks are shown under the corresponding row and column. By convention, the first (i.e., row) player's payoff is listed first. In Table 10.1, each network's payoff is measured by the projected *total* number of viewers (in millions) over the two-hour period. For instance, if each network leads with its hit show at 8 P.M., NBC's audience will be 36 million viewers and CBS's will be 33 million. The table also shows the number of viewers during each hour.[2] Although the disaggregated figures are of some interest in their own right, what ultimately matters to each network is its total audience.

In the ratings battle, each network's sole interest is in maximizing its total audience.[3] With this goal in mind, what is each network's optimal action? Table 10.1 provides a relatively simple answer: Each network should schedule its hit show in the 8-to-9 P.M. slot. To confirm this, first take NBC's point of view. To find its own best course of action, NBC must anticipate the behavior of its rival. Obviously, there are two cases to consider:

[2]The hourly viewer numbers reflect a number of facts. First, the total number of viewers is larger during the 8-to-9 P.M. slot than during the 9-to-10 P.M. slot. Second, during a given hour, the more highly rated a network's show (and the less highly rated its competitor), the larger the network's audience. Third, a portion of viewers watching a network's show from 8 to 9 P.M. continues to stay tuned to that network during the 9-to-10 P.M. slot.

[3]In different contexts, a player's payoff may take many forms: a monetary value (such as revenue, cost, or profit), a litigation victory, the number of electoral votes won, market share, and so on. The general point is that the payoff is meant to capture *everything* the decision maker cares about—his or her ultimate objective or utility to be maximized (or, if a cost, to be minimized). One implication of this point is that comparisons of player payoffs are *not* meaningful. For instance, if player 1 faces the payoff entries (5, −1), he derives no welfare from the fact that the other player makes a loss. The player's welfare is completely captured by his own five units of profit. The player fares better with the payoff (6, 10). In short, his or her motives are neither competitive nor altruistic; they are simply self-interested.

1. If CBS schedules its hit at 8 P.M., NBC should follow suit. By doing so, its total audience is 36 million. NBC's alternative—placing its hit at 9 P.M.—would deliver a smaller total audience of 30 million. Leading with its hit is NBC's best response if CBS leads with its hit.

2. If CBS schedules its hit at 9 P.M., NBC's best response would continue to be leading with its hit. (An audience of 39 million is better than an audience of 32 million.)

In short, regardless of CBS's action, NBC's audience-maximizing response is to schedule its hit at 8 P.M.

A strategy that is a best response to *any* strategy that the other player might pick is called a **dominant strategy**. Thus, we have shown that scheduling its hit at 8 P.M. is NBC's dominant strategy. By similar reasoning, CBS's dominant strategy is to lead with its hit. (If NBC schedules its hit at 8 P.M., CBS prefers a 33 million audience to a 28 million audience; if NBC puts its hit at 9 P.M., CBS prefers a 36 million audience to a 30 million audience.) The predicted outcome of the ratings battle is for each network to use its dominant strategy—that is, schedule its hit at 8 P.M. This results in audience shares of 36 million and 33 million, respectively.

As a simple variation on this example, suppose CBS is aware that scheduling its hit against NBC's hit would be suicidal. (Imagine NBC's hit to be the top-rated show.) To illustrate, change CBS's top-left entry in Table 10.1 from 33 to 25. How does this change CBS's behavior? Now if NBC schedules its hit at 8 P.M., CBS's best response is to put its hit at 9 P.M. (If NBC schedules its hit at 9 P.M., it remains the case that CBS's best response is to put its hit at 8 P.M.) In other words, CBS should set its schedule to avoid a showdown of hit shows. CBS no longer has a dominant strategy; rather, its best response depends on what NBC does. Nonetheless, its optimal action is easy to determine. NBC surely will choose to schedule its hit at 8 P.M., because this is its dominant strategy. Anticipating this move, CBS should place its hit at 9 P.M. as a best response. The network outcomes are audiences of 39 million and 28 million viewers, respectively.

In this variation on the basic example, CBS's optimal action requires a simple kind of *reflexive thinking: putting itself in NBC's shoes*. Notice that the predicted outcome has the property that each player's strategy is a best response against the chosen strategy of the other. Thus, neither network could improve its profit by second-guessing the other and moving to a different strategy.

Consider competition between two department stores, each of which must decide what kind of clothing to promote. Does either store have a dominant strategy? What is the predicted outcome?   **CHECK STATION 1**

		Store 2	
		Promote Girls' Clothes	Promote Women's Clothes
Store 1	Promote Girls' Clothes	0, 0	4, 2
	Promote Children's Clothes	2, 2	2, 4

Equilibrium Strategies

What action should a decision maker take to achieve his objectives when competing with another individual acting in her own interests? The principal answer supplied by game theory is as follows:

> In settings where competitors choose actions independently of one another (and so cannot collude), each player should use an equilibrium strategy, one that maximizes each player's expected payoff against the strategy chosen by the other. This is known as a *Nash equilibrium.*

In both versions of the ratings battle example, the predicted outcome satisfies this definition; that is, it is an equilibrium. The following example illustrates a competitive setting in which *neither* side has a dominant strategy. Nonetheless, each side has an equilibrium strategy, and that is how each should play.

MARKET-SHARE COMPETITION   Consider two firms that compete fiercely for shares of a market that is of *constant* size. (The market is mature with few growth opportunities.) Each firm can adopt one of three marketing strategies in an attempt to win customers from the other. The payoff table in Table 10.2 depicts the percentage increase in market share of firm 1 (the row player). For instance, if both firms adopt their first strategies, firm 1 loses (and firm 2 gains) two share points. The market share competition is a **zero-sum game**. The competitors' interests are strictly opposed; one side's gain is the other side's loss. This being the case, it is customary to list only the row player's payoffs. The row player seeks to maximize its payoff, while the column player seeks to keep this payoff to a minimum. By doing so, firm 2 maximizes its own increase in market share.

In the advertising competition, there is a single equilibrium pair of strategies: R2 versus C2. The resulting payoff (two here) is called the *equilibrium outcome.* To check that this is an equilibrium, consider in turn each firm's options. Against C2, the best firm 1 can do is use R2. Switching to R1 or R3 means suffering a loss of market share. Similarly, the best firm 2 can do against R2 is use C2. If it switches to C1 or C3, it grants firm 1 a greater

TABLE 10.2

Competitive Advertising in a Mature Market

In this zero-sum game, the firms' equilibrium strategies are R2 and C2.

		Firm 2		
		C1	C2	C3
Firm 1	R1	$\boxed{-2}$	−1	④
	R2	5	$\boxed{②}$	3
	R3	⑦	−3	$\boxed{-5}$

share increase, implying a greater loss in market share for itself. Thus, the strategies R2 and C2 are profit maximizing against each other and constitute a Nash equilibrium.

To check that this is the only equilibrium, let's identify each firm's best response (i.e., its most profitable action) to any action taken by its competitor. In Table 10.2, the payoffs from firm 1's best responses to firm 2's possible actions are circled. Firm 1's best response to C1 is R3, to C2 is R2, and to C3 is R1. The circles offer visual proof of the fact that firm 1 has no dominant strategy. (Why? If a strategy were dominant, all the circles would line up along the same row.) The table also identifies firm 2's best responses: Its best response to R1 is C1, to R2 is C2, and to R3 is C3. The resulting payoffs are enclosed in squares. (Firm 2 has no dominant strategy.) The circles and squares make it easy to identify the equilibrium outcome and strategies. A payoff is an equilibrium outcome if and only if it is enclosed by *both* a circle and a square, that is, it must be a best-response strategy for each player. Thus, we confirm that a payoff of 2 is the unique equilibrium outcome; R2 versus C2 are the equilibrium strategies that generate this outcome.

The best a smart player can expect to get in a zero-sum game against an equally smart player is his or her equilibrium outcome. If either side deviates from its equilibrium play, it reduces its own payoff and increases the competitor's payoff. Indeed, there should be no real uncertainty about how the game will be played. Each side should anticipate equilibrium behavior from the other. The resulting equilibrium outcome is called the *value* of the game.[4]

The following payoff table lists the respective market shares of the two firms in the advertising competition. It is derived directly from Table 10.2 under the assumption that the firms' initial shares are 45 percent and 55 percent, respectively. For instance, according to Table 10.2, the play of R1 versus C1 results in a 2-percentage-point loss for firm 1; this translates into 43 percent and 57 percent market shares in the table. Given the form of the payoff table, explain why this competition can be referred to as a constant-sum game. Determine the equilibrium. Is there any strategic difference between a zero-sum game and a constant-sum game? **CHECK STATION 2**

| | | Firm 2 | | |
		C1	C2	C3
	R1	43, 57	44, 56	49, 51
Firm 1	R2	50, 50	47, 53	48, 52
	R3	52, 48	42, 58	40, 60

A REMINDER   It is important to distinguish clearly between a Nash equilibrium that involves dominant strategies and one that does not. Here is the difference:

[4]A zero-sum game always possesses an equilibrium. The value of the game is unique; there cannot be two equilibria having different values. However, equilibrium behavior may require the use of randomized actions (so-called mixed strategies) by the players. We discuss the use of mixed strategies in the appendix to this chapter.

In a dominant-strategy equilibrium, each player chooses an action that is a best response against *any* action the other might take.

In a Nash equilibrium, each player takes an action that is a best response to the action the other takes.

Both kinds of equilibrium share the essential feature of stability. In equilibrium, there is no second guessing; it is impossible for either side to increase its payoff by unilaterally deviating from its chosen strategy.

The concepts differ in one important respect. When a player has a dominant strategy, there is *no circumstance* in which doing anything else ever makes sense. The player always should use this strategy. Of course, in many, if not most, competitive situations, players will not have available a single strategy that is dominant. However, as in the market-share competition, there still will be a Nash equilibrium. Here each side's action is a best response against the other's. As long as each competitor is smart enough to recognize the Nash equilibrium and expect the other to do likewise, this is how each should play.

But what if one player is not so smart? In the market-share battle, suppose the manager of firm 2 is convinced that firm 1 plans to use strategy R3. This might not seem to be a very smart move by firm 1. (Perhaps it is lured to R3 by the mistaken hope of a +7 payoff.) But let's say that there is ample evidence that this is how firm 1 will play. (It has already begun launching the R3 advertising campaign.) Then, surely, firm 2 should choose C3, gaining a 5 percent share increase at firm 1's expense. By changing from C2 to C3, firm 2 can profit from firm 1's mistake. The point is this: In a Nash equilibrium (unlike a dominant-strategy equilibrium), there exist some circumstances where it *might* pay to use a nonequilibrium strategy. If one player deviates from equilibrium (by mistake or for any other reason), the other player might be able to improve its payoff by deviating also.

Are we recommending nonequilibrium play in Table 10.2 for either firm? Certainly not. Equilibrium play is quite transparent and should be grasped readily by both sides. But in a different setting where there is reason to anticipate one player deviating from equilibrium play, the other player may be able to (optimally) exploit this.

CHECK STATION 3   **In Chapter 9's example of dueling suppliers, each firm had constant unit costs $AC = MC = \$6$, and market demand was described by $P = 30 - (Q_1 + Q_2)$, where output is measured in thousands of units. The payoff table lists the firm's profits for three levels of output. Choose one entry and check that the payoffs are correct. Does either firm have a dominant strategy? From the table, the firms appear to prefer outputs of 6 thousand units each. Explain why this is not an equilibrium outcome. Find the firms' equilibrium quantities. (Confirm that this matches the answer derived algebraically in Chapter 9.)**

		Firm 2's Quantity		
		6	8	10
	6	72, 72	60, 80	48, 80
Firm 1's Quantity	8	80, 60	64, 64	48, 60
	10	80, 48	60, 48	40, 40

THE PRISONER'S DILEMMA ONCE AGAIN   Before concluding this section, we take a brief second look at the paradigm of the prisoner's dilemma (PD) introduced in Chapter 9. The top portion of Table 10.3 reproduces the price-war payoffs of Table 9.2. The middle portion of the table portrays a different sort of PD: an arms race between a pair of superpowers. Finally, the bottom portion uses symbolic payoffs to represent the generic features of the prisoner's dilemma.

Although particular payoffs vary, the strategic implications of the three payoff tables are the same. Assuming noncooperative play (i.e., no possibility of communication or collusion), self-interest dictates the play of dominant strategies. In the price war, a low price is most profitable, regardless of the competitor's price. Similarly, an arms buildup is the dominant strategy in the arms race. (Fortunately, events in the former Soviet Union and the end of the cold war have called a halt to the arms buildup.) Finally, in the generic prisoner's dilemma, defection is the dominant strategy. Note that the temptation payoff from defecting is greater than the reward payoff from cooperation. In turn, the penalty payoff if both players defect is greater than the sucker payoff if one player cooperates while the other defects. In short, the logic of dominant strategies inevitably leads to the inferior penalty payoffs under noncooperative play.

TABLE 10.3

Three Prisoner's Dilemmas

In each case, the play of dominant strategies leads to inferior outcomes.

a. A Price War

		Firm 2	
		High Price	**Low Price**
Firm 1	**High Price**	10, 10	5, 12
	Low Price	12, 5	7, 7

b. An Arms Race

		Superpower 2	
		Disarm	**Build Arms**
Superpower 1	**Disarm**	10, 10	−50, 20
	Build Arms	20, −50	−20, −20

c. A Generic PD

		Player 2	
		Cooperate	**Defect**
Player 1	**Cooperate**	R, R	S, T
	Defect	T, S	P, P

T = Temptation
R = Reward
P = Penalty
S = Sucker

$$T > R > P > S$$

What if the rules of the competition allow communication between players, and what if binding agreements are possible? Under these cooperative ground rules, players should agree to take actions to achieve the mutually beneficial "upper-left" payoffs. Thus, firms would want to agree to charge high prices, and superpowers would strive to negotiate a binding and verifiable arms-control treaty. We will say more about the possibilities of reaching such agreements in our later discussion of repeated competition.

Two-Tiered Tender Offers

A common takeover tactic in the 1980s and early 1990s was the "two-tiered" tender offer. Here is a bare-bones example of how this kind of offer works. Suppose that firm A (the acquiring firm) is seeking to gain control of firm T (the target). Firm T's current (i.e., pre-tender) stock price is $50 per share. Firm A offers a price of $55 per share for 50 percent of firm T's outstanding shares. If 50 percent of shareholders (induced by this price) tender their shares, this percentage will be just enough for firm A to gain control of firm T. In keeping with a two-tier strategy, firm A offers only $35 per share for the remaining 50 percent of shares.

Does this two-tiered offer strategy make sense? Will firm A succeed in gaining control? Or will it pay a high $55 price per share but receive only a minority of shares, meaning the takeover will fail? The accompanying payoff table depicts the strategic landscape from the typical shareholder's point of view. The shareholder has two options: to tender her shares or to retain them. The columns show that the shareholder's payoff depends on her action *and* on whether or not the acquisition proves to be successful.

		Tender Fails (S < 50%)	Tender Succeeds (S ≥ 50%)
Typical Shareholder	Tender	$55	$45 – $55
	Retain	$50	$35

Let's check the payoff entries. The first column entries show that if the tender fails, those who tender shares receive $55, while those who retain theirs see their shares' value remain at the preacquisition level of $50. If the tender succeeds, the average price received by those who tender depends on the overall percentage of shares that are offered. If exactly 50 percent of shareholders tender, each tendering shareholder receives $55. At the opposite extreme, what if 100 percent of shareholders tender? Because firm A only buys 50 percent of outstanding shares, each shareholder's offer is *prorated*, meaning that half of its tendered shares are accepted at $55 and the other half are not accepted. After the acquisition is successfully completed, all remaining shares (i.e., all unaccepted shares) are bought for the lower $35 price. Therefore, the *average* price received by a typical tendering shareholder is: $(.5)(55) + (.5)(35) = 45. This explains the $45 to $55 payoff range listed in the upper-right entry.

Now that we've anticipated the possible payoffs facing shareholders, the analysis is straightforward. *Each shareholder should tender all of her shares, regardless of the percentage of other shareholders who tender.* Comparing the entries in the top and bottom rows, we see that tendering is a dominant strategy for every shareholder. (Note that $55 > $50 and $45–$55 > $35.) Because every shareholder can be expected to tender, the acquisition easily succeeds and the typical shareholder (after prorating) obtains an average price of $45 for her shares.

The extraordinary result is that the acquirer, by structuring a two-tiered offer, pays an average price, $45, which is less than the market value of the target, $50. In other words, target shareholders are getting $5 per share less than what the market deems the firm is worth. Collectively, shareholders are caught in a financial "prisoner's dilemma." They would prefer to hold out for a higher uniform price. But the acquirer has made them an offer that they, individually, can't refuse. Although the two-tiered tender offer has been deemed to be coercive, it has not been found to be illegal. Nonetheless, the majority of US states have enacted rules that effectively restrain the practice, and so with the leveling of the financial playing field, the two-tiered strategy has all but disappeared over the last 20 years.

COMPETITIVE STRATEGY

Strategic decisions by managers embrace an interesting mixture of competition and cooperation. Firms compete via price wars, patent races, capacity expansion, and entry deterrence. But they also cooperate through joint ventures, the adoption of common standards, and implicit agreements to maintain high prices. The following competitive situations illustrate this blend of competition and cooperation.

A COMMON STANDARD FOR HIGH-DEFINITION DVDs   Holding several times the amount of information, the current generation of Blu-ray DVDs provides strikingly clear picture quality for movies, videogames, and computer graphics. Moreover, the story of how Blu-ray DVDs became the dominant standard holds important strategic lessons. In 2005, two incompatible technologies battled to become the standard in the United States and worldwide. In one camp, Sony Corporation led a group of companies including Samsung, Matsushita, Philips, Dell Computer, and Hewlett-Packard promoting the Blu-ray format. The opposing side, led by Toshiba Corporation and backed by NEC Corporation and Microsoft, developed the HD format. Each format had its advantages, but each was *incompatible* with the other. For more than two years, the corporate players formed alliances and pushed their preferred formats. The Blu-ray group enlisted movie studios like Twentieth Century Fox and Walt Disney. The HD group counted NBC and Universal studios in its camp, while studios such as Warner Brothers and Paramount Pictures pledged to release movies in both formats. Negotiations concerning the standards dispute were overseen by the DVD forum, an industry group made up of some 200 corporate members. However, with no resolution in sight, the sales of new DVD players and DVDs lagged; consumers were put off by high prices and, more importantly, by the risk that they might be left with an abandoned technology.

Table 10.4 shows the (hypothetical) payoffs to the two opposing camps. Not surprisingly, the Sony group's greatest payoff occurs if all sides adopt the Blu-ray format, whereas the Toshiba group's greatest payoff comes with the HD format. However, *coordination* is

TABLE 10.4

		Toshiba Group	
The Battle for a Common Technology Standard		**Adopt Blu-ray Format**	**Adopt HD Format**
Sony Group	**Adopt Blu-ray Format**	100, 50	30, 20
	Adopt HD Format	0, 0	60, 90

The two equilibria have both sides adopting the Blu-ray format or both sides adopting the HD format.

crucial. Both sides receive much lower payoffs if different, incompatible technologies are chosen (the off-diagonal entries).

The payoff table in Table 10.4 has two equilibria: Both adopt the Blu-ray format (upper-left cell), or both adopt the HD format (lower-right cell). Each is an equilibrium because if one side adopts a given format, the best the other can do is follow suit. (Check this.) Coordination on a common standard is in each side's own best interest. The catch is that the sides have strongly opposed views on which standard it should be. We would expect the outcome to be one of the equilibria—but which one? That is a matter of bargaining and staying power. In general, rational bargainers should agree on a common standard, but such an agreement is far from guaranteed as evidenced by the actual bitter and protracted dispute.

The HD DVD standards dispute was finally resolved in early 2008. The Blu-ray standard emerged as the winning standard due to a cumulative series of factors. First, Sony installed Blu-ray players in its Play Station 3 game consoles and so attracted videogamers. Second, it gained additional purchase by swaying video distributors, Blockbuster and Netflix, and major retailers such as Best Buy and Walmart, to its side. The final tipping point was persuading Warner Bros., the leading video distributor, to release its features exclusively in Blu-ray.[5] With an overwhelming critical mass of studios, distributors, and retailers, the Sony group had effectively claimed the upper-left equilibrium in Table 10.4.

Fortunately, mutual advantage is a strong force behind the emergence of common standards. Thirty years ago, there existed a plethora of operating systems in the emerging personal computer market. Today, Microsoft Windows is the dominant standard with some 80 percent market share. More generally, the world has moved toward a number of common standards: metric measurement, left-hand-steering automobiles, and common principles of international law. (Obviously, countries retain different languages, currencies, customs, and laws, even though English, the US dollar, and most recently the euro serve as de facto, partial standards.)

Competitive situations such as that embodied in Table 10.4 are ubiquitous. In fact, they commonly are referred to under the label "battle of the sexes." In that domestic version, husband and wife must decide whether to attend a ball game or the ballet on a given night.

[5]This account is based on D. Leiberman, "Is the Tug of War over High-Def DVD Format Over?" *USA Today,* February 15, 2008, 1B; and B. Barnes, "Warner Backs Blu-ray, Tilting DVD Battle," *The New York Times,* January 5, 2008, p. B1.

Each strongly prefers the other's company to attending an event alone. The two equilibria have husband and wife making the same choice. But which choice? The wife prefers that they both attend the ball game; the husband prefers the ballet. Based on past experience, we will not hazard a guess as to the outcome of the domestic discussion and negotiations. The general point is that the battle of the sexes is a model applicable to any bargaining situation.

Market Entry

Consider once again Chapter 1's example of market competition between the two office-supply giants—Staples and Office Depot. (In 2013, the "new" Office Depot was created via a merger of equals between Office Depot and Office Max.) Both chains have aggressively expanded their number of superstores across the country. Often the chains are jockeying for the same sites in the same cities.

To model the ongoing competition between the chains, suppose that both are considering a new superstore in a midsize city. Although the city is currently underserved, each chain recognizes that demand is sufficient to support only *one* superstore profitably. There is not enough market room for two stores. If both chains erect new superstores and split the market, both will suffer losses. (Each firm's net cash flow will be insufficient to cover the high fixed costs of opening a new store.) Table 10.5 shows the firms' payoffs. If one firm stays out, it earns zero profit. If it enters, its profit is $4 million or –$4 million depending on whether the other firm enters. Clearly, neither firm has a dominant strategy. However, it is easy to identify the two off-diagonal outcomes as equilibria. If Staples enters, Office Depot's best response is to stay out. Thus, entry by Staples alone is an equilibrium. By the same reasoning, entry by Office Depot is also an equilibrium. ("Both firms entering" is not an equilibrium, nor is "both firms staying out." Check this.)

Rational competitors should reach one of the equilibria, but it is difficult to say which one. Each firm wishes to be the one that enters the market and gains the profit. One way for a player (say, Staples) to claim its desired equilibrium is to be the first to enter. Here there is a **first-mover advantage**. Given the opportunity to make the first move, Staples should enter and preempt the market. Then, Office Depot's best second move is to stay out. By stealing a march on the opposition—that is, being first to market—a firm obtains its preferred equilibrium. Even if the firms require the same amount of time to launch a superstore, Staples can claim a first-mover advantage if it can make a *credible* commitment to enter the market. To be credible, Staples' behavior must convince its rival of its entry commitment; a mere threat to that effect is not enough. A campaign announcing

TABLE 10.5

Market Entry

There are two equilibria. If one firm enters the market, the other should stay out.

		Office Max	
		Stay Out	Enter
Staples	Stay Out	0, 0	0, 4
	Enter	4, 0	–4, –4

and promoting the new store would be one way to signal the firm's commitment; another would be entering into a binding real estate lease. Of course, sometimes both firms commit to entry with disastrous results. [6]

CHECK STATION 4   **Boeing and Airbus (a European consortium) compete to sell similar aircraft worldwide. The following table depicts the players' actions and hypothetical payoffs. What are the equilibrium outcomes? How does the outcome change if European governments pay a $40 million production subsidy to Airbus?**

		Airbus	
		Produce	**Do Not Produce**
	Produce	−20, −20	80, 0
Boeing	**Do Not Produce**	0, 80	0, 0

Bargaining

One of the most fertile domains for applying game theory is in the realm of bargaining and negotiation. The following example is intended to suggest some of the strategic issues that arise in bargaining settings.

BARGAINING OVER THE TERMS OF A TRANSACTION   Two firms, a buyer and a seller, are in negotiations concerning the sale price of a good. Both sides know that the seller's cost to produce the good is $80,000 and that the buyer's value for the good (the maximum amount the firm can pay) is $120,000. Suppose that, before negotiations begin, each side has formulated its final and best offer, a price beyond which it will not concede in the negotiations. In particular, each is considering one of three possible final offers: $90,000, $100,000, or $110,000.

The firms' offers determine the final price as follows. First, if the firms' price offers are incompatible—that is, the seller insists on a price greater than the buyer is willing to pay—there is no agreement, and each side earns a zero profit. Second, if the players' final offers match, then this is the final price. Third, if the buyer's offer exceeds the seller's demand, the final price is midway between the two offers—as if the players simply split the difference.

Table 10.6 lists the payoffs that result from different combinations of final offers in this stylized bargaining game. The three zero-profit outcomes in the upper-left portion of the table are the result of incompatible offers. Alternatively, if the buyer's offer is $100,000 and the seller's offer is $90,000, the final price is $95,000. Therefore, the buyer's profit is 120,000 − 95,000 = $25,000, and the seller's profit is 95,000 − 80,000 = $15,000. These profits are shown in the middle-right entry. The other profit entries are computed in analogous fashion.

---

[6]Competitive situations such as these often are referred to as games of "chicken." Two trucks loaded with dynamite (or two cars loaded with teenagers) are racing toward each other along a one-lane road. The first to swerve out of the way is chicken. The only equilibrium has one side holding true to course and the other swerving. Here the issue of commitment is made in dramatic terms.

TABLE 10.6

A Stylized Bargaining
Game

Even the simplest
bargaining situations
involve multiple
equilibria.

		Seller Final Offers ($000s)		
		110	100	90
Buyer Final	**90**	0, 0	0, 0	㉚, [10]
Offers	**100**	0, 0	⑳, [20]	25, 15
($000s)	**110**	⑩, [30]	15, 25	20, 20

Table 10.6 displays three distinct equilibria. In the middle equilibrium, each side makes a price offer of $100,000, resulting in an agreement in which each side earns $20,000. Facing this offer, the best the player can do is match it. Asking for less diminishes one's profit, and asking for more results in a disagreement and a zero profit. Thus, this is an equilibrium. In the lower-left equilibrium, the final price favors the seller, whereas in the upper-right equilibrium, the final price favors the buyer. Each of these is a legitimate, though not necessarily fair, equilibrium. For instance, against a seller who "plays hard-ball" and sets $110,000 as her final price, the best the buyer can do is concede by offering $110,000 as well. Twenty-five percent of something is better than 50 percent of nothing.

To keep things simple, we have limited the buyer and seller to three offers. Of course, in actual bargaining, each side's final offer could lie anywhere in the range from $80,000 to $120,000. In general, all matching offers in this range constitute equilibria. The problem is that there are *too many* equilibria. The equilibrium concept does rule out certain outcomes. For instance, the bargaining game should never end in a disagreement. Nevertheless, there are matching equilibrium offers that have the bargainers splitting the total gains from an agreement in any proportion (10–90, 40–60, 70–30, and so on). In Chapter 15, we will say much more about how bargaining tactics can influence which equilibrium is reached.

Sequential Competition

In the competitive settings analyzed thus far, players have taken one-shot actions. Of course, many realistic competitive settings involve a series of actions over time. One firm may make a move, its rival a countermove, and so on. In a **sequential game**, players take turns moving. To portray the sequence of moves, we use a **game tree**. As we shall see, when one party makes its current decision, it must look ahead and try to anticipate the actions and reactions of its competitors at their turns in the game tree. To illustrate the method, we start with a compact example.

A multinational firm (MNF) is pondering whether to accept a developing country's (DC) invitation to invest in the development of a copper mine on its soil. Management of MNF is contemplating an agreement in which MNF and DC split the profits from the mine equally. By its estimates, each side's profit is worth about $50 million (in net present value). Both sides are aware that any agreement, being unenforceable, is not really binding. For instance, after MNF has sunk a large investment in the project, DC's leaders could decide to break the agreement and expropriate the mine. Given DC's desperate economic condition, this is

**An International
Mineral Lease**

a real possibility. In such a case, MNF would suffer a loss of $20 million. The value of the nationalized mine—run less efficiently by DC—would be $80 million. Finally, each side must look to the other to launch the mining project. MNF sees no other countries in which to invest, and DC has found no other companies capable of launching the mine.

Given this description, we can use the game tree in Figure 10.1 to portray the sequence of actions by MNF and DC. (Such a depiction is commonly called the *extensive form* of the game.) The first move is MNF's: whether to invest or not. If MNF does invest, the next move (at the time the mine becomes operational) is DC's: whether to honor the 50–50 agreement or to expropriate the mine. In the game tree, squares represent points of decision, and monetary payoffs are shown at the branch tips of the tree. Here both players' payoffs are shown: MNF's first, then DC's. (Political considerations aside, we presume that the monetary payoffs accurately portray the objectives of the parties.) Furthermore, although it is easy to envision other actions and reactions by the parties, we have kept things simple: one move for each player.

At the initial move, should MNF invest in the mine? To answer this question, MNF's management must look ahead to DC's subsequent move and the ensuing payoffs. Once the mine is operational, DC can be expected to expropriate it; DC certainly prefers an $80 million payoff to a mere $50 million from cooperation. Foreseeing this (and the resulting $20 million loss), MNF wisely decides not to invest. The parties find themselves on the horns of a dilemma. Both would gain handsomely from a cooperative agreement. But under the current circumstances, such an agreement is unenforceable. DC's position is particularly vexing. It can promise MNF that it will not expropriate the mine. But talk is cheap. Given the economic stakes, the promise is not credible.

If the desirable cooperative outcome is to be achieved, the parties must structure an agreement that alters DC's incentives to expropriate. DC will honor an agreement only

FIGURE 10.1

Moving toward an
International Agreement

Game trees are solved
from right to left.
Anticipating that DC
will expropriate, MNF
chooses not to invest
in the first place.

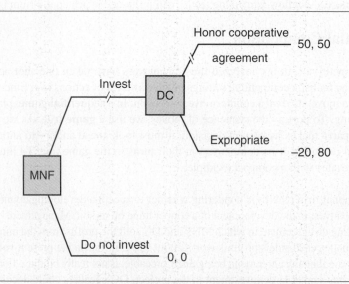

if it is more profitable to do so than to expropriate. This basic point suggests a number of remedies. One solution is for MNF to give DC an 81–19 split of the $100 million total gain from the mine. Although this might not seem particularly fair, it does induce DC's compliance. Thus, MNF can invest confidently, counting on a $19 million return. Alternatively, the 50–50 split can be maintained with a monetary penalty exacted if DC breaches the agreement. For instance, as part of an agreement, DC would place $31 million (let's say) in an account with an international agency, such as the World Bank. This money would be forfeited to MNF if DC were to expropriate the mine. Clearly, DC prefers the $50 million from the agreement to the $80 - 31 = 49 million net profit from expropriation.

ENTRY DETERRENCE   In the earlier example of market entry, two firms made simultaneous decisions whether or not to enter a market. Let's modify the situation and presume that one firm, the incumbent, already occupies the market and currently holds a monopoly position. A second firm is deciding whether to enter. If entry occurs, the incumbent must decide whether to maintain or cut its current price. The game tree in Figure 10.2a depicts the situation. The new firm has the first move: deciding whether or not to enter. (Because of high fixed costs, entry is a long-term commitment. The new firm cannot test the waters and then exit.) The incumbent has the next move: maintaining or cutting its price. As the game tree shows, entry is profitable if a high price is maintained but leads to losses if price is cut.

A natural strategy for the incumbent is to threaten to cut price if the new firm enters. If this threat is believed, the new firm will find it in its best interest to stay out of the market. Without a competitor, the incumbent can maintain its price and earn a profit of 12. Seemingly, the threat alone is enough to preserve the incumbent's monopoly position. However, the game-tree analysis reveals a significant problem with this strategy. Such a threat lacks credibility. If the new firm were to take the first move and enter the market, the incumbent would *not* rationally cut price. Once the market has become a duopoly, the incumbent firm's profit-maximizing choice is to maintain price. (A profit of 6 is better than a profit of 4.) In fact, maintaining price is a dominant strategy for the incumbent; high prices are preferred whether or not entry occurs. Thus, the equilibrium is for the first firm to enter and the incumbent to maintain price.

This example of entry deterrence underscores once again the importance of strategic commitment. If the incumbent could convince the entrant of its commitment to a low price, this would forestall entry. Perhaps one way to accomplish this goal is for the incumbent to cut price *before* the other firm enters—precisely to show its commitment to this low price. If the incumbent can move first and cut its price once and for all, the other firm's best response will be to stay clear of the market. The incumbent certainly would prefer this outcome; its profit is 9, higher than its profit (6) from moving second and accommodating entry. This possibility is depicted in Figure 10.2b's game tree. Be sure to note the reversal in the order of the moves.

Maintaining a lower-than-monopoly price to forestall entry is called **limit pricing**. Cutting price before entry is intended as a signal of the incumbent's price intentions after entry. But is it a credible signal? Again, the real issue is commitment. If the incumbent can bind itself to a low-price policy (now and in the future), the new firm will be convinced

FIGURE 10.2

Deterring Entry

In the upper game tree, E is not deterred by I's empty threat to cut price. In the lower tree, I deters entry by committing to a limit price before entry occurs.

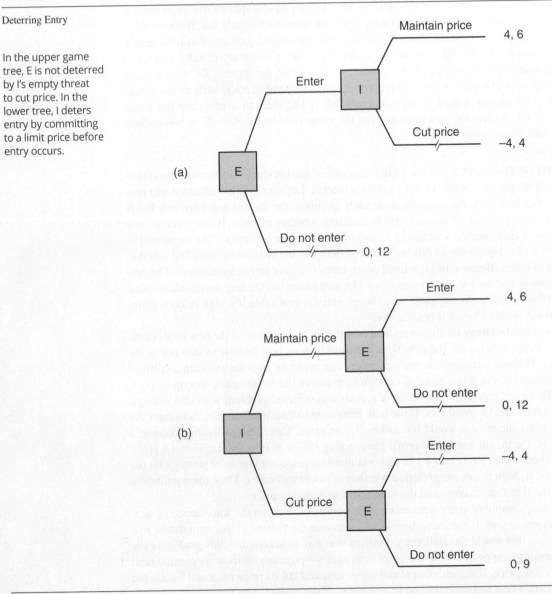

that entry is a losing proposition. This might be accomplished by making long-term price agreements with customers or by staking the firm's reputation on its low prices.[7]

[7]In many cases, however, pricing practices can be undone relatively rapidly and costlessly. The operative question is: If the entrant were to enter, would the incumbent continue to limit price or would it revert to a high price that best serves its self-interest? If the incumbent is expected to revert, limit pricing loses its credibility and its deterrence effect. Reversion can be depicted by adding a final pricing decision in Figure 10.2b's game tree. Clearly, cutting price in advance does no good if the incumbent is expected to undo the price cut after entry.

Strategic entry barriers (first noted in Chapter 8) are defined as any move by a current firm designed to exclude new firms by lowering the profitability of entry. Credible limit pricing is one such strategy.[8] Maintaining excess capacity that allows the incumbent to expand output at a low marginal cost and profitably cut price in response to any potential entrant is another. High levels of advertising, saturating the product space by proliferating the number of brands, or making product improvements that require high levels of R&D are others. Many of these strategies are *not profitable in themselves*. For example, spending on advertising may increase the firm's own costs faster than it increases revenues. However, if such a move raises the cost of entry, it may be profitable overall by excluding new firms (and thus reducing competition). In some circumstances, incumbent firms actually may welcome costly government regulations if these policies have the effect of limiting entry.

Moving beyond these compact examples, one can construct game trees to model more complicated competitive settings, for instance, those that involve multiple sequential moves by more than two players. As long as the number of moves is finite (so the game cannot go on forever) and all players have perfect information about previous moves, the optimal moves of the players can be found by **backward induction**—that is, by solving the game tree from right to left. In other words, to determine a player's optimal action at any point of decision, one must first pin down the optimal plays for all future moves. The resulting sequences of optimal moves constitute the players' equilibrium strategies. Thus, we note an important result in game theory:

Any sequential game with perfect information can be solved backward to obtain a complete solution.

Thinking ahead is the watchword for sequential games. Or, in the words of the philosopher Soren Kierkegaard, "Life can only be understood backwards, but it must be lived forwards."

Repeated Competition

Frequently, firms encounter one another in repeated competition. For instance, duopolists may compete with respect to prices and/or quantities, not just in a single period of time, but repeatedly. Similarly, an incumbent monopolist may encounter a number of would-be entrants over time. How does repetition of this sort affect strategy and behavior?

---

[8]Setting a low price can also serve as a signal to the entrant that the incumbent has low costs. This signal is important when the entrant is uncertain of the incumbent's true costs. Against a high-cost incumbent, entry is likely to be profitable since prices will remain high. But against a low-cost rival (ready and able to lower price), entry would be disastrous. By charging a low price prior to entry, the incumbent can send a credible message that its costs are, indeed, low. To work as a credible signal, the price must be low enough to distinguish a low-cost incumbent from a high-cost one. That is, the high-cost incumbent must have no incentive to imitate this low price. For a thorough discussion, see P. Milgrom and J. Roberts, "Sequential Equilibria," *Econometrica* (1982): 443–459.

Repeated competition introduces two important elements into the players' strategic calculations. First, players can think in terms of *contingent* strategies. For instance, one firm's pricing decision this month could depend on the pricing behavior of its rival during prior months. (The firm might want to punish a rival's price cuts with cuts of its own.) Second, in repeated play, the present isn't the only thing that counts; the future does as well. Accordingly, a player may choose to take certain actions today in order to establish a *reputation* with its rivals in the future. As we shall see, the use of contingent strategies and the formation of reputations serve to broaden the range of equilibrium behavior.

REPEATED PRICE COMPETITION   As one example of a repeated game, suppose the price competition shown in Table 10.3a is played not once, but repeatedly over time. Thus, when the firms independently set prices in January, they know they will face new price decisions in February and in March and in each succeeding month into the indefinite future. Recall that in one-time play, charging a low price is each firm's dominant strategy. As a result, firms find themselves in a low-profit prisoner's dilemma. But what if the game is played indefinitely? One possibility is for the players to charge low prices every period (that is, simply to repeat the single-stage equilibrium). Charging low prices indefinitely is one equilibrium of repeated competition, albeit a very unattractive one. After all, who wants to be trapped in a prisoner's dilemma forever?

Are there other more favorable possibilities? Common sense would suggest that players would strive to coordinate on a cooperative, high-price strategy. The question is how firms can keep this kind of implicit agreement from breaking down. One way is to exploit the power of contingent strategies. Consider the following **punitive** (or grim) strategy:

> The firm (1) sets a high price in the first period, (2) sets a high price in every succeeding period, provided the other firm does likewise, and (3) sets low prices forever after, if the other firm ever charges a low price.

In short, any defection from the cooperative high-price outcome is penalized by immediate and perpetual defections to low prices.

Let's check that the firms' mutual play of this punitive strategy constitutes an equilibrium in the repeated competition. If each firm adheres to this strategy, each charges a high price in the first and all other periods. Each earns a profit of 10 each period forever. Alternatively, could a firm benefit by unilaterally deviating from the punitive strategy? What if the firm deviated by charging a low price, say in the first period (as good a time as any)? In this period, it increases its profits from 10 to 12. However, this triggers low prices from the other firm forever. Thus, the best it can do is to continue with low prices as well, earning a profit of 7 each period henceforth. Clearly, a one-time 2-unit profit increase is not worth a 3-unit profit reduction into perpetuity.[9] Accordingly, the firm's interest is to maintain its reputation for cooperative play throughout the repeated competition. To sum up, the play of punitive strategies, by holding out the threat of retribution, supports a cooperative, high-price equilibrium.

---

[9]The astute reader will recognize that this conclusion depends on how the firm weighs future versus present profits. Firms discount future profits. For discount rates of any reasonable magnitude, neither firm has an incentive to cut price. (However, in the extreme case of an extraordinarily high discount rate, future profits would carry almost no weight and the firm would opt for the immediate price cut.)

The general lesson is that, in infinitely repeated competition, the threat of punishment can be sufficient to enforce a cooperative equilibrium. Indeed, swift but limited penalties may be sufficient to support cooperation. For instance, the strategy "tit-for-tat" is much less drastic than the punitive strategy just described. Under tit-for-tat,

> The firm (1) sets a high price in the first period, and (2) in each succeeding period, echoes (i.e., imitates) the competitor's previous price.

The point of **tit-for-tat** is to deliver a *limited* punishment for defections from cooperation. If the competitor cuts price one period, the firm cuts its price next period. But if and when the competitor returns to a high price, the firm returns to high prices, too. As with the punitive strategies, the mutual play of tit-for-tat supports a cooperative high-price equilibrium. With both using tit-for-tat, the firms cooperate indefinitely. Neither can gain by a unilateral defection; a one-period gain is not worth triggering an ongoing cycle of defections.

The mutual play of tit-for-tat, or of the punitive strategy, succeeds in supporting a cooperative equilibrium. But these are only two of an endless number of possible contingent strategies. Not surprisingly, there has been considerable research interest in strategies for playing the repeated prisoner's dilemma. An intriguing result of this research is how well tit-for-tat performs in achieving cooperation. Tit-for-tat has four virtues. First, it is *nice;* it is never the first to defect. Second, it is *retaliatory*; it immediately punishes an unwarranted defection. Third, it is *clear*; a competitor can immediately see that it doesn't pay to mess with tit-for-tat. Fourth, it is *forgiving*; by mimicking the competitor's previous move, it always is ready to return to cooperation. This last feature is the big difference between the punitive strategy (which satisfies the first three features) and tit-for-tat.[10]

OTHER ASPECTS OF REPUTATION   We have seen that a repeated game allows a player to create and maintain a reputation for cooperation. Reputation can play an analogous role in related contexts.

As a simple example, suppose a seller can produce medium-quality goods or high-quality goods. A typical buyer is willing to pay a premium price for a high-quality item, and the seller could make a greater profit from delivering high quality. The trouble is that the two types of good are indistinguishable at the time of purchase. Only after the buyer has purchased and used the good is the difference in quality apparent. If only a *single*, one-time transaction is at stake, we can argue (without needing a payoff table) that the only equilibrium has the seller offering medium-quality goods at a low price. Why? Because a seller's claim for high quality would not be credible. Any buyer who believed the claim and paid a premium price would be exploited by a self-interested seller who delivered medium quality instead.

---

[10]The political scientist Robert Axelrod has been a pioneer in investigating the repeated prisoner's dilemma. In a famous series of experiments, he asked economists, management scientists, and game theorists to devise strategies to be used in repeated prisoner's dilemmas, such as price competition. What strategy performed best on average when paired in turn against all other strategies? Tit-for-tat! For more on repeated competition and the features of successful strategies, see R. Axelrod, *The Evolution of Cooperation* (New York: Basic Books, 1984).

Of course, you might plausibly protest that honesty should be the best policy for the seller. This is true—*provided* the seller has an incentive to establish a reputation for delivering high-quality goods now and in the indefinite future. Here is a simple way to establish a high-quality equilibrium. If a seller ever delivers a medium-quality item at a premium price, the buyer in question refuses to pay a premium price to that seller ever again and instructs all other buyers to treat the seller the same way. Given this purchasing behavior by buyers, any seller has the incentive to deliver high-quality items and maintain its reputation.

Finally, although reputation provides a basis for repeated cooperation in the pricing and quality contexts, this need not always be the case. In other contexts, a firm's advantage may lie in establishing a reputation for toughness. For instance, in the market-entry game in Table 10.5, we saw that the key to success was to preempt the market by being the first to enter. Now suppose there are a multitude of markets across the country to enter and conquer. How can a firm successfully expand and claim its fair share (or more than its fair share) of these markets? The experience of Wal-Mart Stores Inc. provides a classic example. While other national discount store chains were declaring bankruptcy, Wal-Mart aggressively expanded into small southwestern cities—localities that would support one discount store but not two.

What has been the chain's experience in cities where it has met competition from other retailers? It has relied mainly on its reputation for "staying the course." Thus, Wal-Mart has been willing to suffer losses while waiting for its competitor to exit the market. By maintaining a tough reputation, this "preempt and persist" strategy is credible in each new market Wal-Mart enters. Finally, what has been Wal-Mart's response to new entrants in markets where it already holds a monopoly position? In many cities, the economics are essentially as described in Figure 10.2a's game tree. It is more profitable to maintain price after entry than to cut price. In isolation, Wal-Mart's threat to cut price is not credible and would not deter new entry. But the very fact that Wal-Mart is a chain of stores—more than 4,000 US stores facing an endless number of would-be entrants—profoundly alters its incentives. Wal-Mart credibly can pledge that it will fight entry by *always* cutting prices afterward. According to this pledge, if it once acquiesces to entry, it forever sacrifices its reputation for toughness and will acquiesce to future entrants that challenge its other stores. By staking its reputation in this way, Wal-Mart succeeds in deterring entry in equilibrium; the short-term profit gain from accommodating entry (even once) is not worth the permanent cost (in reduced future profits) from destroying its reputation for toughness.

A FINAL NOTE ON FINITE COMPETITION   We have seen that unlimited repetition can support cooperation in equilibrium. Of course, competition need not go on indefinitely. For instance, one might imagine that there is some probability that the competition will end after any stage. As long as this probability is small enough, the previous analysis, in support of the cooperative equilibrium, continues to hold. However, what happens when the number of periods of competition are *limited* rather than infinite—that is, when the final period (even one very far in the future) is known? Here the logic of cooperation breaks down. To see this, consider once again the example of price competition played over a fixed number of periods. To find each firm's optimal actions, we work backward. In the last period, each firm's dominant strategy is to cut price, so this is what each does. (No threat of future price cuts can change this because there is no tomorrow.) What about the next-to-last period? With prices sure to be low in the last period, each firm's best strategy is to cut price then as well. In general, if low prices are expected in subsequent periods, each firm's best strategy is to cut prices one period earlier. Whatever the fixed number of periods—3 or 300—this logic carries all the way back to period 1. With a fixed endpoint to the game, the only equilibrium is the repeated play of low prices. [11]

The first step for each airline is to prepare estimates of its profits for alternative numbers of departures it might schedule. We know that daily demand is 2,000 trips at a price of $225 per trip. In other words, the airlines are competing for shares of a market having $450,000 in total revenue. The cost for each additional daily departure is $20,000. Let's derive an expression for airline A's profit. We denote the airlines' numbers of departures by *a, b,* and *c,* respectively. Then airline A's profit (in thousands of dollars) can be expressed as

A Battle for Air Passengers Revisited

$$\pi_a = 450\frac{a}{(a + b + c)} - 20a.$$

Here A's share of total revenue is $a/(a + b + c)$. For instance, if all airlines fly identical numbers of flights, they obtain one-third market shares, or $150,000 in revenue each. If airline A provides half the total flights, it claims half the total revenue, and so on. The second term in the profit expression is the total cost of providing this number of departures. (Analogous expressions apply for the other airlines.) Inspection of this equation reveals the airline's basic trade-off: By flying more flights, it claims a greater share of revenue, at the same time incurring additional costs. Moreover, the larger the number of competitors' flights, the smaller the airline's revenue share. If all airlines fly "too many" flights, they all incur large costs, but the result remains a revenue standoff.

Table 10.7 lists the typical airline's payoff table. Note two things about the table. First, it has condensed the decisions of the other two airlines into one variable: the total number of competitor flights. (The columns list numbers of these flights ranging from 5 to 17.) From the profit equation, we observe that an airline's profit depends only on the number of its own flights (*a*) and the total

---

[11]With a fixed end of the repeated competition, optimal play by rational players dictates continual low prices and profits. Is there a way back to the cooperative, high-price outcome? The answer is yes, if one admits the possibility of *near-rational* play. Suppose there is a small chance that one or both sides will play cooperatively because they fail to look ahead to the end of the game. (Perhaps they believe the competition will go on indefinitely.) Injecting this "little bit" of irrationality is a good thing. Now, even a perfectly rational player finds it in his or her self-interest to charge a high price and maintain a cooperative equilibrium (at least until near the end of the competition). For an analysis of the repeated prisoner's dilemma along these lines, see D. Kreps, P. Milgrom, J. Roberts, and R. Wilson, "Rational Cooperation in the Finitely Repeated Prisoners' Dilemma," *Journal of Economic Theory* (1982): 245–252.

number of competitor flights ($b + c$). For example, if airline A mounts five flights and B and C have a total of five flights, A's profit is $(5/10)(450) - (5)(20) = \$125$ thousand, as shown in Table 10.7. Second, only the airline's own profit is listed (to save space). As we would expect, each firm's profit is highly sensitive to the number of flights flown by its competitors. By reading across the payoffs in any row, we see that an airline's profit falls drastically as the number of competing flights increases.

If the three airlines are going to compete month after month, how might they set their number of departures each period? In answering this question, we consider two possible benchmarks: equilibrium behavior and collusive behavior.

To help identify equilibrium behavior, best-response payoffs are highlighted in Table 10.7. For example, if its competitors schedule only 5 total flights, the airline's best response is 6 flights, earning it \$125,500 (the highest payoff in column 1); against 13 flights, the airline's best response is 4 flights; and so on. The table shows that no airline has a dominant strategy. (The more numerous the competitors' flights, the fewer flights the airline should fly.) However, it is striking that the best responses congregate closely around five flights (ranging from three to six). In fact, the unique equilibrium has each of the airlines mounting exactly five flights. To confirm this, note that if the other two airlines fly five each (or 10 total), the airline's best response also is to fly five. (You might want to check by trial and error that no other combination of flights is an equilibrium.) In equilibrium, each airline's profit is \$50,000; total flights number 15, and industry profit is \$150,000.

What if the airlines could tacitly collude in determining the total number of daily departures? Because market revenue is fixed at \$450,000, the best the industry can do is carry the 2,000 passengers at least cost, that is, by using the fewest flights. This requires 10 daily departures (fully loaded), since capacity per plane is 200 passengers. Total industry profit is $450,000 - (10)(20,000) = \$250,000$. If the airlines fly three, three, and four flights, their respective profits are \$75,000,

TABLE 10.7

An Airline's Payoff Table

The airline's best responses are highlighted. In equilibrium, each of the three airlines flies five daily departures.

		Total Number of Competitors' Flights											
		5	6	7	8	9	10	11	12	13	14	15	16	17
	2	50.0	50.0	50.0	50.0	41.8	35.0	29.2	24.3	20.0	16.3	12.9	10.0	7.4
Own	3	75.0	75.0	75.0	62.7	52.5	43.8	36.4	30.0	24.4	19.4	15.0	11.1	7.5
Number	4	100.0	100.0	83.6	70.0	58.5	48.6	40.0	32.5	25.9	20.0	14.7	10.0	5.7
of Flights	5	125.0	104.5	87.5	73.1	60.7	50.0	40.6	32.4	25.0	18.4	12.5	7.1	2.3
	6	125.5	105.0	87.7	72.9	60.0	48.8	38.8	30.0	22.1	15.0	8.6	2.7	-2.6
	7	122.5	102.3	85.0	70.0	56.9	45.3	35.0	25.8	17.5	10.0	3.2	-3.0	-8.8
	8	116.9	97.1	80.0	65.0	51.8	40.0	29.5	20.0	11.4	3.6	-3.5	-10.0	-16.0

$75,000, and $100,000. One possibility is a tacit agreement among the airlines limiting the number of departures—ostensibly to achieve efficient loadings—perhaps alternating delivery of the tenth flight.

Remember, however, that such a tacit understanding is very fragile. If the other airlines limit themselves to six total flights, the last airline's best response is six flights, not four. Although it maximizes industry profit, collusive behavior does not constitute an equilibrium. Any airline can profit by unilaterally increasing its number of departures. Historically, the airlines have competed vigorously for passengers by offering the convenience of frequent departures. Until recently, on many routes the airlines have been plagued by too many competing flights, resulting in lower occupancy and reduced profits for all.

SUMMARY

Decision-Making Principles

1. The formal study of competitive behavior by self-interested players is the subject of game theory. In competitive settings, determining one's own optimal action depends on correctly anticipating the actions and reactions of one's rivals.

2. A dominant strategy is a best response (i.e., maximizes the player's profit) with respect to *any* strategy that a competitor takes. If a dominant strategy exists, a rational individual should play it.

3. In a (Nash) equilibrium, each player employs a strategy that maximizes his or her expected payoff, given the strategies chosen by the others. Game theory predicts that the outcome of any competitive situation will be an equilibrium: a set of strategies from which no player can profitably deviate.

4. In sequential competition, the manager must think ahead. His or her best course of action depends on anticipating the subsequent actions of competitors.

Nuts and Bolts

1. Payoff tables are essential for analyzing competitive situations. A payoff table lists the profit outcomes of all firms, as these outcomes depend on the firms' own actions and those of competitors.

2. In a zero-sum game, the interests of the players are strictly opposed; one player's gain is the other's loss. By contrast, a non-zero-sum game combines elements of competition and cooperation.

3. When players take independent actions (play non-cooperatively), the solution of the game involves the play of equilibrium strategies.

4. When there are multiple equilibria, it is often advantageous to claim the first move.

5. If players can freely communicate and reach a binding agreement, they typically will try to maximize their total payoff.

6. A game tree lists the sequence of player actions and their resulting payoffs. It is possible to solve any game with perfect information by backward induction.

7. In repeated games, the use of contingent strategies and the formation of reputations serve to broaden the range of equilibrium behavior.

Questions and Problems

1. Give a careful explanation of a Nash equilibrium. How is it different from a dominant-strategy equilibrium?

2. Is it ever an advantage to move first in a zero-sum game? When is it an advantage to have the first move in a non-zero-sum game? Provide an example in which it is advantageous to have the second move.

3. Consider the following zero-sum game.

		Player C		
		C1	C2	C3
Player R	R1	13	12	10
	R2	14	6	8
	R3	3	16	7

a. Does either player have a dominant strategy? Does either have a dominated strategy? Explain.

b. Find the players' equilibrium strategies.

4. In mid-2012, Saudi Arabia and Venezuela (both members of OPEC) produced an average of 8 million and 3 million barrels of oil a day, respectively. Production costs were about $20 per barrel, and the price of oil averaged $80 per barrel. Each country had the capacity to produce an extra 1 million barrels per day. At that time, it was estimated that each 1-million-barrel increase in supply would depress the average price of oil by $10.

a. Fill in the missing profit entries in the payoff table.

b. What actions should each country take and why?

		Venezuela	
		3 M barrels	4 M barrels
Saudi Arabia	8 M barrels	____, ____	____, ____
	9 M barrels	____, ____	____, ____

c. Does the asymmetry in the countries' sizes cause them to take different attitudes toward expanding output? Explain why or why not. Comment on whether or not a prisoner's dilemma is present.

5. Firms J and K produce compact-disc players and compete against one another. Each firm can develop either an economy player (E) or a deluxe player (D). According to the best available market research, the firms' resulting profits are given by the accompanying payoff table.

a. The firms make their decisions independently, and each is seeking its own maximum profit. Is it possible to make a confident prediction concerning their actions and the outcome? Explain.

		Firm K	
		E	D
Firm J	E	30, 55	50, 60
	D	40, 75	25, 50

b. Suppose that firm J has a lead in development and so can move first. What action should J take, and what will be K's response?

c. What will be the outcome if firm K can move first?

6. Two firms dominate the market for surgical sutures and compete aggressively with respect to advertising. The following payoff table depicts the profit implications of their different advertising strategies.
   a. Suppose that no communication is possible between the firms; each must choose its ad strategy independently of the other. What actions will the firms take, and what is the outcome?
   b. Suppose firm B moves first in making its advertising decision, then knowing its rivals action, firm A makes its decision. What first move should firm B take? What is firm A's best second move? Relative to the outcome in part (a), how do the firms fare?
   c. If the firms can communicate before setting their advertising strategies, what outcome will occur? Explain.

		Firm B's Ad Spending		
		Low	Medium	High
Firm A's Ad Spending	Low	8, 11	6, 12	5, 14
	Medium	12, 9	8, 10	6, 8
	High	11, 6	10, 8	4, 6

7. Two superpowers are involved in a nuclear arms race. As shown in the payoff table, each can choose to continue to build its weapons stock or alternatively to stop the escalation. The entries show each country's payoff in terms of national security from their joint actions.
   a. Determine the (Nash) equilibrium (or equilibria) of the game. Does the superpower competition constitute a prisoner's dilemma? Explain.
   b. Does your answer to part (a) help explain the "cooling" of the arms race between the United States and the former Soviet Union over the last 20 years? Explain.

		Superpower 2	
		Build	Stop
Superpower 1	Build	3, 4	5, –3
	Stop	–2, 6	6, 8

8. Proctor and Gamble and Kimberly-Clarke dominate the U.S. diaper market with shares of about 50 percent and 35 percent respectively. Both firms invest large sums in R&D to continually reduce the cost of making better performing diapers. The payoff table shows the companies' profits ($millions) from different R&D strategies.
   a. Identify the (Nash) equilibrium of the accompanying payoff table.

		Kimberly-Clark	
		Medium R&D	High R&D
Procter and Gamble	Medium R&D	600, 400	300, 550
	High R&D	700, 150	400, 250

   b. The companies have competed for decades and make R&D decisions every year. If the competition were to go on indefinitely, what strategies might the companies employ to their mutual benefit? (Communication or collusion is not possible.) Explain briefly.

c. R&D competition is quite different from price competition. Price changes can be implemented immediately and are immediately known to the other firm. R&D spending takes time to yield results (sometimes a blockbuster new product) and is much harder to discern by one's rival. For the repetitive competition in part (b), in what ways does R&D competition make things more difficult for the firms to achieve mutual long-term profits?

d. In your view, why aren't there more firms competing in the diaper market?

9. Consider the accompanying zero-sum payoff table.
   a. Does either player have a dominant strategy? Does either have a dominated strategy? Explain.
   b. Once you have eliminated one dominated strategy, see if some other strategy is dominated. Solve the payoff table by iteratively eliminating dominated strategies. What strategies will the players use?

		Firm Z		
		C1	**C2**	**C3**
	R1	−1	−2	4
Firm Y	**R2**	0	2	2
	R3	−2	4	0

10. Firm A and firm B are battling for market share in two separate markets. Market I is worth $30 million in revenue; market II is worth $18 million. Firm A must decide how to allocate its three salespersons between the markets; firm B has only two salespersons to allocate. Each firm's revenue share in each market is *proportional* to the number of salespeople the firm assigns there. For example, if firm A puts two salespersons and firm B puts one salesperson in market I, A's revenue from this market is $[2/(2 + 1)]\$30 = \$20$ million and B's revenue is the remaining $10 million. (The firms split a market equally if neither assigns a salesperson to it.) Each firm is solely interested in maximizing the *total* revenue it obtains from the two markets.
    a. Compute the complete payoff table. (Firm A has four possible allocations: 3-0, 2-1, 1-2, and 0-3. Firm B has three allocations: 2-0, 1-1, and 0-2.) Is this a constant-sum game?
    b. Does either firm have a dominant strategy (or dominated strategies)? What is the predicted outcome?

11. One way to lower the rate of auto accidents is strict enforcement of motor vehicle laws (speeding, drunk driving, and so on). However, maximum enforcement is very costly. The following payoff table lists the payoffs of a typical motorist and a town government. The motorist can obey or disobey motor vehicle laws, which the town can enforce or not.

		Town	
		Enforce	**Don't Enforce**
	Obey	0, −15	0, 0
Motorist	**Don't Obey**	−20, −20	5, −10

    a. What is the town's optimal strategy? What is the typical motorist's behavior in response?
    b. What if the town could commit to a strict enforcement policy and motorists believed that this policy would be used? Would the town wish to do so?
    c. Now suppose the town could commit to enforcing the law part of the time. (The typical motorist cannot predict exactly when the town's traffic police will be monitoring the roadways.) What is the town's optimal degree (i.e., percentage) of enforcement? Explain.

12. The following payoff table lists the profits of a buyer and a seller. The *seller acts first* by choosing a sale price ($9, $8, or $6). The buyer then decides the quantity of the good to purchase (two units, four units, six units, or eight units).
    a. Suppose the buyer and seller transact only once. Does the buyer have a dominant strategy? Depending on the price quoted, what is his best response? What price should the seller set? Explain carefully.

		Buyer Quantities		
		2 units	**4 units**	**6 units**	**8 units**

		2 units	**4 units**	**6 units**	**8 units**
Seller Prices	**P = $9**	10, 6	20, 5	30, 0	40, –8
	P = $8	8, 8	16, 9	24, 6	32, 0
	P = $6	4, 12	8, 17	12, 18	16, 16

b. Suppose the seller and buyer are in a multiyear relationship. Each month, the buyer quotes a price and the seller selects her quantity. How might this change each player's behavior?

c. Now suppose the buyer and seller are in a position to negotiate an agreement specifying price and quantity. Can they improve on the result in part a? Which quantity should they set? What price would be equitable? Explain.

Discussion Question   Over the last decade, the Delta Shuttle and the U.S. Air Shuttle have battled for market share on the Boston-New York and Washington, D.C.-New York routes. In addition to service quality and dependability (claimed or real), the airlines compete on price via periodic fare changes. The hypothetical payoff table lists each airline's estimated profit (expressed on a per-seat basis) for various combinations of one-way fares.

Delta Shuttle Fares	U.S. Air Shuttle Fares		
	$139	**$119**	**$99**
$139	$34, $38	15, 42	$6, $32
$119	42, 20	22, 22	10, 25
$ 99	35, 7	27, 9	18, 16

a. Suppose that the two airlines select their fares independently and "once and for all." (The airlines' fares cannot be changed.) What fares should the airlines set?

b. Suppose, instead, that the airlines will set fares over the next 18 months. In any month, each airline is free to change its fare if it wishes. What pattern of fares would you predict for the airlines over the 18 months?

c. Pair yourself with another student from the class. The two of you will play the roles of Delta and U.S. Air and set prices for the next 18 months. You will exchange written prices for each month and determine your resulting profits from the payoff table. The competition continues in this way for 18 months, after which time you should compute your total profit (the sum of your monthly payoffs). Summarize the results of your competition. What lessons can you draw from it?

Spreadsheet Problems

S1. Four large used-car dealers compete for customers in a city where demand for used automobiles is constant at about 800 cars per month. By an implicit agreement, the dealers set comparable prices on their cars, with the result that price wars and competitive discounting are extremely rare. All dealers claim to have the lowest prices, but the facts say otherwise. The average (variable) cost of a used car to the dealer (procuring and readying it for sale) is $2,400. The average sale price per car is $4,000.

The dealers do compete with respect to the number and types of cars in their showrooms. The typical prospective buyer visits a number of dealers looking for the "right" car. The greater the number of cars a dealer has available, the better is its chance of making a sale. In fact, a particular dealer's share of the total market is proportional to the number of cars it holds in its showroom. Thus, dealer 1's profit can be expressed as $\pi_1 = 3{,}200{,}000[x_1/(x_1 + x_2 + x_3 + x_4)] - 2{,}400x_1$. The profit expressions for the other dealers are analogous.

The partial spreadsheet that follows lists the profit of a typical dealer (for various inventories) when it faces competitors with different average inventories. For instance, if dealer 1 stocks an inventory of 250 cars when the other dealers do likewise, then dealer 1's inventory is 25 percent of the total. Thus, it sells exactly (.25)(800) = 200 cars at a price of $4,000 each, while paying for 250 cars at $2,400 each. Its net profit is $200,000.

a. Create a spreadsheet to complete the entries in the following payoff table. *Hint*: To compute cell G10, enter the formula:

$$= 3200*\$B10/(\$B10 + 3*G\$5) - 2.4*\$B10.$$

Then simply copy this formula into the other cells of the table. (Adding dollar signs creates the appropriate absolute references to the dealers' inventory levels. For the row player's action, the sign always goes before the alphabetical coordinate, $B10. For the column player's action, it goes before the numerical reference, G$5.) Also, in cells D7-D10 and E7, dealer 1 sells its entire inventory; thus, its payoffs are computed accordingly.

b. Find dealer 1's best inventory response to the various inventory actions of the other dealers. (Circle the greatest profit entry in each column of the table.)

c. What is the equilibrium inventory level for each of the four dealers?

d. If the dealers colluded to limit inventories, what would be the maximum monopoly profit they could earn collectively? Would individual dealers have an incentive to cheat on their inventories? Explain.

e. What would be the effect of free entry into the used-car business?

	A	B	C	D	E	F	G	H	I	J	K
1											
2				**USED CAR DEALERS**							
3											
4		Dealer 1's		Average Auto Inventory of the Other Three Dealers							
5		Inventory		175	200	225	250	275	300	325	
6											
7		175		280.0	280.0	238.8	185.4				
8		200		320.0	320.0	251.4	193.7				
9		225		360.0	332.7	260.0	198.5				
10		250		400.0	341.2	264.9	200.0				
11		275									
12		300									
13		325									
14		350									
15											

S2. In Problem 10, suppose that each firm has a $10 million direct sales budget to allocate between the two markets. Again, revenues in the markets are split in proportion to direct sales dollars spent.

a. Create a three-entry spreadsheet to find firm A's total revenue if it spends $7 million in market I (and the remainder in market II) while firm B spends $6 million in market I. Which firm earns the greater total revenue?

b. Use the spreadsheet optimizer to find firm A's optimal spending split when firm B's split is $6 million-$4 million.

c. Find firm A's optimal spending splits, if firm B spends $5 million, $6 million, $6.25 million, $9 million, or $9.5 million in market I. What is the symmetric equilibrium of this spending game? Provide an intuitive explanation for the equilibrium.

Suggested References

The following references are classic treatments of game theory.

Schelling, T. C. *The Strategy of Conflict.* Cambridge, MA: Harvard University Press, 1990.

Von Neumann, J., and O. Morgenstern. *Theory of Games and Economic Behavior.* Princeton, NJ: Princeton University Press, 1944.

A number of texts provide comprehensive and up-to-date treatments of game theory.

Camerer, C. *Behavioral Game Theory.* Princeton, NJ: Princeton University Press, 2003.

Dixit, A., D. H. Reiley, and S. Skeath. *Games of Strategy.* New York: W.W. Norton, 2009.

Fudenberg, D., and J. Tirole. *Game Theory.* Cambridge, MA: MIT Press, 1994.

Myerson, R. *Game Theory.* Cambridge, MA: Harvard University Press, 1997 (Paperback).

Osborne, M. J. *An Introduction to Game Theory.* New York: Oxford University Press, 2004.

Rasmusen, E. *Games and Information,* 4th Ed. Cambridge: Blackwell, 2006.

For applications of game theory to competitive strategy and business problems, we highly recommend

Dixit, A. K., and B. J. Nalebuff. *Thinking Strategically: The Competitive Edge in Business, Politics, and Everyday Life.* New York: W. W. Norton, 1993 (paperback).

McMillan, J. *Games, Strategies, and Managers.* New York: Oxford University Press, 1996.

Game theory resources on the Web include

www.economics.harvard.edu/~aroth/alroth.html. *Professor Alvin Roth's home page has an extensive number of links to game theory sites.*

http://levine.sscnet.ucla.edu/general.htm. *Professor David Levine of UCLA provides some absorbing readings and games.*

www.comlabgames.com. *This site has software for playing and designing games.*

Check Station Answers

1. Store 1 does not have a dominant strategy, but store 2 does. Regardless of store 1's action, store 2's optimal choice is to promote women's clothing. Anticipating this behavior, store 1's best response is to promote girls' clothing. Despite the seeming symmetry of the example, store 1 fares much better than store 2.

2. This competition is a constant-sum game because the players' payoffs in each cell add up to the same sum. (Here the market shares always add up to 100.) The method of circles and squares pinpoints the equilibrium at R2 and C2. This is exactly the same outcome as in the zero-sum version in Table 10.2. There is no strategic difference between a zero-sum game and its constant-sum counterpart.

3. If its rival produces six units, the firm's best response is either eight or ten units. (Actually, an amount not shown, nine units, would be absolutely best.) If its rival produces eight units, the firm's best response is eight units. If its rival produces ten units, the firm's best response is either six or eight units (actually, seven is best). This shows that neither firm has a dominant strategy. The firms might hope to produce six units each, but this is not an equilibrium. Either could gain at the other's expense by increasing output (ideally, to nine units). The sole equilibrium has each firm producing eight units–the same answer as found in Chapter 9.

4. Originally, there are two equilibria: Boeing alone produces or Airbus alone produces. With the government subsidy, Airbus's dominant strategy is to produce. Knowing this, Boeing gives up the market.

Mixed Strategies

LO#1. Discuss situations in which game theory calls for the use of a mixed strategy.

Whenever a player selects a particular course of action with certainty, we refer to this as a *pure* strategy. All of the applications in the main body of this chapter have involved pure-strategy equilibria, for instance, R2 versus C2 in the market-share competition. However, in other settings, optimal play frequently requires the use of *mixed (or randomized)* strategies. Here, a player randomizes between two or more pure strategies, selecting each with fixed probabilities. Consider a second version of the market-share competition.

MARKET COMPETITION REVISITED   Suppose that the firms have only their first and third strategies available. The payoff table in Table 10A.1a is identical to that of Table 10.2 except that the second strategy of each player is omitted. Now, there is no pure-strategy equilibrium. Instead, the players' best responses "cycle" and never settle down to any pair of strategies. For example, beginning at R1, C1, firm 1 would gain by switching to R3. But R3, C1 is not stable since now firm 2 would gain by switching to C3. But R3, C3 will give way to Rl, C3 (after firm 1 switches), and, in turn, this gives way to R1, C1 (after firm 2 switches). We are back to where we began.

Although there is no equilibrium in pure strategies, the payoff table does have a unique equilibrium when players use particular mixed strategies. To qualify as a mixed-strategy equilibrium:

> The player's chosen probabilities must ensure that the other player earns the same expected payoff from any of the pure strategies making up his or her mixture.

This statement is quite a mouthful and requires some explaining. Why must the opponent's pure strategies earn the *same* expected payoff? To see this, let's turn back to the market-share competition. Suppose firm 1 decided to randomize between R1 and R3, each with probability .5. This is a plausible mixed strategy but, as we shall see, is not in equilibrium. Suppose firm 2 anticipates firm 1 using this 50-50 mixture. What is firm 2's best response? Suppose firm 2 considers Cl. Because firm 1's actual action is uncertain, firm 2 must compute its **expected payoff**. From Table 10A.1a, the expected payoff is $(0.5)(-2) + (0.5)(7) = 2.5$. Alternatively, using C3, firm 2's expected payoff is $(0.5)(4) + (0.5)(-5) = -0.5$. Clearly, firm 2 always prefers to play C3. (Remember, firm 2 is trying to *minimize* the expected market-share increase of firm 1.) But if firm 2 always is expected to play C3, then it would be foolish for firm 1 to persist in playing the 50-50 mixture.

TABLE 10A.1

Mixed Strategies in a
Zero-Sum Game

(a)

		Firm 2	
		C1	C3
Firm 1	R1	−2	4
	R3	7	−5

(b)

		Firm 2		Firm 1's
		(1/2)	(1/2)	Expected Payoff
		C1	C3	
(2/3)	R1	−2	4	1
Firm 1 (1/3)	R3	7	−5	1
Firm 2's Expected Payoff		1	1	

Firm 1 should respond to C3 by playing R1 all the time. But then firm 2 would not want to play C3, and we are back in a cycle of second guessing. In short, mixed strategies when one player's pure strategies have different expected payoffs cannot be in equilibrium.

Now we are ready to compute the "correct" equilibrium probabilities for each firm's mixed strategy. Start with firm 1. Let x denote the probability it plays R1 and $1 - x$ the probability it plays R3. If firm 2 uses C1, its expected payoff is: $(x)(-2) + (1 - x)(7)$. If, instead, it uses C3, its expected payoff is: $(x)(4) + (1 - x)(-5)$. Firm 2 is indifferent between C1 and C3 when these expected payoffs are equal:

$$-2x + 7(1 - x) = 4x - 5(1 - x), \qquad [10A.1]$$

or $12 = 18x$. Thus, $x = 2/3$. In equilibrium, firm 1 uses R1 and R3 with probabilities $2/3$ and $1/3$, respectively. Turning to firm 2, let y denote the probability it plays C1 and $1 - y$ the probability it plays C3. If firm 1 uses R1, its expected payoff is: $(y)(-2) + (1 - y)(4)$. If, instead, it uses R3, its expected payoff is: $(y)(7) + (1 - y)(-5)$. Equating these expected payoffs implies:

$$-2y + 4(1 - y) = 7y - 5(1 - y), \qquad [10A.2]$$

or $9 = 18y$. Thus, $y = 1/2$. In equilibrium, firm 2 uses C1 and C3, each with probability $1/2$. In Table 10A.1b, we display these mixed strategies.[1] Finally, what is each firm's

---

[1]There is a simple rule for finding the mixed strategies in a 2-by-2 payoff table like the accompanying one. Firm 1's mixed-strategy proportions are: $x = (d - c)/[(d - c) + (a - b)]$ and $1 - x = (a - b)/[(d - c) + (a - b)]$. Firm 2's proportions are: $y = (d - b)/[(d - b) + (a - c)]$ and $1 - y = (a - c)/[(d - b) + (a - c)]$. To find the R1 chance, take the difference between the entries in the *opposite row* $(d - c)$ and then divide by the sum of the row differences, $(d - c) + (a - b)$. The same opposite-row rule works for the R2 chance, and an *opposite-column* rule works for computing firm 2's mixed strategy proportions.

		y	$1 - y$
		C1	C2
x	R1	a	b
$1 - x$	R2	c	d

expected payoff when it uses its mixed strategy? If we substitute $x = 2/3$ into either side of Equation 10A.1, we find that firm 2's expected payoff is 1 from either of its pure strategies. Thus, the expected payoff for its mixed strategy is also 1. Similarly, firm 1's expected payoff is 1 from either of its strategies. These expected payoffs also are shown in Table 10A.1b. In short, when both sides use their optimal mixed strategies, firm 1's expected gain in market share (and firm 2's expected loss) is 1 percent.

REMARK   In this equilibrium, neither side can improve its expected payoff by switching from its mixed strategy. In fact, a player actually does not lose by switching to some other strategy proportion. For instance, as long as firm 2 uses its 50-50 mixed strategy, firm 1 earns the same expected payoff from *any* mixture of R1 and R3 (one-third/two-thirds, 50-50, etc.). The penalty for switching from equilibrium proportions comes in a different form: A smart opponent can take advantage of such a switch. Using its equilibrium strategy, firm 1 *guarantees* itself an expected payoff of 1 against the equilibrium play of firm 2 or against any other play. If firm 1 were to switch to nonequilibrium strategy proportions (let's say 60-40 proportions), it gives firm 2 the chance to gain at its expense by switching to C3. (Against a 60-40 mix by firm 1, the expected payoff of C3 is .4.) Firm 1's original advantage (an expected payoff of +1 in equilibrium) now would be eroded. In short, wandering from the original equilibrium play is ill-advised.

A GAME OF TRUST   Table 10A.2 depicts a *non-zero-sum* game that might be called a game of trust. Each player has two actions. The players' highest payoffs occur if player 1 is "straightforward" and player 2 is "trusting." The catch is that player 1 might try to take advantage of a trusting partner by playing the "bluff" strategy. In turn, player 2, recognizing this possibility, could take a "skeptical" position, and so on. The greater the incidence of bluffing and/or skepticism, the lower is the sum of the players' payoffs. Thus, this behavior is detrimental. One finds the basic features of this game in many economic settings. For instance, a contractor might be tempted to pass on unexpected cost overruns to a more or less trusting government agency. Alternatively, in an out-of-court settlement, party A might try to extract excessive monetary compensation from party B.

The circles and squares in Table 10A.2 show the best responses for the respective players. We see that there is no pure-strategy equilibrium. To find the mixed-strategy equilibrium, we follow the approach used earlier. Player 1's proportions must leave player 2 indifferent between being trusting or skeptical. It follows that

$$20x - 10(1 - x) = 10x + 0(1 - x).$$

The left side of this equation is player 2's expected payoff from being trusting; the right side is her payoff from being skeptical. The solution is $x = .5$. Thus, player 1 is straightforward or bluffs with equal probability. In turn, player 2's proportions (y and $1 - y$) must leave player 1 indifferent between being straightforward or bluffing. It follows that

$$20y + 10(1 - y) = 50y + 0(1 - y).$$

This reduces to $10 = 40y$, or $y = .25$. Thus, player 2 should be trusting 25 percent of the time and skeptical 75 percent of the time.

Notice that player 2 must be inclined toward skepticism precisely in order to keep player 1 honest. If player 2 were too trusting, player 1 always would bluff. Table 10A.2b

		Player 2	
		Trusting	**Skeptical**
Player 1	**Straightforward**	20, 20	10, 10
	Bluff	50, −10	0, 0

			Player 2		
			(.25)	(.75)	**Player 1's**
			Trusting	**Skeptical**	**Expected Payoff**
Player 1	(.5)	**Straightforward**	20, 20	10, 10	12.5
	(.5)	**Bluff**	50, −10	0, 0	12.5
		Player 2's Expected Payoff		5.0	

shows these mixed strategies and the players' resulting expected payoffs. Both players' expected payoffs fall well short of the 20 in profit each would enjoy in the upper-left cell. However, the straightforward and trusting strategies do not constitute a viable equilibrium.

A fundamental result in game theory holds that every game (having a finite number of players and actions) has at least one Nash equilibrium. Thus, if a payoff table lacks a pure-strategy equilibrium, there will always be a mixed-strategy equilibrium. Deliberately taking randomized actions might seem strange at first. But, as the examples indicate, mixed strategies are needed to sustain equilibrium. Indeed, in a zero-sum game lacking a pure-strategy equilibrium, mixed strategies are required to protect oneself against an opponent's opportunistic play.

Finally, many games may have both pure-strategy and mixed-strategy equilibria. One example is the market-entry game in Table 10.5. We have already identified a pair of pure-strategy equilibria in which one firm enters and the other stays out. There is also a mixed-strategy equilibrium in which each firm enters with probability .5. When the competitor enters with this frequency, the firm's expected profit from entering is 0, the same as if it stayed out. Obviously, this equilibrium is not very desirable for the firms. If they compete for new markets repeatedly, the firms mutually would prefer to divide up the available markets by alternating between the two pure-strategy equilibria.

Problems

1. A stranger in a bar challenges you to play the following zero-sum game. The table lists your payoffs in dollars.

		Him	
		C1	**C2**
You	**R1**	−16	24
	R2	8	−16

What is your optimal mixed strategy? What is your opponent's? How much should you expect to win or lose on average?

2. The following payoff table offers a simple depiction of the strategy choices of the Allies and Germany with respect to the 1944 D-Day invasion during World War II. The Allies can land at either Calais or Normandy, and Germany can focus its defense at one, but not both, locations. Payoffs can be interpreted as the Allies' probability of ultimately winning the war.

   Find the mixed-strategy equilibrium. Explain briefly these optimal strategies. What is the value of the game, that is, the Allies' winning chances?

		Germany	
		Calais	Normandy
Allies	Calais	.6	.9
	Normandy	.8	.6

3. In the game show *Jeopardy*, Bob with $10,000 and Dan with $6,000 are about to place their bets in Final Jeopardy. (The third player has so little money that he cannot possible win.) Each secretly places his bet and then answers a final question, winning his bet with a correct answer, losing it if he is wrong. Both know that either's chance of a correct answer is **.5** (and these chances are independent). After answers are given and bets are added or subtracted, the person with the *most total money* wins (keeping his money and returning to play again the next day). The loser gets nothing.

   This situation is equivalent to a zero-sum game, where Bob seeks to maximize his chance of winning (and Dan wants to minimize Bob's chance). As shown in Table A, Bob's strategic options are to make a shut-out bid, $2,001, giving him an unbeatable $12,001 if he answers correctly, or to bid nothing, $0. Dan's options are to bid his entire winnings, $6,000, or to bid nothing, $0.

   a. In Table A, supply Bob's winning chances for the two missing entries. (For example, the lower-left entry shows that if Bob doesn't bet but Dan does, Bob's winning chance is .5 – i.e., when Dan answers incorrectly.) Then, determine both players' equilibrium strategies and the value of the game (i.e., Bob's winning chances). Does either player use a mixed strategy?

   Table A

	Dan	
Bob	Bet $6,000	Bet $0
Bet $2,001	___	___
Bet $0	.50	1.0

   b. As before, Bob has $10,000, but now suppose that Dan has *$8,000*. Complete the missing entries in Table B, and find both players' equilibrium strategies. Does either player use a mixed strategy? Now, what is Bob's chance of winning?

   Table B

	Dan	
Bob	Bet $8,000	Bet $0
Bet $6,001	___	___
Bet $0	.50	1.0

CHAPTER 11

Regulation, Public Goods, and Benefit-Cost Analysis

How many people does it take to screw in a light bulb?
Economist: None, the market will do it.
Consumer Advocate: None, the regulators will do it.

DENNIS CARLTON AND JEFFREY PERLOFF

LO#1. Describe the three important types of market failure—due to monopoly, externalities, and imperfect information—and outline the appropriate regulatory responses.

LO#2. Discuss the economic rationale for government provision of public goods.

LO#3. Identify the key steps of benefit-cost analysis.

LO#4. Demonstrate how benefit-cost analysis can be applied to a public investment decision.

LO#5. Explain how benefits and costs are valued when they cannot be measured by market prices.

Azidothymidine, or AZT, retards multiplication of the AIDS virus in cells. Scientists discovered AZT in 1964, and Burroughs Wellcome Co. acquired the patent a decade later. When the AIDS epidemic struck, Wellcome sent the drug to the National Institutes of Health for tests and human trials.

The FDA, AZT, and AIDS

In 1987, the Food and Drug Administration approved AZT in a record four months, well under the usual two years. However, soon after AZT's introduction, critics attacked Wellcome for the "excessive" price it set for the drug. The cost of treatment for patients with advanced cases of AIDS ranged between $5,000 and $8,000 per year, making AZT one of the highest-priced drugs ever sold.

In its defense, Wellcome justified the high price as a way of recovering the enormous costs of developing AZT, although the company refused to divulge those costs. Critics contended that the government's sponsorship of the drug's testing significantly reduced the company's costs. In 1989, federal lawmakers sought an investigation of Wellcome's pricing policies. Some called for the government to require the company to lower prices. Ultimately, the company reduced AZT's price by 20 percent.

The story of AZT raises questions. What roles should private firms and government play in bringing therapeutic drugs to market? How should safety be ensured? How should prices be set?

Ours is a mixed economy encompassing both private markets and the public sector. Private markets provide an astonishing variety of goods and services. But there are things markets cannot efficiently provide, including safe streets, clean air, national security, an educated citizenry, and protection from potential carcinogens. Government sets the most basic ground rules without which private markets could not function. Government policies and laws define and enforce basic property and contractual rights of business firms and individuals. The government also acts to ensure open and free competition. Finally, the government produces or buys many public goods, from defense expenditures to highways.

Government decision making encompasses three broad areas: microeconomic, macroeconomic, and distributive. Government's microeconomic role is to provide certain public goods and services, undertake public investments, and regulate operations of private markets. Government's macroeconomic tasks include: reducing the frequency and severity of recessions, promoting economic growth, and maintaining low rates of inflation and unemployment. In its distributive role, government attempts to reduce income inequality; ensure minimum health, education, and living standards; and improve the welfare of the poor. Many government programs serve more than one goal. For instance, increased government spending may stimulate an economy threatened by recession, redistribute income, and fund particular projects.

This chapter focuses on the microeconomic function of government. Here, the government has two main roles: (1) to regulate private markets by providing basic rules and by correcting market failures, and (2) to provide certain desirable public goods and services that are not, or cannot, be provided via private markets. Part I of this chapter focuses on regulation; Part II applies benefit-cost analysis to evaluate public programs.

I. MARKET FAILURES AND REGULATION

Private markets depend on well-defined property rights. One must be able to own something in order to buy or sell it. Property rights are defined by law and enforced by courts and law enforcement authorities. The law of property continues to evolve. For instance, tradable pollution permits and rights in genomic material are new types of property rights. Governments also enforce contractual rights and provide rules for transactions, including rules for disclosure and prohibiting fraud. Well-defined rules allow markets to function. Indeed, when markets fail, there are often calls for greater attention to enforcement of the basic rules of the game. In the aftermath of the savings and loan crisis in the 1980s, hundreds of bank officials went to jail, and there have been calls for equivalent action following the financial collapse of 2007–2008.

In Chapter 7, we showed that perfectly competitive markets are efficient, that is, *competitive markets provide the right amounts of goods and services at minimum cost to the consumers who value them most highly.* While many markets in the United States approximate the requirements of perfect competition, notable cases of market failure also exist. Market failures usually can be traced to three causes: (1) monopoly power, (2) externalities, and (3) imperfect information. In the next three sections, we examine each of these cases in turn.

MARKET FAILURE DUE TO MONOPOLY

In monopolistic markets (pure monopoly, monopolistic competition, or oligopoly), producers have discretion in setting prices. Monopolists raise prices, increasing the monopolist's profit at the expense of consumer welfare.[1] Consumers lose more than monopolistic producers gain, and total welfare falls.

We can see this *deadweight loss* by turning back to Figure 8.3. Deadweight loss is measured by the area of triangle MDE. The perfectly competitive outcome (point E) delivers maximum social benefit in the form of the large consumer-surplus triangle ACE. By contrast, under monopoly (point M), total social benefit is measured as the sum of consumer surplus (triangle ABM) and the monopolist's excess profit (rectangle MBCD). The difference between total social benefit attained under perfect competition and monopoly is measured by the deadweight loss triangle MDE.

Let industry demand be given by $P = 20 - 2Q$ and industry unit cost by $AC = MC = 8$. Find output and price under pure monopoly and under perfect competition. Calculate the deadweight loss due to monopoly.   **CHECK STATION 1**

Similar welfare losses occur in the intermediate cases of monopolistic competition and oligopoly. With a small number of firms, prices are raised above the competitive level but fall short of the pure monopoly level. Accordingly, smaller deadweight losses occur under these market conditions. The size of these losses depends on the number of firms, the kind of oligopolistic behavior exhibited, and the elasticity of market demand, among other factors. Research estimates of monopoly losses vary from .5 to 6 percent of gross domestic product (GDP). Recent estimates have been predominantly in the lower part of this range, below 2 percent of GDP.[2]

RENT SEEKING   Because monopoly allows a firm to earn excess profits, companies will invest resources in order to secure a monopoly position. This includes activities directed at the political system (lobbying), the court system (litigation), and the regulatory system (for example, at the Patent Office). Economists call the excess profits that monopolists earn *rents* and call the quest for these rents *rent seeking*. Economic theory suggests that firms will compete for rents up to the point where it no longer profits them to do so. That is, they will compete until most of the excess profits from monopoly have been dissipated. Rent-seeking activity represents a social loss. (If everyone stopped doing it, social welfare would increase, even if monopoly remained.)

If the monopolist dissipates its excess profits through rent-seeking activity, the total welfare loss of monopoly includes not just the deadweight loss MDE in Figure 8.3 but also the area MBCD. Estimates of rent-seeking losses (including resources spent by society to prevent rent-seeking) are typically higher (sometimes much higher) than the estimated deadweight losses due to actual monopolization of markets.[3]

---

[1] Market power has even entered the health care debate, with some arguing that one driver of high U.S. Health care costs has been the consolidation of hospitals, leading to higher prices. See E. Porter, "Health Care's Overlooked Cost Factor," *The New York Times* (June 12, 2013), p. B1.

[2] For a survey and critique of these results, see A. J. Daskin, "Deadweight Loss in Oligopoly: A New Approach," *Southern Economic Journal* (July 1991): 171–185.

[3] For a good discussion, see J. R. Hines, Jr., "Three Sides of Harberger Triangles," *Journal of Economic Perspectives* (Spring 1999): 167–188.

Government Responses

Antitrust action often is taken to prevent the emergence of monopoly power and restore competition to a monopolistic industry. The US Congress has passed a number of important pieces of antitrust legislation to prevent and attack monopolies. The Sherman Act of 1890 prohibits conspiracies and combinations in restraint of trade, monopolization of any kind, and attempts to monopolize. The Clayton Act of 1914 forbids types of price discrimination aimed at reducing competition. It also prohibits tying agreements. (In such agreements the producer will sell a customer a product only if the customer agrees to buy another product from the producer.) The act also prohibits corporations from buying up competitors' shares of stock or having board members in common with competitors if this practice will lessen competition. The Federal Trade Commission Act of 1914 outlaws "unfair methods of competition" and created the Federal Trade Commission (FTC) to define and enforce this law. In addition, there are a number of other pieces of legislation designed to foster competition.

The government can sue to enforce the provisions of the various antitrust laws. In addition, both the Sherman Act and the Clayton Act allow private parties who are injured ·by anticompetitive behavior to sue for damages. If successful, the suing party receives three times the value of the actual injury. Suits by either the government or private parties have several aims and results.

BREAKING UP EXISTING MONOPOLIES   Under the Sherman Act, the government may sue to break up a corporation that has attained a monopoly or near monopoly. In 1911, the US Supreme Court broke up Standard Oil of New Jersey (which controlled over 90 percent of the refining and sales of petroleum products) into 30 independent corporations. In 1982 AT&T, after being sued, agreed to be broken into 23 independent local telephone companies. These operating companies became seven regional phone companies offering local telephone service. The long-distance service, Western Electric, and Bell Laboratories were retained by AT&T. Other suits by the government have been less successful. The courts refused to break up U.S. Steel in 1920 and IBM in 1982. In 2001, the Bush administration abandoned attempts to break up Microsoft. Currently, several near-monopolies—including Google, Facebook, eBay, and Amazon—continue to exist without government attempts to break them up. Instead, the government has focused on monopolistic practices.

PREVENTING MONOPOLISTIC PRACTICES   The government seeks to ban practices used (1) to acquire and defend monopoly power and (2) to exploit monopoly power. Such practices include bundling and tying arrangements, price discrimination, and predatory pricing.

Illegal predatory pricing occurs when a large company sets price below cost in order to drive smaller companies out of business. The dominant firm then raises prices once the competitors are driven out. (Companies do not reenter since they know that entry will lead to another round of price cutting.) Courts must distinguish predatory pricing from normal price competition. In 1993, the US Supreme Court cleared Brown and Williamson Tobacco Corporation of predatory pricing in a suit brought by a rival seller. In that case, the court required proof that the accused company deliberately priced at a loss, that this behavior had a reasonable chance of driving rivals out of business, and that the accused would profit as a result. Because of this high standard, few predatory cases are brought or won in the United States. In Europe, where the standard of proof is lower, suits have been more successful. In 2009, the European Commission fined Intel $1.45 billion for offering steep price discounts to customers committing to buying 80 to 100 percent of their needs (allegedly excluding rival suppliers). In 2009 and 2010, Intel also settled cases brought by rival AMD and the Federal Trade Commission.

PREVENTING MERGERS THAT REDUCE COMPETITION   The government also has acted to prevent mergers. American merger policy was born in opposition to the great wave of mergers and consolidations at the close of the nineteenth century. The original philosophy of the trustbusters was that market dominance and monopoly were inherently bad. In 1962, the government successfully sued to prevent the merger of Brown Shoe and Kinney Shoe, the fourth and eighth largest manufacturers of shoes at the time. And in 1966, the government stopped the merger of two Los Angeles grocery chains that shared just 8 percent of the local market.

By the 1970s and 1980s, however, the "Chicago School approach" had assumed dominance in the antitrust arena. According to this philosophy, the forces of free-market competition are far more effective at limiting monopolies than government regulators. Absent prohibitive barriers to entry, a firm's monopoly power is temporary. High profits would attract new entrants, eroding the monopolist's power. Following this approach, the Reagan and Bush administrations used their antitrust powers sparingly.

In the 1990s, antitrust thinking accepted new reasons for government action. Size was not the first concern but, rather, the ability to raise prices. For instance, the combination of Staples and Office Depot would have claimed only about 4 percent of the national office supply market. However, the government's economic analysis predicted that prices would rise by 15 percent or more in markets where the stores formerly competed head to head, so the merger was denied. Under this approach, antitrust intervention proceeds on a case-by-case basis.

Following this philosophy, Clinton administration regulators blocked proposed mergers of Rite-Aid and Revco (prescription drug suppliers), and Microsoft's acquisition of Intuit (maker of Quicken financial software). In 1998, the Justice Department blocked the proposed merger of the defense giants Lockheed Martin and Northrop Grumman. However, finding no significant adverse competitive effects, regulators approved the mega-mergers of Kimberly-Clark and Scott Paper; Chase Manhattan and Chemical Bank; Citicorp and Travelers Group; and Boeing and McDonnell-Douglas.

After 2000, merger enforcement in the United States again returned to a more permissive philosophy by both courts and the administration.[4] In 2004 the court refused to enjoin the acquisition of PeopleSoft by Oracle, even though the firms were the leaders in top-end financial and human resources management software. In 2006, the government approved the acquisition of Maytag by Whirlpool, with 20 percent and 51 percent market shares in washing machines. Likewise, Delta Airline's 2008 acquisition of Northwest

---

[4]For a comprehensive discussion of recent antitrust policy, see J. B. Baker and C. Shapiro, "Reinvigorating Horizontal Merger Enforcement," in R. Pitofsky (ed.), *How the Chicago School Overshot the Mark: The Effect of Conservative Economic Analysis on Antitrust* (Oxford: Oxford University Press, 2008).

Airlines was uncontested. For multinational firms, much of the action moved to Europe. In 2001 the European Union's Antitrust Commission blocked a proposed merger between General Electric and Honeywell International, although it had the blessing of US authorities. Likewise, European regulators blocked a music joint venture between Time Warner and EMI Group.

The Obama administration has closely scrutinized numerous proposed mergers, approving many (often with conditions) while rejecting a few. In 2010, regulators approved the takeover of the world's largest concert promoter, Live Nation, by Ticketmaster, the world's largest ticket seller, on condition that Ticketmaster licensed its ticket-selling software to two competitors and that it would divest itself of its sports-ticketing subsidiary. (Many artists, including Bruce Springsteen, opposed this merger.) In the same year, the merger of United and Continental Airlines was approved. In 2011, the administration approved (with conditions) Comcast's acquisition of a majority stake in NBC Universal and Google's bid to acquire ITA, a travel software developer but blocked tax-preparer H&R Block's acquisition of TaxACT. In the same year, the government blocked the proposed acquisition by AT&T (second largest US carrier) of T-Mobile (fourth largest), but in 2013 approved the merger of T-Mobile and Metro PCS (fifth largest) to form a larger, though still fourth largest, T-Mobile. In 2012, Western Digital and Hitachi merged to create the largest hard-disk company in the world, reducing the major players from five to four. A year later, the government initially opposed but eventually approved the merger of American Airlines and US Airways to form the world's largest airline. Also in 2013, regulators approved the merger of Office Max and Office Depot as well as Anheuser-Busch InBev's acquisition of Grupo Modelo, on condition that InBev would transfer the right to sell Corona beer in the United States to a rival distributor.

Too Big to Fail

The financial meltdown of 2007–2008 brought another concern about mergers and the creation of mega-firms.[5] When major financial institutions were near collapse in 2008, their default would have driven hundreds of other companies out of business and threatened the entire US economic system. The US government had little recourse but to bail many of them out. They were "too big to fail."

In the aftermath, many economists advocated breaking up large financial institutions into smaller units, arguing that when managements know that their institution will not be allowed to fail, they take unreasonable risks. The Obama administration took the view, however, that the US economy needed large financial institutions. The Dodd–Frank Act allowed too-big-too-fail institutions to exist, but designated them as "systemically significant" and thus subject to additional regulation. Banks with assets greater than $50 billion are so designated and a newly created Financial Stability Oversight Council has included other institutions based on their size and their degree of leverage and interconnectedness. It has also created regulations to limit the risk-taking activity of their managements. Of course, such regulation is controversial. The debate is far from over.

[5]This account is based on a variety of sources including S. M. Davidoff, "The Too Big to Fail Quandary," *New York Times* (February 23, 2011), p. B1.

PREVENTING COLLUSION Firms need not be monopolies to exercise monopoly power. Firms can form cartels and collaborate to reduce output and to fix prices. Such cartels have the same effect on social welfare as do monopolies, and such behavior is illegal. In 1927 the court found that the makers of toilets had acted illegally when they met to fix prices and limit quantities. Even absent an explicit agreement to fix prices, the court may find *conscious parallelism*—that is, a situation in which all producers act in the same way at the same time while being aware that other producers are doing likewise.

In the 1990s, the government successfully challenged the practice of Ivy League universities meeting and exchanging information on planned tuition increases, faculty salaries, and financial aid policies. In 1996, the giant agribusiness firm Archer Daniels Midland pleaded guilty to fixing the price of citric acid (a food additive) and lysine (a feed additive) and paid a $100 million fine. In 1997, 30 brokerage firms paid $900 million to settle claims that they fixed prices.

In the last 15 years, antitrust authorities in the United States and Europe continued to vigorously pursue price-fixing cases. In 2004, Infineon Corporation agreed to pay $160 million for its role in fixing the prices of memory chips. In 2006, European authorities fined 30 producers of pipe-fittings almost $400 million. In 2007, US authorities fined British Airways and Korean Airlines $850 million for colluding to fix fuel surcharges in airfares. In 2008, three Asian producers of flat screens for television paid $585 million in fines, and in 2010, six microchip makers paid the state of California $175 million in fines for price fixing. In 2011, the European Commission fined Procter & Gamble and Unilever a total of $456 million for operating a laundry-detergent cartel. In 2013, a judge ordered Dow Chemical to pay $1.2 billion in damages for conspiring to fix urethane prices. In the same year, Apple was found guilty of conspiring with publishers to fix the price of e-books, resulting in price increases of as much as 50 percent. (The case is currently under appeal.)

The granddaddy of all price-fixing cases involved the manipulation of trillions of dollars of variable-rate financial instruments pegged to the London Interbank Offered Rate (LIBOR), the interest rate that banks charge one another. In 2008, evidence surfaced suggesting that banks might be colluding to manipulate these rates. Even small rate changes could mean enormous profits earned on interest-linked portfolios held by these financial institutions. Subsequent investigations ensnared some of the largest institutions in the finance industry, including Deutsche Bank, the Royal Bank of Scotland, Citigroup, Societe Generale, J.P. Morgan, HSBC, and Credit Agricole. To date, US and European authorities have levied over $5 billion in fines, and the investigations and lawsuits are far from over.

The United States versus Microsoft

The most important test of antitrust regulation in the digital age was the Justice Department's landmark antitrust suit against Microsoft. The Microsoft case featured network externalities and the control of standards. Recall from Chapter 3 that network externalities exist when users obtain greater value with a larger network of other connected customers. As a result, there is a strong tendency for one dominant standard to emerge to the exclusion of others. With over 90 percent of the PC market, the Windows operating system established itself as the dominant standard.

But despite its market dominance, Microsoft was not immune from the forces of competition. In the mid-1990s, the most important threats to Microsoft were posed by Sun Microsystems' Java language and by Netscape's Internet browser. Widespread use of Java could have effectively sapped the monopoly power Microsoft derived from control of the Windows standard. With Java, any other operating system (working with Java) could compete with Windows on equal terms. Similarly, Netscape's browser, because it could operate as an intermediary between the operating system and applications (particularly Internet applications), posed its own challenge. If the browser succeeded in becoming a standard, Microsoft would find its market power diluted.

Microsoft argued that it faced strong competition and that its strategy of integrating more and more functions into its operating system met this competition by delivering maximum value to consumers. The company's opponents claimed that Microsoft's intention was not to produce a better product at a lower price, but to limit new competition and prohibit future entry. By bundling its own browser, Internet Explorer, with Windows, Microsoft gave Explorer prominence on the desktop, creating an effective barrier against users choosing Java or Netscape. The company also used leverage against hardware producers. For example, Microsoft warned PC manufacturers that if they did not favor Internet Explorer, they would lose their Windows licenses. Similarly, it required PC makers to install and prominently display Internet Explorer. By threatening to turn to rival chipmaker Advanced Micro Devices, Microsoft prevented Intel from joining with Sun to improve the performance of Java on Intel's chips. Finally, Microsoft's leverage extended to software applications developers. Any developer doing business with the company (and receiving advanced information about new versions of Windows) was contractually required to use Internet Explorer and Microsoft's proprietary version of Java.

In April 2000, Judge Thomas Jackson ruled that Microsoft had used anticompetitive means to maintain a monopoly for its PC operating system and had attempted to monopolize the Web-browser market.[6] He ordered that Microsoft should be divided into two entities: an operating systems company and a software applications company. The split would prevent Microsoft from using its monopoly in the former area to extend its market power into other markets. In June 2001, the Appeals Court upheld the trial court's findings of monopolization but overruled the proposed breakup. Under a negotiated settlement of the case, Microsoft agreed to (1) sell Windows under the same terms to all PC makers, (2) allow PC makers to install non-Microsoft software as they pleased, and (3) disclose technical information to software rivals so that their products could run smoothly on Windows. Microsoft was not restricted from entering new markets or from adding any features it wanted to its operating system.[7]

---

[6]For a variety of economic views, see D. S. Evans et al., *Did Microsoft Harm Consumers? Two Opposing Views* (Washington, DC: AEI Press, 2000).

[7]European authorities pressed for more aggressive regulations. In 2004, the European Commission ordered Microsoft to supply information on its operating system to its software rivals so that they could design software to run on Windows in competition with Microsoft's own application software. To date, European authorities have fined Microsoft more than $2.5 billion for violations and noncompliance.

MARKET FAILURE DUE TO EXTERNALITIES

An **externality** is a cost or benefit that is caused by one economic agent but borne by another. For example, pollution is a cost caused by a producer but experienced by others—such as local residents who suffer deteriorated air quality or who must endure aircraft noise. Externalities can be negative, as in the case of pollution, or positive. For instance, the pursuit of basic science and research (often government sponsored) generates a host of spin-off benefits to others.

The difficulty posed by externalities is that the party producing the externality has no incentive to consider the external effects on other affected parties. The general rule is this:

> Left to its own devices, a party will produce too much of a negative externality and too little of a positive externality.

In short, externalities—either positive or negative—are a potential source of economic inefficiency.

To see this, consider the production of a chemical that generates air pollution as a byproduct. Figure 11.1 shows the competitive market supply and demand for the chemical. The market equilibrium occurs at the intersection of demand and supply, here at price $P_c = \$4$ per liter and industry output $Q_c = 10$ million liters. In the absence of any externality, this competitive outcome would be efficient.

Suppose, however, that an externality, pollution, is present. To keep things simple, we assume that a known, fixed amount of pollution—say 1 cubic foot of noxious gas is generated per liter of chemical produced and that each cubic foot causes $1 in harm. In Figure 11.1, the $1 external cost associated with pollution is added on top of the chemical industry supply curve, MIC (marginal internal cost), to form the new curve, MTC (marginal total cost). The original supply curve embodies the *internal* costs of producing the chemical, that is, those borne by producers. This marginal cost is simply $4 per liter. However, the true, full cost of producing the chemical is the sum of all costs per unit, internal and external. Thus, the full cost of expanding output comes to: $MIC + MEC = \$4 + \$1 = \$5$. In the figure, this is shown by the curve MTC.

Once the externality is recognized, we can pinpoint the industry's efficient level of output using the logic of marginal benefits and costs. Optimal industry output occurs at the intersection of the demand curve (marginal benefit) and the MTC curve, at output level $Q^* = 8$ million liters. Thus, the efficient level of output is lower than the competitive outcome, $Q_c = 10$ million liters. By failing to recognize the externality, the competitive market produces too much output and pollution, relative to the efficient outcome. Figure 11.1 also shows the deadweight loss from the excess production, $Q_c - Q^*$—the triangular shaded area where marginal benefits to consumers fall below the full marginal costs of supply.

The inefficiency problems associated with externalities are caused by incorrect pricing. The competitive price of $4 reflects only the marginal internal costs of the chemical. But the full marginal cost is higher by the amount of the marginal external cost (here, $1). In the figure, the efficient price is actually $5, where $P^* = MB = MTC$. This simple

FIGURE 11.1

Production Accompanied
by an Externality

An unregulated
competitive market
produces too much
of the externality. In
contrast, the optimal
outcome occurs
where demand
equals MTC.

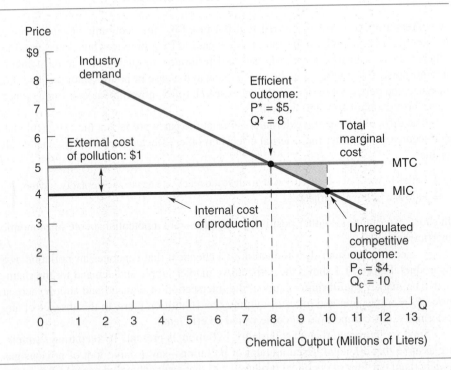

observation suggests a direct way for a government regulator to implement the efficient
outcome:

> An efficient means of regulation is to tax the producer of a negative externality an
> amount exactly equal to the associated marginal external cost.

In our example, the external cost of pollution is $1 (per extra cubic foot of pol-
lutant), so this is the appropriate tax. In other words, each chemical firm pays a tax,
$T = \$1$, for each cubic foot of pollution it discharges. What is the effect of this tax on
the typical chemical producer? By continuing to produce the chemical with pollution as
a by-product, the firm incurs an out-of-pocket cost (per additional unit of output) equal
to $MIC + T = MIC + MEC$. Because the tax is set exactly equal to the marginal external
cost (MEC), the producer of the externality is made to pay its true social cost. Setting
the right tax ($T = MEC$) serves to "internalize the externality." With the tax in place,
the relevant industry supply curve is MTC (up from MIC, the pretax curve), and the
competitive market equilibrium becomes $P* = \$5$ and $Q* = 8$ million liters, precisely
the efficient outcome.[8]

---

[8]Note that the full cost increase due to the externality is passed on in the form of a higher price to purchasers
of the chemical. This should not be viewed as somehow unfair. Rather, before the pollution tax, consumers
were enjoying an unduly low price, one that did not reflect the full social cost of producing the chemical.
Internalizing the externality means that the competitive price will now (fairly) reflect all relevant production
costs.

Suppose the $1 pollution tax is instituted. Among the affected groups—chemical consumers and suppliers, the government, and the general citizenry—who gains and who loses from the program, and by how much? What is the net gain to society as a whole?

Now suppose the firm has available the technology to chemically treat and eliminate harmful pollutants. Suppose that the cleanup costs $.50 per unit of pollution. Note first that absent any pollution fee or tax, there is absolutely no incentive for the firm to engage in cleanup. Cleanup simply means incurring additional costs. However, suppose the $1 tax per unit of pollution is in place. Now the firm's cleanup incentive is obvious. It is cheaper to eliminate the pollution (a $.50 per unit cost) than to pollute and pay the government tax. Thus, the firm's cost-minimizing strategy is 100 percent cleanup. How does this affect price and output in the chemical market? In Figure 11.1, the (external) cost of pollution is replaced by the (internal) cost of cleanup. The market price becomes $4.50 (reflecting the full cost of production and treatment), and total production increases from 8 million to 9 million liters.

With a $1 tax and a treatment cost of $.50, complete cleanup is both privately and socially efficient. From a societal viewpoint, it is less costly for the firm to expend resources for cleanup than for society to suffer the external costs of pollution. Instead, what if the cost of cleanup is $1.50 per unit? Facing a $1-per-unit pollution fee, the typical firm finds it cheaper to pay the tax than to clean up, so no pollution treatment occurs. This result is also efficient. Because the cost of cleanup exceeds the resulting benefit, it simply is not worth eliminating the pollution.

Remedying Externalities

The adverse effects of externalities can be ameliorated by a number of means, including: (1) taxes, (2) government standards, (3) permits (either tradable or not), (4) liability rules, and (5) bargaining among affected parties. (Some of these methods may work together as when parties bargain under the threat of court or regulatory action.)

We have already seen the argument for imposing taxes and fees on the economic agent causing the externality. Let's take a closer look. Figure 11.2 reconsiders pollution cleanup separately from its implications for the output of the chemical industry. As with most activities, the marginal cost of cleanup rises with increasing levels of cleanup. (The cheapest forms of cleanup are undertaken first.) Because of diminishing returns, marginal benefits decline with rising levels of cleanup. (Note that the marginal benefit of cleanup simply reflects, i.e., is exactly the same as, the marginal external cost caused by the pollution.) The optimal amount of cleanup occurs at Q^*, where $MB = MC$, well short of complete cleanup. Beyond this level, the extra benefits are not worth the costs. [9]

The government can promote cleanup Q^* through either pollution fees or quantity standards. The appropriate fee is set at the value of the marginal benefit of pollution reduction. Alternatively, the regulator could mandate Q^* as the minimum standard. When the regulator has perfect knowledge of marginal benefits and costs, either method can be used to attain the desired result.

[9]This economic point may seem patently obvious. Nonetheless, it is at odds with the Environmental Protection Agency's legislative mandate to promote and improve the quality of the environment without regard for cost.

FIGURE 11.2

Optimal Regulation of an
Externality

The optimal amount
of cleanup is
determined at Q^*,
where the marginal
benefit of cleanup
matches the
marginal cost.

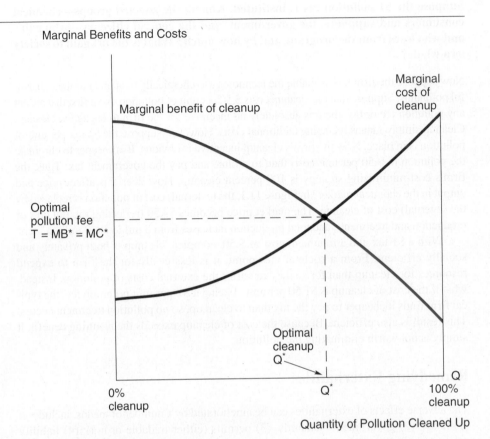

Marginal Benefits and Costs

Marginal benefit of cleanup

Marginal
cost of
cleanup

Optimal
pollution fee
$T = MB^* = MC^*$

Optimal
cleanup
Q^*

0%
cleanup

Q^*

100%
cleanup

Quantity of Pollution Cleaned Up

When imperfect information is the rule, however, externality fees have certain advantages over standards. With fees, regulators need only know marginal benefit. With standards, the regulator needs to know both marginal costs and marginal benefits. If the regulator overestimates cleanup costs, the standard will be too lax; if it underestimates these costs, the standard will be too stringent. The enormity of this problem stems from the myriad sources of pollution. Could a regulatory body, no matter how well informed, be expected to know the pertinent cleanup costs associated with each pollution source and set optimal standards everywhere? Clearly, such individual standards would be subject to considerable error.

In contrast, under the tax approach, all generators of a given externality are charged the same fee. This uniform fee is set to reflect the estimated marginal benefit of cleanup (equivalently, the externality cost). Whatever their differing costs of abatement, each firm cleans up pollution to the point where its marginal cost equals the tax: $T = MC_1 = MC_2 = \ldots = MC_n$. (Firms for which cleanup is cheap undertake greater pollution abatement.) Marginal costs are equated across all firms, ensuring that the total amount of pollution is eliminated at least cost. The fee system achieves full efficiency when the tax matches MB^*.

Pollution fees, while also subject to error, are far easier to adjust and correct. Suppose the regulator mistakenly sets too low a tax; let's say that $T < MB^*$ in Figure 11.2. Because firms clean up only to the point where the marginal cost equals the tax, the result will be relatively little cleanup. The regulator will see that marginal benefit is above the tax, and thus above marginal cost. Thus, it can adjust the tax upward until, by trial and error, the resulting level of cleanup satisfies $MB^* = T$ (and thus $MB^* = MC^*$), thereby achieving the social optimum. The regulator needs only to observe marginal benefit and the tax, and not the marginal costs of each pollution source.

Regulators have used externality fees in a variety of areas. London, for example, has imposed a congestion fee for driving in the central city. Analysts credit this fee (about $20 per day for driving downtown) with reducing traffic, shortening wait times, and more than doubling average speed in the city.[10] Many countries use taxes to reduce gasoline consumption. This approach is more efficient than imposing fuel-efficiency standards, which do not significantly change consumer behavior and which producers try to game. Some economists and policy makers have suggested using taxes to shift America's dietary patterns, by taxing high-sugar and high-fat foods and to address gun violence by taxing guns and ammunition to compensate innocent victims of gun violence.[11]

Another regulatory response to an externality, such as pollution, is the introduction of **transferable emissions permits**. The regulator issues permits corresponding to a fixed total quantity of pollution, and allows these permits to be freely tradable among firms. One would expect a ready market for these permits to emerge. Which firms would end up buying the permits? Those with the highest cleanup costs. By contrast, those with lower costs engage in cleanup and instead sell permits.

Under a trading system, the required amount of pollution is cleaned up at least total cost. (The regulator still faces the problem of determining the allowable total amount of pollution.) A number of such markets have been set up. In the United States, trading permits for sulfur dioxide (the pollutant responsible for acid rain) has been responsible for a 50 percent drop in these emissions. The Chicago Climate Exchange, which operated from 2003 until the end of 2010, allowed corporations to trade greenhouse gas emission credits. In 2008 the Regional Greenhouse Gas Initiative, comprising a dozen US northeastern states, began auctioning off CO_2 permits. The goal is to reduce permits (and thus emissions) by 10 percent by 2018. In 2010, California regulators approved rules to implement the cap-and-trade system established by the state's landmark 2006 Global Warming Solutions Act. The European Union Emissions Trading System, established in 2005, is the largest carbon emissions trading program in the world.

PRIVATE PAYMENTS   When the affected parties are few in number and property rights are clearly defined, externalities can be resolved efficiently without government intervention.

---

[10]See "Lessons from London's Congestion Charge," *The Economist* (February 22, 2007), p. 51.

[11]See E. Porter, "Taxes Show One Way to Save Fuel," *The New York Times* (September 12, 2012), p. B1; M. Bittman, "Bad Food? Tax It, and Subsidize Vegetables," *The New York Times* (July 24, 2011), p. WK1; and L. Finley and J. G. Culhane, "Make Gun Companies Pay Blood Money," *The New York Times* (June 24, 2013), p. A21.

TABLE 11.1

Private Remedies for an
Externality

	Mills' Action	Mill's Cost	Fishery's Cost
Fifty percent cleanup is the course of action that minimizes the parties' total cost. This efficient outcome can be reached via self-interested bargaining between the parties.	0% cleanup	$0	$100,000
	50% cleanup	50,000	30,000
	100% cleanup	120,000	0

Consider an upstream mill that releases pollutants into a waterway to the detriment of a downstream fishery. Table 11.1 depicts three abatement actions the mill might take and the resulting costs to each party. The efficient solution is 50 percent abatement because this minimizes the total cost incurred by the parties. How might this come to pass? The Coase theorem (developed by Ronald Coase) provides an answer: *Bargaining between the parties will result in an efficient outcome, regardless of the property-rights assignment.*[12] To illustrate, suppose the fishery has the right to clean water. Thus it can demand 100 percent cleanup. However, both sides can gain from an agreement at 50 percent cleanup. The mill saves $70,000 in cleanup costs, while the loss to the fishery is only $30,000. Thus, a payment of, say, $50,000 from mill to fishery in exchange for the right to 50 percent discharge would benefit both and is socially efficient.

Suppose, instead, that the mill has the right to pollute. Now the fishery must pay the mill to reduce its pollution. Nonetheless, the efficient agreement remains 50 percent cleanup. A payment by the fishery of, say, $60,000 (or, more generally, any payment between $50,000 and $70,000) for 50 percent cleanup is again mutually beneficial and socially efficient. No matter where they start, the parties always have an economic incentive to bargain to an efficient outcome.

Another solution is to give the party harmed by the externality the right to sue for damages. If an externality is produced, the injured party brings the case to court and will be awarded monetary damages (from the defendant) equal to the economic cost it suffers. This system of private damages is exactly analogous to an externality tax. The initiator of the externality is made to pay the full external cost of his or her actions. The difference is that the payment is private; it goes to the injured party, not the government. As an illustration, suppose the fishery holds the right to clean water and can sue for full damages. The mill has three options: 100 percent cleanup at a cost of $120,000 and no damages paid; 50 percent cleanup, costing it $50,000 while paying damages of $30,000 (reflecting the harm done to the fishery); or 0 percent cleanup and damages of $100,000. Clearly, the mill's cost-minimizing action is 50 percent cleanup. This is precisely the efficient outcome.

[12]R. Coase, "The Problem of Social Cost," *Journal of Law and Economics* (1960): 1–31.

The world faces an environmental problem of unprecedented complexity. Across the globe, countries contribute to global warming through the emission of greenhouse gases (GHG)—primarily carbon dioxide (CO_2), but also methane and nitrous oxides. Sources of these gases include fossil-fuel energy use, industrial and agricultural processes, and forest burning. Surface temperatures have risen almost 1.5 degrees Fahrenheit over the past century, and the rate of increase has increased in recent years. Potential consequences of global warming are significant coastline regression, extreme regional climate changes (from disturbances in global wind patterns and ocean currents), and changes in agricultural yields.

Global Warming

Global warming represents the ultimate externality. GHGs entering the atmosphere from any particular point source are distributed equally around the globe within 12 months, thus, affecting everyone. Countries can reduce emissions by a variety of means: reining in heavy industry (at the cost of reducing the rate of economic growth), switching from fossil fuels to cleaner energy sources (including nuclear power), using more fuel-efficient technologies, adopting conservation measures, and replanting forests. However all of these measures are costly, and it's in no single country's interest to institute *unilateral* reductions in GHGs. Yet, all countries potentially could benefit if *multilateral* reductions were undertaken.

Starting with the 1992 Environmental Summit in Rio de Janeiro, the nations of the world have explored various means of achieving efficient reductions, including the setting of standards and timetables for reductions, the implementation of a global "carbon" tax whereby producers of CO_2 are taxed according to the amount they contribute to the atmosphere, and the creation of carbon markets.

However, the uncertainty about the magnitudes of benefits and costs make the setting of standards and taxes difficult. Some experts have called for 25 to 40 percent cuts by 2050 while others call for more modest reductions. The Obama administration has pledged to cut US emissions 17 percent (relative to 2005 levels) by 2020 with even greater cuts farther in the future. There is currently no consensus on the optimal amount of GHG reductions worldwide.[13] A second problem is distributional. The wealthy, developed countries, having already achieved material prosperity, are the loudest in calling for action, while less-developed countries are more interested in economic development. (In other words, environmental protection is a normal good; as income increases, more of it is desired.)

Although developed countries produce the lion's share of emissions, many of the opportunities for low-cost emission reductions reside in the developing world. Thus, payments (especially development aid) from industrial nations to developing ones in exchange for reducing pollution would seem to be most essential to achieve an efficient outcome.

The Kyoto Treaty, supported by more than 160 nations in 1997 (but not the United States) and reaffirmed in 2001 and 2007 included promises by major industrialized nations to reduce emissions by an average 5.2 percent below 1990 levels by 2012 and also included a call for the establishment of carbon markets in which developing

[13]According to a 2010 estimate by William Nordhaus, an optimal worldwide emissions plan would have total global emissions stabilizing by 2045 with a resulting average global temperature increase (relative to 2002) of about 3.5 degrees Fahrenheit. For more on the economics of global warming, see W. Nordhaus, *The Climate Casino: Risk, Uncertainty, and Economics for a Warming World* (New Haven: Yale University Press, 2013); and R. S. Tol, "The Economic Effects of Climate Change," *Journal of Economic Perspectives* (Spring 2009): 29–51.

countries could collect significant monetary sums for GHG reductions. Still, progress has been slow. The UN Conference on Sustainable Development, held in Rio de Janeiro in 2012, produced little in the way of concrete proposals.

Promoting Positive Externalities

A positive externality occurs when an activity has beneficial side effects on parties other than those producing the activity. Efforts to improve literacy and education levels in a particular segment of the population benefit not only the individuals themselves but also society as a whole. By limiting the onset and spread of disease, vaccination programs protect the general population, including those who are not vaccinated.

Economic agents in unregulated markets tend to undertake too few activities that generate positive externalities. The appropriate government intervention is either to mandate or to subsidize greater levels of these beneficial activities. In the United States, education is publicly provided and is mandatory through certain grade levels. Similarly, vaccinations against common diseases are provided for free to the public.

PROMOTING RESEARCH   Consider a firm that is contemplating embarking on an R&D program to produce a superior flame-retardant fabric. The firm estimates the expected gross profit of the program (in present-value terms) to be $12 million. It also knows that the program will benefit society as a whole (both consumers and other firms who develop copycat fabrics). Suppose that the external benefits come to an estimated $6 million. Finally, the firm's total cost of undertaking the R&D program is $15 million.

The program's net profit to the firm is $12 − $15 = −$3 million. Thus, the firm will choose not to undertake the program. But net social benefits are $12 + $6 − $15 = $3 million.

The profit motive alone is not enough to induce the firm to go ahead even though the program benefits society as a whole. The problem is that the firm faces paying the entire cost of the R&D program but reaps only two-thirds of the total benefit ($12 million of the $18 million total). Accordingly, the remedy is a "one-third" subsidy. For every $1.00 of the firm's R&D expenditures, the government reimburses or pays for $.33. With the subsidy, the firm's net R&D cost becomes $(2/3)(15) = 10 million. Therefore, its net profit becomes $12 − $10 = $2 million, and the firm undertakes the program.

The general rule (of which this example is a specific case) is this: *To induce efficient behavior, the subsidy should be set equal to the ratio of external benefit to total benefit.*

In addition to subsidizing companies, governments around the world do their own research or pay for research through grants to universities and research institutions. For example, clean energy creates a positive externality. Governments have spent hundreds of billions of dollars on clean energy research, resulting in sharply falling costs.

THE PATENT SYSTEM   In the United States, patent law grants the holder exclusive rights to an invention for 20 years. The rationale for patents is to provide incentives for firms (and individuals) to pursue inventions and innovations. Without patent protection, a firm that creates an invention would be able to claim only a small portion of the profit generated by the invention since copycat producers would get the rest. Patent protection allows the inventor to capture a greater portion of the benefits created.

Patent laws may provide incentives for research, but because they grant the successful inventor a monopoly, they allow the inventor to set a high monopoly price. Thus the new product or service will not be used as widely as it might be. As in any monopoly, there is a deadweight loss. Thus, patent protection represents a trade-off between (1) encouraging invention (and the dissemination of knowledge, since the patent makes public the details of the invention) and (2) the welfare losses caused by monopoly.

COPYRIGHT   Copyright law provides protection for expressive works, such as music, drama, literature, film, and even software. The Copyright Act of 1790 protected material for 14 years, renewable for another 14 years while the author was still alive. By 1998, this protection had been raised to the life of the author plus 70 years.

Copyright law continues to evolve, especially in the music domain, where technological advances have made copying and downloading easy and inexpensive. In the late 1970s, Universal Pictures and Disney sued Sony and other makers of video recorders to prohibit the sale of the recorders. Sony won and the courts allowed the production of these devices. On the other hand, in 2001, the Court of Appeals (Ninth Circuit) effectively shut down Napster, a popular music and file exchange service. The court objected to Napster making copyrighted songs available from its main server. Still, illegal downloads continue to dominate the market. The media industry has responded by aggressively promoting paid download services such as iTunes, MusicMatch, Rhapsody, and even a new, paid Napster.

Regulatory Reform and Deregulation

Efficient regulation depends on a careful consideration of benefits and costs. Regulatory reforms in the 1980s and 1990s have made slow but steady progress in this direction. Initially, benefits were not explicitly traded off against costs. For example, the 1970 Clean Air Act specifically excludes a consideration of costs in setting air-quality standards, and the Food and Drug Administration is not obligated to use benefit-cost tests in ascertaining product safety. However, over time regulatory agencies have increasingly turned to a comparison of benefits and costs.

One important area of reform is deregulation.[14] Critics have pointed out that regulation frequently reduces true competition, that regulators are often "captured" by the firms they are supposed to regulate, and that government intervention has spread into many areas that are a far cry from natural monopolies: trucking, airlines, and banking, for example. Beginning in the late 1970s, policy makers increasingly embraced deregulation in a wide variety of industries, including airlines, banking, brokerage firms, cable television, natural gas, railroads, trucking, and telecommunications. Mainly, the results have been positive. Once freed of restrictive regulations, railroads, trucking firms, banks,

---

[14]For economic assessments of regulation and deregulation, see R. W. Hahn and P. T. Tetlock, "Has Economic Analysis Improved Regulatory Decisions?" *Journal of Economic Perspectives* (Summer 2008): 67–84; C. Winston, *Last Exit: Privatization and Deregulation of the U.S. Transportation System*, (Washington, DC: The Brookings Institution, 2010); and C. Winston, "US Industry Adjustment to Economic Deregulation," *Journal of Economic Perspectives* (Summer 1998): 89–110.

and brokerage firms, have engaged in vigorous price competition and have become more efficient. In the airline industry, deregulation produced entry by no-frills airlines, greater competition along high-traffic routes, lower average fares, greater variety and frequency of service, and increased airline efficiency with some reduction in service quality. Overall, consumers have benefited significantly.

Nevertheless, deregulation does not fit all industries. The financial market collapse and the consequent deep recession of 2007–2008 have been tied to the deregulation of financial markets. Congress subsequently enacted broad legislation to more tightly regulate financial markets and institutions.

MARKET FAILURE DUE TO IMPERFECT INFORMATION

The efficiency of markets depends on consumers having good information. Unfortunately, some economic transactions involve significant uncertainties as to product quality, reliability, or safety. In these markets, consumers may not have sufficient information to make efficient choices.

There are numerous cases of market inefficiencies due to imperfect information, ranging from the routine to the dramatic. As a simple example, consider two hypothetical lines of household batteries marketed by competing firms. The first firm's battery is a best seller; it is cheaper to produce and thus carries a lower price (10 percent lower) than the competition. However, the second firm's battery lasts 18 percent longer on average. If consumers knew this, the second battery brand could well be the better seller because it delivers more power per penny. However, lacking this information, uninformed consumers will buy the cheaper battery. In the absence of good information, the less efficient product would dominate the market.

More serious examples of information failures involve product safety. Suppose that a toy, a miniature missile launcher, is popular in Europe where it has produced a large number of serious injuries. The prudent regulatory response might be to ban the product in the United States altogether.

When consumers lack information, market outcomes typically will fail to be efficient. Government regulators, with superior information, may be able to mandate better outcomes than would occur in an unregulated market. Thus, the government bans some drugs, taxes alcohol and cigarettes, mandates compulsory education up to a certain grade, and prohibits the sale of unsafe products. Government can also require producers to provide information, such as nutritional labeling on foods or warning labels on cigarettes and wine. Restaurants in Los Angeles and New York City are required to post letter grades reflecting their inspection results in their front windows. The impact has been strongly positive, with restaurateurs improving cleanliness and food-safety standards. The FDA has recently proposed warnings on tanning beds, which have been linked to increased risks of melanoma.

However, government regulation is not always an ideal remedy even in the presence of market failure. Sometimes, the choice is between imperfect markets and imperfect regulation or between market failure and regulatory failure. For instance, automobile regulations govern performance, reliability, safety, fuel economy, and emissions. Most of these regulations respond effectively to market imperfections. But almost all these regulations are costly, and not all constitute unambiguous improvements.

II. BENEFIT-COST ANALYSIS AND PUBLIC GOODS PROVISION

Benefit-cost analysis is a method of evaluating public projects and programs.[15] It is used in planning budgets, building dams and airports, controlling disease, planning for safety, spending for education and research, and evaluating the costs and benefits of regulation. Almost any government program is fair game for the application of the benefit-cost approach. We begin by discussing the economic rationale for the government's provision of certain kinds of public goods. We then go on to outline the basics of benefit-cost analysis.

PUBLIC GOODS

Why are some goods and services provided by government rather than by private markets? What features characterize public goods? A **pure public good** is one that is nonrival and nonexclusive. Roughly speaking, it can be said that "if anyone enjoys the public good, everyone enjoys it." We can think of a pure public good as the extreme case of an externality: All benefits are external. The prototypical example of a pure public good is national defense. Defense is nonrival; that is, all citizens within the protected area enjoy the benefits of defense. (One state's enjoyment of national defense does not subtract from another state's enjoyment.) Furthermore, national defense is nonexclusive: It is impossible (or certainly impractical) to single out and exclude a particular town or region from the national-defense network. A considerable range of other goods, from local police protection to municipal mosquito abatement, share these two properties of pure public goods.

Whether or not exclusive, a nonrival public good has the feature that increased benefits can be provided to additional people at zero (or negligible) marginal cost. An uncongested highway or bridge has this property. The marginal cost of additional users is nearly zero. Even though exclusion is feasible, it should not be employed. Thus, the greatest collective benefit occurs when the highway is toll-free. Each additional user benefits at no cost to society.

Public Goods and Efficiency

Under the basic benefit-cost rule, the government should undertake a project or program if and only if its total benefits, summed over all its users, exceed its total costs. Thus, we should build a highway if and only if collective benefits to users (discounted over its life) exceed its total costs—land, construction, and maintenance.

---

[15]By some historical accident, there is no clear agreement on the proper term for this method of analysis; *benefit-cost analysis* and *cost-benefit analysis* are used interchangeably.

Going further, we can also ask what is the optimal size highway to build? For example, a longer span of multilane, high-speed roadway delivers faster and more numerous trips to more destinations but at an additional construction cost. Consider the planning problem depicted in Figure 11.3. The horizontal axis lists highways of different lengths (in miles) that might be built. The MC curve shows the marginal cost (in millions of dollars) of constructing additional miles of highway. The figure also presents demand curves for highway trips for commercial users (business trucks, vans, and the like) and

FIGURE 11.3

Optimal Output of a Pure Public Good

A highway of optimal length (17.5 miles) equates the total marginal benefit of users to the marginal cost of construction.

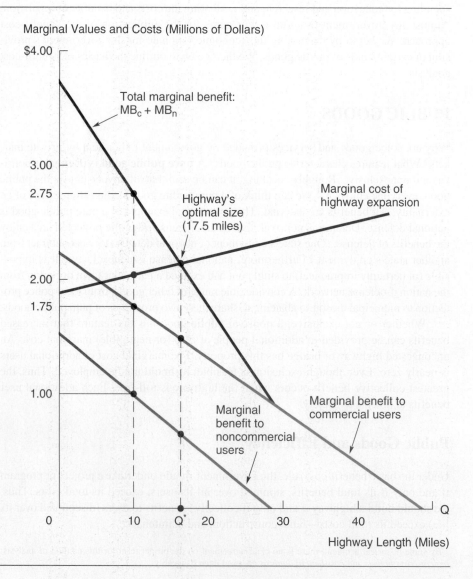

$MB_c + MB_n$

Total marginal benefit: $MB_c + MB_n$

Highway's optimal size (17.5 miles)

Marginal cost of highway expansion

Marginal benefit to noncommercial users

Marginal benefit to commercial users

noncommercial users (*ordinary* drivers). Each demand curve measures the marginal benefit for the group afforded by extra miles of highway.

We determine optimal highway size by comparing marginal benefit and marginal cost. Note that *the total marginal benefit to the groups together is found by taking the vertical sum of the separate marginal benefit (demand) curves.* For instance, according to Figure 11.3, a 10-mile-long highway delivers a marginal benefit of $1.75 million per mile to commercial vehicles and $1 million per mile to ordinary drivers. Since these trips are nonrival (i.e., the highway has more than enough capacity for both groups), the total marginal benefit is $2.75 million. More generally, the uppermost demand curve shows the sum of the groups' marginal benefits by size of highway. We can now determine the optimal size of the public project in the usual way. In Figure 11.3, a 17.5-mile highway generates the maximum social net benefit. At this size, total marginal benefit equals marginal cost.

Two observations are in order. First, there is the issue of financing the project. As pointed out earlier, to optimize usage (and therefore benefits), the highway should be toll-free.[16] Consequently, highway costs must be paid through taxes or government borrowing. Second, to evaluate this project we need accurate estimates of marginal benefits. To get this information we could survey potential users. However, our sample may be unrepresentative, and some potential users, eager for the project, may deliberately exaggerate their values. Others who oppose the project may report zero or even negative values—to block spending on the highway. To the extent that marginal benefits (and marginal costs) are in error, so, too, will be the provision of the public good.

Not surprisingly, spending decisions on public goods frequently are determined as much by politics as by benefit-cost analyses. For instance, the highway decision could be voted on directly by state representatives. The virtue of voting is that it is broadly representative of constituents' preferences. However, a voter's ballot, yea or nay, cannot reflect the magnitude of the individual's true benefit or cost from the project. A project may receive majority approval even though the dollar gains of the majority fall well short of the total cost incurred by the minority. Conversely, an economically worthwhile project with benefits diffused over a vast, nonvoting constituency may well be blocked by a special interest group that gets out its vote.

THE BASICS OF BENEFIT-COST ANALYSIS

It is best to think of benefit-cost analysis in three steps: (1) identify all impacts (pro and con) on all affected members of society; (2) value these various benefits and costs in *dollar terms;* and (3) recommend undertaking the program if and only if doing so produces a positive total *net* benefit to society—that is, if and only if total social benefits exceed total social costs.

---

[16]Governments do set highway tolls to pay back the cost of construction or to raise revenue even after all borrowing has been retired. To the extent that these tolls reduce usage, they are economically inefficient.

Applying the Net Benefit Rule

According to the third step in benefit-cost analysis, the program should be undertaken if and only if

$$\text{Net benefit} = \text{Total benefit} - \text{Total cost} > 0,$$

that is, only if total benefit exceeds total cost. (As we shall see, if benefits and costs occur over time, we must calculate the present discounted value of each using an appropriate rate of interest.)

We can extend this basic rule to the case of several mutually exclusive public programs. For instance, suppose the Department of the Interior is considering building a dam along a major river in the Pacific Northwest. The dam can be built in one of two locations, according to one of three designs. Thus, there are six possible dam plans: seven alternatives, including the option of not building. Among these mutually exclusive alternatives, the one with the *maximum net benefit* should be selected. (If all dam plans imply negative net benefits, not building the dam delivers the highest net benefit, namely zero.)

A second variation on the basic rule is applicable to public investment decisions involving resource constraints. Suppose that if the dam is built, it will generate 1.5 million acre-feet of water per year. This water can be employed in a number of competing uses, including allocation to city residents, to local industry, or to farmers. The water should be allocated in a way that maximizes total net social benefit. To attain this goal, we first compute the *net benefit per acre-foot* of water in each use. Suppose that benefit is \$100/acre-foot for city residents, \$120/acre-foot for industry, and \$60/acre-foot for farmers. Thus industry's demand should be satisfied first, followed by the city's demand, and finally the farmers' demand.

Dollar Values

Critics of benefit-cost analysis point out the difficulty (and perhaps impossibility) of estimating dollar values for many impacts. How does one value clean air, greater national security, unspoiled wilderness, or additional lives saved? Proponents of benefit-cost analysis do not deny these difficulties; rather, they point out that any decision depends, explicitly or implicitly, on some kind of valuation. For instance, suppose a government agency refuses to authorize \$240 million for spending on highway safety programs that are projected to result in 50 fewer highway deaths annually. The implication is that the lives saved are not worth the dollar cost—the value of each such life saved is less than \$4.8 million. Virtually all economic decisions involve trade-offs, issues of dollar values and costs. The strength of the benefit-cost approach is that it highlights these trade-offs, at the same time acknowledging that many values are imprecise or uncertain.

Efficiency versus Equity

In benefit-cost analysis, only total benefits and costs matter, not their distribution. But benefits and costs are almost always unequally distributed across the affected population. For almost any public program there are gainers and losers. Shouldn't decisions concerning public programs reflect distributional or equity considerations?

Benefit-cost analysis justifies its focus on efficiency rather than equity on several grounds. First, efficiency and equity need not conflict, provided appropriate compensation is paid among the affected parties. Suppose a public program generates a benefit of $5 million to group A but causes group B to suffer a loss of $3 million. The immediate impact of the project is clearly unequal. Nonetheless, if the gainers pay the losers, say, $4 million, both groups will profit from the program.

Compensation frequently occurs. For example, the extension of a highway inevitably means that the government takes land and private homes by eminent domain. The government compensates the owners by paying fair market value for the properties. (Still, in the vast majority of public programs, compensation is the exception rather than the norm.)

The second argument for ignoring equity relies on a form of division of labor. Distribution is better addressed via a progressive tax system and through transfer programs that direct resources to low-income and other targeted groups. It is much more efficient to use the tax and transfer system directly than to pursue distributional goals via specific public investments. Blocking the aforementioned project on equity grounds has a net cost: forgoing a $5 million gain while saving only $3 million in cost. Redistribution via taxes and transfers conserves dollars; there is no net loss. A third argument contends that by following the benefit-cost rule over a large number of projects, long-run net benefits are maximized *and* project-specific inequities will tend to even out. Sometimes you win, sometimes you lose, but on average you benefit. Critics counter that wealthy, politically connected players win much more than they lose. Clearly, this is an empirical issue.

Finally, although it is not common practice, it is possible to account for distribution in benefit-cost analysis. In standard benefit-cost analysis, when costs and benefits are added, *all groups' benefits or costs carry equal dollar weight.* One could, however, employ *unequal* weights to account for distributional concerns. For instance, if group B in the preceding example consists of low-income residents, their dollars might be accorded twice the weight of group A's dollars. With these weights, the benefit-cost analysis now becomes $5 - (2)(\$3) = -\$1$ million. Thus, the program would not be implemented because of its effect on distribution. A similar distributional analysis would support investing in a program (even if its net benefit is negative) if its benefits accrue to the neediest in society and its costs fall on the most affluent.

EVALUATING A PUBLIC PROJECT

In this section, we apply benefit-cost analysis to a public investment decision: building a bridge. The analysis considers several questions: Is the public investment better than the alternative of regulating the private transport market? Would private investment and control of the bridge be a still better alternative?

Public Investment in a Bridge

A task force of state and city planners is considering the construction of a harbor bridge to connect downtown and a northern peninsula. Currently, most residents of the peninsula commute to the city via ferry. Preliminary studies have shown there is considerable demand for the bridge. The question is whether the benefit to these commuters is worth the cost.

The planners have the following information. The ferry currently provides an estimated 5 million commuting trips annually at a price of $2 per trip; since the ferry's average cost per trip is $1, its profit per trip is $1. The bridge will cost $85 million to build, and with proper maintenance will last indefinitely. The bridge will cost $5 million a year to operate and maintain. Plans are for the bridge to be toll-free. This will price the ferry out of business. The planners estimate that the bridge will furnish 10 million commuting trips per year. The discount rate (in real terms) appropriate for the project is 4 percent. Based on this information, how can the planners construct a benefit-cost analysis to guide its investment decision?

We can begin by tabulating one benefit-cost analysis for the status quo (the ferry) and another for the bridge. Figure 11.4 shows the demand curve for commuter trips and the resulting benefit-cost calculations for the ferry and bridge. The demand curve shows that, at the ferry's current $2 price per trip, 5 million trips are taken (point F). If a toll-free bridge is built, 10 million trips will be made (point B). The planning board believes demand is linear; consequently, the demand curve is determined to be: $Q = 10 - 2.5P$, or equivalently, $P = 4 - .4Q$, where Q is measured in *millions* of trips.

Now we can use the demand curve to compute net benefits for the ferry and bridge alternatives. Currently, the ferry delivers benefits to two groups: the ferry itself (its shareholders) and commuters. As indicated in Figure 11.4, the ferry's annual profit is: ($2.00 - $1.00)(5) = $5 million. The commuters' collective benefit takes the form of *consumer surplus*—the difference between what consumers are willing to pay and the actual price charged. The triangular area between the demand curve and the $2 price line (up to their point of intersection at 5 million trips) measures the total consumer surplus enjoyed by ferry commuters. The area of this triangle is: (.5)($4.00 - $2.00)(5) = $5 million. Thus, the sum of profit plus consumer surplus is $10 million per year. Supposing this continues indefinitely, the resulting net present value is: 10/.04 = $250 million.[17]

Now let's consider the benefit-cost calculation for the bridge in Figure 11.4. The first line under the bridge's accounting shows a profit of zero for the ferry, since it will be put out of business. The last two lines show the burden on taxpayers; they must foot the bill for the construction and maintenance costs of the bridge. Because the bridge charges no toll, it generates no revenue. The second line makes the key point: *The entire benefit of the bridge takes the form of consumer surplus,* the dollar benefits commuters enjoy above the (zero) price they pay. Consumer surplus is given by the triangle inscribed under the demand curve and above the zero price line. The dollar value is: (.5)(4.00)(10) = $20 million per year. In present-value terms, this benefit comes to $500 million against a total cost (also in present-value terms) of $210 million. Thus, the net benefit of the bridge is $290 million. Since this is greater than that of the status quo (the ferry), the bridge should be built. The advantage of the bridge relative to the ferry is: $290 million − $250 million = $40 million.

---

[17]The present value of a perpetual annuity is $PV = CF/r$, where CF is the annual cash flow and r is the yearly interest rate. In the present example, it probably would be more realistic to predict annual traffic (on the ferry or the bridge) to grow at some rate per year, (g). In this case, the present value is given by $PV = CF/(r - g)$.

FIGURE 11.4

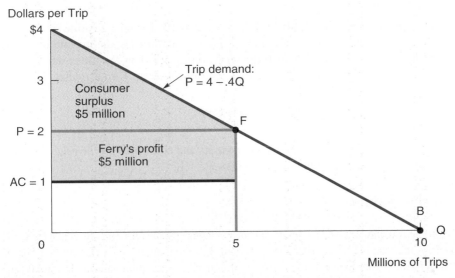

Alternative	Affected Groups	Annual Flow	Net Present Value
Ferry:	Ferry Operator	$ 5.0 (profit)	$125
	Ferry Commuters	$ 5.0 (consumer surplus)	$125
	TOTAL NET BENEFIT	$ 10.0	$250
Bridge:	Ferry Operator	$ 0.0 (profit)	$ 0
	Bridge Commuters	$ 20.0 (consumer surplus)	$500
	Taxpayers	–$ 5.0 (maintenance cost)	–$125
		(capital cost:)	–$ 85
	TOTAL NET BENEFIT		$290

A Benefit-Cost Analysis of Building a Bridge

The bridge should be built because its projected net benefit exceeds that of the current ferry operation.

PUBLIC PRICING   Here's a point that should not be overlooked: The decision to build the bridge crucially depends on charging the "right" toll. In the present example, the right price is zero because there is a negligible cost (no wear and tear or congestion) associated with additional cars crossing the bridge. Setting any positive price would exclude some commuters and reduce net benefit. But what if there were significant costs associated with additional use? The general principle behind optimal pricing is simple: *The optimal price should just equal the marginal cost associated with extra usage.* For instance, because large tractor-trailer trucks cause significant road damage to highways, they should pay a commensurate toll. In general, user fees should be set at a level that just covers the marginal cost of the service being delivered.

Suppose the planning authority sets a $2 toll per trip on the bridge (the same price as the ferry). Compute the net (discounted) benefit of the bridge and compare it to that of the ferry. In what sense is this pricing policy self-defeating?

CHECK
STATION 3

REGULATING THE FERRY   Before concluding that building the bridge is warranted, government decision makers should consider another option: regulation of the private market, for example, by limiting the price the ferry operator can charge. The optimal regulated price is simply the price that would prevail in a perfectly competitive market. With free entry of competitors into the market, the ferry's price would be driven down to the zero-profit point, $P = \$1$. This is the price the government should set for the (natural monopolist) ferry operator.

At a $1 price, the ferry delivers 7.5 million trips and makes a zero profit. Commuters realize total consumer surplus that comes to: $(.5)(4.00 - 1.00)(7.5) = \$11.25$ million per year. The present value of the net benefit associated with ferry regulation is: $\$11.25$ million$/.04 = \$281.25$ million. Building the bridge, with a discounted net benefit of $290 million, has a slight edge over the regulatory alternative and continues to be the best course of action.

CHECK STATION 4　**Could a private firm profitably build and operate the bridge? Assume it faces the same costs and interest rate as the government. In addition, the private bridge is expected to share the market with the ferry, unless it prices the latter out of business. What toll should the private bridge operator charge? Can it realize a profit?**

VALUING BENEFITS AND COSTS

The main issues with respect to valuing benefits and costs concern the role of market prices and ways of valuing nonmarket items.

Market Values

In most cases, market prices provide the correct values for benefits and costs. In Chapter 7, we saw that competitive markets are efficient. In such markets, the price of the good or service is an exact measure of its marginal benefit to consumers and its marginal cost to producers: $P = MB = MC$. For instance, if construction of the bridge requires 50,000 cubic yards of concrete and the price of concrete is $100 per cubic yard, the total cost of this input is $5 million. The same principle applies to other inputs—capital, labor, land, and so on. It also applies to valuing the benefits of program outputs. For instance, suppose the chief benefit of constructing a water project is the irrigation of new tracts of land. The market value of water would represent the dollar benefits of the project.[18]

Nonmarketed Benefits and Costs

Critics of benefit-cost analysis point out the difficulty (and perhaps impossibility) of estimating dollar values for many impacts. How does one value clean air, greater national security, unspoiled wilderness, additional lives saved, or a benefit or cost that will occur generations from now? Difficult valuation problems arise when benefits and costs are highly uncertain, nonmarketed, intangible, or slated to occur in the distant future.

---

[18]In some cases, market prices may be "distorted" so they do not accurately reflect the social marginal costs and benefits. For instance, the presence of monopoly, externalities, and taxes all create distortions, requiring valuation adjustments to any benefit-cost analysis.

Consider, for example, the benefits of public schools. Should performance be judged by average test scores? Dropout rates? Because public education is provided collectively (i.e., financed out of local tax revenues), there is no "market" value for this essential service. Parents do not pay market prices for their children's education. Contrast this with private schools. Here the value is at least as much as the price parents actually pay in tuition. There is no need to study the determinants of school performance; the market price is enough. If a private school fails to deliver a quality education, parents will stop paying the high market price.

All nonmarket goods are difficult to value, including national security, pollution, health risks, traffic congestion—even the value of a life. In the absence of market prices, other valuation methods are necessary.

DIRECT ELICITATION   One way to find out what people really want is to ask them. For instance, consider a program of subsidized "free" day care for low-income, single parents. Cost estimates for such a program are available, but the dollar value of benefits is more elusive. A direct approach is to identify and survey the recipient population: "How much would 20 hours of day care per week, located within 20 minutes of your residence, be worth to you? What about 40 hours per week?" Policy makers use surveys as a means of valuation in a host of public projects and programs—from air-quality improvement to public transit systems to the risks of occupational hazards.

Direct elicitation is current, relatively uncomplicated, controllable, and politically appealing. On the other hand, it is costly and not immune from error. It is subject to sampling bias (asking the wrong people), sampling error (people unsure of how they feel), and response bias (people trying to manipulate the decision by giving inaccurate responses).[19]

INDIRECT MARKET MEASURES   A second approach looks to *related* markets. Three examples illustrate the method:

1. To measure the value of a public secondary school education, analysts estimate the difference in labor earnings (in present-value terms) between high school graduates and ninth-grade dropouts.

2. To measure an individual's value of time (for example, to find the value of not having to sit in traffic for x hours) we can look at the hourly wage one can earn on the job.

3. To measure the cost of pollution we can compare property values in high-pollution areas versus those in otherwise comparable low-pollution areas.

---

[19]Surveys of low-income groups face an additional problem. For these groups, value responses reflect both willingness to pay and ability to pay. Consider two alternative survey questions: (1) If a new day-care facility were built in your neighborhood, how much would you be willing to pay for 20 hours of day care per week? (2) You are currently using 20 hours of day care per week. If the facility were to close down, how much money per week would be needed to compensate you for the loss of day-care services? The answer to the first question (constrained by the respondent's ability to pay) might be much lower than the answer to the second ($3 per hour, say, compared to $6 per hour). Since the goal of the day-care program is to efficiently address the needs of the local, low-income population, many would argue that the second response (free of the income constraint) represents the superior benefit estimate.

SOCIALLY DETERMINED VALUES   Society, via its norms and laws, places monetary values on many nonmarketed items. Workers' compensation laws determine monetary payments in the event of industrial injuries. Judges and juries set damages and compensation in contract and tort proceedings. In divorce cases, the court may be asked to determine the monetary value of a homemaker's contribution to the family. Government regulations implicitly determine societal values. For instance, federal law requires special access for the handicapped in public buildings and public transit. Presumably, the social value is at least as high as the cost of meeting this requirement.

CHECK STATION 5   How might each of the preceding approaches provide dollar values in the following situations: (a) the costs (across all dimensions to all affected parties) of accidents in the chemical industry and (b) the cost of noise pollution for residents near busy airports?

VALUING LIVES   Perhaps the most controversial application of benefit-cost analysis occurs in the valuation of lives. Many of us believe that human life is priceless and beyond monetary measure. Yet many government programs involve determining whether enhanced safety, not only in the form of injuries prevented but also in terms of lives saved, is worth the cost. As noted earlier, the decision *not* to spend $240 million on a program expected to save 50 lives implies that the value of a life is less than $4.8 million. Such implications are inevitable in decision making. Virtually all economic decisions involve trade-offs. A sound benefit-cost analysis highlights these trade-offs.

A number of approaches to estimating the dollar value of a life have been taken. One approach to valuing lives, the *earnings* method, appeals to the labor market for an answer. Boldly stated, the value of a life is measured by the present value of an individual's lifetime wage earnings. Depending on the precise assumptions, studies using the earnings approach have produced estimates in the range of $3 million to $4 million per life. Of course, many would argue that the presumption "you're worth what you earn" constitutes a gross understatement of a life's value. (One would never want to apply this method to unemployed or retired people.)

A second approach examines the amounts of compensation individuals demand for bearing the risk of death. Other things being equal, high-risk jobs—law enforcement, firefighting, skyscraper construction, mining, lumberjacking, oil drilling, to name a few—pay higher wages. The wage premium that people demand for taking on a greater risk of death, gives us an idea of how they value increased or decreased risk of death. For example, for skyscraper construction workers, the additional mortality risk is approximately .2 percent *per year.* Suppose the wage premium paid to such workers (again relative to a comparable low-risk job) is $12,600 per year. Thus, if a construction firm hires, say, 1,000 workers, it pays a total wage premium (due to risk) of $12.6 million and 2 deaths will occur on average. The implied value of a life is $12.6 million/2 = $6.3 million.

Proponents argue that the risk-cost trade-off embodied in private markets is the best guide to valuing lives when it comes to government decisions. But, for several reasons, the method is likely to underestimate a life's dollar value. An individual who chooses a high-risk occupation is likely to be more risk loving than the average person and, therefore, demand a lower wage premium. (If compensation for the average person were closer to $15,000, the value of a life would be $7.5 million.) In addition, workers in dangerous occupations may be inadequately informed about the true risks. Values for lives inferred from such decisions may reflect (at least partially) poor judgment, as well as calculated risks. Also, many high-risk jobs may go to people who, due to their socioeconomic status, have few other options.

Under the Obama administration, the Environmental Protection Agency has put the value of life at $9.3 million, up from $6.8 million under the Bush administration, and has suggested a figure 50 percent higher for cancer deaths, which are slow and painful. (Homeland Security has suggested doubling the amount for terrorism deaths.) The Food and Drug Administration has raised the value from $5 million to $7.9 million. Of course, higher values tip the scales toward more safety-related regulation.[20]

The FDA, AZT, and AIDS Revisited

The regulation of therapeutic drugs, such as AZT, poses particularly difficult problems because three kinds of market failure are present at once. First, external benefits associated with new drugs are enormous. Strong patent protection for developers of new drugs provides incentives for investment in high-cost and risky R&D, along with the subsidies provided by government-funded research. But patent laws remedy one kind of market failure at the expense of a second. Under patent protection, the developer has a 20-year monopoly on the sale of the drug and, naturally, attempts to establish monopoly prices in order to maximize available profit. Prices are thus inefficiently high and output too low.

The market also suffers from imperfect information. On their own, consumers cannot assess the benefits and risks of new drugs. Thus, the government requires laboratory and clinical studies to confirm its benefits and to identify potential side effects and risks. The medical research community, in conjunction with drug companies, carries out these tests. The FDA evaluates the test results and decides whether or not to approve the drug. The FDA relies on two basic benefit-cost rules: (1) approve the drug if and only if its expected benefits exceed its costs, and (2) design the tests so that the expected benefit of additional information justifies the cost. Conducting extensive tests accounts for most of the lengthy approval process.

How should the government react to these multiple market failures? Ideally, the government should grant the developer the right to sell a new drug at a price that offers the firm a normal rate of return given the risks of the development process. Thus, this prescription parallels the rule of average-cost pricing, discussed earlier in the context of natural monopoly (Chapter 8). This rate of return, however, must average in the costs of unsuccessful research efforts. After all, only a small fraction of the drugs on which R&D efforts are devoted are brought to market.

Because of the difficulty in measuring average costs in such a risky environment, most health analysts are reluctant to move toward formal price regulations

---

[20]On valuing lives, see W. K. Viscusi, "How to Value a Life," *Journal of Economics and Finance*, 32 (October 2008): 311–323; and B. Applebaum, "As U.S. Agencies Put More Value on a Life, Businesses Fret," *The New York Times* (February 17, 2011), p. A1.

for new drugs.[21] Research studies show some evidence of above-normal returns earned by pharmaceutical companies. But price regulations designed to eliminate excess profits could go too far, leaving drug companies with below-normal returns and severely retarding new drug development. More modest government strategies aimed at increasing the availability of new drugs include (1) increasing government subsidies to needy individuals to pay for the costs of drugs, (2) disseminating information about generic drug substitutes, and (3) using managed-care purchasing arrangements to negotiate lower drug prices.

The government does play a significant role on other fronts. Given the enormous external benefits of new drug development, the government should continue to sponsor and subsidize scientific studies by universities, private firms, and its own research groups. Finally, for many new drugs, such as AZT, the FDA should accelerate its approval process (notwithstanding the high costs of doing so). For the most promising drugs, the considerable benefits of early introduction and dissemination justify these additional costs.

SUMMARY

Decision-Making Principles

1. There are three main causes of market failure: monopoly power, externalities, and imperfect information. Each case offers a potential role for government regulation.

2. Benefit-cost analysis identifies all impacts (pro and con) on all affected members of society, values these benefits and costs in dollar terms, and sums all benefits and subtracts all costs to determine net benefit. A project should be adopted or a regulation enacted if, and only if, it has a positive net benefit.

3. This last rule does not formally account for distributional effects. Nonetheless, the cataloguing of costs and benefits should alert the policy maker to the equity and distributional consequences of the program.

Nuts and Bolts

1. Deadweight loss measures the reduction in net benefits when the level of output differs from the efficient (i.e., competitive) outcome. Under monopoly, the deadweight loss triangle stems from the production of too little output. Rent seeking measures the costs that occur when firms expend resources to obtain monopoly power. Measures to promote and/or restore competitive behavior are the most effective remedies for monopoly.

2. An externality is an impact or side effect that is caused by one economic agent and incurred by another agent or agents. An efficient means of regulation is to tax the producer of a negative externality an amount exactly equal to the associated marginal external cost. Under conditions conducive to bargaining, externalities also may be resolved via monetary payments between the affected parties.

---

[21]For economic assessments of drug development and policy recommendations, see F. M. Scherer, "Pharmaceutical Innovation," in B. Hall and N. Rosenberg (eds.), *Handbook of the Economics of Technological Innovation* (North Holland: 2010), 540-574; F. M. Scherer, "A Note on Global Welfare in Pharmaceutical Patent Policy," *The World Economy* (July 2004), 1127–1142; and E. Porter, "Do New Drugs Always Have to Cost So Much?" *The New York Times* (November 14, 2004), p. BU5.

3. Pure public goods are nonrival and nonexclusive. The optimal quantity of a pure public good is determined where the sum of the marginal benefits to all affected groups equals the good's marginal cost.

4. The basic benefit-cost decision rules are as follows:

   a. Distributional consequences aside, undertake a single public investment if and only if the present value of net benefits is positive.

   b. In a choice among mutually exclusive alternatives, select the one with the highest present value of net benefits.

   c. In public decisions involving resource constraints, select combinations of programs that maximize total net benefits subject to the constraints.

5. When efficiently functioning markets exist for a program's inputs and outputs, we can value the associated benefits and costs at market prices. The valuation of nonmarketed impacts and "intangibles" follows one of three approaches: (a) direct elicitation of values, (b) values based on indirect market values, and (c) values based on public policy.

Questions and Problems

1. Suppose Coca-Cola and Pepsi were to announce plans to merge into a single global soft-drink company. What would be the possible effects on soft-drink consumers? What kind of regulatory scrutiny should the US government cast on the proposed merger?

2. Two firms in a city compete as duopolists and face the industry demand curve: $P = 120 - .2Q$, where Q denotes total output (in thousands of units). For each firm, $LAC = LMC = \$60$ per unit. In equilibrium, each firm produces: $Q_1 = Q_2 = 100$ thousand units.

   a. Compute total industry profit and consumer surplus.

   b. Now suppose that the two firms have decided to merge to take advantage of economies of scale that will drive long-run average cost down to $LAC = \$50$ per unit for the merged firm. With no other rivals, the merged firm will act as a monopolist. Determine the monopoly price and quantity.

   c. Antitrust authorities are considering blocking the merger on the grounds that it is anticompetitive. The firms argue that the merger is pro-competitive because of the significant cost reductions. Is *total welfare* (accounting for both the effect on consumers and the effect on industry profit) higher or lower after the merger than before?

3. A state in the northwestern United States faces a number of problems concerning the production of its paper products. The wood pulp industry (from which paper is made) is a monopoly that generates a significant amount of pollution. As the state's secretary of commerce, you have hired three analysts to help you think through several government policy alternatives. The demand for wood pulp is given by: $P = 500 - 10Q$, where Q is measured in thousands of units. The long-run cost of production exhibits constant returns to scale: $LAC = LMC = 150$. Producing a unit of wood pulp generates one unit of pollution. The marginal external cost is estimated to be 100 per extra unit of pollution.

   a. Analyst A advises no government intervention at all. In this case, what quantity and price will prevail in the (monopolized) industry?

   b. Analyst B is mainly worried about the monopolization of the industry, and, therefore, recommends that you promote competition through regulation and antitrust policy. What quantity of pulp would a perfectly competitive industry produce?

   c. Analyst C is worried about the pollution externality and, therefore, recommends a tax of 100 per unit of pulp output (on the currently monopolized industry). What quantity of pulp will the monopolized industry produce under the tax?

   d. Which of the analysts' recommendations would you support? Do you have a better policy? Explain. (*Hint*: Identify the socially efficient level of pulp production to help clarify your answer.)

4. In each of the following situations, explain whether an externality is present.

   a. Mine safety has improved in recent years. Nonetheless, mining accidents result in 50 to 100 deaths per year and thousands of lost workdays due to injury.

   b. Large brokerage and financial service companies conduct intensive introductory training programs for new hires, many of whom, once trained, leave the company within the first year to work for competitors.

c. The volume of e-mail spam has grown exponentially in the last five years.

d. A husband and wife who have put off buying a house suddenly find themselves priced out of the market by rocketing real-estate prices.

5. Consider the market for studded snow tires. Industry demand is given by $P = 170 - 5Q$, where Q is the number of tires in thousands. Studded tires are supplied in a competitive market at an average cost of $60 per tire.

    a. Determine the competitive price and quantity of studded tires.

    b. Over their lifetimes, studded tires cause considerable road damage. The best estimate of total road damage is: $C = .25Q^2$. Consequently, the marginal cost of an extra studded tire on the road is given by: $MC = .5Q$. Accounting for this road damage, a regulator seeks to determine the quantity of tires that will maximize net social benefit. Find this quantity. At this quantity, what is the resulting market price? Compute the net social benefit.

    c. By what regulatory means could this outcome be obtained? Explain.

    d. Suppose firms can manufacture low-impact studded tires that do negligible road damage at an extra cost of $12 per tire. Assuming optimal regulation, as in part (b) or part (c), which type of tire will be produced? Explain.

6. Explain whether you agree or disagree with each of the following statements. In each case, indicate whether your position is based (implicitly or explicitly) on benefit-cost analysis or on some other criterion.

    a. The Consumer Product Safety Commission should uphold strict safety standards for all children's toys.

    b. OSHA should relax many of its workplace safety regulations, for instance, by relying on workers to take precautions rather than requiring expensive safety devices on machines and tools.

    c. All public buildings owned by those receiving federal funds must be modified where necessary to ensure access for disabled individuals.

    d. The Department of Agriculture should curtail the use of pesticides by farmers.

    e. Given its large projected deficit, the federal government should postpone capital spending to repair 80-year-old bridges.

7. Two large manufacturing firms are major sources of airborne pollutants in a metropolitan area. Currently, each firm generates about 15 million units of pollution per year. The firms' costs of reducing pollution are $C_1 = 2Q_1 + .1Q_2^2$ and $C_2 = .15Q_2^2$, where Q_1 and Q_2 denote the amounts of pollution cleaned up by the respective firms. The social benefit of reducing pollution is estimated to be $B = 9Q - .2Q^2$, where Q denotes the total amount of pollution cleaned up; that is, $Q = Q_1 + Q_2$.

    a. Write the expressions for the marginal benefit and marginal costs of cleanup, that is, MB, MC_1, and MC_2.

    b. Suppose the EPA seeks to implement pollution standards that maximize net benefits to society $(B - C_1 - C_2)$. Find the optimal values of Q_1 and Q_2 by setting $MB = MC_1 = MC_2$. Explain why the firms face different quantity standards.

    c. Suppose, instead, that the regulator sets a uniform pollution tax of $4 per unit. How much pollution will each firm clean up?

    d. What tax should the regulator set to implement the optimal cleanup amounts in part (b)? Explain.

8. Three blocs of nations are beginning negotiations aimed at reducing the emissions of greenhouse gases (GHGs). The blocs are the United States, the European Community, and a coalition of developing nations (DNs). Table A shows each bloc's current GHG emissions and the annual cost of reducing emissions to lower levels. The extent of global warming depends on the *total* GHG emissions of the three blocs. Each bloc would benefit from global emission reductions. Table B lists these benefits (measured vis-a-vis the status quo). In both tables, emissions are measured in billions of tons per year.

    a. Is global warming a kind of prisoner's dilemma? Is it in the self-interest of any of the blocs to reduce emissions unilaterally? Explain briefly.

    b. In preliminary talks, Europe has sought an agreement calling for *shared sacrifices*—that is, multilateral emission reductions. However, because of large budget deficits, neither the United States nor Europe is prepared to extend monetary aid to the developing world in compensation for its reductions. Does there exist a multilateral reduction plan that benefits all blocs?

    c. Suppose, instead, that financial payments between blocs are feasible. Identify the efficient, global reduction plan. How much reduction should each bloc undertake, and what sort of compensation is necessary? (*Hint*: Any incremental emission reduction should be undertaken as long as the *additional* global benefit exceeds the *extra* cost.)

Costs of Reducing Emissions ($ Billions per Year)

	United States		Europe		Developing Nations	
Population:	350 million		440 million		2 billion	
National Income:	$15 trillion		$16 trillion		$6 trillion	
	Emissions	**Cost**	**Emissions**	**Cost**	**Emissions**	**Cost**
Status Quo	1.2	$ 0	1.0	0	1.4	0
	1.0	22	.8	18	1.2	12
	.8	60	.6	42	1.0	30
	.6	100	.4	80	.8	48

Benefits from Emission Reductions ($ Billions per Year)

Total Emissions	United States	Europe	DNs	Total Emissions	United States	Europe	DNs
3.6	0	0	0	2.6	28	40	46
3.4	6	8	10	2.4	32	45	54
3.2	12	16	20	2.2	36	50	60
3.0	18	24	30	2.0	40	55	66
2.8	24	32	38	1.8	44	60	72

9. Real World Enterprises (RWE) provides a variety of "backroom" business services to other companies. It operates eight different facilities that employ large numbers of workers undertaking clerical tasks. The firm has become aware that a significant number of its workers suffer from hand and wrist injuries associated with repetitive motion on the job. These injuries result in productivity losses, increased health care costs (RWE provides generous health benefits to its employees), and reduced employee morale.

RWE has undertaken a study of the extent of the problem. The study finds that the firm would incur a cost of about $150,000 per facility to create a health and safety program. The study also notes that the problem is much greater at some facilities (because of differing clerical tasks) than at others. The following table estimates the relation between *total benefits* to RWE and the number of facilities participating in the safety program:

Number of Facilities in Program	Total Benefit to RWE
1	$500,000
2	$975,000
3	$1,375,000
4	$1,600,000
5	$1,700,000
6	$1,800,000
7	$1,850,000
8	$1,875,000

    a. At how many facilities (if any) should RWE offer the health and safety program? What is the net gain for the company, given this investment in the program?

    b. A study by the Occupational Safety and Health Administration (OSHA) finds that health and safety programs like that contemplated by RWE also benefit society *beyond* RWE and its workers (e.g., the programs also benefit the families of injured workers). In the case of RWE, these *additional* benefits to society would add about $75,000 in benefit for *each* facility in the program. What does the OSHA study imply about the optimal number of RW facilities that should receive the health and safety program relative to your answer in part (a)? Explain.

    c. One group in OSHA wants to require that a universal health and safety program requirement be implemented for *all* workplaces (in RWE's case, all eight facilities would be required to adopt the health and safety program). What would be the social welfare impact of this requirement in RWE's case?

    d. How might OSHA provide an effective and direct incentive system to induce RWE to implement programs for the optimal number of facilities as in part (b)? Explain.

10. a. A commonly used benefit-cost rule is to undertake a program if and only if its ratio of benefits to cost (both in present–value terms) is greater than 1 (B/C > 1). Does this rule make sense?

    b. A city is deliberating what to do with a downtown vacant lot that it owns. Should it build a parking garage or a public library? According to its studies, the benefit-cost ratio for the garage is 2 and the ratio for the library is 1.5. Accordingly, the city decides to build the garage. Is this conclusion justified, or is additional information needed? Explain carefully.

    c. A state must decide which of its deteriorating bridges to repair within its limited budget. The total number of such bridges (some currently closed for safety reasons) is between 450 and 500. The state has gathered estimates of repair costs and projected traffic benefits for each bridge. It has decided to repair those bridges with the greatest benefit-cost ratios until its budget is exhausted. Does this strategy make sense? Explain carefully.

11. A city must decide whether to build a downtown parking garage (for up to 750 cars) and what rate to charge. It is considering two rates: a flat $1.50 per-hour rate or an all-day rate averaging $1 per hour (based on a $10 daily rate and an average 10-hour stay). Parking demand is $Q = 900 - 300P$, where Q is the number of cars in the garage each hour and P is the hourly rate. The capital cost of the garage is estimated to be $20 million and its annual operating cost to be $.62 million (regardless of the number of cars utilizing it) over its estimated 40-year life. The city's discount rate is 8 percent. At 8 percent, $1 per year for 40 years has a present value of $11.90. (Use the factor of 11.9 to multiply yearly net benefits to obtain present values.)

    a. Sketch the demand curve (per hour) and calculate total benefits—the sum of consumer surplus and revenue—from the garage under either rate. (Multiply by 10 hours per day and 260 working days per year to find annual values.) Should the city build the facility? If so, which of the two rates should it charge?

    b. Could a private developer profitably build and operate the garage? Which of the two rates would it set? (Assume it faces the same demand, costs, and discount rate as the city.)

12. A state highway safety agency must allocate its budget for the next fiscal year. A total funding of $32 million has been granted for reducing fatalities and property damage due to automobile accidents. However, detailed funding decisions concerning specific programs remain to be made. The following table lists pertinent data on four major programs.

    To solve its budget problem, the council still must formulate a trade-off between lives saved and property damage prevented. The council is aware that a certain government agency employed $4.8 million as the value of a life saved. To make a start on its decision, members of the council have agreed to use this figure, enabling it to put a dollar value on the total benefits (from lives and property saved) of a given expenditure on each program.

    a. Find the budget allocation that generates the greatest total benefits. (*Hint*: Where should the first dollars be spent, the next dollars, and so on?)

b. Suppose the council increases the value of a life to $7.2 million. How does the value placed on a life influence the council's budget allocation? Explain briefly.

Project	Upper Limit on Expenditures	Expected Fatalities Prevented per Millions of Dollars Expended	Expected Reduction in Property Damage per Millions of Dollars Expended
Seatbelt advertising	$14,000,000	1.0	$0
Research in improved highway safety	12,000,000	.2	3,200,000
Research in improved auto design	9,000,000	.5	1,500,000
Dollars spent lobbying for tougher drunk-driving penalties	16,000,000	.75	200,000

Discussion Question   Everyone has tales to tell about the ups and downs of air travel. The industry has been deregulated for nearly 40 years. Over this time, few airlines have consistently earned profits. Though competition has kept airfares low, many consumers have not been happy with the travel experience and the countless fees. Over the last decade, mergers and consolidation have been the norm in the United States.

In 2013, the US Justice Department approved the merger between American Airlines and US Air, making the combined entity the world's biggest airline. Utilizing information drawn from the business press and other sources, (1) present the economic case in favor of the merger; or (2) make the economic case against the merger. In your view, should the merger have been approved?

Spreadsheet Problem

S1. Consider once again the combination of market failures outlined in Problem 3. Recall that the demand for wood pulp is described by $P = 500 - 10Q$, where Q is measured in thousands of units. The long-run cost of production exhibits constant returns to scale: $LAC = LMC = 150$. Producing a unit of wood pulp generates one unit of pollution, and the marginal external cost is estimated to be 100 per extra unit of pollution.

a. Create a spreadsheet similar to the one shown to model this setting. In the spreadsheet, cells B10, C10, and D10 contain numerical values. The entries in rows 15 and 19 and cell E10 are computed by formulas linked to the numerical cells. *Hints*: Remember that consumer surplus is found by using the formula for the area of a triangle, in this case: .5*(500-E10)*B10. Total benefit is the sum of consumer surplus, net profit, and government tax revenue minus the external costs associated with pollution.

b. Using the spreadsheet, confirm the output and price results for each of the analyst's recommendations in Problem 3. Then find the optimal regulatory policy using the spreadsheet's optimizer. That is, maximize total benefit by adjusting the output and tax cells.

	A	B	C	D	E	F	G	H
1								
2		COPING WITH AN EXTERNALITY						
3								
4			Market Demand		LMC = LAC		MCEXT	
5			P = 500 − 10Q		150		100	
6								
7								
8		Quantity	Tax	Clean Up (u)	Price			
9								
10		10	0	0	400			
11								
12								
13		Con Surp	Net Profit	Govt Rev	External Cost		Total Benefit	
14								
15		500	2,500	0	1,000		2,000	
16								
17			Gross Profit	tax + Clnup cost	tax − MCu			
18								
19			2,500	0	0			
20								

c. Now suppose that the wood pulp producers can clean up part or all of their pollution at a cost. The total cost of cleaning up u units of pollution is: $5u^2$; that is, it increases quadratically. By cleaning up pollution, producers avoid any tax. Thus, the government's tax revenue is given by $R = t(Q − u)$, and the firms' total pollution-related costs are $t(Q − u) + 5u^2$ (cell D19). Find the optimal output, tax, and cleanup. (*Hint*: Maximize total benefits subject to cell E19 equaling zero. Remember that the firms will reduce pollution up to the point that the tax per unit equals the MC of cleaning up an extra unit and note that $MC = 10u$.) Explain your results.

Suggested References

The following references provide advanced discussions of the theory and practice of regulation.

Hahn, R. W., and P. C. Tetlock. "Has Economic Analysis Improved Regulatory Decisions?" *Journal of Economic Perspectives* (Winter 2008): 67–84.

"Symposium on Antitrust Policy." *Journal of Economic Perspectives* (Fall 2003): 3–50.

"Symposium on the Microsoft Case." *Journal of Economic Perspectives* (Spring 2001): 25–80.

Viscusi, W. K., J. M. Vernon, and J. E. Harrington. *The Economics of Regulation and Antitrust.* Cambridge, MA: MIT Press, 2005.

The following articles are classic treatments concerning the difficulties of regulation and the remedies provided by private negotiation.

Coase, R. R. "The Problem of Social Cost." *Journal of Law and Economics* (October 1960): 1–44.

Stigler, G. J. "The Theory of Economic Regulation." *Bell Journal of Economics* (Spring 1971): 3–21.

The following references survey the state of environmental regulation.

Nordhaus, W.D. *The Climate Casino: Risk, Uncertainty, and Economics for a Warming World.* New Haven: Yale University Press, 2013.

Stavins, R. N. (ed.). *The Economics of the Environment: Selected Readings.* New York: W.W. Norton & Company, 2012.

"Stern Review on the Economics of Climate Change." *Journal of Economic Literature* (September 2007), reviewed by W. Nordhaus (pp. 686–702) and M. Weitzman (pp. 703–724).

The following reference provides several case studies of benefit-cost analysis.

Gramlich, E. M. *A Guide to Benefit-Cost Analysis.* New York: Waveland Press, 2000.

The following article discusses how to value lives.

Viscusi, W. K. "How to Value a Life." *Journal of Economics and Finance* (October 2008): 311–323.

Comprehensive online guides to antitrust policy include: http://www.ftc.gov/bc/antitrust/index.shtm, and http://www.antitrustinstitute.org/content/antitrust-primers.

For the economic merits of energy and carbon taxes, see:

http://www.globalpolicy.org/social-and-economic-policy/global-taxes-1-79/energy-taxes.html

Check Station Answers

1. Under competition, $P_c = AC = 8$ and $Q_c = 6$. Under monopoly, MR = MC. Therefore, $MR = 20 - 4Q = 8$, so $Q_m = 3$ and $P_m = 14$. The deadweight loss is $(1/2)(P_m - P_c)(Q_m - Q_c) = 9$.

2. Who gains and who loses from instituting the pollution tax? Chemical suppliers continue to earn zero profits. The government collects ($1)(8) = $8 million. Pollution is reduced from 10 million to 8 million units for a social benefit of $2 million. Consumers suffer from the increase from $P = $4 to $P = $5. Their loss in consumer surplus is given by the trapezoidal area between these price lines and under the demand curve. This area is computed as ($1)(8 + 10)/2 = $9 million. Thus, the total net benefit is $8 + 2 - 9 = $1 million.

3. At a $2 toll with 5 million trips, the bridge generates $10 million in revenue and creates $5 million in consumer surplus. After subtracting the maintenance cost, the bridge's annual total net benefit is $10 million, so its net present value is 10/.04 - 85 = $165 million. By limiting traffic, the toll sacrifices consumer surplus. As a result, the bridge is not worth building with this pricing policy; its net benefits are lower than the status quo, the ferry.

4. The best the firm can do is to price the ferry out of the market by charging $P = $1 (or a penny below). At this price, demand is 7.5 million trips, so the firm's annual profit (net of maintenance) is $2.5 million. The net present value of profit is: 2.5/.04 - 85 = -$22.5 million. Building the bridge is a losing proposition for a private firm.

5. a. (1) A survey would provide direct information on workers' risk perceptions.

   (2) An indirect market approach would examine the wage premium in risky jobs. For example, wages might be $5,000 per year higher for a chemical worker than for a comparable factory worker as compensation for job risk.

   (3) Workers' compensation might represent societal values. (If the government, via medical insurance, pays part of the costs of accidents, this cost also should be included.)

   b. (1) A survey would attempt to evaluate the severity of noise problems based on the testimony of residents.

   (2) The cost of noise pollution would be reflected in lower property values near airports.

   (3) Unfortunately, society does not compensate affected homeowners for noise-related costs. However, the government sets restrictions on airline routes to reduce the worst incidences of noise pollution.

CHAPTER 12

Decision Making under Uncertainty

If Hell is paved with good intentions, it is largely because of the impossibility of foreseeing consequences.

ALDOUS HUXLEY

LO#1. Review the fundamentals of uncertainty, probability, and expected value.

LO#2. Detail the structure and use of decision trees for decision making under uncertainty.

LO#3. Describe the characteristics of sequential decisions.

LO#4. Discuss how risk aversion affects decision making under uncertainty.

Gearing Down for a Recession

Sales of pleasure boats are highly cyclical. In a booming economy, large increases in personal disposable income greatly expand the demand for motorcraft, sailboats, and luxury yachts. In the midst of a recession, sales of boats sink and a sizable percentage of dealers go out of business. You own a maritime dealership and have made handsome profits during the good times. Currently, you are in the process of deciding on the number of motorcraft to order from the manufacturer for the coming season. If the economy continues to grow as in the past, your order will be roughly the same as in the previous year. However, a number of economic forecasters are predicting a significant chance—40 percent—of a recession in the next six months. If a recession occurs, you can expect to sell no more than half the number of boats sold in the past. Should you order for a rising economy or scale back for a recession? A wrong decision means large losses (in an unexpected recession) or forgone profits (in an unanticipated boom).

In this chapter, we focus on decisions involving risks—situations in which the consequences of any action the decision maker might take are uncertain because unforeseeable events may occur that will affect relevant outcomes. To analyze this type of problem, the decision maker should begin by taking four steps:

1. List the available alternatives, not only for direct action but also for gathering information on which to base later action.

2. List the outcomes that can possibly occur (these will depend on chance events as well as on the decision maker's own actions).

3. Evaluate the chances that any uncertain outcome will occur.

4. Value each possible outcome.

As this list indicates, decision making under certainty and uncertainty share a number of features. Whatever the setting, the manager should be aware of all available actions, determine the consequences of each action, and formulate a criterion for assessing each outcome. The introduction of uncertainty, however, requires additional analysis and judgment. First, the manager must be aware of these uncertain events and how they will affect the outcome of any action chosen. Moreover, after accounting for these uncertainties, the manager must assess or estimate the likelihood of alternative outcomes. Second, in decisions under risk, the manager has a course of action that is missing in decisions under certainty: the option to acquire additional information about the risks before making the main decision. Third, the manager must carefully assess the firm's attitude toward risk, that is, formulate a criterion that determines which risks are acceptable. This criterion then can serve as a guide for choosing among risky alternatives.

In this chapter, we begin our study of decision making under uncertainty. First, we review the fundamentals of uncertainty, probability, and expected value. Then we examine the use of decision trees as a guide for managerial choices, especially in sequential decisions. Finally, we explore the effect of risk aversion on managerial decisions: how a manager can assess attitudes toward risk and apply the expected-utility criterion as a decision guide.

UNCERTAINTY, PROBABILITY, AND EXPECTED VALUE

Uncertainty lies at the heart of many important decisions. For example, introducing a new product entails a multitude of risks, including the cost and timetable of development, the volume of sales in the product's first and subsequent years, and competitors' possible reactions. The example that opens this chapter suggests that uncertainty concerning the future course of the macroeconomy—consumer and business spending, price inflation, interest rate movements—is an important factor for many industries and firms.

Uncertainty (or *risk*) is present when there is more than one possible outcome for a decision.[1] Roughly speaking, the greater the dispersion of possible outcomes, the higher the degree of uncertainty. The key to sound decision making under uncertainty is to recognize the range of possible outcomes and assess the likelihood of their occurrence. Uncertainty is acknowledged in expressions such as "it is likely," "the odds are," and "there is an outside chance." The difficulty with such qualitative expressions is that they are ambiguous and open to different interpretations. One is prompted to ask, "How likely is likely?" The essential means for quantifying statements of likelihood is to use *probabilities*. It is far more useful for a meteorologist to state that there is a 60 percent chance of rain tomorrow than to claim that rain is likely. Probability has been described as the mathematical language of uncertainty. The key is to have a sound understanding of what probabilities mean.

Probability

The **probability** of an outcome is the odds or chance that the outcome will occur. In the usual parlance, we speak of probabilities as ranging between 0 and 1. (An event

[1]Throughout the discussion, we use the terms *risk* and *uncertainty* interchangeably.

having a probability of 1 is a certainty; an event having a probability of 0 is deemed impossible.) Whatever the probability, the relevant question is: What is the basis for this assessment? Frequently there is an *objective* foundation for the probability assessment. The chance of heads on a single toss of a fair coin is 50 percent, or one-half. In a random draw, the chance of picking the lone black ball from a hat containing five balls is one in five, and so on.

The main basis for assessments such as these is the notion of a probability *as a long-run frequency*. If an uncertain event (like a coin toss or a random draw) is repeated a very large number of times, the frequency of the event is a measure of its true probability. For instance, if a fair coin is tossed 1,000 times, the frequency of heads (i.e., the number of heads divided by the total number of tosses) will be very close to .5. If the actual long-run frequency turned out to be .6, we would be justified in asserting that the coin was unfair. The frequency interpretation applies to most statistical data. For example, if annual employment in the mining industry totals 40,000 workers and 80 workers die in mining accidents each year, the annual probability of a representative mine worker dying on the job is 80/40,000 or .2 percent.

It should be evident that in many (and perhaps most) situations, there is no chance that a situation will be repeated and therefore no way to assess probabilities on frequency grounds. In its development of a new product (one that is unique to the marketplace), a firm knows that the product launch is a one-shot situation. The firm may believe there is a 40 percent chance of success, but there is no way to validate this by launching the product 100 times and watching for 40 successes. Similarly, a company about to enter into patent litigation faces the problem of predicting the likely outcome of a one-time legal suit.

In dealing with such situations, decision makers rely on a *subjective* notion of probability. According to the *subjective* view, the probability of an outcome represents the decision maker's degree of belief that the outcome will occur. This is exactly the meaning of a statement such as "The chance of a successful product launch is 40 percent." Of course, in making a probability assessment, the manager should attempt to analyze and interpret all pertinent evidence and information that might bear on the outcome in question.[2] For the new product, this would include consumer surveys, test-market results, the product's unique qualities, its price relative to prices of competing products, and so on. The point is that a subjective probability is not arbitrary or ad hoc; it simply represents the decision maker's best assessment, based on current information, of the likelihood of an uncertain event. In this sense, all probabilities—even those based on frequencies or statistical data—represent the decision maker's degree of belief.

---

[2]Any probability forecast is based on the decision maker's currently available information. Consequently, if this information changes, so will the probability assessment. Thus, a disappointing market test would lead management to lower its probability assessment of product success. The point is that probability assessments are not engraved in stone; rather, they are constantly being revised in light of new information. In addition, various "experts" often hold different subjective probability assessments about an event based on different information or different interpretations of common information. (In contrast, the objective probability of heads in a single coin toss is immutable; that is, it is always one-half. Assuming there is no doubt about the fairness of the coin, this probability will not change with new information, nor will it be subject to dispute.) We take up the subjects of information acquisition and probability revision in Chapter 13.

Expected Value

The manager typically begins the process of analyzing a decision under uncertainty by using a probability distribution. A **probability distribution** is a listing of the possible outcomes concerning an unknown event and their respective probabilities. For example, the manager might envision the probability distribution shown in the table for the first year's outcome of a new-product launch.

Outcome	First-Year Sales Revenue	Probability
Complete success	$10,000,000	.1
Promising	7,000,000	.3
Mixed response	3,000,000	.2
Failure	1,000,000	.4

This probability distribution provides the best available description of the uncertainty surrounding the market's reception of the product. Note the considerable range of outcomes and the high likelihood of failure. (Revenue of $1 million is not enough to justify continuing the product.) Failure is the norm for even the most promising new products.

From the probability distribution, we can compute the **expected value** of the uncertain variable in question. In the preceding example, expected revenue is calculated as: $(.1)(\$10) + (.3)(\$7) + (.2)(\$3) + (.4)(\$1) = \$4.1$ million.

More generally, suppose the decision maker faces a risky prospect that has n possible monetary outcomes, $v_1, v_2, \ldots, v_n$, predicted to occur with probabilities $p_1, p_2, \ldots, p_n$, where these probabilities must sum to 1.0. Then the expected monetary value of the risky prospect is

$$E(v) = p_1v_1 + p_2v_2 + \cdots + p_nv_n.$$

In the preceding numerical example, we have applied exactly this formula with respect to the four possible outcomes. In the decision trees of the following section, expected values will play a key role.

DECISION TREES

The **decision tree** is a convenient way to represent decisions, chance events, and possible outcomes in choices under risk and uncertainty. In fact, this simple diagram can incorporate all the information needed to "solve" the decision problem once the specific objectives of the decision maker have been established. The method is extremely versatile. When first encountered, choices under risk appear messy, ill defined, and puzzling. The actual choices, the potential risks, and the appropriate objective to pursue may all be far from clear. The individual should not be blamed for regarding his or her choice as "a riddle wrapped in a mystery inside an enigma," to borrow a phrase from Winston Churchill. However, sketching a crude decision tree almost always helps clarify the risks and options. The structure of the tree emphasizes the ingredients (choices, outcomes, and probabilities) necessary for making an informed decision. The more precise the tree becomes (after drawing and redrawing), the more precise one's thinking becomes about the problem. The "finished" tree can then be evaluated to "solve" the decision problem. Probably more important, the decision tree provides a visual explanation for the recommended choice. One easily can pinpoint the "why" of the decision: which circumstances or risks weighed in favor of which course of action. And one can undertake any number of sensitivity analyses, altering the facts of the decision to determine the impact on the recommended course of action.

Decision trees can be simple or complex, spare or "bushy," small enough to evaluate by hand or large enough to benefit from software programs for depiction and solution. To illustrate the method, we start with a concise example.

An Oil Drilling Decision

An oil wildcatter must decide whether to drill at a given site before his option period expires. The cost of drilling is $200,000. This sum will be completely lost if the site is "dry," that is, contains no oil. The wildcatter estimates that, if he strikes oil, the total profit (before drilling costs) over the well's life will be $800,000. Thus, if there is a strike, the wildcatter will earn a $600,000 profit.

Figure 12.1 shows the decision tree for the wildcatter's problem. The tree depicts the sequence of events in the decision, reading from left to right. The problem starts with a point of decision, by convention represented by a square, from which emanate two branches: the decisions to drill or not to drill. If the choice is not to drill, the story ends there. The final profit outcome is $0, as indicated at the tip of the branch. If the choice is to drill, a chance event, represented by a circle, occurs. The chance event summarizes the risk associated with drilling. The two possible outcomes, a strike or a dry well, are shown on the branches emanating from the circular chance node. The respective monetary outcomes, $600,000 and −$200,000, are listed next to the branch tips.

We need one final piece of information to complete the description of the decision problem. This is the probability, in the wildcatter's best judgment, that the site will have oil. Suppose this probability is .4 (or a 40 percent chance). This is listed on the chance

FIGURE 12.1

The Wildcatter's
Drilling Problem

By drilling, the
wildcatter earns an
expected profit of
$120,000.

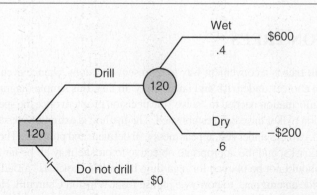

branch corresponding to "wet." Obviously, the probability of dry must be .6, because wet and dry sites are the only two outcomes. For the moment, let us suppose the wildcatter's probability assessment is based on a completed geological survey of the site, his judgment of how this site compares with other sites (with and without oil) that he has drilled in the past, and any other pertinent information. (In Chapter 13, we will say much more about interpreting, estimating, and revising probability projections of uncertain outcomes.)

All that remains is to specify a criterion by which the decision maker can choose a course of action under uncertainty. The criterion we employ at the outset of this chapter is expected value.

> The **expected-value criterion** instructs the manager to choose the course of action that generates the greatest expected profit.

Let's apply the expected-value criterion to determine the wildcatter's best course of action. The "do not drill" option results in a certain outcome of $0. The expected profit from the "drill" option is

$$(.4)(600,000) + (.6)(-200,000) = \$120,000.$$

Note that this expected profit is a weighted average of the possible outcomes, the weight for each outcome being its probability. The greater an outcome's probability, the more weight that outcome has in determining the overall expected profit (i.e., the expected profit moves closer to it). For instance, if the strike chances were .5, the expected value would be a straight average of the possible profit and loss, or $200,000. Better strike odds produce a higher expected profit.

In Figure 12.1, the expected profit of $120,000 has been recorded at the chance node of the tree. This indicates that, before the chance event has been resolved (i.e., before the true outcome, oil or no oil, has been revealed), the expected value of the risky drilling prospect is $120,000. According to the expected-value criterion, the wildcatter's optimal decision is to drill. The double slashes through the decision tree's "do not drill" branch show that this choice has been ruled out.

A firm supplies aircraft engines to the government and to private firms. It must decide between two mutually exclusive contracts. If it contracts with a private firm, its profit will be $2 million, $.7 million, or −$.5 million with probabilities .25, .41, and .34, respectively. If it contracts with the government, its profit will be $4 million or −$2.5 million with respective probabilities .45 and .55. Which contract offers the greater expected profit?   **CHECK STATION 1**

GOOD AND BAD DECISIONS AND OUTCOMES   Suppose the wildcatter follows the expected-value criterion and drills the site. Unfortunately, the site turns out to be dry. The resulting $200,000 loss is a *bad outcome*. But this does not mean that the choice to drill the site was a *bad decision*. Given what the wildcatter knew then, the risk was worth taking. Roughly speaking, the chance of a very large profit outweighed the chance of a smaller (although sizable) loss. Drilling was a good decision that happened (unluckily) to end in a bad outcome.

The point is that a good decision must be judged on the basis of the information available before the fact, that is, at the time the choice must be made. Of course, hindsight is 20–20, but this is of no avail to the manager. Moreover, 20–20 hindsight is misleading when it comes to evaluating past decisions. A bad outcome does not brand the decision as bad, nor does a good outcome mark a decision as good. What matters are the chances of the foreseeable good and bad outcomes at the point of decision. No matter how basic this point, it is surprising how often it is forgotten by decision makers in business and government. Perhaps the greatest virtue of using decision trees in evaluating and comparing risks is that it reminds us of the difference between good decisions and good outcomes.

Features of the Expected-Value Criterion

The depiction of the risk in Figure 12.1 is stark and simple. Thus, it comes as no surprise that the expected-value calculation is automatic, indeed, almost trivial. Nonetheless, it is important to recognize the general properties of this criterion, properties that apply equally to simple and complex risks.

The first (and most basic) feature of the expected-value standard is that it values a risky prospect by accounting not only for the set of possible outcomes, but also for the probabilities of those outcomes. For instance, suppose the wildcatter must decide whether to drill on one site or another. (There are insufficient resources to drill on both.) The first site's possible monetary outcomes are 800, 600, 160, −60, and −200 (all in thousands of dollars); these outcomes occur with probabilities .05, .15, .2, .25, and .35, respectively. Consequently, the expected profit from drilling this site is $(.05)(800) + (.15)(600) + (.2)(160) + (.25)(−60) + (.35)(−200) = \$77$ thousand. The second site has the same five possible outcomes as the first but with probabilities .05, .2, .25, .2, and .3. Notice that the second site offers greater probabilities of "good" outcomes than the first site. Clearly, then, the second site should have a higher value than the first. The expected-value standard satisfies this common-sense requirement. Performing the appropriate computation will show that the second site's expected profit is $128 thousand, a significantly higher figure than the expected profit of the first site.

Second, the expected value of a risky prospect represents the average monetary outcome if it were repeated indefinitely (with each repeated outcome generated independently of the others). In this statistical sense, the expected-value standard is appropriate for playing the long-run averages. Indeed, many managers employ the expected-value criterion when it comes to often-repeated, routine decisions involving (individually) small risks. For instance, suppose you have the chance to bet on each of 100 tosses of a coin. You win a dime on each head and lose a nickel on each tail. This, you'll no doubt agree, is the epitome of a routine, often-repeated, low-risk decision. Here the expected-value criterion instructs you to bet on each toss. If you choose this profitable (albeit somewhat boring) course of action, your expected gain in the 100 tosses is $2.50. Your actual profit will vary in the neighborhood of $2.50, perhaps coming out a little above, perhaps a little below. The statistical *law of large numbers* applied to the independent tosses ensures that there is no real risk associated with the bet.

Third, in decisions involving multiple and related risks, the expected-value criterion allows the decision maker to compute expected values *in stages*. Figure 12.2 makes this point by presenting a "bushier" (and more realistic) tree for the wildcatter's drilling decision. The tree incorporates three risks affecting drilling profits: the cost of drilling and recovery, the amount of oil discovered, and the price of oil per barrel. As the tree depicts, the cost of drilling and recovery is the first uncertainty to be resolved and depends on the depth at which oil is found (or not found). In the wildcatter's judgment, oil may be struck at one of two depths or not at all. Thus, the tree depicts three branches emanating from the initial chance node. As an example, let's consider the second branch: oil found at 5,000 feet. This branch ends in a chance node from which three new branches emerge. These branches show the possible amounts of oil (barrels per year) that might be recovered; the third branch, for instance, has a total recovery of 16,000 barrels. Finally, each recovery branch ends in a chance node from which three new branches sprout. These indicate the possible different values of average oil prices over the life of the well. For example, the third branch lists a $55-per-barrel price. At the end of this branch, the last uncertainty is resolved and the wildcatter's profit, in this case $180 thousand, is finally determined. (Simply take the profit figures at face value. We have not supplied the revenues and costs on which they are based.)

The path from the leftmost chance node to the $180,000 profit outcome indicates one particular scenario that might occur: finding a 16,000-barrel oil field at 5,000 feet and selling it at a two-year average price of $55 per barrel. However, this outcome is but one of many possible outcomes contingent on the resolution of the multiple risks. In all, there are $(2)(3)(3) + 1 = 19$ possible profit outcomes, one for each branch tip. The combination of multiple risks, each with multiple outcomes, means that the corresponding decision tree will be bushy indeed.

The bushy tree also requires a lengthier process of probability assessment, because the wildcatter must evaluate probabilities for three distinct risks. The first three branches of the tree show his chances of striking (or not striking) oil at different depths. If he finds some oil at a given depth, the next question is how much. The secondary branches of the tree list the chances of finding different oil quantities. Note that the likelihood of different recovery amounts depends on the depth at which oil is first found, and the likelihood of very large deposits is better at 3,000 feet than at 5,000 feet. (Remember that these recovery probabilities are conditional on some oil being found at all. Shallow fields are likely to be large fields, but the chance of finding oil at 3,000 feet is only .13 in the first place.) Finally, once the recovery quantity is ascertained, the sole remaining uncertainty concerns the market price of oil. The chances listed on the third-level branches have been obtained from an expert's prediction of future prices. Note that the chances of different market prices per barrel are independent of the quantity of oil recovered (i.e., the chances are the same regardless of the recovery amount).

What is the wildcatter's expected value from drilling in the face of these multiple risks? To answer this question, we calculate the expected value in stages by "averaging back" the tree, starting at the branch tips and working to the left. To illustrate, consider the chance node D on the tree: a 5,000-barrel-per-year oil reserve at a depth of 3,000 feet. The three branches list the profit outcomes for this field depending on the (uncertain) oil price. The expected profit from such a field is simply the average of the possible profit outcomes weighted by the respective probabilities. Thus, the expected profit is: $(.2)(700) + (.5)(350)$

FIGURE 12.2

A More Complicated Drilling Decision

This decision tree contains multiple risks that generate 19 possible outcomes.

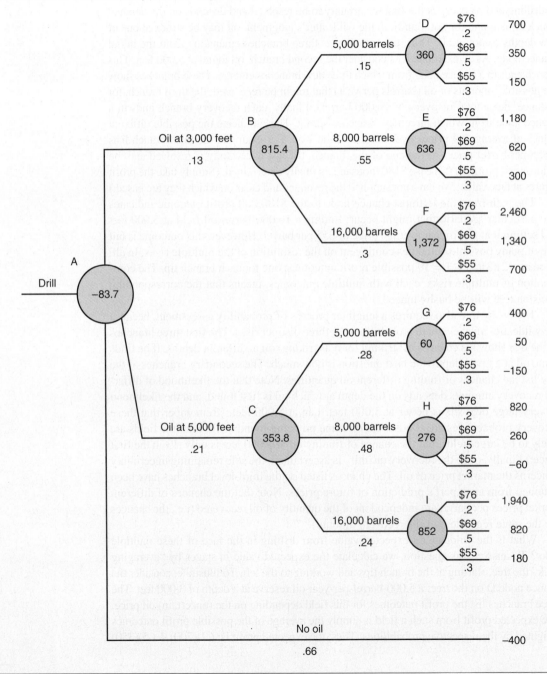

+ (.3)(150) = $360 thousand, listed in chance node D. But what if the field had yielded 8,000 barrels per year? By an analogous calculation, we find the expected profit to be $636 thousand in this case, as shown in chance node E. The expected profits for the chance nodes F through I (corresponding to different-sized fields at different depths) have also been computed and listed on the tree. At this point, we have "averaged out" the price uncertainty.

In the next step, we average over the possible quantities of oil found. Chance node B shows the expected profit if oil is found at 3,000 feet, computed by averaging the expected profits at nodes D through F:

$$(.15)(360) + (.55)(636) + (.3)(1,372) = \$815.4 \text{ thousand.}$$

Node C lists the expected profit ($353.8 thousand) for a field found at 5,000 feet.

The last step is to compute the overall expected profit of drilling. This is shown in the initial chance node A and is the average of the expected profits at B and C and the $400 thousand loss if no oil is found. As always, this expected value is computed using the branch probabilities as weights. Therefore, the expected profit from drilling is

$$(.13)(815.4) + (.21)(353.8) + (.66)(-400) = -\$83.7 \text{ thousand.}$$

The wildcatter has solved his decision problem by calculating in stages the expected profit of drilling. Since this is negative, the wildcatter should choose not to exercise his option on the site.

Suppose the chief executive of an oil company must decide whether to drill a site and, if so, how deep. It costs $160,000 to drill the first 3,000 feet, and there is a .4 chance of striking oil. If oil is struck, the profit (net of drilling expenses) is $600,000. If oil is not struck, the executive can drill 2,000 feet deeper at an additional cost of $90,000. Her chance of finding oil between 3,000 and 5,000 feet is .2, and her net profit (after all drilling costs) from a strike at this depth is $400,000. What action should the executive take to maximize expected profit?

CHECK STATION 2

For the last 30 years, globalization of business has been an enduring trend. Consumers in all parts of the world buy an increasing proportion of foreign goods, and a growing number of firms operate across national boundaries. The prospects of rapid growth and high profits from untapped foreign markets are attractive to large firms. The fast-growing Chinese economy and the resulting unleashed consumer demand have been the target of multinational firms in telecommunications, mining, financial services, automobiles, and fast food. Ford has invested $6 billion in developing a "world" car to be marketed and sold all over the globe. Procter & Gamble and Kimberly-Clark compete for the disposable diaper market in Brazil. For US movie producers, international box-office results are as important as domestic revenues.

The Perils of International Business

If opportunity is one side of the international business coin, the other side is risk. Leveraging successes enjoyed in local markets to far-flung foreign operations is far from certain. These risks come in many categories.

ECONOMIC CONDITIONS   The financial crises in Southeast Asia, Argentina, Iceland, Ireland, and, of course, the 2008 global recession and the painfully slow recovery have caused dramatic falls in business and consumer spending around the world. Global firms with sales concentrated in the hardest hit regions saw profits evaporate and losses mount.

UNCERTAIN COSTS   Because of low-skilled workforces, lack of capital, and primitive distribution systems, the costs of doing business in developing countries are frequently high and uncertain. Foreign firms assembling electronics goods in Russia have been plagued by low worker productivity, vandalism, and crime.

DIFFERENT CULTURES   Brazilians spend a higher percentage of income on their children than do citizens of neighboring countries. They are eager for disposable diapers, while Argentines are largely indifferent. Consumers in Southeast Asia are accustomed to buying light meals from street vendors, not from fast-food restaurants. To cite an extreme case of cultural miscalculation, General Motors introduced its popular Nova car model into South America. Only after disastrous sales did the company realize that *no va* means "does not go" in Spanish.

POLITICAL RISK   Tax and regulatory burdens, government bureaucracy and even corruption, and changing political parties and governments all contribute to the risk of doing business abroad. Over the past 50 years, international businesses have been decimated by unrest and civil war in places such as Cuba, Lebanon, El Salvador, Vietnam, the Balkans, and most recently, in Iraq, Egypt, Syria, and Ukraine. Today, outright expropriation is much less frequent but remains a risk.

EXCHANGE-RATE RISK   A firm that earns a significant part of its revenues abroad is subject to exchange-rate risk when converting these to its home currency. For instance, a depreciating Japanese yen means lower dollar profits from revenues earned in Japan. Similarly, the costs incurred by a foreign subsidiary are subject to exchange-rate risk. Thus, the depreciating currencies of Southeast Asia (by lowering the dollar-equivalent costs) make production in that part of the world more attractive to global firms.

Even the most experienced international firms face unforeseen risks and suffer missteps in foreign markets. Despite its marketing muscle and well-tested formula for operating its eating places, McDonald's has gained little market share in India, South Africa, and the Philippines. Instead, it has been humbled by well-established local competitors catering to local tastes.

The lesson to take from these companies' experience is that international businesses, if they are to be successful, must be especially vigilant in identifying myriad risks and capturing them in carefully conceived, bushy decision trees.

SEQUENTIAL DECISIONS

Some of the most interesting and important business and economic problems call for a series of decisions to be made over time. For example, suppose a chemical firm is considering a large capital investment in a new petrochemical facility. The profitability of such an investment depends on numerous uncertain factors: future market demand, reactions of close competitors, and so on. Profits also depend on the future product and pricing decisions of the firm itself. It is not simply that the firm faces many decisions over time; the more important point is that the sequence of decisions is interdependent. A correct investment decision today presupposes that the company will make optimal (i.e., profit-maximizing) pricing decisions tomorrow if the plant is built. The following example illustrates this general point about sequential decisions.

In Chapter 1, we sketched a decision problem facing a pharmaceutical firm that must choose between two research and development approaches. Suppose the profits and probabilities of the competing methods are summarized in the following table:

An R&D Decision Revisited

R&D Choice	Investment	Outcomes	Profit (excluding R&D)	Probability
Biochemical	$100 million	Large success	$ 900 million	.7
		Small success	500 million	.3
Biogenetic	200 million	Success	$2 billion	.2
		Failure	0 million	.8

All profit figures are expressed in terms of present discounted values and thus are directly comparable to investment figures.

We observe that the biogenetic (G) approach requires a greater initial investment and is significantly riskier than the biochemical (C) alternative. In the worst case, the firm will write off the R&D effort, earning no commercial profit and therefore losing its $200 million investment. The biochemical approach is also uncertain but far less risky. A commercially viable drug is guaranteed. Even in its worst case, the firm makes a $400 million net profit. Straightforward calculations show that

$$E(\pi_C) = (.7)(900) + (.3)(500) - 100 = \$680 \text{ million,}$$

whereas

$$E(\pi_G) = (.2)(2,000) - 200 = \$200 \text{ million,}$$

where $E(\pi)$ denotes expected profit. Of the two methods, the company should pursue the biochemical approach.

However, the firm's decision analysis should not end here. It has a considerably wider range of options than first appears. Resources permitting, the firm might do well to hedge its bet by pursuing *both* R&D programs simultaneously. Depending on the results, the firm can then decide which method to commercialize.

The decision tree in Figure 12.3 depicts the simultaneous R&D option. The tree lists four distinct possible R&D outcomes: one, both, or neither effort may be successful. The probability of each joint outcome is the product of the probabilities of the individual outcomes because these risks are assumed to be independent. Thus, the chance that both methods will succeed is $(.7)(.2) = .14$, and so on. Note that the probabilities of the four possible outcomes sum to 1, as they must.

FIGURE 12.3

Simultaneous R&D
Investments

By investing in both
R&D methods, the
company earns an
expected profit of
$724 million.

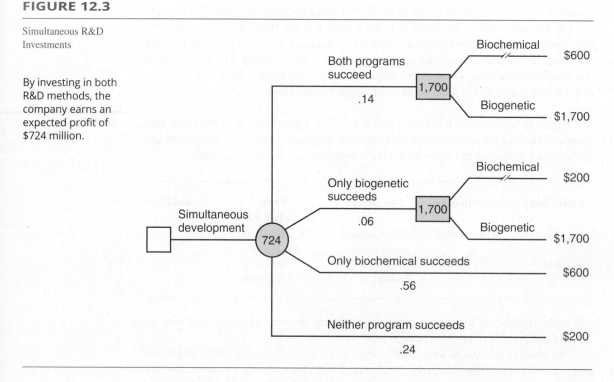

When the results of both R&D programs are in, the firm must decide which method to commercialize. If the biogenetic research effort fails (the lower two branches), the firm has no choice; it must go the biochemical route. If the biogenetic research is successful, the firm should commercialize this method because it offers the greater profit. (Note that the firm will produce the drug with only a *single* method—whichever is more profitable.) Thus, in the upper two branches, the drug is produced biogenetically. The profit is $2,000 million minus $300 million (the total investment on both methods), or $1,700 million. The other profit outcomes are computed in analogous fashion.

What is the firm's expected profit at the start of the simultaneous R&D effort? Multiplying the possible monetary outcomes by their respective probabilities, we compute this to be

$$(.14)(1,700) + (.06)(1,700) + (.56)(600) + (.24)(200) = \$724 \text{ million.}$$

Simultaneous development offers a larger expected profit than the next-best alternative, pursuing the biochemical approach exclusively. By undertaking both programs, the firm enjoys the security of biochemical's "sure thing" profits while still testing the biogenetic waters—a long shot that could provide a huge profit. Even in the likely event that the biogenetic option fails, the firm makes a profit. The decision tree instructs us that pursuing both approaches simultaneously increases the firm's expected profit by 724 − 680 = $44 million vis-a-vis pursuing the biochemical method alone.

However, the firm has not yet exhausted its options. Now it considers pursuing the R&D methods sequentially: one first, then (if necessary) the other. This raises an obvious question: Which method should it pursue first?

The decision tree in Figure 12.4 depicts the sequential strategy: biochemical R&D first, then biogenetic R&D. After the outcome of the first R&D effort is known, the firm can choose to commercialize it or invest in the second program. (If the biogenetic program is subsequently pursued and fails, the firm goes back and completes development of the biochemical approach.) The top square shows the firm's decision in the event the biochemical program is successful. Contrary to one's intuition, the firm should *not* proceed to immediate development; rather, its best course of action is also to invest in the biogenetic R&D program, see the result, and, if it fails, fall back on the biochemical approach. The resulting expected profit from making this second R&D investment is $820 million—$20 million better than immediately commercializing a biochemically based drug. What if the biochemical program is less successful? The lower decision square provides the answer. Clearly, the firm's best action is to invest in the biogenetic R&D program; the expected profit of $500 million is $100 million greater than the alternative. Thus, regardless of the outcome of the biochemical program, the biogenetic program also should be pursued.

The drug company's overall expected profit at the outset, that is, at the tree's initial chance node is: $(.7)(820) + (.3)(500) = \$724$ million. The expected profit from this sequential strategy is *exactly the same* as under simultaneous development. This result may seem surprising until we note that the two strategies call for the company to take exactly the same

FIGURE 12.4

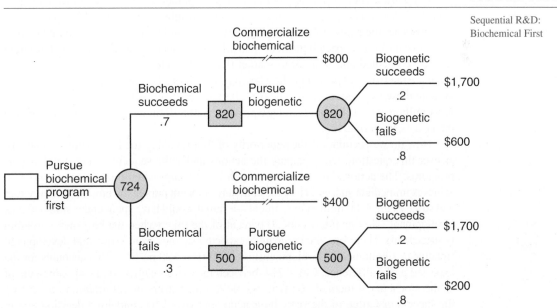

Sequential R&D:
Biochemical First

FIGURE 12.5

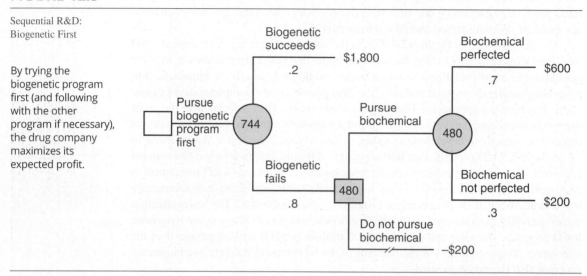

Sequential R&D:
Biogenetic First

By trying the biogenetic program first (and following with the other program if necessary), the drug company maximizes its expected profit.

Biogenetic succeeds
$1,800
.2

Pursue biogenetic program first   744

Biogenetic fails   480
.8

Pursue biochemical   480

Biochemical perfected
$600
.7

Biochemical not perfected
$200
.3

Do not pursue biochemical
−$200

actions. Even under sequential development, the company's best strategy is to pursue both R&D methods, just as under simultaneous development. Despite the apparent differences in the decision trees, the strategies must have the same expected profit because they call for the same actions in all cases. Thus, this sequential strategy offers no advantage over committing to simultaneous development in the first place.

In contrast, the reverse sequential strategy—pursue the biogenetic program first, then the biochemical program if necessary—is advantageous. Figure 12.5 depicts this strategy. The tree shows that if the biogenetic program is successful, it should be commercialized (for an expected profit of $1.8 billion). Otherwise, the biochemical program should be pursued and brought to market (for an expected profit of $480 million). To calculate the firm's expected profit when it first embarks on this sequential program, we average these two results. Thus, the overall expected profit is $(.2)(1,800) + (.8)(480) = $744 million. This sequential strategy provides $20 million more profit on average than the next-best alternative.

How do we account for the superiority of first pursuing the biogenetic method? To answer this question, let's compare the actions under the sequential and simultaneous programs. The actions are the same in each case, except when the biogenetic program achieves immediate success. Here the company need not pursue the biochemical program and so saves the $100 million investment—a sum it would have spent under simultaneous development. This saving occurs 20 percent of the time (when the biogenetic program is successful). Therefore, the company's expected savings from sequential development (relative to simultaneous development) is $(.2)(100) = $20 million. This accounts for the expected profit difference, 744 − 724, between the two strategies. By postponing pursuit of the biochemical method, the firm is able to profit from the information concerning the success or failure of the risky biogenetic approach. The condensed decision tree in Figure 12.6 summarizes the expected profits for all of the company's possible actions.

FIGURE 12.6

Summary of Pharmaceu-
tical Company's R&D
Options

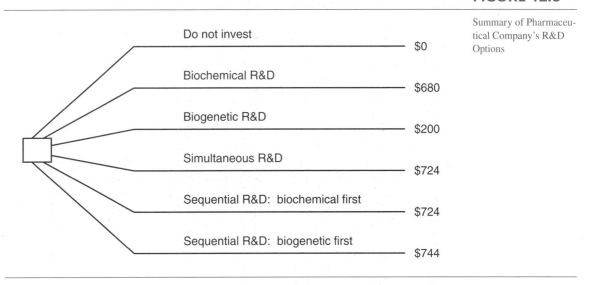

Do not invest	$0
Biochemical R&D	$680
Biogenetic R&D	$200
Simultaneous R&D	$724
Sequential R&D: biochemical first	$724
Sequential R&D: biogenetic first	$744

Firm A is deliberating whether to launch a new product. If firm B (its main compet- **CHECK**
itor) does not bring out its own product (a 40 percent probability), firm A expects **STATION 3**
to earn $20 million over the product's life. If firm B introduces its own product,
there is a 50 percent chance that the market will view it as superior to A's, in which
case firm A will lose $30 million on the launch. If A's product is superior, its profit
will be $10 million. Presuming its goal is to maximize expected profit, should firm
A launch the product?

Research shows that individuals have difficulties identifying and evaluating risks. Too **Business Behavior:**
often they rely on intuition, rules of thumb, and experience to make risky decisions. **Risky Decisions**
Managers' three most common pitfalls include:

1. *Seeing too few possibilities.* That is, they take too narrow or a "myopic" view of
   the future. While successful firms astutely foresee possible future consequences
   and act appropriately, many firms suffer losses by failing to foresee coming events.
   Too often managers simply extrapolate the current status quo into their forecasts
   for the future, thus ignoring upside and downside possibilities alike. Professor Max
   Bazerman of Harvard Business School calls these risks "predictable surprises"
   (the disasters you should have seen coming). It is like drawing a decision tree with
   whole sections of chance branches missing (because those possibilities have been
   completely missed or overlooked) but not knowing it.

2. *Relying on verbal expressions of probability.* Losing the patent case is *unlikely*. There
   is a *reasonable chance* that our product will beat our rival's to market. Although
   expressions such as these come naturally, they are surprisingly imprecise. Researchers have asked scores of individuals, including businesspeople, what such expressions mean in terms of probability. For instance, "unlikely" conveys a probability of
   anywhere between 11 and 39 percent, with a median response of 25 percent. In turn,

"a reasonable chance" can mean a probability as high as 80 percent or as low as 50 percent. As decision trees remind us, determining reasonable probabilities for the risks that matter is crucial for crafting profit-maximizing decisions. A pessimistic view of "unlikely" could well lead to a very different decision than an optimistic view. It's far better to try to pinpoint and agree on reasonable probability estimates in the first place.

3. *Holding optimistic beliefs.* Here, optimism means overstating the probability of favorable outcomes and downplaying the chances of unfavorable ones. By nature confident, many managers unconsciously engage in wishful forecasting: What they want to have happen they believe is likely to happen. Clearly, overoptimistic, unrealistic beliefs can lead to poor or even disastrous decisions. A constructive remedy to unfounded optimism is to insist on realistic assessments based on external benchmarks. Nobel prize winner Daniel Kahneman calls this "taking the outside view." For instance, a management team might believe and claim a 60 percent chance of success for a new product, based purely on an internally focused assessment. But of all new product launches surveyed each year, only about 10 to 15 percent are successfully being sold two years later. Even if impressive internal factors justify elevating the product's success rate to, say, three times this base rate, a realistic revised probability is only 30 to 45 percent—a far cry from 60 percent.

The BP Oil Spill Disaster Revisited

On April 20, 2010, in the Gulf of Mexico, the *Deepwater Horizon* drilling rig exploded, killing 11 workers and unleashing one of the largest oil leaks and environmental disasters in US history. BP had leased the rig to drill an exploratory well at a water depth of approximately 5,000 feet and was in the process of temporarily shutting down the well. Offshore drilling at great depth involves a myriad of operational risks. According to the preliminary report of the commission investigating the disaster, BP and its contractors Halliburton Co. and Transocean Ltd. repeatedly took risky actions in the interests of saving time and money. Leading up to and precipitating the disaster, the three parties —due to poor communications, conflicting assessments, and confusion about responsibilities—made a series of costly mistakes and misjudgments. The available evidence indicates that the explosion was not an unavoidable fluke but, rather, a result of management decisions stemming from a culture within BP that downplayed safety risks.[3] Not until September 9, after repeated failed attempts to stem the leak, was the well finally shut down.

The overview of the BP oil spill in Chapter 1 concluded with a key question: What decision-making pitfalls and mistakes contributed to the accident? Research in behavioral economics points to a number of psychological decision traps as potential contributors to BP's excessive risk taking. In highly uncertain settings, self-serving **overoptimism** and **overconfidence** can blind management to the true risks they face. Given a 20-year record of aggressive oil exploration with many successes and few mishaps, BP's top management could easily convince itself that its margins of safety (even if not great by industry standards) were more than adequate. Overoptimism would

---

[3]This account is based on numerous published sources, including "The Report on Causes of the Deepwater Horizon Oil Rig Blowout and Ways to Prevent Such Events," U.S. Department of the Interior, November 16, 2010; G. Chazan, "BP's Safety Drive Faces Rough Road," *The Wall Street Journal* (February 1, 2011), p. A1; S. Lyall, "In BP's Record, a History of Boldness and Costly Blunders," *The Wall Street Journal* (July 13, 2010), p. A1; J. Nocera, "BP Ignored the Omens of Disaster," *The New York Times* (June 19, 2010), p. B1; and I. Urbina, "In Gulf, It Was Unclear Who Was in Charge of Rig," *The New York Times* (June 6, 2010), p. A1.

lead BP to see a spill risk as a less than "one in a thousand" probability, whereas the objective risk might be closer to one in one hundred. Overconfidence could convince decision makers that if untoward risks developed, they could be managed and controlled. Though there were numerous instances in which workers, engineers, and middle managers raised safety concerns, top managers, in the thrall of **Group Think**, could downplay these concerns and maintain an unshakeable consensus in favor of the company's aggressive strategic plan.

Finally, BP should have drawn strong lessons from a decade of experience marred by a series of disasters stemming from the company's aggressive risk-taking attitude. In March 2005, BP's Texas City plant exploded, killing 15 people and injuring 170 others, making it the worst industrial accident in a generation. Later that year, a series of cost-cutting decisions, shoddy operations, and mistakes nearly sank one of BP's $1 billion rigs in another part of the Gulf. In 2006, BP suffered a nearly 300,000-gallon oil leak in its pipeline in Prudhoe Bay, Alaska. Though BP changed its top leadership in 2007 and pledged to recommit itself to improving safety, the company's core culture did not significantly change.

RISK AVERSION

Thus far, we have used the concept of expected monetary value as a guide to making decisions under uncertainty. A decision maker who follows the expected-profit criterion is said to be **risk neutral**. This standard is appropriate for a manager who is willing to play the averages. The evidence suggests, however, that individuals and firms are not neutral toward risks that are large relative to their financial resources. When it comes to significant risks, individuals and institutions adopt an attitude that is conservative toward losses. Thus, the use of the expected-profit criterion must be qualified.

A COIN GAMBLE   You are offered the following choice: You can receive $60 for certain (the money is yours to keep), or you can accept the following gamble. A fair coin is tossed. If heads come up, you win $400; if tails come up, you lose $200. Would you choose the sure $60 or accept the gamble on the coin toss? In answering, imagine that real money (your own) is at stake.

When given this choice, the majority of individuals prefer the sure $60 to the gamble. This is not surprising, given the magnitude of the risk associated with the coin toss. Notice, however, that choosing $60 is at odds with maximizing expected profit. The expected profit of the coin toss is: $(.5)(400) + (.5)(-200) = \$100$. Thus, a risk-neutral decision maker would prefer the gamble to the sure $60. Refusing the bet shows that you are not risk neutral when it comes to profits and losses of this magnitude.

A precise way to express one's evaluation of the coin toss (or any risky prospect) is to name a certainty equivalent. The **certainty equivalent (CE)** is the amount of money for certain that makes the individual exactly indifferent to the risky prospect. Suppose that, after some thought, you determine you would be indifferent to the options of receiving $25 for certain or facing the risk of the coin toss. You are saying that your CE for the coin toss is $25. This CE is significantly smaller than the expected value of the bet, $100. This being the case, we would say that you are risk averse. An individual is **risk averse** if his or her certainty equivalent for a given risky prospect is less than its expected value.

Loosely speaking, the magnitude of one's aversion to risk is indicated by the shortfall of the CE below the expected value of the risky prospect; this difference (sometimes referred to as a *discount for risk*) measures the reduction in value (below expected value) due to a prospect's riskiness. Here the risk discount is $100 - 25 = \$75$. The discount depends on individual preferences as well as on the size of the risk. For instance, a second individual might prefer to avoid the coin toss altogether; that is, in a choice between the coin toss and receiving $0 for certain, this individual prefers $0. This preference makes good sense for someone who does not wish to bear the downside risk of the coin toss. Suppose this individual is indifferent to the options of *paying* $20 for certain or taking the coin toss. (He or she is willing to pay $20 to avoid the risk of the gamble.) Here the CE is −$20, and the risk discount is $\$100 - (-20) = \$120$. Clearly, the second decision maker is more risk averse than the first.

THE DEMAND FOR INSURANCE   Risk aversion directly explains the demand for insurance. Insurance companies stand ready to compensate their policyholders in the event of losses (specified in the insurance contract) at a price in the form of the premium paid by the customer to the company. Risk-averse individuals are willing to give up monetary income to avoid risks. In effect, this is what they do when they purchase insurance.

To make the argument concrete, consider a couple who is about to purchase fire insurance to protect their home (which is valued at $250,000). The risk of a fire destroying their house is very small—about 1 in 500 in any given year. Nevertheless, the loss of their house would mean financial ruin. Thus, the couple finds it prudent to purchase insurance. In return for payment of a $500 annual premium, a 100 percent fire policy promises to pay whatever amount is necessary to rebuild and replace the house in the event of fire. In purely financial terms, the couple faces the following options. If they do not buy the policy, their housing wealth at the end of the year will be $250,000 if there is no fire or $0 if a fire occurs (a 1-in-500 chance). Their expected loss from fire is: (1/500) ($250,000) = $500. The premium is priced to exactly cover the expected loss—that is to say, the policy is actuarially fair. By purchasing the policy at this fair premium, the couple is guaranteed against loss. Regardless of whether a fire occurs, they will have their house (or the money to rebuild it). Because they are risk averse, the couple greatly prefers to fully insure at the cost of the $500 premium rather than bear the risk of losing everything in a fire.

How are insurance companies able to offer actuarially fair insurance? Because of their large size and ability to pool different risks, insurance companies generally behave as though they are risk neutral. To illustrate, suppose the company insures 500,000 houses in a state against fire. Although it is impossible to predict which houses will be struck by fire, the law of large numbers indicates that very close to 1,000 homes in total will have fire losses. Thus, the total premiums ($250 million) will closely match the company's actual payout on the losses. Because of administrative costs in writing the policies, insurance companies typically charge premiums that exceed their expected losses. (Of course, competition among insurance companies limits the premiums any one company can charge.) But higher premiums do not eliminate (although they may reduce) the demand for insurance. Even if the fire insurance premium were $1,000 per year, in all likelihood, the risk-averse couple would still be willing to buy coverage rather than go unprotected.[4]

Risk Management at Microsoft

"Microsoft sees risk everywhere, in a dozen broad categories: financial, reputational, technological, competitive, customer, people (employees and contractors), operations, distributions, business partners, regulatory and legislative, political and strategic."[5] This might seem an unusual statement. After all, what could be more secure than the company's near-monopoly position in PC operating systems?

Yet, Microsoft's risk managers see things quite differently. Their job is to identify, quantify, and manage literally hundreds of risks, of which 20 to 30 may be most important at a given time. Of particular importance are regulatory risks (government antitrust actions) and uncertainties surrounding intellectual property rights. In the longer term, the emergence of new software markets and Microsoft's ability to influence or control the accompanying standards and platforms are crucial. Once managers have identified key risks, they can address the best way to manage them: via insurance, or via a shared-risk joint venture, by diversification, or (in the extreme case) by ceasing the risky activity altogether.

Risk management is becoming a pervasive part of big business. When faced with enormous uncertainties, management's stance is decidedly not risk neutral. Invariably, it is risk averse. Beyond the expected monetary returns associated with the separate risks on its radar screen, management must be concerned about its combined risk exposures. As noted earlier, it is wise to diversify by pursuing multiple risky R&D initiatives, instead of putting all eggs in one basket. Firms operating in "dirty" industries must continuously assess the risks posed by changing environmental regulations. In the wake of the monumental losses associated with Hurricanes Andrew, Katrina, and Sandy, disaster insurers have reassessed their risk portfolios. Using computer models, they sift through decades of data on storm patterns and earthquakes to estimate risk probabilities. While watching out for excessive geographic concentration of insurance coverage, the insurers are also reassessing shoreline properties, scrutinizing building codes, raising premiums, dropping policies, reinsuring portions of their risks, and offloading a portion of their risks with reinsurers.

An important insight offered by risk management is that many risks are interdependent. Decisions made in one area create (or mitigate) risks in another. Alerted to the risks of mass tort litigation for repetitive stress injury, Microsoft incorporated this cost ($2.82 per unit) when setting the licensing fee for its new innovative keyboards, thereby providing a prudent monetary reserve for this risk.

---

[4]The general rule is that a risk-averse individual always will insure fully against a risk if offered actuarially fair insurance. At higher premiums, a range of outcomes is possible: full insurance, partial insurance, or no insurance. A popular type of partial insurance involves provision for deductibles. With a deductible, the company pays only for the portion of losses above a specified monetary threshold. Thus, the policyholder buys insurance (at a reduced premium) for large losses but self-insures for small ones.

[5]This quotation and the synopsis in the text are drawn from E. Teach, "Microsoft's Universe of Risk," *CFO Magazine* (March 1997), 69–72.

Expected Utility

How can a manager formulate a criterion, reflecting the firm's attitude toward risk, to guide his or her decisions? The formal answer to this question was developed by mathematical economists John von Neumann and Oscar Morgenstern, and is called the expected-utility rule. (At the same time, von Neumann and Morgenstern developed the field of game theory, which we encountered in Chapter 10.)

The use of expected utility proceeds in two steps. First, the decision maker must think carefully about the firm's preferences concerning risks: what risks it is willing to accept and how to value those risks. In the process, the manager constructs a utility scale that describes this risk tolerance. Second, the manager analyzes the decision problem in much the same way as before: that is, he constructs a decision tree showing relevant probabilities and possible monetary outcomes and then evaluates the tree. However, there is one crucial difference: In contrast to the risk-neutral manager, who averages *monetary values* at each step, the risk-averse decision maker averages the *utilities* associated with monetary values. At each point of decision, the manager selects the alternative that supplies the maximum expected utility. With this summary in hand, let's see exactly how the method works.

A RISK-AVERSE WILDCATTER   Once again, let's consider the wildcatter's basic decision problem, reproduced in Figure 12.7. Now suppose the wildcatter is risk averse; he is unwilling to rely on expected profits as his choice criterion. Instead, he seeks to determine a criterion for choosing among risky prospects that reflects his own attitude toward risk. We now show how he can construct a utility function that measures his own degree of risk aversion and how he can use this function to guide his choices.

The wildcatter begins by attaching a utility value to each possible monetary outcome. Let's start with the decision to drill. Here the outcomes are $600,000 and −$200,000; these are the best and worst possible outcomes, respectively. The wildcatter is free to set these utility values arbitrarily as long as the best outcome receives the higher value. The usual choice is to assign the worst outcome a utility value of zero. Thus, we would write U(−200) = 0; that is, the utility associated with a loss of $200,000 is zero. In turn,

FIGURE 12.7

The Wildcatter's Drilling
Problem Revisited

Given his degree of
risk aversion, the
wildcatter chooses
not to drill.

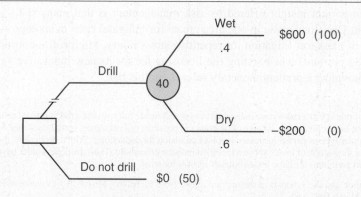

let's arbitrarily set U(600) = 100. This establishes a range of utility values from 0 to 100 for monetary outcomes between the worst and best possible outcomes.

Using these utility values, the wildcatter evaluates the option to drill by computing its expected utility. The **expected utility** is the probability of each outcome times its utility, summed over all outcomes. Thus, the expected utility of drilling is

$$E(U_{drill}) = (.4)U(600) + (.6)U(-200)$$
$$= (.4)(100) + (.6)(0) = 40.$$

Now consider the "do not drill" option. In this case, the wildcatter's monetary result is $0 for certain. What utility value should the wildcatter assign this outcome? To determine U(0), the wildcatter compares $0 for certain with a gamble offering $600,000 (with probability p) and −$200,000 (with probability $1 - p$). The wildcatter measures his relative preference for $0 by finding the probability, p, that leaves him indifferent to the options of $0 and the gamble. Suppose that, after some mental trial and error, he judges his indifference probability to be $p = .5$; that is, he is indifferent to a certain $0 and to a 50-50 risk between $600,000 and −$200,000. The fact that he is indifferent (at $p = .5$) allows us to find U(0). The expected utility of the 50-50 gamble is

$$(.5)U(600) + (.5)U(-200) = (.5)(100) + (.5)(0) = 50.$$

Since the wildcatter is indifferent to $0 for certain and this gamble, the two alternatives must have the same utility; that is, U(0) = 50.

Finally, the wildcatter uses expected utility as a guide for his decision. The simple rule is this:

| The decision maker should choose the course of action that maximizes his or her expected utility.

The expected utility of drilling is 40, whereas the utility of not drilling is 50. Thus, the wildcatter should elect not to drill the site. The decision tree in Figure 12.7 shows how the expected utility rule is applied. Beside each monetary value in the tree is its associated utility. The expected utility of drilling is computed and listed by the chance circle. Finally, the "drill" decision branch has been crossed out because it has the lesser expected utility. The wildcatter's preferred option is not to drill.

In the more complicated examples to come, there will be many opportunities to practice the mechanics of expected utility. For the moment, the key point to remember is this: The decision maker's job is to assess utilities that express his or her attitude toward risk. There is no "formula" for determining the "right" utilities; they are purely personal and subjective.

In the preceding example, the wildcatter's key assessment is that $0 for certain is equivalent (in terms of his preferences) to a 50-50 risk between $600,000 and −$200,000. Notice that this assessment reflects risk aversion on his part. The 50-50 risk has an expected value of $200,000. Yet the wildcatter's stated CE for this risk is $0; this is a considerable risk discount. With this assessment in hand, it becomes a simple matter to compare expected utilities: 40 for drilling versus 50 for not drilling. We also should note an equivalent way to explain the decision not to drill. Given his degree of risk aversion, the wildcatter prefers to drill only if the chances of striking oil are greater than .5 (his indifference probability). Because the actual probability of an oil strike on this site is only .4, he naturally chooses not to drill.

A MORE COMPLICATED OIL DRILLING PROBLEM   Figure 12.8a depicts a more complicated drilling prospect involving four possible monetary outcomes and associated probabilities. In addition, the wildcatter's utility value is listed beside each monetary outcome. He continues to set U(600) = 100 and U(−200) = 0. Accordingly, U(0) remains 50. The wildcatter also has assessed U(200) = 70 and U(−120) = 25. In other words, he is indifferent to the options of $200,000 for certain and a 70–30 risk between the outcomes, $600,000 and −$200,000. Similarly, he is indifferent to *losing* $120,000 for certain or a 25–75 risk between the same two outcomes.[6] Therefore, these utilities are U(200) = (.7)(100) + (.3)(0) = 70 and U(−120) = (.25)(100) + (.75)(0) = 25.

Now the wildcatter is ready to compare his two options. The expected utility of drilling is (.2)(100) + (.18)(70) + (.32)(50) + (.3)(25) = 56.1. The utility of not drilling is U($0) = 50. Thus, drilling offers the higher expected utility and should be elected.[7]

Why the Expected-Utility Method Works

The preceding discussion shows *how* the expected-utility rule works. It is also worth checking *why* it works. Figure 12.8b demonstrates the reasoning behind the expected-utility rule. Beside each monetary outcome is listed an equivalent (in terms of preference) risk over the best and worst outcomes. By his own admission, the wildcatter is indifferent to a given monetary outcome versus the equivalent risk. Therefore, we can substitute the equivalent risk for each monetary outcome in the decision tree. Substituting equivalent risks will not change how the wildcatter feels about the drill option. (This assumption usually is called the *substitution principle*.) We make the substitution by (mentally) deleting the monetary outcome and, in its place, connecting the equivalent risk to the branch tip. Although the decision tree looks very bushy, the substitution has an important implication: Now the only outcomes in the tree are $600,000 and −$200,000, the best and worst outcomes. If we add up the *total* probability of obtaining $600,000, we obtain the reduced tree on the right. The probability is computed as

$$(.2)(1.0) + (.18)(.7) + (.32)(.5) + (.30)(.25) = .561.$$

(Note that four branch paths on the tree end in $600,000. Each path involves a pair of chance branches, so we use the product rule for probabilities.) Thus, the actual drilling risk is equivalent (has been reduced) to a simpler risk offering a .561 chance at $600,000 and a .439 chance at −$200,000.

Now the wildcatter's decision is straightforward: Drilling is preferred to not drilling because, by his own admission, the wildcatter rates $0 for certain as equivalent to a .5

---

[6]Notice that −$200,000 is not an actual drilling outcome. (The worst actual outcome is −$120,000.) However, this fact makes no substantive difference in assigning utilities. The wildcatter is free to assign any outcome as the lowest or "zero-utility" value as long as this monetary outcome is lower than all actual outcomes.

[7]We note in passing that the original drilling site and the second drilling site have identical expected profits: $120,000. (Check the expected value of the second site.) Loosely speaking, the original site is more risky than the second. (It has a greater upside potential as well as greater downside risk.) Here the risk-averse wildcatter rejects the first site while choosing to drill the second.

FIGURE 12.8

A More Complicated
Drilling Prospect

The decision tree in
part a summarizes the
risks of drilling. The
wildcatter chooses
to drill because the
expected utility of this
option exceeds the
utility of not drilling.
Part b reduces the
drilling decision tree
to an equivalent tree.

Do not drill

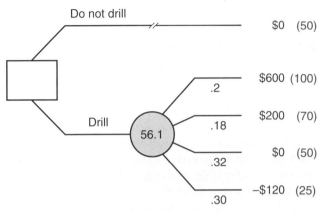

$0   (50)

$600 (100)
.2

$200 (70)
.18

Drill
56.1

$0   (50)
.32

−$120 (25)
.30

(a) Basic Decision Tree

(b) Reducing the Drill Option to an Equivalent Risk

chance of the best outcome, and this is less than the .561 equivalent chance offered by drilling. We have gone to some trouble to see through the logic of the wildcatter's choice. But notice that applying the expected-utility rule determines the decision in *exactly* the same way (albeit more compactly). We found the expected utility of drilling to be 56.1. Since this is greater than the utility of not drilling (50), drilling is the better option.

Henceforth, we can apply the expected-utility rule with confidence that it properly evaluates the relative risks of different courses of action.

Expected Utility and Risk Aversion

Figure 12.9 shows the wildcatter's utility curve over a range of monetary outcomes. This curve is constructed by plotting utilities for particular monetary values and then drawing a smooth curve through those points. As pictured, the utility curve is concave: that is, it becomes less and less steep. The concavity of the curve reflects the wildcatter's risk aversion. To see this, consider a simple two-outcome risk—say, a 50-50 chance of $600,000 or −$200,000. By definition, the expected utility of this risk is $(.5)(100) + (.5)(0) = 50$. Pinpoint 50 on the vertical utility scale, read over to the curve, and then read down to the certainty equivalent value. As we saw earlier, this is $0. Now, instead of reading off the curve at $U = 50$, read over to the dashed line connecting the endpoints of the curve. Reading down, we arrive at the monetary value $200,000. This is exactly the expected value of the risky prospect:

FIGURE 12.9

The Wildcatter's Utility
Curve

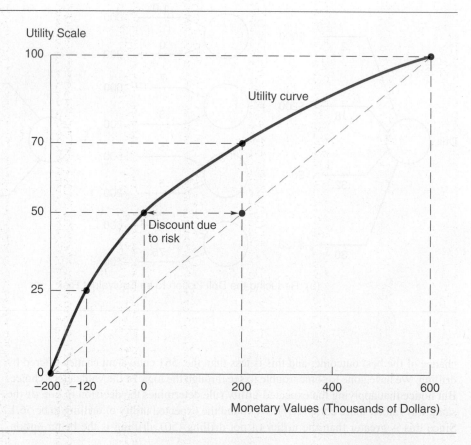

(.5)(600) + (.5)(−200) = $200 thousand. The point is that the expected value of any risky prospect always lies along a straight-line utility curve. *A risk-neutral manager has a linear utility graph.* In fact, the horizontal gap between the CE (read off the curve) and the expected value (read off the line) exactly measures the discount due to risk aversion. For any concave curve, it is always true that the CE falls to the left of (i.e., is lower than) the corresponding expected value.

Figure 12.10 shows three typical utility curves. The concave curve reflects risk aversion, and the linear graph reflects risk neutrality. The third curve is convex: that is, it becomes steeper and steeper. It is easy to check that an individual displaying such a curve is **risk loving** and prefers to bear risk. More precisely, the individual's CE for any risk is greater than (lies to the right of) its expected value.

With the utility graph in hand, the decision maker can supply requisite utility values and routinely evaluate decision trees. Besides assigning utility values to outcomes, the decision maker can use the graph in reverse. For instance, the expected utility of the second oil site (56.1) merits drilling. A direct expression of how much the site is worth to the wildcatter is given by its certainty equivalent. To find the CE, start at a utility of 56.1 in Figure 12.9, read over to the utility curve, and then read down to the corresponding monetary value—in this case, about $50,000. This is the value the wildcatter places on the site. Thus, he would not sell out if offered $30,000 but would do so readily if offered a certain $60,000 (or any sum greater than $50,000).

Consider a 50-50 risk between $600,000 and $0. Check that the expected utility of this risk is 75. Using the utility graph, find the CE of this risk. Compare the risk's CE and its expected value. Why is the gap between the two relatively small?

CHECK STATION 4

Once a utility curve has been assessed, the manager can use the expected-utility rule repeatedly and routinely to guide his or her decisions. Each particular decision carries accompanying profits and losses. But what ultimately matters is the impact of the firm's many decisions on its monetary wealth position. As a general rule, it is best to assess a utility function over final monetary wealth. For example, suppose the wildcatter begins the year with $1.8 million. He thinks about the potential range of his realized *wealth* two years from now. (This range depends on the number and riskiness of sites he might explore.) In a worst-case scenario he might end with debts of $1.5 million. In the best case, his wealth might reach $5 million. Thus, he should assess his utility curve over this wide range.

To sum up, the manager must think hard about tolerance for risks over different final wealth positions. In doing so, the manager assesses a utility graph that best represents his or her attitude toward risk.[8] Once the utility curve is in hand, the manager can analyze any decision problem by means of the usual decision tree after supplying utility values for possible final monetary wealth positions. Finally, the manager averages back the tree and selects the course of action that has the highest expected utility.

[8]Decision makers can use a variety of methods to assess utility curves. One such method is presented in Problem 12 at the end of this chapter. In the process of utility assessment, the manager can gain considerable insight about his or her risk preferences. For instance, a common finding is that decision makers become considerably less risk averse when starting from a high (rather than a low) financial wealth base.

FIGURE 12.10

Three Utility Functions

A risk-averse individual (part a) has a concave utility function. A risk-neutral individual (part b) has a linear utility function. A risk-loving individual (part c) has a convex utility function.

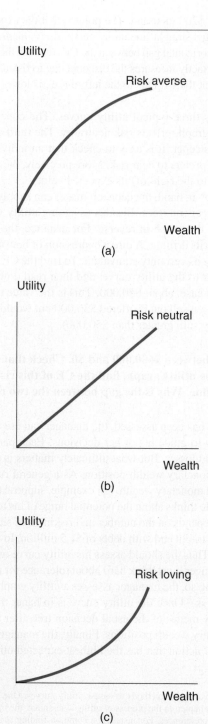

Utility

Risk averse

Wealth

(a)

Utility

Risk neutral

Wealth

(b)

Utility

Risk loving

Wealth

(c)

To solve the boat dealer's problem posed at the beginning of the chapter, we supply the following information. The dealer incurs fixed costs amounting to $150,000 per year and obtains motorcraft from the manufacturer at an average cost of $10,000 each. In a growing economy, the demand for motorboats is described by $P = 20 - .05Q$; in a slumping economy, demand is $P = 20 - .1Q$, where P is measured in thousands of dollars.

Gearing Down for a Recession Revisited

Let's start by finding the dealer's profit-maximizing boat order for each type of economy. Setting MR = MC, we find the dealer's optimal quantity and price to be $Q_G = 100$ and $P_G = \$15,000$ for a growing economy; the resulting profit is $\pi_G = \$350,000$. For the recession economy, we find $Q_R = 50$, $P_R = \$15,000$, and $\pi_R = \$100,000$. Of course, the dealer must place the order now, before knowing the true direction of the economy. Let's suppose the dealer must choose to order a round lot of either 50 or 100 boats. (Other possibilities are considered in Problem 13 at the end of the chapter.) In light of a 60 percent chance of growth, which order, 50 or 100, has the higher expected profit?

The decision tree in Figure 12.11 answers this question. If 100 boats are ordered, the dealer's profit is either $350,000 or −$150,000. Under slumping demand, the best the dealer can do is sell all 100 boats at a price of $10,000 each. (At this quantity, revenue is maximized; that is, MR = 0.) If 50 boats are ordered, the possible outcomes are $225,000 and $100,000. The first outcome occurs when the dealer plans for a recession but is pleasantly surprised by growing demand and sells the 50 boats at a price of $17,500 each. (Note that this price is obtained from the demand curve for a growing economy.)

Direct calculation shows that ordering 50 boats generates an expected profit of $175,000, whereas ordering 100 boats produces only $150,000. Thus, a risk-neutral dealer prefers the smaller (50-boat) order. (A risk-averse dealer shares this preference,

FIGURE 12.11

Ordering Boats under Uncertainty

The dealer's better course of action is to order 50 boats.

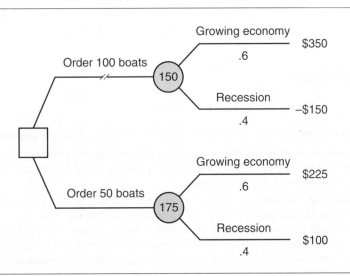

because ordering 50 boats is less risky than ordering 100.) This result might conflict with one's intuition. After all, a growing economy is more likely than not, and ordering 100 boats is optimal in this case; therefore, one would judge 100 boats to be the better choice. What's wrong with this reasoning? The key point is that the cost of making a wrong decision differs across the two actions. Taking a large boat order is very costly (generates a large loss) if a slumping economy causes inventory to be sold at bargain prices. The "cost" of placing a limited order and having too little inventory to accommodate a growing economy is relatively small. (At least the dealer can raise prices.) As a result, the expected profit associated with the small order is significantly greater than that of the large order.

SUMMARY

Decision-Making Principles

1. In choices among risky prospects, sound decision making means assessing the foreseeable good and bad outcomes and their respective chances. Thus, decisions must be judged according to the information available at the time the choice is made, not with the benefit of 20-20 hindsight.

2. When a series of related decisions are to be made, an optimal initial choice depends on foreseeing and making optimal choices for the decisions that follow.

3. To make sound decisions, the manager must also assess his or her own (or the company's) attitude toward risk. A risk-averse decision maker assesses a (certainty equivalent) value for a risky prospect that is smaller than the prospect's expected value.

Nuts and Bolts

1. The decision tree is the basic tool for making decisions under uncertainty. The tree must include branches for (a) all possible actions of the decision maker and (b) all chance events that can affect outcomes. Each chance branch should be assigned a probability. In decisions involving profits and losses, each branch tip should be assigned a monetary value.

2. The decision tree should accurately depict the chronology of the decision setting, that is, the sequence of decision nodes and chance nodes.

3. The expected-value criterion values a risky prospect by taking a weighted average of the possible monetary outcomes, the weight for each outcome being its probability:

$$E(v) = p_1v_1 + p_2v_2 + \cdots + p_nv_n.$$

The expected-value criterion is appropriate for a risk-neutral decision maker, one who is willing to play the averages.

4. More generally, the principle of expected-utility maximization provides a consistent guide to decisions. In applying this principle, the manager constructs a utility graph that portrays his or her attitude toward risk. If the manager is risk neutral, this graph will be linear; if risk averse, it will be concave.

5. Whatever his or her attitude toward risk, the manager "solves" the decision tree by a process of "averaging and eliminating"—starting from the right and moving left. The expected utility (profit) at any chance node is found by averaging—that is, by multiplying branch utilities (or profits) by probabilities. At any decision node, the decision maker selects the alternative having the greatest expected utility (profit). All inferior decision branches are eliminated. The movement from right to left means that the last uncertainties are averaged first and the last decisions are evaluated first.

Questions and Problems

1. a. Average back the decision tree below, supplying expected monetary values for points A through E.
   b. One of your fellow managers is worried that there are no probabilities given for the branches leading from point D. In order to solve the tree, he decides to assign a .5 probability to each branch. Do you agree with this procedure or not? Explain.

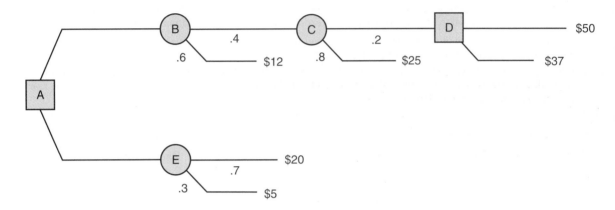

2. The parents of a seven-year-old boy sued a New York hospital for $10 million. The boy was blinded shortly after he was born two weeks premature. His parents claimed that hospital doctors administered excessive oxygen to the baby and that this caused the blindness. The case went to trial, and just as the jury announced it had reached a verdict, the lawyers for the two sides arrived at an out-of-court settlement of $1,500,000.
   a. If you were the parents, how would you decide whether to accept the settlement or wait for the jury's decision? What probability assessments would you need to make? Would you have accepted the settlement?
   b. Answer the questions in part (a), taking the hospital's point of view.

3. For five years, a firm has successfully marketed a package of multitask software. Recently, sales have begun to slip because the software is incompatible with a number of popular application programs. Thus, future profits are uncertain. In the software's present form, the firm's managers envision three possible five-year forecasts: maintaining current profits in the neighborhood of $2 million, a slip in profits to $.5 million, or the onset of losses to the tune of −$1 million. The respective probabilities for these outcomes are .2, .5, and .3.
      An alternative strategy is to develop an "open," or compatible, version of the software. This will allow the firm to maintain its market position, but the effort will be costly. Depending on how costly, the firm envisions four possible profit outcomes: $1.5 million, $1.1 million, $.8 million, and $.6 million, with each outcome considered equally likely.
   a. Which course of action produces greater expected profit?
   b. Roughly speaking, which course of action appears to be less risky? If management were risk averse, would this fact change its preferred course of action?

4. A European consortium has spent a considerable amount of time and money developing a new supersonic aircraft. The aircraft gets high marks on all performance measures except noise. Because of flight noise, the consortium's management is concerned that the US government may impose restrictions on some of the American airports where the aircraft can land. Management judges a 50-50 chance that there will be some restrictions. Without restrictions, management estimates its (present discounted) profit at $125 million; with restrictions, its profit would be only $25 million. Management must decide now, before knowing the government's decision, whether to redesign parts of the aircraft to solve the noise problem. The cost of the redesign program is $25 million. There is a .6 chance that the redesign program will solve the noise problem (in which case, full landing rights are a certainty) and a .4 chance it will fail.
      Using a decision tree, determine the consortium's best course of action, assuming management is risk neutral.

5. A firm faces uncertain revenues and uncertain costs. Its revenues may be $120,000, $160,000, or $175,000, with probabilities .2, .3, and .5, respectively. Its costs are $150,000 or $170,000 with chances .6 and .4, respectively. (Revenues and costs are independent.)
   a. How many possible profit outcomes exist? Draw a decision tree listing these profit outcomes at the branch tips. Compute the firm's expected profit by folding back the tree. (It does not matter which uncertainty, demand or cost, is resolved first in the tree.)
   b. Without a decision tree, calculate *separately* the firm's expected revenue and expected cost. What is the firm's expected profit? (This result underscores a great computational convenience of the expected-value criterion. Expected profit is equal to expected revenue minus expected cost; that is, expectations can be taken separately.)

6. Global Studios is thinking of producing a megafilm, *Aqua World*, which could be a megahit or a megaflop. Profit is uncertain for two reasons: (1) the cost of producing the film may be low or high, and (2) the market reception for the film may be strong or weak. There is a .5 chance of low costs (C) and a .5 chance of high costs. The probability of strong demand (D) is .4; the probability of weak demand is .6. The studio's profits (in millions of dollars) for the four possible outcomes are shown in the table.

Low C/Strong D	Low C/Weak D	High C/Strong D	High C/Weak D
80	10	0	−70

   a. Should the studio produce the film? Use a decision tree to justify your answer.
   b. The studio is concerned that Kevin Costmore, the film's director and star, might let production costs get out of control. Thus, the studio insists on a clause in the production contract giving it the right to terminate the project after the first $30 million is spent. By this time, the studio *will know for certain* whether total production costs are going to be low (i.e., under control) or high (out of control). How much is this termination clause worth to the studio vis-a-vis the situation in part (a)?

7. As noted in the text, top management of BP adopted a "lax" approach to safety in its aggressive pursuit of oil discovery. Consider two alternative safety stances it could have adopted. Emulating Exxon Mobil, BP might have taken an "ultraconservative" approach to safety, implementing extensive training of personnel, allowing for generous margins of error, closely monitoring drilling operations, and formulating backup systems and contingency plans in the event of an emerging drilling problem. Or it could have taken a "standard" middle-of-the-road approach, closely following accepted safety practices of other firms in the industry.

   Consider an oil drilling site that is expected to yield $2 billion in profit over its economic life, if no unforeseen disasters or spills occur. By following standard safety practices, BP can limit the risk of a disastrous spill to a 1 percent probability. The cost of adopting standard safety practices (in terms of time and money) at the site is $160 million. Instead, adopting an ultraconservative approach (at a cost of $240 million) would reduce the disaster risk to .5 percent. Finally, BP's lax safety approach costs only $40 million and implies a disaster risk of 3 percent.
   a. If a disaster were to occur, the best estimate of the ultimate cost to BP is $10 billion. This expected-value estimate considers a range of costs—from the tens of millions if an oil spill is immediately plugged by emergency measures to as high as $40 billion (BP's estimated cost of the 2010 spill) in the worst-case scenario. Of the three operating options, which is most profitable? Equivalently, which has the *lowest* net expected cost?
   b. How would BP's operating choice change if, because of wishful thinking, it (wrongly) believed that its lenient safety policy implied only a 2 percent disaster risk? Or if it believed that its expected disaster cost would be $5 billion (instead of $10 billion)?

8. Firm A is facing a possible lawsuit by legal firm B. Firm B represents the family of Mr. Smith, who was killed in a motel fire (allegedly caused by faulty wiring). Firm A was the builder of the motel. Firm A has asked its legal team to estimate the likely jury award it will be ordered to pay in court. Expert legal counsel anticipates three possible court

outcomes: awards of $1,000,000, $600,000, or $0, with probabilities .2, .5, and .3, respectively. In addition to any awards, firm A's legal expenses associated with fighting the court case are estimated to be $100,000.

Firm A also has considered the alternative of entering out-of-court settlement negotiations with firm B. Based on the assessments of its lawyers, A envisions the other side holding out for one of two settlement amounts: $900,000 (a high amount) or $400,000 (a much more reasonable amount). Each demand is considered equally likely. If presented with one of these settlement demands, firm A is free to accept it (in which case, firm B agrees to waive any future right to sue) *or* reject it and take its chances in court. The legal cost of pursuing a settlement (whether or not one is reached) is $50,000.

Determine the settlement or litigation strategy that minimizes firm A's expected total cost (any payment plus legal fees).

9. Some years ago, McDonald's (MD) launched Campaign 55, reducing the prices of its "flagship" sandwiches with the objective of regaining market share. Before the launch, suppose MD's management envisioned two possible outcomes: a strong customer response or a weak response. Industry experts were not very optimistic about the campaign. They assessed the probability of a strong response to be .4. MD predicted an expected profit of $50 million if the response proved to be strong. If the immediate customer response was weak, management believed that all was not lost. If MD could persuade the majority of its franchisees to back and help fund the campaign, the resulting profit would be $20 million. However, if the majority rose up against the campaign, the red ink would fly, and McDonald's profit would be −$100 million. MD considered these two outcomes to be *equally likely*.
   a. Given these assessments, construct a decision tree to determine MD's expected-profit-maximizing course of action.
   b. Suppose that MD has the flexibility to try the campaign but to terminate it if the initial response is weak, thereby limiting its total loss to $20 million. (It must pull the plug before knowing whether the franchisees are for or against the campaign.) Again, construct a decision tree to determine MD's expected-profit-maximizing strategy.

10. As CEO of firm A, you and your management team face the decision of whether to undertake a $200 million R&D effort to create a new mega-medicine. Your research scientists estimate that there is a 40 percent chance of successfully creating the drug. Success means securing a worldwide patent worth $550 million (implying a net profit of $350 million). However, firm B (your main rival) has just announced that it is spending $150 million to pursue development of the same medicine (by a scientific method completely independent of yours). You judge that B's chance of success is 30 percent. Furthermore, if both firms are successful, they will split equally the available worldwide profits ($275 million each) based on separate patents.
   a. Given its vast financial resources, firm A is risk neutral. Should it undertake the $200 million R&D effort? (Use a decision tree to justify your answer.)
   b. Now suppose that it is feasible for firm A to delay its R&D decision until after the result of B's R&D effort (success or failure) is known. Is it advantageous for firm A to wait and claim this "second move"? (Use a decision tree to justify your answer.)
   c. Instead, suppose that the two firms can form a joint venture to pursue either or both of their R&D programs. What is the expected profit of simultaneously pursuing *both* programs? *Hint:* Be sure to compute the probability that *both efforts fail* (in which case the firms' combined loss is 200 + 150 = $350 million). Could the joint venture profitably pursue a *single* program?

11. Consider once again the R&D strategies of the drug company. Suppose the company's management is risk averse and has assessed the following utility values for the set of possible outcomes (in millions of dollars).

Outcome	Utility	Outcome	Utility
$2,000	100	$700	59
1,800	95	600	55
1,700	92	500	50
1,000	71	400	44
800	64	200	32
		0	0

Compute the expected utility of pursuing the biochemical approach alone. Next, find the expected utility of pursuing the biogenetic approach first, then continuing with the biochemical approach if necessary. In light of these calculations, what action do you recommend for the company? How has the company's risk aversion influenced its decision?

12. In attempting to quantify its attitude toward risk, top management of the pharmaceutical company has reported certainty equivalent values for a variety of 50-50 risks. These are summarized in the following table.

Outcomes of 50-50 Risk	Certainty Equivalent
$2,000 and $0	$500
$2,000 and $500	$1,120
$500 and $0	$130
$2,000 and $1,120	$1,530
$1,120 and $500	$780
$500 and $130	$280
$1,120 and $130	$500

For instance, the company's CE for a 50-50 risk between $2,000 million (i.e., $2 billion) and $0 is $500 million, and so on.

a. Use these responses to determine utility values for each of the monetary values in the second column. *Hint*: Set U($2,000) = 100 and U($0) = 50. Show that U($500) = 50, U($1,120) = 75, and so on. Construct a utility graph by plotting points and drawing a smooth curve. (You may wish to check the utility values in Problem 11 against your curve.)

*b. Consider the mathematical utility function U = 2.24$\sqrt{y}$, where U is the utility value corresponding to monetary outcome y. Check that this function is an accurate description of the pharmaceutical company's attitude toward risk. Is the company very risk averse?

*13. Put yourself in the boat dealer's shoes. You currently are considering other order quantities in addition to 50 and 100. Find the optimal order quantity, that is, the exact quantity that maximizes your expected profit. (*Hint*: From the two demand curves, find the expected price equation, that is, the expected sale price for any given quantity of boats. Given this expected-price equation, apply the MR = MC rule to maximize expected profit.)

Discussion Questions Consider the following examples.

1. In 1997, after spending more than $500 million in development and after extensive test marketing, Procter & Gamble launched a series of snack food products made with Olestra, a "no fat" substitute. Although touted as a miracle product, Olestra faced a number of uncertainties concerning taste and shelf life; regulatory approval; and, most important, medical side effects (stomach cramps and the ugly specter of diarrhea in some consumers). Four years later and buffeted by heavy losses, P&G abandoned the fat substitute.

2. In 2010, the California utility, PG&E (formerly, Pacific, Gas, and Electric) suffered a fatal gas pipeline explosion in San Bruno. The company was found to have inadequate inspection and safety programs. The combination of lawsuits, regulatory penalties, and increased testing requirements has cost the company more than $2 billion and counting.

3. Walt Disney Pictures vowed it would learn from its mistakes after suffering a loss of more than $100 million on the film *John Carter*. (The studio had ceded creative control to a maverick director, allowed production costs to spiral out of control, and pursued an ill-conceived marketing campaign.) In planning its two major film releases of 2013, it chose to bet on a bankable star, Johnny Depp, starring in a legendary western, and on a heartwarming, 3-D animated feature made on a moderate budget. The studio got half of what it hoped for. While *The Lone Ranger* quickly bled $160 million in losses, *Frozen* emerged as a surprise holiday hit, generating well over $1 billion box office worldwide and spawning related branded products and a future musical stage production.

Use these examples and other management cases reported in the business press to make a list of the many categories of risks facing managers. In particular lines of business, what categories of risks are the most crucial for the firm's profit? How might firms eliminate, mitigate, or insure against these risks?

Suggested References

The following texts are among the best and most complete treatments of decisions under uncertainty.

Brown, R. *Rational Choice and Judgment: Decision Analysis for the Decider.* Hoboken, NJ: John Wiley and Sons, 2005.

Raiffa, H. *Decision Analysis.* New York: McGraw-Hill, 1997 (paperback).

Savage, S. *Decision Making with Insight.* Belmont, CA: Thomson Learning, 2003.

Practical ways of using decision analysis are discussed in:

Keeney, R. L. "Making Better Decision Makers." *Decision Analysis* (December 2004): 193–204.

Watkins, M. D., and M. H. Bazerman. "Predictable Surprises: The Disasters You Should Have Seen Coming." *Harvard Business Review* (March 2003): 72–88.

The next two references survey the experimental evidence on decision making under uncertainty.

Camerer, C. "Individual Decision Making." in J. H. Kagel and A. E. Roth (eds.), *The Handbook of Experimental Economics.* Princeton, NJ: Princeton University Press, 1995.

Davis, D. D., and C. A. Holt. *Experimental Economics.* Chapter 8. Princeton, NJ: Princeton University Press, 1993.

The following reference is the fascinating account of the many risks and decisions involved in Ford's redesign of its popular Taurus model.

Walton, M. *Car Wars.* New York: Norton, 1999 (paperback).

The following references offer comprehensive guides to decision-tree applications and software:

Buckshaw, D. "Decision Analysis Software Survey. *OR/MS Today* (October 2012): 42–53, also available online at http://www.lionhrtpub.com/orms/surveys/das/das.html.

Keefer, D. L., C. W. Kirkwood, and J. L. Corner. "Perspectives on Decision Analysis Applications, 1990–2001." *Decision Analysis* (March 2004): 4–22.

Internet sites dealing with decision making under uncertainty include Sam Savage's wonderful guide to risk at www.analycorp.com/uncertainty/, and Decision-tree software published by Decision Support Services, www.treeplan.com/.

Check Station Answers

1. The firm's expected profit under the private contract is: $(.25)(\$2) + (.41)(\$.7) + (.34)(-\$.5) = \$.617$ million. Under the government contract, the firm's expected profit is: $(.45)(\$4) + (.55)(-\$2.5) = \$.425$ million. In terms of expected value, the private contract is the better alternative.

2. The executive's expected profit of drilling to *only* 3,000 feet is: $(.4)(600) + (.6)(-160) = \$144$ thousand. By quitting after 3,000 feet, the executive takes a loss of $160,000. What is her expected profit it she drills deeper? It is: $(.2)(400) + (.8)(-250) = -\$120$ thousand. The expected loss from drilling deeper is smaller than that from quitting. Finally, the expected profit from drilling 5,000 feet (if necessary) is $(.4)(600) + (.6)(-120) = \$168$ thousand. This is the executive's best course of action.

3. We calculate firm A's expected profit from launching the product in two steps. If firm B brings out its own product (probability 60 percent), A's expected profit is $(.5)(\$10) + (.5)(-\$30) = -\$10$ million. If B does not bring out a product (probability 40 percent), A's profit is $20 million. Thus, firm A's overall expected profit is $(.4)(\$20) + (.6)(-\$10) = \$2$ million. To maximize expected profit, the firm should launch the product.

4. The expected utility of a 50-50 risk between $600,000 (U = 100) and $0 (U = 50) is (.5)(100) + (.5)(50) = 75. From Figure 12.9, we see that the CE of this risky prospect is about $220,000. In contrast, the expected value of this risk is $300,000. To determine this expected value using the figure, draw a line between the $600,000 and $0 points on the graph. Then find .75 on the utility scale, read over to the line, and read down to the monetary value of $300,000. Note that the risk discount (the horizontal gap between the utility curve and the dashed line) is smaller here than for the $600,000 versus −$200,000 risk. This illustrates a general principle: The smaller the range of risk, then the smaller is the curvature of the utility graph and the closer the CE is to the expected value.

CHAPTER 13

The Value of Information

The race isn't always to the fastest nor the battle to the strongest, but that is the way you should bet.

DAMON RUNYAN

LO#1. Explain when a decision maker should seek additional information.

LO#2. Show how to revise probabilities to accommodate new information.

LO#3. Identify pitfalls to avoid in using information to make forecasts.

LO#4. Discuss auctions and the kinds of decisions under uncertainty facing buyers and the auctioneer.

The Stock Market and the Economy

Forecasting the economy is big business. Scores of forecasters, many using econometric models that contain hundreds of equations, are paid handsomely by private businesses for predictions of the future course of the economy. Like the boat dealer in the previous chapter, businesses strive for early warnings of changes in the course of the economy. The fluctuation in stock market prices is one such early signal. Steady and sustained increases in stock prices (as summarized by the Dow Jones Industrial Average or the S&P 500 index) point to a growing economy over the next six to nine months. Stock market drops signal a coming recession. In fact, stock market movements have been a key leading indicator of recessions. Each of the seven postwar US recessions has been preceded by a sustained fall in stock prices. (These price drops have come between 6 and 12 months in advance of the onset of the recession.) How should a decision maker (the boat dealer, for instance) judge the chances of a recession after observing a rising stock market or after a falling market?

Future historians will remember the last half of the twentieth century as the dawning of the Age of Information. Information is the business of a significant and growing portion of the private sector. A key question is how information can be used to make better plans and decisions in business, government, the sciences, and even in personal matters. The pervasive role of information in decision making is illustrated by the following questions: Should a consumer products firm undertake an expensive test-market program before launching a new and highly promising product? What scientific research approaches should the government support in the long-term war on cancer? How should a firm use macroeconomic forecasts of the economy to make inventory and capacity decisions?

What do polls and statistical analyses indicate about the likely outcome of the upcoming presidential election? What tests are appropriate during pregnancies of older women to screen for severe fetal genetic defects? How can information on public risks—such as those posed by nuclear power, steel fatigue in aging bridges or aircraft, coastal hurricanes, environmental pollution, the spread of infectious diseases—be used to prevent disasters?

These are all broad and important questions. The aim of this chapter is to provide a way of thinking about information—in particular, about how it can be used to make better decisions. We consider a trio of questions:

1. When should a manager acquire additional information before making his or her main decision?

2. How should the manager modify probability assessments of uncertain events in light of this information?

3. How should he or she make decisions with this information in hand?

Together, the answers to these questions provide the foundation for determining the value of information in decisions under uncertainty.

THE VALUE OF INFORMATION

The Oil Wildcatter Revisited

Let's return to the oil-drilling decision of the previous chapter, but with one additional option: Suppose that the wildcatter forms a partnership with a well-known geologist to explore for oil. At a cost, the partnership can take a seismic test to obtain better information about the site before drilling. To begin, we consider the extreme case of a *perfect* seismic test. Suppose that the geologist conducts the test and that she categorizes its outcome as either "good" or "bad." By "good" she means that oil is present (the site is wet) for certain; by "bad" she means the site is definitely dry. (Another way to say this is that wet sites always test good and dry sites always test bad.) It should be clear that, for decision-making purposes, this perfect test is very valuable. If the outcome is good, the partnership drills, strikes oil with certainty, and gains a $600,000 profit. If it is bad, it knows there is no oil and so avoids a loss by choosing not to drill.

The decision tree in Figure 13.1 displays this strategy. Notice that the tree begins not with a decision square but with a chance circle. The outcome of the test is resolved first: good or bad. Then two decision squares appear because a choice must be made in two separate cases: after a good seismic test or after a bad one. The course of action—drill if and only if the test is good—is also shown on the tree.

How well off is the partnership with the perfect seismic test? In Figure 13.1, we have computed the expected profit at the outset, before the test result is in. Recall that the partners judge the probability of oil to be $\Pr(W) = .4$. Since good tests occur precisely when the site is wet, the frequency of a good test is also .4. Similarly, $\Pr(B) = .6$. Therefore, the initial expected value is $(.4)(600,000) + (.6)(0) = \$240,000$. Forty percent of the time, the seismic result is good, and there is a $600,000 drilling profit. The rest of the time, the result is bad, no drilling occurs, and the profit is zero.

FIGURE 13.1

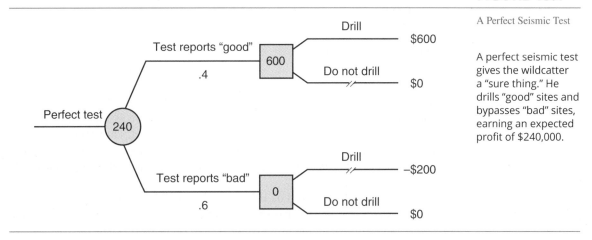

A Perfect Seismic Test

A perfect seismic test gives the wildcatter a "sure thing." He drills "good" sites and bypasses "bad" sites, earning an expected profit of $240,000.

How much is the test information worth to the partnership? The answer is provided by the concept of the expected value of information. The **expected value of information (EVI)** is simply the difference between the decision maker's expected value with the test information and without it. Thus, we can write the expected value of information as

$$EVI = \text{Expected value with information}$$
$$- \text{Expected value without information.}$$

Recall from the discussion in Chapter 12 that, without the test, the best decision was to drill, and the resulting expected profit was $120,000. In the present decision, the EVI is $240,000 − $120,000 = $120,000.

The EVI measures the benefit of the test. So far we have not specified the test's cost. Suppose the test costs $50,000. Since the benefit exceeds the cost, the partners should elect the test. Their expected net gain is EVI − (Test cost) = $120,000 − $50,000 = $70,000. If the cost were $150,000, however, the test would not be worth its expense. The general rule is

A decision maker should acquire costly information if and only if the expected value of the information exceeds its cost.

Before leaving this simple example, let's check exactly where the increase in expected profit came from. Refer once again to Figure 13.1. As the tree indicates, only good sites are drilled. But now consider the effect if all sites, good and bad, were drilled, as would be the case if the test information were not available. From the tree, we see that the partners would lose $200,000 from drilling bad/dry sites. Thus, the advantage of the test is that it saves this amount by screening out these sites. This savings occurs 60 percent of the time, because this is the frequency of dry sites. The partner's expected gain from the seismic test (compared to always drilling) is (.6)(200,000) = $120,000. This is exactly the EVI calculated earlier. The test allows the partners to resolve the uncertainty, wet or dry, before committing to a decision—to drill or not to drill. In this way, they save the cost of drilling dry sites.

Imperfect Information

Although illustrative, the preceding example is unrealistic because it is unlikely that the partners ever could obtain perfect information before drilling. We now consider the decision to drill in light of an *imperfect* seismic test. Again, we assume the test results are categorized as "good" or "bad," but now the test is imperfect. The partners are aware of the recent record of test outcomes, listed in Table 13.1. We address the same questions as before: Should the partners invest in the test, and, if so, what drilling decision should they make based on its result?

Table 13.1 provides a record of 100 past sites (judged to be roughly similar to the current site) where seismic tests have been conducted. It provides a two-way classification of each site's outcome: the result of the test (good or bad) versus the true state of the site (wet or dry). The top left-hand entry shows that 30 of the 100 sites tested good and proved to contain oil. The other entries have similar interpretations. Loosely speaking, there is a correlation between the test and the actual outcomes, demonstrated by the preponderance of cases lying on the main diagonal of the table: Good tests (G) are likely to be associated with wet sites (W) and bad tests (B) with dry sites (D). However, there are a significant number of false reports ($G\&D$ and $B\&W$). The test results, therefore, are far from perfect.

Let's use the historical frequencies in the table as an easy way to develop a number of probabilities essential for evaluating the seismic test option. First, note that the overall frequency of wet sites is 40 out of 100, or 40 percent. (See the total at the bottom of the column labeled "Wet.") Thus, this past record is consistent with the initial probability assessment of the site under consideration. Second, it is natural to inquire as to the chances of striking oil if the site has tested good or, alternatively, if it has tested bad. Looking at the first row of the table, we find that among 50 sites that tested good, 30 also turned out to be wet. The notation $\Pr(W|G)$ is used to denote the probability that the site is wet given (or conditional on) a good test. From the table, we find that $\Pr(W|G) = 30/50 = .6$. Alternatively, if the test is bad, what are the chances of finding oil? Of the 50 sites that tested bad, 10 were wet. Therefore, we have $\Pr(W|B) = 10/50 = .2$.

TABLE 13.1

Past Seismic Test Record (100 Sites)

		Actual State of the Site		
		Wet (W)	Dry (D)	Total
Seismic	Good (G)	30	20	50
Result	Bad (B)	10	40	50
	Total	40	60	100

Let's review what the table is telling us. Before taking the test, the best estimate of the chance of striking oil is $\Pr(W) = .4$. This usually is termed the *prior probability* (i.e., before new information is obtained). After taking the test, the partners will revise their probability assessment based on the test outcome. One of two *conditional probabilities* will be relevant. The initial assessment is revised upward after a good test, $\Pr(W|G) = .6$, and downward after a bad result, $\Pr(W|B) = .2$. Another important piece of data in the table is that 50 out of 100 sites tested good and 50 tested bad. That is, the probability that a site will test good is .5.

One other point should be made. As presented, Table 13.1 lists the number of cases in each cell. By placing a decimal point before each entry, we give the cells a slightly different interpretation. Now each is understood to be a frequency or probability. For instance, the upper-left entry becomes .3; that is, 30 percent of all sites tested good and proved to be wet. We use the notation $\Pr(W\&G) = .3$ to denote the probability of this joint outcome. Similar interpretations and notation hold for the other entries. This new interpretation has no effect on the conditional probabilities found earlier. For example, the chance that the site is wet after a bad test is $\Pr(W|B) = .1/.5 = .2$, exactly the same as the preceding result. Because of its flexibility and wide application, we employ a probabilistic interpretation in the remainder of this chapter.

It is important to see how the seismic information can improve the partners' decision. Figure 13.2 makes this point by depicting the new decision tree, which incorporates the seismic results. We start by emphasizing the sequence of events in the tree. As in Figure 13.1, the first event is the test result: good or bad. This is represented by the chance node (the circle) from which the possible test results emanate. After seeing the result, the partners must decide whether or not to drill. These decisions are denoted by the two squares appearing on the good and bad test branches. Finally, for the "drill" option, the

FIGURE 13.2

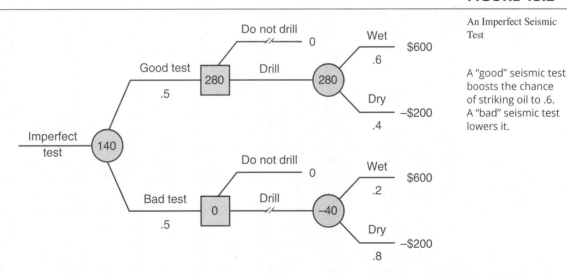

An Imperfect Seismic Test

A "good" seismic test boosts the chance of striking oil to .6. A "bad" seismic test lowers it.

tree shows the chance event, wet or dry, along with the revised probabilities. After a good test, striking oil carries a 60 percent chance; after a bad test, the chance is only 20 percent. (In contrast to the case of a perfect seismic test, a good result does not guarantee oil, nor does a bad result rule it out.)

With the decision tree in hand, the optimal decision strategy is easy to determine. Consider the upper decision square. If the test is good, drilling offers an expected profit of $280,000 and should be undertaken. By contrast, after a bad test, drilling has an expected profit of −$40,000 (since the chance of finding oil is only 20 percent). Thus, the partners should employ a contingent strategy: Drill the site if the seismic test is favorable and forgo it if the test is unfavorable. How much profit do they stand to gain using this strategy? To answer this question, we simply calculate the expected profit at the initial chance node, before the test outcome is known. As we noted earlier, a good test is expected to occur 50 percent of the time, in which case drilling earns an expected profit of $280,000. The other 50 percent of the time, a bad test occurs, no drilling takes place, and the profit is $0. Thus, the expected profit at the initial chance node is simply $(.5)($280,000) + (.5)(0) = $140,000$. Remembering that the expected profit without the test is $120,000, we find the test has an EVI of $140,000 − $120,000 = $20,000. This test is much less valuable than the perfect seismic test examined earlier. Nonetheless, if the test is inexpensive enough (costs less than $20,000), the partners should elect it.

REVISING PROBABILITIES

In many situations, the decision maker possesses potentially valuable information, but in a form that is not readily usable. Typically, the decision maker must ask: How does this piece of information alter my assessment of an uncertain event? Does it make the event more or less likely? By how much should I revise the event's probability? A considerable body of research has studied the ways in which individuals make probabilistic predictions. The overwhelming evidence from these studies is that one's intuition often is a poor guide when it comes to probability assessment and revision. (See the discussion of intuitive prediction later in the chapter.) Fortunately, some basic results in probability provide a formal method for handling this task.

To illustrate the method, suppose the partners lack the seismic record listed in Table 13.1. Instead, they have the following summary information about *the accuracy* of the seismic test. The vendor of the test certifies that, in the past, sites that were actually wet tested "good" three-quarters of the time and dry sites tested "bad" two-thirds of the time. In algebraic terms, we have $\Pr(G|W) = 3/4$ and $\Pr(B|D) = 2/3$. As before, the partners assess a 40 percent chance that the site is wet based on their information prior to the seismic test, $\Pr(W) = .4$.

How can the partners derive $\Pr(W|G)$ and $\Pr(W|B)$, the two key probabilities they need to solve their decision tree? The most direct way is to compute the table of joint probabilities in Table 13.1. Consider the calculation of one such joint probability, $\Pr(W\&G)$, appearing in the upper-left corner of the table. The partners reason as follows: According to their prior judgment, the site is wet 40 percent of the time. A wet site can be expected to test good three-quarters of the time. Therefore, the site is both wet and good three-quarters of 40 percent of the time, or 30 percent of the time. In algebraic terms, we have $Pr(W\&G) = (3/4)(.4) = .3$. What is the probability that the site is dry and falsely tests good (the upper right cell in the table)? Since $Pr(D) = .6$ and only one-third of dry sites test good, the joint probability is $Pr(D\&G) = (1/3)(.6) = .2$. The other joint probabilities are computed in similar fashion. The basic result is that any joint probability can be expressed as the product of a prior probability and a conditional probability reflecting the accuracy of the test. In the first calculation, we made use of the result

$$Pr(W\&G) = Pr(G|W)Pr(W). \qquad [13.1]$$

Once we have the table of joint probabilities, it is a simple matter to compute the probabilities needed for the decision tree. The probability of a given test result—say, $Pr(G)$— is found by adding across the appropriate row. In algebraic terms,

$$Pr(G) = Pr(W\&G) + Pr(D\&G), \qquad [13.2]$$

so that $Pr(G) = .3 + .2 = .5$. Note that a good test can occur when the site is really wet *and* when the site is really dry.

Next, we calculate revised probabilities. The chance that the site is wet given a good seismic test is computed as

$$Pr(W|G) = \frac{Pr(W\&G)}{Pr(G)}, \qquad [13.3]$$

so that $Pr(W|G) = .3/.5 = .6$. Similarly, we have $Pr(W|B) = Pr(W\&B)/Pr(B) = .1/.5 = .2$. Of course, these are precisely the answers we found earlier from the joint probability table. But in this case, the partners did not begin with the table in front of them; rather, they started with a prior probability, $Pr(W)$, and with information on the accuracy of the test, $Pr(G|W)$ and $Pr(B|D)$. From these facts, they were able to calculate the necessary probabilities: $Pr(G)$, $Pr(W|G)$, and $Pr(W|B)$.

Suppose the partners face the same seismic test just discussed but are less optimistic about the site; the prior probability now is $Pr(W) = .28$. Construct the joint probability table, and compute $Pr(W|G)$ and $Pr(W|B)$.   **CHECK STATION 1**

Bayes' Theorem

With a little practice, the step-by-step mechanics of calculating revised probabilities become routine. In fact, the sequence of steps can be condensed into a single formula. For example, if we replace $Pr(W\&G)$ in Equation 13.3 with the right-hand side of Equation 13.1, we obtain

$$Pr(W|G) = \left[\frac{Pr(G|W)}{Pr(G)}\right][Pr(W)] \qquad [13.4]$$

This equation is the most common form of **Bayes' theorem** (named after Reverend Thomas Bayes, who wrote an essay on the subject in 1763). Bayes' theorem expresses the conditional probability needed for the decision in terms of the reverse conditional probability and the prior probability.[1]

Bayes' theorem is more than a numerical formula. More generally, it expresses the way new information affects a decision maker's probability assessments. The decision maker begins with a prior probability assessment; this is the second bracketed term in Equation 13.4. He or she revises this prior assessment in light of new information. Note that the revised probability, $\Pr(W|G)$, depends directly on the prior probability, $\Pr(W)$. Other things being equal, the larger one's prior probability, the larger will be one's revised probability. (The only exception is in the case of *perfect* information, where $\Pr(W|G)$ is unity regardless of the prior assessment.)

Of course, the other factor affecting the revised probability is the new information itself (the first bracketed term in Equation 13.4). If the factor $[\Pr(G|W)/\Pr(G)]$ is greater than 1—that is, if $\Pr(G|W)$ is greater than $\Pr(G)$— the information will cause the partners to revise upward their probability of striking oil. But this is exactly what we would expect. If the frequency of a good test is greater for wet sites than the overall frequency of good results (for all sites, wet and dry), this means that a good test is a positive indicator of oil. The bigger the ratio $\Pr(G|W)/\Pr(G)$, the larger the upward revision. Let's look at a quick example illustrating Bayes' theorem.

HEALTH RISKS FROM SMOKING   About 1 in 12 American adults is a heavy smoker. One way to assess the health risk of heavy smoking is to study the population of individuals who have lung cancer. Among individuals suffering from lung cancer, the proportion of heavy smokers is 1 in 3. Based on these facts, by what factor does the risk of lung cancer increase due to heavy smoking?

Using Bayes' theorem is the key to answering this question. Analogous to Equation 13.4, we write

$$\Pr(LC|S) = \left[\frac{\Pr(S|LC)}{\Pr(S)} \right] \Pr(LC),$$

where LC denotes lung cancer and S a heavy smoker. We know that $[\Pr(S|LC)/\Pr(S)] = (1/3)/(1/12) = 4$. Then, from the preceding equation, we conclude that $\Pr(LC|S) = 4\Pr(LC)$. In words, the risk of lung cancer for a smoker is *four* times the overall risk of lung cancer (for smokers and nonsmokers together).

CHECK STATION 2   **The partners face the same seismic test as earlier and (as in Check Station 1) hold the prior probability $\Pr(W) = .28$. Determine the optimal actions in light of the test, and calculate the resulting expected profit. What is the value of the test?**

---

[1]An expanded version of Bayes' theorem is obtained by taking the right-hand side of Equation 13.2 and substituting it for the denominator in Equation 13.4:

$$\Pr(W|G) = \frac{\Pr(G|W)\,\Pr(W)}{\Pr(G|W)\,\Pr(W) + \Pr(G|D)\,\Pr(D)}.$$

The partners have available numerical values for all the right-hand-side variables and thus can calculate $\Pr(W|G)$ directly. Note that the numerator is $\Pr(G\&W)$, and this term is repeated in the denominator along with $\Pr(G\&D)$. From this version of Bayes' theorem, we see that the magnitude of $\Pr(W|G)$ depends directly on the frequency of the event "good and wet" relative to the frequency of "good and dry."

VALUELESS INFORMATION   Not all new information is of value to the decision maker. The key question in evaluating new information is: What impact does it have in revising the decision maker's initial probability assessment? Consider again Bayes' theorem (Equation 13.4) in the context of the oil-drilling problem:

$$\Pr(W|G) = \left[\frac{\Pr(G|W)}{\Pr(G)}\right] \Pr(W).$$

Suppose the test's past track record is such that $\Pr(G|W) = \Pr(G)$. In words, this says the chance of getting a good test for sites containing oil is no greater than the overall frequency of good tests at all sites, wet and dry. Clearly, the test would appear to have little predictive value; its result is completely uncorrelated with the true condition of the site, wet or dry. Bayes' theorem confirms that the test is *valueless*. Since the first factor in Equation 13.4 is 1, it follows that $\Pr(W|G) = \Pr(W)$. The new probability is identical to the prior probability; there is no probability revision. This being the case, the partners' decisions will not be affected by the outcome of the test. Obviously, then, their expected profit also will be unchanged; that is, the expected value of this new information will be zero. Such information is worthless.

The partners wish to evaluate the quality of a new seismic test before deciding to pay for it. They assess the following joint probabilities: $\Pr(W\&G) = .32$, $\Pr(B\&D) = .12$, $\Pr(B\&W) = .08$, and $\Pr(G\&D) = .48$. What is the value of the test?   **CHECK STATION 3**

There is one other important case in which new information or a test result would have no value. This occurs when the decision maker's optimal decision is unaffected by the test result even though the test outcome may cause him or her to revise key probabilities. The decision maker takes the same actions with or without the test and so earns the same expected profit in each instance. Again, the EVI is zero. Here's an illustrative example.

A NEW SEISMIC TEST   Suppose the quality of a new seismic test is summarized in the table. What is the EVI of this test?

	Wet (W)	Dry (D)	Total
Good (G)	.1	.1	.2
Bad (B)	.3	.5	.8
Total	.4	.6	1.0

From the table, we calculate that $\Pr(W|G) = .1/.2 = .5$ and $\Pr(W|B) = .3/.8 = .375$. After seeing a good test, the partners drill and attain an expected profit of 200,000. After a bad test, what expected profit would drilling bring? The requisite calculation is:

$$E(\pi) = (.375)(600,000) + (.625)(-200,000) = \$100,000.$$

Since drilling is profitable, the partners should drill even in light of a bad test result.

What is the overall expected profit with the test? After good tests (20 percent of the time), the partners drill and earn $200,000. After bad tests (the other 80 percent of the time), they also drill and earn $100,000. Thus, their expected profit is: (.2)(200,000) + (.8)(100,000) = $120,000. It should not come as a surprise that this is exactly the same profit they would earn without the test. Without the test, the optimal action is to drill. With the test, the optimal action is to drill. Since they take the same actions with or without the test, they earn the same expected profit in each instance.

What is the general lesson to be learned from this example? Acquiring new information is beneficial if and only if it has the potential to affect the manager's actual decisions. If it does not, the information is of no value.[2]

OTHER APPLICATIONS

For pedagogical purposes, we have made intensive use of the oil-drilling example. However, it is important to stress the *general* application of information issues in all types of business and public policy decisions. In a host of settings, the decision maker is confronted with the task of quantifying his or her uncertainty, that is, estimating a probability. Here are some examples:

- The largest consumer-products firms launch between 15 and 25 new products each year from a potential pool of 50 to 100 candidates. How can the firms' product managers judge the likely success rates of different products? Which kinds of products (and marketing campaigns) have been most successful in the past? Based on surveys and market tests, how should the companies reassess their products' chances of success?

- In the relentless pursuit of quality, a parts supplier for the automobile industry seeks to reduce its rate of product defects. How does it estimate its defect rate? How can it identify the key factors that affect this rate? Would modifying its production-line process reduce the rate?

- Do a chemical company's emissions into the air (at levels within legal standards) pose a health risk for its workers or the surrounding residents? Are they responsible for an increased rate of certain types of cancer in the community? Is the cancer rate actually elevated, and, if so, what other factors (age or other characteristics of the population, or even chance) would account for this?

In the preceding examples and in most other similar problems, there is no shortage of historical data that may have a bearing on the probability being estimated. The tough questions are: What is the best way to interpret the data? How can the manager identify factors that distinguish when a risk will be high or low? These are not easy questions to answer. Nonetheless, the road to the answers almost always begins with constructing two-dimensional tables of probabilities. Such tables look much like those in the wildcatter example. The column headings list the actual risk or uncertain event of concern to

---

[2]This point holds regardless of the decision maker's attitude toward risk. Given the opportunity to acquire information, a risk-averse manager solves the same decision tree as his or her risk-neutral counterpart but uses expected utility as a guide. Information is valuable if the expected utility with the information (after accounting for its cost) exceeds the expected utility without it.

the decision maker. The row headings summarize the way in which the decision maker has categorized the data—identifying factors that influence the relevant risk. The next section presents a typical example.

Predicting Credit Risks

How can a bank assess and accurately predict the creditworthiness of a new business customer? In recent years, banks have increasingly turned to statistical measures, compiling computerized composite credit scores for customers. The bank's aim is to distinguish high- and low-risk accounts, closing or reducing credit limits on the former and increasing limits on the latter.

Consider how the method works in screening traditional business loans. The loan division of a bank has spent considerable time and energy developing a scoring system for predicting the default rates on different loan accounts.[3] The scoring formula incorporates key characteristics of the customer, the type and purpose of the loan, and forecasts of future economic conditions, all of which influence or indicate the risk of default. Bank officers put each loan into one of four categories on the basis of these scores. After a year's experience with the system, the bank is ready to assess its performance. In doing so, it has constructed the data in Table 13.2a. The table shows the breakdown of "performing" (paying) loans in the four categories and defaulted loans (also by category) over the past year.

Last year, the overall rate of default by the bank's business customers was 1 in 10 loan accounts. The overall quality of business customers seeking loans this year is expected to be unchanged from last (as is the general business climate). How should the bank use this information in making loan decisions? Table 13.2b provides the answer. This table computes the joint probabilities of all possible events by multiplying prior and conditional probabilities. For example, the proportion of all loans that are designated in class A and that default is

$$\Pr(\text{default \& } A) = \Pr(A|\text{default})\Pr(\text{default}).$$
$$= (.1)(.1) = .01$$

The other entries in the joint probability table are calculated in similar fashion.

The bank's final step (Table 13.2c) is to compute revised probabilities: the default risk for each designated loan category. These risks are approximately 5, 5, 13, and 25 percent for the respective categories. We can draw several observations from these results. First, as we might expect, loans identified as "high-risk" (class D) have by far the greatest probability of default. Presumably these loans were extended under much stricter conditions—higher interest rates, stiffer collateral conditions, lower loan amounts—because of their risk. Still, it is natural to ask whether the bank's loan officers (at the time of granting) recognized exactly how risky class D loans were. (Perhaps at the time they saw them as 15 to 20 percent risks.) In light of the actual 25 percent default rate, the

---

[3]For an account of banks' scoring methods, see M. Quint, "Banks Raise Scrutiny of Credit Cards," *The New York Times* (March 27, 1991), p. D1, and R. Simon, "Looking to Improve Your Credit Score? Fair Isaac Can Help," *The Wall Street Journal* (March 19, 2002), p. A1.

TABLE 13.2

Assessing Loan Risks

Part a lists the frequency of loan categories by actual default experience. Part b lists the joint probabilities of all outcomes.

(a) Frequencies of Loan Categories by Actual Default Record

Category	Performing Loan	Defaulted Loan
A ("zero" risk)	.2	.1
B (solid)	.4	.2
C (uncertain)	.3	.4
D (high risk)	.1	.3
Total	1.0	1.0

For example, 10 percent of all defaulted loans were (incorrectly) judged to be "zero" risk at the time the money was lent.

(b) Joint Probabilities

Category	Performing Loan	Defaulted Loan	Total
A ("zero" risk)	.18	.01	.19
B (solid)	.36	.02	.38
C (uncertain)	.27	.04	.31
D (high risk)	.09	.03	.12
Total	.90	.10	1.00

(c) Conditional Probabilities

$Pr(default|A) = .01/.19 = .05$

$Pr(default|B) = .02/.38 = .05$

$Pr(default|C) = .04/.31 = .13$

$Pr(default|D) = .03/.12 = .25$

bank may be well advised to stop making class D loans altogether (or make them under even more stringent conditions).

A second observation is that the actual default risks for class A and class B loans are indistinguishable. The scoring system seemingly does not work very well in gauging small risks; that is, it makes a distinction when none exists. This suggests taking a closer look at the class A (zero-risk) loans that actually failed. Do these loans share common attributes? Could the scoring system be modified to identify these loans as low-risk class B loans? To sum up, the scoring system provides valuable information bearing on actual loan performance. However, the bank probably has further work to do in refining the system.

Business Behavior and Decision Pitfalls

By now you should be familiar with and practiced in the simple mechanics of computing probabilities based on new information. Of course, the typical manager (and, to be sure, the average person) does not have Bayes' theorem memorized; rather, the manager probably uses informal prediction methods based on personal judgment, experience, and intuition. However, there are two main problems with informal approaches.

The first difficulty is that the logic underlying the prediction often is uncheckable, or at least hard to pin down. What factors led the individual to make that prediction? How would this forecast change under different circumstances or assumptions? Some sort of logical analysis is necessary to answer these questions. Even forecasters with track records of accurate predictions must be able to explain their methodology to others. Again, formal analysis is essential. To take an extreme case, how confident would you be in a forecaster, no matter how accurate the track record, if he or she confessed to using astrological tables or a Ouija board?

The second difficulty is that forecasts based informally on intuition, judgment, and experience frequently are inaccurate or biased. For instance, a common layperson's belief is that a large head, forehead, or brain is a sign of intelligence. But scientific evidence shows this hypothesis to be false. Perhaps the best way to understand the difficulties in making probabilistic predictions is to test yourself on some short (but subtle) examples.

For each of the following examples, use your informal judgment to come up with your own best probability estimate of the event in question. After recording your intuitive responses, you may wish to use a formal method (a joint probability table or Bayes' theorem) to find solutions. Keep yourself honest by writing down your responses before turning to the answers that follow.

EXAMPLE 1   An individual, picked at random from the US labor force, is described in the following short psychological sketch:

> Steve is shy and withdrawn, with little interest in people or the world of reality. He has a need for order and structure and a passion for detail.

Which of the following is Steve's most likely occupation: (1) farmer, (2) salesperson, (3) librarian, (4) airline pilot, or (5) doctor?

EXAMPLE 2   You are presented with three boxes. Each box has two compartments. In one box there is a gold coin in each compartment. In the second, there is a silver coin in each compartment. In the third, there is a gold coin in one compartment and a silver coin in the other. The compartments are closed, and the boxes (identical from the outside) are randomly mixed. You choose one box and are allowed to open one compartment. Suppose you see a silver coin. What are the chances that the coin in the other compartment is silver?

EXAMPLE 3   During his annual medical examination, a 59-year-old man was found to have blood in his stool, a possible indication of cancer of the bowel. This cancer is relatively rare; for a man this age, the incidence of bowel cancer is about 1 in 1,000. It is also quite curable provided it is identified early, while still small. In answer to his questions, the man is told that a sophisticated cancer test is available, and this test is 95 percent accurate. (If cancer is present, the test will be positive with 95 percent probability. Likewise, if there is no cancer, the test will be negative 95 percent of the time.) Suppose the test result is positive. What is the chance that the man has cancer of the bowel?

EXAMPLE 1   For this question, the most common response by far is librarian, followed by farmer and airline pilot. Apparently, the psychological sketch fits the commonly perceived stereotype of a librarian. Overlooked in this answer is one crucial fact: The individual has been picked at random from the labor force. This being the case, one's prior probability (before reading the sketch) should be heavily weighted toward salesperson. Salespeople comprise roughly 15 percent of the labor force; farmers are next, at under 3 percent; and librarians comprise only a fraction of 1 percent. How much should the sketch alter these prior probabilities? Surely very little, since we have but two sentences about Steve, and they are not very informative or discriminating. Perhaps half of all persons might be described as orderly and passionate about detail. Up to a quarter of the population might regard themselves as "shy." Moreover, not all librarians are shy, nor are all salespersons gregarious. In short, the observation that the worker has been picked at random is the overriding determinant of his likely occupation. Nonetheless, most people overlook this fact and invest too much confidence in the relatively uninformative sketch.

EXAMPLE 2   The nearly unanimous answer to this question is 50 percent. One reasons that the draw rules out the gold-gold box, leaving either the silver-silver or gold-silver boxes as equally likely. Despite its overwhelming intuitive appeal, this answer is wrong. The chances are two in three that the other coin will be silver. An easy way to see this is to note that there are a total of three silver coins in the boxes, and the coin you see is equally likely to be any of the three. But two of these coins reside in the all-silver box, meaning its neighbor is silver. Only one of the silver coins has a gold neighbor. Thus, upon seeing a silver coin, the odds are two to one against the other coin being gold. Bayes' theorem provides a neat confirmation of this correct answer:

$$\Pr(SS \text{ box}|S) = \left[\frac{\Pr(S|SS \text{ box})}{\Pr(S)} \right] \Pr(SS \text{ box}).$$

On the right-hand side, the first term is 1.0 (a silver coin is a certainty from the SS box), the second term is .5 (the overall chance of picking a silver coin is $1/2$), and the last term (the prior chance of picking the SS box at random) is $1/3$. Thus, we find $\Pr(SS \text{ box}|S) = (1.0/.5)(1/3) = 2/3$.

EXAMPLE 3   On the basis of the near-perfect test, most respondents see cancer as very likely, in the range of 50 to 95 percent. However, the correct chance is only about 2 percent. This surprising answer can be confirmed by using Bayes' theorem or applying the following simple reasoning. Suppose 1,000 59-year-old men were to be tested. According to the prior probability, one man actually would have cancer; with near certainty, he would test positive. Of the remaining 999 healthy men, 95 percent would test negative. But 5 percent, or 50 men, would record false positives. In all, one would expect 51 positives, 1 true and 50 false. Thus, $\Pr(\text{cancer}|+) = 1/51$, or about 2 percent. Why is this probability so low? It is because the disease is very rare in the first place. Because the test is not quite perfect, the false positives tend to swamp the true positives. Thus, the revised probability is much lower than intuition would suggest. We should note that the test caused a large probability revision: a 20-fold increase from 1 in 1,000 to 2 in 100. In this sense, the test is quite informative. Thus, it may be very valuable in guiding subsequent medical treatment.

These examples are representative of a host of applications (used by economists and psychologists in their research) showing the systematic errors individuals make in predicting probabilities. A number of important conclusions emerge from this research. First, individuals are *overconfident* in their abilities to make such predictions. Consequently, their prediction mistakes (large and recurrent as they may be) always come as a surprise. (Even for professional forecasters, the common saying is "often wrong, never in doubt.") Second, individuals make mistakes in combining new and old information. In many cases, individuals put too much weight on seemingly compelling information (the psychological sketch or the positive medical test) and too little weight on the underlying prior probability of the event in question. In other cases, they fail to appreciate the weight that should be given statistical information (particularly when based on large, random samples).

To sum up, the evidence on individual intuitive prediction delivers a cautionary message. The use of formal analysis guided by Bayes' theorem offers a much better guide to probabilistic prediction.

Based on 20 years of hiring experience, a small business owner swears that job candidates who were varsity athletes in high school make the best salespeople. How would you go about assessing this conclusion?

CHECK STATION 4

The *Challenger* Disaster and NASA's Risk Analysis

On January 28, 1986, the space shuttle *Challenger* exploded 74 seconds after take-off, killing schoolteacher Christa McAuliffe and the six astronauts on board. The presidential commission that investigated the disaster faulted a series of decisions by NASA surrounding the flight.[4] Beset by escalating costs and three previous launch delays, NASA went ahead with the January launch despite the knowledge of potential risks.

Indeed, the commission's principal criticism focused on NASA failures to recognize and accurately assess key launch risks. The explosion was caused by a blow-out of the O-ring seal between two sections of the booster rocket. Moreover, on the basis of their experience with earlier shuttle flights, NASA and Morton Thiokol, the maker of the booster rocker, were aware of possible O-ring problems. O-ring wear had been observed on 7 of the 24 previous shuttle launches. Of course, the rockets had always done the job on the previous launches. So who could argue with a run of 24 successes?

If some O-ring damage was occurring, what was the proximate cause? NASA scientists had some concerns about the link between low launch temperatures and O-ring failures. These concerns became more salient when a cold front and temperatures of 30 degrees Fahrenheit were forecast for January 28. Because of the cold, a prominent Morton Thiokol engineer recommended against the launch. But this advice was overruled, and the warning was not communicated to top NASA officials. The temperature was 36 degrees Fahrenheit at launch time.

---

[4]This account is drawn from a number of sources: W. Biddle, "What Destroyed the Challenger?" *Discover Magazine* (April 1986): 40–47; D. L. Chandler, "NASA's System for Assessing Risks Is Faulted," *Boston Globe* (March 5, 1988), p. 26; and J. E. Russo and P. J. Schoemaker, *Decision Traps* (New York: Simon and Schuster, 1990), pp. 196–198.

The following temperature line shows the data that NASA scientists gathered on the eve of the launch. The diagram shows the launch temperatures for

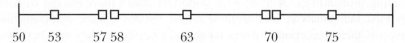

the previous seven shuttle flights that had experienced O-ring wear. These "problem" launches occurred at both high and low temperatures, so the diagram reveals no discernible association between low launch temperatures and O-ring wear. Five of the seven flights had shown wear on a single O-ring, but the launch at 53 degrees Fahrenheit had experienced wear on three rings. An indication of low-temperature problems, perhaps? However, the launch at 75 degrees also exhibited abnormal wear, this time on two O-rings. It is not surprising that NASA scientists, based on this evidence, saw no real O-ring risks from low-temperature launches.

Was there evidence available that NASA overlooked? The answer is yes. NASA's crucial error was its failure to appreciate the evidence of the 17 "uneventful" flights. In fact, every one of the launches that were free of O-ring damage occurred at temperatures of 65 degrees and above. Against this background, the incidence of O-ring wear at relatively low temperature looks quite damning. For instance, it is instructive to list the outcomes of all 24 launches in a simple two-by-two table. (The table uses 65° as a dividing line but the results are unaffected if 63° or 67° degrees was chosen instead.)

	O-Ring Wear	No O-Ring Wear	Total
Temperature > 65°	3	17	20
Temperature < 65°	4	0	4
Total	7	17	24

The message of the table should be clear. Once we have separated out the most frequent outcome, high-temperature launches showing no wear, we are left with four launches made at lower temperatures (below 65°), *all of which experienced O-ring damage.* Thus, the table offers strong evidence that low-temperature launches entail O-ring risks.

By failing to incorporate the results of the "uneventful" flights in addition to the "problem" flights, NASA came up short in its risk assessment. To put this as simply as possible, data in all four cells of a two-by-two table are needed to establish an association between any two factors. Why did NASA miss such an apparently simple association? The investigative panel pointed to one important reason. NASA diligently compiled a checklist of over 4,500 "critical" risk factors. However, all these factors were treated equally, with no effort to distinguish the "most critical" factors. NASA should have set priorities according to the likelihood of each factor leading to system failure. Indeed, tests conducted for the presidential panel after the shuttle disaster showed that O-ring failure was much more sensitive to changes in temperature than had been previously imagined. If NASA had recognized the need to acquire this test information in advance, it would have certainly abandoned the cold-weather launch.

AUCTIONS AND COMPETITIVE BIDDING

Auctions are a common means of selling goods (and also buying goods, in the case of competitive procurements). Auctions thrive in economic settings marked by uncertainty. Because a well-developed market does not already exist, auctions are used to determine the best final price, what the "market will bear." Auctions involve two kinds of decisions under uncertainty. As a competitor, how should a firm bid to maximize its expected profit from the auction? In turn, how can the auctioning party design competitive bidding institutions to maximize the expected price it obtains?

To address these questions, we need to describe the kind of uncertainty present in the auction environment and the auction method used:

1. In the **private-value** auction setting, each bidder knows his own private value or *reservation price* for the item at auction but is uncertain about the possible valuations of competing bidders. For instance, a potential buyer has closely examined an antique Persian rug up for auction and has determined that her reservation price for the rug is $1,000. She has only a general idea of the possible values other bidders might place on the rug. The private-value model applies to all kinds of personal items that are for the buyer's private use and are not intended for resale.

2. In the **common-value** setting, the item at auction has mainly the same, but unknown, value to all bidders. However, each bidder typically holds differing information about the item's value. An oil lease, an office building, a company that is a target of competitive tender offers—all of these examples fit the common-value model. In all these cases, would-be buyers might hold different opinions on the value of the item up for bid, and this true value will only become known in the future. In the case of the oil lease, this value won't be determined until after the site is drilled.

Next, we need to consider the type of auction method. The two most frequently used methods are the **English** and **sealed-bid** auctions. In the familiar English ascending auction, the auctioneer calls for higher and higher bids, and the last and highest bid claims the item. By contrast, in a sealed-bid auction, buyers submit private bids, bids are opened, and the highest bidder claims the item and pays its bid. As we shall see, these methods imply very different strategies on the parts of bidders.

Private-Value Auctions

THE ENGLISH AUCTION   Suppose that a Persian rug is to be sold by English auction, and there are six bidders, each of whom has determined its private value for the rug. Call these values, $v_1, v_2, \ldots v_6$. If buyer 1 were to win the bidding at price P, his profit from the purchase would be $v_1 - P$, the difference between what it's worth to him and the price he pays. Optimal bidder strategies in the English auction turn out to be remarkably simple:

> When buyers hold private values, each buyer's dominant strategy in an English auction is to bid for the item up to the buyer's reservation price if necessary.

In the English auction, a buyer should never place a bid above his or her true value; this would imply a loss if the bid were to win. Nor should the buyer stop and be outbid short of his or her value; this needlessly precludes earning a profit should a slightly higher bid win. Bidding up to full value (if necessary) is optimal regardless of the competitors' values or the bid strategies they might use; that is, this is a dominant strategy. Notice that the bidding stops when the price barely rises above the next-to-last bidder's value. Thus, the winning English price is at a level approximately equal to the second-highest reservation price: $P_E = v_{2nd}$. The bidder holding the highest value, v_{MAX}, wins the item and gains a profit of $v_{MAX} - v_{2nd}$. For instance, if $v_{MAX} = \$1,000$ and $v_{2nd} = \$800$ among the six bidders, the final auction price will be (just over) $800.

THE SEALED-BID AUCTION   Bidding strategy in a sealed-bid auction—given the inherent uncertainty about rivals' sealed bids—is considerably more complicated. Any bidder (buyer 1, for instance) should submit a sealed bid that is well below her true reservation price in order to earn a profit, $v_1 - b_1$, if she should win. But in determining how low a bid, the buyer faces a fundamental trade-off between the probability and profitability of winning. In lowering her sealed bid, the buyer increases her profit from winning but lowers the probability that she beats the highest competing bid. (Similarly, in a competitive procurement where the lowest price wins, raising one's bid increases the supplier's winning profit but lowers the firm's chance of being selected.) Given this trade-off, it is natural to ask: What constitutes a profit-maximizing bid?

To keep things simple, suppose that there are only two bidders in the rug auction. Each knows his or her own value and believes that the others' sealed bid is sure to fall in the range $600 to $900, with all values in this range equally likely. The first bidder's self-assessed reservation price is $1,000. Then, we can show that her profit-maximizing sealed bid is $b_1 = \$800$. To see this, consider her expected profit:

$$E(\pi) = [1,000 - b_1][\Pr(b_1 \text{ wins})].$$

Because the possible bids of the rival, buyer 2, are distributed uniformly between $600 and $900, a particular bid b_1 wins with probability: $(b_1 - 600)/300$. For instance, a bid of $700 wins with probability one-third, a bid of $750 (at the median of the range) wins with probability .5, and a bid of $900 wins with certainty. Substituting the probability expression into the expected profit equation yields

$$E(\pi) = (1,000 - b_1)\left(\frac{b_1 - 600}{300}\right).$$

The bidder's marginal profit is $M\pi = dE(\pi)/db_1 = [1{,}000 - 2b_1 + 600]/300$. Setting this equal to zero implies: $b_1 = (.5)(600) + (.5)(1{,}000) = \$800$, as claimed. Note that buyer 1's expected profit is zero for the extreme bids, \$600 (so low that she never wins), and \$1,000 (so high that she makes no profit). Buyer 1's optimal bid is exactly halfway between these extremes.

If the number of bidders increases, we would expect this to cause all buyers to increase their sealed bids in order to have any chance of beating rival bids. This is, indeed, the case. For example, suppose there are three bidders. Buyer 1 believes that each of the rival's bids will fall in the \$600 to \$900 range, and that these bids are drawn *independently* in this range. (So the actual value of the second buyer's bid has no influence on the likely value of the third buyer's bid and vice versa.) Buyer 1 is thinking of bidding \$750, which happens to be at the midpoint of this range. Although the chance of beating a single rival bid is .5, the chance of beating both bids is only: $(.5)^2 = .25$. If buyer 1 is to have any real chance of winning and securing a maximum expected profit, she must raise her sealed bid.

In fact, in this example, we can write down the buyer's profit-maximizing bidding strategy as it depends on the number of bidders (N). The firm's optimal bidding strategy is: $b_1 = [1/N](600) + [(N-1)/N](1{,}000)$. Note for $N = 2$, $b_1 = \$800$ as shown before. By comparison, if $N = 4$, then $b_1 = \$900$, and if $N = 8$, then $b_1 = \$950$.

Here is the general rule. When there are N risk-neutral bidders and each bidder's value is independently and uniformly drawn from a range with lower bound L and upper bound U, the typical buyer's optimal sealed-bid strategy is:

$$b_1 = [1/N]L + [(N-1)/N]v_1.$$

Note that a buyer's optimal bid is a weighted average of the lowest possible value and bid ($L = \$600$ in our example) and the buyer's own reservation value, v_1. As the number of bidders increases, buyers bid closer and closer to their reservation values. (For instance, with 10 bidders, the coefficient multiplying v_1 becomes .9). These optimal sealed-bid strategies also constitute a Nash equilibrium. Each buyer's bid strategy maximizes its expected profit against the strategies of the others.

Common-Value Auctions

THE SEALED-BID AUCTION   The US government periodically sells offshore oil tracts via sealed-bid auctions. The value of any tract is highly uncertain, depending on whether oil is found, at what depth and at what cost, and future oil prices. Except for differences in costs, the profit from the tract is likely to be similar across firms. Thus, to a greater or lesser degree, the tract has a **common value** for all bidders. The difficulty is that this value is unknown. In making its bid, typically the bidding firm will form an estimate of the tract's potential value. Obviously, this estimate will be subject to error, and firms may hold very different estimates of value. How should a profit-maximizing firm bid in this situation?

Figure 13.3 depicts sealed bidding behavior when the item for bid has a common unknown value. The true (but unknown) value is labeled V. Centered at V is the distribution of possible bidder estimates (curve E). The figure depicts a normal distribution of

FIGURE 13.3

The Winner's Curse

When the value of
the item is highly
uncertain, a winning
bid drawn from the
right tail of the bid
distribution may
exceed the true value
of the item.

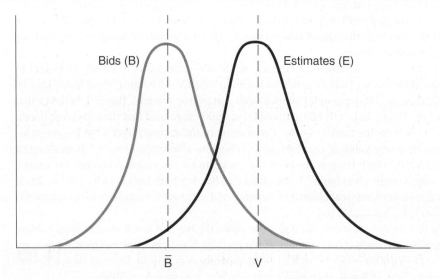

estimates. On average, estimates reflect the true value, *V*, but there is considerable dispersion. Some buyers underestimate and others overestimate the true value. The figure also depicts a typical distribution of bids (curve B). Clearly, each bidder, seeking a profit, submits a bid well below its estimate of value. This explains why the bid distribution is centered well to the left of (i.e., below) the estimate distribution.

Here is an important observation to draw from Figure 13.3. A winning bid drawn from the right tail of the bid distribution may exceed the true value of the item. The shaded tail shows the portion of the distribution of bids that exceeds the true value. For a bid in this region, the buyer is said to fall prey to the **winner's curse**. After the fact, the auction winner finds that the good obtained is worth less than the price paid for it. The source of the winner's curse lies in the fact that the winning bidder has been too optimistic and has grossly overestimated the good's value. When the firm's (upward) estimation error exceeds its bid discount, it buys the good at a price greater than its value. For instance, suppose the true value of the oil tract is $2 million, but the most optimistic bidder believes it's worth $3 million. Hoping to win the lease at a profit, this firm bids $2.3 million (discounts its estimate by $.7 million) but still ends up overpaying and experiencing a $.3 million loss on the tract.

The key to avoiding the winner's curse is for the bidder to recognize that the act of winning conveys information about the bidder's estimate relative to others. In all likelihood, winning means that the bidder probably overestimated the true value. Put another way, *conditional on winning the auction, the buyer should figure the item's true value to be significantly less than its original estimate.* The upshot is that each buyer should estimate the tract's value by first discounting its original estimate before making a bid.

The potential size of the winner's curse depends on two factors: the degree of uncertainty surrounding the item's value and the number of bidders. Obviously, the winner's curse is impossible if there is no uncertainty. No firm knowingly will bid above the item's true value. The larger the dispersion of estimates and therefore the dispersion of bids, the greater the degree of overbidding by the winning buyer. A more subtle point is that an increase in the number of bidders raises the frequency of the winner's curse. As the number of bidders rises, so will the range of actual estimates and bids. If there are only two bidders, it is unlikely that either will hold an estimate in the extreme right tail. But when there are many bidders, the presence of one or more optimistic, right-tail bidders becomes much more likely.

How much should a buyer discount his original estimate to assess correctly the item's true acquisition value and so avoid the winner's curse? First, the buyer's bid discount depends on the degree of uncertainty surrounding the item's value. If uncertainty is great so that an optimistic estimate is likely to be 30 percent too high on average, the bid discount must be at least this large. Second, as the number of bidders increases, the bid discount should increase—that is, a buyer's sealed bid should be reduced. Winning against a greater number of bidders means that the buyer's estimate is farther in Figure 13.3's right tail. To avoid overpaying, the buyer must fashion a bid that is at a greater discount to its original estimate. Against more rivals, the buyer should bid more conservatively, not more aggressively.

THE ENGLISH AUCTION   When the item up for bid has a common but unknown value, bidding at an English auction becomes more subtle and complex than in a private, independent value setting. Because of winner's curse considerations, the bidder cannot simply plan to bid up to its value estimate. Observing the number of active bidders and when they drop out conveys information about competitors' estimates and, therefore, the item's unknown value. Thus, the buyer's upper bid limit should incorporate these observations. If many rivals have already dropped out and only a few are left bidding, the buyer should significantly temper his estimate of the tract's value.

Expected Auction Revenue

Research in both the theory and practice of auctions indicates a number of ways in which the seller can maximize its expected revenue when auctioning items for sale.

1. The seller should always enlist as many bidders as possible. In either the English or sealed-bid auction, more numerous bidders means greater competition—higher sealed bids or a greater chance of continually rising English bids—and therefore, a higher expected final price.

2. In either auction, the seller should always set a reserve price—a minimum price below which the item will not be sold. If competition is relatively weak at the auction, this reserve protects the seller from parting with the item at too low a price. Typically, the reserve should be set strategically, at a level greater than the seller's true reservation value.

3. Depending on the setting, the English auction or the sealed bid auction might deliver the greater expected revenue.

   A. **Revenue equivalence**—whereby the two auctions deliver the same expected revenue—holds in the symmetric, independent, private-value setting. The term "symmetric" means that all buyers are risk neutral and that their private values are drawn independently of one another from the *same* common distribution. Remember that bidding in the English auction stops at a price equal to the *second highest* buyer value, v_{2nd}. By comparison, in the sealed bid auction, the seller gains the *highest* sealed bid. So, one's first impression might be that the sealed-bid auction is superior. But remember that buyers behave strategically in shading their sealed bids well below their true reservation prices. How much do they shade on average? Just enough to cause the level of the highest sealed bid to match, on average, the second-highest value among the buyers.

   B. If bidders are risk averse or if values are asymmetrically distributed (some buyers are known to likely hold higher values than others), the sealed- bid auction generates greater expected revenue than the English. Conversely, in the common-value setting, the English auction attenuates the risk of the winner's curse, so savvy buyers can afford to bid higher than in the sealed-bid auction. Here, the English auction enjoys an expected revenue advantage.[5]

The Stock Market and the Economy Revisited

As noted at the beginning of the chapter, the stock market has dropped precipitously prior to all seven postwar recessions. In light of a sustained stock market drop, some analysts have concluded that there will be a forthcoming recession. Do you agree?

The answer is not a simple yes. As a famous economist once said, "The stock market has predicted 12 of the last 7 recessions." Thus, in at least five instances, stock prices have fallen without a subsequent economic recession. In these cases, stock price movements were a false indicator of the future course of the economy.

Table 13.3a illustrates the point. While the US economy has suffered seven periods of recession in the postwar period, the norm has been a growing economy. (The table shows that the economy grew in 30 out of 37 periods, or roughly 81 percent of the time.) The stock market fell prior to all seven recessions, but it also fell prior to periods of economic growth.

Now let's return to the boat dealer's decision introduced in Chapter 12. Recall that the dealer assessed a .6 chance for a growing economy. This is more pessimistic than historical experience would suggest. Based on this forecast, the dealer's optimal course of action was to order 50 boats, thereby earning an expected profit of $175,000. We now can ask, How should the dealer revise this forecast of economic conditions in light of stock market movements? How many boats should the dealer order?

[5]However, if buyers tend to bid naively (rather than optimally), they will be much more likely to fall prey to the "winner's curse" in a sealed-bid auction (where they are in the dark about competing bids) than in an English auction. In this case, the sealed-bid auction would hold a revenue advantage for the seller. For empirical evidence on auction revenues, see: W. Samuelson, "Auctions: Advances in Theory and Practice," in K. Chatterjee and W. Samuelson (eds.), *Game Theory and Business Applications,* Chapter 13 (New York: Springer Academic Publishers, 2014).

TABLE 13.3

The Stock Market as a
Leading Indicator of the
Economy

a. The Historical Record	Economy Grows (G)	Recession (R)	Total
Stocks Rise (S+)	25	0	25
Stocks Drop (S−)	5	7	12
Total	30	7	37

b. The Boat Dealer's Assessed Probabilities	Economy Grows (G)	Recession (R)	Total
Stocks Rise (S+)	.5	0	.5
Stocks Drop (S−)	.1	.4	.5
Total	.6	.4	1.0

From Table 13.3a, we have $\Pr(S- |R) = 7/7 = 1.0$ and $\Pr(S+ |G) = 25/30 = .833$. Using this information, we construct Table 13.3b. Note that the table is based on the dealer's prior probability, $\Pr(G) = .6$. The upper-left entry lists the joint probability that stocks rise $(S+)$ and the economy grows (G). This is computed as

$$\Pr(S+\&G) = \Pr(S+ |G)\Pr(G) = (.833)(.6) = .50.$$

Similarly,

$$\Pr(S-\&G) = \Pr(S- |G)\Pr(G) = (.166)(.6) = .10.$$

The second column is self-explanatory. We can readily compute revised probabilities from Table 13.3b:

$$\Pr(G|S+) = .5/.5 = 1.0$$

and

$$\Pr(G|S-) = .1/.5 = .20.$$

The decision tree in Figure 13.4 completes the solution. In light of a rising stock market, there is no chance of a recession. Accordingly, the dealer should order 100 boats, anticipating an expected profit of $350,000. If the stock market falls, there is an 80 percent chance of a recession. The best the dealer can do is to order 50 boats, earning an expected profit of $125,000. Averaging the cases of rising and falling stock prices, the dealer can anticipate an overall expected profit of $(.5)(350,000) + (.5)(125,000) = \$237,500$. The dealer does well to gear the size of the order to future prospects of the economy as signaled by stock movements. Chapter 12's analysis indicated, without any additional information, the dealer's best action was to order 50 boats, for an expected profit of $175,000. Accordingly, the dealer's expected value of information is: EVI = $237,500 − $175,000 = $62,500.

FIGURE 13.4

Yacht Orders and the
Stock Market

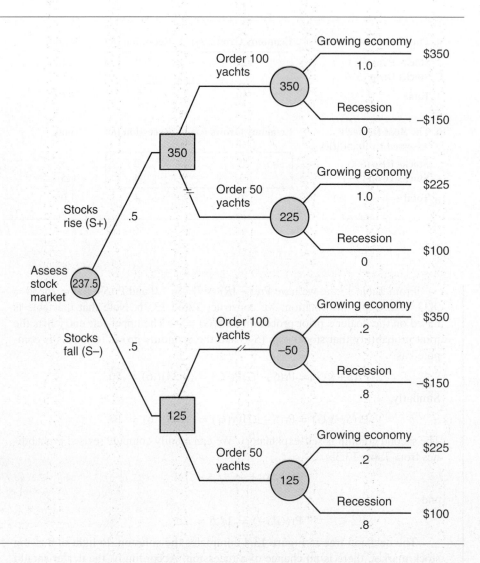

SUMMARY

Decision-Making Principles

1. Any new information source is potentially valuable in influencing forecasts of uncertain events and thus guiding better decisions.
   a. The decision maker should acquire additional information if and only if its expected value (in making better decisions) exceeds its cost.
   b. The decision maker should not commit needlessly to a single course of action for the foreseeable future. By crossing bridges only when he or she comes to them, the decision maker can expect to make better-informed decisions.

2. The logic of Bayes' theorem shows that any probability forecast is based on a combination of the decision maker's previous information (his or her prior probabilities) and newly acquired information.
   a. The greater the initial degree of uncertainty or the stronger the new evidence, the greater the subsequent probability revision.
   b. Information is valueless if it results in no probability revisions or, even with such revisions, if it does not change the individual's optimal decisions.
3. Although most business and government decision makers rely on informal prediction methods, evidence shows that these methods are prone to error and bias.

Nuts and Bolts

1. Calculation of revised probabilities is accomplished using a joint probability table (with rows listing the test results and columns listing the uncertain outcomes) or employing Bayes' theorem.
2. New information (such as a test result) appears at the beginning of the decision tree, prior to the main decision. A decision square follows each possible test outcome.
3. As always, the decision tree is solved by averaging out and folding back. The expected profit computed at the beginning of the tree measures the expected benefit from making decisions based on the acquired information.
4. The expected value of information is the difference between the decision maker's expected profit with the information and without it.

Questions and Problems

1. It is time to buy a new car, and you have done a considerable amount of research on the matter over the past weeks. From consumer magazines and various online sources, you have reviewed an impressive body of information on different models' repair records, road handling, specifications and features, comfort, customer satisfaction, and so on. You have test-driven a half-dozen candidates and discussed prices with several dealers for each model. All things considered, you have decided to buy a Model M and will finalize purchase in the next few days. However, after attending a party last night, you are less certain. An acquaintance spent the better part of the evening recounting the disastrous experience he had with his new Model M. He got rid of the car after six months of electrical, steering, and handling problems. He is considering suing the dealer and claims you are crazy to consider buying the Model M. What do you do now?

2. Just prior to baseball's spring training season, you are asked to assess the probability that a particular baseball team will win the coming World Series.
   a. How would you go about making this assessment? In what sense is this assessment subjective?
   b. If you knew absolutely nothing about baseball, what would be the appropriate probability assessment? As an avid sports fan, how would you modify this "naive" assessment? How would your assessment change day by day as the season progressed?

3. A health club has sent promotional material to a mailing list consisting of local college students, area doctors, and lawyers. The following table shows the record of individuals taking up the club's introductory offer in the first 10 days of the promotion.

	Frequency of Respondents		
	Responded	Did Not Respond	Total
Students	.08	.16	.24
Doctors	.05	.13	.18
Lawyers	.09	.49	.58
Total	.22	.78	1.00

    a. What is the chance that a typical college student will respond to the promotion? A typical doctor? A typical lawyer? With respect to which group is the promotion most effective?

    b. How might information, such as shown in the table, be useful to marketing and advertising managers?

4. The following table (compiled from police reports) shows the record of automobile accidents for three age groups over the last year in a five-county region.

	Number of Drivers Having:		
	No Accidents	1 Accident	2 or > Accidents
Age 17–30	90,243	12,050	1,822
Age 31–55	243,125	21,443	2,822
Over 55	149,674	16,621	2,293

    a. An analyst points out that of 57,051 drivers involved in accidents last year, drivers aged 31 to 55 accounted for 24,265 cases, or some 43 percent of the total—a far greater proportion than any other age group. Should one conclude that this age group has the highest-risk drivers?

    b. Which age group has the worst accident record? The best? Explain.

    c. A separate analysis shows that for drivers aged 35 to 45, the rate of accidents (one or more per year) is 9.3 per 1,000 drivers. For drivers aged 65 to 75, the rate is 8.4 per 1,000 drivers. However, most studies show that members in the younger group are much safer drivers than those in the older group. Why might a simple comparison of accident rates per driver be misleading? What other important factor should be taken into account?

5. Consider once again the decision to redesign an aircraft (Problem 4 in Chapter 12).

    a. Find the expected value of perfect information about the redesign program. Calculate separately the expected value of perfect information about the US government's decision.

    b. Suppose that management of the consortium questions its engineers about the success or failure of the redesign program prior to committing to it. Management recognizes that its engineers are likely to be biased in favor of the program. It judges that if the program truly will succeed, the engineers will endorse it 90 percent of the time, but even if the program will fail, they will endorse it 50 percent of the time. What is the likelihood of success in light of an endorsement? What if the engineers do not endorse the program?

6. Consider the following simplified version of the television game show *Let's Make a Deal*. There is a grand prize behind one of three curtains; the other two curtains are empty. As a contestant, you get to choose a curtain at random. Let's say you choose curtain 3. Before revealing what's behind the curtain, the game show host always offers to show you what one of the other curtains contains. She shows you that curtain 2 is empty; in fact, she always shows you an empty curtain. (You know that's how the game works; so do the audience and everybody else.) Now you must decide: Do you stick with your original choice, curtain 3, or switch to curtain 1? Which action gives you the better chance of finding the grand prize?

7. Opening a multimillion dollar musical on Broadway is the ultimate financial gamble. Hits such as *The Phantom of the Opera* can earn millions in profit. Disasters too numerous to name have meant millions in losses. In the 2011 season, the producers of the musical *Spider-man, Turn Off the Dark* with state-of-the-art special effects and music and lyrics by Bono and The Edge faced high hopes and an important decision: whether to mount the usual series of out-of-town previews or to open directly on Broadway. A direct opening would save considerable costs (estimates for the Broadway run alone were spiraling above $60 million) but would give up the valuable opportunity to revise and craft the show based on audience reactions in tryouts.

    a. A direct Broadway opening is projected to have three possible outcomes: a "Hit" (implying net profit of $30 million), a "solid show" ($10 million in profit), or a "bomb" ($50 million in losses). The producers' best probability estimates of these outcomes are .3, .5, and .2, respectively. What is the expected profit of a direct Broadway opening?

b. Alternatively, the producers could test the production in a series of out-of-town previews at an added cost of $7 million. By carefully taking the pulse of the audience, the producers can expect one of three findings. If the show is "well-received" (probability .35), then only mild tweaking will be needed and estimated Broadway profits from an extended run will be $24 million. If the show has definite "kinks" (probability .45), then besides being less appealing to audiences, the show will require fixing and reworking, reducing the estimated Broadway profit to $12 million. Finally, if the production turns out to have "major problems" in front of the preview audiences (probability .2), then the producers should cut their losses and not open on Broadway at all (so they are only $7 million in the red).

What is the expected overall profit from previewing the show out of town? Is this more profitable than opening on Broadway directly?

8. Recall the earlier example of assessing the risk of loan defaults. Suppose the bank's top managers are divided on whether to adopt the scoring system permanently. A number of top officers believe their intuitive judgment about risks is superior to an "artificial" score. Accordingly, the bank decides to test its judgment against the scoring system. The managers will make their own designations of loans to the four categories and see how well they can identify problem loans. Their track record over the past year is shown in the accompanying table. For instance, the table shows that of all defaulting loans, 45 percent of them are categorized as class C (uncertain).

Category	Performing Loan	Defaulted Loan
A ("zero" risk)	.25	.20
B (solid)	.30	.25
C (uncertain)	.40	.45
D (high risk)	.05	.10
Total	1.00	1.00

a. Predict the probability of default for each loan category. (Assume the overall default rate is 10 percent, $Pr(default) = .1$.)

b. How do these risk assessments, based on judgment and intuition, compare with the earlier predictions based on credit scores? Which approach seems to provide more valuable information? Explain.

9. Firm B is considering whether to pursue an R&D effort to develop a powerful new microchip. One concern with the design is that the chip might generate too much heat operating at high speeds. Indeed, there is the risk that the heat problem will doom the R&D effort. Firm B's scientists believe that there is a .5 chance that the R&D effort will succeed (S) and a .5 chance it will fail (F). If the effort succeeds, there is a second risk. Firm B has filed several patents concerning the design of the chip. If these patents are upheld in court, it will have the exclusive right to produce the chip. However, a competitor, firm Z, has been pursuing a similar chip design and has filed its own patents. If the courts decide in favor of firm Z, both firms will be free to produce similar chips and will share the market. Firm B's legal department estimates a .6 chance that its patents will be upheld, giving it exclusive production rights.

The following table lists firm B's possible profit outcomes.

Failed R&D investment	−$40 million
Successful R&D/Exclusive production rights	$50 million
Successful R&D/Shared production rights	$5 million

a. Firm B must decide now whether to undertake the R&D investment. What course of action maximizes its expected profit? (Use a decision tree to justify your answer.)

b. Suppose instead that firm B can postpone its R&D decision for six months, by which time it will have learned the court's ruling on its patent. What is its expected profit if it waits? Depending on the court outcome, what actions should it take?

c. Suppose, instead, that firm B can build a 75 percent speed, prototype chip before committing to the full-scale R&D investment. The prototype chip will either run cool (C) or hot (H). The firm's scientists believe that the prototype will certainly run cool if the R&D effort is to succeed: $\Pr(C|S) = 1.0$. If the R&D effort is doomed to fail, the scientists believe that the prototype chip will run hot with probability $2/5$: $\Pr(H|F) = .4$. Find $\Pr(S|C)$ and $\Pr(S|H)$.

d. Should the firm build the prototype chip at a cost of $2 million? Use a decision tree to justify your answer. (Assume that the firm *cannot* wait for the patent outcome.)

*10. A government agency suspects that one of the firms it has hired under a cost-plus contract is padding its bills. If padding is going on and if the agency can prove its case in court, it estimates it could save $2 million in disallowed costs. However, the cost of bringing a large-scale legal action against the firm is considerable, about $500,000. The agency's auditors believe that there is a 20 percent chance that padding is going on. Its lawyers reckon that there is a 75 percent chance of proving and winning the legal case (if padding is indeed taking place).

a. Assuming the agency is risk neutral, use a decision tree to determine its best course of action.

b. Suppose the agency can conduct a preliminary investigation (conduct audits and interview dozens of employees) before deciding whether to bring a case. From the investigation, the agency can expect one of two results: a "clean" outcome (C) or a "questionable bill of health" (Q). If cost padding really is going on, there is a 75 percent chance that the investigation will signal Q. If there really is no cost padding, then the chance of C is 80 percent. (There is a 20 percent chance that would-be whistleblowers, such as disgruntled employees, will allege questionable practices even when no padding is going on.) If an investigation results in outcome Q, what is the chance that cost padding is going on?

c. Use a decision tree to determine the expected value to the agency of conducting an investigation.

11. On behalf of your company, you are preparing a price bid to supply a fixed quantity of a good to a potential buyer. You are aware that a number of competitors also are eager to obtain the contract. The buyer will select the lowest bid. Your cost is $100,000. If yours is the winning bid, your profit is the difference between your bid and your cost. If not, your profit is zero. You are considering three possible bids:

Bid $110,000; the probability of winning is .9.

Bid $130,000; the probability of winning is .5.

Bid $160,000; the probability of winning is .2.

a. Assuming your company's aim is to maximize its expected profit, which bid should you submit?

b. In part (a), your cost is $100,000 for certain. Now suppose it is uncertain: either $80,000 or $120,000, with each cost equally likely. Will this fact change your bidding behavior in part (a)? Explain briefly.

c. Suppose it is possible to gain information about the cost so that you will know exactly what the cost will be ($80,000 or $120,000) before submitting a bid. Use a decision tree to find the value of this information.

12. Private companies frequently approach your consulting firm to undertake special projects and provide advice to management. As a senior consultant, one of your jobs is to quote a price for these projects based on an estimate of cost and firm resources (i.e., consultants available to work on them). Your firm recognizes that it is competing with other consulting firms for its potential clients' business.

Over the last six months, you have bid on 10 separate projects and have won 9 of them. You are establishing a reputation as someone who really can bring in business. Some managers in the firm are worried, however, about a

---

* Starred problems are more challenging.

shortage of resources (i.e., available consultants) to complete these jobs. Is yours a "good" bidding record? Describe carefully how you would make this assessment.

13. A half-dozen firms are competing to secure a highway contract from a local government via sealed bid. When bids are opened, the winning firm's bid is 40 percent below the next-lowest bid.
    a. How might you explain such a low bid? Given such a bid, what risks does the winning bidder face? Explain.
    b. Is such a low bid unambiguously "good" for the local government? What potential risk does the government face? (In terms of the auctioning party's risk, how does a procurement differ from an auction sale?) How might the government protect itself from this risk?

Discussion Question In August 1999, Bridgestone/Firestone Inc. recalled 6.5 million tires in the wake of a number of tire-related rollover accidents in the Explorer SUV produced by Ford Motor Company. Although Firestone tires have an admirable overall quality record and the Explorer ranks second in its safety record among eight leading brands of SUV, 88 fatalities in the United States and as many as 50 fatalities overseas have been linked to the combination of Firestone tires (three particular brands) mounted on the Explorer. A review of the Firestone/Ford debacle shows that both companies (as well as the National Highway Safety Administration) lacked the data to permit early recognition of this accident risk. (To this day, there is no way to "prove" the exact causes of the tire failures. Evidence and analysis of the safety risk is purely statistical.)

   a. Ironically, the low overall rate of tire-related accidents made it more difficult to detect the particular Firestone/Ford risk. Why would this be the case? Until 1999, Firestone relied exclusively on the low rate of tire claims under warranty to conclude that its tires were safe. Why might reliance on warranty data alone be a mistake?
   b. The rate of tire failure is associated with multiple factors. The Explorer accidents with Firestone tires tended to occur at high speeds and at high temperatures. In addition, low tire pressures, recommended by Ford to increase ride comfort, tended to create more road friction and heat. (Carrying heavy loads has the same effect.) Precisely because the risk was associated with multiple, simultaneous factors, it was much more difficult to detect. Why would this be the case? (*Hint*: Screening factors *individually* produced no obvious warning signals.)
   c. Ford believed that the major fault was with Firestone's tires. Firestone contended that its tires were absolutely safe under its recommended operating conditions, and that the Explorer's design and operation were the major culprits. What kind of information would one gather to assess these rival arguments? Explain.

Spreadsheet Problems

S1. Individual investors face a daunting choice of thousands of stock and bond funds and fund managers. The following (stylized) spreadsheet example tries to distinguish superior fund managers from the throng of average managers based on their past track records of performance. Suppose there are three types of mutual fund managers: Superior (20 percent of the population), Average (60 percent), and Inferior (20 percent). In any six-month period, superior managers earn positive returns 70 percent of the time, average managers 60 percent of the time, and inferior managers just 50 percent of the time. At the risk of oversimplifying, we assume an average six-month gain of 25 percent (at an annual rate) versus a possible loss of 15 percent. Thus, the superior manager's expected return is calculated as: $(.7)(25) + (.3)(-15) = 13$ percent. Similarly, an average fund manager's expected return is 9 percent, and an inferior manager's expected return is only 5 percent. These rates of return mimic real-life fund performance and are listed in the top of the spreadsheet.

Consider the strong 10-year track record of manager G. This fund has had positive returns in 15 (six-month) periods and negative returns in only 5 periods. This long and strong track record suggests that G is a superior manager. Using the spreadsheet, our task is to compute the revised probability: $\Pr(S|15$ of $20)$. To do this, we first compute the converse probability: Pr(15 of 20|S), the likelihood of such a track record if Manager G is truly superior (i.e. has a .7 chance of earning a positive return in any particular six-month period). This likelihood follows a binomial probability and is shown to be about .18 in cell D15. This probability is computed using the following Excel formula:

$$= \text{BINOMDIST}(C15, B15, D9, 0).$$

Here, the first argument (cell C15) is the number of binomial successes, the second argument is the total number of trials, the third argument is the probability of success on each trial, and the last argument is always zero. By similar formulas, we compute Pr(15 of 20|A) and Pr(15 of 20|I) in cells E15 and F15. (Notice, it is much less likely that such a strong track record would be recorded by an average fund or especially by an inferior fund.)

	A	B	C	D	E	F	G	H	I	J	K
1											
2			EVALUATING FUND MANAGERS								
3											
4				Possible Annual Returns							
5				25	or	−15					
6											
7				Fund Manager Types							
8				Superior	Average	Inferior					
9			Prob(Up)	0.7	0.6	0.5					
10			Exp Return	13	9	5					
11											
12				Likelihood							
13			Track Record	Superior	Average	Inferior					
14		Years	Ups								
15		20	15	0.179	0.075	0.015					
16											
17				Joint Probability							
18			Track Record	Superior	Average	Inferior					
19		Years	Ups					Total			
20		20	15	0.036	?	?		?			
21										Expected	
22			Prior Prob	0.2	0.6	0.2				Return	
23											
24			Revised Prob	?	?	?		1.000		?	

a. Complete the joint probability table by computing the missing entries in cells E20 and F20. (Cell D20 has been calculated for you.) In turn, compute the revised probabilities (i.e., Pr(S|15 of 20) and so on) in row 24.

b. Even with an impressive past performance record, how confident are you that manager *G* is of the superior type? If you invest your money with manager *G*, what return would you predict on average? Compute the expected return in cell J24 using the revised probabilities found in part (a).

c. Experiment with different performance records (cells B15 and C15) and greater differences between types of fund managers (cells D9 and F9). What effect does each factor have on one's ability to identify superior managers?

Suggested References

Borison, A., and G. Hamm. "How to Manage Risk (after Risk Management Has Failed)." *Sloan Management Review* (Fall 2010): 51–57.

Camerer, C. "Individual Decision Making." In J. H. Kagel and A. E. Roth (eds.) *The Handbook of Experimental Economics.* Princeton, NJ: Princeton University Press, 1995.

Clemin, R. T., and T. Reilly. *Making Hard Decisions with Decision Tools Suite Update.* Belmont, CA: Thomson Learning, 2003.

Howard, R. A., J. E. Matheson, and D. W. North. "The Decision to Seed Hurricanes." *Science*, June 16, 1972, pp. 1191–1202. *This article is a classic application concerning the value of information.*

Kahneman, D., P. Slovic, and A. Tversky. *Judgment under Uncertainty: Heuristics and Biases.* Cambridge: Cambridge University Press, 1982. *This volume contains many classic articles on the pitfalls of intuitive probability assessments.*

Lawrence, D. B. *The Economic Value of Information.* New York: Springer-Verlag, 1999.

Salop, S. C. "Evaluating Uncertain Evidence with Sir Thomas Bayes: A Note for Teachers," *Journal of Economic Perspectives* (Summer 1987): 155–160. *Salop argues strongly for the application of probabilities and statistical techniques in the evaluation of legal evidence.*

Savage, S. L. *Decision Making with Insight.* Belmont, CA: Thomson Learning, 2003.

The following selections analyze common-value and private-value auctions respectively.

Milgrom, P., and R. Weber. "The Theory of Auctions." *Econometrica* (1982): 1089–1122.

Riley, J. G., and W. Samuelson. "Optimal Auctions." *American Economic Review* (1981): 381–392.

Empirical and experimental evidence on auction performance is discussed in the following selections.

Klemperer, P. *Auctions: Theory and Practice*, Princeton, NJ: Princeton University Press, 2004.

Samuelson, W. "Auctions: Advances in Theory and Practice," in K. Chatterjee and W. Samuelson (eds.), *Game Theory and Business Applications,* Chapter 13. New York: Springer Academic Publishers, 2014.

Check Station Answers

1. The joint probability table can be written as follows:

	Wet (W)	Dry (D)	Total
Good (G)	.21	.24	.45
Bad (B)	.07	.48	.55
Total	.28	.72	1.0

For example, $\Pr(G\&W) = \Pr(G|W)\Pr(W) = (3/4)(.28) = .21$. From the table, we find: $\Pr(W|G) = .21/.45 = .47$ and $\Pr(W|B) = .07/.55 = .13$.

2. With a good test, the partners drill and gain an expected profit of: $(.47)(600) + (.53)(-200) = \$176$ thousand. If the test is bad, they do not drill and earn \$0. Thus, their overall expected profit is: $(.45)(176) = \$79.2$ thousand. Without the test, the expected profit from drilling is $(.28)(600) + (.72)(-200) = \$24$ thousand. Therefore, the value of the test is: \$55.2 thousand.

3. This test is valueless: $\Pr(W|G) = .32/.8 = .4$, and $\Pr(W|B) = .08/.2 = .4$. The test never causes a probability revision. It reports "good" 80 percent of the time, whether or not the site is wet: $\Pr(G|W) = \Pr(G|D) = .8$.

4. To assess this conclusion, there are a number of questions to ask. How large is the sample of hires? Five hires over the 10 years? Fifteen hires? Were the hires predominantly high school athletes, or was there a mix of backgrounds allowing for relative performance comparisons? Was the business owner biased toward athletes (giving them better assignments or forgiving/forgetting their mistakes)? What does an objective reading of the hiring and performance data really say? (Or is the owner exhibiting "confirmation" bias—seeing what he wants to see?)

CHAPTER 14

Asymmetric Information and Organizational Design

I was to learn later in life that we tend to meet any new situation by reorganizing, and what a wonderful method it can be for creating the illusion of progress while producing confusion, inefficiency, and demoralization.

PETRONIUS ARBITER, 210 B.C.

LO#1. Define asymmetric information, and describe how it can lead to adverse selection and moral hazard.

LO#2. Show how asymmetric information influences decision making in organizations.

Incentive Pay at DuPont's Fiber Division

Beginning in January 1989, DuPont's fiber division began an experiment that the *Wall Street Journal* characterized as the "most extensive and innovative ever tried at a major U.S. corporation." Under the plan, managers and employees at the division would receive salary raises based on their division's overall performance relative to an annual profit goal.[1]

To see how the plan would work, consider a worker making $50,000 per year and expecting wage increases of 4 percent per year for the next three years, raising the worker's salary to about $56,200 in year three. Under the plan, if the worker's division attained 100 percent of its annual profit goal in the three years, this is exactly what the worker would receive. If the division achieved 150 percent or more of its profit goal, workers would earn raises of 8 percent per year for a third-year wage of about $63,000. However, if the division achieved only 80 percent of its profit goal, workers would receive 2.9 percent raises, reaching only $54,500 in third-year salary. Finally, if the division came in below 80 percent, annual raises would fall to 1.9 percent, for a third-year salary of only $52,900.

At its introduction, nearly all of the fiber division's 20,000 employees (and four of the five affected labor unions) adopted the plan. (The first-year profit goal was set at a modest level, and partial-year sales results almost guaranteed beating it.) The salary incentives seemed to affect workers' behavior, prompting many to suggest ways to cut costs and enhance revenues. Some workers said the plan would change their viewpoints: from fixation on their particular jobs to the big picture of company performance.

In Chapters 12 and 13, we considered decision making under uncertainty and the value of information solely from the individual manager's point of view. Many managerial

[1]L. Hayes, "All Eyes on Du Pont's Incentive-Pay Plan," *The Wall Street Journal* (December 5, 1988), p. A1.

decisions involve *asymmetric* information—situations in which one party knows more than another about key economic facts. In such cases, managers must be careful to draw correct inferences from the behavior of others. Asymmetric information can create incentive problems and even lead to market failures.

The first section of this chapter considers the effects of asymmetric information, and the second explores how firms can best organize themselves to deal with asymmetric information.

ASYMMETRIC INFORMATION

In situations characterized by asymmetric information, one party knows more than another about key economic facts. The presence of asymmetric information can lead to *adverse selection* and *moral hazard,* each of which we take up in turn.

Adverse Selection

Managers must make accurate probability assessments to make well-informed decisions. But as the next example shows, these assessments must take into account the likely behavior of other decision makers.

A BENEFITS PROGRAM   A company's human resources department has introduced a premium medical insurance program for its employees and their spouses. Employees who elect this coverage pay more than with the standard plan. Unlike the standard plan, the premium plan will pay for maternity-related health expenses. From records of the last ten years, the firm estimates that 1 in 20 of its employees will have a new baby in a given year. Accordingly, the company has set the higher premium to cover its expected payouts at this 1-in-20 rate. Postscript: In the first two years of the program, the company lost an enormous amount of money on the program. Employees covered by the plan are having babies at the rate of 1 in 10 per year. Is this bad luck or bad planning?

The company's losses are not due to bad luck, but instead due to *adverse selection.* The following table lists the hypothetical, but plausible, numbers for the first year of the program.

	Baby	No Baby	Total
Policy	100	900	1,000
No policy	100	2,900	3,000
Total	200	3,800	4,000

The overall rate of new babies is 200/4,000 or 1 in 20, exactly the average rate of the previous 10 years. However, *among policyholders*, the rate of having babies is 1 in 10 (100/1,000); among non-policyholders, it is 1 in 30. This result should not surprise us. Couples who are planning to add to their families will tend to elect the policy; those who are not will forgo the coverage. This behavior is termed *self-selection.* From the company's point of view, the result is called **adverse selection**. Couples who are most likely to have babies (and know this) are most likely to elect the coverage.

Adverse selection occurs because individuals have better information about their true risks than the insurance provider does. As a result, individuals at the greatest risk elect insurance coverage. Insurance companies must anticipate this behavior and set their premiums accordingly. In the preceding example, the company would have to double its premium to break even.

A "LEMONS" MARKET   The used-car market is a famous example of asymmetric information.[2] New cars drop significantly in value immediately after being sold. Why? People whose new car turns out to be a "lemon" are much more likely to sell than those who got good cars. Used-car buyers know this and thus offer less.

To see this, consider someone trying to sell a one-year-old car. Suppose that the value of the car to the seller ranges from $8,000 to $14,000, with all values in this range equally likely. The lemon's value is $8,000; a prize car is worth $14,000. Furthermore, suppose potential used-car purchasers are eager to buy. On average, they are willing to pay $1,000 more for the typical used car than the seller's value.

If both sides know a given car's true value, buyer and seller can conclude a mutually beneficial sale. A car valued by the seller at, say, $11,000 would be worth $12,000 to the typical buyer, and both parties know this. Thus, the sides could bargain to a price between these two values—say, $11,500—and both would benefit.

Now suppose that the potential seller knows the quality of the car but a potential buyer does not. Consider an $11,000 price. If *all* cars were sold at this price, sellers on average would just break even and buyers would obtain an average profit of $1,000 (since their average value is $12,000). However, a seller will not sell a car for $11,000 if it is worth more. Consequently, only cars with seller values between $8,000 and $11,000 will be offered for sale. With all values in this range equally likely, the average seller value is $9,500 (the midpoint of this range), and the buyer's average value for these cars is $9,500 + $1,000 = $10,500. Rational buyers should *not* pay $11,000; this is more than their expected value.

It turns out that $10,000 is the market equilibrium. At this price, only cars with seller values between $8,000 and $10,000 are offered for sale. Thus, buyers can expect to obtain cars worth (to them) between $9,000 and $11,000, or $10,000 on average, so this lower price level is sustainable. In equilibrium, lower-value cars dominate the market and only one third of the potential supply of cars is sold. Asymmetric information and adverse selection have severely limited the market.

Adverse selection is a common phenomenon. Banks, credit-card companies, and other lenders face the problem of distinguishing between low-risk borrowers and high-risk borrowers. If a bank charges the same interest rates to both types of borrowers, it will tend to attract the worst credit risks. This will force interest rates up and further worsen the pool of credit risks.

Adverse selection also operates in health insurance markets. People in poor health are much more likely to purchase insurance; thus, the proportion of this group in the

---

[2]The classic article on this topic is G. A. Akerlof, "The Market for 'Lemons': Quality Uncertainty and the Market Mechanism," *Quarterly Journal of Economics* (1970): 488–500.

insured pool increases, forcing up premiums. (The increased premiums may induce the healthiest people to drop their coverage, further worsening the proportions.) One way to contain adverse selection is to limit or eliminate consumer discretion. For instance, the Affordable Care Act of 2010 requires all citizens to purchase health insurance or to pay a fine. With nearly all citizens buying insurance, insurers do not have to worry that only the unhealthy will sign on. Medicare achieves the same goal, by subsidizing medical care for residents over 65 years of age. (Because care is effectively free to the user, all citizens opt in regardless of their health status.)

CHECK STATION 1   **Used-car dealers serve as middlemen, procuring large numbers of vehicles from many sources and reselling them to the public. Is adverse selection present when the dealer buys vehicles? When the dealer sells vehicles? In each case, what measures might the dealer take to mitigate adverse consequences?**

Signaling

In the presence of asymmetric information, managers gather information to better gauge risks. For instance, auto insurers place drivers into different risk classes according to age and past driving record and set premiums accordingly. A used-car buyer might have a licensed mechanic thoroughly check out a prospective purchase. Banks and other lenders devote significant time and resources to assessing borrowers' computerized credit histories. By obtaining better information (albeit at a cost), the manager can go a long way toward reducing or even eliminating the problem of adverse selection.

Asymmetric information poses a problem for the informed party as well. For instance, a seller might know he or she has a high-quality used car but might be unable to sell it for its true value due to adverse selection. Similarly, an individual who cannot prove he or she is a good credit risk may have to pay the same (high) interest rates as high-risk candidates. In general, "high-quality" individuals wish to distinguish themselves from their "low-quality" counterparts. They can do this in several ways. One way is by developing a reputation. For example, a seller may seek to build and maintain a reputation for delivering high-quality goods and services. A business that depends on repeat purchases and word of mouth will find its long-term interest served by accurately representing the quality of its goods.

An alternative method is to offer warranties. A warranty both protects customers against quality problems and signals product quality. A producer of a high-quality product can afford to offer an extensive warranty because it will cost the producer very little. A producer of a low-quality product will choose not to offer such a warranty because it is too expensive to do so. Warranties provide a (low-cost) way for high-quality producers to distinguish themselves from low-quality producers and allows high-quality producers to charge higher prices.

Signaling is a common response to the presence of asymmetric information. Consider the job market. At the time of hiring, a firm may find it difficult to predict how productive different job candidates will be. Management will have much better information after the worker has been on the job for six months or a year, but by that time, it may have invested considerable resources in on-the-job training. (Also, terminating unproductive workers is difficult and costly.) Workers themselves are well aware of their abilities, skills, and energy. High-productivity workers would like to *signal* their true abilities to potential employers and thereby obtain higher-paying jobs.

One way to signal their true value is via education.[3] Education not only provides knowledge that can increase an individual's productivity, it also serves as a signal. Individuals of high innate ability find school easier and perform better. Thus, productive persons will invest more heavily in education than will their less productive counterparts. Other things being equal, the higher an individual's educational achievement, the stronger the productivity signal.

For signaling to work, high-quality individuals must have an incentive to use the signal while their lower-quality counterparts choose not to. This means that signaling must be less costly for the former group than for the latter. Moreover, signaling is never costless. Students sometimes pursue college or higher degrees simply to earn a "job credential" rather than for the education itself. As long as signaling is part of the equation, individuals will have an incentive to overinvest in education.

Principals, Agents, and Moral Hazard

The preceding examples share the feature that the actions of one party affect the welfare of a second party. The **principal–agent problem** occurs when a principal (with limited information) relies on a self-interested agent (who has better information) to take actions on the principal's behalf.

Examples of principal–agent relationships abound. A physician (agent), who has superior knowledge, acts on behalf of her patient (principal). A supplier (agent) may or may not live up to his or her contractual obligations to serve a buyer (principal). Within the firm, employees (agents) know a lot more about their work effort than their employers (principals). Top managers (agents) with intimate knowledge of the firm are meant to serve stockholders (principals).

The problem of **moral hazard** occurs when an agent has incentives to act in its own interests, *contrary* to the interests of the principal. The following principal–agent setting combines the dual problems of moral hazard and adverse selection.

A BUILDING CONTRACT   A business firm (the principal) has entered into a building contract with a construction firm (the agent) to build a new corporate headquarters. The estimate of the final cost is $6.5 million. Both sides acknowledge that this estimate is highly uncertain; final cost could range from $6 million to $7.5 million. Recognizing this uncertainty, the parties have drawn up a cost-plus contract whereby the firm will reimburse the builder for all allowable costs, plus a normal rate of profit. The contract sets the completion date for two years from commencement of the project, but this target is also uncertain.

---

[3]The classic treatment of this topic is A. M. Spence, *Market Signaling* (Cambridge, MA: Harvard University Press, 1974). Professors Spence and Akerlof (see Footnote 2) shared the 2001 Nobel Prize in economics (with J. Stiglitz) for the cited research in asymmetric information.

The business firm is less well-informed about the contractor's likely capabilities and completion cost than the contractor itself. This information asymmetry exposes the business firm to the risk of adverse selection in choosing a contractor. Some contractors will give honest estimates and others will low-ball—that is, give an estimate below what they know the real cost will be. The cost-plus contract attracts the low-ballers, who may in the end cost the firm more than the honest contractors.

The business firm faces a second risk due to moral hazard. Under the cost-plus contract, the contractor is not responsible for any cost overruns and does not benefit from any cost underruns. Thus, it has no incentive to complete the project at minimum cost. It might instead indulge in various kinds of managerial "slacking" or in the extreme case might exaggerate or "pad" its stated costs. In short, the contractor has an incentive to act in its own interests to the detriment of the client.

In this example, the business firm faces the twin, but logically distinct, risks of adverse selection and moral hazard. Here is the distinction:

> Adverse selection occurs when the agent (whose interests are at odds with the principal's) holds unobservable or hidden *information*.
>
> Moral hazard occurs when an agent (whose interests are at odds with the principal's) takes unobservable or hidden *actions*.

Generally speaking, adverse selection occurs at the time the agent enters into a relationship, while moral hazard occurs after a relationship has been established. At the outset, the agent uses his or her private information to decide whether to enter into the relationship. Once in the relationship, the agent decides which (unobserved) self-interested actions to take. For example, a life insurance policy may attract those with serious health problems (adverse selection) and may cause those covered to begin to engage in more risky behavior (moral hazard). Likewise, a poorly designed employment contract may attract lower-productivity employees (adverse selection) and give those workers incentives to engage in self-serving actions at the expense of the employer (moral hazard). As the next two examples show, the problem of moral hazard is pervasive.

Health Insurance and Medical Costs

The United States offers some of the most sophisticated health and hospital care in the world. However, health-care costs continue to rise and now comprise over 17 percent of US gross domestic product.

Paradoxically, the very benefit that health insurance bestows is also partly responsible for the escalation of health expenditures.[4] With the patient's payment share as low as 10 percent of true costs, patient and physician have an incentive to overspend on health-care services, resulting in higher insurance premiums and increased burdens on government-sponsored programs. This is the moral hazard.

What are the ways out of this dilemma? One approach is to make doctors aware of costs. Traditionally, medical education has isolated doctors from considerations of cost.

[4]For a close analysis of health care insurance and health costs, see M. McClellan, "Reforming Payments to Healthcare Providers: The Key to Slowing Healthcare Cost Growth While Improving Quality?" *Journal of Economic Perspectives*, 25 (Spring 2011): 69–92. The health spending problem is not only about overutilization, but also about prices. Other developed countries have either single-payer systems or a nationalized health service that allows them to bargain effectively for lower prices.

However, since 2007, medical licensing standards have required residency programs to teach doctors about "cost awareness" and "risk-benefit analysis."[5] A second approach is to monitor and regulate the choices of patient and physician. These efforts range from promulgating voluntary standards of medical practice to controlling which medical procedures in which circumstances insurance will reimburse. These practices can reduce medical expenditures but at the risk of compromising the discretion of physicians and patients. Since the mid-1990s, many health insurers, health maintenance organizations (HMOs), and hospitals have aggressively pursued cost-containment strategies, often sparking conflicts with physicians and patients.

A third response is to improve the *incentives* for cost control. For example, insurers might make the patient pay a greater percentage of the cost. Advocates of this approach argue that raising patient payment rates to 20 to 30 percent would provide stronger incentives for reduced expenditures and help eliminate spending on unnecessary tests and ineffective treatments. Whole Foods Market, Inc. has adopted a program in which employee premiums are low (zero for most workers), but the deductible (the amount an employee must pay before the insurance kicks in) is $1,500. To cover this, Whole Foods puts a fixed amount of money into a medical account for each employee each year. If the employee does not use this money, it is carried forward to future years. Thus, workers should begin acting as if they are spending their own money, at least up to the amount of the deductible.[6]

An alternative approach targets physician incentives. Coupled with insurance, the traditional fee-for-service approach simply reimburses doctors for the cost of treatment. When ordering outside tests or treatments, doctors are often unaware of the cost of the tests. When ordering inside tests or treatments, doctors have a financial incentive to prescribe costly treatments, even if less costly treatments would be more effective. Moreover, the threat of malpractice suits encourages doctors to practice defensive medicine—to overprescribe costly tests and treatments.

In contrast to a fee-for-service approach, *fixed* payments for treatments, separated into diagnosis-related groups, provide strong cost-control incentives. For instance, a hospital that receives a fixed payment for a surgical appendectomy has a strong incentive to keep down costs. An increasingly popular payment scheme, the *capitation* approach, takes this concept to the limit. Under capitation, an insurer pays a group of doctors one fixed annual payment per patient, set at the estimated cost of caring for each enrollee. Doctors receive less compensation if costs get out of hand but profit if they keep costs low.[7]

---

[5]College professors face a similar problem. Most professors have no idea how much a textbook will cost students and so rarely take textbook costs into account. As a result, textbook publishers are free to set high prices for leading texts.

[6]For a discussion of the Whole Foods program, see R. Lieber, "New Way to Curb Medical Costs: Make Employees Feel the Sting," *The Wall Street Journal Online* (June 23, 2004), p. A1. In some cases, however, incentive plans calling for higher co-pays can lead to worse health decisions. Studies have documented that some individuals stop taking highly effective medicines (and eschew other preventive tests and measures such as mammograms) when they perceive the financial cost to be too high. This reaction, termed "behavioral hazard," is the exact opposite of moral hazard. See, S. Mullainathan, "When a Co-Pay Gets in the Way of Health," *The New York Times* (August 11, 2013), p. BU6.

[7]Still another approach is known as pay-for-performance (P4P) which gives doctors and hospitals financial rewards or bonuses for achieving key objectives, such as reduced infection rates or shorter waiting times. See B. Keller, "Carrots for Doctors," *The New York Times* (January 28, 2013), p. A17.

CHECK
STATION 2 **The capitation approach gives full decision-making control to physicians. One result might be a greater focus on preventive care. Explain why. Might adverse selection (exercised by the physician group) and moral hazard (also exercised by the physician group) be a problem? What risks do doctors face under capitation? On the patients' side, might there be a risk of compromised health-care quality? Explain.**

The Financial Meltdown

The US financial crisis of 2007–2008 was marked by a "perfect storm" of asymmetric information, moral hazard, and misaligned incentives. Consider the home lending market where some of the worst abuses occurred.[8] Thirty years ago, most home loans were a matter between individual borrowers and their bank lender. The lender would carefully assess a borrower's risk and set terms and conditions on the loan accordingly. Both sides then had a mutual objective in making the loan work and seeing it successfully paid off. These days, the lending market involves many competing loan originators (not simply one's local bank), and home loans are "securitized," that is, packaged together to be sold as securities to investors. Securitization shares risk and lowers financial costs. However, it also creates moral hazard and misaligned incentives.

In the booming economic times of 2002 to 2006, borrowers and lenders alike were seduced by the belief that housing prices could only go up. Loan originators profited by signing up borrowers, including many subprime borrowers with questionable ability to repay. Since other financial institutions and investors would assume the risks of the loans, originators paid little heed to financial worthiness and whether the loans could be paid back. In extreme cases, originators issued low- or zero-down-payment loans or "stated-income loans" in which borrowers simply stated their income without the requirement of verification. There was ample room for moral hazard by borrowers and loan originators alike.

Asymmetric information and moral hazard appeared at other stages of the financial process, as well. The major ratings agencies such as Moody's and Standard and Poor's gave these mortgage-backed securities optimistically high ratings—partly because they failed to appreciate their true risks and undoubtedly because the agencies received their revenues from the very institutions whose securities they were rating. The giant insurance company, American International Group (AIG), issued default insurance on these mortgage-backed securities (in return for hefty premiums). Brokers promoted the securities to investors as being high return with tolerable risk. After all, the housing market was booming, and the securities were A-rated and backed by AIG insurance.

In 2007, the music stopped. Housing prices plateaued then fell; the economy slowed; and subprime borrowers first began missing payments, then defaulting and walking away. The market unraveled, causing staggering losses in the credit industry. The Federal Reserve and the US Treasury stepped in to shore up or rescue a host of financial institutions. In 2008, Congress established the $700 billion Troubled Assets Relief Program (TARP) to bail out financial institutions through the purchase of non-performing assets. In that same year, Bank of America, Goldman Sachs, and other

---

[8]For an analysis of the financial crisis paying special attention to the housing market, see R. Shiller, *The Subprime Solution: How Today's Global Financial Crisis Happened, and What to Do about It* (Princeton, NJ: Princeton University Press, 2008).

major financial institutions received monetary infusions, and AIG was rescued by an $85 billion loan.

The unwinding of the financial meltdown revived the doctrine of "too big to fail." Under this doctrine, some major financial institutions are considered so important to the economic health of the financial system that the government will not allow them to fail. However, such a policy may induce these banks and financial institutions to take excessive risks, a form of moral hazard that increases the chance of insolvencies—the very disasters that intervention seeks to prevent.

The Dodd–Frank Act, passed in the aftermath of the financial crisis, designated certain financial institutions as "systemically significant" (too big to fail), but subjected them to additional capital requirements and regulation.[9] Another part of the law requires originators to retain a percentage of the loans they make to better incentivize them to scrutinize loan recipients.

PAYING FOR RESULTS   Frequently the problem of moral hazard can be mitigated by paying careful attention to incentives. Historically, most law firms and advertising agencies charged for their services on an hourly basis. Principal–agent theory predicts that "you get what you pay for"—in this case, these firms have every incentive to expend excessive hours on the contracted tasks. The more time spent, the more hours billed. An alternative is to pay for results. In the legal profession, one option is the contingency arrangement, whereby the law firm gets a percentage of the attained settlement amount or court award. Indeed, contingency fee payments have been an increasing trend. (In 2011, General Electric converted almost all of its offensive patent litigation from hourly to contingency-fee arrangements.) Still another arrangement for legal services is flat-rate billing—that is, a flat rate for a particular task regardless of the number of hours spent. In the earlier example of building the corporate headquarters, the firm and contractor might agree to enter into a fixed-price contract. In receiving a fixed price, the contractor has an obvious incentive to keep costs under control.

Of course, paying for results is not without problems. The building contractor might lower costs by sacrificing quality or finishing behind schedule. Investment bankers get paid for bringing acquisition targets to clients. The problem is that they get paid only when a deal is completed. They earn nothing if the deal is abandoned or if they steer a client away from a bad deal. (Financier Warren Buffett has likened taking advice from investment bankers to asking a barber if you need a haircut.) This applies to stockbrokers and real-estate agents as well.

SUMMING UP   The message of this section is that the principal–agent relationship comes with an associated cost. Agents, though possessing better information, have interests that conflict with those of the principal. Accordingly, the parties will attempt to mitigate these problems. This might mean monitoring or limiting the agent's decision-making discretion or improving the agent's incentives. Nonetheless, asymmetric information imposes real **agency costs,** both from nonoptimal actions on the part of

---

[9]For views on financial reform, see A. R. Sorkin, "Dodd–Frank Dissenters Sound Off," *The New York Times* (May 10, 2011), p. B1; and S. M. Davidoff, "In F.D.I.C.'s Proposal, Incentive for Excess Risk Remains," *The New York Times* (April 2, 2011), p. B9.

agents and expenses incurred by the principal to limit such actions. An important task of managers is to organize firms in ways that minimize these agency costs.

ORGANIZATIONAL DESIGN

Having examined the economics of different market structures in previous chapters, we now take a closer look at the organization of firms. What economic factors determine the size, breadth, and organization of firms? Why do some economic transactions take place within firms, whereas others are transacted via markets? This section considers each of these questions.

The Nature of the Firm

As recently as 100 years ago, the typical firm was a very small concern, managed by its owner and employing a small number of workers. Only the railroads, steel producers, and a handful of other manufacturers constituted the realm of large firms. Today, there are over 50 corporations of more than 250,000 employees each, including Walmart, which has more than 2 million. Although firms range in size from the single proprietor to the largest *Fortune* 500 companies, the vast majority of managers work for firms with 50 or more employees. Thus, we focus primarily on this category.

Consider the following proposition first articulated by Ronald Coase.[10]

| Firms will be organized to minimize the total cost of production including transaction | costs. |

That is, competition among firms will ensure that only the most efficient organizational forms survive and prosper.

In applying Coase's proposition, let's start with the owner-managed firm, the norm in the nineteenth century and still represented today. Consider a small clothing producer, run by a sole proprietor who is both owner and manager. The proprietor has procured the necessary equipment, hired workers, and made all important decisions. As sole owner, the proprietor claims all profits (and pays all losses) from the business. The proprietor holds the relevant information about how to run the business, as well as a strong incentive to take optimal actions. With management and ownership vested in one individual, the informational and moral hazard problems are minimized.

Contrast this with today's large-scale firm. Because of economies of scale and scope, average costs decline at higher levels of output. This offers a first explanation for large firm size. Of course, the increase in scale makes the business of transforming inputs into outputs much more complicated. No longer can a single owner-manager take on all management and decision-making responsibilities. The modern firm distributes information and management responsibilities among a wide group of inside managers.

---

[10]R. Coase, "The Nature of the Firm," *Econometrica* (1939): 386–405.

14.1

	Factors Favoring In-House Production	Factors Favoring Outsourcing
between roduction and ng	1. Firm-specific good or service	1. Standardized good or service
	2. Outside risks: input quality, supply disruptions	2. Competitive market available
	3. High degree of coordination required	3. Low degree of coordination required

order to have a more reliable supply of inputs or markets for outputs.[11] Table 14.1 lists the most important factors favoring in-house production over outsourcing. Besides the factors already discussed, the presence of outsourcing uncertainty confers an advantage to taking activities in-house. Thus, for a state-of-the-art high-tech component, the firm may not be able to ensure the same quality through outsourcing that it can achieve through in-house production. In addition, the firm may find it easier to handle redesigns in-house than through outsourcing. In short, when risks loom large, the firm might want to fall back on the maxim: If you want something done right, do it yourself.

Assigning Decision-Making Responsibilities

A general principle guides the division of management responsibilities within the firm.

> A firm should assign decision responsibilities to those managers with the best information on which to act.

This maxim reminds us of Chapter 13's principal message. Superior information is valuable precisely because it supports better decisions. Thus, good organizational design places decisions as close as possible to the relevant information.

A corollary to this proposition follows. Organizations should distribute tasks to best generate and utilize specialized information. After all, division of labor and specialization characterize the modern firm. Indeed, specialization not only enhances productivity in the traditional sense but also greatly improves the quality of decisions. Consider two contrasting cases. You are a manager whose calendar for today requires you to make six crucial decisions: from solving a production problem in your West Coast plant to deciding on a new marketing plan, to dealing with federal regulators. You are woefully unprepared to decide any of these issues. (This is sort of like the nightmare about the exam no one told you about and for which you never studied.) By comparison, suppose instead your calendar calls for six big decisions in your bread-and-butter area of

---

[11] There are numerous examples of vertical integration. In 2008, Apple purchased a key producer of custom microchips used in its products. That same year, steel producer ArcelorMittal bought mines in Brazil. In 2009, Boeing acquired a key producer of fuselage parts, and in 2010, Oracle, a software producer, purchased Sun Microsystems whose servers run Oracle products. For a discussion, see B. Worthen, C. Tuna, and J. Scheck, "Companies More Prone to Go 'Vertical,'" *The Wall Street Journal* (December 1, 2009), p. A1. For a study of Japanese auto production, see S. Nagaoak, A. Takeishi, and Y. Noro, "Determinants of Firm Boundaries: Empirical Analysis of the Japanese Auto Industry from 1984 to 2002," *Journal of the Japanese and International Economies* (2008): 187–206.

TABLE

The Choic
In-House
Outsource

The large firm presents an interesting and important trade-off. On the one ha
increases in scale and scope offer the advantage of declining average costs. On the oth
hand, the division of management responsibilities raises myriad principal–agent problems. Thus, top management must design an organizational structure that preserves the
advantages of large-scale production while mitigating the attendant agency problems
and agency costs.

The design of organizational structure involves three issues:

1. *Determining the boundaries of the firm,* that is, deciding which activities the firm
   should undertake internally and which it should leave to outside contractors and
   suppliers.

2. *Dividing decision-making responsibilities within the firm,* including determining
   the degree to which decision making should be centralized or decentralized.

3. *Crafting mechanisms for monitoring and rewarding managers* and other firm
   employees, including hiring, promotion, and remuneration.

Note that these three issues are usually interrelated. In addition, organizational structures
can be either formal or informal. Formal structures carefully define decision-making
authority and set up specific mechanisms to monitor and reward. Informal structures,
often known by the term *corporate culture,* create goals and expectations and foster a
social environment that informally rewards good performance.

The Boundaries of the Firm

Any firm must decide whether to undertake an economic activity in-house or to outsource the activity. Most firms rely on outside markets to procure their most basic inputs,
everything from telephone service and office equipment to automobiles and fuel. We
know from Chapter 7 that competitive markets ensure efficient provision of standardized
goods and services at the lowest sustainable prices. Thus, the firm can likely procure
these standardized inputs from outside suppliers more cheaply than producing them
itself.

Which circumstances might favor undertaking an activity in-house? Roughly speaking, the firm will undertake those activities that require extensive coordination in production or make use of specialized inputs. For example, a large law firm will procure
its office space via the commercial real-estate market and purchase routine supplies and
equipment. However, the firm's bread-and-butter legal services will be coordinated and
provided in-house. Complex cases require lawyers of many specialties (from first-year
associates to senior partners) working together to meet clients' needs. Established relationships within the firm make this easier to do.

Empirical studies bear this out. A study of the Japanese automobile industry found
that the more specialized and interdependent a component is, the more likely it is to be
produced in-house. Moreover, as production and supply chain operations have become
more interdependent and complex over the last decade, many firms have pursued a
strategy of **vertical integration**—acquiring either suppliers or corporate customers in

The large firm presents an interesting and important trade-off. On the one hand, increases in scale and scope offer the advantage of declining average costs. On the other hand, the division of management responsibilities raises myriad principal–agent problems. Thus, top management must design an organizational structure that preserves the advantages of large-scale production while mitigating the attendant agency problems and agency costs.

The design of organizational structure involves three issues:

1. *Determining the boundaries of the firm,* that is, deciding which activities the firm should undertake internally and which it should leave to outside contractors and suppliers.

2. *Dividing decision-making responsibilities within the firm,* including determining the degree to which decision making should be centralized or decentralized.

3. *Crafting mechanisms for monitoring and rewarding managers* and other firm employees, including hiring, promotion, and remuneration.

Note that these three issues are usually interrelated. In addition, organizational structures can be either formal or informal. Formal structures carefully define decision-making authority and set up specific mechanisms to monitor and reward. Informal structures, often known by the term *corporate culture,* create goals and expectations and foster a social environment that informally rewards good performance.

The Boundaries of the Firm

Any firm must decide whether to undertake an economic activity in-house or to outsource the activity. Most firms rely on outside markets to procure their most basic inputs, everything from telephone service and office equipment to automobiles and fuel. We know from Chapter 7 that competitive markets ensure efficient provision of standardized goods and services at the lowest sustainable prices. Thus, the firm can likely procure these standardized inputs from outside suppliers more cheaply than producing them itself.

Which circumstances might favor undertaking an activity in-house? Roughly speaking, the firm will undertake those activities that require extensive coordination in production or make use of specialized inputs. For example, a large law firm will procure its office space via the commercial real-estate market and purchase routine supplies and equipment. However, the firm's bread-and-butter legal services will be coordinated and provided in-house. Complex cases require lawyers of many specialties (from first-year associates to senior partners) working together to meet clients' needs. Established relationships within the firm make this easier to do.

Empirical studies bear this out. A study of the Japanese automobile industry found that the more specialized and interdependent a component is, the more likely it is to be produced in-house. Moreover, as production and supply chain operations have become more interdependent and complex over the last decade, many firms have pursued a strategy of **vertical integration**—acquiring either suppliers or corporate customers in

TABLE 14.1

The Choice between In-House Production and Outsourcing

Factors Favoring In-House Production	Factors Favoring Outsourcing
1. Firm-specific good or service	1. Standardized good or service
2. Outside risks: input quality, supply disruptions	2. Competitive market available
3. High degree of coordination required	3. Low degree of coordination required

order to have a more reliable supply of inputs or markets for outputs.[11] Table 14.1 lists the most important factors favoring in-house production over outsourcing. Besides the factors already discussed, the presence of outsourcing uncertainty confers an advantage to taking activities in-house. Thus, for a state-of-the-art high-tech component, the firm may not be able to ensure the same quality through outsourcing that it can achieve through in-house production. In addition, the firm may find it easier to handle redesigns in-house than through outsourcing. In short, when risks loom large, the firm might want to fall back on the maxim: If you want something done right, do it yourself.

Assigning Decision-Making Responsibilities

A general principle guides the division of management responsibilities within the firm.

A firm should assign decision responsibilities to those managers with the best information on which to act.

This maxim reminds us of Chapter 13's principal message. Superior information is valuable precisely because it supports better decisions. Thus, good organizational design places decisions as close as possible to the relevant information.

A corollary to this proposition follows. Organizations should distribute tasks to best generate and utilize specialized information. After all, division of labor and specialization characterize the modern firm. Indeed, specialization not only enhances productivity in the traditional sense but also greatly improves the quality of decisions. Consider two contrasting cases. You are a manager whose calendar for today requires you to make six crucial decisions: from solving a production problem in your West Coast plant to deciding on a new marketing plan, to dealing with federal regulators. You are woefully unprepared to decide any of these issues. (This is sort of like the nightmare about the exam no one told you about and for which you never studied.) By comparison, suppose instead your calendar calls for six big decisions in your bread-and-butter area of

---

[11] There are numerous examples of vertical integration. In 2008, Apple purchased a key producer of custom microchips used in its products. That same year, steel producer ArcelorMittal bought mines in Brazil. In 2009, Boeing acquired a key producer of fuselage parts, and in 2010, Oracle, a software producer, purchased Sun Microsystems whose servers run Oracle products. For a discussion, see B. Worthen, C. Tuna, and J. Scheck, "Companies More Prone to Go 'Vertical,'" *The Wall Street Journal* (December 1, 2009), p. A1. For a study of Japanese auto production, see S. Nagaoak, A. Takeishi, and Y. Noro, "Determinants of Firm Boundaries: Empirical Analysis of the Japanese Auto Industry from 1984 to 2002," *Journal of the Japanese and International Economies* (2008): 187–206.

responsibility. Well prepared by years of experience and accumulated knowledge, you eagerly tackle these challenges.

Modern firms typically divide responsibilities along functional lines—production, marketing, finance, and so on. This type of structure has obvious advantages and less obvious disadvantages. One risk is that functional managers may lose sight of the bigger picture. Obviously, a materials manager must communicate with a production manager. The latter cannot plan to increase jeans production without the necessary denim and thread on order. Similarly, a product designer greatly benefits by learning of customers' needs and complaints from the marketing manager.

An alternative organizational design divides responsibility by line of product or service. Product lines represent natural profit centers. Consequently, a product manager oversees many functional areas for his or her product and makes decisions to maximize profitability. Midlevel managers would still occupy functional jobs within this product division. Management can also be organized by the type of customer (business versus residential, for instance) or by geographical regions.

The Airbus Industrie consortium was formed to produce commercial aircraft in 1970.[12] The commercial aircraft manufacturer lived the first 30 years of its existence as a consortium of French, British, German, and Spanish aerospace companies, plus a marketing unit charged with negotiating the aircraft sales. During the 1990s, the Airbus consortium succeeded in increasing its market share to about 40 percent of the global commercial aircraft market (to Boeing's 60 percent). However, critics claimed that Airbus bought market share by selling aircraft at a loss, all the while receiving financial transfusions from its national governments.

Under its original organizational structure, Airbus was its own worst enemy. According to a long-standing political compromise, the construction of each new aircraft was carved up in fixed shares among the partners. Germany and France (each with 37.9 percent stakes) built parts of the fuselage and assembled finished planes. Britain (20 percent stake) built the main wings, and Spain (4.2 percent stake) built parts of the tail. (General Electric produced the engines in a joint venture with a French company.) This slice-and-dice organizational approach produced inefficiency, duplication, and waste. The partners regarded each other as unreliable outside suppliers. Management meetings among the members resembled games of "liar's poker." Each member tried to charge the highest possible prices to other members for parts it supplied and to pay the lowest prices to other members for parts it bought. Each fanatically guarded and kept secret its financial information.

In 2000, after much infighting, Airbus was reorganized as a corporation. Although it continued to produce its aircraft components in different European locations, it tightly integrated production, assembly, scheduling, and delivery, cutting costs, centralizing procurement, and expanding sales. In 2003, Airbus delivered more planes than Boeing

Airbus's Dysfunctional Organization

[12]This account is based on "EADS: Peace on the Rhine," *The Economist* (January 1, 2011), p. 78; N. Clark, "France and Germany Agree to Streamline Airbus's Parent," *The Wall Street Journal* (July 17, 2007), p. C5; D. Michaels, "Airbus Revamp Brings Sense to Consortium, Fuels Boeing Rivalry," *The Wall Street Journal* (April 3, 2001), p. A1; and D. Michaels, "Europe's Airbus Ready to Spread Wings as a Company," *The Wall Street Journal* (June 23, 2000), p. A15.

for the first time in its history. In 2007, continuing its management reforms, Airbus's parent corporation (EADS) abandoned its dual French–German management structure in favor of a unitary executive.

DECENTRALIZATION   Dividing organizations along functional and product lines creates pockets of specialized information dispersed throughout the business organization and assigns decision-making responsibility as closely as possible to holders of this information. Presumably, an experienced regional sales manager with his or her ear close to the ground can best make periodic marketing, promotion, and pricing decisions. In general, as the number of contingencies grows, so does the importance of decentralized decision making. A single decision maker might do a credible job identifying a profit-maximizing price in a peaceful, unchanging market. However, with scores of ever-changing market segments, setting prices centrally becomes daunting, perhaps even hopeless for a single decision maker.

Let's now consider the contrary point of view and ask, under what circumstances does efficiency favor centralized decisions? The answer: when decisions are highly interdependent, that is, when managers must coordinate choices. For instance, management's optimal output decision depends on both demand and cost. Thus, neither a production manager nor a marketing manager has all of the relevant information to determine optimal output, Q^*. Accordingly, the output decision should be made by centralized managers who use demand and cost information from both departments. However, once centralized management has determined output, it can delegate other decisions, such as the details of input decisions or the advertising campaign to the appropriate functional areas.

Greater centralization may also be appropriate in the face of significant principal-agent problems. Imagine that a regional manager has the best information to make a particular decision, but that the manager's interests conflict with the firm's objectives. In such cases, upper-level management should make the decision, even with imperfect information. Table 14.2 summarizes factors bearing on the choice between centralization and decentralization.

COORDINATION THROUGH TEAMS   Teams are often used to combine the advantages of centralization and decentralization. Teams pool information and perspectives. A 2007 study documented that the percentage of large firms with 20 percent or more of their employees in teams grew from 37 percent in 1987 to 66 percent in 1999.[13]

TABLE 14.2

The Choice between Centralization or Decentralization	Factors Favoring Centralization	Factors Favoring Decentralization
	1. High degree of coordination required	1. Low degree of coordination required
	2. Concentration of decision-relevant information	2. Dispersion of decision-relevant information
	3. Significant principal–agent problems	3. Compatible interests and objectives

[13] See E. P. Lazear and K. L. Shaw, "Personnel Economics: The Economist's View of Human Resources," *Journal of Economic Perspectives* (Fall 2007): 91–114.

Though DuPont is organized with independent subsidiaries, each responsible for its own performance, the company also uses committees containing executives from across its subsidiaries to develop strategies and products. Accenture, IBM, and Google have all used teams with great success. ICU Medical has probably taken the team concept as far as any company. Any group of employees may form a team to solve a problem or to take on a project. Successful teams are rewarded monetarily and many have made substantial contributions.

Of course, team decision making is costly in terms of human resources and risks difficulties in reaching a decision consensus; thus it should not be used indiscriminately.

In principle, how would an organization determine the optimal size of a team?

CHECK
STATION 3

COORDINATION VIA TRANSFER PRICES   The divisions of large firms often provide goods or services to each other. For instance, a firm's automotive division might receive finished engines from its parts unit. **Transfer prices**—the prices that selling divisions charge to buying divisions within the firm—help coordinate internal actions. (See the appendix to Chapter 6 for a full discussion and analysis.) The key to maximizing the firm's total profit is to s*et each transfer price equal to the marginal cost* of the good or service in question. For instance, the automotive division should pay a transfer price to the engine division that reflects the marginal cost of producing each engine. (If the firm's engines are also sold on external markets, the transfer price should be set at the going market price.) With prices set this way, profit-maximizing decisions of the separate divisions will maximize total profits of the firm.

As we saw in the case of Airbus, setting appropriate transfer prices is not always easy. The supplying division often pushes for a higher transfer price to enhance its own profit while the receiving division wants a lower price for the same reason. Overstating or understating the transfer price can lead to incorrect decisions, resulting in lower profits for the firm. Setting correct transfer prices is essential for efficient coordination within the multidivision firm.

In the mid-1990s, DHL Worldwide Express was the leader in international document and parcel delivery, claiming over 40 percent of the worldwide market.[14] Recognized for its premium services (speedy delivery, package customs clearance, and tracking), the company also charged premium prices. However, corporate headquarters was concerned about its pricing policies. Regional managers exercised wide discretion in offering discounts (small or steep) to particular customers for different types of deliveries. Indeed, some multinational customers complained of widely different rates for deliveries of comparable distance.

DHL Worldwide Express

Should DHL move to greater centralization of pricing decisions? Consider the economics of the global delivery market. First, demand conditions (and cost conditions) varied significantly in different parts of the world. Some routes experienced much higher volumes of shipments than others. Competition was absent in some parts of the world, cutthroat in others. DHL held a virtual monopoly in most of Africa but faced a price war with TNT and FedEx in Southeast Asia. Demand also varied across services. Because

[14]This account is based on "DHL Worldwide Express," Harvard Business School Case, 1997.

of customers' urgent need for documents, the document segment was less price sensitive than the package segment and, therefore, commanded higher markups. Demand also varied by customers. Banks and financial institutions typically displayed much less elastic demand than a wholesaler shipping spare parts.

In light of these facts, DHL headquarters acknowledged that regional managers had the best information to make pricing decisions and thus retained a decentralized decision approach but with two limitations. First, large discounts from the list price would first require higher-level approval. Second, to ensure consistency and customer goodwill, local managers would have only limited pricing discretion on important multinational accounts. Headquarters also implemented a sophisticated centralized information system to estimate delivery costs anywhere in the world. Using the new centralized information system, regional managers could access data on marginal cost by route and price accordingly.

Monitoring and Rewarding Performance

The modern firm is built on formal and informal systems of carrots and sticks to motivate managers and other employees to act in the interest of the organization. These include merit evaluations, raises, bonuses, promotions, lateral transfers, perquisites, admonishments, pats on the back, and even firings. Here we focus on the following question: To what degree can pay-for-performance mechanisms mitigate moral hazard problems in organizations? In our answer, we examine two specific problems: motivating workers and maximizing executive performance.

MOTIVATING WORKERS   Probably the most pervasive form of principal-agent relationship is that of employer and worker. For a successful relationship, the firm (the principal) must motivate the worker (the agent) to act in the employer's interests. Workers have knowledge and abilities advantageous to their companies, but their needs and desires may differ from the firm's objectives. For example, workers control the effort they put into a job. Increased effort raises the firm's output and profitability. However, working harder generates disutility for the worker.

Tying compensation to effort is one way to induce higher effort levels. If both the employer and employee can observe effort, they can design an optimal contract. First, employer and worker should agree to an effort level that maximizes the total net benefit of the firm and the worker. This total net benefit is just $\pi - D$, where π is the firm's profit attributable to the worker and D denotes the worker's *disutility*. Suppose that a second-year associate at a small law firm works 55 hours per week in return for a $55,000 annual salary and that this work generates $80,000 in additional net revenue for the firm. Suppose also that the associate experiences a personal disutility from working of $40,000. Then, the total net benefit from the employment relationship is $80,000 − $40,000 = $40,000. The firm's share of this is $80,000 − $55,000 = $25,000, and the associate's share is $15,000 (the difference between the actual pay and the least amount he would accept in compensation for the disutility of the job). If the employee worked longer hours, could both the firm and the employee do better? Suppose that working 70 hours a week would increase net revenue to $90,000, but it would also imply disutility to the worker of $60,000, reducing the total net benefit to $30,000. Even with the firm compensating the worker for the longer hours, sharing the smaller net benefit cannot be mutually beneficial. The optimal work plan (i.e., the value-maximizing plan) is 55 hours per week.

Asymmetric information introduces potential complications. Frequently, the firm cannot observe and measure the worker's effort. Let's start with two pieces of good news.

> If effort is observable, then the parties can always implement an optimal contract even if output can only be measured approximately.

To see why, suppose that output depends not only on the worker's effort but also on uncertain elements beyond the worker's control. In this case, the optimal contract will specify the level of effort that maximizes the *expected* net profit from the relationship. As long as the worker complies with this level of effort, he or she receives the stipulated monetary compensation and the firm maximizes expected profit. This is sometimes referred to as a *forcing* contract. The contract terms are designed to force the worker to take the optimal level of effort; otherwise the worker is penalized.

A second result follows:

> If output is observable and depends *deterministically* on effort, then the parties can always implement an optimal contract even if effort is unobservable.

Simply by observing the worker's output, the employer can infer the worker's effort. Thus the employee will receive compensation if the output (and thus the effort) goal is met.

Here is the bad news associated with asymmetric information:

> If effort is not observable and if observable output is not deterministically related to effort, then the parties will be unable to implement an optimal employment contract because of moral hazard.

The stylized example in Table 14.3 demonstrates this result. The worker can choose one of four effort levels—low, medium, high, or super. The additional gross profit attributed to the worker depends *probabilistically,* not deterministically, on the level of effort. Gross profits are uncertain, either $100,000 or $50,000. Increasing effort raises the probability of achieving the high-profit outcome and increases expected gross profit. However, the employer cannot infer the worker's effort level from the profit outcome. (Even a super effort might result in a low profit result.)

From Table 14.3a, we see that high effort generates the greatest net profit, $40,000. If both employer and employee could observe effort, the employee would agree to high effort and the employer would compensate accordingly. Item 1 in Table 14.3b lists the terms of such a contract. The firm pays $60,000 in salary to the worker if and only if the effort level is high. (In general, the exact wage bargain struck would depend on labor market conditions.)

Now suppose that the employer cannot observe effort and continues to pay the worker $60,000. The outcome is shown in item 2 of Table 14.3b. The worker naturally chooses a low level of effort, the employer's expected profit is reduced to $0, and the parties' total expected profit falls to $25,000. There is no incentive for the employee to work harder; to do so means no increase in compensation (merely increased disutility). This is the essence of the moral hazard problem.

What can the employer do? One option is simply to anticipate low effort and adjust the salary down to $45,000, securing a $15,000 net profit from the employment relationship. This outcome (item 3 of Table 14.3b) is better than $0 but still far short of the $25,000 that is possible when effort is observable. A second option is to offer an *incentive* contract. What if the employer offers to pay the worker a base salary of $10,000 plus one-half of all gross profits the employee generates on the job? This arrangement creates an incentive to supply extra effort. As shown in item 4 of Table 14.3b, the worker maximizes his or her benefit (salary less disutility) by choosing a *medium* level of effort. The incentive contract has induced additional effort and has increased the total profit pie. This is an improvement, but the worker still does not have sufficient incentive to adopt optimal behavior, that is, exert high effort. (Be sure to check this for yourself.)

Raising the worker's profit share is the key to inducing extra effort. Going further, allowing the worker to keep 100 percent of his or her contribution to profit, ensures an optimal choice of effort. Now the worker's interest is aligned with the firm's—to maximize profits. Unfortunately, even this solution has problems. First, 100 percent profit participation is very risky for the worker. The gross profit outcome will be either $100,000 or $50,000. Any risk-averse worker will demand a premium for bearing this risk. If the worker's disutility of this risk is, say, $5,000, then imposing this risk on the worker shrinks the total pie by this amount. Second, under this contract, the worker guarantees the employer a certain profit of $25,000. Because the employer now has a

TABLE 14.3

Employment Contracts	**(a) Effort and Profits**

Effort Level	Gross Profits $100K or $50K	Expected Gross Profit	Disutility	Expected Net Profit
Super	.8 and .2	$90,000	$60,000	$30,000
High	.7 and .3	$85,000	$45,000	$40,000
Medium	.5 and .5	$75,000	$39,000	$36,000
Low	.2 and .8	$60,000	$35,000	$25,000

(b) Different Contracts

	Effort Level	Compensation	Employer Profit	Worker Profit	Total Profit
Observable Effort					
1. Forcing Contract	High	$60,000	$25,000	$15,000	$40,000
Unobservable Effort					
2. Fixed Wage	Low	$60,000	$0	$25,000	$25,000
3. Fixed Wage	Low	$45,000	$15,000	$10,000	$25,000
Incentive Pay					
4. (1/2 Profit + $10,000)	Medium	$60,000/$35,000	$27,500	$ 8,500	$36,000
5. (Profit − $25,000)	High	$75,000/$25,000	$25,000	$15,000	$40,000

guaranteed profit, the employer lacks incentives to do its part to maximize profits. Now, the moral hazard shoe is on the other foot. Will the employer adopt optimal behavior? The answer is problematic.

In general, we expect high-powered incentives (such as profit-sharing) in settings where effort is unobservable and profits depend significantly on the agent's effort (rather than on external, uncontrollable factors).

Should a firm sell its product in its own stores or instead by franchising? As we noted in Chapter 2, the franchise arrangement creates high-powered incentives for the franchisee; the franchise manager's profits depend directly on his or her efforts. By contrast, under an employment relationship, the employee typically faces low-powered incentives with less managerial discretion and little (or zero) profit sharing.

Integration or Franchising?

A recent survey that reviewed research studies on franchising shows that the "real world" accords well with the theoretical models.[15] Across all sectors, the incidence of franchising consistently increased when the main determinant of profit was the agent's effort (rather than other uncontrollable factors). Conversely, researchers found that the traditional employment relationship prevailed when the firm could monitor employee effort levels and decisions at low cost. (Franchising's high-powered incentives were unnecessary when effort could be monitored and controlled directly.) Finally, franchising was more common when management decisions depended on information about local markets. As noted earlier in Table 14.2, the dispersion of decision-relevant information favors decentralized decisions—that is, external franchising.

Using the facts in Table 14.3, show that the worker's profit share must be just greater than 60 percent to ensure that the worker adopts an efficient level of effort.

CHECK STATION 4

EVALUATING INDIVIDUAL PERFORMANCE   An understanding of incentives in the principal–agent problem leads to an additional result.

> All information bearing on an individual's effort and contribution to profit should be included in the measure of performance. Any variables not bearing on effort or profit contribution should be excluded.

This proposition is sometimes called the *informativeness* principle. In other words, the more precise the measure of performance (combined with the appropriate incentive structure), the more efficient will be the agent's behavior (and the smaller will be the resulting agency cost). The challenge is in accurately monitoring and measuring performance. Frequently, it is difficult to disentangle the contribution of a particular worker from other economic factors and from the contributions of fellow workers. Imperfect performance measurement not only reduces the incentives for efficient behavior, it also exposes the worker to significant risks in the compensation scheme.

Facing this problem, many companies turn to subjective measures to evaluate individual employee performance. Supervisors may evaluate the performance of employees

---

[15]See F. Lafontaine and M. E. Slade, "Incentive and Strategic Contracting: Implications for the Franchise Decision," Chapter 6 in K. Chatterjee and W. Samuelson (eds.), *Game Theory and Business Applications* (New York: Springer, 2014).

on an annual or semiannual basis, giving them numerical ratings (say, on a 10-point scale) for various aspects of job performance. Alternatively, the employer may give the worker a number of annual goals and then evaluate the employee on whether and how well he or she accomplished these goals.

But how does the evaluation system set realistic benchmarks for performance? Industrial engineers and efficiency experts could perform studies that examine efficient ways of completing tasks. Alternatively, firms can use past performance as a benchmark. One worry with benchmarks is that employees could slack off to avoid higher benchmarks in the future. To overcome this, firms frequently base benchmarks on the historic average performance of a large group of comparable workers.

EVALUATING GROUP PERFORMANCE   Frequently, group performance is easier to measure than individual performance. In addition, rewarding group performance may encourage cooperation among employees who can all share in the fruits of their collective achievement. However, rewarding group performance introduces new risks to employees. Now compensation and advancement depend on the uncertain efforts of others. Also, rewarding group performance may discourage optimal effort (indeed, encourage shirking), especially when the firm cannot easily observe individual effort.

For example, consider a team of five workers whose annual bonuses depend on the success of the group. Individual effort is unobservable. However, if all team members exert 15 percent extra effort, group performance will rise by a like amount and each member will reap an additional $25,000 in bonus. If only four members exert 15 percent effort, then output rises by 12 percent and each member receives $20,000. Suppose the disutility of extra effort is $10,000 for each worker. (Have you spotted the prisoner's dilemma yet?) It is better for all to exert extra effort than for none to do so. (Each receives $25,000 with a disutility of $10,000.) However, it is even better for a worker to slack off while his or her coworkers put in the extra effort. The slacking worker receives $20,000 extra compensation and no disutility from extra effort. Each member's personal incentive is to "free ride" on the efforts of the others. As a result, no one exerts extra effort.

Smaller groups naturally have fewer of these free-riding problems than larger groups, since it is easier to monitor effort by group members. In addition, mutual trust that all will do their part is easier to achieve in small groups. Despite potential problems with group compensation, the percentage of large firms that base some compensation on group performance has grown, as has the use of teams.

Separation of Ownership and Control in the Modern Corporation

An important example of the principal–agent problem occurs in large publicly held corporations. Such corporations are owned by vast numbers of shareholders (principals) and managed by directors (agents). Shareholders elect the board of directors, who oversee corporate management (agents).

This organizational form confers significant benefits in the financing of the firm. In issuing shares, the corporation gets access to a vast supply of financial capital, funds that would be difficult or impossible to secure from a single owner or even from a limited number of partners. Investors can diversify across many firms and business sectors with the added protection of limited liability. (Limited liability means that creditors cannot pursue the personal assets of shareholders.)

Shareholders own the company, but they do not have the right to manage it. Setting day-to-day management decisions according to shareholder votes, besides being extraordinarily costly and impractical, would surely generate poor decisions. Rather, the organization is controlled by a cadre of professional managers acting on behalf of shareholders.

In large publicly held firms, shareholders have little practical control over the selection of top management or how top management performs once in place. Two roadblocks prevent shareholders from wielding voting power over the board and top management. First, management controls the voting and proxy process. In most elections there is only one slate of nominees, the slate chosen by management, and management can use corporate assets to support this slate. By contrast, insurgent shareholders (those seeking to change management) must use their own funds to challenge incumbent management and are reimbursed only if successful.

Second, there is often little incentive to challenge the incumbent management team. A typical shareholder often owns a very small fraction of the outstanding voting shares of a large corporation. This shareholder recognizes that his or her vote will have a negligible effect on the outcome of any voting contest. Consequently, few shareholders will take the considerable time, effort, and cost of understanding the competing solicitations in a proxy battle. Most shareholders simply cast their votes for current management.

For example, suppose a group of shareholders holding 1 percent of shares is convinced (and rightly so) that a change in top management would increase the value of the firm by $10 million. Thus, if the group succeeds, its gain from the change would be $100,000. Suppose that a reasonable estimate of the challengers' cost of waging a proxy fight is $150,000. Given the difficulties in educating and subsequently enlisting hundreds of poorly informed small shareholders, the chances of winning the fight might be 30 percent at best. In this case, the group's expected gain from waging the battle is $(.3)(100,000) + (.7)(-\$150,000) = -\$75,000$. (If the proponents win, they are reimbursed for their solicitation costs.) The challenger group has absolutely no incentive to launch this fight, despite the $10 million collective benefit from a management change. As a result, challenges are rare and, of those that happen, most fail.

Frequently, an inventor-entrepreneur who launches a new firm occupies the role of chief officer and owns greater than 50 percent of the firm. Ten years later, the same inventor-entrepreneur might have reduced his or her ownership share to well below 50 percent and transferred decision-making responsibilities to a cadre of other top managers. Explain why.   **CHECK STATION 5**

LIMITING THE POWER OF TOP MANAGEMENT   Because shareholders have limited control over the selection and performance of top management, one would expect significant principal–agent problems. Managers may pursue their own agendas and take actions that conflict with the interests of shareholders. For instance, executives might engage in *empire building,* thereby, incurring unnecessary costs (inflated management salaries, executive jets, and the like). Alternatively, in pursuit of the prestige of being market-share leaders, executives might expand the firm's operations far past the point of profit maximization. As the classical economist Adam Smith so eloquently put it:

> The directors of such companies . . . , being the managers rather of other people's money than of their own, it cannot well be expected that they should watch over it with the same anxious vigilance with which the partners in a private copartnery frequently watch over their own. . . Negligence and profusion, therefore, must always prevail, more or less, in the management of the affairs of such a company.[16]

Consider executive compensation which is often set by a committee of the executive's own colleagues. In 2012, average CEO pay in the top 350 US companies was $14.2 million, 272.9 times the average worker pay in these companies.[17] (In 1963, this ratio was 20 to 1.) Particularly high levels of compensation have been associated with lax corporate governance. Because of these concerns, three mechanisms have arisen to mitigate the principal–agent problems inherent in large corporations:

1. **Disclosure requirements**. Justice Louis Brandeis famously said, "Sunlight is the best disinfectant." Federal and state securities acts have rigorous disclosure requirements encompassing quarterly and annual reporting and disclosures in conjunction with proxy solicitation and tender offers. In 2006, in response to ballooning executive pay, the Securities and Exchange Commission mandated greater disclosure of executive compensation.

2. **External enforcement of managerial duties**. In the United States, both private parties and government can sue if directors violate duties of care or loyalty or engage in fraud, deception, or insider trading. Private attorneys have ample incentives through attorneys' fees to prosecute such cases on behalf of shareholders.

3. **The market for corporate control**. The market itself may discipline managers. For instance, suppose that poor management causes the firm's stock price to fall to $40 per share. By changing management, a would-be acquirer could increase firm value to, say, $65 per share. Such an acquirer decides to make a tender offer (offering to buy shares from the public) at $50 per share (a $10 premium over market price). If stockholders tender a majority of their shares, then the acquiring firm can remove current management and install its own team. The ever-present threat of a takeover forces managers to maximize firm value or risk a takeover and the loss of their jobs. However, this mechanism has been diluted in recent years by courts and state legislatures that have erected barriers to hostile takeovers.

Two other mechanisms strive to reduce the principal–agent problems:

1. **Shareholder empowerment**. A variety of reforms aim at giving shareholders more power. Some would alter voting rules to provide for binding shareholder resolutions. Other measures seek to reduce the cost of shareholder challenges (e.g., by allowing shareholders to use limited corporate resources in their challenges or

---

[16]Adam Smith, *The Wealth of Nations,* Book 5, Chapter 1, Part 3, Article 1, 1776.

[17]Mishel and Natalie Sabadish, "CEO Pay in 2012 Was Extraordinarily High Relative to Typical Workers and Other High Earners," Economic Policy Institute, June 26, 2013. Available at http://www.epi.org/publication/ceo-pay-2012-extraordinarily-high/.

allowing solicitation and voting through the Internet). Still other proposals seek to encourage cooperation among large institutional shareholders (pension funds, insurance funds, and investment funds), which frequently hold large numbers of shares. In 2011, the SEC promulgated new "say on pay" rules requiring that executive compensation be subject to a nonbinding shareholder vote at least every three years.

2. **Corporate governance reforms.** In the United States, corporate boards are typically composed of inside and outside directors. Inside directors are full-time executives who run the day-to-day operations of the corporation. Outside directors are part-time business people who provide general oversight of the corporation. Outside directors are much more likely to put shareholders' interests ahead of their own.

As an example, consider a hostile takeover in which both inside and outside directors will lose their jobs. For the inside directors, this loss can be enormous, including surrender of an executive position and the large income, important responsibilities, and prestige that go with it. An outside director loses a very part-time job and a very part-time salary. Thus, the inside director might strongly oppose the tender offer, whereas the outside director, largely free from a conflict of interest, would act more objectively.

As critics point out, strong outside directors often cannot control top management. Outside directors are typically chosen by inside directors, and their continued employment depends on getting along with the insiders. In addition, inside directors typically control the flow of information to outsiders. Many corporate governance reform proposals aim at increasing the independence and influence of outside directors and include increasing the number of outside directors (to a majority); removing inside directors from nominating new directors and from setting directorial compensation; allowing shareholders to nominate competing slates of directors; setting mandatory retirement ages or term limits for directors; and prohibiting interlocking directorships (where inside directors of one company are outside directors of another and vice versa).

FINANCIAL INCENTIVES By crafting pay-for-performance compensation plans, the firm can provide managers greater incentives to maximize share value. Consider a corporation whose stock is currently trading at a price of $100 per share. Now compare three possible executive compensation schemes. At year end, executive 1 receives a flat bonus of $200,000 cash. Executive 2 receives $100,000 cash plus 1,000 shares (worth $100,000). These restricted shares cannot be traded for three years. Finally, executive 3 receives $100,000 cash plus $100,000 worth of warrants (options). Each warrant gives the holder the right to purchase a share of the corporation's stock at $100 per share. Suppose that warrants are trading at $10 per warrant. Executive 3 thus receives 10,000 warrants.

The three schemes have the same cash value, but differ in their incentives. Executive 1 received no equity interest in the firm, so has no direct financial incentive to maximize share value. Executive 2 holds 1,000 shares. For every dollar that he raises the share price, executive 2 profits by $1,000.[18] Finally, executive 3 holds 10,000 warrants. For each $1 increase in share price above $100, executive 3's 10,000 warrants increase in value by $10,000. This gives by far the greatest incentive to maximize share value.

---

[18] The financial wizard Warren Buffett owns almost 45 percent of Berkshire Hathaway, the conglomerate he controls. Obviously, Buffett has a keen incentive to increase his company's value.

Linking executive compensation to the firm's performance serves to align management's interests with those of shareholders. Executive compensation during the 1980s and 1990s varied little with company performance. However, over the last 15 years, compensation paid to top executives has been linked more closely to firm performance. In addition, boards have been more likely to penalize executives for poor company performance, and firings (though still infrequent) have become more common.[19]

Still, pay-for-performance (PFP) systems are not without problems. Companies cannot easily measure executive performance; PFP schemes often reward the wrong types of behavior; and monetary compensation does not always sufficiently motivate behavior. Fluctuations in corporate outcomes outside the control of the manager can produce large variations in the manager's compensation, causing risk-averse behavior and requiring additional compensation to bear these risks. Indeed, PFP schemes may be used to mask excessive executive compensation. In general, structuring an optimal PFP scheme depends on a trade-off between fostering the desired incentives and insuring the agent against undue monetary risks.[20] This task is easier in principle than in practice.

ENRON, WORLDCOM, AND TYCO   What do the spectacular failures of some of our largest corporations say about the organizational design of the modern firm? Business failure in itself does not necessarily imply organizational failure. Even with the most able management and the most efficient organization, business carries numerous risks. Nevertheless, faulty organizational design and poor decision making can have devastating effects.

Prior to its collapse in December 2001, Enron earned over $100 billion in revenues and had 20,000 employees. It had pioneered online energy trading and had moved into other areas such as broadband communications. However, to hide its exposure to risk and increase its access to cheap credit, Enron illegally moved many of its risky activities to affiliated companies, often run by Enron personnel. This removed the activities from Enron's books but did not remove the risk from the corporation. In late 2001, some of these assets began to perform poorly, exposing the company's hidden fragile capital structure. The firm's credit rating fell. Investors began selling its stock, and Enron collapsed.

By 1997, WorldCom, Inc., through internal growth and its acquisition of MCI, had become the second-largest long-distance provider in the country. After the collapse of Enron, investors at WorldCom, Inc. became suspicious of accounting irregularities and filed a class-action suit that ultimately exposed one of the biggest fraudulent accounting schemes of all time. Accounting fraud also undid Tyco International, a conglomerate that produced a wide variety of products. Tyco's chief executive officer, chief financial officer, and general counsel stole hundreds of millions of dollars from the company through fraudulent accounting and illegal stock transactions.

---

[19]There is a lively debate on the causes of large executive salaries and how closely executive pay is tied to corporate performance. See K. J. Murphy, "Executive Compensation: Where We Are, and How We Got There," in G. M. Constantinides, M. Harris, and R. M. Stoltz (eds.) *Handbook of the Economics of Finance* (Oxford, UK: Elsevier, 2013), 211–356; L. Bebchuk and J. Fried, *Pay without Performance: The Unfulfilled Promise of Executive Compensation* (Cambridge, MA: Harvard University Press, 2006); S. N. Kaplan, "Executive Compensation and Corporate Governance in the U.S.: Perceptions, Facts, and Challenges," *Journal of Applied Corporate Finance* (Spring 2013): 8–25; and M. Jensen and K. J. Murphy, "Performance Pay and Top-Management Incentives," *Journal of Political Economy* (April 1990): 225–264.

[20]For a lucid analysis of this trade-off, see John McMillan, *Games, Strategies, and Managers* (New York: Oxford University Press, 1996), Chapter 9.

These are principal–agent problems run amuck. The participants in these schemes were able to remove transactions from the view of their principals, the investing public. Without proper monitoring, the participants could then act in their own interests to the detriment of their principals.

The government policy response to these scandals has focused on increased monitoring and penalties. In 2002, Congress passed the Sarbanes-Oxley Act, which raised firm reporting requirements and increased fines and jail time for violations. For example, the act mandates that the chief executive officer and the chief financial officer personally certify the firm's financial statements. It also requires real-time disclosure of changes in a firm's financial condition. Fines for violations can now reach $5 million (plus disgorgement), and violators can go to prison for up to 20 years.[21]

In October 1990, only two years into its three-year plan, DuPont announced that it was ending its experiment to link workers' compensation in its fibers division to division profits.[22] Although it promised to give workers and managers a greater sense of responsibility for (and stake in) the success of the fiber business, the plan had a number of unintended, though predictable, consequences. Instead of becoming more deeply involved and paying greater attention to profitability, many workers grew more alienated, believing they had little or no control over profits. Tensions increased among employees whose bonuses now depended on the efforts of others. Many workers blamed management for wasting money and being a drag on profits. They resented the fact that managers were protected by other bonus plans geared to firm-wide profits.

Incentive Pay at DuPont's Fiber Division Revisited

The failure to achieve the 1990 profit goal (set 4 percent above the 1989 goal), sealed the fate of the plan. With its principal customers—the automobile and housing industries—crippled by the 1990 economic recession, the fiber division's profit prospects were dismal. After earning a modest bonus in the first year, employees stood to lose 2 to 4 percent of their pay in the second.

The aforementioned problems are exactly in line with this chapter's analysis. In effect, the bonus system created a 20,000-person team! Although one could spew bromides on how everyone should work together, the incentive effects drove people apart. Any individual employee had virtually no impact on the division's profits and thus had little personal incentive to pay attention to profitability. Instead, the worker's compensation was placed at risk, determined by factors beyond his or her control. Indeed, many workers rebelled at pay cuts triggered by the economic downturn, a factor they deemed irrelevant as far as their performance was concerned. For all these reasons, the plan failed.

---

[21]In response to the scandals, Congress also strengthened the role of the United States Sentencing Commission, which establishes penalties for organizations that violate federal laws. The guidelines permit reduced penalties for firms that report illegal activities, take responsibility for them, and cooperate with the prosecuting authorities. These rules are meant to provide strong incentives for firms to prevent illegal behavior (and to expose it should it happen).

[22]See R. Koenig, "Du Pont Plan Linking Pay to Fibers Profit Unravels," *The Wall Street Journal* (October 25, 1990), B1.

SUMMARY

Decision-Making Principles

1. Many business relationships involve an agent, in possession of superior information, taking actions for a principal. The principal must provide incentives or controls to induce the agent to act in the principal's behalf and to mitigate potential problems posed by adverse selection and moral hazard.

2. Modern firms divide information and management responsibilities among a wide group of managers.

3. Business firms will be organized to minimize the total cost of production, including transaction and information costs. Designing an efficient organization involves determining the boundaries of the firm, assigning decision responsibilities to managers with the best information on which to act, and providing control and incentive systems to minimize agency costs.

Nuts and Bolts

1. Adverse selection occurs when the agent who has information that is unavailable to the principal self-selects in a manner detrimental to the principal. Warranties, contingent agreements, reputation building, and signaling can help mitigate adverse selection problems.

2. Moral hazard occurs when an agent takes unobservable or hidden actions detrimental to the principal. Principals can design controls and incentives to mitigate (though not eliminate) moral hazard problems. The resulting reduction in welfare from moral hazard is frequently called an agency cost.

3. A firm will choose to undertake an activity in-house rather than rely on outsourcing when the activity requires a high degree of coordination or where the input is highly specialized.

4. A firm will benefit from decentralized decision making when specialized information is dispersed among different management segments and when delegated decisions exhibit a low degree of interdependence.

5. Firms require control and incentive systems when an agent's objective differs from the firm's. Compensating the agent the exact amount he or she contributes to profit solves the incentive problem but exposes the agent to additional risk.

6. The modern corporation is characterized by separation of ownership and control. The owner-shareholders have little direct control over management. However, performance incentives, the external enforcement of executive duties, corporate governance reforms, and the market for corporate control can help mitigate principal–agent problems.

Questions and Problems

1. Carmakers acknowledge that a small percentage of new automobiles are "lemons." Chrysler Corporation succeeded in winning back lost market share by offering buyers the chance to return their new cars for up to 30 days if they were not satisfied. In this way, the "new" Chrysler sought to demonstrate its confidence in product quality. Suppose Chrysler made the following estimates for the program: (1) 4 percent of its new cars were lemons; (2) one-half of all lemons would be discovered and returned; and (3) 1 out of every 16 normal-quality cars would be returned because of minor problems, buyer change of heart, and so on.
   a. Of all the cars returned, what portion are lemons? For a buyer satisfied after month 1, what is the chance that that person will later find that he or she owns a lemon?
   b. How might Chrysler decide whether the program's benefits in screening for quality are worth its costs?

2. In the early 1990s, lawsuits charged Sears with massive fraud in its auto repair centers, alleging that mechanics were convincing customers that they needed expensive repairs when, in fact, they were unnecessary. Sears entered into a

multimillion-dollar agreement to settle the case out of court. In a bid to win back business it had lost during the highly publicized case, Sears announced that its sales staff would no longer be paid on commission.

   a. In your view, were the abuses by the mechanics a result of adverse selection, moral hazard, or both?

   b. The management of Sears stated that it was unaware of the abuses. What are the incentives for management to monitor its employees to prevent such wrongdoing?

   c. What is the disadvantage of ending the commission system?

3. Suppose prospective clerical workers fall into one of two categories in equal numbers: high productivity (HP) and low productivity (LP). An HP worker's value to the firm is $45,000 per year; an LP worker's value is $30,000 per year. A firm hires workers who stay an average of five years.

   a. At the time of hiring, the firm cannot distinguish HP and LP workers. In this case, what wage will it offer its new hires?

   b. One option is for workers to attend college before taking a job. Suppose college has no effect on clerical productivity (its other virtues notwithstanding). For an HP worker, the expected total cost of attending a four-year college (accounting for possible scholarships) is $60,000. The expected cost for an LP worker is $90,000. Can HP workers effectively signal their productivity by attending college? What if the average job stay is only three years?

4. As a benefit to employees, many universities offer their clerical and administrative employees free tuition for themselves and their families. Why might universities prefer this to simply offering the employees more money?

5. Five couples are having dinner at a fancy French restaurant. They expect that the total dinner bill will be split evenly five ways. How might this prior knowledge affect the diners' menu selections? (What if one couple mistakenly believes there are to be separate checks?)

6. Each year, almost 200,000 men are diagnosed with prostate cancer. Decision making is complicated because there are up to five potential treatments, ranging from aggressive surgery to radiation to "watchful waiting" (that is, carefully monitoring slow-growing cancers). One recently developed treatment is IMRT, a sophisticated technology that delivers radiation to kill and (hopefully) eliminate cancerous cells. The treatment mainly takes place in hospitals that are reimbursed by insurance programs. However, in more than a dozen states, private urology practices have emerged that not only diagnose and advise patients, but also own IMRT equipment and hire radiologists to administer the treatment. These practices are reimbursed by private insurers and Medicaid.

   a. Private urologists cite the advantages of their carrying out IMRT. What kinds of advantages are possible?

   b. Citing IMRT's high cost, critics claim that putting IMRT in private urologists' hands is leading to cost escalation. Why might this be the case? Under this setup, is there a danger of overtreatment? Why or why not?

7. Firm X has promised to deliver an order of industrial parts to firm Y. However, there is a small chance that firm X will have so many orders from customers that it cannot fulfill them all. If its order is not filled, firm Y's profit will fall by $100,000. If customer demand exceeds capacity, firm X's cost of fulfilling firm Y's order might turn out to be anywhere between $50,000 and $150,000.

   a. Consider a contract in which firm X must guarantee delivery to firm Y. Explain when and why such a contract leads to inefficient actions and outcomes.

   b. Alternatively, suppose the contract has a penalty provision: If firm X doesn't deliver, it pays a penalty of $50,000 to firm Y. Does this contract lead to efficient outcomes? Why or why not? What if the penalty for nondelivery is set at $100,000 instead?

8. When a corporation offers shares of stock or other securities to the public, it hires an underwriter to conduct the sale. (The underwriter is an investment bank such as Morgan Stanley or Goldman Sachs.) Most commonly, firms and investment bankers use a procedure known as *firm commitment* underwriting. The underwriter buys the shares from the company and then sells them to the public. If the offering is under-subscribed or if the price must be subsequently lowered to unload the shares, the underwriter, not the firm, suffers the loss. Why do firms and underwriters use this procedure? What's in it for each? How does this means of sale affect the buying public?

9. Since the mid-1980s, baseball teams have bid vigorously for free agents— players with six or more years of service who are free to sign with a new team. After signing a five-year contract with a new team for an exorbitant amount, a free-agent pitcher has had three consecutive lackluster seasons.

a. How might adverse selection explain this outcome?

b. How might moral hazard cause this outcome? Explain.

c. What advice would you give owners in bidding for free agents?

10. Many companies give out perquisites (the corner office, company cars, etc.) strictly on the basis of seniority. Likewise, companies frequently allocate tasks based on seniority. For example, many airlines assign routes to pilots and flight attendants based on seniority. What are the advantages and disadvantages of the seniority system?

11. Team decision making frequently mitigates information and coordination problems. What are some of the costs of teams?

12. For planning purposes, company headquarters seeks to obtain accurate information about the productive capacity of one of its plants. The plant manager knows that the facility's capacity is $Q = 10,000$ units, but knows that headquarters is in the dark. Using a bonus system, headquarters also wants to encourage the manager to strive for maximum plant output.

a. Headquarters decides to use the bonus system:

$$B = .5(Q - Q_T),$$

where the plant manager forecasts the likely output Q_T. If actual output Q exceeds Q_T at the end of the year, the bonus increases. If Q falls short of Q_T, the bonus is reduced. Under this system, will the manager report the plant's true capacity, 10,000 units? Explain.

b. Suppose instead that headquarters uses the following bonus system:

$$B = .4Q_T + .3(Q - Q_T), \text{ if } Q > Q_T, \text{ and}$$
$$B = .4Q_T + .5(Q - Q_T), \text{ if } Q < Q_T.$$

Will the manager report the plant's true capacity? Will the manager strive for maximum output? Explain.

Discussion Question

The last 20 years have witnessed a revolution in information technology. The emergence of low-cost information storage, retrieval, sharing, and transmission systems has begun to change the organization of firms in numerous ways.

a. What effect might the IT revolution have on the large-scale firm's choice between undertaking an activity in-house or outsourcing it?

b. Top managers have ever increasing amounts of information ("knowledge capital") at their disposal, but a common lament is that this knowledge is not always available at the "right place" in the organization. An ideal IT system would promote efficient information sharing. In what respects would low-cost information sharing favor a centralized organization? A decentralized one?

c. In what ways might improved IT facilitate the management-worker relationship within the firm? How might IT be labor saving?

Spreadsheet Problem

S1. Suppose that the gross profit generated by a particular worker is given by $\pi = 1,000e + u$, where e denotes the worker's effort (measured as an index between 0 and 50) and u is a random variable with a mean of zero and a positive standard deviation. Thus, profit depends not only on the worker's effort but also on random factors beyond his control. The worker's disutility associated with effort is given by $D = 10e^2$. The employer compensates the worker with an incentive contract of the form $P = W + b\pi$, where W is a fixed wage component and b is the worker's profit share. For concreteness, let $e = 30$, and suppose that the contract calls for $W = \$10,000$ and $b = .3$. Then the expected gross profit attributable to the worker is $\$30,000$. The employer's expected wage payment is $\$10,000 + (.3)(\$30,000) = \$19,000$, and the employer's expected profit is $\$30,000 - \$19,000 = \$11,000$. In turn, the worker's expected profit (net of any disutility) is $\$19,000 - 10(30)^2 = \$10,000$.

Under an incentive contract, the variability in the worker's wage (i.e., the risk) increases with the profit share b. A risk-averse worker will *discount* the expected profit listed earlier by a risk premium to account for the burden of risk. To be precise, we suppose that the risk premium takes the form $R = 10,000b^2$. The maximum premium, $10,000, occurs under 100 percent profit sharing ($b = 1$). Of course, for $b = 0$, the wage is fixed, so there is no risk and no risk premium. For $b = .3$, the premium is $900, so the worker's risk-adjusted profit is $10,000 − $900 = $9,100. In general, the worker's risk-adjusted profit is given by:

$$\pi_w = W + b(1,000e) - 10e^2 - 10,000b^2.$$

a. Create a spreadsheet similar to the example given. For the contract with $W = \$10,000$ and $b = .3$, find the worker's optimal level of effort. (*Hint*: Use the spreadsheet's optimizer to maximize the worker's risk-adjusted profit in cell E12. Alternatively, adjust the worker's effort until $M\pi_w = 1,000b - 20e$ in cell E17 is exactly equal to zero.)

b. Find the worker's optimal effort levels for sharing rates of .4, .6, .8, and 1.0. What pattern do you detect?

	A	B	C	D	E	F
1						
2		AN OPTIMAL INCENTIVE CONTRACT				
3						
4		Fixed	Profit	Worker's	Expected	
5		Wage (W)	Share (b)	Effort	Gross Profit	
6						
7		10,000	0.30	30	30,000	
8						
9		Expected	Worker's	Worker's	Risk-adjusted	
10		Compensation	Risk Premium	Disutility	Profit	
11						
12		19,000	900	9,000	9,100	
13						
14		Employer's	Total		Worker's	
15		Profit	Profit		Marginal Profit	
16						
17		11,000	20,100		−300	
18						

c. Using the optimizer, find the sharing rate and level of effort that together maximize the employer and worker's total profit. (*Hint*: Adjust cells C7 and D7 to maximize cell C17 subject to the constraint that $M\pi_w$ in cell E17 is equal to zero.) Does this optimal contract carry a strong or weak profit incentive?

d. If e were observable, then the parties could write a forcing contract with a fixed wage ($b = 0$) payable as long as the worker delivers an optimal level of effort. What level of effort maximizes total profit? Compare the total profits attained in this case with the total profits in part (c).

Suggested References

The following articles are some of the classic treatments of asymmetric information, principal–agent problems, and organizational design:

Akerlof, G. "The Market for 'Lemons': Quality Uncertainty and the Market Mechanism." *Quarterly Journal of Economics* (1970): 488–500.

Brynjolfsson, E., and L. M. Hitt. "Beyond Computation: Information Technology, Organizational Transformation, and Business Performance." *Journal of Economic Perspectives* (2000): 23–48.

Coase, R. "The Nature of the Firm." *Economica* (1937): 386–405.

Jensen, M. C., and W. Meckling. "Theory of the Firm: Managerial Behavior, Agency Costs and Ownership Structure." *Journal of Financial Economics* (1976): 305–360.

Lazear, E. P., and K. L. Shaw. "Personnel Economics: The Economist's View of Human Resources." *Journal of Economic Perspectives* (Fall 2007): 91–114.

Riley, J. G. "Silver Signals: Twenty-Five Years of Screening and Signalling." *Journal of Economic Literature* (2001): 432–478.

The following works discuss the problem of incentives in contracting and finance, respectively:

LePatner, B. B. *Broken Buildings, Busted Budgets: How to Fix America's Trillion-Dollar Construction Industry.* Chicago: University of Chicago Press, 2007.

Shiller, R. *The Subprime Solution: How Today's Global Financial Crisis Happened, and What to Do about It.* Princeton, NJ: Princeton University Press, 2008.

The following texts offer superb treatments of organizational design:

Brickley, J. A., C. W. Smith, and J. L. Zimmerman. *Managerial Economics and Organizational Architecture.* New York: McGraw-Hill, 2008.

Milgrom, P., and J. Roberts. *Economics, Organization and Management.* Englewood Cliffs, NJ: Prentice-Hall, 1992.

An interesting place to begin an Internet search is Erik Brynjolfsson's home page (with links to research on organizational structure and information technology): http://ebusiness.mit.edu/erik.

Check Station Answers

1. A used-car dealer faces two types of adverse selection problems. First, the dealer is in the business of buying cars and must take care to avoid low-quality vehicles. Thus, it is wise to have staff mechanics to inspect vehicles before purchase. The dealer must also sell used cars to the suspecting public. By developing a good reputation and by offering warranties, the dealer can mitigate these adverse selection problems as well.

2. Under capitation, after being paid its up-front fees, the physicians' group pays for all costs. Therefore, it has the strongest possible incentive to practice preventive care (provided, of course, that it is cost-effective). A possible problem with this approach is the presence of adverse selection. A doctors' group has an incentive to enlist the healthiest segments of the population and to turn its back on those in poor health. Under capitation, doctors face substantial financial risks. (At the end of the year, the costs paid out may exceed the capitation revenues received.) This raises a new moral hazard problem. Heightened cost incentives might induce doctors to compromise the quality of care (to maintain their incomes).

3. Optimizing the size of a team involves trading off the marginal benefits of adding another member (another perspective and source of information) against the additional cost. Besides the cost in human resources, added costs would include the difficulty in communicating and reaching consensus and the heightening of free-rider problems. As always, the optimal trade-off occurs where MB = MC.

4. Suppose the worker's profit share is exactly 60 percent. Now if the worker changes from medium effort to high effort, his expected compensation increases by $(.6)(\$85,000 - \$75,000) = \$6,000$, according to Table 14.3. The resulting change in disutility is $\$45,000 - \$39,000 = \$6,000$. Thus, the worker is exactly indifferent to exerting the extra effort. Raising the profit share slightly above 60 percent tips the decision to high effort (the optimal choice).

5. This is a classic manifestation of the growing separation of management and control in successful, growing firms. Formerly, the inventor was best equipped to shepherd the firm's new product. At this later stage in the product life cycle, efficiency may dictate the institution of professional managers. The drop in the entrepreneur's ownership stake is probably also a reflection of efficient financial diversification on his or her part.

CHAPTER 15

Bargaining and Negotiation

To get to the Promised Land, you have to negotiate your way through the wilderness.

H. COHEN

LO#1. Describe the economic factors that create opportunities for mutually beneficial agreements.

LO#2. Explain how the presence of multiple issues affects negotiations.

LO#3. Discuss the balance of competition and cooperation in negotiation strategy.

Sanofi's Bid for Genzyme

In Spring 2010, Christopher Viehbacher, CEO of the French pharmaceutical giant, Sanofi-Aventis SA, set his sights on acquiring Genzyme Corporation, a pioneering biotechnology company based in Cambridge, Massachusetts. A year and a half on the job, Viehbacher's mandate was to turn around Sanofi by cutting costs and finding new sources of revenue to replace the loss in sales from its series of drugs losing their patent protection. Known for its research, Genzyme had a number of profitable drugs in its sales pipeline (particularly ones treating rare diseases) and a potential blockbuster drug in development for treating multiple sclerosis. However, in the past year Genzyme's profit and stock price had taken huge hits due to contamination problems that temporarily shut down its main production site.

Throughout 2010, Viehbacher carried out secret talks with Henri Termeer, the CEO of Genzyme. However, Veihbacher's irresistible force was met by Termeer's immovable object. Backed by his directors, Termeer, who had been with the company since its creation, saw no economic reason for Genzyme to be acquired. Moreover, the two sides could not come close to agreeing on Genzyme's proper valuation and on a mutually agreeable sale price. Finally, in October 2010, Sanofi announced a hostile takeover bid for Genzyme at a price of $69 per share, some 38 percent above the company's stock price in previous months. But Termeer, Genzyme's board, and its shareholders showed no interest in selling out at that price.

Amidst the sides' conflicting assessments of the acquisition and given its potential risks, could a mutually beneficial deal be achieved? If so, how should it be negotiated and structured?

Negotiation and bargaining are important features of many economic settings. Examples include negotiating the terms of a sales transaction, management-labor bargaining, and settling a dispute out of court, to name just a few. Generally speaking, these are situations in which both parties stand to benefit from a cooperative agreement. Nonetheless, a significant degree of conflict remains because each side seeks to secure an agreement at terms most favorable to itself.

Many economic transactions are completed by means of bargaining under bilateral monopoly—that is, in settings in which a single seller faces a single buyer. In contrast to organized markets, in which competition among large numbers of buyers and sellers determines price and quantity, in bargaining settings the competition is one on one. Although the analysis of market competition obviously deserves attention (see Chapters 7, 8, and 9), it is worth remembering that there are other important means of resource allocation.

Our objectives in this chapter are twofold. In the first two sections, we analyze the economic forces underlying the bargaining setting: What economic factors create the opportunity for mutually beneficial agreements? What form do economically efficient bargains take? In answering this question, we revisit the David Letterman negotiations introduced in Chapter 1. Next, we examine bargaining strategy from the perspective of decision making under uncertainty: What bargaining strategy maximizes management's expected profit from the transaction? What are the risks of such a strategy? We conclude by examining settings calling for repeated negotiations and consider the many reasons why negotiations may fail.

THE ECONOMIC SOURCES
OF BENEFICIAL AGREEMENTS

It takes two to tango and three to form a ménage à trois. In other words, economic agents enter into transactions because the transactions are mutually beneficial. A well-crafted agreement is better for both parties than no agreement at all. Moreover, some agreements are better (for both parties) than others. Given this observation, it is natural to explore the economic factors that create the opportunities for mutually beneficial agreements. We begin our discussion by considering a typical negotiated transaction involving a buyer and a seller.

SELLING A WAREHOUSE   Two firms are locked in negotiations concerning the sale of a warehouse, the equipment therein, and a considerable inventory of industrial machinery. The main issue is price. The present owner is closing down its current operation in a move to redirect its resources into other businesses. The warehouse is in a valuable location for the would-be buyer, who also could make direct use of the equipment and machinery inventory. The buyer has examined the warehouse and contents and, after considerable figuring, has estimated its value for the transaction at $600,000; that is, the potential buyer is indifferent to the options of paying $600,000 to complete the purchase or forgoing the transaction altogether. The seller sets its value for the transaction at $520,000; this is the net amount the firm estimates it would obtain, on average, from selling the warehouse and contents via a broker or at auction. The buyer and seller values are referred to as **reservation prices** or **walk-away prices**.

Given the values held by buyer and seller, it is evident that a mutually beneficial agreement is possible. In particular, both parties would prefer an agreement at a price between $520,000 and $600,000 to the alternative of no agreement at all. For convenience, we denote the sale price by P. The seller's profit from such a transaction is $P - \$520,000$, whereas the buyer's gain is $\$600,000 - P$. If there is no agreement on a price (and, therefore, no sale), each party earns zero profit. Clearly, any price such that $\$520,000 \leq P \leq \$600,000$ affords positive profits for both parties. This price range between the buyer and seller walk-away prices is referred to as the **zone of agreement**. Observe that the total gain (the sum of buyer and seller profit) from such a transaction is

$$(\$600,000 - P) + (P - \$520,000) = \$600,000 - \$520,000 = \$80,000.$$

The total gain (or trading gain) is measured by the difference between the buyer and seller values—that is, the size of the zone of agreement.

Figure 15.1 presents two views of the buyer-seller transaction. Part (a) shows the zone of agreement and possible negotiated prices within it. A price of $540,000 is shown at point A. At this price, the buyer claims $60,000 in profit and the seller claims $20,000. Obviously, at higher negotiated prices, the seller's profit increases and the buyer's profit falls dollar for dollar. Part (b) displays this profit trade-off explicitly. The parties' profits from transactions at various prices are graphed on the axes. The profits from a $540,000 price appear at point A. Prices of $560,000 and $580,000 (and the corresponding profits) are listed at points B and C, respectively. The downward-sloping line shows the profit implications for all possible prices within the zone of agreement. This is commonly called the **payoff frontier**. If the parties fail to reach an agreement, they obtain zero profits, as marked by point 0 at the origin of the graph.

Figure 15.1 reemphasizes a simple but important point about the gains from a negotiated agreement. An agreement at any price between $520,000 and $600,000 is better for both parties than no agreement. The "no agreement" outcome is said to be *inefficient* because there exists one or more alternative outcomes that are better for both parties. We say that *an outcome is efficient if no other outcome exists that is better for both parties.*[1] By this definition, all of the outcomes along the payoff frontier are efficient. For instance, consider an agreement at a $520,000 price. Any change in price that makes one party better off necessarily makes the other worse off; that is, there is no other agreement that is better for both parties. Thus, this agreement is efficient.

This example, simple as it is, illustrates the mixture of cooperative and competitive elements in bargaining. The parties must cooperate to reach some mutually beneficial agreement. But, of course, the price at which an agreement occurs is a matter of competition: The buyer prefers a low price, the seller a high price. In the negotiation literature this situation is called a *distributive* bargain, because the parties can be thought of as bargaining (via price) over the distribution of the total profit (in this case, $80,000)

---

[1]More precisely, an agreement is efficient if there is no other agreement that makes one party better off without making the other worse off.

FIGURE 15.1

The Zone of Agreement
and the Payoff Frontier

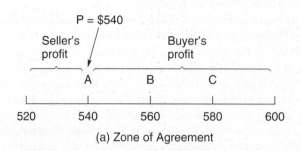

(a) Zone of Agreement

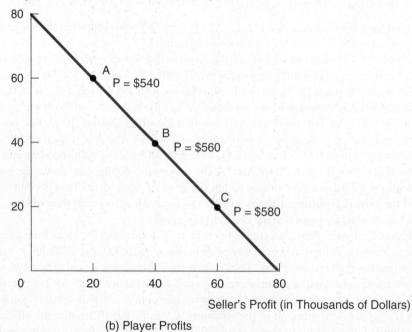

(b) Player Profits

available from the transaction. The actual price they negotiate depends in part on the bargaining abilities of the parties and on notions of equity and fairness. For instance, a final price in the vicinity of $560,000 (implying $40,000 in profit for each side) might be negotiated by equally matched bargainers who are in agreement that the total bargaining profit should be divided equitably. For the moment, however, our analysis has identified the zone of agreement without offering a prediction of which price within this zone will be the agreement terms.

Two additional points can be drawn from the example. First, the source of the trading gains is the difference in the parties' values. Because the seller's value for the warehouse and items is less than the buyer's value, completion of the transaction creates a trading gain that both sides share. In contrast, if the agent values were reversed (i.e., the seller's value was $600,000 and the buyer's value $520,000), no mutually beneficial transaction would be possible. Second, the values or reservation prices of the parties are influenced by the alternative transactions available to them. In the present circumstances, for instance, the buyer estimates the monetary value for the warehouse at $600,000. Clearly, if the buyer learned of the availability of another warehouse at a comparable location at an unexpectedly low price, its walk-away price for the current transaction would fall markedly. Similarly, if the buyer revised downward its estimate of the potential profit from the warehouse operation (because of adverse economic conditions in general), its walk-away value also would fall. Of course, the importance of outside opportunities pertains equally to the seller. These outside opportunities are often referred to as each side's BATNA—best alternative to a negotiated agreement. The alternative transactions available to the parties directly or indirectly set the respective walk-away prices between which negotiated agreements can occur.

CHECK STATION 1

***Fifty Shades of Grey* by British Author E.L. James has been a remarkable worldwide best seller. The erotic romance novel was originally published in paperback by a small Australian print-on-demand publisher. The eBook version was self-published by the author, and favorable "word of mouth" sent eBook sales soaring. In 2012, James sold Random House, Inc. the paperback and eBook rights to the *Fifty Shades* Trilogy after negotiating with various major publishers. What was the economic basis for this mutually beneficial agreement?**

Resolving Disputes

As we have seen, negotiation is a frequent means of securing new transactions. It also plays an essential role in dispute resolution. Examples include management–labor negotiations, international negotiations, conflicts between government regulators and business, and legal disputes. As we will see, the resolution of an ongoing dispute offers exactly the same kind of mutual benefits as the forging of a new agreement. The following typical example makes the point.

A PATENT CONFLICT   A small manufacturer of a specialty pump used in oil refineries and nuclear reactors has filed a $4 million lawsuit against a leading pump company for patent infringement. Three years after the small firm successfully introduced its pump, the large firm began to sell a similar pump at lower prices. The small firm claims its rival *reverse engineered* its pump and then copied it, making only small modifications. The small firm holds numerous patents on the pump's "unique" valves and circuitry—patents that it claims have been infringed upon. The large company has filed its own patents and claims the pump it developed is unique (and, indeed, is more similar in design to its own 10-year-old model than to the small firm's model).

The firms' legal representatives are conducting negotiations aimed at reaching an out-of-court settlement. Both sides recognize that a full-scale trial will be very costly—in all likelihood, more costly for the small firm. How should each side approach the negotiations? Can the parties reach a mutually beneficial out-of-court agreement?

For either side, an optimal negotiating strategy depends critically on its best estimate of the expected monetary outcome if the case goes to court. After all, the court outcome is the relevant alternative to a negotiated agreement. The problem is that the court outcome is highly uncertain. The court's award of monetary damages (if any) can vary over a wide range. Under a "no infringement" ruling, the large firm would owe zero damages. Alternatively, if a broad infringement is found, the large firm could be ordered to cease sale of the pump altogether and pay maximum damages. Outcomes in between include narrowly defined infringements (of a particular valve, for instance), with damages based on larger or smaller estimates of the resulting economic loss suffered by the small company.

Given these multiple uncertainties, each side would be well advised to take a cue from Chapters 12 and 13 and construct a decision tree incorporating the sequence and probabilities of the different possible outcomes and monetary consequences. Suppose each side has done this and has averaged back its tree to compute the expected litigation value of the case (i.e., the amount on average that the court will order the large firm to pay the small firm). Let v_S and v_L denote the small and large firms' respective expected values. Because the two sides are likely to see the risks and possible outcomes differently, these estimates will also differ from each other. In addition, the firms have in hand estimates of the total costs (legal and other) of fighting the case in court. We denote these costs by c_S and c_L, respectively.

With this information in hand, we can evaluate the monetary implications for each side of going to court. The small firm's expected profit, net of court costs, is $v_S - c_S$. The large firm's expected expense, including court costs, is $v_L + c_L$. Thus, a proposed out-of-court settlement (call this P) is beneficial for both sides if and only if

$$v_S - c_S \leq P \leq v_L + c_L.$$ [15.1]

This range of out-of-court settlements constitutes the zone of agreement. To illustrate, suppose the firms' assessments of the case are identical. Let's say that the expected litigation value is $v_S = v_L = \$1$ million, and court costs are $c_S = \$200,000$ and $c_L = \$160,000$, respectively. Then any out-of-court settlement (i.e., a payment from the large firm to the small firm) between $800,000 and $1.16 million is mutually beneficial. As always, the size of the zone of agreement measures the total benefit at stake in reaching an agreement.

The collective benefit from an agreement is simply the sum of the court costs the disputants save by avoiding litigation. (Let's check this: The size of the zone of agreement is $\$1,160,000 - \$800,000 = \$360,000$, which is exactly the sum of the court costs.) The exact terms of the agreement dictate how this benefit is split. For instance, under an agreement at $P = \$1$ million, the parties settle for what each agrees is the expected litigation outcome. In the process, each side saves its court costs. (Under an agreement at $P = \$980,000$, each side saves $180,000 relative to its expected litigation outcome.)

Differences in Values

The preceding discussion and examples illustrate a basic principle:

> Differences in values create opportunities for parties to craft mutually beneficial agreements.

The following applications involve decisions under uncertainty and explore two sources of value differences: differences in probability assessments and differences in attitudes toward risk.

PROBABILITY ASSESSMENTS   Even if two parties have identical preferences, they may assess different values for a transaction due to different probability assessments and forecasts. For instance, an agreement may be supported by each side's *optimistic* belief that the transaction is substantially better than no agreement at all. As Mark Twain said, "It is differences of opinion that make horse races." Many transactions involve an element of a bet: Each side believes it has a better assessment of the transaction's value than the other and will gain (possibly) at the other's expense. Of course, differences in probability assessments also can work against negotiated agreements. The following application makes the point.

SETTLEMENT NEGOTIATIONS REVISITED   Let's return to the patent dispute, but now suppose the firms hold different, conflicting assessments about the litigation value of the case. The small firm believes there is a .6 chance that its side will win the case (i.e., there will be a finding of patent infringement). The large firm assesses a .6 chance that *it* will win the case (i.e., no infringement will be found). Both sides estimate an expected damage award of $2 million for an infringement finding and no damages otherwise. Therefore, the parties' expected values are: $v_S = (.6)(\$2.0) = \$1.2$ million and $v_L = (.4)(2.0) = \$.8$ million. Accounting for the parties' legal costs (as in constraint 15.1), the least the small firm will accept out of court is $1 million, whereas the most the large firm will offer is $960,000. Thus, there is no zone of agreement. In general, a negotiated settlement is possible if and only if there is some price, P, such that constraint 15.1 is satisfied. An equivalent constraint is

$$v_S - v_L \leq c_S + c_L, \qquad\qquad [15.2]$$

which is derived by rearranging constraint 15.1. A mutually beneficial settlement is possible if and only if the difference between the parties' litigation expectations is smaller than the combined court costs.

RISK AVERSION   Recall from the discussion in Chapter 12 that a risk-averse agent assesses the value for an uncertain outcome to be significantly lower than its expected value (*EV*). This value is termed the outcome's certainty equivalent (*CE*). In algebraic terms, $CE < EV$. The greater the agent's risk aversion and/or the riskiness of the outcome, the greater the gap between the certainty equivalent and expected value.

The presence of risk aversion motivates transactions that minimize and/or share risks among the parties. For instance, consider the patent dispute once again. We saw that, when each side assessed its winning chances at 60 percent, the parties' expected payoffs (court costs included) were $1 million and −$960,000; thus, no settlement was possible. However, because the litigation outcome is highly uncertain, we can expect each risk-averse disputant to value going to court at a *CE* value considerably below its EV. For example, suppose the small firm judges its *CE* value for going to court at $800,000 (including court costs), and the large firm sets *CE* = −$1.1 million. Now there is a $300,000-wide zone of agreement in the settlement negotiations. The presence of risk aversion makes a *certain* out-of-court settlement more attractive than a risky outcome in court (even though each side is optimistic about the outcome at trial).

As a general principle, transactions should be designed so that risks are assumed by the party best able to bear them. Consider the wildcatter in Chapter 12 who holds an option to drill for oil on a geological site. Suppose the wildcatter estimates the expected profit of the site to be $140,000 but, being risk averse, assesses the CE value of the site to be considerably less than this—say, $100,000. Should the wildcatter explore the site or sell the option to a giant exploration company that drills scores of wells in all parts of the world? Suppose the large drilling company is risk neutral. If its geologists agree with the wildcatter's probabilistic assessments, the company's value for the site is $140,000. Consequently, the option can be sold at a mutually beneficial price between $100,000 and $140,000. The option should be transferred to the risk-neutral party because that party values the site more highly.

A classic case of a transaction designed for optimal risk bearing is the cost-plus contract used in high-risk procurements. The risks concerning performance, cost, and timetable of delivery in defense procurement—for instance, in the development of a new weapons system or aircraft—are enormous. As a result, the usual fixed-price contract, in which the defense contractor is paid a fixed price and bears all production risk, is impractical (that is, the firm would set an extremely high fixed price—add a substantial risk premium—to compensate for possible cost overruns). Given its vast financial wealth, the federal government arguably can be characterized as risk neutral. The government, rather than the firm, should bear the contract risk. Under a cost-plus contract, the government reimburses the firm for all allowable costs and pays it a fixed profit amount in addition. The large variability in cost is borne by the government buyer, whereas the contractor's profit is guaranteed. The government benefits by paying the firm a much lower profit fee than would be required if the firm were the risk bearer.[2]

When both parties are risk averse, the optimal response to uncertainty is **risk sharing**. Returning to the oil example, suppose a second drilling firm is identical to the first; that is, it is equally risk averse and holds the same probability assessments. Then the site has a CE value of $100,000 to either party. Because there is no difference in value, there is no possibility of mutual benefit from an outright sale. But consider what happens if the two companies form a partnership to share equally (i.e., 50-50) all profits and losses from drilling. The expected value of each side's 50 percent profit share is, of course, $70,000. What is each side's CE for its share? Because each outfit now is exposed to considerably smaller risks, this CE will be *higher* than $50,000 (one-half the

---

[2]One disadvantage of the cost-plus contract is that it offers the firm very little incentive to keep costs down.

CE of 100 percent ownership), though still lower than $70,000. In effect, each firm is more nearly risk neutral when its risk is reduced proportionally. Let's say each outfit's CE is $60,000. Then the total value of drilling as a partnership is $60,000 + $60,000 = $120,000. By selling a 50 percent profit share (for, say, $50,000), the original option holder is better off (its total value increases from $100,000 to $110,000), as is the purchaser (with an expected profit of $60,000 – $50,000 = $10,000). Thus, risk sharing has promoted a mutually beneficial transaction.[3]

Suppose five identical, risk-averse wildcatters form a partnership to share equally the profit or loss from the site discussed earlier. What is the effect on each outfit's expected profit and CE? What about the total value of the partnership (i.e., the sum of the individual CEs)? As a thought experiment, extend the example to a 20-member syndicate. What happens to the total value of the syndicate as the risk is split among more and more firms?

CHECK
STATION 2

Contingent Contracts

Agreements containing contingency clauses are a widespread response to the presence of risk and uncertainty in economic transactions. Under a contingent contract, the terms of the sale depend, in clearly defined ways, on the outcomes of future events. Cost-plus contracts designed for high-risk procurements constitute one broad class of contingent contracts. The widespread use of variable-rate mortgages is another important example. Such contracts facilitate risk sharing; the use of contingent pricing typically means that both sides' returns depend on the outcomes of uncertain economic variables. Contingent contracts also can facilitate transactions when parties hold conflicting probability assessments. The following example makes the point.

CONTINGENT PRICING IN AN ACQUISITION   Firm A is negotiating to buy a division of firm T. The difficulty is that the value of the division depends on whether it wins the bidding for a major contract from the government. If it wins, the division will be worth $20 million under current management and $22 million if acquired by firm A. If it loses, it will be worth $10 million under current management and $12 million if acquired by firm A. In either case, the division is worth more to firm A than to firm T, due to synergies with firm A's other operations. Firm T judges a 0.7 probability that the division will win the contract, but firm A judges this probability to be only 0.4. Is a mutually beneficial agreement possible?

To answer this question, first consider a straight cash buyout. Firm T values the division at $(.7)(20) + (.3)(10) = \$17$ million. The price must be at least this high to be acceptable. Firm A computes the expected value at $(.4)(22) + (.6)(12) = \$16$ million, so it will pay no more than this. Consequently, a cash buyout is impossible. Both sides

---

[3]Since the two firms are identical, 50-50 risk sharing constitutes an optimal (i.e., value-maximizing) contract.

agree that the division will be worth more under firm A than under firm T (regardless of the contract outcome). But the parties' different, conflicting probability assessments make a straight cash purchase impossible.

However, the acquisition can be consummated if a contingent-pricing clause is included. Suppose the parties agree that the purchase price will be $21 million if the government contract is won and $11 million if it is not. Clearly these price terms provide each side a $1 million profit regardless of the government contract outcome. Contingent pricing neatly overcomes the obstacle posed by conflicting probability beliefs.

The use of contingent contracts is a common response to risk and uncertainty in purchase and sale arrangements. Warranties and guarantees are obvious examples. Here the terms of the agreement are adjusted in light of future events. Another response to uncertainty is the use of incentive contracts, which call for both buyer and seller to share the burden of cost overruns. Acquisition of an enterprise at a purchase price that depends on the firm's future earnings is still another example. Corporate acquisitions paid for with securities of the acquiring firm embody an element of contingent pricing. If the acquisition is truly valuable, the securities of the merged company will appreciate.

MULTIPLE-ISSUE NEGOTIATIONS

Thus far, we have considered single-issue agreements in which price is the only object of the negotiation. Here an agreement within a range of prices is mutually preferred to no agreement at all. The negotiation setting becomes more complicated when the terms of an agreement involve multiple issues, such as performance specifications, service requirements, or product attributes, as well as price. When multiple issues are at stake, the parties cannot be satisfied in simply finding an agreement; rather, the goal is to uncover an optimal agreement—one that, roughly speaking, is best for both parties.

Even if the parties have conflicting interests on each of many separate issues, diligent negotiations can arrive at a well-crafted agreement that is better for both sides than alternative agreements. The simplest of examples suffices to make the point. Consider two members of a legislative committee whose interests are directly opposed on each of two issues. Ms. A strongly favors issue 1 and weakly opposes issue 2. Mr. B strongly favors issue 2 and weakly opposes issue 1. Can these members fashion a mutually beneficial voting agreement? The answer is yes. They should agree to "swap votes" so that both vote affirmatively on each issue. By gaining a vote on the issue that is more important to him or her, each member is better off after the swap (even though the member votes against his or her strict self-interest on the unimportant issue). This example illustrates a principle that is applicable to bargaining in general:

> In multiple-issue negotiations, as long as there are differences in the value (importance) parties place on issues, there will be opportunities for mutually beneficial agreements of a *quid pro quo* nature.

In multiple-issue bargaining involving monetary transfers, the key to the attainment of efficiency is to structure agreements to maximize the *total* value the parties derive from the transaction. The logic of this result is quite simple. The transacting parties should form an agreement that maximizes the size of the profit "pie" to be split. Then negotiation of an overall price for the transaction has the effect of dividing the pie between the parties. Any such division of the maximal total value is efficient; one side cannot gain without the other side losing. In turn, any division of a less-than-maximal total value is necessarily inefficient. An appropriately priced maximal-value agreement delivers higher profits for both sides. Here is a concrete example.

A COMPLEX PROCUREMENT   The Department of Defense (DOD) is in the process of negotiating a procurement contract for aircraft engines with an aeronautics firm. The contract will specify the number of engines to be delivered, the time of delivery, and the total price to be paid by DOD to the contractor. The firm has assessed its total cost of supplying various quantities of engines by different deadlines. For its part, DOD has assessed monetary values (its maximum willingness to pay) for different contracted deliveries. Table 15.1 lists the parties' costs and values.

Suppose DOD and the firm are considering a contract for 40 engines in four years at a price of $39 million. Is this contract mutually beneficial? Could both parties do better under a different contract at the right price? Of the nine possible combinations of order sizes and delivery dates, which should the parties adopt?

From Table 15.1, we find the parties' profits under the 40-engine, four-year contract ($39 million price) as follows: The firm's profit is $39 − $36 = $3 million; DOD's profit is $42 − $39 = $3 million. Clearly, this is a mutually beneficial agreement. However, it is evident from the table that the parties can improve on these contract terms. The value-maximizing contract calls for 80 engines to be delivered in three years. This contract offers a total profit of $85 − $70 = $15 million. (This is just the difference between

TABLE 15.1

A Multiple-Issue Procurement Contract

(a) The Firm's Costs (Millions of Dollars)

Number of Engines	Time of Delivery		
	2 Years	3 Years	4 Years
40	40	38	36
60	60	55	51
80	80	70	65

A contract calling for 80 engines to be delivered in three years provides the greatest total profit ($15 million) to the parties.

(b) Department of Defense Values (Millions of Dollars)

Number of Engines	Time of Delivery		
	2 Years	3 Years	4 Years
40	50	46	42
60	72	69	63
80	90	85	78

DOD's value and the firm's cost.) At a $77.5 million price, each side earns a $7.5 million profit—some two-and-one-half times the profit under the four-year, 40-engine agreement. The three-year, 80-engine contract is efficient. All other contracts offer lower total profits and, therefore, are inefficient.

CHECK STATION 3   In negotiating a contract, firm A and firm B are considering three options. Firm A can supply firm B with a 97 percent pure compound, a 98 percent pure compound, or a 99 percent pure compound. Raising purity by 1 percent increases firm A's cost by $50,000. Firm B's potential profits are $200,000, $280,000, and $320,000 for the 97 percent, 98 percent, and 99 percent compounds. Which of the three options constitutes an efficient agreement (i.e., that maximizes the parties' total value or "pie")? Why?

Wooing David Letterman Revisited

In 1993, David Letterman faced the most difficult decision of his life. Should he agree to a renegotiated contract with NBC or take a new path and move to CBS? In the early 1990s, NBC's unbeatable late-night lineup, *The Tonight Show* with Johnny Carson and *Late Night* with Letterman, accounted for huge net revenues of some $100 million per year. But in 1992 NBC chose the comedian Jay Leno, instead of Letterman, to succeed Johnny Carson as the host of *The Tonight Show* in an effort to keep its lock on late-night programming. CBS, a nonentity in late-night television, saw its chance to woo David Letterman to a new 11:30 P.M. show on its network. After extensive negotiations, CBS offered Letterman a $14 million salary to do the new show (a $10 million raise over his salary at NBC). In addition, Letterman's own production company would be paid $25 million annually to produce the show. (By comparison, NBC produced *The Tonight Show* in house at an annual cost of $15 million.)

However, NBC was unwilling to surrender Letterman to CBS without a fight. The network entered into secret negotiations with Letterman's representative, Michael Ovitz, exploring the possibility of dumping Leno and giving *The Tonight Show* to Letterman. One group of NBC executives stood firmly behind Leno. Another group preferred replacing Leno to losing Letterman to CBS. Giving Letterman *The Tonight Show* would mean paying him much more, as well as buying out Leno's contract. Moreover, the network still would face certain risks: Would Letterman's brand of irreverent comedy appeal to the more mainstream television audience in the earlier time slot? What show would replace *Late Night*? Even if it retained Letterman as host of *The Tonight Show*, NBC had to face the fact that its new lineup (with an undetermined late-night entry) would produce only about $75 million in annual net revenue.

In the end, NBC offered *The Tonight Show* to Letterman—but with the condition that he wait a year until Leno's current contract was up.[4] Letterman yearned for a chance to showcase his talents in the earlier time slot. But he had been hurt and angry when NBC bypassed him for *The Tonight Show* in the first place. Now, NBC's last-ditch offer was too little too late. He decided to leave NBC. CBS executives were elated. Over a

---

[4]This account is based on B. Carter, *The Late Shift: Letterman, Leno, and the Network Battle for the Night* (New York: Hyperion, 1994); K. Auletta, "Late-Night Gamble," *The New Yorker* (February 1, 1993), pp. 38–46, and B. Carter, "A Letterman Deal with ABC Was Just a Signature Away," *The New York Times* (March 18, 2002), p. C1.

five-year horizon, they expected the new Letterman show to generate $35 million in net revenue per year. Over a longer period (assuming the establishment of a second show following Letterman), net revenues surely would increase, perhaps substantially.

When Willie Sutton was asked why he robbed banks, he replied, "Because that's where the money is." In some sense, this advice applies to the Letterman bargaining. Good negotiators should find their way to where the money is—that is, they should conclude value-maximizing deals. Let's step back and evaluate Letterman's possible deals with NBC or CBS.

Table 15.2 lists the main possibilities and the monetary consequences to each of the parties in the negotiations. (Values are annual estimates over the three years of Letterman's contract.) For comparison purposes, the first agreement shows the original status quo. NBC obtains $100 million in revenue and clears $63 million in profit after

TABLE 15.2

	NBC	CBS	Letterman	Total	The Letterman Negotiations
1. Dave at NBC, 12:30					
Revenue	100	0			
Dave's salary	−5		5		
Leno's salary	−2				
Cost of two shows	−30				
	63	0	5	68	
2. Dave to CBS, 11:30					
Revenue	50	35	9*		
Dave's salary		−14	14		
Leno, 1 new host	−3				
Shows: costs, profits	−30	−25	10 (25 − 15)		
	17	−4	33	46	
3. Dave to NBC, 11:30					
Revenue	75	0	9		
Dave's salary	−14		14		
Buy out Leno	−5				
Shows: costs, profits	−41		10		
	15	0	33	48	
4. Dave gets big raise					
Revenue	100	0			
Dave's salary	−25		25		
Leno's salary	−2				
Shows: costs, profits	−40		10		
	33	0	35	68	
5. Dave to CBS, 12:30					
Revenue	60?	40?			
Dave's salary		−14	14		
Leno 1 new host	−3				
Shows: costs, profits	−30	−25	10		
	27	1	24	52	

*Letterman's personal value for the 11:30 P.M. slot.

paying star salaries and $15 million to produce each show. Letterman earns $5 million, and CBS is out of the late-night business.

Now consider the new agreement. According to analysts' projections, NBC's net revenue was expected to drop to about $50 million per year. With its revenue cut in half (and only a modest savings in star salaries), NBC's profit is decimated. CBS's projected revenues are not quite sufficient to cover its costs. Did Michael Ovitz squeeze out the best deal for Letterman from CBS? The answer certainly seems to be yes. Clearly, CBS viewed snagging Letterman as an investment: Future revenue growth from Letterman is judged to be worth the initial loss.

The third column shows Letterman's good fortune. Besides his own salary, Letterman's production company stands to earn $10 million in profit ($25 million in revenue, minus $15 million in "normal" production costs). The "top" entry of $9 million requires some explanation. This estimate represents the personal value Letterman put on getting the 11:30 slot. Again and again during the negotiations, Letterman stated how much being able to perform for the broader mainstream audience meant to him. The $9 million is a guesstimate of how much the 11:30 slot was worth to him. In short, the total value of the deal to Letterman includes not only his monetary compensation but also the value he put on moving to 11:30.

What if NBC had dumped Leno and offered Letterman the earlier time slot at terms matching CBS's offer? The third agreement shows the consequences. NBC preserves most of its original revenue but must pay Letterman's price and also must buy out Leno (his salary plus about a $3 million annual penalty). NBC's profit from this option is even less than its profit if Letterman defects to CBS. Thus, in addition to its loyalty to Leno, NBC seems to have had a financial reason for not matching CBS's deal.

What is harder to explain is why NBC did not pay what was necessary to keep Letterman in his 12:30 slot. The fourth agreement has NBC giving Letterman $35 million per year, thereby beating CBS's deal. By doing so, NBC retains its $100 million late-night gold mine and earns $33 million in net profit. This is nearly twice the profit NBC can hope for if it loses Letterman. Given the monetary estimates in Table 15.2, this is the value-maximizing agreement. In this agreement, the parties' combined value is $68 million. By comparison, the combined value is somewhat less than $50 million in either the second or third agreements. Keeping NBC's late-night lineup intact appears to be where the money is.[5] CBS's entry into the late-night sweepstakes (via the second or third deals) has two value-reducing effects. First, it slices up the market, thus lowering total revenue. (Indeed, ABC's competing news show, *Nightline*, was probably the main beneficiary of the talk-show wars.) Second, adding a third show raises the networks' total costs. For completeness, the table shows a fifth possible deal in which Letterman agrees to a 12:30 show with CBS. Although such a move avoids an 11:30 head-to-head battle, the parties' total value is still significantly less than a don't-rock-the-boat agreement.

If money were the only thing that mattered, Letterman and NBC appear to have missed a mutually beneficial agreement. Of course, one can argue over the exact revenue and cost implications of the deals. (However, a quick sensitivity analysis shows that

---

[5]Note that the fourth agreement produces exactly the same total value ($68 million) as the original status quo. Of course, the main difference is how this profit is divided. By virtue of CBS's competitive offer, NBC is forced to concede a substantial payoff to Letterman.

NBC's retaining Letterman at 12:30 would have been the efficient agreement, short of drastic alterations in the revenue and cost figures.) Nonmonetary factors, particularly Letterman's disappointment when he was spurned as Johnny Carson's successor, may offer the best explanations for the ultimate negotiated outcome.

Does history ever repeat itself? In 2002, ABC made an aggressive effort to lure Letterman from CBS after negotiations to renew his contract had become acrimonious. At the same time, CBS set in motion a contingency plan to attract late night host Conan O'Brien from NBC should it lose Letterman. In the end, Letterman decided to stay with CBS, and in 2009, O'Brien took over hosting *The Tonight Show* when NBC decided to move Leno to an earlier slot. This was short-lived, as both time slots suffered. NBC moved Leno back to 11:35. After some negotiation, O'Brien reached a settlement with NBC and began his own late night show, *Conan,* on TBS.

Jay Leno retired in 2014, and NBC replaced him with Jimmy Fallon. A few months later, Letterman announced his retirement as well, and CBS named Stephen Colbert as the new host for *The Late Show*.

We can sum up our discussion in this section with the following proposition:

> When there are available monetary transfers that redistribute bargainers' payoffs dollar for dollar, an efficient agreement is one that maximizes the parties' total value from the transaction.

NEGOTIATION STRATEGY

Negotiations inevitably produce tension between the forces of competition and cooperation. To reach a mutually beneficial agreement, both sides must cooperate. More than that, they must strive to uncover better agreements. Yet each side's ultimate objective is to secure the most favorable agreement for itself. Thus far, our discussion has focused on identifying efficient agreements, that is, outlining the best the parties can do together. However, for a variety of reasons, bargaining as actually practiced often falls far short of optimal outcomes. In his seminal work on bargaining, *The Strategy of Conflict,* Thomas Schelling puts the problem this way:

> Most bargaining situations ultimately involve some range of possible outcomes within which each party would rather make a concession than fail to reach agreement at all. In such a situation any potential outcome is one from which at least one of the parties, and probably both, would have been willing to retreat for the sake of agreement, and very often the other side knows it. Any potential outcome is therefore one that either party could have improved by insisting; yet he may have no basis for insisting, since the other knows or suspects that he would rather concede than do without an agreement. Each party's strategy is guided mainly by what he expects the other side to insist on; yet each knows that the other is guided by reciprocal thoughts. The final outcome must be a point from which neither expects the other to retreat.[6]

[6] T. C. Schelling, *The Strategy of Conflict* (Cambridge, MA: Harvard University Press, 1990).

To put this another way, any set of terms falling inside the zone of agreement can be supported as an *equilibrium* outcome. As an example, consider two parties bargaining over the division of the total profit from a mutually beneficial transaction. Bargaining takes place in the simplest possible way: Each side makes a *single* offer, naming his or her share of the total profit. If the offers are compatible (i.e., they add up to less than 100 percent of the total profit), there is an agreement (each party getting his or her offer); otherwise, there is no agreement. Here any pair of offers summing to exactly 100 percent constitutes an equilibrium. For instance, offers of 50 percent each are in equilibrium. Neither side can profit by (1) demanding more, because this leads to a disagreement and zero profit, or (2) demanding less, because this directly lowers his or her profit. In turn, the offers 80 percent and 20 percent (or any other pair of compatible offers, no matter how inequitable) are also in equilibrium. The cold truth is that, against an opponent whose nonnegotiable demand is for 80 percent of the profit, the best one can do is settle for the remaining 20 percent. To sum up, any division of the profit (equitable or inequitable) is an equilibrium outcome.

Via the dynamic process called bargaining, parties will arrive at some final outcome. But the multitude of equilibrium outcomes makes it difficult to predict which one. Clearly the final outcome depends significantly on the bargainers' expectations—expectations that are modified via the exchange of offers and counteroffers during the negotiations. In some sense, bargaining ceases when expectations converge, at a point where neither side can expect the other to concede further. Then either an agreement is signed or, if the sides stubbornly hold to conflicting expectations, a disagreement results.

Perfect Information

If both sides have perfect information—that is, there is no uncertainty about the economic facts of the negotiation—profit-maximizing bargainers always should reach an efficient agreement. The reason is simple. To settle for an inefficient agreement is to leave money on the table. This cannot be profit maximizing; there exist alternative terms providing greater profit for *both* parties. As we saw earlier, if the disputants in a conflict are sure of the disposition of the case if it goes to court, they should settle the case in the first place with both benefiting from saving the collective costs of going to court. At the same time, we should emphasize that what is true in theory does not always hold in practice. Even under perfect information, identifying and implementing efficient agreements is far from easy.

CHECK STATION 4   Two students are chosen at random and are given a $10 bill. They have two minutes to negotiate how to divide the money. If they reach an agreement, they keep their agreed-upon shares. Otherwise, each receives nothing.

a. What agreement (if any) do you think they will reach?

b. Suppose both know that in the event of a disagreement one of the students will still receive $2 while the other receives $0. How might this change the negotiations?

Imperfect Information

A more realistic description of the bargaining setting posits imperfect information on the part of the bargainers. Typically, each side has only limited information about its own values for potential agreements and, at best, will have only probabilistic information about the other side's values. Under imperfect information, issues of bargaining strategy become increasingly important. In a simple price negotiation, for instance, neither side knows for certain how far it can push the other before an agreement becomes impossible. Indeed, neither can be certain whether there is a zone of agreement. The negotiation process itself conveys information about possible acceptable agreements, but this information cannot be taken at face value. In everyday bargaining, the parties typically start with exaggerated and incompatible demands. It would be foolish for one side to concede immediately to the other's opening offer. Similarly, it would be unwise for one side to "lay its cards on the table" and reveal its true value for the transaction at the outset. In short, bargaining strategy calls for a significant element of bluff.

The theory of negotiation under uncertainty yields an important result:

> In bargaining settings under imperfect information, optimal bargaining behavior is incompatible with the attainment of efficient agreements all of the time.

Imperfect information presents a barrier to the attainment of efficient agreements both during and after the actual negotiations. As a general rule it is in the self-interest of each side to keep its values private—indeed, to misrepresent its values during the negotiations for the purpose of assuming a "tough" bargaining stance. The result is a predictable number of missed and/or inefficient agreements. The presence of uncertainty *after* an agreement is signed also poses problems. For instance, if agreements are difficult to monitor or enforce, there may be insufficient incentives for one or both parties to fulfill the terms of the agreement. The following example shows clearly how optimal bargaining behavior can result in a failure to attain certain beneficial agreements.

A TENDER OFFER   Firm A (the acquirer) is about to make a first-and-final price offer for the outright purchase of family-owned firm T (the target). Firm A is confident the target will be worth $1.6 million under A's own management. It has only a vague idea of firm T's reservation price, that is, the minimum price current management will accept. Its best guess is that this value (denoted by v) is *uniformly distributed* between $1 million and $2 million; that is, all possible values in this range are equally likely. What is the firm's best offer? How often will a sale be concluded?

Clearly the acquirer can confine its attention to offers in the $1 million to $1.6 million range. Firm A faces an obvious trade-off between the probability and profitability of agreements. The higher its offer, the greater the chance of acceptance, but the lower the transaction profit. The firm's expected profit from offer P is

$$E(\pi) = [1.6 - P]\Pr(P \text{ is accepted})$$
$$= (1.6 - P)(P - 1) = -1.6 + 2.6P - P^2. \qquad [15.3]$$

Here, we have used the fact that $\Pr(P$ is accepted$) = P - 1$. For instance, as predicted by this expression, the offer, $P = \$1.5$ million, is accepted half the time (by a target with a value anywhere between \$1 million and \$1.5 million). The higher offer, $P = \$1.8$ million, is accepted with probability .8, and so on. To maximize expected profit, we set

$$M\pi = dE(\pi)/dP = 2.6 - 2P = 0.$$

Thus, the optimal offer is: $P^* = \$1.3$ million. The probability that this price will be accepted is .3, implying that the acquirer's maximum expected profit is \$90,000. The point to underscore is this: The acquirer maximizes its expected profit by taking a calculated risk; it shades its offer well below its true value, even though this tactic poses the risk of missing possible agreements (whenever the target's value is between \$1.3 million and \$1.6 million).

The lesson of this example carries over to the case of multiple offers and counteroffers. In equilibrium, a self-interested bargainer should always hold out for terms that are strictly better than its true reservation price, thereby incurring the risk that some possible agreements are missed. Put another way, suppose one side always is willing to concede up to its true value, if necessary, to reach an agreement. Clearly, the other side could take advantage of this purely cooperative behavior by "waiting the player out"—agreeing to terms only after the player has made full concessions. To protect itself against this "waiting" strategy, a player must be willing to risk disagreement. As movie producer Sam Goldwyn once said, "The most important thing in acting is honesty. Once you've learned to fake that, you've got it made." To a degree, the same can be said of bargaining. Under imperfect information, a certain amount of dissembling, playing one's cards close to the vest, is essential. Otherwise, one is prone to the danger of being read like an open book by an opponent.

Repetition and Reputation

Thus far, we have focused on a one-time negotiation between a pair of interested parties. As a natural consequence, the parties' bargaining behavior has been motivated solely by the immediate profit available from an agreement. Now let's consider the effect if one or both parties are expected to face different bargaining situations repeatedly. For instance, labor contracts typically are no longer than three years. Thus, even when the current contract is signed and sealed, labor and management are well aware that they will be negotiating a new contract in two or three years' time. Alternatively, one side may find itself repeatedly negotiating with scores of different parties over time. As an example, representatives of insurance companies negotiate hundreds of tort and liability claims each year.

Repeated negotiation (with the same or different parties) introduces the key strategic element of *reputation*; that is, the firm recognizes that its behavior in the current set of negotiations can influence the expectations of its future bargaining partners. In a one-time bargaining setting, in contrast, the firm's actions are motivated solely by immediate profit; issues of reputation do not enter.

One important effect of reputation formation in repeated negotiations is to limit the scope of purely opportunistic behavior. To illustrate, consider current contract negotiations between two firms, A and B. Due to many bargaining factors in its favor, A is confident it can negotiate a contract giving it 90 percent of the total profit from an agreement. If it expects never to bargain with B again, A surely will push for these favorable terms. But what if B and A are likely to bargain with each other over many subsequent contracts? Negotiating too good a contract poses the risk of souring the entire bargaining relationship. (Perhaps B would spurn A and seek out a new bargaining partner in the future.) Accordingly, A may rationally choose not to take full advantage of its short-term bargaining power.

Reputation effects also suggest that B, the weaker bargaining party, may be unwilling to concede the lion's share of the short-term gain to A. In a one-shot bargain, accepting 10 percent of something is better than nothing. But in repeated bargaining, B must be concerned about its reputation. Large concessions now may spur the other party to take a tougher bargaining stance in the future. Thus, B has an interest in establishing a reputation as a tough but fair bargainer. Sometimes this reputation effect means sacrificing or delaying short-term agreements. For instance, strikes frequently occur because one or both sides seek to establish their long-term reputations. Insurance companies typically take a tough stance toward settling claims of uncertain merit. Viewing the claim by itself, the company might find it cheaper to settle than to go to court. Nonetheless, on reputation grounds, it pays to fight to deter questionable claims in the future.

Finally, the repeated bargaining relationship has a *disciplining* role—a role we already noted in Chapter 10 in our discussion of the repeated prisoner's dilemma. Recall that, in the one-shot prisoner's dilemma, the dominant-strategy equilibrium calls for noncooperation. In contrast, in the infinitely repeated prisoner's dilemma, continual cooperation is an equilibrium. The key to this equilibrium is one side's credible threat to punish the other's noncooperation with a retaliatory response. Similarly, bargaining partners that are "married" to each other have obvious incentives to maintain a cooperative relationship.

Business Behavior
Failed Agreements

In actual business practice, negotiation behavior mainly follows economic predictions. For instance, when both bargainers have complete information about the mutual benefits to be had from a successful transaction or deal, an agreement should soon follow. Contrary to the notion of the litigious American legal system, most disputes (some researchers estimate more than 90 percent) end in amicable settlement agreements rather than costly court proceedings. Deal makers routinely trade off multiple issues and include contingent clauses as needed in order to increase the total value of an agreement, which the parties can then share.

Nonetheless, there are instances when bargaining behavior and outcomes diverge from the textbook predictions advanced by economic principles. High-profile disputes occur even when there is strong evidence of mutual benefit from a timely agreement. Though less frequent today, costly strikes persist. Examples are the lengthy screenwriters strike in Hollywood in 2007–2008; management–player disputes in the National Football League, the National Hockey League, and the National Basketball Association (causing canceled games in the latter two leagues); and the 2012 Chicago teachers strikes. Most strikes are ultimately settled at terms that could have been concluded much earlier, without incurring the attendant economic costs to both sides. Frequently, top management of a target company rebuffs a merger or takeover advance, even when it would deliver a large price premium to shareholders. Chief executive officers (the venerable Jack Welch included) find themselves entangled in costly and public divorce disputes. The death of a business mogul triggers an ugly dispute about how his or her inheritance and control of the family business should be divided among layers of the family tree.

Recall our earlier point that disputants who hold the same information about the case under contention should always find their way to an efficient, mutually beneficial agreement (assuming one exists). But several factors impede agreements in practice. First, research by psychologists has documented a key impediment to agreements: self-serving bias. For instance, consider a bargaining experiment in which participants are assigned the roles of plaintiff and defendant in a legal case and are given *exactly the same* facts and information. The economic prediction is that the parties (sharing the same valuation of the case) should always agree to a settlement to avoid the legal costs of going to court. The results are quite the contrary. Invariably, the plaintiff sees a much greater court award than does the defendant—on exactly the same evidence. One's prediction is biased (consciously or unconsciously) by one's self-interest. Therefore, disputants in these experiments frequently litigate and incur the associated court costs. A second source of missed agreements occurs when there are multiple mutually beneficial bargaining equilibria. Recall the conflict over the standard for high-definition DVDs described in Chapter 10, Table 10.4. For years, each side adamantly held to its preferred incompatible format, severely impeding adoption of either new technology. Here, the problem was a failure to agree on either equilibrium. Third, notions of fairness can aid or impede agreements. On the one hand, the fairness of a transparent 50-50 split can offer an obvious point of agreement. On the other, there might be many possible candidates for a fair agreement, among which the bargainers disagree. Suppose that agreement A is one such candidate that both sides prefer to their disagreement outcomes. Nonetheless, it is not unusual for bargaining to end in disagreement, simply because one side finds agreement A unacceptable on grounds of fairness.

Finally, as we have noted, when bargainers hold imperfect information, self-interested negotiation behavior leads to missed agreements, at least some of the time. Thus, some frequency of disagreements should not be surprising in settings where each side has only partial information about potential agreements. Indeed, other means of dispute resolution such as mediation and arbitration are sometimes invoked to facilitate the prospect of reaching an accord. To sum up, bargaining is a valuable, but not perfect, means of reaching agreements.

Sanofi's Bid for Genzyme Revisited

While top management of Sanofi believed that acquiring Genzyme would add considerable value to its operations, the question remained, At what price? CEO Viehbacher was fond of saying, "I'm an accountant, not a scientist." Yes, Genzyme offered promising drugs in development, top scientific capabilities, a US beachhead, and proximity to research talent at MIT and Harvard University. But Sanofi saw Genzyme with its ongoing production problems as something of a fixer upper.

Proper valuation of Genzyme was key, and the marketplace, as demonstrated by the firm's depressed stock price, was not bullish. Viehbacher and Sanofi's board had no intention of overpaying for the acquisition.[7]

Genzyme's own assessment of its intrinsic value was in sharp conflict with Sanofi's view. Earnings were recovering, production problems were being fixed, new blockbuster drugs were in the pipeline, and longer-term cash flows would support an increasing market valuation for the company. Not surprisingly, the two sides were far apart in their valuations during private discussions during 2010. For months, little in these conversations was moving them closer together. Having acquired two seats on Genzyme's board, activist investor Carl Icahn began pushing for a sale at a favorable price. But Sanofi's September cash offer of $69 per share (valuing the company at $17.5 billion) was soundly rebuffed by Genzyme's management. In October, Sanofi launched a hostile tender offer directly to Genzyme's shareholders, also at $69 per share.

The public offer triggered withering attacks (reported in the press) by both sides. According to Genzyme's CEO Termeer, during a September meeting, Viehbacher had revealed that Sanofi might be willing to pay between $69 and $80 per share. Viehbacher strongly denied any suggestion of this higher price range. He chastised Termeer for refusing to share any company financial information that might narrow the gap between the sides' conflicting value assessments, and accused the Genzyme side of refusing to bargain altogether.

The close of 2010 saw Genzyme presenting investors with exuberant next-year earnings projections, and Sanofi retorting that these forecasts, far higher than analyst estimates, were "pie in the sky." The key points of disagreement between the sides were: (1) the speed in which sales of two key Genzyme drugs would recover once ongoing production problems had been overcome, and (2) the revenue prospects of Lemtrada, Genzyme's multiple sclerosis drug awaiting Food and Drug Administration (FDA) approval. In 2011, the key breakthrough in the negotiations centered on these twin points. After much work, the final terms of the deal set a $74 base price (worth $20.1 billion) plus a "contingent value right" that would sweeten the price if specific revenue goals were met in the near future. These goals included reaching a specific benchmark for sales of the two aforementioned drugs, FDA approval of Lemtrada, and its reaching a series of benchmarks. (The Lemtrada benchmarks represented a key contingency, since Genzyme estimated $3.5 billion in peak sales for the drug, while Sanofi expected $1 billion or less.) In the end, this contingent pricing plan—which could add as much as $14 per share to the sale price if all benchmarks were met—was the key to unlocking a mutually beneficial deal.

[7]This account is based on R. Weisman, "Genzyme Deal Survived a Culture Clash," *Boston Globe* (February 12, 2011), p. A1; C. V. Nicholson, "Sanofi Agrees to Buy Genzyme for $20.1 Billion," *The New York Times* (February 17, 2011), p. B10; R. Weisman, "Sanofi's Chief Questions Genzyme's Price," *Boston Globe* (October 29, 2010), p. B7; and J. Whalen and D. Cimilluca, "Sanofi's Genzyme Bid Turns Hostile," *The Wall Street Journal* (October 5, 2010), p. B3.

SUMMARY

Decision-Making Principles

1. The impetus for all negotiations is mutual gain—to forge an agreement that is better for both sides than a disagreement. This is true whether the sides are attempting to form a new agreement or to resolve a long-standing dispute.

2. The zone of agreement lies between the parties' values for the transaction (assessed relative to what each would get in a disagreement). In terms of negotiation strategy, the amount of profit one side can claim from an agreement depends on an assessment not only of its own walk-away value but also that of the other side (because this sets a limit on the other side's ability to compromise).

3. Negotiations involve a mixture of competition and cooperation. They are as much about value "creating" as value "claiming." An efficient agreement maximizes the parties' total value from the transaction. Value is created by trading on differences. Parties should adopt an issue as part of an agreement, provided the benefits to one side exceed the costs to the other.

Nuts and Bolts

1. Mutually beneficial transactions are based on differences in bargainer values. In single-issue transactions, the difference between the bargainers' reservation prices determines the total profit available from an agreement. Differences in values can result from differences in preferences, probability assessments, or attitudes toward risk.

2. An outcome is efficient if there exists no other alternative that is better for both parties. The payoff frontier shows the set of efficient agreements. For any movement along the frontier, any gain for one bargainer necessitates a loss for the other.

3. When monetary transfers are freely available, an agreement is efficient if and only if it is value maximizing—that is, generates the greatest total profit to the bargainers together. The size of the transfer determines the distribution of the total profit between the bargainers.

4. Under perfect information, rational bargainers always should achieve an efficient agreement. Moreover, any agreement on the payoff frontier (provided it is preferred by both parties to a disagreement) can be supported as an equilibrium bargaining outcome.

5. In bargaining settings under imperfect information, optimal bargaining behavior may preclude the attainment of efficient agreements. For instance, disputants will prefer to incur the cost of going to court if the difference in their litigation expectations exceeds their collective court costs. In simple price bargaining, a buyer strategically understates its true value, while the seller overstates its value (or cost), with the result that mutually beneficial agreements may be lost. Similarly, strategic considerations in multiple-issue negotiations can prevent the attainment of value-maximizing agreements.

Questions and Problems

1. A plaintiff is suing a defendant for $100,000. The cost of going to court is $15,000 for each side.
   a. The parties agree there is a 50 percent chance of the plaintiff's winning the case. What is the range of mutually beneficial agreements that the parties might negotiate in an out-of-court settlement? What if each side believes *its* winning chance is 60 percent?
   b. Suppose the damages are $200,000, and each side sees its winning chance at 60 percent. What are the prospects for an out-of-court settlement?
   c. Suppose the plaintiff is bringing a nuisance suit. The plaintiff has no chance of winning in court, and both sides know it. Would it be rational for the defendant to settle the case out of court nonetheless? Explain. What legal rules can you suggest that might serve to deter nuisance suits?

2. In labor negotiations, failure to reach a contract agreement frequently results in a labor strike or work slowdown. In each of the following situations, identify which side—labor or management—is better positioned to obtain favorable contract terms from the other.

   a. Demand for the firm's products is booming, and the firm is earning record profits.

   b. The labor union has over $20,000 per worker in its strike fund.

   c. A recession in the region has led to increased unemployment.

3. The developer of a new shopping mall is negotiating the terms of a store lease with a sporting goods firm. The developer is pressing the store for an increase in monthly rent. The store offers to pay the developer 1 percent of its first year's revenues in return for a lower monthly rent, and the developer agrees. Why might this more complicated contract be mutually beneficial? Explain briefly.

4. Firm S supplies inputs to firm B. Because producing the input is quite complicated, some defects are inevitable. Firm S can reduce the rate of defects at a cost. In turn, defective parts lower firm B's profits (because of lost sales and unhappy customers). The firms' profits and costs (in thousands of dollars) are shown in the table.

   a. Should firm B insist on 0 percent defects? Why or why not?

   b. What level of product quality is part of an efficient agreement? Explain.

	B's Profit	S's Cost		B's Profit	S's Cost
0% Defects	100	80	6% Defects	50	25
2% Defects	86	58	8% Defects	26	20
4% Defects	72	37	10% Defects	24	16

5. An upstream paper mill releases moderate amounts of pollutants into a waterway. A downstream fishery suffers an economic cost from this pollution of $100,000 annually. This cost burden would fall to $30,000 if the pollution were reduced by 50 percent. Complete (100 percent) cleanup would cost the mill $120,000, whereas a 50 percent cleanup would cost $50,000.

   a. Currently, the mill has the legal right to pollute. Can the parties come to a mutually beneficial agreement to reduce pollution? If so, how much pollution should be reduced?

   b. Answer part (a) assuming the fishery has the legal right to clean water.

6. The United Mine Workers (UMW) and the Association of Coal Producers are attempting to negotiate a new contract in which the issues at stake are a wage increase, the introduction of a right-to-strike clause, and a proposal that non-mining jobs at sites be opened up to nonunion workers. Each $1.00 increase in the hourly wage would raise the association's total wage bill by $40 million. Besides the wage issue, the UMW feels very strongly about the right-to-strike clause; in fact, it would be willing to give up $.75 in wage increases to secure it. It feels less strongly about reserving nonmining work for the union and is willing to give up only $.50 in wages to retain this provision. For its part, the association has attempted to calculate the impact of each of these provisions. It judges that accepting the right-to-strike clause might increase its costs by $50 million in the long run and that opening site work to nonunion labor would save it $60 million.

   a. Under an efficient agreement, how should the parties decide the right-to-strike and reserved-work issues?

   b. As a variation on this example, suppose the current administration in Washington has invoked emergency legislation to freeze mining wages (as well as other prices and wages in the economy). The result is that the right-to-strike and reserved-work clauses are the only issues under negotiation; any wage change is prohibited. Now how should the parties decide these issues to mutual advantage?

7. Firm B and firm S are in the process of negotiating a contract whereby S will synthesize a hormone for B. Besides the payment from B to S, three issues are involved: (1) whether the hormone will be 95 percent or only 80 percent pure, (2) whether the target date for completion will be three or five years, and (3) whether B will lend two of its expert

biochemists to S to aid in the development. Firm B has estimated its values for various combinations of issues, and firm S has estimated its costs. These amounts are shown in the table.

	B's Values		S's Costs	
	3 Years	5 Years	3 Years	5 Years
95%	180	100	140	80
80%	160	60	90	50
No Biochemists	0	0	0	0
Biochemists	−30	−30	−40	−20

Lending the biochemists is purely an additive factor; doing so reduces B's value but also reduces S's cost. For example, a three-year contract for a 95 percent pure hormone with the loan of the biochemists has a value to B of $180 - 30 = 150$ and a cost to S of $140 - 40 = 100$.

a. With three issues (two outcomes each), there are eight possible contracts. Which contracts are inefficient (i.e., produce worse outcomes for both sides than some other contract)?

b. Given that dollar-for-dollar compensation can be paid between the parties, which of the eight contracts is optimal? Explain.

8. Firm A seeks to acquire (privately owned) firm T whose ultimate dollar value is uncertain because of its possible liability for the past production of hazardous waste. The table shows A's and T's respective values (in $ millions) for the firm conditional on whether the firm is found to be liable. Note that A and T have different contingent values and different probability assessments (shown in parentheses) as to T's liability. Both firms are risk neutral.

	Value of Firm T	
	T Not Liable	T Liable
A's Value	50 (.5)	20 (.5)
T's Value	40 (.8)	30 (.2)

a. Firm A is hoping to acquire T in a 100 percent cash transaction. Is a mutually beneficial 100 percent cash transaction possible? Explain.

b. Instead, suppose that firm A considers acquiring T, paying all or in part with its own stock. (The owners of T are prohibited from selling the stock they receive for two years.) If A acquires T and subsequently T is found liable, both sides expect that A's stock price will fall by 50 percent. Is a mutually beneficial *100 percent stock* transaction possible? (Provide an example to show whether the answer is yes or no.)

c. The firms are considering a provision in the acquisition allowing T's senior managers (who will continue to work for the combined firm) to buy back (at a predetermined price) ownership of T in the event that the firm is found liable. Does such a provision make sense? Provide a qualitative explanation.

*9. A buyer has value v_b for a potential acquisition and believes the seller's reservation price has the cumulative probability distribution $F(v)$. The buyer chooses P to maximize its expected profit:

$$\pi_b = (v_b - P)\Pr(P \text{ accepted}) = (v_b - P)F(P).$$

Find the buyer's marginal profit and set it equal to zero. Show that the buyer's optimal price satisfies $P = v_b - F(P)/f(P)$, where $f(v) = dF(v)/dv$ is the associated density function. Note that the buyer shades down its value in making its optimal bid.

*Starred problems are more challenging.

10. Firms A and B are negotiating to conclude a business deal worth $200,000 in total value to the parties. At issue is how this total value will be split. Firm A knows B will agree to a 50-50 split, but it also has thought about claiming a greater share by making a take-it-or-leave-it offer. Firm A judges that firm B would accept a 45 percent share with probability .9, a 40 percent share with probability .85, and a 35 percent share with probability .8. What offer should A make to maximize its expected profit?

*11. Firm A is attempting to acquire firm T but is uncertain about T's value. It judges that the firm's value under current management (call this v_T) is in the range of $60 to $80 per share, with all values in between equally likely. A estimates that, under its own management, T will be worth $v_A = 1.5v_T - 30$. (Note that v_A is strictly greater than v_T except when v_T equals 60 when the two values are the same.) Firm A will make a price offer to purchase firm T, which T's current management (knowing v_T) will accept or reject. Show that all possible offers result in an *expected loss* for firm A, even though T is always worth more under A's control than under T's. (In this example, asymmetric information implies an adverse selection problem similar to those discussed in Chapter 14.)

12. In December 2005, Time Warner (TW) was the subject of two different news stories. Its AOL division was pursuing an online advertising alliance with Microsoft, while continuing to have discussions with its current partner Google. It was also confronted by dissident shareholder Carl Icahn who challenged management to break up TW.

   a. TW's board estimated that a 6-month continuing conflict with Icahn would reduce TW's value by $200 million on average. The cost to Icahn and his backers of mounting a full challenge to the board would be about $50 million. Some financial pundits believed that Icahn's real motive was to induce TW's board to pay him *greenmail*, buying his stock (about 3% of shares) at a premium to be rid of his challenge. Under these circumstances, do you expect Icahn to go through with his challenge? What if there is a provision in TW's charter stating that any price premium paid for a special purchase must also be extended to any and all shareholders owning more than .1% of TW shares?

   b. AOL and Google's partnership at the time generated annual profits of about $250 million and $70 million for the respective parties. Analysts estimated that an AOL-Microsoft alliance would generate an annual total profit of $500 million. Losing AOL as a partner would also undermine Google's competitive position—meaning a reduction in its overall profit of $50 million (on top of the foregone $70 million alliance profit).

      In an **efficient** negotiated agreement, should AOL partner with Microsoft or with Google? Explain.

   c. In the AOL-Microsoft negotiations, Microsoft believed that online ad revenue was mainly driven by the overall number of site visitors and users (an area where Microsoft's MSN site is strong), while AOL believed ad revenue would depend on customers undertaking searches (Microsoft's search engine is weak and less popular). How might these different opinions affect how an agreement is structured (and whether there is an agreement at all)?

Discussion Question   Traditionally, negotiation and litigation have been the two prevailing methods of dispute resolution. These alternative methods lie at opposite extremes of a spectrum. The negotiation process is private, voluntary, informal, and unstructured, aimed at reaching a mutually beneficial agreement involving only the parties themselves. The litigation (or adjudication) process is public and follows formal rules whereby both sides of the dispute are heard and a binding outcome is determined by a third party (judge or jury).

The last 20 years have seen increased use of alternative methods for resolving disputes—mediation and arbitration, in particular. In mediation, a third party is engaged to help the parties reach a mutually beneficial agreement. In arbitration, a third party hears the dispute and renders a binding decision.

   a. Using available reference sources (in print or on the Internet), provide summaries of the mediation and arbitration processes.

   b. Provide a critical assessment of the advantages and disadvantages of each method in reaching efficient agreements (and in terms of time and cost). How do the methods compare to the alternatives of negotiation and litigation?

*Starred problems are more challenging.

Spreadsheet Problem

S1. A US firm (company U) is negotiating to buy aircraft engines from a British firm (company B). Under discussion is the price to be paid (in British pounds), quality (high or low), warranty (full or partial), and the delivery schedule (two, three, or five years). The spreadsheet that follows shows company U's values in dollars and company B's costs in British pounds for possible agreements. For instance, delivery of high-quality engines under full warranty in two years implies a cost (in pounds) to company B of 68 + 10 = £78 million. Company B receives £110 million (cell H13), implying a profit of 110 – 78 = £32 million (cell L13). In turn, company U's value (in dollars) for the deal is $238 + $18 = $256 million. The exchange rate is $2 for each pound. Thus, company U's final profit is 256 – (2)(110) = $36 million (cell K13).

a. Create a spreadsheet similar to the sample spreadsheet given. Put the numerical value of 1 in cell C7, C9, I7, *or* I9, and put zeros in the remaining three cells. The placement of the 1 (a so-called dummy variable) specifies the exact agreement. For instance, putting the 1 in cell C7 indicates high-quality engines under full warranty. Similarly, put a 1 in cell C12, C13, *or* C14 to indicate the delivery schedule. Then compute company U's profit (cell K13) according to the formula

$$= (C7*D7 + C9*D9 + I7*G7 + I9*G9$$
$$+ C12*D12 + C13*D13 + C14*D14) - 2*H13.$$

This formula works because all zero-valued dummies disappear, leaving only the values (238 plus 18) for the actual agreement. Company B's profit is computed as its revenue payment minus its cost by an analogous formula.

	A	B	C	D	E	F	G	H	I	J	K	L	M
1													
2		A BRITISH-AMERICAN CONTRACT											
3													
4					Warranty								
5		Quality		Full			Partial						
6			Co U	Co B		Co U	Co B						
7		High	1	238	68		180	42	0		Sum		
8											1		
9		Low	0	178	24		92	18	0				
10													
11		Delivery	Co U	Co B		U's Payment to B					Co U's	Co B's	
12		2 Years	1	18	10		(Pounds)				Profit	Profit	
13		3 Years	0	0	0		110				36	32	
14		5 Years	0	–24	–18								
15													
16		Sum	1										
17													

b. Find the zone of agreement by maximizing company U's profit subject to company B's profit being equal to 0, and vice versa. Use your spreadsheet's optimizer, listing U's payment and the seven dummy variables as the adjustable cells. Include the constraints that all dummies must be greater than or equal to 0. In addition, the sum of the first four dummies (computed in cell K8) must equal 1, and the sum of the last three dummies (computed in cell C16) must also equal 1. Finally, do not forget the constraint that one firm's profit is equal to 0.

c. Find one or more points on the efficient frontier, setting one company's profit equal to a positive value and maximizing the other's profit. What agreement terms are efficient? Explain.

Suggested References

The following books offer practical guides to reaching mutually beneficial agreements:

Bazerman, M. H., and J. J. Gillespie. "Betting on the Future: The Virtues of Contingent Contracts." *Harvard Business Review* (September 1999): 155–160.

Fisher, R., W. Ury, and B. Patton. *Getting to Yes*. New York: Houghton Mifflin, 1992.

Shell, R. *Bargaining for Advantage: Negotiation Strategies for Reasonable People*. New York: Penguin, 2006.

The following are rigorous and readable texts on bargaining:

Brams, S. J. *Negotiation Games: Applying Game Theory to Bargaining and Arbitration*. New York: Routledge, 2003.

Raiffa, H. *The Art and Science of Negotiation*. Cambridge, MA: Harvard University Press, 1982.

Roth, A. (ed.). *Game-Theoretic Models of Bargaining*. Cambridge, MA: Cambridge University Press, 1985.

(See especially the chapters by Chatterjee, Myerson, Samuelson, and Wilson.)

Schelling, T. C. *The Strategy of Conflict*. Chapters 2 and 3. Cambridge, MA: Harvard University Press, 1990.

A rigorous treatment of bargaining theory is contained in

Kennan, J., and R. Wilson. "Bargaining with Private Information." *Journal of Economic Literature* (March 1993): 45–104.

Experimental and empirical evidence on bargaining is provided in

Babcock, L., and G. Loewenstein. "Explaining Bargaining Impasse: The Role of Self-Serving Biases." *Journal of Economic Perspectives* 11 (Winter 1997): 109–126.

Camerer, C. F. *Behavioral Game Theory,* Chapters 2 and 4. Princeton, NJ: Princeton University Press, 2003.

Cramton, P., and J. S. Tracy. "Strikes and Holdouts in Wage Bargaining: Theory and Data." *American Economic Review* 82 (1992): 100–121.

Roth, A. E. "Bargaining Experiments," in J. H. Kagel and A. E. Roth (Eds.), *The Handbook of Experimental Economics*, Princeton, NJ: Princeton University Press, 1995.

There are numerous Web sites offering negotiation resources and support. Among the best are

Harvard Law School's Project on Negotiation, www.pon.harvard.edu/.

Stanford University's Center on Conflict and Negotiation, www.stanford.edu/group/sccn/.

Check Station Answers

1. The original paperback arrangement was appropriate for a low-volume release. Once *Fifty Shades* emerged as a blockbuster, Random House with its marketing clout and scale economies of production, could deliver much greater total profit to be split with retailers and the author. (Random House also substantially cut the paperback price to increase sales.) Thus, transferring the paperback rights to Random House, by increasing the "pie" made obvious economic

sense. Why James agreed to relinquish the eBook rights is less obvious. Many experts argued that the real money was in eBooks, and that Random House had relatively limited scope to increase these sales. Therefore, James would have been better off continuing to self-publish the eBook version of the trilogy.

2. The smaller the portion of risk he or she holds, the more risk neutral the decision maker becomes. Thus, with risks split five ways, the gap between the prospect's expected value and its CE value (the sum of the CE values of syndicate members) will shrink. If risk were shared by a large number of members (say, 100), the individual risk would be trivial, and the total CE value would approach the prospect's expected value.

3. Increasing purity by 1 percent has a MC to Firm A of $50,000. For Firm B, the extra benefit is $80,000 (going from 97 percent to 98 percent) and $40,000 (going from 98 percent to 99 percent). The change to 98 percent increases total value (because MB > MC), but a further increase to 99 percent does not make sense (MC > MB). Therefore, 98 percent is the efficient outcome.

4. a. Given perfect information about the zone of agreement, the students should always be expected to negotiate a mutually beneficial split. The obvious focal point is a 50-50 split giving each $5.

   b. One player's walk-away price (or BATNA) has improved from $0 to $2, so the size of the zone of agreement shrinks from $10 to $8. With perfect information an agreement should be reached, but now the "fair division" is less clear. A split of $6-$4 would leave each student an equal $4 gain relative to their walk-away price, so this would be fair. But, a 50-50 split still has an equitable appeal.

CHAPTER 16

Linear Programming

Management is the art of doing the best one can within constraints and occasionally getting around them.

ANONYMOUS

LO#1. Show how to analyze managerial decisions using linear programming.

LO#2. Explain the importance of sensitivity analysis and shadow prices in linear programming problems.

LO#3. Understand how to formulate larger-scale linear programming problems and solve them using standard spreadsheet programs.

A portfolio manager has $20 million to invest in a fund consisting of the following bonds:

Bond Category	Quality Rating	Maturity (Years)	Yield (Percent)
Treasury bills	5.0	0.4	4.0
Treasury bonds	5.0	4.0	6.0
Corporate bonds	3.5	3.2	4.4
Municipal bonds	3.0	2.0	5.6
Junk bonds	1.0	2.5	8.0

He has listed the bonds in descending order of quality rating (US Treasury securities carry the lowest risk, junk bonds are most risky). The second column lists average maturity (in years) for each category. The final column shows the expected return or yield (in percent per year, after tax) for each bond. Junk bonds have the greatest expected return, followed by US Treasury bonds.

The manager intends to create a bond fund by investing proportions of the $20 million in the different securities and has announced an investment goal of a high-quality, medium-maturity portfolio. In particular, the fund's average quality rating should be at least 3.5, and its average maturity should be no shorter than 1.5 years and no longer than 2.5 years.

The portfolio manager seeks to create a bond fund that offers the highest expected return subject to the quality and maturity requirements given. To accomplish this goal, what proportion of the $20 million should she invest in each bond?

Linear programming (LP) is a method of formulating and solving decision problems that involve explicit resource constraints. Analysts use the LP method to solve problems such as the investment decision and a host of other decision questions: How should a firm allocate its advertising expenditure among various media? What quantities of two jointly manufactured goods should a firm produce with a fixed amount of labor and inputs? How should a federal agency allocate its limited budget between two competing safety programs? What quantities of output should a consumer-products firm transport from each of its factories to each of its retail outlets to minimize transportation cost?

What do these problems have in common? First, all seek to find the best values of certain variables: the right advertising mix, the most profitable product quantities, the appropriate budget allocation. These values, which the decision maker controls, are **decision variables**. Second, each decision has an explicit objective, be it maximum profit, minimum cost, or maximum number of lives saved. Third, constraints limit the possible values of the decision variables. For example, limited labor supply may constrain the quantity of output. Similarly, the federal agency cannot spend more than its available budget, and the consumer-products firm must supply the quantities to its retail outlets subject to its factories' production capacities. Thus, in each case, the heart of the problem is finding (calculating) values for the decision variables that best meet the given objective while satisfying various constraints.

With respect to the first two features, decision variables and objectives, the LP method resembles the optimization methods we have encountered already. Like the pricing and output decisions of Chapters 2 and 3, LP decisions rely on marginal analysis (of a special kind) for their solution. Unlike those decisions, however, LP problems incorporate explicit resource constraints. The interplay of these constraints creates new and interesting economic trade-offs.

In this chapter, we take a systematic approach to managerial decisions involving economic constraints. First, we describe a number of constrained decision problems and show how they can be formulated and solved mathematically as linear programs. Next, we examine the important concept of shadow prices for resources. Then we introduce more complex linear programming decisions and illustrate the kinds of solutions furnished by computer programs.

LINEAR PROGRAMS

We can analyze a host of managerial decisions using linear programming. Here is a representative example.

FINDING AN OPTIMAL COMPUTER MIX   Consider a personal computer (PC) manufacturer that produces two versions of its popular desktop computer. The standard version has a high-capacity (80-gigabyte) hard disk, and an optical DVD drive. The economy version, which sells at a lower price, has a 40-gigabyte hard disk and does not include a DVD drive. The prices, variable costs, and contributions of the models are shown in the table.

	Standard PC	Economy PC
Price	$1,600	$1,000
Variable cost	1,100	700
Contribution	500	300

The firm has ample components (such as monitors and keyboards) from which to assemble PCs, but a limited capacity (given available factory space and necessary equipment) for producing DVD drives and hard-disk drives. The firm's maximum weekly outputs are 200 DVD drives and 20,000 total gigabytes of hard-drive capacity. The firm can split its hard-drive capacity in any way between the two models. For instance, it could devote all of its hard-drive capacity to 250 standard models or, alternatively, to 500 economy models. Or it could produce other combinations—for instance, 200 standard models and 100 economy models. In addition, the firm assembles computers using a 50-person labor force that supplies 2,000 hours of labor per week. The two models require roughly equal assembly time—an average of 5 labor-hours each.

How many computers of each type should the firm produce to maximize its profit? Answering this question requires two steps: (1) formulating the firm's decision as a linear program; that is, a set of mathematical equations that precisely describe the firm's available options; and (2) solving these mathematical equations.

The formulation stage begins with the identification of the relevant decision variables. The firm must determine two key quantities: the number of standard models (S) and the number of economy models (E). The firm seeks to maximize the total contribution (π) it obtains from these products. We can express this contribution algebraically as

$$\pi = 500S + 300E. \qquad \text{[OF]}$$

The goal to be maximized—in this instance, total contribution—is the **objective function (OF)**.

Next we identify the production constraints. The company cannot produce an unlimited number of computers. It faces three principal constraints. First, the firm can produce only 200 DVD drives a week. This means that, at most, it can produce 200 standard models. Also, it can produce a maximum of 20,000 gigabytes of hard drives. Finally, the firm has only 2,000 hours of labor to devote to production of PCs. The algebraic representations of these constraints are

$$S \leq 200 \qquad \text{[D]}$$
$$80S + 40E \leq 20,000 \qquad \text{[H]}$$
$$5S + 5E \leq 2,000. \qquad \text{[L]}$$

As the labels in brackets indicate, the inequalities correspond to the DVD drive, hard-disk drive, and labor constraints, respectively. The right-hand side of each inequality lists the total capacity (or supply) of the particular input. The left-hand side shows the total amount used of each resource if the firm produces quantities S and E of the models. For instance, producing S standard models requires S number of DVD drives—one drive per machine. Thus, according to the first constraint, DVD capacity limits the weekly output of standard models to 200.

Next consider the hard-disk constraint. Production of the models in the quantities S and E together requires $80S + 40E$ gigabytes of hard-disk capacity. For instance, producing 100 of each model per week would require a total of $(80)(100) + (40)(100) = 12,000$ gigabytes of capacity, which is safely within the 20,000 gigabytes available. Finally, consider the labor constraint. Here, the firm uses a total of $5S + 5E$ hours of labor. The total amount of labor cannot exceed 2,000.

The complete mathematical description of the problem consists of the objective function (to be maximized), the three resource constraints, and two nonnegativity constraints, $S \geq 0$ and $E \geq 0$. These last two constraints simply reflect the impossibility of producing negative quantities. Although obvious (even trivial) to the decision maker, we must include them to get the right answer. (Computer programs don't have the same intuition as managers.)

We now have a fully formed linear program. What makes it linear? All of the expressions, for both the objective function and the constraints, are linear. In a linear expression, we can multiply the variable by a constant, we can add or subtract these multiplied variables, and we can add a constant to the expression. (But this is all; we cannot multiply two variables together, we cannot raise variables to powers, we cannot take square roots of variables, or anything else.) Roughly speaking, the linearity assumption requires that the key quantities in the actual managerial problem— revenues, costs, and profits—vary proportionally with changes in the firm's decision variables. For instance, if the firm can sell its product at fixed prices, its revenue is proportional to output, thus satisfying linearity. However, if the firm faces a downward-sloping demand curve (the usual circumstance in Chapters 2 and 3), revenue is a nonlinear function of output; that is, the revenue graph is curved. The linear programming method cannot handle this case. (Instead, we can use a related method, nonlinear programming.)

Graphing the LP Problem

We can solve small-scale linear programs, like the PC example, using graphical methods. This approach provides the numerical solution and offers insight into the factors that determine the optimal decision. The method consists of the following steps:

1. Construct a graph, placing a decision variable on each axis.

2. Graph each constraint as though it were binding, that is, as if it held with strict equality.

3. Find the feasible region, the area of the graph that simultaneously satisfies all constraints.

4. Superimpose contours of the objective function on the feasible region to determine the optimal corner of the region.

5. Solve the appropriate equations of the LP problem to determine the optimal values of the decision variables at the corner solution.

FIGURE 16.1

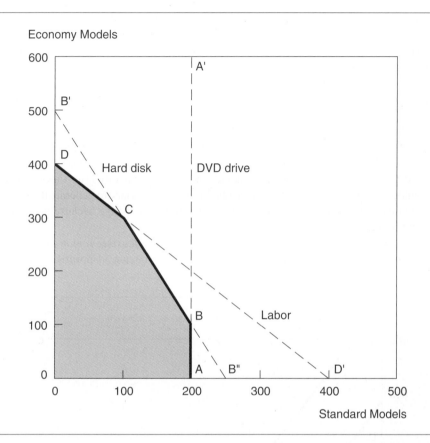

Economy Models

The feasible combinations of standard and economy model PCs lie within the region OABCD.

Standard Models

Let's apply this procedure to solve the computer company's production problem. Figure 16.1 plots the firm's decision variables, S and E, on the horizontal and vertical axes, respectively, and plots the three resource constraints as straight lines. The area OABCD represents the **feasible region** of all *possible* combinations of the two computer models. For each resource, the constraint line in the graph depicts model combinations that use up exactly the available resource. Any point lying to the right of any of the resource constraint lines represents quantities that the firm cannot produce. For example, if the point lies to the right of the DVD constraint, it represents an output combination that requires more than 200 DVD drives. Any point to the left of this line requires fewer than 200 drives. In turn, the equation $80S + 40E = 20,000$ describes the binding hard-disk constraint and appears on the graph as the line B′B″.[1] Finally, the binding labor

[1]The easiest way to graph any constraint line is to pinpoint its two intercepts; that is, set one of the decision variables equal to zero and solve for the other. Doing this for the hard-disk equation, we find $E = 0$ with $S = 250$ and, in turn, $S = 0$ with $E = 500$. Thus, the horizontal intercept is 250 (at B″) and the vertical intercept is 500 (at B′).

constraint is given by the equation $5S + 5E = 2,000$ and is graphed as DD'. The firm's feasible region of production consists of S and E combinations that simultaneously satisfy all three constraints: the shaded area bounded by OABCD.

The company still has to determine the output combination (the point in the feasible region) that maximizes total contribution. To find this point, we draw in contribution contours—lines indicating combinations of S and E that yield a fixed value of contribution. For instance, we can graph the contour corresponding to a contribution of $75,000 by using the equation $500S + 300E = 75,000$. This contour is shown in Figure 16.2. (Check this by noting that the horizontal intercept is $S = 150$, since the firm can earn $75,000 by producing only standard models. In turn, the vertical intercept is $E = 250$.) Figure 16.2 also depicts contours corresponding to contributions of $120,000, $140,000, and $200,000. Note that increasing the contribution causes a parallel (northeast) shift in the contour. Obviously, larger production quantities are necessary to generate the greater contribution. Note, however, that the contour slopes do not change because the ratio of contributions is always $500 to $300.

The optimal solution is found at the corner of the feasible region that touches the highest contribution contour. In Figure 16.2, this occurs at point C. Here, the

FIGURE 16.2

Production Constraints with Contribution Contours

The firm's profit-maximizing combination of computers occurs at point C, where the highest contribution contour touches the feasible region.

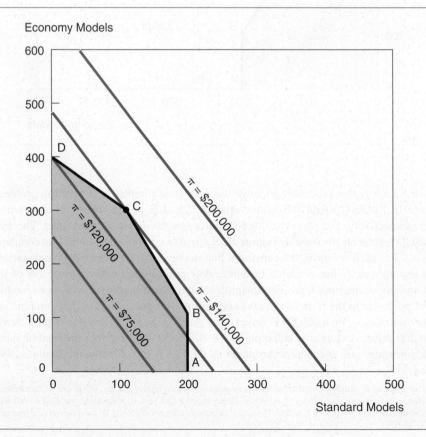

contour corresponding to $140,000 contribution just touches the feasible region. As the figure shows, this is the best the firm can do. The firm can consider other feasible production plans, but any such plan lies on a lower contribution contour. For instance, point B's plan (200 standard models and 100 economy models) produces only $130,000 in contribution (i.e., lies on a lower contour). At point D the firm earns even less. However, "pie in the sky" production plans are irrelevant. The firm cannot attain a higher contribution—say, $200,000—because such a contour lies wholly outside the feasible region.

We can reinforce the visual solution to the LP problem by using marginal analysis. Suppose the firm takes point D as a candidate for its optimal production plan. Using marginal analysis, the firm asks whether it could increase its contribution by moving to some other point on the edge of the feasible region. Suppose it considers moving in the direction of C, producing more standard models and fewer economy models. (Note that segment DC portrays the binding labor constraint.) To produce an extra standard model requires 5 additional hours of labor; with all labor utilized, this means producing one fewer economy model (which frees up 5 labor-hours). Would such a move improve the firm's profit? It certainly would! The net increase in contribution is $200. (The gain is $500 in contribution for the extra standard unit minus $300 in lost contribution from the economy unit that is no longer produced.) Thus, the firm should make the one-unit switch. But having switched one unit, it can increase its profit by switching a second unit (by exactly the same logic). It can continue to increase its profit by moving along segment DC until it attains the production plan corresponding to point C. Here, it can no longer improve its profit because it runs up against the hard-disk capacity constraint. Having exploited all its options for increasing its profit, the firm has arrived at its optimal product mix.[2]

What are the precise model quantities at point C? Since point C lies on the constraint lines corresponding to hard disks and labor, we know that these constraints are binding; that is, the optimal mix uses up all available hard-disk capacity and labor. Thus, S and E satisfy the constraints, $80S + 40E = 20,000$ and $5S + 5E = 2,000$. Solving these two equations in two unknowns, we find that $S = 100$ and $E = 300$. Total contribution is $\pi = (\$500)(100) + (\$300)(300) = \$140,000$ after inserting the optimal quantities into the objective function.

CHECK STATION 1 **A farmer raises two crops, wheat and barley. Wheat sells at $6 per bushel and barley at $3.75 per bushel. The production of each crop requires land and labor in differing amounts. Each 1,000 bushels of wheat requires one acre of farmland and 40 labor-hours per week. An equal quantity of barley also requires 1 acre but requires only 20 hours of labor per week. The farmer has 10 acres of land and an average of 320 hours of hired labor per week to devote to wheat and barley production. How much of each crop should the farmer produce? In your answer, formulate and graph the appropriate LP problem.**

[2]Check for yourself that, starting from point B, the firm also profits by moving toward point C. How much does contribution increase if it produces an extra economy unit?

A Minimization Problem

The production problem the PC company faces is typical of a large class of profit-maximization problems. A second important class of decisions involves cost minimization. The next example illustrates the point.

REGULATION AT LEAST COST   An environmental regulatory agency is launching a program to reduce water pollution in one of the region's major rivers. As a first step, it has set standards for two key measures of water quality. It seeks (1) to increase the level of dissolved oxygen (essential to fish and other life in the estuary) by 6 milligrams (mg) per liter and (2) to reduce the concentrations of chlorides by 70 mg per liter. Its aim is to meet both these standards at minimum cost by allocating funds between two programs.

Program 1: Direct treatment of effluents. Each $1 million spent in this program will increase dissolved oxygen by 3 mg/liter and reduce chlorides by 10 mg/liter.

Program 2: Flow regulation. Each $1 million spent in this program will increase dissolved oxygen by 1 mg/liter and reduce chlorides by 20 mg/liter.

How much should the agency spend on one or both programs to meet its goals?

Let's formulate and solve the agency's problem. Here, the agency must choose how much to spend on direct treatment and how much to spend on flow regulation. We label the spending (in millions of dollars) on the respective programs by D and F. The agency seeks to minimize the total cost (C) of the programs, subject to meeting its goals.

$$\text{Minimize: } C = D + F. \qquad \text{[OF]}$$

The goals it must meet can be expressed by the following inequalities.

$$\text{Subject to: } \quad 3D + F \geq 6 \qquad \text{[O]}$$
$$10D + 20F \geq 70. \qquad \text{[C]}$$

The first inequality reflects the fact that the programs together must increase oxygen by 6 mg/liter. The right-hand side lists this minimum requirement. The left-hand side shows the total amount of oxygen generated by the programs. For instance, spending $2 million on each program ($D = F = 2$) would increase oxygen by $(3)(2) + 2 = 8$ mg/liter, which would more than meet the goal. In turn, the left-hand side of the second constraint shows the reduction in chlorine: 10 mg per million spent on the first program plus 20 mg per million on the second. The nonnegativity constraints, $D \geq 0$ and $F \geq 0$, complete the formulation.

Figure 16.3 shows the graph of the feasible region. The main point to observe is the impact of the "greater than or equal to" constraints. The feasible region lies above the two-sided boundary AZB. (Make sure you understand that the constraint lines are properly graphed. Check the intercepts!) Obviously, large values of F and D (i.e., greater spending on the programs) will make it easier to meet the dual improvement goals, but the point is to do it at *minimum* cost. When it comes to cost contours, the object is to get to the lowest one (i.e., the one farthest to the southwest) while meeting both goals. Figure 16.3 shows the relevant part of the "least-cost" contour. Note that it touches the feasible

FIGURE 16.3

Amount Spent on Program F

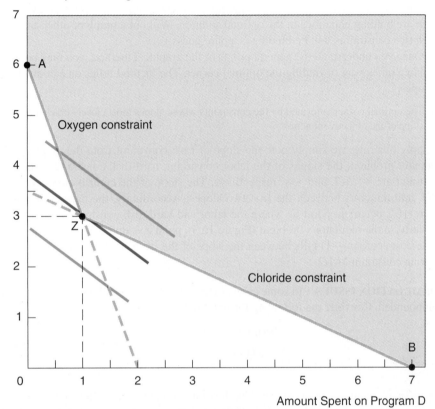

At point Z, $1 million is spent on program D and $3 million on program F. This plan meets the oxygen and chloride constraints at minimum total cost.

region at point Z, the corner formed by the binding oxygen and chlorine constraints. The precise amounts to spend on each program are found by solving the equations: $3D + F = 6$ and $10D + 20F = \$70$ million. The solution $D = 1$ and $F = 3$ is the result.[3] In short, $1 million and $3 million should be spent on the respective programs. The least-cost total outlay is $4 million.

ALGEBRAIC SOLUTIONS   The mathematics for solving small-scale linear programs involves two main steps: (1) identifying the correct set of simultaneous equations and

[3]Recall that there are two equivalent ways to solve simultaneous equations. The first method is by *substitution*. For instance, in the regulator's problem, we transform the equation $3D + F = 6$ to the form $F = 6 - 3D$. Then we insert this expression for F into the second equation, $10D + 20F = 70$. We are left with one equation in one unknown: $10D + 20(6 - 3D) = 70$. The solution is $D = 1$. Putting this value back into the first equation, we find $F = 6 - (3)(1) = 3$. The second method is by *elimination*. It is easiest to eliminate F by multiplying both sides of the first equation by 20 to obtain $60D + 20F = 120$. Then we subtract the second equation from this expression. Note that $20F$ in each equation cancels out, leaving $60D - 10D = 120 - 70$; this implies $D = 1$ and $F = 3$. Either method works equally well.

(2) solving these equations for the optimal values of the decision variables. In the preceding example we used simple graphics to solve the first step. (*Caution*: We cannot simply *assume* certain constraints will be binding and go ahead and solve them. In the computer example, there are five inequalities, including the nonnegativity constraints, only two of which are binding equalities in the optimal solution. Without a graph or other analysis, which two constraints will be binding is a pure guess.)

Once you understand the general points of the graphical method, you may be interested in a quick way of finding the optimal corner. The method relies on a comparison of slopes:

> The optimal corner is formed by the constraints whose slopes most closely bracket the slope of the objective function.

To apply this rule, we simply note the slope of each constraint from the graph. In the computer problem, the slopes of the labor constraint, hard-disk constraint, and DVD constraint are -1, -2, and $-\infty$, respectively. The slope of the contribution contour is $-5/3$, and this falls between the first two slopes. Accordingly, the optimal output in Figure 16.2 occurs at point C, where the labor and hard-disk constraints are binding. Similarly, in the regulator's problem (Figure 16.3), point Z is optimal because the slope of the cost contour (-1) falls between the slope of the oxygen constraint (-3) and the chlorine constraint ($-1/2$).

FORMULATION ISSUES   In some cases, LP problems have no solution or the solution is unbounded. Consider the following formulation:

$$\text{Maximize: } 3x + y$$
$$\text{Subject to: } x + 2y \leq 12$$
$$x + y \geq 15.$$

The difficulty here lies in the constraints. It is impossible to find values of the decision variables that simultaneously satisfy both inequalities. (Graph the constraints to confirm this.) In short, the problem itself is infeasible. It lacks a feasible region and, therefore, has no possibility of an optimal solution.[4]

A different formulation difficulty arises if we make a slight modification in the preceding example. Suppose that the variable y is omitted in the first constraint so that the inequality reads $x \leq 12$. The new problem has a feasible region—in fact, too large a region. The feasible region consists of all points to the left of the vertical line $x = 12$ and above the downward-sloping line $x + y = 15$. Now the feasible region is unbounded; it extends vertically indefinitely. Clearly, we can make the value of the objective function as large as we like by making y as large as possible—all the while keeping x below 12. This linear program has an unbounded solution, which tells us that we have poorly formulated the problem. After all, in the real world, no firm has the opportunity to make an infinite profit. Somehow we have omitted the real constraints that limit the firm's profitability.

---

[4]This kind of infeasibility can arise quite naturally. In this problem, for instance, let the decision variables denote the quantity of two products. Total production is limited due to fixed capacity (the first constraint). At the same time, the firm has contracted to deliver a minimum of 15 total units to a buyer (the second constraint). Here, there is no solution, because the firm has contracted to deliver more than it possibly can supply.

SENSITIVITY ANALYSIS AND SHADOW PRICES

The solution of the basic linear program provides management with its optimal decision. The solution is also the starting point for considering a range of related decisions and what-if questions. For instance, managers of the computer firm recognize that changing market prices are a fact of life in the PC industry. How might the firm change its production mix in response to changes in product prices? As a second example, the firm might consider increasing (at a cost) one or more of its production capacities (labor or hard-drive capacity, for instance). How much would such an increase in capacity be worth, and would it be worth the cost?

Sensitivity analysis is important in almost all decision contexts, but especially so in LP problems. As we shall see, analysts use computers to solve almost all medium- and large-scale LP problems. Standard computer output provides not only the numerical solution to the problem in question but also a wide variety of sensitivity analyses. Thus, a solid understanding of sensitivity analysis is essential in order to take full advantage of the power of linear programming.

Changes in the Objective Function

It is natural to ask how changes in the coefficients of the objective function affect the optimal decision. In the computer firm's production problem, for instance, the current contributions are $500 and $300 per unit of each model type. Obviously, if market prices or variable unit costs change, so will the contributions. How would such changes affect the firm's optimal production mix?

As a concrete example, suppose the firm anticipates that the current industry price for an economy model, $1,000, will fall to $900 in the coming months. Thus the firm expects that contribution per unit of the economy model will fall to $900 − $700 = $200 as a result. Assuming an unchanged contribution for model S, the firm's new objective function is

$$\pi = 500S + 200E.$$

With the sizable drop in E's contribution per unit, intuition suggests that the firm should reduce the output of E and increase the output of S. Figure 16.4 indicates that this is indeed the case. It shows the same feasible region as Figure 16.2. But the slopes of the contribution contours change. In Figure 16.4, the highest contribution contour touches the feasible region at point B, where the hard disk and DVD constraints are binding. (The slope of the new contribution contour is $-500/200 = -2.5$, and this falls between the slopes of these two constraint lines, -2 and $-\infty$.) We find the values of the decision variables at optimal corner B by solving the equations $S = 200$ and $2S + E = 500$. The resulting values are $S = 200$ and $E = 100$, and maximum contribution is $120,000. In contrast, if the firm were to maintain its old production mix, $S = 100$ and $E = 300$ (at point C), it would earn a contribution of only $110,000. To sum up, the firm should respond to the fall in economy model contribution by shifting to a greater quantity of standard models.

FIGURE 16.4

Production Constraints with New Contributions

A fall in the unit contribution of economy PCs causes the contribution contour to steepen and the optimal mix of PCs to move from point C to point B.

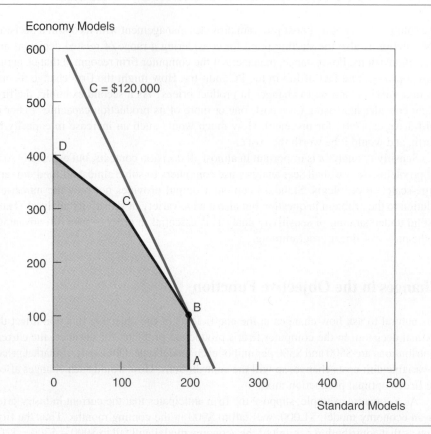

A general conclusion emerges from this example: The optimal production plan depends on the *relative* contributions of the two models. To see this, write the objective function in the form $\pi_S S + \pi_E E$, where π_S and π_E denote the contribution per unit for the respective models. The slope of the contribution contour is $\Delta E/\Delta S = -\pi_S/\pi_E$. Depending on the ratio of model contributions, one of the following three plans is optimal:

Point B ($S = 200, E = 100$)   provided $-\infty < -\pi_S/\pi_E \leq -2$

Point C ($S = 100, E = 300$)   provided $-2 \leq -\pi_S/\pi_E \leq -1$

Point D ($S = 0, E = 400$)   provided $-1 \leq -\pi_S/\pi_E \leq 0$

Note that a small change in the contribution ratio has no effect on the optimal plan as long as the requisite inequality continues to hold. For instance, if the price cut is to $960 (only 4 percent), the new contribution ratio will be 500/260. Production plan C will continue to be optimal because the second inequality still will be satisfied. (Of course, with the fall in price, the firm's profit will drop; nonetheless, the firm should stick to plan C.) If the contribution of model *E* falls below half that of model *S*, production plan

B will become optimal.[5] Finally, if the contribution of E exceeds that of S, producing model E exclusively will produce the most total contribution. In other words, as production of one model becomes relatively less and less profitable, the optimal plan shifts to increasing amounts of the other model.

How will the farmer's mix of crops be affected if the price of wheat increases to $8? If it falls to $3.20? What if both crop prices fall by 15 percent? How high would the ratio P_W/P_B have to be to induce the farmer to produce only wheat? How low would the ratio have to be for him to produce only barley?   **CHECK STATION 2**

Shadow Prices

Let's return to the original version of the computer firm's problem. Management is operating according to its optimal production plan: 100 standard models and 300 economy models per week, which together generate $140,000 in contribution. At this solution, production uses 100 percent of hard-disk capacity and all of the firm's current labor supply. This prompts some natural questions for management to contemplate: How much would profits increase by increasing hard-disk capacity? What about by increasing the labor force? As we shall see, the notion of shadow prices for resources provides the answers to these questions.

The **shadow price** of a resource measures the change in the value of the objective function associated with a unit change in the resource. To illustrate, let's compute the shadow price associated with hard-disk capacity. Suppose the firm increases this capacity from 20,000 to 22,000 gigabytes. Figure 16.5 shows the capacity increase as a rightward shift in the hard-disk constraint line. With the increase in capacity, point C moves to the southeast. Nonetheless, the newly positioned point C remains the optimal corner; that is, the firm should continue to utilize all of its disk capacity and labor. The hard-disk and labor constraints are $80S + 40E \leq 22,000$ and $5S + 5E \leq 2,000$, respectively. Solving these as binding constraints, we find the optimal production plan to be $S = 150$ and $E = 250$. The firm's new contribution is ($500)(150) + ($300)(250) = $150,000. The 2,000-unit increase in disk capacity has resulted in a $10,000 profit increase. Thus, the shadow price of an extra unit of capacity is $10,000/2,000 = $5.

To find the shadow price associated with additional hours of labor, we set up an analogous calculation. Suppose the firm expands its labor force to 2,100 hours per week. The binding constraint equations are now $5S + 5E = 2,100$ and $80S + 40E = 20,000$. Thus, the optimal production plan is $S = 80$ and $E = 340$. The new contribution is ($500)(80) + ($300)(340) = $142,000. The addition of 100 labor-hours per week increases contribution by $2,000. (Remember, the old contribution was $140,000.) Therefore, the shadow price of labor (per hour) is $2,000/100 = $20.

Each individual resource constraint has a shadow price. Each shadow price measures the change in the objective function from a change in that resource *alone,* that is, with the amounts of all other resources held constant. As is usual in sensitivity analyses,

---

[5] If the slope of the objective function contour happens to be identical to the slope of a given constraint, any production point along the constraint is optimal. For instance, if $-\pi_S/\pi_E = -2$, maximum total contribution is attained at points B and C and any other point along segment BC.

FIGURE 16.5

The Shadow Price of
Hard Disks

If the firm can
increase its hard-disk
capacity by 2,000
gigabytes, it will
operate at point C and
increase its profit by
$10,000.

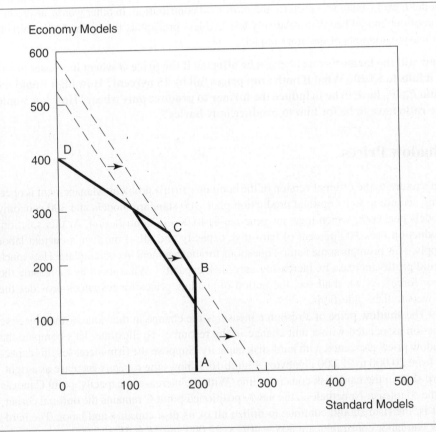

we trace the impact of one effect at a time. Also, *each shadow price is constant as long as the same constraints are binding in the optimal solution.* This price measures both the benefit of added capacity and the cost of reduced capacity. For instance, we saw that a 2,000-unit increase in hard-disk capacity raised profit by $10,000 (implying a shadow price of $5). By the same token, we can confirm that having 3,000 extra units of capacity raises profit by $15,000, whereas 1,000 extra units raises profit by $5,000. In fact, a 2,000-unit drop in capacity (a move from 20,000 to 18,000) causes a $10,000 fall in contribution (from $140,000 to $130,000). In each case, the shadow price per unit change in capacity is $5—a constant.

Now consider what happens if we expand hard-disk capacity beyond a total of 24,000 units—say, from 24,000 to 24,400 units. If we were to draw the new constraint in Figure 16.5, we would find that it lies entirely outside (i.e., to the right of) the downward-sloping labor supply constraint. Clearly, the hard-disk constraint is no longer binding. Instead, the DVD and labor constraints are binding, implying $S = 200$ and $5E + 5S = 2,000$. Thus, the optimal product mix is $S = 200$ and $E = 200$. The optimal mix remains the same when hard-disk capacity is increased beyond 24,000 or any higher amount. Any additions to capacity beyond 24,000 go unused. What is the shadow price of each extra unit of capacity beyond 24,000? Zero! The extra capacity has no effect on the feasible region, the firm's optimal plan, and its maximum profit. Because the change in profit from the extra units is zero, the shadow price is zero as well.

Thus, we have demonstrated a third property concerning shadow prices: *Any resource that is not used fully in the optimal solution (i.e., has a nonbinding constraint) has a shadow price of zero.* For example, in the original version of the problem (Figure 16.2), C is the optimal corner, where $S = 100$ and $E = 300$. Because this production plan uses only 100 DVD drives, and 200 units of capacity are available, the shadow price of DVD capacity is zero. Clearly, the firm would be no worse off with less capacity (unless capacity were reduced below 100, in which case the shortage of capacity would affect the optimal production plan).

To sum up, a constraint's shadow price measures the improvement in the objective that results from relaxing the constraint or, conversely, the decline in the objective from tightening the constraint.

For the farmer's problem, compute the shadow prices of land and labor. How   CHECK
many additional hours would the farmer have to expend before the shadow price   STATION 3
of labor fell to zero?

Optimal Decisions and Shadow Prices

Shadow prices that emerge from a linear program's optimal solution measure implicit values for the firm's limited resources. In the short run, these resources may be fixed. But in the longer run, the firm frequently can expand or contract its resources, usually at some cost. Shadow prices are essential for making these decisions. For instance, suppose the computer producer can hire extra labor at a cost of $15 per hour (wages plus fringe benefits). Should it do so? The answer is yes. The additional contribution per labor-hour is $20 (simply the shadow price for labor found earlier). Because the cost is only $15, the firm makes a net profit of $20 − $15 = $5 per labor-hour hired. It profitably can hire extra labor up to the point where labor's shadow price falls below $15. This occurs at a total labor supply of 2,500 labor-hours. At this point, the labor constraint becomes nonbinding (lies just outside the DVD and hard-disk constraint lines); thus, its shadow price falls to zero. Therefore, starting from 2,000 labor-hours, the firm could profit from hiring as many as 500 extra hours.

Now, suppose the firm could engage a subcontractor to provide an extra 2,000 units of hard-disk capacity *and* 100 hours of labor for a fixed fee of $18,000. Should the firm accept this deal? Again, the answer is derived directly from knowledge of the resource shadow prices. The total value to the firm of the extra capacities is simply ($5)(2,000) + ($20)(100) = $12,000. Here, the values of the separate capacity increases (using the respective shadow prices) are summed to arrive at the firm's total benefit. Because this benefit is less than the $18,000 cost, the firm should refuse the deal.

Finally, shadow prices play a crucial role in evaluating new activities. To illustrate, suppose the firm is contemplating the production and sale of a new super-turbo computer (*T*). Each unit of this model has an expected contribution of $700, contains a

120-gigabyte hard disk and one DVD drive, and requires 10 hours of labor. Should the firm produce this model? One way to answer this question is to formulate the new, larger LP problem as follows:

$$\text{Maximize:} \quad 500S + 300E + 700T$$
$$\text{Subject to:} \quad S + T \leq 200$$
$$80S + 40E + 120T \leq 20{,}000$$
$$5S + 5E + 10T \leq 2{,}000.$$

Using an LP computer program to solve this problem, we find that $S = 100$, $E = 300$, and $T = 0$. Despite the higher unit contribution, no units of the turbo model should be produced because its assembly would require a large quantity of "expensive" labor.

We can reach the same conclusion much more quickly using the shadow prices from our original problem. Suppose the firm considers producing one turbo unit, $T = 1$. The direct benefit is simply the unit's contribution, $700. What is the implicit cost of this unit? Because producing the unit uses the firm's limited resources, the firm will be able to produce fewer units of the other models, and total contribution from those models must fall. This loss in contribution is an **opportunity cost**. Measuring this cost is straightforward. Producing a single turbo unit uses 120 gigabytes of hard-disk capacity valued at $5 per unit (its shadow price), one unit of DVD capacity valued at $0 (remember, its shadow price is zero), and 10 hours of labor valued at $20 each. The total cost is

$$(\$5)(120) + (0)(1) + (\$20)(10) = \$800.$$

Thus, if the firm produced this turbo unit, the change in its total contribution would be $700 - $800 = -$100$. Producing a single turbo unit (or indeed any number of units) is a losing proposition. (If the firm produced 10 units, it would generate 10 times the loss, -$1,000.) Of course, if the unit contribution were predicted to be $900, a comparison of benefit and opportunity cost would show that the firm *should introduce* the turbo PC. This benefit–cost comparison would not indicate how many turbo units the firm should produce. The precise, optimal value of T can be determined only by solving the new linear program just illustrated.

Thus, we have the following general rule:

> A firm can profitably introduce a new activity if and only if the activity's direct benefit exceeds its opportunity cost, where opportunity cost is the sum of the resources used, valued at their respective shadow prices.

CHECK STATION 4   **The farmer considers planting a third crop, soybeans. The price of soybeans is $13.50 per bushel. Growing 1,000 bushels of soybeans requires 4 acres of land and 80 hours of labor per week. Is soybean production profitable? Explain.**

In closing this section, it is worth making one further point about the relationship between marginal analysis and the optimal solutions of linear programs. Earlier we saw that a new activity is excluded (its quantity is set equal to zero) if its unit benefit is less than its unit cost. What about activities that are *included* in the optimal solution? Recall that both standard and economy computers are part of the PC firm's optimal production mix. The marginal benefit of producing an extra standard model is $500 (its contribution). Using the resource shadow prices, its marginal cost is computed as

$$(\$5)(80) + (\$0)(1) + (\$20)(5) = \$500.$$

In the optimal solution, marginal benefit and marginal cost are identical. Similarly, for the economy model, marginal benefit is $300 and marginal cost is

$$(\$5)(40) + (\$0)(1) + (\$20)(5) = \$300.$$

Again marginal benefit and marginal cost are identical. The following general result holds for any linear program:

> For any decision variable that is positive in the optimal solution, its marginal benefit equals its marginal cost, where the latter is computed according to the resource shadow prices.

Thus, once again we find that the relationship, MB = MC, holds at the optimum solution.

Allocating HIV Resources

In the fall of 1999, the Centers for Disease Control and Prevention called for a panel of health scientists, economists, and policy experts to formulate a framework and strategy for HIV prevention in the United States. A member of that panel, Edward Kaplan of Yale University, has described the work of the panel in analyzing the problem of HIV prevention.[6] The panel concluded that a key goal was "to prevent as many new HIV infections as possible within the resources available for HIV prevention." Although this broad goal might seem obvious, current health-care measures often pursue other ends. As Kaplan noted, formulating the problem as a constrained maximization problem was, at least at first, foreign to many on the panel who were not economists.

The panel modeled the strategy for HIV prevention as an LP problem. The key question was: How should the budget for prevention ($412 million in 1999) allocate funds across dozens of alternative prevention programs, with myriad constraints, to maximize the number of HIV cases prevented? Prevention programs ranged from counseling at-risk populations to screening blood donations to preventing mother-to-child transmissions to funding needle exchanges for intravenous drug users. The panel marshaled the available economic and medical data to solve a variety of LP problems under different scenarios (from pessimistic to optimistic). They found that an optimal resource policy could prevent about 3,900 new HIV infections per year at the $412 million funding level. Investigation of the relevant shadow prices showed that increasing funding would lead to greater HIV prevention but at a diminishing rate.

In contrast to the optimal plan, US prevention policy at the time allocated funds to different programs, regions, and targeted populations roughly in proportion to reported AIDS cases and prevented only an estimated 3,000 infections. (Although spending more dollars where there are more AIDS cases probably makes sense for *treatment*, it is not the best plan for maximum *prevention*. Proportional allocation also embodied a perverse incentive: The allocation tended to target additional funds to programs reporting the most AIDS cases rather than to health programs that successfully prevented or reduced cases.)

[6]E. Kaplan, "Allocating HIV Resources," *OR/MS Today* (February 2001): 26–29.

Overall, the most cost-effective prevention programs (derived with the LP approach) were able to increase prevention by some 30 percent compared to current programs of the time. Kaplan also noted that if the allocation included funds for needle-exchange programs (at the time, federal law prohibited funding for such programs), annual preventions would increase to some 5,300. To sum up, Kaplan credited the resource allocation model with organizing the tough thinking needed to combat AIDS.

FORMULATION AND COMPUTER SOLUTION FOR LARGER LP PROBLEMS

Skill in recognizing, formulating, and solving linear programming problems comes with practice. This section presents four decision problems that represent a cross section of important management applications of linear programming. Once you are comfortable with these applications, the other decision problems you encounter will begin to look familiar, and their formulation and solution will become almost automatic. In addition, you will be able to formulate larger-scale problems and then solve them using standard computer programs. The final two problems display the kinds of LP solutions such programs provide, with emphasis on interpreting the computer output.

Production Decisions

We begin with two production problems.

PRODUCTION FOR MAXIMUM OUTPUT   A manufacturing firm can produce a good using three different production methods, each requiring different amounts of labor and capital—two inputs in fixed supply. The firm has 60 machine-hours and 90 labor-hours per day to devote to the product. The processes require the following inputs to produce one unit of output.

	Process 1	Process 2	Process 3
Machine-hours	.5	1	2
Labor-hours	2	1	.5

The firm seeks to maximize output by using the processes singly or in combination. How much output should it produce, and by which processes?

The LP formulation is as follows:

$$\text{Maximize:} \quad x_1 + x_2 + x_3$$
$$\text{Subject to:} \quad .5x_1 + x_2 + 2x_3 \leq 60$$
$$2x_1 + x_2 + .5x_3 \leq 90.$$

All decision variables are nonnegative.

The decision variables (x_1, x_2, and x_3) denote the quantities of output produced via each process. The firm wishes to maximize total output, the sum of the outputs produced by each process subject to the constraints that the total amounts of labor and capital used to produce total output cannot exceed available supplies of inputs.

This problem involves two constraints (plus three nonnegativity constraints) and three decision variables. Here, the previous graphical method will not work because there are more decision variables than axes of the graph. However, we can find the solution graphing the two *constraints* on the axes instead. The method is shown in Figure 16.6, where available input supplies—rather than decision variables—are placed on the axes. The rectangle OLMK represents the feasible region, whose sides indicate the available amounts of capital and labor (60 and 90 units, respectively).

The next step is to graph a contour of the objective function. Figure 16.6 shows two such contours. The inner contour shows combinations of inputs necessary to produce 40 units of output; the outer contour corresponds to producing 70 units. For instance, if the firm seeks to produce 40 units, it can do so via process 1, using 20 machine-hours and 80 labor-hours; this input combination is shown as point A in the figure. Alternatively,

FIGURE 16.6

Maximum Output with
Limited Inputs

With 60 machine-hours and 90 labor-hours, the firm can produce its maximum output, 70 units, at point M by using processes 1 and 2 in combination.

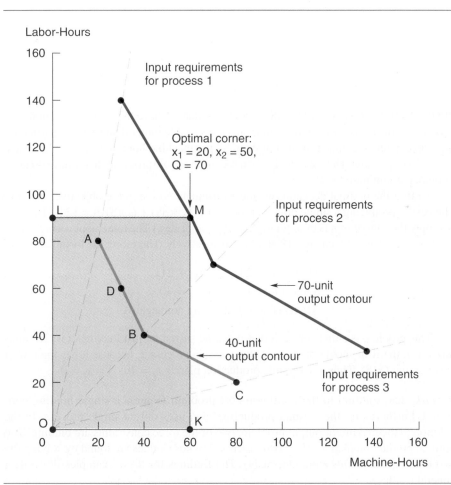

it could use process 2, using 40 units of each input (point B), or process 3, using 80 and 20 units (point C).

To complete the production contour we draw the segments connecting these points. For instance, the firm could produce the 40 units using a combination of processes 1 and 2. Consider the outputs $x_1 = 20$, $x_2 = 20$, and $x_3 = 0$. Total production is 40 units, using a total of $10 + 20 = 30$ machine-hours and $40 + 20 = 60$ labor-hours. This pair of inputs occurs at point D in Figure 16.6, halfway along the segment joining A and B. In general, by using processes 1 and 2 in various proportions to produce 40 units in total, we trace out the line segment AB. Similarly, combinations of processes 2 and 3 use inputs described by the line segment BC.

To complete the graphical solution, we find the highest production contour attainable given the fixed supply of inputs. The highest contour touches the corner of the feasible region at point M, where each input is fully utilized. At this point, the firm produces output using only processes 1 and 2. Returning to the mathematical formulation, we know from the graph that $x_3 = 0$ and that

$$.5x_1 + x_2 = 60$$
$$2x_1 + x_2 = 90$$

because both constraints are binding. Solving these equations simultaneously, we find $x_1 = 20$, $x_2 = 50$, and maximum total output is 70.

PRODUCTION AT MINIMUM COST   Suppose that we have the same production processes as in the previous example, but inputs are variable rather than fixed. In particular, the firm can rent machine time at a price of \$8 per machine-hour and can hire labor at a wage of \$10 per hour. How should the firm use the available processes to produce 40 units of output at minimum cost?

To find the optimal decision, we must formulate correctly the objective function. The cost of producing a single unit via process 1 is $(.5)(\$8) + (2)(\$10) = \$24$. (The cost is simply the sum of inputs used multiplied by their prices.) The total input costs per unit for processes 2 and 3 come to \$18 and \$21, respectively. Therefore, the formulation is

Minimize: $24x_1 + 18x_2 + 21x_3$
Subject to: $x_1 + x_2 + x_3 = 40$.
All decision variables are nonnegative.

This problem is simple enough that it can be solved by just looking at it. To minimize cost, the firm should produce exclusively via process 2, because it has the lowest cost per unit (\$18). Thus, the optimal production plan is $x_2 = 40$, $x_1 = x_3 = 0$.

Remark: The solution to the minimum-cost problem features a single binding constraint. Furthermore, the optimal production plan uses only a single process. In the solution to the maximum-output problem, two of the three constraints are binding. The optimal production plan involves two processes (whose values are found by solving the two binding constraints simultaneously). The findings for these examples illustrate a general result:

In any linear programming problem, the number of decision variables that take nonzero values in the optimal solution always is equal to the number of binding constraints.

Therefore, in decision problems in which the number of decision variables (call this number N) greatly exceeds the number of constraints (call this M), at least $N - M$ decision variables will be zero in the optimal solution.

Computer Solutions

Solving LP problems graphically is impractical for problems in which there are three or more decision variables and constraints. Fortunately, many computer programs are available to solve large-scale LP problems. Indeed, a major airline routing its aircraft can find itself facing a linear programming problem involving thousands of decision variables and hundreds of constraints. Computers can efficiently solve even problems this large. In its broad description, the computer solution is much the same, however large the problem. Typically, the user inputs a mathematical formulation of the problem, that is, the objective function and all constraints. The computer program then produces optimal values of all decision variables, the optimal value of the objective function, and the shadow prices associated with the constraints.

The last 30 years have seen the development of dozens of *spreadsheet-based* linear programming packages.[7] The user enters basic data, including constraints, directly into a spreadsheet. The program then carries out all arithmetic calculations and displays the optimal solution and shadow prices in the original spreadsheet. A key advantage is that this output can be used as inputs into larger, related spreadsheets. The following examples illustrate a typical spreadsheet-based LP program.

A STAFFING PROBLEM   A major city has minimum requirements for the number of police officers on duty during each four-hour period (see the following table). Because split shifts are prohibited, each officer must work eight consecutive hours.

Officers receive standard pay rates for shifts 1 and 2, time and a quarter for shifts 3 and 4, and time and a half for shifts 5 and 6. How can the police department find a daily work schedule that will minimize its total wage cost?

Shift	Time	Required Number of Police Officers
1	8 A.M.–12 P.M.	150
2	12–4 P.M.	100
3	4–8 P.M.	250
4	8 P.M.–12 A.M.	400
5	12–4 A.M.	500
6	4–8 A.M.	175

[7]For a review of these software packages, see R. Fourer, "Linear Programming Survey," *OR/MS Today* (June 2013): 44–53. (An updated version of this comprehensive survey of LP software packages is available online at http://lionhrtpub.com/orms. Click on "software surveys.")

The formulation of this decision problem is as follows:

Minimize: $x_1 + 1.125x_2 + 1.25x_3 + 1.375x_4 + 1.5x_5 + 1.25x_6$

Subject to: $x_1 + x_6 \geq 150$

$x_2 + x_1 \geq 100$

$x_3 + x_2 \geq 250$

$x_4 + x_3 \geq 400$

$x_5 + x_4 \geq 500$

$x_6 + x_5 \geq 175$

All decision variables are nonnegative.

Here $x_1, x_2, \ldots, x_6$ denote the number of officers who *begin* duty with shift 1, 2, . . . , 6. The objective function lists the total number of regular-time salaries of the force. (The city pays an officer beginning duty in shift 1 regular time for eight hours. One beginning in shift 2 receives four hours of regular-time pay and four hours at time and a quarter; overall, he or she counts as a 1.125 officer. We similarly calculate the pay for officers beginning shifts 3 through 6.) The left-hand side of the first constraint lists the number of police on duty during the 8 A.M. to 12 P.M. period. (This is the sum of x_1 and x_6, the number of officers beginning shifts at 8 A.M. and ending shifts at noon.) This number must be no fewer than the 150-person requirement. We express the other five constraints in the same way.

The manager enters the objective function and the relevant constraints into the spreadsheet. Table 16.1 shows the completed spreadsheet (including the problem's optimal solution and shadow prices). In the table, the decision variables appear in row 6 and are in colored type for easy identification. We can vary these as we wish and observe the effect on the objective. The values shown here are the optimal values generated by executing Excel's optimization program, Solver. In actual practice, the user is free to enter any initial values. For instance, the user could begin by setting all six variables at 300 officers—values that far exceed required staffing levels. The manager can also experiment with other values. Cell I5 lists the objective, the total number of regular-time police officers (the value of which the manager wants to minimize). The value in this cell has been computed by using the objective function equation in the LP formulation.

Rows 8 and 10 represent the constraints. The fixed values in row 10 denote the required number of officers on the six shifts (the right side of the preceding inequalities). The computed values in row 8 list the number of officers actually present during the time periods. For instance, the value in cell C8 is the sum of cells B6 and C6, and so on. Finally, each value in row 12, the so-called extra officers, is the difference between the actual (row 8) and required (row 10) number of personnel.

To direct the computer to solve the LP problem, one must complete the Solver menu (shown below the spreadsheet in Table 16.1). In the menu, we have entered target cell I5 (total cost) to be minimized by varying cells B6 to G6 (the numbers hired beginning in each time period). The constraints specify that cells B12 through G12 must be greater than or equal to zero, so there cannot be a shortage of officers (i.e., a negative number of extra officers) on any shift. The final constraint states that all decision variables must be nonnegative.

Upon execution, the spreadsheet-based optimization program instantly computes all optimal values consistent with satisfying all constraints. From the spreadsheet solution in Table 16.1, we see that the minimum total number of regular-time officers is 1,150, as shown in cell I5. Note that the bare minimum number of officers is present on five of the six shifts; only the second shift has excess numbers. Moreover, officers begin

TABLE 16.1

Linear Programming Solution for Police Staffing Problem

The department meets its hourly staffing requirements at minimum total cost.

	A	B	C	D	E	F	G	H	I	J
1										
2		8AM–12	12–4 PM	4–8 PM	8 PM–12	12–4 AM	4–8 AM			
3										
4	Shift Costs	1	1.125	1.25	1.375	1.5	1.25		Total Cost	
5									1,150	
6	# of Officers	150	175	75	325	175	0			
7										
8	# per 8-hour shift	150	325	250	400	500	175			
9										
10	Officers required	150	100	250	400	500	175			
11										
12	Extra Officers	0	225	0	0	0	0			
13										
14	Shadow Price	1.0	0	1.125	0.125	1.25	0.25			

Solver Parameters ? X

Set Target Cell: $I$5

Equal to: ○ Max ● Min

By Changing Cells:

$B$6 : $G$6

Subject to Constraints:

$B$12 : $G$12 ≥ 0
$B$6 : $G$6 ≥ 0

Solve

Close

Options

Add

Change

Delete

work on five of the six shifts; no officers begin work on shift 6 at 4 A.M. (This illustrates the earlier general result: Since there are five binding constraints, there are exactly five nonzero decision variables.)[8]

The spreadsheet also lists the shadow price associated with each constraint. For instance, the shadow price of requiring an extra officer on the fourth shift (moving from 400 to 401 officers) is .125. How can this extra officer be obtained for only a *fractional* increase in the workforce? The answer is by hiring one fewer officer beginning in shift 2 (where we already have surplus personnel) and hiring one more officer beginning in shift 3. This trade satisfies the new constraints. The net increase in cost comes from the difference between the hourly costs on shifts 2 and 3: $1.25 - 1.125 = .125$. This confirms the shadow price.

Clean Coal

Energy production—whether to provide electric power, heat homes and buildings, or fuel all kinds of transportation—is a dirty business. The most abundant and economical forms of energy, coal and oil, are also the most harmful to the environment. As energy demand surges in China, India, and other fast-developing nations, the risks of environmental harm and global climate change only increase. Consequently, developing "green" technologies and alternative energy sources is one of the paramount economic challenges and opportunities of the new century. Rapid innovation has raised the promise of technologically feasible solar and wind power. Though use of these and other renewable energy sources has more than tripled during the last decade, they still account for less than 5 percent of electricity production in the United States. Moreover, they are costly; for instance, in generating electricity, solar power is more than five times as costly as coal.

To understand the energy challenge, one must come to grips with a fundamental *constraint*. Absent a miraculous technological breakthrough (and the evidence makes such a leap extremely unlikely), the share of alternative green sources in energy production will be very small, and green energy is and will be expensive. Instituting a carbon tax would help level the "playing field" where dirty and clean fuels compete with respect to cost. But clean fuels would still be severely constrained by the problem of scale. (Spreadsheet problem S2 at the end of the chapter models the choice among alternative energy sources as a linear program.)

Arguably, the best immediate means for reducing environmental harm (and, in particular, the rate of global warming caused by greenhouse gas emissions) is to institute incremental improvements in the combustion of traditional fossil fuels, which are cheap and abundant.[9] Electric utilities in China and the United States have begun development of underground coal gasification processes that leave much of the pollutants and greenhouse gases such as carbon dioxide under the ground. Over the next 20 years, China's challenge is to provide enough electricity—the equivalent of the entire US electrical grid—for some 300 million people who will live in its newly developed cities and towns. Dependent on coal and aware of the limitations of large-scale hydroelectric projects, China's planners are undertaking the world's largest and most aggressive experiment in

[8] This is not the only optimal plan. A second solution of the LP problem is $x_1 = 75$, $x_2 = 250$, $x_3 = 0$, $x_4 = 400$, $x_5 = 100$, and $x_6 = 75$. This plan also requires the minimum number of regular-time officers (1,150).

[9] For a discussion of clean coal, see J. Fallows, "Dirty Coal, Clean Future," *The Atlantic* (December 2010), 64–78.

developing clean coal processes for generating electricity. Conservation, smarter electricity pricing, renewable energy sources, even nuclear power—these many initiatives will all offer (limited) contributions to the world's energy needs. But how fast China travels down the clean-coal learning curve and how willingly it shares its advances with the rest of the world will also be crucial.

A SCHOOL BUSING PROBLEM   Each year, a municipality contracts with a private bus company for the transportation of students in the primary grades to and from school. As a management consultant to the city, you must structure a busing plan. The city's annual payment to the bus company will depend on the number of "kid-miles" the company carries. (For instance, carrying 20 children 2 miles each amounts to 40 kid-miles, as does carrying 8 children 5 miles each.)

The city's three elementary schools draw students from four distinct geographic neighborhoods. The city's planning department has furnished figures on the number of students in each neighborhood, the capacity of each school, and the distance from each school to each neighborhood. Figure 16.7 shows a map of the school district and provides the pertinent data. You must formulate a busing plan that will minimize total transportation cost. Before turning to the LP formulation and the computer solution in Table 16.2, try coming up with an optimal bus plan on your own, using the information in Figure 16.7.

From the data in Figure 16.7, we can develop the following LP formulation:

$$\text{Minimize:} \quad 2.0N1 + 3.0E1 + \ldots + 13.0W3 + 2.2S3$$

$$\text{Subject to:} \quad N1 + E1 + W1 + S1 \leq 360$$
$$N2 + E2 + W2 + S2 \leq 400 \qquad \text{School capacities}$$
$$N3 + E3 + W3 + S3 \leq 260$$

$$N1 + N2 + N3 = 240$$
$$E1 + E2 + E3 = 120 \qquad \text{Neighborhood}$$
$$W1 + W2 + W3 = 400 \qquad \text{Enrollments}$$
$$S1 + S2 + S3 = 200$$

All decision variables are nonnegative.

The formulation begins with recognizing that a busing plan has 12 decision variables: the number of children from each of four neighborhoods bused to each of three schools. For instance, the variable $N1$ denotes the number of students from the north neighborhood bused to school 1, and so on. Remember that the city wants to minimize the total number of kid-miles traveled. As the formulation shows, the objective function is found by multiplying the number of students along a given route by the distance along the route ($2.0N1$, for instance) and summing. The first three constraints pertain to school capacities: The total number of students going to each school cannot exceed the school's capacity. The last four constraints pertain to neighborhood enrollments: For each neighborhood, all school-age children ride the bus to some school. (If the left-hand side of the equality fell short of the right-hand side, many happy children would be left on street corners without being picked up for school.)

FIGURE 16.7

Data for a School Busing
Problem

The number of
elementary school-
children in the neigh-
borhoods and the
student capacities of
the schools are listed
in parentheses.

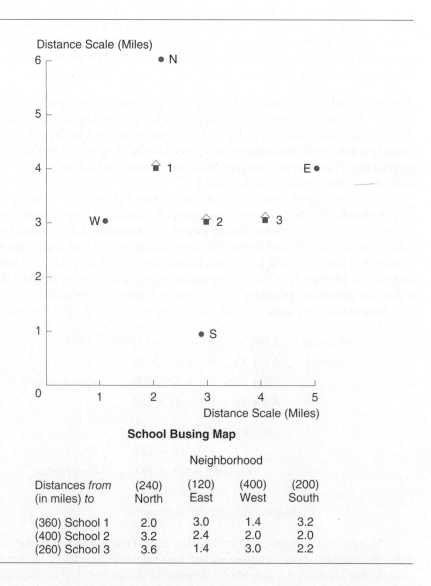

School Busing Map

Distances *from* (in miles) *to*	Neighborhood			
	(240) North	(120) East	(400) West	(200) South
(360) School 1	2.0	3.0	1.4	3.2
(400) School 2	3.2	2.4	2.0	2.0
(260) School 3	3.6	1.4	3.0	2.2

Table 16.2 shows the computer solution. Note that the north and east children go to the schools closest to them, and the west and south students go to either their nearest and second-nearest schools. School 3 has extra spaces. The city pays for the minimum number of kid-miles: 1,792. The table also lists shadow prices associated with each school and each neighborhood. For instance, the shadow price associated with busing an extra child from the north neighborhood is 2.8; this results from busing the student to school 1 (2 miles). Because school 1 already is at capacity, however, the extra north child displaces a west child who goes to school 2 instead of school 1 (an extra distance of 0.6 miles).

TABLE 16.2

Linear Programming Solution for Busing Problem

The least-cost solution shows the numbers of children bused on six routes between neighborhood and schools.

	A	B	C	D	E	F	G	H	I	J
1										
2			Distances				Total			
3		North	East	West	South		Kid Miles			
4	School 1	2.0	3.0	1.4	3.2		1,792			
5	School 2	3.2	2.4	2.0	2.0					
6	School 3	3.6	1.4	3.0	2.2					
7										
8										
9			Students			Total in	Capacity	Extra	Shadow	
10		North	East	West	South	School	of School	Space	Prices	
11										
12	School 1	240	0	120	0	360	360	0	0.8	
13	School 2	0	0	280	120	400	400	0	0.2	
14	School 3	0	120	0	80	200	260	60	0	
15										
16	Total Kids Bussed	240	120	400	200					
17	Students in District	240	120	400	200					
18	Difference	0	0	0	0					
19	Shadow Prices	2.8	1.4	2.2	2.2					
20										

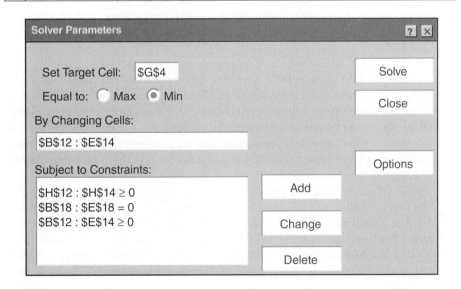

In turn, the extra west child going to school 2 displaces a south child who now travels an extra distance of .2 miles to school 3. Thus, the listed shadow price represents a total increase in miles of: $2.0 + .6 + .2 = 2.8$.

CHECK STATION 5 **Confirm that the shadow prices associated with school 1 and the west neighborhood are correct.**

An Investment Problem Revisited

Recall that the manager wants to construct a portfolio of securities that offers the highest expected after-tax return, subject to the following requirements: (1) The portfolio's average quality rating is at least 3.5, and (2) the portfolio's average maturity is at least 1.5 years but no greater than 2.5 years.

Bond Category	Quality Rating	Maturity (Years)	Yield (Percent)
Treasury bills	5.0	0.4	4.0
Treasury bonds	5.0	4.0	6.0
Corporate bonds	3.5	3.2	4.4
Municipal bonds	3.0	2.0	5.6
Junk bonds	1.0	2.5	8.0

The LP formulation is

Maximize: $4.0B + 6.0T + 4.4C + 5.6M + 8.0J$

Subject to: $5B + 5T + 3.5C + 3M + 1J \geq 3.5$

$.4B + 4.0T + 3.2C + 2.0M + 2.5J \geq 1.5$

$.4B + 4.0T + 3.2C + 2.0M + 2.5J \leq 2.5$

$B + T + C + M + J = 1.0.$

All decision variables are nonnegative.

The portfolio manager must determine the proportions of the individual's total dollar investment to invest in the securities. These proportions are denoted by B, T, C, M, and J for the respective securities. (For instance, if the manager divided the portfolio equally among the five assets, the values would be $B = T = C = M = J = .2$.) The actual size of the manager's investment fund does not enter into the formulation. The optimal proportions will be the same whether the manager is investing \$20,000 or \$20 million.

The objective function lists the average (or expected) return of the portfolio. The first constraint indicates that the portfolio's average risk rating must be at least 3.5. The second and third constraints list the bounds on the portfolio's average maturity. The final constraint ensures that the portfolio proportions sum exactly to 1.

What portfolio will maximize the investor's expected return, subject to the risk and maturity constraints? From Table 16.3, we see that the optimal portfolio puts

TABLE 16.3

Linear Programming Solution for an Optimal Portfolio

By dividing funds among Treasury bills, Treasury bonds, and junk bonds, the investor earns a maximum expected return (6.23 percent) while meeting three investment requirements.

	A	B	C	D	E	F	G	H	I	J	K	L
1												
2		T-Bills	T-Bonds	C-Bonds	Munis	Junk		Portfolio				
3												
4	Proportions	0.260	0.365	0	0	0.375		1				
5												Shadow
6	Returns	4	6	4.4	5.6	8		6.23		Goal	Gap	Price
7												
8	Ratings	5	5	3.5	3	1		3.5	>	3.5	0	0.708
9												
10									>	1.5	1	0
11	Maturities	0.4	4	3.2	2	2.5		2.5				
12									<	2.5	0	0.555
13												

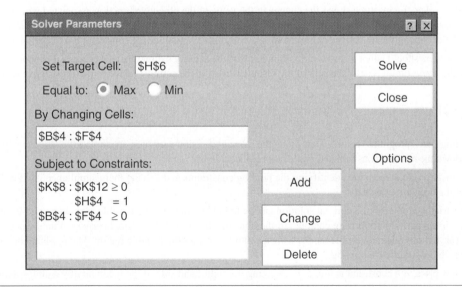

26 percent of the individual's total dollar investment in Treasury bills, 36.5 percent in Treasury bonds, and the remainder in junk bonds. This portfolio has a risk rating of exactly 3.5 (which just meets this constraint), has a maturity of exactly 2.5 years (which just meets the upper maturity constraint), and delivers a maximum portfolio return of 6.23 percent.

The spreadsheet also lists the relevant shadow prices as calculated by the LP program. The shadow prices associated with the risk and maturity constraints are of some interest. The former shadow price shows that allowing a unit reduction in the portfolio's risk index (reflecting a tolerance for greater risk) would raise the portfolio's expected return by .708 percent. According to the latter shadow price, increasing the average maturity of the portfolio by a year would increase the expected return by .555 percent. (In either case, the portfolio would shift toward a greater share of junk bonds and a smaller share of Treasury bills.)

SUMMARY

Decision-Making Principles

1. Linear programming is a method of formulating and solving decision problems that involve explicit resource constraints. The range of LP problems includes product mix, cost minimization, transportation, scheduling, inventory, and financial and budgeting decisions.

2. To qualify as a linear program, all decision variables must enter linearly into the objective function and into all constraints. As long as the LP problem is feasible, an optimal solution always exists at one of the corners of the feasible region. The optimal corner can be found by graphical means or by computer algorithms.

3. The shadow price of a resource shows the change in the value of the objective function associated with a unit change in the resource. Thus, the shadow price measures the improvement in the objective from relaxing a constraint or, conversely, the decline in the objective from tightening a constraint. A nonbinding constraint has a shadow price of zero.

4. Decision makers should adopt a new activity if and only if the activity's direct benefit exceeds its opportunity cost. We measure this opportunity cost by the sum of the resources used in the activity valued at their respective shadow prices.

Nuts and Bolts

1. Formulating linear programs requires identifying the relevant decision variables, specifying the objective function, and writing down the relevant constraints as mathematical inequalities.

2. Solving linear programs requires identifying the binding constraints and solving them simultaneously for the optimal values of the decision variables.

3. For two-variable problems, the optimal solution can be found by graphing the feasible region (framed by the binding constraint lines) and superimposing contours of the objective function. The optimal corner is found where the highest contour (or, for minimization problems, the lowest contour) touches the feasible region. The optimal corner determines which constraints are binding.

4. The shadow price of a constraint is found by changing the right-hand side of the inequality by a unit, solving the binding constraints for the decision variables, and recomputing the objective function. The shadow price is simply the change between the new and old values of the objective.

Questions and Problems

1. Explain whether LP techniques can be used in each of the following economic settings:
   a. There are increasing returns to scale in production.
   b. The objective function and all constraints are linear, but the number of decision variables exceeds the number of constraints.
   c. The firm faces a downward-sloping linear demand curve. (To sell more output, it must lower its price.)
   d. The firm can vary the amounts of two basic chemicals in producing a specialty chemical, but, for quality control reasons, the relative proportions of chemicals must be between 40/60 and 60/40.

2. Which of the following formulations can be solved via the LP method?
   a. Maximize: $x + 2y$, subject to: $x + y \geq 2$ and $3x - y \geq 4$.
   b. Maximize: xy, subject to: $x + y \leq 2$ and $3x - y \geq 4$.
   c. Maximize: $x + 2y$, subject to: $x + y \leq 2$ and $3x - y \geq 4$.
   d. Maximize: $x + 2y$, subject to: $x + y \leq 2$ and $3x + y \geq 8$.
   e. Maximize: $x + 2y$, subject to: $x + y \leq 2$ and $x/(x + y) \leq .7$.

3. A manager has formulated the following LP problems. Use graphical methods to find the optimal solutions. (In each, all variables are nonnegative.)
   a. Maximize: $10x + 15y$, subject to: $2x + 5y \leq 40$ and $6x + 3y \leq 48$.
   b. Minimize: $.75x + y$, subject to: $x + .5y \geq 10$ and $x + y \geq 16$.

4. Consider an LP problem in which a firm produces multiple goods (A and B) using two inputs (X and Y) in limited supply. Suppose a technological advance increases the amount of good A that can be produced per unit of input X. How will this change the feasible region? How will this affect the quantities of the goods produced in the profit-maximizing solution to the LP problem? (To answer these questions, be sure to graph the two resource constraints.)

5. An athlete carefully watches her intake of calcium, protein, and calories. Her breakfast diet consists mainly of milk and cereal, whose prices and nutrient contents appear in the following table:

	Milk (1 oz.)	Cereal (1 oz.)
Calcium	2	2
Protein	2	6
Calories	6	2
Price	$.10	$.15

She seeks a diet that supplies at least 50 units of calcium, 90 units of protein, and 66 calories at minimum cost.
   a. Formulate, graph, and solve this decision problem. What is the minimum cost of meeting the nutrient requirements?
   b. Calculate and provide an economic interpretation of the shadow price associated with calcium.

6. A firm produces tires by two separate processes that require different quantities of capital (K), labor (L), and raw materials (M). Process 1 requires one unit of K, four units of L, and two units of M to produce a tire yielding a $4 profit. Process 2 requires one unit of K, two units of L, and four units of M to produce a tire yielding a $6 profit. The available supply of capital is 10; of labor, 32; and of raw materials, 32.
   a. Formulate and solve (by graphing) the firm's profit-maximization problem.
   b. Find the shadow prices of raw materials and labor.

7. Consider again the investment problem that opened the chapter.
   a. Suppose the portfolio manager limits the portfolio to Treasury bills and Treasury bonds. Using a graph, find the proportions of each type of bond that maximize expected return subject to the risk and maturity constraints.
   b. Now suppose the manager can invest in any of the five securities but cares only about the risk constraint. Determine the optimal portfolio.
   c. Answer part (b), assuming the manager cares only about the maturity constraints.

8. A soft-drink producer must decide how to divide its spending between two forms of media: television advertising and magazine advertising. Each 30-second commercial on prime-time network television costs $120,000 and, by the company's estimate, will reach 10,000 viewers, 5,000 of whom are in the prime consumer age group, 15 to 25. A single-page ad in a leading human-interest weekly magazine costs $40,000 and reaches 5,000 individuals, 1,000 of whom are in the 15-to-25 age group. In addition, the company plans to hold a sweepstakes contest to promote its new soft drink. (A requirement for entry is to enclose the coded label from the new drink.) The company believes the print ad will be more effective in generating trial purchases and entries. Each magazine spot is expected to produce 500 entries and each television spot 250 entries. Finally, the company's goal in its promotion campaign is to reach at least 600,000 total viewers and 150,000 young viewers and to generate 30,000 or more contest entrants.

   How many spots of each kind should it purchase to meet these three goals and do so at minimum cost?

9. A lumber company uses labor (L) and capital (K) to produce joint products, hardwood (H) and plywood (P). These items can be produced by one of two processes:

   Process 1: 1 unit of L and 2 units of K to yield 2 units of H and 1 unit of P

   or

   Process 2: 2 units of L and 2 units of K to yield 2 units of H and 4 units of P

   Profit contribution is $2 per unit of H and $1 per unit of P. The firm has 110 units of L and 160 units of K available.

   a. Formulate and solve the firm's profit-maximization problem. (*Hint*: Don't be distracted by the fact that the processes produce joint products. The correct decision variables are the levels of each process.)

   b. Find the shadow price of labor.

   c. Answer part (a), assuming the contribution of P rises to $3 per unit.

10. A 30-year-old investment analyst has been experimenting with Optimum *Eating*, a new iPhone app. The app shows you how to divide the proportion of your weekly meals among the four categories listed in the following table. The table's bottom two rows list the health attributes of the meal categories. The row labeled "BMI" (standing for Body Mass Index) rates the categories in terms of maintaining a trim and healthy body weight. Healthy meals deliver a maximum BMI score (100); fast-food meals deliver the worst score (20). The "Heart" row uses a similar scale to rate the meals as to their impact on cardiovascular factors such as blood pressure and cholesterol. Both scales have been developed by the Office of the US Surgeon General. The last column lists the Surgeon General's recommended goals for a healthy weekly diet, 70 for BMI and 80 for heart.

Portions	Healthy .25	Standard .25	Fast Food .25	Restaurant .25	Diet Score	
Value	$3.00	$8.00	$12.00	$28.00	$12.75	Goals
Cost	$6.00	$5.00	$8.00	$20.00	$9.75	$10.00
BMI	100	70	20	50	60.00	70
Heart	100	70	40	70	70.00	80

   The Cost row lists the average cost per meal (from a database of cities across the United States. (The costs in the table are those for Milwaukee, Wisconsin.) Finally, the values in the first row are purely personal and have been entered by the financial analyst himself. (Notice that the analyst's taste buds are quite averse to healthy meals. He rates a healthy meal that costs $6.00 as worth only $3.00 in value.)

   At the outset, the app sets the meal proportions by default at .25 across the board. For these default proportions, the diet column calculates the average cost, BMI score, and heart score per meal. (These scores are computed by multiplying each meal category proportion by its score and then adding these products over the four categories.) Note that the default diet falls short of meeting both the BMI and heart goals listed in the last column.

a. On a spreadsheet, recreate this app in the form of a linear program.

b. Use your spreadsheet's optimizer to find the meal proportions that meet the BMI and heart goals at minimum cost. Which meal category is *not* a part of the least-cost weekly meal plan?

c. Instead, the analyst wants to adopt a plan that maximizes his value per meal while meeting both health goals and spending no more than $10 per meal on average. Use the optimizer to determine this meal plan. How does the plan change if the analyst is able to budget $15 per meal?

11. A Boston-based middle manager recently received an exciting e-mail offer from American Airlines. Because of her long-time loyalty, she is eligible to obtain LIFETIME Platinum elite status on American if she fulfills a special "challenge"—flying 20,000 miles and 12 segments between October 1 and December 31. She covets the perks that come from Platinum status: priority check-in and boarding, lounge access, 100 percent bonus on miles flown. The challenge is definitely doable; she has friends and family to visit in Los Angeles (5,200 miles roundtrip), Miami (2,520 miles), and Durham, North Carolina (1,224 miles)—all of which have American direct flights from Boston. (Each roundtrip counts as two flight segments.)

a. She is ready to book her trips, and the cheapest American roundtrip fares to the three cities are $425, $300, and $200, respectively. How should she plan her numbers of trips to these destinations to meet the mile and segment challenge at minimum total cost? Using a spreadsheet and optimizer, formulate and solve her linear program. (In the optimizer menu, be sure to include the constraint that the number of trips to each destination must be an integer.)

b. How would her trip plan and total cost change if 25,000 flown miles were required? What if only 10 segments (and 20,000 miles) were needed?

Discussion Question   Following the example in the text, consider two HIV prevention programs: (1) intensive counseling of high-risk individuals and (2) instituting a needle-exchange program for intravenous drug users. Counseling has an estimated cost of $1,500 per individual per year and is expected to prevent .2 new HIV cases per individual helped. The needle-exchange program costs $500 per individual and prevents .1 new HIV cases per individual.

a. Which program is more effective at HIV prevention *per individual treated*? Which program is more cost effective, that is, more effective *per dollar spent*? Do your answers raise a dilemma as to which program to fund?

b. Suppose that a regional health organization has a total budget of $450,000 to spend on the two programs and has identified 1,000 high-risk individuals. In coordinating the two prevention programs, it sets two variables, C and N, for the respective numbers to be counseled or furnished clean needles. (Given their very different orientations, the programs are mutually exclusive; each individual is enrolled in a single program.) If the authority's goal is to prevent as many new HIV cases as possible, how many individuals should it enroll in each program?

c. What is the authority's optimal allocation if the at-risk population numbers only 250? Show that it will have unused funds.

d. Finally, what is the authority's optimal allocation if the at-risk population numbers 500? Be sure to show the appropriate LP formulation.

Spreadsheet Problems

S1. An electronics firm has production plants in Oregon and Tennessee. It ships its products overseas from three ports: Los Angeles, New Orleans, and New York. Transportation costs between plants and seaports are shown in the table.

	Los Angeles	New Orleans	New York
Oregon	$14	$26	$30
Tennessee	24	10	12

The maximum capacity of the Oregon plant is 9,000 tons; the capacity of the Tennessee plant is 10,000 tons. The minimum daily quantities shipped overseas from Los Angeles, New Orleans, and New York are 5,000, 7,000, and 6,000 tons, respectively.

a. The company's objective is to minimize the cost of transporting its product from plants to ports while fulfilling its daily overseas shipping requirements. Formulate the appropriate LP problem.

b. Attempt to solve the LP problem by inspection. Find the company's minimum-cost transport plan using a standard LP computer program.

c. Determine and interpret the shadow price associated with the 6,000 minimum daily shipment to New York.

S2. The accompanying spreadsheet lists six different means of generating electricity in the United States. Row 6 lists the estimated megawatt hours produced in 2010 by power plants of each kind. In turn, row 7 lists the maximum capacity for each, while row 9 shows the proportion of the US total (3.8 billion MWh) for each source. (For instance, coal-burning facilities account for 46 percent of electricity generation.) As discussed earlier in the chapter, the different energy sources vary with respect to average cost per megawatt, carbon dioxide emissions, and environmental and health consequences. (This last category combines diverse impacts: environmental damage from strip mining or damming rivers, the consequences of securely storing nuclear waste, worker and residential safety risks, and so on.) These costs and impacts—expressed per megawatt hour of electricity—are shown in rows 12, 13, and 14. Finally, cells H12, H13, and H14 show the cost, carbon emissions, and environmental/health impact associated with *total* US electricity production averaged across all US facilities. (Note that computing the average cost in cell H12 uses the formula: $= B9*B12 + C9*C12 + \ldots G9*G12$.)

	A	B	C	D	E	F	G	H	I
1									
2	Options for US Electricity Generation								
3									
4		Coal	Clean Coal	Nat Gas	Nuclear	Hydro	Renewable	Total	Goal
5									
6	Output (MWh)	1.75	0	0.87	0.75	0.26	0.17	3.80	3.80
7	Maximum	2.6	0.5	1.9	0.75	0.44	0.25		
8									
9	Proportion	46.1%	0.0%	22.9%	19.7%	6.8%	4.5%	100%	
10									
11							Cost inc tax:	$66.12	
12	Cost	$40	$60	$50	$115	$100	$150	$66.12	
13	CO_2	1.1	0.5	0.62	0	0	0	0.65	.50
14	Environ/Health	100	50	80	65	15	15	78.89	65
15									
16	Carbon Tax								
17	$0	$0	$0	$0	$0	$0	$0	$0	
18									

a. Re-create the spreadsheet. Ignoring the carbon and environmental impacts, what proportions of the energy sources would minimize the nation's average cost per megawatt hour (cell H12) while generating 3.8 billion MWh in total? Explain.

b. Answer the question in part (a) with the added constraint that carbon emissions should be no greater than .5 tons per MWh of electricity generated—that is, cell H13 must be smaller or equal to cell I13. What roles do clean coal and renewable energy sources play? Is it possible to reduce carbon emissions below .35 tons per MWh? Explain.

c. Suppose that government regulations dictate that twin goals—.4 tons of CO_2 per MWh (cell I13) and an environmental/health score no greater than 65 (cell I14)—must both be met. Determine the cost-minimizing mix of energy sources. Proponents of nuclear power argue that this source could provide a total capacity of 1.25 MWh of electricity if enough new plants were built over the next 30 years. Is such a nuclear expansion warranted?

d. An alternative to a CO_2 emission standard is a carbon tax. Policy makers have proposed a tax of \$80 per ton of CO_2 emissions to reflect the expected cost of increased global warming. Such a tax would raise the total cost per MWh of the first three energy sources. For instance, an \$80 tax (inserted in cell A17) would imply an added $(80)(1.1) = \$88$ cost per MWh for coal-fired electricity (in cell B17). Under the \$80 tax, what mix of generating plants minimizes the average cost of electricity? (*Hint*: In cell H17, compute the average tax per MWh; then minimize cell H11, computed as the sum of cells H12 and H17.) How high would the carbon tax have to be to spur expansion of renewable energy sources?

Suggested References

The following reference is one of many fine, applied programming texts.

Gass, S. I. *An Illustrated Guide to Linear Programming*. New York: McGraw-Hill, 1990.

The following articles describe typical managerial applications.

Bollapragada, S. et al. "NBC's Optimization Systems Increase Revenues and Productivity." *Interfaces* (January–February 2002): 47–60.

Higle, J. L., and S. W. Wallace. "Sensitivity Analysis and Uncertainty in Linear Programming." *Interfaces* (July–August 2003): 53–60.

Kaplan, E. "Allocating HIV Resources." *OR/MS Today* (February 2001): 26–29. The panel's full report is available online at: www.nationalacademies.org (search for "No Time to Lose" full text). The direct link is www.nap.edu/books/0309071372/html/

Kimes, S. E., and J. A. Fitzsimmons. "Selecting Profitable Sites at La Quinta Motor Inns." *Interfaces* (March–April 1990): 12–20.

LeBlanc, L. J. et al. "Nu-kote's Spreadsheet Linear Programming Models for Optimizing Transportation." *Interfaces* (March–April 2004): 139–146.

Linear programming software is surveyed by

Fourer, R. "Linear Programming: Software Survey." *OR/MS Today* (June 2013): 44–53, also available online at http://www.lionhrtpub.com/orms/surveys/LP/LP-survey.html.

Check Station Answers

1. The formulation of the farmer's problem is

$$\text{Maximize:} \quad R = 6W + 3.75B$$
$$\text{Subject to:} \quad W + B \leq 10 \quad \text{(land)}$$
$$40W + 20B \leq 320 \quad \text{(labor)},$$

where W and B denote the amounts (in thousands of bushels) of wheat and barley, respectively. Graphing the problem reveals that both constraints are binding. Solving simultaneously the equations $W + B = 10$ and $40W + 20B = 320$, we find $W = 6$ thousand bushels and $B = 4$ thousand bushels. The resulting revenue is: $(\$6)(6) + (\$3.75)(4) = \$51$ thousand.

2. As long as P_W/P_B is between 1 and 2, the crop mix $W = 6$ and $B = 4$ is optimal. (For instance, a 15 percent fall in both prices has no effect on the ratio.) A rise in the price of wheat to $8 puts the ratio outside this range, causing the farmer to produce only wheat. The new solution is $W = 8$ and $B = 0$, with only the labor constraint binding. A fall in the price of wheat to $3.50 causes the farmer to produce only barley. Now the solution is $B = 10$ and $W = 0$.

3. To find the shadow price of land, solve the equations $W + B = 11$ and $40W + 20B = 320$ to arrive at $W = 5$ thousand bushels and $B = 6$ thousand bushels. The farmer's new revenue is $52,500. Land's shadow price is the difference between the old and new revenues, $52,500 - $51,000 = $1,500 per acre. To find the shadow price of labor, solve the equations $W + B = 10$ and $40W + 20B = 330$ to arrive at $W = 6.5$ and $B = 3.5$. The farmer's new revenue is $52,125. Therefore, labor's shadow price is $1,125/10 = $112.50 per hour. Labor's shadow price becomes zero when the supply of labor increases to 400 hours per week. At this level, the labor constraint line lies (just) outside the land constraint line.

4. Producing 1,000 bushels of soybeans has an opportunity cost of

$$($1,500)(4) + ($112.5)(80) = $15,000.$$

The direct revenue from selling the 1,000 bushels is $13,500. Since this revenue falls short of the cost, soybeans (in this or any other amount) should not be grown.

5. a. *School 1's shadow price:* The extra spot in school 1 will be filled by a west student who was attending school 2. This saves .6 kid-miles, because school 1 is this much closer to the west neighborhood than is school 2. In turn, the freed space in school 2 is filled by a south student (who was attending school 3) for a .2 kid-mile savings. The total gain is: $.6 + .2 = .8$ kid-miles.

   b. *West neighborhood's shadow price:* The extra west student attends school 2 (an extra 2.0 kid-miles), displacing a south student who now moves to school 3 (an extra .2 kid-miles). Thus, the total increase in kid-miles is 2.2.

Index

A

Abbott Laboratories, 13
Accounting profit, 178
Acquisitions, contingent pricing in, 483–484
Adjusted R-squared, 111–112
Advanced Micro Devices Inc., 249
Adverse selection, 446–448
Advertising, 53, 290–293
Africa, drug prices in, 14
Agency cost, 453–454
Agreements, failed, 493–494
AIDS medications, 13–14, 341–342, 369–370
Air passenger battle, 303–304, 327–329
Airbus, 247, 268, 318, 457
Airline deregulation, 275
Airline ticket pricing, 59–60, 84–85, 275
Algebraic solutions, linear programming and, 511–512
Alternatives, exploration of in decision making, 8
Amazon, 39, 182, 198, 233, 234, 344
America Online (AOL), 87, 234
American International Group (AIG), 452
Apple, 87, 88, 234, 249, 287, 347, 456
Assessments, probability, 481
Asymmetric information.
   adverse selection and, 446–448
   benefits program and, 446–447
   building contracts and, 449–450
   financial meltdown and, 452–454
   health insurance and medical costs and, 450–451
   incentive pay and, 445, 469
   "lemons" market and, 447–448
   moral hazard and, 449–450
   principal-agent problems and, 449–454
   signaling and, 448–449

AT&T, 344, 346
Automobiles
   aluminum *vs.* steel in, 167
   parts production and, 148
Average-cost pricing, 256–257
Average fixed costs, 187
Average total cost, 183–185
Average variable cost, 183, 185, 187
Azidothymidine (AZT), 341, 369–370

B

Bank of America, 452
Bargaining and negotiation. *See also* Negotiations
   bargaining power, 269
   beneficial agreements and, 476–479
   competitive strategy and, 318–319
   contingent contracts and, 483–484
   contingent pricing in an acquisition, 483–484
   failed agreements and, 493–494
   multiple-issue negotiations, 484–489
   negotiation strategy, 489–495
   patent conflict and, 479–480
   probability assessments and, 481
   resolving disputes and, 479–480
   risk aversion and, 481–483
   Sanofi's bid for Genzyme, 475, 494–495
   selling a warehouse and, 476–479
   settlement negotiations, 481
   value differences and, 481–483
Barnes & Noble, 181
Barometric models, 127–128
Barriers to entry, 245, 247–250
   capital requirements and, 247
   economies of scale and, 247

Barriers to entry (*continued*)
  legal barriers, 248
  product differentiation and, 248
  pure quality and cost advantages and, 247–248
  resources control and, 248
  strategic barriers and, 248–249
Baseball, winning in, 156
Bayes' theorem, 419–422
Bazerman, Max, 393
Behavioral economics, 11
Beneficial agreements, economic sources of, 476–484
Benefit-cost analysis, 7, 14–15, 359–369
  basics of, 361–363
  direct elicitation and, 367
  dollar values and, 362
  efficiency *vs.* equity and, 362–363
  indirect market measures and, 367
  market values and, 366
  net benefit rule and, 362
  nonmarketed benefits and costs, 366–369
  public goods and efficiency, 359–361
  public project evaluation and, 363–366
  valuing lives and, 368–369
Berkshire Hathaway, 467
Bertrand, Joseph, 286
Bertrand price competition, 286–287
Best Buy, 269, 316
Bezos, Jeff, 39
Blockbuster, 316
Blu-Ray DVD format, 315
Boeing, 195, 198, 247, 268, 318, 345, 457
Book publishers, E-book pricing and, 182
Boundaries, firm, 455–456
BP, 4, 7, 8, 394–395
Brandenberger, Adam, 269
Bridges, public investment in, 363–366
Bristol-Myers, 13, 293
British Airways, 347
Budget constraints, 95
Buffet, Warren, 453, 467
Building contracts, 449–450
Bundling, 299–301
Burger King, 19
Burroughs Wellcome Co., 341
Business behavior
  decision pitfalls and, 424–427
  pricing in practice, 77
  starting business, 178–179

C
Cable TV subscribers, forecasting and, 123
Calculus
  marginal analysis and, 28–31
  optimization techniques and, 47–55
Capital One, 103
Capital requirements, entry barriers and, 247
Capitation approach, 451
Carson, Johnny, 486
Cartels, 252–254
CBS, 486–489
Certainty equivalent, 395, 481
Challenger disaster, 427–429
Chicago School approach, 345
Cigarette industry, 77
Citicorp, 345
Clayton Act of 1914, 344
Clean Air Act of 1970, 357–358
Coal, clean, 526–527
Coase, Ronald, 454
Coase theorem, 354
Cobb-Douglas function, 162–164
Coca-Cola, 102, 248
Coefficient of determination, 110–111
Collusion prevention, 347
Comcast, 346
Comparative advantage, international trade and, 189–191
Competition, repeated, 323–327
Competitive bidding. *See* Auctions and competitive bidding
Competitive equilibrium, 219–225
  decisions of competitive firm and, 220–222
  firm's supply curve and, 220–222
  long-run equilibrium, 222
  long-run market supply and, 224–225
  market equilibrium, 223–225
  price taking and, 220
Competitive situations. *See also* Game theory
  communication and agreement among competitors, 306
  cooperative, 306
  degree of mutual interest and, 305–306
  information amount and, 307
  noncooperative, 306
  number of competitors and, 305
  outcomes and payoffs and, 304–305
  players and their actions, 304
  repeated or one-shot competition, 306–307

sizing up of, 304–307
  underlying rules and, 305
Competitive strategy
  bargaining and, 318–319
  duration and, 326–327
  entry deterrence and, 319–321
  first-mover strategy and, 317
  high-definition DVD standards and, 315–317
  international mineral lease and, 319–321
  limit pricing and, 321
  market entry and, 317–318
  mixed strategies, 337–340
  punitive strategy and, 324
  repeated competition and, 323–327
  reputation and, 324, 325–326
  sequential competition and, 319–323
  strategic entry barrier and, 323
  tit-for-tat and, 325
  two-tiered tender offers and, 314–315
Competitor communication, 306
Complementary goods, 64, 269
Complex procurements, 485–486
Computer solutions, linear programming and, 523–526
Concentration, oligopoly and, 273–275
Concentration ratios, 269–271
Conditional probabilities, 417
Constant average cost, returns to scale and, 192
Constant-cost industry, 224
Constant elasticity, 114
Constant returns to scale, 153, 187
Constrained optimization, 53–55
  Lagrange multipliers and, 54–55
  profits from multiple markets and, 53–54
  supply commitment and, 53
Consumer experiments, 101
Consumer preferences and demand, 93–99
  budget constraint and, 95
  consumer's problem and, 93–98
  demand curves and, 98–99
  indifference curves and, 93–95
  marginal rate of substitution and, 97–98
  optimal consumption and, 96–98
  price-consumption curve and, 98–99
Consumer surplus, 226
Consumer surveys, 101–102
Contingent contracts, 483–484
Contingent strategies, 324
Contracts, contingent, 483–484

Controlled market studies
  cross-sectional data and, 102
  time-series data and, 102
Cooperative competitive situations, 306
Coopetition, 269
Coordination
  through teams, 458–459
  via transfer prices, 459–460
Copyrights, 248, 357
Corporate control market, 466
Corporate culture, 455
Corporate governance reforms, 467
Cost, surveys and, 101
Cost advantages, entry barriers and, 247–248
Cost allocation, 175, 203–204
Cost analysis
  allocating costs, 175, 203–204
  comparative advantage and international trade, 189–191
  cost of production and, 182–191
  e-commerce and cost economies, 195–196
  economies of scope, 196–197
  fixed and sunk costs, 179–182
  flexibility and innovation, 197–198
  multiple products and, 202
  opportunity costs and economic profits, 176–179
  optimal decisions and, 199–202
  relevant costs and, 176–182
  returns to scale, 191–196
  shut-down rule and, 200–202
  single product and, 199–200
Cost awareness, 451
Cost control incentives, 451
Cost function, 25, 182
Cost uncertainty, international business and, 388
Cournot, Augustin, 278
Cournot equilibrium, 279
Credit risks, predicting, 423–424
Cross-price elasticity, 89
Cross-sectional data, 102
Customized pricing and products, 83–84

D
Data collection
  consumer surveys and, 101–102
  controlled market studies and, 102–103
  uncontrolled market data and, 103–104
Data-driven business, 103–104
Data mining, 103

Day care, 225–231
Deadweight loss, 252, 343
Decentralization, 458
Decision making
    alternative exploration and, 8
    behavioral economics and, 11
    building a new bridge and, 3
    drug prices in Africa and, 13–14
    economic view and, 11–15
    examples of, 2–5
    making choices and, 9–10
    market entry and, 3
    multinational production and pricing and, 2
    objective determination and, 6–7
    oil exploration risks and, 4–5
    predicting consequences and, 8–9
    problem definition and, 5–6
    public decisions and, 14–15
    regulatory problems and, 3–4
    research and development decisions and, 4
    responsibilities for, 456–460
    sensitivity analysis and, 10–11
    six steps to, 5–11
    using models and, 9
    value maximization and, 12–13
Decision making under uncertainty
    BP oil spill and, 394–395
    decision trees and, 381–388
    expected value and, 381
    international business and, 387–388
    management pitfalls and, 393–394
    Microsoft risk management example, 397
    probability and, 379–380
    probability distribution and, 381
    recession and, 378
    risk aversion and, 395–404
    sequential decisions and, 388–395
    uncertainty defined, 379
Decision trees, 381–388
Declining average cost, returns to scale and, 192–193
Decreasing returns to scale, 154, 188
Deepwater Horizon, 4, 394–395
Degrees of freedom, 111–112
Demand analysis
    airline ticket pricing and, 59, 84–85
    business behavior pricing in practice, 77
    complementary goods, 64
    cross-price elasticity and, 69–70

demand curve and shifting demand, 61–63
demand determinants, 60–64
demand function, 60–61
elasticity of demand, 64–71
income elasticity and, 69
inferior goods, 63
information goods and, 81–84
maximizing revenue and, 74–75
multinational production and pricing, 79–80
normal goods, 63
optimal pricing and, 71–84
price discrimination and, 78–81
price elasticity, revenue, and marginal revenue, 71–74
price elasticity and prediction, 70–71
sensitivity analysis and, 38
substitute good, 63–64
Demand-based pricing, 80
Demand curves, 20–23, 61–63, 98–99, 216
Demand determinants, 60–64
Demand estimation and forecasting
    data collection and, 101–104
    forecasting, 125–130
    movie demand, 100, 131–132
    regression analysis and, 104–118
Demand function, 60–61
Department of Defense procurements, 485–486
Dependent variables, 106
Deregulation, 357–358
Deterministic demand curves, 23–24
Deterministic models, 9
DHL, 459–460
Direct elicitation, 367
Disclosure requirements, 466
Discount for risk, 396
Disney, 357
Dispute resolution, 479–480
Disruptive innovation, 198
Distributive bargain, 477
Dodd-Frank Act, 346, 453
Dominant firm, oligopoly and, 276–278
Dominant strategy, 309
Drug prices in Africa, 13–14
Dueling suppliers, oligopoly and, 278–280
Duopoly equilibrium, 279–280
DuPont, 445, 459, 469
Durbin-Watson statistic, 116, 118
Dutch auctions, 547
DVD standards, 315–317

E

E-book pricing, 182
E-commerce, cost economies and, 195–196
EasyJet, 275
eBay, 82, 83, 195, 196, 234, 248, 276, 344
Economic profit, 177–178
Economies of scale, 187, 247
Economies of scope, 196–197
Economy, stock market and, 331, 434–436
Effective monopoly, 272
Effectively competitive market, 272
Efficiency, public goods and, 359–361
Ehrlich, Paul, 214
Elasticity of demand, 64–71
Enron, 468
Entry barriers, strategic, 248–249
Entry deterrence, 321–323
Enumeration, 10
Equation specification, 114
Equilibrium, 279–280
Equilibrium price, 217
Equilibrium strategies, 310–315
    market-share competition, 310–312
    Nash equilibrium and, 311–312
    prisoner's dilemma and, 313–314
Estimation error, 107
Euro Disney, 128–130
European Union Antitrust Commission, 346
Exchange-rate risk, international business and, 388
Exchange rates, sensitivity analysis and, 38–39
Executive compensation, incentives and, 467–468
Expected utility, 398–404
Expected value, 381
Expected value of information (EVI), 415
External enforcement of managerial duties, 466
Externalities and market failure, 349–358
    copyright and, 357
    global warming and, 355–356
    patent system and, 356–357
    private payments and, 353–354
    promoting positive externalities, 356–357
    regulatory reform and deregulation, 357–358
    remedying, 351–356

F

F-statistic, 112
Facebook, 195
Failed agreements, 493–494

Fast-food franchising, 19–20, 40–41
Fat-Cat strategy, 289
FDA drug approval, 341
Federal Trade Commission Act of 1914, 344
Ferry regulation, 366
Films, bundling, 299–300
Financial crisis of 2007 and 2008, 452–453
Financial incentives, 467–468
Firm boundaries, 455–456
Firm nature, 454–455
First-degree price discrimination, 80
First-mover advantage, 317
Five-forces framework, 268–269
Fixed costs, 179–180, 183
Fixed inputs, 147
Fixed-price contracts, 562
Fixed proportions, production with, 161
Flexibility, innovation and, 197–198
Football, winning in, 156
Ford Motor Company, 198
Forecasting, 125–130
    accuracy and, 129–130
    barometric models and, 127–128
    Cable TV subscribers and, 123
    demand for toys, 123–125
    Euro Disney and, 128–130
    fitting a simple trend and, 120–123
    housing bubble and crash and, 126–127
    performance and, 130
    time-series models, 118–120
Formulation issues, linear programming and, 512
Franchising, 463
Fudenberg, Drew, 289
Full-cost pricing, 77
Functional lines, 457

G

Game of trust, 339–340
Game theory. *See also* Competitive situations
    air passenger battle and, 303–304, 327–329
    analyzing payoff tables and, 307–315
    dominant strategy and, 309
    equilibrium strategies and, 310–315
    non-zero-sum games, 306, 339–340
    sizing up competitive situations and, 304–307
    TV ratings game and, 307–309
    two-tiered tender offers and, 314–315
    zero-sum game, 306, 311

Game tree, 319

General Agreement on Tariffs and Trade (GATT), 235

General Electric, 346, 453, 457

General Motors, 276, 302, 388

Genzyme Corporation, 475, 494–495

GlaxoSmithKline, 13, 198

Global airfares, 275

Global warming, 355–356

Goodness of fit, 110

Goods necessity, price elasticity and, 68

Google, 56, 82, 103, 104, 195, 196, 248, 287, 344, 346, 459, 499

Government decisions, 14–15

Government regulation. *See* Regulation

Government spending programs, sunk costs and, 181

Graphing, linear programming and, 506–509

Group performance evaluation, 464

Group think, 395

H

HD DVD format, 315–317

Health insurance, 447–448, 450–451

Herfindahl-Hirschman Index (HHI), 273

Hermes, 287

Heteroscedasticity, 116

Hewlett-Packard, 315

High-definition DVDs, 315–317

HIV resource allocation, 519–520

Home lending market, 452

Hostile takeovers, 467

Housing bubble and crash, 126–127

I

IBM, 196, 249, 344, 459

Icahn, Carl, 495

Imperfect information, 416–418

    market failure and, 358–359

    negotiations and, 491–492

Incentive contracts, 462, 562

Incentive pay, 445–446

Income elasticity, 69

Income proportion, price elasticity and, 68

Increasing average cost, returns to scale and, 193

Increasing-cost industry, 225

Increasing returns to scale, 154, 187

Independent private value setting, 544

Independent variables, 106

Index of Leading Indicators, 128

Indifference curves, 93–95

Indirect market measures, benefit-cost analysis and, 367

Individual performance evaluation, 463–464

Industry concentration, oligopoly and, 269–273

Inelastic demand, 66

Infant formula industry, 266–267, 292–293

Inferior goods, 63

Information, asymmetric. *See* Asymmetric information

Information amount, competitive situations and, 307

Information goods and services

    customized pricing and products, 83–84

    demand analysis and, 81–84

    network externalities and, 82–83

Information value

    Bayes' theorem and, 419–422

    business behavior and decision pitfalls, 424–427

    Challenger disaster and, 427–429

    expected value of information, 415

    imperfect information, 416–418

    oil-drilling decisions and, 414–416

    predicting credit risks and, 423–424

    revising probabilities and, 418–422

    stock market and, 413, 434–436

    valueless information, 421

Informational advertising, oligopoly and, 291–292

Informativeness principle, 463

Innovation

    disruptive, 198

    flexibility and, 197–198

    incremental, 198

Input

    marginal cost of, 151

    optimal use of, 151–153

Insurance demand, 396–397

Intel, 247, 249–250, 276

International business

    different cultures and, 388

    economic conditions and, 387–388

    exchange-rate risks and, 388

    perils of, 387–388

    political risks and, 388

    uncertain costs and, 388

International trade, 235–237

    comparative advantage and, 189–191

    restricted trade in watches, 235–237

    tariffs and quotas and, 235–237

Internet

    barriers to entry and, 234

    consumer information and, 232

    geographic range and variety and, 233

lower costs and, 233
 market competition and, 232–234
 perfect competition and, 234
Inverse demand equation, 22
Investment problem, linear programming and, 503,
  530–532
iPad, 287
Isocost line, 159
Isoquant, 157–159

J
Jackson, Thomas, 348

K
Kahn, Alfred, 257
Kahneman, Daniel, 394
Kindle, 39
Kinked demand curves, 280–282
Kinney Shoe, 345
Kyoto Treaty, 355–356

L
Labor specialization, 192
Lagrange multipliers, 54–55
Law of diminishing marginal returns, 151
Law of diminishing returns, 185
Law of one price, 220
Leading indicators, 127–128
Learning curve, price cutting and, 287
Least-cost production, 154–160
Legal barriers, monopolies and, 248
"Lemons" market, 447–448
Leno, Jay, 5, 486, 488
Letterman, David, 5, 8, 486–489
Limit pricing, 321–322
Linear production function, 160–161
Linear programming
 algebraic solutions and, 511–512
 allocating HIV resources and, 519–520
 changes in objective function and, 513–515
 clean coal and, 526–527
 computer solutions and, 523–526
 finding an optimal computer mix and, 504–506
 formulation and computer solutions and, 520–530
 formulation issues and, 512
 graphing and, 506–509
 investment problem and, 503, 530–532
 larger problems and, 520–530
 minimization problem and, 510–512
 production at minimum cost and, 522–523

 production for maximum output and, 520–522
 regulation at least cost and, 510–511
 school busing problem and, 527–530
 sensitivity analysis and, 513–515
 shadow prices and, 515–519
 staffing problem and, 523–526
Lives, valuation of, 368–369
Lockheed Martin, 345
Long-run costs, 187–189
 constant returns to scale and, 187
 cost variability and, 187
 decreasing returns to scale, 188
 economies of scale, 187
 increasing returns to scale, 187
 vs. short-run costs, 188–189
Long-run equilibrium, 222
Long-run frequency, probabilityand, 380
Long-run market supply, 224–225
Long-run production, 153–160. *See also* Production
 constant returns to scale and, 153–154
 decreasing returns to scale and, 154
 graphical approach and, 156–160
 increasing returns to scale and, 154
 isocost line and, 159
 isoquants and, 157–159
 least-cost production and, 154–160
 marginal rate of technical substitution and, 157
 output elasticity and, 154
 returns to scale and, 153–154
Loose oligopoly, 272

M
Management pitfalls, risky decisions and, 393–394
Marginal analysis, 19–41, 48–52
 calculus and, 28–31
 cost analysis and, 25
 differential calculus and, 49–50
 in fast-food franchising, 19–20, 40–41
 marginal cost and, 33
 marginal profit and, 27–28
 marginal revenue and, 31
 marginal revenue and marginal cost, 52
 microchip manufacturer and, 21–27
 model of the firm and, 20–27
 profit analysis and, 25–26
 profit maximization and, 33–35
 revenue analysis and, 21–25
 second derivative and, 51–52
 sensitivity analysis and, 35–39

Marginal benefit curve, 228
Marginal cost, 33, 52, 185–187
Marginal cost of an input, 152
Marginal-cost pricing, 256
Marginal product, 148–149
Marginal profit, 27–28
Marginal rate of substitution, 97–98
Marginal rate of technical substitution (MRTS), 157
Marginal revenue, 33, 52, 71–74, 151
Market competition, Internet and, 232–234
Market data, uncontrolled, 103–104
Market demand, price cutting and, 286–287
Market efficiency, 225–234
    day-care market and, 227–231
    dynamic, marketwide efficiency, 231–232
    efficiency and equity, 232
    marginal benefit curve and, 228
    private markets and, 225–234
Market entry, 3
Market equilibrium, 223–225
Market failure
    externalities and, 349–358
    imperfect information and, 358–359
    regulation and, 342–348
Market-share competition, 310–311
Market skimming, price cutting and, 287
Market structures, 215
Market studies, controlled, 102–103
Market supply, long-run, 224–225
Markup rule, 76
Material costs, sensitivity analysis and, 38
Maximizing total sales, 12
Maximum profit, 28–31
McDonald's, 19, 40, 41, 302, 388
McDonnell-Douglas, 195, 345
Mean, 104
Medical costs, 450–451
Merck & Co., 13
Merger prevention, monopolies and, 345–346
Method of Lagrange multipliers, 54–55
Microchips market, 27–27, 212–213
Microsoft, 82, 195, 198, 234, 276, 287, 302, 315, 345, 347–348, 397
Microsoft antitrust case, 347–348
Mineral lease, international, 319–321
Minimization problem, linear programming and, 510–512
Minimum efficient scale, 193–195
Mixed bundling, 300–301

Mixed competitive strategies, 337–340
    game of trust and, 339–340
    market competition and, 337–339
Model of the firm, 20–27
Models, decision making and, 9
Monopolistic competition, 257–259
Monopoly
    average-cost pricing and, 256–257
    barriers to entry and, 247–249
    breaking up existing, 344
    cartels and, 252–254
    government responses and, 344–348
    Intel's monopoly, 249–250
    marginal-cost pricing and, 256
    monopolistic competition, 257–259
    natural monopolies, 255–257
    New York City taxicabs and, 244, 260–261
    perfect competition vs. puremonopoly, 250–257
    preventing collusion and, 347
    preventing mergers and, 345–346
    preventing practices and, 344–345
    price and output decision and, 244–245
    product differentiation and, 248
    pure monopoly, 244–249
    regulation and, 344–348
    rent-seeking activity and, 343
Moral hazard, 449–450, 453
Morgenstern, Oskar, 304, 398
Motivation, 460–463
Movie demand, 100, 131–132
Multicollinearity, 115
Multinational production and pricing, 2, 79–81
Multiple-issue negotiations, 484–489
    complex procurement and, 485–486
    wooing David Letterman, 486–489
Multiple market profits, 53–54
Multiple plants, production decisions and, 164–165
Multiple products, 166–167, 202
Multiple regression, 108–109, 142–143
Multivariate function maximization, 52–53
Murphy, Kevin, 468
Mutual interest, competitive situations and, 305–306
Myopic viewpoints, 393

N
Nalebuff, Barry, 269
Nash, John, 279
Nash equilibrium, 279, 310–312
Natural monopolies, 193, 255–257

NBC, 5, 315, 486–489
Negotiations. *See also* Bargaining and negotiations
   failed agreements and, 493–494
   imperfect information and, 416–418
   multiple-issue, 484–489
   perfect information and, 490
   repetition and reputation and, 492–494
   strategy and, 489–494
   tender offer and, 491–492
Net benefit rule, 362
Netflix, 316
Network externalities, 82–83
New Coke, 102
New York City's taxicabs, 244, 260–261
Non-zero-sum games, 306, 339–340
Noncooperative competitive situations, 306
Nonmarketed benefits and costs, 366–369
Normal good, 63
Northwest Airlines, 345–346
Nuclear power plant construction, 180

O
Objective determination, decision making and, 6–7
Objective function, 505, 513–515
Office Depot, 345
Oil drilling decisions, 382–384, 398–404, 414–416
Oil exploration risks, 4
Oligopoly
   advertising and, 290–292
   Bertrand price competition and, 286
   bundling and tying and, 299–302
   concentration and prices and, 273–275
   concentration ratios and, 269–273
   dominant firm and, 276–278
   dueling suppliers and, 278–280
   duopoly equilibrium and, 279–280
   five-forces framework and, 268–269
   global airfares and, 275
   Herfindahl-Hirschman Index and, 273
   industry concentration and, 269–273
   infant formula industry and, 266–267, 292–293
   informational advertising and, 291
   loose oligopoly, 272
   mixed bundling, 300–301
   price competition and, 280–287
   price cutting and, 286–287
   price rigidity and kinked demand, 280–282
   price wars and, 282–284
   prisoner's dilemma and, 284–285
   product differentiation and, 291
   quantity competition and, 276–280
   relevant market and, 272
   strategic commitments and, 288–290
   strategic complements and, 288
   strategic substitutes and, 288
   symmetric firms and, 278–280
   tight oligopoly, 272
Omitted variables, 115
One-shot competition, 306–307
Opportunity costs
   economic profits and, 176–179
   starting a business and, 178–179
Optimal advertising, 290–291
Optimal computer mix, linear programming and,
   504–506
Optimal consumption, consumer preferences and
   demand, 96–98
Optimal decisions
   cost analysis and, 199–202
   shadow prices and, 517–519
Optimal markup pricing, 75–77
Optimal output, 199–200
Optimal pricing, demand analysis and, 71–84
Optimal reaction function, 279
Optimal use of an input, 151–153
Optimistic beliefs, holding, 394
Optimization techniques
   constrained optimization and, 53–55
   marginal analysis and, 48–52
   maximizing multivariable functions, 52–53
   maximizing profit and, 47
   using spreadsheets, 56–58
Oracle, 195, 234, 345, 456
Ordinary least-squares regression, 104–109
Organization of Oil Exporting Countries (OPEC),
   252–254
Organizational design, 454–469. *See also* Asymmetric
   information
   Airbus's dysfunctional organization, 457–458
   boundaries of the firm, 455–456
   coordination through teams and, 458–459
   coordination via transfer prices, 459–460
   corporate control market and, 466
   corporate governance reforms and, 467
   decentralization and, 458
   decision-making responsibilities and, 456–460
   DHL Worldwide Express and, 459–460
   disclosure requirements and, 466

Organizational design (*continued*)
external enforcement of managerial duties and, 466
failures and, 468–469
financial incentives and, 467–468
group performance evaluation and, 464
individual performance evaluation and, 463–464
integration or franchising, 463
limiting top management power and, 465–467
monitoring and rewarding performance, 460–464
nature of firm and, 454–455
outsourcing and, 456
ownership and control separation and, 464–469
shareholder empowerment and, 466–467
vertical integration and, 455
Output elasticity, 154
Outside directors, 467
Outsourcing, 456
Overconfidence, 394–395, 427
Overhead, sensitivity analysis and, 36, 38
Overoptimism, 394–395
Ovitz, Michael, 5, 486
Ownership
limiting top management power, 465–467
separation of control and, 464–469

P
Paramount Pictures, 315
Patent conflict, 479–480
Patent system, 248, 356–357
Pay-for-performance systems, 468
Payoff frontier, 477
Payoff tables, 307–315
Perfect competition
competitive equilibrium and, 219–225
four conditions of, 219
international trade and, 234–237
Internet and, 232–234
market efficiency and, 225–234
price and output under, 221
supply and demand basics and, 216–219
vs. pure monopoly, 250–257
Perfect information, negotiations and, 490
Perfect price discrimination, 80
Perfect substitutes, 161
Perfectly elastic demand, 66, 220
Perfectly inelastic demand, 66
Performance
forecasting, 130

group evaluation, 464
individual evaluation, 463–464
motivating and rewarding, 460–463
Physician incentives, 451
Players, competitive situations and, 304
Point elasticities, 65
Political risk, international business and, 388
Pollution, 349–358
Polynomial functions, 161–162
Porter, Michael, 234, 267
Positive externalities, promoting, 356–357
Predatory pricing, 344–345
Predictable surprises, 393
Prediction mistakes, overconfidence and, 393
Price and advertising, 53
Price competition
oligopoly and, 280–287
repeated, 323–325
Price-consumption curves, 98, 99
Price cutting
boosting sales of related products and, 287
learning curve and, 287
market demand changes and, 286–287
market skimming and, 287
strategic price cuts, 287
Price discrimination, 78–81
first-degree or perfect price discrimination, 80–81
second-degree price discrimination, 81
third-degree price discrimination, 80
Price elasticity, 64–67
adjustment time and, 68
goods necessity and, 68
income proportion and purchase, 68
prediction and, 70–71
revenue and marginal revenue and, 71–74
substitute availability and, 68
Price rigidity, oligopoly and, 280–282
Price taker, 220
Prices, oligopoly and, 273–275, 282–284
Principal-agent problems, 449–454, 466–467
Prior probability, 417
Prisoner's dilemma, 284–285, 313–314
Private markets, benefits and costs and, 225–234
Probabilistic models, 9
Probability
assessments and, 481
conditional probabilities, 417
distribution and, 381

outcome and, 379–380
prior probability, 417
revisions and, 418–422
Problem definition, decision making and, 5–6
Procter & Gamble, 196, 198, 276, 347, 387
Product differentiation
entry barriers and, 248
monopolistic competition and, 257
oligopoly and, 291
Production
aluminum *vs.* steel in cars and trucks, 167
auto parts and, 148–150
basic production concepts, 147
Cobb-Douglas function, 162–163
estimating production functions, 163–164
fixed inputs and, 147
fixed proportions and, 161
law of diminishing marginal returns, 151
linear production function, 160–161
in long run, 153–160
long-run costs and, 197–199
marginal product and, 148
marginal rate of technical substitution, 157
for maximum output, 520–522
measuring functions of, 160–164
at minimum cost, 522–523
multiple plants and, 164–165
multiple products and, 166
optimal use of an input, 151–153
polynomial functions, 161–162
returns to scale and, 153–154
sales force allocation and, 146, 167–169
short-run and long-run production, 147–151
short-run costs and, 183–187
Profit
analysis, 25–26
function, 26
maximization, 6–7, 33–35, 47–48
Public decision, 14–15
Public goods
efficiency and, 359–361
pure public goods, 359
Public pricing, 365
Public project evaluation, 363–366
Punitive strategy, 324
Pure monopoly. *See* Monopoly
Pure public goods, 359
Pure selling problem, 74

Q
Quantity competition, oligopoly and, 276–280
Quotas, 235–237

R
R-squared statistic, 110–111
Random fluctuations, time-series models
and, 118
Recession, 378, 405–406
Reflexive thinking, 309
Regression analysis, 104–118
adjusted R-squared, 111–112
Durbin-Watson statistic and, 116, 118
equation specification and, 114
F-stat istic and, 112
heteroscedasticity and, 116
interpreting regression statistics and, 109–114
mean and, 104
multicollinearity and, 115
multiple regression, 108–109
omitted variables and, 115
ordinary least-squares regression, 104–109
potential problems in, 114–118
R-squared statistic, 110–111
sample variance and, 104
serial correlation and, 116
simultaneity and identification and, 115–116
standard deviation and, 105
standard error of the regression, 114
standard errors of the coefficients, 112
t-statistic, 113
Regression using spreadsheets, 140–143
multiple regression, 142–143
simple regression, 140–142
Regulation
copyright system, 357–358
externalities and, 349–358
FDA drug approval, 341, 369–370
global warming and, 355–356
imperfect information and, 358–359
at least cost, 510–511
market failures and, 342–348
Microsoft antitrust case, 347–348
monopolies and, 343–346
patent system, 356–357
predatory pricing and, 344–345
regulatory reform and deregulation,
357–358

Relevant costs
  fixed and sunk costs, 179–181
  opportunity costs and economic profits,
    176–179
Rent-seeking activity, monopolies and, 343
Repeated competition, 306–307, 323–327
Repeated negotiation, 492–494
Reputation, 324, 325–326, 492–494
Research and development (R&D)
  decisions regarding, 389–393
Reservation prices, 477
Resource control, entry barriers and, 248
Response accuracy, surveys and, 101
Response bias, surveys and, 101
Returns to scale, 153–154, 191–195
  constant average cost and, 192
  declining average cost and, 192–193
  increasing average cost and, 193
  minimum efficient scale and, 193–195
Revenues
  analysis of, 21–25
  equivalence theorem, 557
  maximization, 74–75
  price elasticity and, 71–74
  revenue function, 25
Revised probabilities, 418–422
Risk
  Challenger disaster and, 427–429
  decision making and, 7
  risk-benefit analysis, 451
  sharing of, 482
Risk aversion, 395–404, 481–483
  coin gamble and, 395–396
  expected utility and, 398–403
  insurance demand and, 396–397
  Microsoft risk management, 397
  wildcatting and, 398–400
Rite-Aid, 345
Root mean squared error (RMSE), 129
Rules, competitive situations and, 305
Ryanair, 275

S
Sales force allocation, 146, 167–169
Sales maximization, 12
Sample bias, surveys and, 101
Sample variance, 104
Samsung, 315
Sanofi-Aventis SA, 475, 494–495

Sarbanes-Oxley Act, 469
Satisficing, 12
Scale, returns to, 191–195
Schelling, Thomas, 489
School busing problem, 527–530
Schultze, Charles, 3–4
Scope, economies of, 196–197
Seasonal variations, time-series models and, 118
Second-degree price discrimination, 81
Self-selection, 446–447
Self-serving bias, 494
Sensitivity analysis, 35–41
  decision making and, 10–11
  exchange rates and, 38–39
  increased demand and, 38
  increased material costs and, 38
  increased overhead and, 36, 38
  linear programming and, 513–515
Sequential competition, 319–323
Sequential decisions, 388–395
Sequential game, 319
Serial correlation, 116
Settlement negotiations, 481
Shadow prices, 515–519
Shareholder empowerment, 466–467
Sherman Act of 1890, 344
Shifting demands, demand curve and, 61–63
Short-run costs
  average fixed costs, 187
  average total cost, 183, 184
  average variable cost, 183, 185
  fixed costs, 183
  marginal cost, 185–187
  production and, 182–187
  variable costs, 183
  vs. long-run costs, 188–189
Short-run production, 147–153
Shut-down rule, 200–202
Signaling, 448–449
Simon, Julian, 214
Simple regression, spreadsheets and, 140–142
Simultaneity, 115–116
Single product, profit maximization and,
    199–200
Smith, Adam, 225, 461
Smoking health risks, 420
Social responsibility, 12
Sony Corporation, 315, 357
Specialization of labor, 149

Spreadsheets
  optimization using, 56–58
  regression using, 140–143
Staffing problem, 523–526
Standard deviation, 105
Standard error of a coefficient, 112
Standard error of the regression, 114
Standard Oil, 344
Statistical tables, 144–145
Steel production, 38
Stock market, economy and, 413
Stock repurchases, 542–543
Strategic commitments, oligopoly and, 288–290
Strategic complements, 288
Strategic entry barrier, 323
Strategic price cuts, 287
Strategic substitutes, 288
Subjective notion of probability, 380
Substitute availability, price elasticity and, 68
Substitute good, 63–64
Substitution principle, 400
Sun Microsystems, 456
Sunk costs, 180–181
Supply and demand
  basics of, 216–219
  demand curve, 216
  equilibrium price, 216
  shifts in, 117, 217–219
  supply curve, 216
Supply curves, 216, 220–222
Surprises, predictable, 393
Surveys
  consumer, 101–102
  cost and, 101
  response accuracy and, 101
  response bias and, 101
  sample bias and, 101
Switching costs, 248
Symmetric firms, oligopoly and, 278–280

T
t-statistic, 113
Taking the outside view, 394
Tariffs, 235–237
Team coordination, 458–459
Television ratings game, 307–309
Tender offers, 314–315, 491–492
The Tonight Show, 5, 486–489
Theory of the firm, 11

Third-degree price discrimination, 80
Ticketmaster, 346
Tight oligopoly, 272
Time-series data, 102
Time-series models, 118–120
  component parts of, 120
  fitting a simple trend and, 120–122
  random fluctuations and, 118
  seasonal variations and, 118
  trends and, 118
Time Warner, 346
Tirole, Jean, 289
Tit-for-tat, 325
Top management
  corporate control market and, 466
  corporate governance reforms and, 467
  disclosure requirements and, 466
  external enforcement and, 466
  financial incentives and, 467–468
  limiting power of, 465–467
  shareholder empowerment and, 466–467
Toshiba Corporation, 315
Total costs, 184
Toys, demand for, 123–125
Transfer pricing, 211–213, 459
Transferable emissions permits, 353
Trends, time-series models and, 118
Troubled Assets Relief Program (TARP), 452
Trucks, aluminum *vs.* steel in, 167
Twain, Mark, 481
Two-part pricing, 81
Two-tiered tender offers, 314–315
Tyco International, 468
Tying, 301–302

U
Uncertainty, decision making and, 7
Uncontrolled market data, 103
Unilever, 347
Unitary elastic demand, 66
United States Sentencing Commission, 469
U.S. Steel, 276, 344
U.S. Treasury, 541
Used-car market, 447–448

V
Value asymmetry, auctions and, 559
Value differences, 481–483
Value maximization, decision making and, 12–13

Valueless information, 421
Variable costs, 183
Verbal expressions of probability, 393–394
Versioning, 84
Vertical integration, 455
Vickrey auction, 545
Von Neumann, John, 304, 398

W
Walk-away prices, 477
Walmart, 247, 269, 276, 316, 326, 454
Walt Disney Co., 128–129, 315
Warehouse sale, 476–479
Watches, restricted trade in, 235–237
Welch, Jack, 494
Whirlpool, 345

Whole Foods Market, 451
Wildcatting, oil, 398–404, 414–416
Winner's curse, 432–433, 555
Worker motivation, 460–463
World Health Organization, 13, 14
WorldCom Inc., 468

X
Xerox, 301–302

Y
YouTube, 195

Z
Zero-sum game, 306, 310
Zone of agreement, 477